TEN CITIES
Clubbing in Nairobi, Cairo, Kyiv,
Johannesburg, Naples, Berlin,
Luanda, Lagos, Bristol, Lisbon
1960 – March 2020

Edited by
Johannes Hossfeld Etyang,
Joyce Nyairo, Florian Sievers

A project of Goethe-Institut
Published by Spector Books

Playlists

Nairobi

1963	Fadhili William, 'Malaika'
1963	Sal Davis, 'Makini'
1965	Daudi Kabaka and Fadhili with Sonko, 'Harambee, Harambee'
1972	Gabriel Omolo & Apollo Komesha, 'Lunch Time'
1976	Jingo, 'Fever'
1976	Orchestre Les Mangelepa, 'Embakasi'
1976	Slim Ali & Famous Hodi Boys, 'You Can Do It'
1980	Orch. Les Wanyika, 'Sina Makosa'
1980	Kelly Brown, 'Higher'
1981	Nguashi Ntimbo and Orchestre Festival du Zaire, 'Shauri Yako'
1988	Musikly Speaking, 'Jamriambo'
1997	Kalamashaka, 'Tafsiri Hii'
1999	Poxi Presha, 'Otonglo Time'
2003	E-Sir ft. Nameless, 'Boomba Train'
2004	Necessary Noize, 'Kenyan Gal, Kenyan Boy'
2004	Esther Wahome, 'Kuna Dawa'
2009	Just A Band, 'Ha-He'
2011	Jaguar, 'Kigeugeu'
2011	Camp Mull ft. Collo, 'Party Don't Stop'
2018	King Kaka ft. Kristoff & Magix Enga, 'Dundaing'

Cairo

1965	Umm Kulthum, 'Enta Omri'
1969	Medhat Saleh, 'Kawkab Tany'
1980	Al Massrieen, *Banat Keteer*
1988	Ali Hamida and Hameed El Shaary Band, *Lolaaky*
1989	Ahmed Adaweya, *Teegy*
1992	Hosam Hosni, *Kol El Banat*
1993	Warda, *Harammt Ahebak*
1993	Angham, 'Shantet Safar'
1995	Hamid El Shaeri, 'El Koha'
2012	Abu Assala, 'Moulid Talatet'
2014	Maurice Louca, *Benhayyi Al-Baghbaghan*
2014	Hassan El Shafei ft. Abla Fahita, 'Mayestahlushi'
2015	Hassan El Prince, 'Mafish Sa7eb Yetsa7eb'
2016	DJ Zeina Ezz, *HDNSM #170*
2016	Donia Samir Ghanem ft. Abdelbaset Hamouda, 'Bab El Hayah'
2016	Ahmed Sheba, 'Ah Law Laebt Ya Zahr'
2017	Nadah El Shazly, *Ahwar*
2018	Sadat El 3alamy ft. Weegz & DJ Haha, 'Kharban'
2018	Dina El Wedidi, 'Alive'
2018	Zuli ft. Abanob, Abyusif, Mado $am, R-Rhyme, 'Nari'

Kyiv

1974	Арніка, Естрадний Ансамбль Арніка
1978	Водограй, Водограй
1980	Назарій Яремчук, Незрівнянний Світ Краси
1982	Vadim Khrapachov, *Polyoty Vo Sne I Nayavu OST*
1992	Shake Hi Fi, *Bananas Whole Year*
1995	Город Супутник, O*urgl-gurgl-gurgl*
1996	Da Sintezatoros!, *More Realistic Then*
1996	Taran, *Mod and Mini and Space Age*
1998	Various, *Who's Next?*
1998	Катя Chilly, *Русалки in da House*
2000	DJ Derbastler & Danilkin, *Summer SALEction 2000*
2002	Max Chorny, *Gde Trava?*
2003	Various, *Music for Space Lorry Drivers*
2005	Zavoloka, *Plavyna*
2007	Ivan Samshit, *Essential Shit*
2013	Vakula, *You've Never Been to Konotop*
2015	Onuka, *Onuka*
2016	Cape Cod, *Cult*
2017	King Imagine, 'Approximate Time Left'
2018	Voin Oruwu, *Big Space Adventure*

Johannesburg

1959	Manhattan Brothers, 'Vuka Vuka'
1967	Miriam Makeba, 'Pata Pata'
1969	Philip Tabane and his Malombo Jazzmen, *The Indigenous Afro-Jazz Sounds of…*
1974	Dollar Brand, *Mannenberg – 'Is Where It's Happening'*
1983	Sipho 'Hot Stix' Mabuse, 'Jive'
1983	Via Afrika, 'Hey Boy'
1983	Brenda & The Big Dudes, 'Weekend Special'
1994	Boom Shaka, 'Kwere Kwere'
1995	Arthur, 'Kaffir'
1998	TKZee, *Halloween*
1998	Bongo Maffin, *The Concerto*
2000	Lebo Mathosa, 'Tsodiyo'
2001	B.O.P., *Zabalaza: Project B*
2004	Thandiswa, *Zabalaza*
2008	Mujava, 'Township Funk'
2011	Spikiri, *The King Don Father 2.5*
2012	Dirty Paraffin, 'Papap! Papap!'
2013	Mafikizolo, 'Khona'
2014	K.O, 'Caracara'
2017	DJ Maphorisa & DJ Shimza ft. Moonchild, 'Makhe'

Naples

1972	Balletto di Bronzo, *Ys*
1973	Osanna, *Palepoli*
1975	Napoli Centrale, *Napoli Centrale*
1976	Roberto de Simone / Nuova Compagnia di Canto Popolare, *La Gatta Cenerentola*
1977	Pino Daniele, *Terra Mia*
1984	Tony Esposito, 'Kalimba de Luna'
1984	Tullio de Piscopo, 'Stop Bajon'
1986	Enzo Avitabile, 'Black Out'
1993	99 Posse, *Curre Curre Guagliò*
1995	Almamegretta, *Sanacore*
1998	Marco Carola, *Fokus*
2001	Retina.it, *Volcano.Waves.1–8*
2001	Gaetano Parisio, *Advanced Techno Research Selection 98/00*
2002	Danilo Vigorito, 'Imaginary Boy EP1'
2004	Terrae and Defrag Sound Processing, 'Mutter EP'
2007	Lucio Aquilina, 'Magic M'
2008	Rino Cerrone & Joseph Capriati, 'Orange EP'
2013	Davide Squillace, 'The Love Story Teller'
2018	Riva Starr, *Curveballs*
2018	Nu Guinea, *Nuova Napoli*

Berlin

1970	Tangerine Dream, *Electronic Meditation*
1977	David Bowie, *Low*
1980	Conrad Schnitzler, 'Auf dem Schwarzen Kanal'

1981	Einstürzende Neubauten, *Kollaps*	
1982	Malaria, 'Kaltes Klares Wasser'	
1984	Manuel Göttsching, *E2-E4*	
1984	Pond, *Planetenwind*	
1988	Westbam, 'Disco Deutschland'	
1992	3 Phase ft. Dr. Motte, 'Der Klang der Familie'	
1993	Basic Channel, 'Domina (C. Craig's Mind Mix)'	
1994	Atari Teenage Riot, 'Raver Bashing'	
1997	Jazzanova, 'Fedime's Flight'	
2000	Divérse, *Staedtizism*	
2001	Rhythm & Sound w/ Cornell Campbell, 'King in My Empire'	
2006	Ricardo Villalobos, 'Fizheuer Zieheuer'	
2009	Paul Kalkbrenner, 'Sky & Sand'	
2013	Marcel Dettmann, *Dettmann II*	
2015	The Howling, *Sacred Ground*	
2016	Fjaak, 'Pray For Berlin'	
2018	Planningtorock ft. Dashius Clay, 'Somethings More Painful Than Others'	

Luanda

1960	Lourdes Van-Dúnem with N'gola Ritmos, 'Monami'
1968	Luis Visconde, 'Chofer de Praça'
1972	Os Kiezos, 'Milhórró'
1973	Urbano de Castro, 'Rosa Maria'
1973	David Zé, 'Rumba Zatukine'
1974	Jovens do Prenda, 'Lamento da Mãe'
1978	Belita Palma, 'Astronauta', or 'Manazinha'
1979	Os Merengues, 'Sessa Mulemba'
1987	S.O.S., 'Carnaval'
1989	Paulo Flores, 'Cherry'
1992	Ruca Van-Dunem & Ricardo Abreu, 'Manhã de Domingo'
1993	Eduardo Paim, 'Rosa Baila'
1993	Gabi Moy, 'Vizinha Zongola'
1997	Versáteis, 'Casamento'
1998	S.S.P., 'Canta Comigo (Essa Keta)'
1999	Sebem, 'Felicidade'
2001	Virgilio Faia, 'Kazucuta Dança'
2010	Cabo Snoop, 'Windeck'
2015	Kyaku Kyadaff, 'Tanta Nkento'
2015	Yuri da Cunha ft. C4 Pedro, 'De Alma Na Paixão'

Lagos

1961	Victor Olaiya & His All-Stars, 'Moonlight Highlife'
1966	Ambrose Campbell, 'Yolanda'
1969	Sir Victor Uwaifo & His Melody Maestroes, 'Joromi'
1971	Fela Ransome Kuti & His Nigeria '70, 'Jeun K'oku (Chop and Quench)'
1974	Sunny Ade & His African Beats, 'Esubiri Ebo Mi'
1975	The Funkees, 'Ole'
1978	Sonny Okosuns, 'Fire in Soweto'
1986	Onyeka, 'One Love'
1988	Chief (Dr.) Sikiru Ayinde Barrister, *Fuji Garbage*
1998	The Remedies, 'Shako Mo'
2004	2face Idibia, 'African Queen'
2006	Weird MC, 'Ijoya'
2008	Jazzman Olofin ft. Adewale Ayuba, 'Raise The Roof'
2011	Daddy Showkey, 'Dyna'
2012	D'banj, 'Oliver Twist'
2015	Wizkid, 'Baba Nla'
2016	Runtown, 'Mad Over You'
2017	Davido, 'If'
2017	Tiwa Savage ft. Wizkid, 'Ma Lo'
2018	Burna Boy, 'On The Low'

Bristol

1979	The Pop Group, 'She Is Beyond Good and Evil'
1981	Talisman, 'Dole Age'
1981	Black Roots, 'Bristol Rock'
1982	Rip Rig & Panic, 'You're My Kind of Climate'
1989	Fresh 4 ft. Lizz.E, 'Wishing on a Star'
1990	Massive Attack, 'Any Love'
1991	Massive Attack, 'Unfinished Sympathy'
1993	Gary Clail & On-U Sound System, 'These Things Are Worth Fighting For'
1993	DJ Krust, 'The Resister'
1994	Portishead, 'Glory Box'
1995	Tricky, 'Aftermath'
1997	Roni Size/Reprazent, 'Brown Paper Bag'
2002	Smith & Mighty, 'B-Line Fi Blow'
2006	Pinch, 'Qawwali'
2007	Joker, 'Kapsize EP'
2007	RSD, 'Corner Dub (Blue & Red Mix)'
2008	Appleblim & Peverelist, 'Circling'
2013	Young Echo, 'Umoja'
2015	Ossia, 'Red X'
2018	Beak>, >>>

Lisbon

1981	Heróis do Mar, 'Brava Dança dos Heróis'
1982	António Variações, 'Estou Além'
1987	Pop Dell'Arte, 'Querelle'
1989	Ik Mux, 'Novo Estado Novo'
1991	Repórter Estrábico, 'Pois, Pois'
1992	LX-90, 'Da/Wha EP'
1994	Underground Sound Of Lisbon, 'So Get Up'
1994	Urban Dreams, 'An Urban Dream of Love'
2002	Spaceboys, 'Moonshrine/Eclipse EP'
2004	Kalaf + Type, 'Fado Superstar'
2008	Buraka Som Sistema, 'Sound of Kuduro'
2010	Gala Drop, 'Rauze'
2010	Tiago, 'Disambiguation'
2010	Photonz, 'Aquarian Ball'
2012	The Discotexas Band, 'The Undertaker'
2012	Batida, 'Alegria'
2013	Branko ft. Zebra Katz, 'Rolling'
2014	Nigga Fox, 'Zen'
2017	Switchdance, 'O Amolador'
2018	DJ Lilocox, 'Paz & Amor EP'

TEN CITIES
Clubbing in Nairobi, Cairo, Kyiv, Johannesburg, Naples, Berlin, Luanda, Lagos, Bristol, Lisbon 1960–March 2020

Edited by
Johannes Hossfeld Etyang,
Joyce Nyairo, Florian Sievers

A project of Goethe-Institut
Published by Spector Books

Preface p.9
Johannes Ebert

Editorial p.11
Johannes Hossfeld Etyang, Joyce Nyairo, Florian Sievers

In the Labs of the Century
Part 1: Music/Spaces p.17
Johannes Hossfeld Etyang

NAIROBI

MUSIC/SPACES
Ngoma Nites
From Rumba and Benga to NuNairobi

| Ngoma Nites – From Rumba and Benga to the digital revolution Joyce Nyairo and Bill Odidi | Nairobi, 2018 Mukami Kuria and Sellanga Ochieng' (Blinky Bill) |

 P.37

SPACES/POLITICS
A Matter of Salvation
Politics of Music and Space in Nairobi

| The 1960s: An Evolving City Peter Wafula Wekesa | The 1970s–1990s: A Mobile City Joyce Nyairo | The 2000s–2010s: A Multiple City Mukami Kuria |

 P.63

CAIRO

MUSIC/SPACES
The Cacophony of Cairo
A Battle of Narratives
Maha ElNabawi P.87

SPACES/POLITICS
Clubbing in an Oppressive City
Musical and Social Spheres from Al-Haram Street to Tahrir Square
Ali Abdel Mohsen P.113

KYIV

MUSIC/SPACES
It's So Sad I Want to Dance
The Fractions of Kyiv's Club Music
Vitalii Bard Bardetski P.145

SPACES/POLITICS
Metallists and Neformaly
From Soviet Enculturation to Recent Night Economies
Kateryna Dysa P.167

JOHANNESBURG

MUSIC / SPACES
Dangerous Combinations and Skeem Sam Foundations
The Most Beautiful Black City in Africa?
Rangoato Hlasane  P.193

SPACES / POLITICS
Imaginary Republics
Dancing after Dark in Johannesburg
Sean O'Toole P.215

NAPLES

MUSIC / SPACES
Under the Volcano
From Caruso to Neapolitan Power and Vesuwave to Techno
Danilo Capasso P.241

SPACES / POLITICS
Neapolitan Nights
From Vesuvian Blues to Planetary Vibes
Vincenzo Cavallo and Iain Chambers  P.263

BERLIN

MUSIC / SPACES
Dancing in the Niches
How the City's Free Spaces Nurtured Avant-Garde Music
Florian Sievers P.289

SPACES / POLITICS
Do it Yourself
Looking for Freedom in Constant Collapse
Tobias Rapp  P.311

LUANDA

MUSIC / POLITICS
Hums and Buzzes
From Semba to Kuduro
Marissa J. Moorman  P.337

SPACES / POLITICS
Movements on a Map of Sounds
Luanda's Dual Urban Matrix
Ângela Mingas  P.359

LAGOS

MUSIC / SPACES
Throw to Me and I Throw Back to You
From Jùjú and Fuji to Afrobeat and 9ja Lamba

Mallam Mudi Yahaya  P.387

SPACES / POLITICS
Circadian Rhythms
The Many Layers of Lagos

Mallam Mudi Yahaya  P.409

BRISTOL

MUSIC / SPACES
A Village Dancing to its Own Beat
Dub-rooted Values in a Tightly Knit Music Scene

Tony Benjamin  P.437

SPACES / POLITICS
Bristol Mixes
Underground, Identity, and the City

Rehan Hyder and Michelle Henning  P.459

LISBON

MUSIC / SPACES
The Soundtrack of a City, the Pulse of a Country
From Yé-Yé to African Lisbon

Rui Miguel Abreu P.487

SPACES / POLITICS
Time Capsule Lisbon
Revolution, Hangovers, Hedonism

Vítor Belanciano P.509

In the Labs of the Century
Part 2: Spaces / Politics   p.537
Johannes Hossfeld Etyang

Preface

I first met Mahmoud Refaat in 2003 when I was director of the Goethe-Institut in Cairo. He was working with musicians from Berlin, weaving sounds from Germany and Egypt into a global soundscape of new West-Eastern stories. This collaboration was part of our attempt to reinterpret the cultural exchange between Europe and the Arab world in response to the speechlessness that followed the events of September 11, 2001. We worked with independent cultural centres, made our facilities available to the local communities as open spaces of exchange, and started co-productions between these communities. Some seven years later, around 2010, the Goethe-Institut in Nairobi initiated a project in which Mahmoud Refaat played a crucial role again, now both as a music curator for his hometown, Cairo, and as a musician with his band Bikya. Ten Cities, carried out by Goethe-Institut in Nairobi together with other Goethe-Institut branches and their partners, even surpassed our approach, with the degree of co-production and interconnectedness, but also with the extent of research and critical reflection. Ten Cities created a network of music and knowledge production between Berlin, Bristol, Cairo, Johannesburg, Kyiv, Lagos, Lisbon, Luanda, Nairobi, and Naples.

Ten Cities was a co-production project for club music. Between 2012 and 2014, the project brought together fifty club music producers, DJs, and musicians from the ten cities in Africa and Europe. They were selected by a local curator in each city – Refaat was the curator for Cairo – to produce new music. The music project resulted in an album (*Soundway Records*, London, 2014).

However, Ten Cities was also a research project, charting a global narrative between Europe and Africa. A story in which a well-known hub of club culture, such as Berlin, is an important protagonist, but only one among ten, each of them in possession of their own pop music roots, each of them recording their own history. After periods of research and work, starting in 2010, the authors and publishers met during the music production phase in April 2013 at the Goethe-Institut in Nairobi for a seminar to share their experiences before parting again to continue their work back home. The research project resulted in this book with the title *Ten Cities*.

This book tells the story of pop music in these ten cities from 1960 to the present. Well-known cities of music appear alongside places whose musical history had been little researched to date. When I arrived in Kyiv, as a young director of the Goethe-Institut in the mid-1990s, I knew nothing about the vibrant club scene that was emerging, even though encounters between German and Ukrainian DJs or experimental electronic productions had already started to play an important role in our programme. The book *Ten Cities* addresses such ignorance and proves the idea that music cultures are much more local, differentiated, equal, and exciting than many might expect.

As well as this, *Ten Cities* draws intimate portraits of cities, of their music cultures, their club cultures and thus, also of the societies from which they evolve and which they, in turn, influence. In this respect, the book is enlightening and helps us to appreciate something that is easily overlooked in these hidden cultures of the night. Something which I have also merely glimpsed during my time in Kyiv and Cairo. Club cultures create free spaces that can be laboratories for future societies, laboratories for experimentation with attitudes and ways of life, which slowly permeate into wider society and may even, at some point, determine the mainstream: Today you can hear Techno in every taxi in Kyiv.

The Goethe-Instituts around the world see themselves as platforms of cultural exchange bringing together artists and cultural producers. *Ten Cities* is an example of this, both in its structure and its content. Just as musicians from the different localities collaborated on a joint production for the music project, authors from within the local scenes wrote for this book, sharing their expertise in the respective music and pop cultures of their cities. This results in representations of high credibility and authenticity that offer new insights and perspectives to the reader.

The last time I met Mahmoud Refaat was in the Ritter Butzke club in Berlin in 2015. It was the conclusion of the music part of Ten Cities, the launch of the album, and musicians from all ten cities who had taken part in the project had come together for one night. We were both enthusiastic about the reunion, the intensity of the networks that had developed between musicians and DJs, the diversity of the music, and the freedom that perhaps only club cultures can offer. We were looking forward to this book, which invites us to immerse ourselves in ten club cultures and their stories from the 1960s to the present day.

Johannes Ebert, Secretary General, Goethe-Institut

Editorial

Johannes Hossfeld Etyang, Joyce Nyairo, Florian Sievers

When the sun sets behind the horizon, the same scene can be observed all over the world these days: people get ready to go out into the night, they visit clubs or bars, some with makeshift dance floors, and they throw their hands in the air, swaying to dance music; momentarily forgetting their activities and worries of the day. Nocturnal raving, partying, and clubbing has become a global phenomenon, it seems. It is everywhere.

But what is this everywhere? And is it the same everywhere? The histories of House music and Techno that currently dominate the narratives of nightlife in the global media, follow a mostly exclusive North Atlantic lineage along the centres Detroit-Chicago-Manchester-London-Berlin–and perhaps the Bass Culture branch in, and from, the Caribbean. This mainstream narrative suggests the existence of centralised hubs and more remote appendices. Viewed from this perspective, many Northern hemisphere cities between Novosibirsk and Vancouver, Reykjavík and Tel Aviv, are peripheral. Among those are European cities like Naples, Kyiv, or Lisbon. Equally important, this tale of the North-Atlantic mainstream ignores urban centres in other parts of the world –especially African cities.

The latter omission is particularly problematic. Africa has enjoyed a contemporaneity that consists of a multitude of the most diverse and active club cultures for more than sixty years. While the traffic, balance of trade and cultural influence might continue to favour the West, soundtracks link Africa and the rest of the world in a continuous flow from the southern hemisphere to the North and vice versa. African cultures have constantly added ideas, genres, and sounds into the global clubbing mainstream. It could even be argued that many of the elemental components of contemporary clubbing were first practised in Africa. This book challenges the prevailing image of centres and periphery in both the North and the South by examining the circulation, flows, and transnationalism that attend to music. To do this, *Ten Cities* tells the story of club music and club culture in portraits of ten club cities in Africa and Europe.

We set the starting point for this study around the year 1960–a time of youth subcultures, of social movements, and political upheavals on both continents. 1960 is sometimes referred to as the 'Year of Africa', the year when Independence swept across the continent in many places. In the North, the new social movements and dissident movements of opposition were shaking up their societies, often aligning themselves with the anti-colonial struggle for Independence in the South.

We chose ten cities–in alphabetical order, they are Berlin, Bristol, Johannesburg, Cairo, Kyiv, Lagos, Lisbon, Luanda, Nairobi, and Naples, which we present in the order of their geographical situation from East to West. In twenty essays and photo series, *Ten Cities* (re)constructs the musical narratives of these cities, piecing together different scenes, subcultures, and their global networks. In addition, this book offers a two-part essay on the overall theoretical framework of our approach.

Our approach was developed from the perspective of a certain place and time: Nairobi around the year 2010. Ten Cities was a project of the Goethe-Institut Nairobi.[1] Music production was a focus of the activities at the institute, which was—together with its partners in the scene, in Kenya and elsewhere—fascinated by the past and present of club music in East Africa and beyond: its barely fathomable complexity, its multi-local belongings, cosmopolitanisms, and transnational networks. It was clear that this music was not just a soundtrack to mindless partying and irrelevant quotidian practice, leaving behind nothing but the remains of the night; a bleak, quiet room, and a hangover. Instead, these cultures of clubbing opened up sound spaces in the city and thereby generated political relevance. From this perspective, the connection between club cultures, the political, and the urban condition came into view: to journey into the sound worlds of club cultures also means to journey into city worlds and political worlds of cities. The result is an urban and political rhythm-analysis from the viewpoint of sound and night.

Writing music history in combination with political and urban history corresponds with the structure of this book. It forms a matrix of twenty essays in two sets. The first set, which is the first essay on each city, recounts the music histories and the stories of different scenes, subcultures, and spaces. This essay series is a response to the fact that club culture has a legendary significance in most cities, but—with the exception of Berlin and perhaps Bristol and Johannesburg—neither the presence of club music nor its history has ever been documented in detail. Those who were there at the time are, of course, in the know, but beyond this limited circle, little knowledge has been handed down. There is nothing new to 'discover' here, but there is a lot to document and to share, because you have to know about it in order to hear, choose, and value what is there. This first set of essays cover the fields of music, pop, and the subcultures' histories. It is tagged 'Music/Spaces'.

The sound spaces are the connecting element to the second essay on each city. This second set explores the meaning of the previously described music genres, scenes, and spaces. The meaning is always interpreted in relation to the political nature of that urban society. Club cultures are read as prisms and laboratories of society and the city. The sonic spheres of clubs are regarded as public spheres—albeit different to the public spheres as understood in the common concept of the political sphere. This second set is tagged 'Spaces/Politics', and the essays draw from urban studies, and social and political theory.

The choice of these ten cities had to be arbitrary since our approach would have qualified many cities for the selection. Our selection also stems from a localisation: from the two places where the editors, as well as the organisers of the music co-productions, lived at the launch of the project: Nairobi and Berlin. From there we followed our networks and identified people we could collaborate with. We chose cities with a rich subculture and a vibrant political life. The revolutionary changes that were

---

[1] The project Ten Cities consisted of a research section that led to this book as well as a practical programme of musical co-productions. For the latter, fifty club music producers, DJs, and musicians selected by local curators from the ten cities visited each other between 2012 and 2014 to produce new music together. The programme was organized by the Goethe-Institut Nairobi and the Berlin music collective Adaptr.org in collaboration with the Goethe-Instituts in Sub-Saharan Africa. The resulting compilation, *Ten Cities*, has been released on CD, vinyl, and digitally by Soundway Records in London.

taking place in several of the cities examined here, while we worked on this book, are telling. Prominent cities with an established music industry were to be included, but also those that are less obvious and where the cities' imagination is circulated less widely in the global media.

As mentioned before, it was important to us that the selection would counteract the mainstream North Atlantic narrative of club cultures. This reframing, the choice of African and European cities, seemed timely to us because the African stories, in particular, are underrepresented in the mainstream history of club cultures. It is important to recognise, in this regard, that almost all of Africa today is a post-colony. Recognising this fact acknowledges the legacies of colonialism that still linger on the continent. It also salutes the residual ethnic cultures, which have percolated over the years and across physical landscapes to invade cities and turn urbanism into a colourful blend of past and present.

The issue hereby is not whether or not Africans in cities see themselves as peripheral to the economic and cultural practices of the West. The issue is that they regard themselves in communion with these practices. On the one hand, able to match or mimic these practices, to challenge them, to appropriate and re-institute them in ways that give these Western practices new meanings within African lives. On the other hand, that communion happens when Africans feed their own practices back into the global circulations of club music and cultures.

Lastly, it was important to us to explore differences and commonalities in patterns of cultural practices at the moment in time when the Mediterranean had become a more, and more heavily policed border and death zone between Africa and Europe; when cross-border exchanges seem increasingly precarious even within Europe. Now more than ever, we would like to remind ourselves of these locally specific cultures of music that have simultaneously been part of one of the most intense trans-local and transnational contexts that culture had to offer over the last sixty years, if not longer.

As this book goes to print, the Covid-19 pandemic has taken an unfathomable toll on creative communities around the world. Club culture, as we knew it, has been eclipsed, at least for now. This book is also a testimony to a convivial spirit that is sure to outlive the pandemic.

—

This book is the project of a group of three editors and twenty-five authors: cultural scientists, music journalists, club activists, musicologists, urbanists, and historians. Since 2013, they have collaborated in a collective and parallel process. They did not write as explorers from the outside but, from within their own scenes, whose networks their research is based on, and scenes to which they remain committed. They are born in these cities, they live in them, or at least have a long research relationship with the scene and city.

Although the authors write from within the different scenes, they were all challenged by a conjecture that is typical of our research topic: club cultures may be strongly referential to the past, but at the same time they are ephemeral – of the moment, of experience in the here and now, often also of the secret life. Club nights are not about documentation.

Recording, and quite often even photography, is prohibited. Thus, club cultures are more short-lived, and more evanescent than other cultures. Nowadays only a few scenes have begun, sometimes with a delay of several years or decades, to collect their oral history and record it as their own narrative. Most of the stories, however, are hardly documented, recorded, and made available on the basis of a broader knowledge base. Nor are they fed into the circuits of knowledge economies. So, these stories have never reached a local audience that was not there at the time nor an audience in distant places that is dedicated to music and its different cultures.

Often, archives have not helped – not in Europe and certainly not in Africa. Archives are sites for the performance of power; the power to determine what is remembered and what is forgotten; archives become a law that determines what can and cannot be said. Invariably then, archives have been limited to official state discourse, disinterested in the quotidian ways in which people express and define their identities and aspirations. This is particularly so in the context of post-colonial Africa – outside of South Africa and parts of Northern Africa – where reflecting on popular culture is a race against amnesia and erasure. This book then aims to be a monument to forgotten histories.

Beyond the politics of archives, there lies the additional challenge of the nature of popular culture as transient and fleeting. Trends change just as quickly as newspaper reports of them are scattered and lost. Thus, the authors who worked to trace records on popular music dating back to the 1960s used a variety of methods that affirm the legitimacy of both popular music and private remembrances – whether oral or written in letters and diaries – as history.

No wonder then that many authors in this book entered uncharted territory with their research. They had to unravel the narratives of a scene, identify and interview key players, scour through newspaper archives, and unearth music libraries – if indeed there were any. In this respect, this book cannot be more than an incomplete contribution. There simply is no room here to include the further research that would be required for a complete account, the surfeit of topics that would have to be pursued and expanded on, the multitude of perspectives that would have to be considered. Nothing that is written here claims to be conclusive, exhaustive, or even official and authoritative.

Both methodically and stylistically, the essays are as different as their authors. They do, however, share a common consensual framework of inquiry which underpins both essay sets of the book, with each author employing it in his or her own way. There is an overlap in their subject areas and fields of reference, they complement each other or often engage in lively dialogue. Because of its conception as a block of twenty essays, this book can be used to immerse oneself fully in one of the cities, or read comparatively through both sets. Thus, you can stay with the musical narratives with the first set and jump from one city to the next. Or, readers who would rather follow the books' further idea that club cultures are always also a narrative of 'other families' (of the political sphere) and of spatial life with sound (of the city) can move on to the second set of texts. Finally, anyone who wants to know what motivated this book is invited to read the two parts of the essay 'In the Labs of The Century' that is included here. It outlines the questions and problems of thinking dance music-politics-city, which set this book in motion.

In the Labs of the Century – Part 1: Music/Spaces

Johannes Hossfeld Etyang

The South African musician and author Todd Matshikiza was one of the central figures of the Sophiatown Renaissance of the 1950s. This period of abundant cultural production was concentrated in the Johannesburg suburb of the same name, and Matshikiza's 1959 Jazz opera, *King Kong*, was seen as one of its highlights. He also wrote for the legendary South African magazine *Drum* about music and the urban life in Johannesburg. It was specifically through his music criticism that Matshikiza created his own style of pop writing, which his colleagues called Matshikese. In one of his music reviews from 1957, Matshikiza recalled a party from the 1930s, during his childhood growing up in the Eastern Cape, thrown by the local Marabi musician Boet Gashe:

> *The location slept peacefully all night till just after midnight. At something like twenty past midnight the residents began to shift uneasily in their beds because the sound of the church bell at the Moravian Mission in Scanlan Street was clanging loud … And d'you know who was ringing the bell? GASHE … His organ was carted on a donkey truck from house to house, and wherever it moved, the people went … And the miners' veins were full with Jazz, as they were with women, and they got both at Gashe's Jazz sessions … Gashe's dances were called 'I-Tswari' where you paid at the*

door and entered into a dingy, stuffy room where the dust from the dancers' feet smothered the solitary paraffin lamp which flickered in the shadows of dancing partners who could hardly see or didn't know each other … But actually one saw nothing in that dust. Not even Gashe, who was bent over his organ in one corner, thumping the rhythm from the pedals with his feet, which were also feeding the organ with air; choking the organ with persistent chords in the right hand, and improvising for an effective melody with his left hand. He would call in the aid of a cuestick to hold down a harmonic note, usually the tonic (doh) or the dominant (son), both of which persist in African music, and you saw the delirious effect of perpetual motion. Perpetual motion. Perpetual motion in a musty hold where man makes friends without restraint.[1]

At the moment there is much talk of a 'global' club culture, both in the Northern and the Southern hemispheres. The image of the DJ jetting around the world with his case full of vinyl records, his laptop, or flash memory, calling a uniform audience to raise their hands in the air, is a stereotype of our time. The EDM industry, the US reinterpretation of Techno as a mainstream spectacle, is also opening up markets in the Global South; it is said to have turned over more than four billion US dollars in 2014 alone.[2] However, beneath this mainstream surface, club cultures, as hidden nocturnal cultures, are much more diverse, specific, and local than is suggested by the

[1] Todd Matshikiza, 'The Stars of Jazz', *Drum*, June 1957, 37–41; On the 'sad note of depravity, self-abandon, sweet, sensuous dissipation' of Marabi cf. Es'kia Mphahlele, *Down Second Avenue* (London and Boston: Faber and Faber, 1959), 96f.

[2] Jim Poe, 'Electronic Music Conference celebrates Australia's booming dance scene', *The Guardian*, 6 December 2013, http://www.theguardian.com/music/australia-culture-blog/2013/dec/06/electronic-music-conference-flume-dance accessed 1 May 2014.

narrative of 'global' club culture – and they draw on a long history.

Dance and club cultures formed when people living in the anonymity of the city began to liberate themselves from old (rural and familial) dependencies and began to celebrate their new freedoms in the nightlife. In the cities of Europe, which grew due to industrialization and labour migration, this process started in the nineteenth century.[3] Since then, many European cities saw waves of 'dance fever', for example, around 1900 and after the First World War.

In African cities, it is not different. The Marabi party, as described by Todd Matshikiza, was organized for South African miners who stopped overnight in Queenstown on their commute between the rural Eastern Cape province and Johannesburg in the 1930s. This story is not a gateway to the exotic, rather an early and accurate example of the very same social practices that began to take on an increasingly global dimension. By the early 1960s, it was clear that a global phenomenon had emerged in urban centres of post-war Europe and various African states, many of which had just gained independence. Es'kia Mphahlele, who worked as a fiction editor for *Drum* from 1955 to 1957, made this point in 1964 when he wrote about music and clubbing in South Africa: 'And so an urban culture has evolved.'[4]

This social and cultural practice, clubbing, is a culture of music, as well as a culture of space. The party described by Matshikiza is evidence of that. The physical sounds,

[3] This process was accelerated by an increase in the disposable income and leisure time of young people that allowed them to establish their own music cultures. On the early history of teenagers cf. Jon Savage, *Teenage: The Creation of Youth Culture* (New York: Viking Books, 2007); on London street culture and the Twopenny-hops of the Costermongers around 1850 cf. Henry Mayhew, *London Labour & London Poor* (Hertfordshire: Wordsworth Classics, 2008), 16.

[4] In 1964, Mphahlele calls dance cultures 'urban culture' as part of the 'fabric of African culture' cf. Es'kia Mphahlele, 'The Fabric of African Culture', *Voices in the Whirlwind* (New York: Hill and Wang, 1972), 154; on the biography of the South African intellectual and founder of the African Literature Department at the University of the Witwatersrand cf. his two autobiographies *Down Second Avenue* (1957) and *Africa, My Music* (1984).

the vibrations, and frequencies of dance music, demarcate an inner and outer sphere. This form of inner sphere can come about anywhere. It does not necessarily require dedicated spaces such as dance halls, music clubs, ballrooms, or discos. The club can be any 'dingy, stuffy room' and 'musty hold' (as in the case of the Queenstown party remembered by Matshikiza) or rooms that are temporarily repurposed, like township *shebeens*, a pub, or a coffee bar (always with a jukebox), restaurants, cafés, school halls, barbershops, and in Africa, above all, churches.[5] Or private locations such as the blues parties in Bristol, the *stokvel* parties in Johannesburg or wedding celebrations in Cairo and Luanda. It can also be mobile spaces such as *felucca* boats in Cairo, or mini-bus taxis equipped with sound systems and music video screens that are a staple of musical life in almost all African cities. Outdoor areas: roads, taxi parking lots, markets, beaches or fields, like those used for raves, are also used as clubbing venues. Whatever the case, it is not the visible and physical walls that delineate the inner sound sphere, but the tangible walls made from the sound's materiality that establishes the space. This may occur at night or, less frequently, during the day.[6]

A multitude of sounds can be responsible for forming this space. The music may come from an organ, as the one Boet Gashe played for the miners, from a live band, a jukebox, a portable sound system, or the subwoofers of a mega club with a DJ spinning the decks. All of this – the diversity of the public culture of going out and dancing in

[5] That revellers are called to the Marabi party with church bells is no coincidence. The relationship between churches and clubs is so multi-layered, at least in African cities, that it would require its own investigation cf. inter alia the role of churches as music locations in Lagos in Mallam Mudi Yahaya's essays in this book.

[6] On the day/lunch time sessions in London in the 1960s cf. Tom Wolfe, 'The Noonday Underground', *The Pump House Gang* (New York: Farrar, Straus & Giroux, 1968).

spaces created by music – we call 'club culture'. In this book, 'club' is a shorthand for the totality of sound spaces people set up with dance music to get together and dance, in the absence of a better word. Whenever, and wherever this occurred. Whatever that meant or might mean in any one place at a time.

The musical histories of club cultures are worth writing about: This is the basic assumption of the first set of essays in this book, which are marked by the running header 'Music/Spaces'.[7] This overview essay introduces and elaborates some of the thoughts that characterise these locally specific music histories from ten cities. At the same time, we believe that the spatial histories that attend club cultures are just as important as the music histories of particular cities, and so this book features a second series of essays gathered the running header 'Spaces/Politics'. The motivations for this complementary focus on space, politics and the urban everyday are discussed in the second part of this overview essay (see pp. 537–554).

Asymmetries

The history of club music – the music that makes up club spaces – has been exhaustively told, occasionally with remarkable historical depth. This narrative is often centred around cities that serve as gateways: Kingston, Detroit, Philadelphia, Chicago, Manchester, Berlin, and so on. It is the subject of magazines, fanzines, and books.[8] There is no

[7] Cf. the essays by Rui Miguel Abreu, Vitalii Bard Bardetski, Tony Benjamin, Danilo Capasso, Maha ElNabawi, Rangoato Hlasane, Marissa J. Moorman, Joyce Nyairo and Bill Odidi, Florian Sievers, and Mudi Yahaya in this book.

[8] An overview of publications in English can be found at http://www.djhistory.com/books. For the study of electronic dance music culture, the excellent journal dj.dancecult.net. deserves a mention.

lack of literature, club music timelines, or topographies. Nevertheless, as the mainstream narratives continue to reiterate the known map of music, one cannot fail to notice blank spaces. Usually, the music map I refer to shows a North Atlantic axis between the industrialized north of the US and some central cities (and holiday islands) in Europe, plus perhaps the Bass Culture line in, and from the Caribbean. It is a history of just a few cities.

Take Europe, for example. You can read a lot about the UK rave scene from London to Manchester, Techno in Berlin, and there is the odd book about cities like Bristol, Munich, and Düsseldorf. But what about Lisbon, Naples, or Kyiv? It is not uncommon to hear tracks from many different places in Europe, including lesser-known ones. Nevertheless, even from places like Lisbon and Naples, this doesn't amount to much; only a few names are familiar. Not much is known about the breadth of contemporary club scenes, let alone those of the past. All of the cities featured in this book were club cities. Music was produced in each of them. They were nodes in trans-local networks and circuits of people, recordings, and equipment; in all these cities people danced. They are just missing from the standard narrative and its topography.

Another omission is even more perspicuous: The mainstream narrative of continuous transatlantic bass and beat does not contain any of the central hubs of club life on the African continent.[9] If African cities are marked on some of the maps, it is only as a mythical motherland of a vaguely distant past of music that had to become real

[9] Of course, while there are special niches of discourse for local research such as the anthropology of music, ethnomusicology, and African Studies, there is also extant knowledge on local scenes, e.g. published in fanzines. This book draws from such sources; more information can be found in the individual essays and their bibliographies. On the other hand, by 'traditional mainstream narrative' I mean those narratives that enjoy wide circulation across scenes and are often read as a comprehensive history of music.

music elsewhere, before it could make an impact on the world. Even after the 'origin' of 'traditional African music' the lines on the maps consistently bypass African cities.[10] As a general rule, the history of club culture is told without the African musical metropoles.

It is obvious that this is a dangerous erasure. The example of the Marabi party with which I started this essay is not a laboured exception. The club cultures in the areas between Cape Town and Cairo count among the most intense in the world. These cities have always been focal points for complex cosmopolitanisms and transcultural interchanges of music. They were points of exchange within a highly productive and intricate network of sounds and practices that were formed through the transit of recordings, instruments, and practices along with the journeys and tours of musicians, as well as their forced migration and exile.[11]

The same connections linked back from the cities into the trans-continental network. This exchange was often facilitated by individual intermediaries such as Ghanaba, who in the 1950s tried 'to underline the important part that Africa has played, and is still playing, to give depth to Jazz music' in the African Room in New York,[12] or Miriam Makeba, Hugh Masekela, or the aforementioned Todd Matshikiza, who emigrated to London in 1960.[13] This is about an elaborate trans-continental musical connection that contains far more than the 'Black Atlantic';[14] the Mediterranean Sea is a part of it, its African shore having always been portrayed as a 'negated elsewhere'.[15] In this

[10] All music histories are implicit cartographies. Some are also presented as maps. Significant examples include Osman Khan's map *How Music Travels–The Evolution of Western Dance Music*, <http://www.thomson.co.uk/blog/wp-content/uploads/infographic/interactive-music-map/index.html> which records 'traditional African music' as the starting point for a profusion of developments which then bypass the continent. Another example is *City of Pop*, the map of the world published in 2008 by the German radio station Zündfunk. It was supposed to be a 'musical street map of the world'. But in spite of its breadth, it contains only few names from the African scenes, such as DJ Mujava from South Africa and Esau Mwamwaya from The Very Best.

[11] The ten cities are also characterized by the same technical developments. Dance music has been universally electrified since the 1960s: electromechanical sounds from electric guitars and Bass define dance music in all ten cities, and PA systems define the sonic spaces of dance. The advent of synthesizers in the 1960s, drum computers, sequencers, and samplers in the 1980s and digital production software in the 1990s revolutionized dance music in all the cities covered in this book, albeit in slightly different timescales.

[12] Cf. Ghanaba's letter to *Time Magazine* in October 1962 cf. Guy Warren, *I have a story to tell* (Accra: Ghanaian Press, 1962), 169.

[13] Cf. Todd Matshikiza, *Chocolates for my Wife* (London: Hodder & Stoughton, 1961).

[14] This book obviously owes a lot to Paul Gilroy's work. On the critique of the lack of African contexts in Gilroy's book on the Black Atlantic as well as the hint that cultural contexts ought to be recognized beyond the Atlantic cf. Neil Lazarus, 'Is a Counterculture of Modernity a Theory of Modernity?', *Diaspora* 4, no. 3 (1995), 323–339.

[15] On the Mediterranean as a zone of exchange cf. Iain Chambers, *Mediterranean Crossings: the Politics of an Interrupted Modernity* (Durham: Duke University Press, 2008), 52; on the Black Mediterranean cf. Cedric Robinson, *Black Marxism: The Making of the Black Radical Tradition* (Chapel Hill, NC: University of North Carolina Press, 1999), viz. the foreword by Robin D.G. Kelly, xiv.

regard African cities have always been connected; they were coeval.[16] In a complex way, dance music was already plural and global at the time, long before it became digital.

The fact that, in a global context, the here and now of African cities does not play any role in the narratives of club culture is bizarre. Anyone who has set foot in any African city today will hear the importance club and dance music hold straight away. Take Nairobi's mini-bus taxis, or *matatus*.[17] They are already like mobile clubs, music videos play inside, disco lights flash outside, and the bass booms. *Matatus* are part of the infrastructure used by the clubbers in Nairobi to move on their trajectories around the city, from club to club. On a Friday evening, this circuit is also a circuit through the music cultures of Nairobi. Inside one club, Kenyan Benga sounds out onto the street, from the next, Congolese Rumba, which the band has played there unchanged for decades; you see the clubbers dancing with style and a sense of history. Around the corner you hear the basses of Kenya's latest club hits, the omnipresent autotune Naija pop, Tanzanian Bongo Flava, South African House, with all styles from the complex circuits of continuous bass and beats of the Black Atlantic, plus the international charts. On these trajectories from sound sphere to sound sphere, the clubbers appropriate their musical city in a nocturnal community, which is bound together by sound.

If you were to compare the number of music and club choices on the average weekend in an African city – be it

[16] Cf. Johannes Fabian's classic *Time and the Other* (New York: Columbia University Press, 2014), 31.

[17] Just A Band's Blinky Bill Sellanga remembers his musical education in Nairobi's matatus in Bill Sellanga, 'Nairobi–Matatus and a Lack of Dancefloors', 2 July 2013, <http://blog.goethe.de/ten-cities/archives/22-Nairobi-Matatus-and-a-Lack-of-Dancefloors-by-Bill-Sellanga.html>; Mbũgua wa Mũngai also writes about mini-buses being musical locations and public spheres in Nairobi in *Nairobi's Matatu Men*, no. 7 (Nairobi: Contact Zones NRB, 2013); For Luanda's 'taxis' cf. Ângela Mingas' essay in this book; for Johannesburg and its car-music-culture cf. Xavier Livermoon, 'Sounds in the City', in Sarah Nuttall and Achille Mbembe (eds.), *Johannesburg* (Durham, N.C.: Duke University Press, 2008), 274f.

Nairobi, Lagos, or Johannesburg – with that of a similarly sized European city, the first would come out on top. And it is not as if only chart Hip-Hop or mainstream EDM was danced here. Local music is produced everywhere. Dance styles and club practices are developed and become trends that spread across the cities and throughout the diaspora. The cities stand for local and regional music styles and genres – while simultaneously chasing after the latest trends from other parts of the world that suit their local audiences. The products of music industries like that of Nigeria and South Africa, which are listened to all over the continent, play an important role in the economy of their respective countries. Club music cultures have always been a lot more differentiated, and thus more versatile, more specific, and more local, than the term 'global' club culture implies.

Selectors and selections

From time to time, sounds and beats from the global South appear in the supposed music capitals of the North and are played in New York, London, and Berlin – audience dance to it, even beyond using 'Africa as a gimmick'.[18] A cogent example may have been the moment when DJ Mujava's 'Township Funk' became a small hit in Europe and one caught a glimpse of South African DJs being massive stars in their country. Or perhaps when Angolan Kuduro was played in European and US clubs and Buraka Som Sistema produced for Santigold, when the Nigerian

[18] Warren, *I have a story to tell* (see n.12), 170.

superstar D'Banj appeared on the UK charts and Wizkid was even more successful. Or when the *New York Times* wrote about the Kenyan group Just A Band and took the opportunity to talk about a 'creative ferment' south of the Sahara.[19]

The article on Just A Band was well informed and important to the group, but it also revealed a deeper truth: the reception framework for music and art from Africa. The excellent blog africaisacountry.com ran the title: '#Breaking: *New York Times* discovers African artists use the Internet'.[20] Reading between the lines of the NYT article, it is clear that the newspaper's reading public is oblivious to what has happened culturally in African cities over the past few decades. When it does find out, it prefers to read such messages within a certain logic. The NYT article packages the topic of music and literature with the narrative of modernisation and technological advancement. Within the universal logic of modernist progress, whose normative standard is the North, coevalness is immediately denied. Yet, there was nothing 'new' to discover; one could have started listening and dancing a long time ago.

From the opposite point of view, looking from the South at the North, the situation is quite different. Musicians, producers, bookers, and club operators in African cities have always cultivated extensive networks with the global North.[21] They know more about the North than the North knows about the South. But they are also selective. The current hits of Dancehall, Hip-Hop, and Charts in

[19] Nicholas Kulish, 'African Artists, Lifting the Promises of Democracy and the Web', *New York Times*, 1 September 2014.

[20] Zachary Rosen, '#Breaking: *New York Times* discovers African artists use the Internets', africaisacountry.com, 17 January 2014, https://africasacountry.com/2014/01/breaking-new-york-times-discovers-african-artists-use-the-internets/ accessed 1 May 2014; on the subject of the discovery of supposedly exotic club cultures cf. Boima Tucker, 'Global Genre Accumulation', africasacountry.com, 22 November 2011, <http://africasacountry.com/2011/11/22/globalgenre-accumulation> accessed 1 May 2014, my regards to Ntone Edjabe for the reference.

[21] On the subject of transnational cultural activity cf. George Lipsitz, *Dangerous Crossroads* (New York: Verso Books, 1997).

North America are played on loop in African clubs. Electronic club music, however, is still relatively new. The more experimental varieties from Europe and the USA are hardly played. If a map were to be drawn with Nairobi at its centre, it would be surrounded by other Kenyan cities with musical links. The next major music capitals marked on the map might be Kampala, Dar es Salaam, and Kinshasa. Other major cities, a bit more distant, would be Lagos, Durban, and Johannesburg. The international capitals, however, would be the US cities of the Hip-Hop continuum and, above all, Kingston. From this perspective, Detroit-Berlin-London would be a musical periphery; an irrelevant suburbia.

We are dealing with two blind spots here. One has to do with how club music works. Club cultures are local; they operate as locally selective cultures. Whether in Nairobi or New York: selectors are always looking for the latest trends worldwide and the best rediscoveries if they are able to detect them. But the discoveries have to stand the test before their own audience, and in their own space. Until recently, the straight beats of Techno and House have not stirred much interest in Kenyan audiences in Nairobi, precisely because they were unsuited to local club culture with its dance styles, spaces, and social practices. They seemed clumsy and unsexy, without any sense of movement, music history, or style.[22] In recent years, the influence of House has changed this: but in the South African variant, which is more syncopated.

[22] See also Mphahlele's observation of dancers at Cy Laurie's Club in London in 1959: *The African Image* (New York: Frederick A. Praeger Publisher, 1962), 211.

Even relationships in the dub continuum often do not work directly. For the African club scenes, the underwater dancehall, as it arrives from places like Bristol, is too dark and trippy. Even in terms of technology, the clubs are designed for different sound frequencies. Similarly, for the European club audience, Kuduro was one of the few African music styles that break through into clubbing communities. Club cultures are fussy, taste-conscious cultures that frequently thrive on distinctions and create their very particular trans-local networks. They are aware of this. It is all the more important to know as much as possible and to be able to draw on the greatest possible archive and understanding.

The second blind spot has to do with the North's perception of the South: the club scenes of the North barely register the club scenes in African cities. The relationship is asymmetrical.[23] Yet this also depends on which narratives circulate beyond the specialized niches of academia. It is a question of a knowledge economy. Those who usually draw the maps, write music history from the vantage point of prominent cities of the North.[24] From there they write about their networks; they draw maps from their particular perspective. And it is usually only they who can then feed these stories into global circuits via the media. Thus, they define the status (and universality) of music scenes. Their stories appear as world history, based on the effect of simple availability and the domination of certain stories over others. However, the story could be told quite differently

[23] For general notes on the asymmetric ignorance of the global North (of 'Europe' in Chakrabarty) cf. Dipesh Chakrabarty, *Provincializing Europe* (Princeton: Princeton University Press, 2000), 29.

[24] On omissions and revisionism in music history cf. Greg Tate, *Everything But the Burden: What White People Are Taking From Black Culture* (New York: Broadway Books, 2003); on the restitution of places like black Detroit cf. Dan Sicko, *Techno Rebels: The Renegades of Electronic Funk* (New York: Billboard, 1999).

from a different perspective, and then other music, other people, other styles would become important; other geographies and other centres would become relevant.

In digital modernity, this changes quite a bit, especially due to platforms such as africaisacountry.com or musicinafrica.net. But it is not nearly enough. It is all the more important to know more, to make more music archives accessible, to tell more stories – to write counter-narratives, to feed them into the circuits of knowledge economies. This book is such a project. *Ten Cities* is for local audiences interested in their cities' music histories; it is also for audiences in distant places, for people interested in club music and its many cultures.

Writing club cultural histories

The essays marked by the running header 'Music/Spaces' describe music history, which is always a history of music spaces as well. They are drafts towards a mainstream narrative of music histories from cities largely without such narrative. The locations in this framework include music histories that have largely been written,[25] as well as music histories that are barely documented and little known beyond their discrete communities (who maintain and circulate them). In addition, we diverge from the exclusively North Atlantic music history and turn the frame to bring ten cities – five in Africa and as many in Europe – into view. 'Africa' and 'Europe' are terms that must be used in quotation marks within this approach, because in this

[25] For Berlin cf. the exemplary books by Tobias Rapp, Theo Lessour, Wolfgang Farkas, Stefanie Seidl, Heiko Zwirner; for Bristol cf. the books of Chris Burton, Gary Thompson, and Phil Johnson; for Nairobi cf. the works of Joyce Nyairo as well as the CD series on Kenyan music history published by Ketebul Music; for Johannesburg cf. the books of David B. Coplan and Christopher Ballantine.

complex (concurrently local and translocal) context there is no 'essential unification or identification, especially not the geographical'.[26] Or if so, then it is in a decidedly strategic sense.

[26] Cf. Jacques Derrida's lecture in Cotonou in 1979: 'The Crisis in the Teaching of Philosophy', *Who's afraid of Philosophy? Right to Philosophy I* (Stanford: Stanford University Press 2002), 108; on the problem of origins, roots, and authenticity – and a specific definition of family cf. Paul Gilroy, *The Black Atlantic* (London: Verso, 1993), 96.

This book is not an attempt to redraw – and finally correct – the music topography, or to provide music history with an accurate geography of centrality. It does not poll, rank, or explicitly compare club scenes, whatever form that should take, which would also allow a modernist history of development and progress to creep in, again. The selection of ten cities is based on an attempt at telling coeval music histories in ten locations, all of which have at one stage or another been hubs in the complex networks of a global nexus forged by dance music and its cultures of clubbing.

The fact that we go back more than half a century and start around 1960 (this varies from text to text) is important for the music histories; without this deeper sense of reflection, they would be incomplete and superficial. The glorious past of dance music in the ten cities must be part of the histories. Sometimes it is necessary to reach back even further, for example to the Jazz scene of 1950s Sophiatown in Johannesburg, to Halim El-Dabh and the Big Four in 1940s Cairo or to Oskar Sala in 1930s Berlin. To evoke and to love that period's music is valuable not only in terms of the re-examination of contemporary electronic dance music whose retromania and hauntology cannot be understood otherwise. It is a past that has never been forgotten by present club culture. Dance music blends the layers of time – and not just because the past has been rendered conveniently accessible in the form of samples.

The authors of the various music histories in the first set of essays – as the authors of the second set of essays in this book – either live in the cities they write about, or have researched them thoroughly over a significant period of time. Because of this, they are not outsiders reporting on exotic musics; rather, they write from within the club scenes themselves. This is in recognition of the fact that 'there is always an ongoing discourse'.[27] If there is a sense of discovery present, it is one of self-discovery. For the position taken by this book, this is crucial.

Writing from within, the authors command a synoptic overview of their local or chosen club scenes. They offer a broad view of their club scenes rather than of individual heroes.[28] Their essays mention many protagonists and locations. As a result, the essays marked by the running header 'Music/Spaces' often resemble sourcebooks rather than polished linear narratives. Of course, they do not want to be seen as complete or final – and certainly not as official and canonical. The essays are intended as stopovers and starting points; they collate club-scene knowledge and aggregate detailed research; rhetorically, they favour breadth over depth.

One outcome of this sonic mapping is the essays tend to replicate the imbalances within the club scenes, notably

[27] Oli Oguibe, editorial, 'Heart of Darkness', *Third Text* 7, no. 23 (June 1993); also, in *The Culture Game* (Minneapolis: University of Minnesota, 2004).

[28] On the 'scenius' of club music scenes cf. Brian Eno, 'Luminous Media Conference', 26 May 2009, <http://www.moredarkthanshark.org/feature_luminous2.html> accessed 5 August 2012.

when it comes to gender in the field of production. The underrepresentation of women in music production, especially in electronic dance music, is evident in all the polls, leaderboards and discourses of club scenes[29] – and is also reflected in the names, lists, and essays in this book. For this reason the attempt at creating an overview – which we believe will be useful – always corresponds with the need for more research and more representation. There is a need for more music-historical and music-sociological writing on the ten cities profiled in this book, and a need for more research on the complex biographies flagged in this book; the lives of these vital protagonists merit being recorded and remembered.

The sphere of urban club cultures and its musical archives are limitless – and in its unforeseeable local and translocal dynamics, it is always one step ahead of any attempt at cataloguing it in a publication. Even the most contemporary moments referred to in this book will already be outdated and sampled as an archive by the time it reaches its public. This is unavoidable, and joyously so. 'You and I know there's no stopping the music,' says club manager Faith to Taneba, the night runner and first-person narrator of Nigerian author Maik Nwosu's 2001 novel *Alpha Song* about the 'believer[s] in the rhythm of the night' in Lagos. 'Music wants to go on and on, beyond all of us. Even when God decides to end the world, if Armageddon is not a fable, the water or whatever will make music on the bodies of the dead.'[30]

---

[29] Cf. the many important works by Angela McRobbie; Rebekah Farrugia, 'Sisterdjs in the House: Electronic/Dance Music and Women-centered Spaces on the Net', *Women's Studies*, communication 27, no. 2 (2004), 236–262; Birgit Richard, 'DJ-Jane Kicks und Acid Chicks', *Gendertronics* (Frankfurt am Main: edition suhrkamp, 2005); Fiona Hutton, *Risky Pleasures? Club Cultures and Feminine Identities* (Aldershot: Ashgate 2006); Rebekah Farrugia, *Beyond the Dance Floor: Female DJs, Technology and Electronic Dance Music Culture* (Bristol and Chicago: Intellect, 2012); Victoria Armstrong, *Technology and the Gendering of Music Education* (Farnham and Burlington: Ashgate 2011).

[30] Maik Nwosu, *Alpha Song* (Lagos: House of Malaika & Beacon Books, 2001), 172.

Bibliography

Armstrong, Victoria, *Technology and the Gendering of Music Education* (Farnham and Burlington: Ashgate, 2011).

Chakrabarty, Dipesh, *Provincializing Europe* (Princeton: Princeton University Press, 2000).

Chambers, Iain, *Mediterranean Crossings: The Politics of an Interrupted Modernity* (Durham: Duke University Press, 2008).

Fabian, Johannes, *Time and the Other* (New York: Columbia University Press, 2014).

Farrugia, Rebekah, 'Sisterdjs in the House: Electronic/Dance Music and Women-Centered Spaces on the Net', *Women's Studies*, communication 27, no. 2 (2004).

Farrugia, Rebekah, *Beyond the Dance Floor: Female DJs, Technology and Electronic Dance Music Culture* (Bristol and Chicago: Intellect, 2012).

Gilroy, Paul, *The Black Atlantic* (London: Verso, 1993).

Hutton, Fiona, *Risky Pleasures? Club Cultures and Feminine Identities* (Aldershot: Ashgate, 2006).

Jacques Derrida, 'The Crisis in the Teaching of Philosophy', *Who's afraid of Philosophy? Right to Philosophy I* (Stanford: Stanford University Press, 2002).

Kulish, Nicholas, 'African Artists, Lifting the Promises of Democracy and the Web', *New York Times*, 1 September 2014.

Lazarus, Neil, 'Is a Counterculture of Modernity a Theory of Modernity?', *Diaspora 4*, no. 3 (1995), 323–339.

Lipsitz, George, *Dangerous Crossroads* (New York: Verso Books, 1997).

Livermoon, Xavier, 'Sounds in the City', in Nuttall, Sarah and Mbembe, Achille (eds.), *Johannesburg* (Durham, NC: Duke University Press, 2008).

Matshikiza, Todd, 'The Stars of Jazz', *Drum*, June 1957, 37–41.

Matshikiza, Todd, *Chocolates for my Wife* (London: Hodder & Stoughton, 1961).

Mayhew, Henry, *London Labour & London Poor* (Hertfordshire: Wordsworth Classics, 2008)

Mphahlele, Es'kia, 'The Fabric of African Culture', *Voices in the Whirlwind* (New York: Hill and Wang, 1972).

Mphahlele, Es'kia, *Down Second Avenue* (London and Boston: Faber and Faber, 1959).

Mphahlele, Es'kia, *The African Image* (New York: Frederick A. Praeger Publisher, 1962).

Mūngai, Mbūgua wa, *Nairobi's Matatu Men:* Portrait of a Subculture (Nairobi: Contact Zones NRB, 2013).

Nwosu, Maik, *Alpha Song* (Lagos: House of Malaika & Beacon Books, 2001).

Oguibe, Oli, editorial, 'Heart of Darkness', *Third Text 7*, no. 23 (June 1993); also in *The Culture Game* (Minneapolis: University of Minnesota, 2004).

Poe, Jim, 'Electronic Music Conference celebrates Australia's booming dance scene', *The Guardian*, 6 December 2013, <http://www.theguardian.com/music/australia-culture-blog/2013/dec/06/electronic-music-conference-flume-dance> accessed 1 May 2014.

Richard, Birgit, 'DJ-Jane Kicks und Acid Chicks', *Gendertronics* (Frankfurt am Main: edition suhrkamp, 2005).

Robinson, Cedric, *Black Marxism: The Making of the Black Radical Tradition* (Chapel Hill, NC: University of North Carolina Press, 1999).

Rosen, Zachary, '#Breaking: *New York Times* discovers African artists use the Internets', africaisacountry.com, 17 January 2014, <https://africasacountry.com/2014/01/breaking-new-york-times-discovers-african-artists-use-the-internets/> accessed 1 May 2014.

Savage, Jon, *Teenage: The Creation of Youth Culture* (New York: Viking Books, 2007).

Sicko, Dan, *Techno Rebels: The Renegades of Electronic Funk* (New York: Billboard, 1999).

Tate, Greg, *Everything but the Burden: What White People Are Taking From Black Culture* (New York: Broadway Books, 2003).

Tucker, Boima, 'Global Genre Accumulation', africasacountry.com, 22 November 2011, <http://africasacountry.com/2011/11/22/globalgenre-accumulation> accessed 1 May 2014.

Warren, Guy, *I have a story to tell* (Accra: Ghanaian Press, 1962).

Wolfe, Tom, 'The Noonday Underground', *The Pump House Gang* (New York: Farrar, Straus & Giroux, 1968).

NAIROBI

MUSIC / SPACES
Ngoma Nites

From Rumba and Benga to NuNairobi

Ngoma Nites – From Rumba and Benga to the digital revolution
Joyce Nyairo and Bill Odidi

Nairobi, 2018
Mukami Kuria and Sellanga Ochieng' (Blinky Bill)

P.37

SPACES / POLITICS
A Matter of Salvation

Politics of Music and Space in Nairobi

The 1960s: An Evolving City
Peter Wafula Wekesa

The 1970s–1990s: A Mobile City
Joyce Nyairo

The 2000s–2010s: A Multiple City
Mukami Kuria

P.63

Ngoma Nites – From Rumba and Benga to NuNairobi

Joyce Nyairo & Bill Odidi, Mukami Kuria & Sellanga Ochieng' (Blinky Bill)

Ngoma Nites – From Rumba and Benga to the digital revolution
Joyce Nyairo and Bill Odidi

[1] Unless otherwise indicated, all song titles will be translated from Kiswahili or Swahili into English. Kishwahili and Swahili are the same language.

'Kenya Free!' proclaimed the headline of the *Daily Nation* on the morning of Independence Day, 12 December 1963. Amongst the liberties to look forward to, with this new political dawn, was the freedom to sing and dance without restriction or restraint. Kenya entered the ranks of independent nations with all-night celebrations, punctuated by dance music across the land. Predictably, the merrymaking was most pronounced in Nairobi, the capital city. Initially named Ewaso Nai'beri or 'a place of cool waters' by the Maasai, Nairobi came to be described, in English, as 'the green city in the sun'. It emerged from a half-way point, so to speak, chosen by colonial authorities during the construction of a railway line from the coast to the interior of East Africa. Nairobi has since become a magnet for all sorts of people from all sorts of places. The manifestations of its cultural life, including recorded popular dance music, represent the apex of a young country's response to nationhood, a response shaped constantly by the interaction of internal and external influences.

On Independence Day, the sounds of hits like Fundi Konde's 'Ajali Haikingiki' [calamity cannot be insured against][1] and 'Majengo Siendi Tena' [I'm not going to Majengo any more] kept revelers 'twisting the night away'. The Twist, coming all the way from the US – courtesy of pop singers like Chubby Checker – was a popular dance and music style of the day. Without doubt the most well-known song from that time is 'Malaika' [angel]. The writing and composition of this song is attributed to Fadhili Williams, lead vocalist of the Equator Sound Band. However, Grant Charo, another band member, was also to become a claimant to that distinction. Be that as it may, 'Malaika' soared away from dance spaces in Kenya to become an international hit. South African singer Miriam Makeba sang it on Kenya's Independence Day. She had come to Nairobi together with American Calypso legend, Harry Belafonte, who was part of the official US delegation to the celebrations. Years later, the German group, Boney M, would also provide a successful cover version of 'Malaika'.

In the early 1960s, dance music in Nairobi was characterized by a sedate Rumba beat, coming from Cuba via the Democratic Republic of Congo, which was known between 1971 and 1997 as Zaire. Peter Tsotsi, an immigrant from Zambia, as well as Zaireans Edouard Masengo and John Mwale were the stellar guitarists of the time adding the South-African Kwela beat to their sound and scoring big successes with a string of Twist numbers. Englishman Charles Worrod is credited with the development of this African Twist sound as a producer. Under his tutelage,

Daudi Kabaka released the fast-paced love song 'Helule Helule', arguably the most successful of the local Twist numbers. Thanks to Worrod's networks, 'Helule' made its way to the UK, and the British band The Tremeloes released a remix version, which reached number fourteen in the UK charts in 1968.[2]

In comparative terms, this outward flow of Nairobi's dance music was miniscule compared to the volume of records that were flowing into the capital from Europe, the US, Southern Africa and, more and more, from Zaire. Right from the early 1950s, Kenyan students studying at Makerere College in Uganda's capital city, Kampala, had been bringing home scores of Rumba records by Zairean musicians. And thus it was that Congolese or 'Lingala music', as it is more commonly known after Zaire's ethnic language of the same name, became a staple on Kenya's airwaves and dance floors. It was this faster paced Lingala music which spawned similar songs in Kiswahili, the emerging lingua franca of East Africa. Imitation was, indeed, the sincerest form of flattery, and this was not the last time that this would be a feature of Kenya's dance music scene.

By 1965, the Starlight Club, off Nairobi's Valley Road, was well established as the go-to place for an emerging city elite.[3] The Starlight had a majestic air, with a stage large enough to host a fifteen-man-band and a dance floor which could accommodate more than two hundred people. The outside grounds had ample parking space, particularly since few patrons drove in those days and relied more so on taxis. One regular at the Starlight was Barack Hussein Obama senior, who had just returned from studying in the US. He was joined a few months later by Ruth Baker, a young woman whom he had befriended in Boston and who had promised to join him in Kenya. They got married in 1964, on Christmas Eve, and quickly became regulars at the Starlight. According to the biographer Sally Jacobs, it was their addiction to the club that got Ruth fired from her job as a typist at the *Daily Nation* newspaper.

In 1969, Starlight patrons were dancing to Daudi Kabaka's 'Pole Musa' [be gentle, Musa]. As a reflection of the scarcity of female musicians at the time, Kabaka himself took on the persona of a woman abused by an alcoholic husband: 'Musa nimevumilia sana / kupigwa pigwa kama mimi punda / na sura yangu imeharibika / na ngumi zako za kila siku, Musa' [Musa, I've put up with it a lot / being beaten constantly as if I was a donkey / and my beauty has been ruined by your daily blows, Musa]. With equal delight, patrons at the Starlight Club were rocking to the Calypso beat, originally from Trinidad, of a 1968 song titled 'Mr. Walker' by Calypsonian legend Mighty Sparrow: 'Good morning Mr. Walker, I've come to see your daughter / sweet Rosemarie, she promised she go marry me / and now I tired waiting / I come to fix the wedding!'

In the 1970s the go-to dance place in Nairobi was Club 1900. The revellers there were slightly younger than those at the Starlight, but their aspiration to western lifestyles was just as intense. When East African Airways, the region's international airline, began to recruit black African crew members, the venue was assured a speedy supply of records from the West.

---

[2] The Tremeloes were founded in 1958. At the time of recording 'Helule' the group was comprised of Chip Hawkes, Alan Blakely, Rick West, and Dave Munden. Their 'Helule Helule' came from the 1968 album *My Little Lady*.

[3] To learn more about the places and diverse social strata of Nairobi please refer to the second essay on the city in this book.

The 1970s: from Boogies to Benga and Disco

In 1974, Sam Kahiga released the number one hit song 'Sugar Mummy', co-written with David Maillu.[4] Both men were published authors. The song, which described the newly visible African woman who had the material largesse to pay for the attentions of younger men, provided startling social commentary on the changing nature of male-female relationships: 'There's a woman, a very rich woman with many, many flats! Many what? / Flats! / She has no Christian name we call her "Sugar Mummy" / "Sugar" what? / "Mummy!"' Social commentary was to become yet another recurrent feature throughout the years, 'Sugar Mummy' fuelled raging debates, going all the way to parliament, on morality and the assault of urban mores on traditional culture. The emergent new female dress code, as evidenced by mini-skirts and hot pants, did not relax these discussions either.

Then there was yet another disturbing development amongst Nairobi's youth: the daytime dances, which came to be known as 'Boogies'. At these events, the music was always loud and the dance of the day was the Bump, which called on dance partners to bring parts of their bodies into rhythmic collision.

Amongst the local sensations at these Boogies was a young lad, born in the coastal city Mombasa, called Abdulkadir Mohammed Ali, who went by the stage name Kelly Brown, in homage to the US musician James Brown.[5] His nation-wide fame came from cover versions of Kool & the Gang's 'Funky Stuff' as well as Sam and Dave's 'When Something Is Wrong With My Baby'. Ishmael Jingo, who was also from the coast but who had spent some time in the UK, shook up the scene with 'Fever', a fusion of the coastal Chakacha rhythm and US Soul.[6] Faisal Brown of the Hodi Boys and Steele Beauttah were also star performers of the day, with songs like 'Mpenzi Rudi' [Come back, my love] and the funky 'What's That Sound?' In addition to local hits, the popular playlist featured foreign numbers like Fela Kuti's 'Lady', Tanzania's Afro 70 Band 'Dirishani' [at the window], and 'Photo Majedsi' by the Zaire based Orchestre Sosoliso. From beyond Africa, the Hue Corporation's 'Rock the Boat' and Johnnie Taylor's 'Who's Making Love?' urged all-out social rebellion.

Somewhat predictably, older Kenyans perceived Boogies as being decadent and a serious threat to the moral fabric of society. In December 1972, the Nairobi Provincial Commissioner declared a ban on all Boogies. But was an administrative fiat going to succeed where persistent lyrical cautioning had evidently already failed?

The foremost modern musician from the Kikuyu ethnic group, Joseph Kamaru, had for several years been singing about the havoc that urban life was wreaking on family values. He had come to provincial fame in 1966 with the song 'Njohi Ndiri Mwarimu' [Gikuyu for 'Alcohol is no teacher']—a cynical take on alcohol abuse. Three years later, Kamaru hit the big time with 'Ndari Ya Mwarimu' [teacher's darling]. Sung yet again from a female perspective, the song condemns a teacher who takes advantage of his pupil, a young girl, in more ways than one. 'Ndari Ya Mwarimu' remained at the top of the charts for three months in a row. Kamaru continued to lobby, through song, for the preservation of traditional values and rights—although, ironically, innovations in his own music

[4] Cf. Joe Mwenda's chart review, 'Sweet Success for the Cousins', *Daily Nation*, 14 August 1974. Sam Kahiga had also co-written 'In the Park' with Kenneth Watene, which was probably the first all-English song ever written by Kenyans—thus inspiring David Amunga to write his own hit, 'America to Africa'. In 1974 David Amunga recorded another very successful English song: 'Jane Is Pretty'.

[5] For more on Kelly Brown's international career see the multi-media pack *Retracing Kenya's Funky Hits* by Ketebul Music, 2011.

[6] 'Fever' features in the soundtrack of the 2006 Hollywood movie *The Last King Of Scotland*.

reflected culture as a dynamic hybrid. Kamaru was not to be the only one to take on the role of social commentator. Others were to follow his example by being exponents of music that provoked people not only to dance but also to think.

—

Like in many places around the world at the time, the jukebox, a coin-operated machine loaded with vinyl discs, made it possible for any bar to double up as a dance space in direct competition to established clubs. Unlike the radio, it played music on demand, uninterrupted by advertisements, news bulletins, or banter from presenters. Jukeboxes were a must-have in nearly all of the bars along River Road, Nairobi's oldest entertainment street. The names of these bars reflected proud ethnic citizenship. For example, a choice of venue had to be made either to hear Joseph Kamaru's aforementioned 'Ndari Ya Mwarimu' [teacher's darling]. or D.O. Misiani and his Shirati Luo Jazz Band singing 'Luo Union', titled after the ethnic group of the same name.

Popular uptown venues were places like the Rainbow Night Club, Sans Chique, the Big Five at the Intercontinental, and The Pub at Brunner's Hotel. Out in Ziwani, in the heart of Nairobi's Eastlands, was the Highlife Bar. And Kaloleni Social Hall remained a favourite for local bands. A big moment in the history of dance music in Nairobi was the opening of the Dambusters Club in 1970. There was also the evergreen Arcadia Club. The Acardia changed names several times over the years, becoming Gloria Africana, then Sal Davis' Night Spot, and eventually the New Florida Club.

1970 was a good year for the Jamhuri Jazz Band from Tanzania with their mega hit 'Shingo Ya Upanga' [praise of woman's long, stunningly beautiful neck] and their compatriots, the Morogoro Jazz Band, with 'Africa, Hoyee!' Also topping the local jukeboxes in 1970 was Gabriel Omolo, a Kenyan, with 'Keep Change'. Omolo would hit it even bigger in 1972, selling over 30,000 copies of 'Lunch Time', an upbeat number in the local Benga music style, which despite its English title was sung in Kiswahili and lamented the high cost of living and its effects on Nairobi's unemployed. Omolo was riding the crest of the wave for the Benga sound, championed by producer Oluoch Kanindo. Moving progressively from its origins in western Kenya on the shores of Lake Victoria, the Benga beat was adopted by musicians elsewhere in the country, giving rise to hits like 'I Love You' from the young Kikuyu musician D.K. Mwai in 1975. Daniel Owino 'D.O.' Misiani laid claim to being the King of Benga.[7] The genre also provided a breakthrough for several female artists who, until then, had been mere additions to male-dominated bands. It was through Benga that female hit-makers like Queen Jane emerged. However, it would be Princess Jully who would come to stand tallest in this group of female Benga greats with her memorable mega-hit 'Dunia Mbaya' [bad world], which in the early 2000s addressed the reality of HIV/AIDS.

From the international music scene in the 1970s, Jamaican Reggae singer Jimmy Cliff was rocking Nairobi's jukeboxes with his 'Wonderful World, Beautiful People'. The Congolese onslaught gained momentum as Orchestre Veve with its lead singer Verckys, hit it big with 'Mfumbwa'

[7] In later years, a seminal name in the production and archiving of Benga would be Tabu Osusa of the label Ketebul Music.

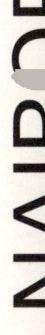

Just a Band: Richard Wandati and Bill Sellanga, Africa Salon at Yale University, New Haven, 2015, photo: Joe Were

Florida Nightclub aka Madhouse, Market Street/Koinange Street, Nairobi, 2013, photo: Stefan Schneider

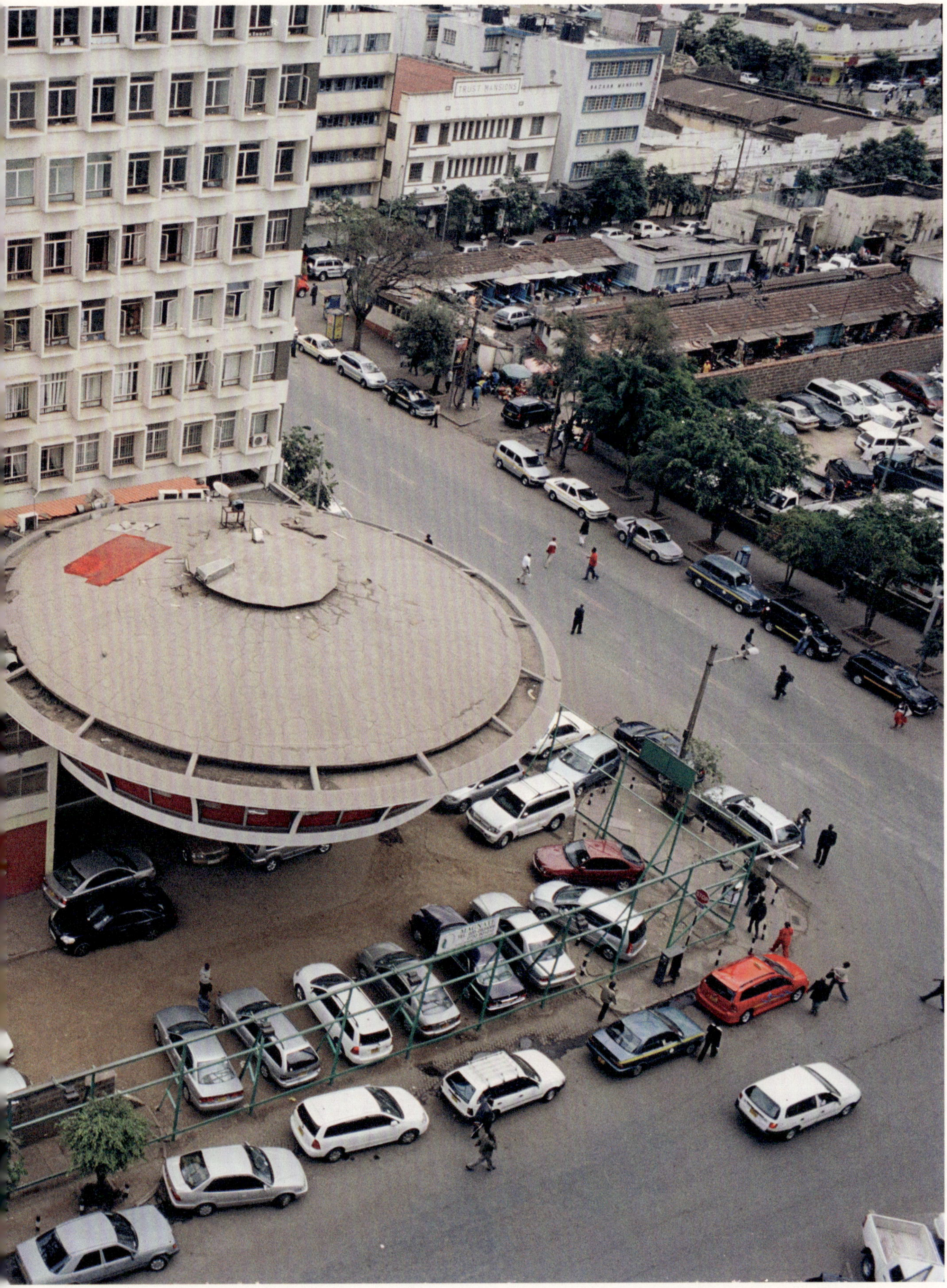
TRUST MANSIONS

Ismail Jingo, photo: unknown

The car park where Florida Nightclub used to be, Market Street/Koinange Street, Nairobi 2015, photo: Stefan Schneider

PLATES

President Records Ltd present Matata, London, 1971, photo: unknown

NAIROBI

Sauti Sol, 2018, photo: Emmanuel Jambo

46

Steele Beauttah, photo: unknown

Jaaziyah Satar, Muthoni Ndonga The Drummer Queen, & Karungari Mungai, Africa Nouveau Festival, Nairobi, photo: Royce Bett

Kelly Brown, photo: unknown

[popular vegetable; wild spinach made into a stew in the Congo]. Their countrymen from the group Boma Liwanza were playing at the Starlight. Such was the concern that in July 1970 a member of parliament sought to know why local artists were so busy imitating Congolese musicians. Meanwhile, the Kenya National Union of Musicians hosted the 'Beat Competition' where the band Matata emerged as winners with the Hodi Boys and the Cavaliers as worthy challengers. Matata was big then with songs like 'African Stomp' and 'Maendeleo Ya Kenya' [development in Kenya]. In 1971 the band went on tour in the UK after winning a competition at the BBC World Service. Anglo-Kenyan singer-songwriter Roger Whitaker was another musician from Nairobi to gain international recognition. In 1970 he enjoyed massive airplay with 'I Don't Believe in it Anymore', but bigger fame would come with 'Indian Lady' (1976) and the patriotic 'My Land Is Kenya' (1982).

It is worth mentioning the tangential and abiding influence of film as a trendsetter, not only on the playlists on Nairobi's airwaves, but also on fashion and dance styles on the club circuit. Early examples of this are the Bruce Lee films which inspired Carl Douglas' 1974 song, 'Kung Fu Fighting'. And, of course, 1978 belonged to *Saturday Night Fever* featuring the Bee Gees' mighty dance hit 'Staying Alive'.

The next significant year in the evolution of Nairobi's dance music was 1979. This was the year when Disco music fully arrived with Donna Summer's hit songs 'Hot Stuff' and 'Bad Girls'. And the Disco sound further prevailed, with songs like Anita Ward's 'Ring My Bell', 'Saturday Night' by T-Connection, or the all-time anthem of women's liberation 'I Will Survive' by Gloria Gaynor, originally released a year earlier. 1979 also marked the entry of Rap/Hip-Hop with the US group Sugarhill Gang's 'Rapper's Delight', one of the first Rap songs worldwide. Local hits of the time included 'Malako' by the Congolese group Les Kinois, the soulful ballad 'Mola' by local group Makonde, and 'Charonyi Ni Wasi', about the challenges of living in the city by the Maroon Commandos, a group comprised of soldiers from the Kenyan military.

Congolese groups like Orchestre Les Mangelepa owed much of their success in Nairobi to the then Commercial Attaché at the Embassy of Zaire, Baba Gaston Wa Illunga, who released his own music under the name Baba Gaston. At the end of 1979, Gaston earned a silver disc for the high sales of 'Viva Christmas', and his other big hit was 'Mapenzi Ya Peremende', a criticism of fickle, exploitative love. His years in Nairobi led to the huge rise in Congolese bands and several concerts by top Lingala musicians such as Tabu Ley Rochereau and Franco with Orchestre TPOK Jazz. It was in that same year 1979, that the venue Golf Range, later to become The Carnivore, burst into the limelight.

The 1980s: from curfew to Chakacha

As the 1970s drew to an end, in every dance space in Nairobi's Eastlands, from Park Inn to Club 1900 and Cantina, the slow dance section of party night belonged to 'Sweet Love' by The Commodores and 'Embakasi' [first international airport in Nairobi] by Orchestre Les Mangelepa. The latter was a Congolese band resident in Nairobi whose fans went wild to hits like 'Nyako Konya'[8] [Nyako is Luo for girl, Konya is Luo for help] and

8
Producer Tabu Osusa, a native Luo who is fluent in Lingagla, insists however that the non-Luo speaking Mangelepa were unaware of these meanings and only picked the words for the rhythmic force as a reversible anagram – listen to the song.

'Maindusa' [real name of Mustang who was a band member of Orchestre Les Mangelepa], delicately balancing on platform shoes and sporting the wide-flared bell-bottom trousers that were so desirable throughout Kenya as a nod to black US fashion. At the Bombax Club, Ibeba System showed off their signature red bell-bottom trousers as they sang hits like 'Ibeba' [things have fallen apart] and 'Pitié, je veux la reconciliation' [have mercy, I want us to make up].

More than any other song, the early 1980s belonged to the Congolese musician Tabu Ley and his song 'Maze' [a pet name for a beautiful woman]. However, 1982 became a significant year for Kenya's club and dance scene for a totally different reason: the attempted coup of 1 August and the subsequent month long dawn to dusk curfew that was imposed on Nairobi and Nanyuki. After a week of stunned inactivity, club owners hit on the survival formula of afternoon dance sessions.[9] Orchestre Virunga, the Starlight's resident band, led the way in the quest for rejuvenation. But it took another twenty-five years for the central business district scene to truly reclaim its crown as the Dance district.

Other mega hits of the early 1980s, both driven by the perennial Rumba beat, were 'Sina Makosa' [I did nothing wrong], first released in 1979 by Les Wanyika from Tanzania, and 'Shauri Yako' [it's your problem], first recorded by Nguashi N'timbo with Orchestre Festival du Zaire. The group later became Super Mazembe. A local ingredient to dance music, Chakacha, a fast-paced, percussion heavy beat from the coast came into its own. This music fused traditional rhythms with modern instruments and transformed what was originally a wedding dance for women into a national craze. Foremost among the groups that carried this sound from the coast to the city were Mombasa Roots and Them Mushrooms, famous for the tourist circuit sensation 'Jambo, Bwana' [hello Mister].

The 1990s: from Gospel to Hip-Hop

By the 1990s, another popular coastal rhythm – Taarab – also came into the mainstream, thanks to the hit 'Vidonge' [their portion] by Malika (Asha Abdow Suleiman). The Taarab singer from Mombasa won over a whole new audience with a sound that combined the traditional coastal flavour with elements of Hip-Hop and electronic music. Her major breakthrough was with the national hit 'Penzi Kwetu' [our love]. In the year 2000, another young singer from Mombasa named Nyota Ndogo (Mwanaisha Abdalla) hit the limelight thanks to her hypnotizing Taarab vocals on the song 'Nataka Toa' [I wish to give], on the first album by Hip-Hop group Necessary Noize,[10] which swept through the country's radio stations and clubs. That formula worked brilliantly again when Nyota was paired with Genge[11] artist Nonini for the single 'Nibebe' [carry me], produced by Andrew 'Madebe' Burchell in Mombasa.

To recall the early 1990s is also to recall the 'Win-a-Car National Dance Championships'. Groups of dancers from around the country brought their choreographed styles before a panel of judges and an audience of fans in a bid to be crowned national champions – and with it win the top prize of a brand new motor vehicle. The organizers of these afternoon competitions did not bother to put a cap on the age of competitors, and some of the dancers were as young as ten years. The ensuing outrage was reminiscent of the hysteria over Boogies in the 1970s.

[9] Cf. Joyce Nyairo, 'The day a coup sneaked up on us', *Daily Nation*, 3 August 2013, <http://www.nation.co.ke/lifestyle/weekend/The-day-a-coup-sneaked-up-on-us/-/1220/1935246/-/8rqagkz/-/index.html> accessed 20 August 2017.

[10] Consisting of the three rappers Nazizi 'The First Lady', Bamzigi 'The African Superman', and Wyre 'The Love Child'.

[11] A Kenyan derivative of Hip-Hop, an urban musical form, sung in Sheng (slang), Kiswahili, or local dialects.

Ironically, the top selling song in the country at that time was not a Disco track or any of the Soukous[12] hits from Paris – but a Gospel song titled 'Ahadi Ya Bwana' [the promise of the Lord], by the Ushindi Choir. In a manner that would reach its peak in the new millennium, the popularity of this song transcended radio and churches, into bars and the *matatu* public mini vans[13], while cassette retailers struggled with the high demand of a reported 300 copies a day on average. Like other Gospel songs emerging at the time, the beat of this song was quite revolutionary with the presence of keyboards, rhythm and bass and drums. The magnetic voice of singer Mary Wambui ensured runaway chart success throughout 1991 and catapulted the eighteen-year-old to national fame.

Consequently, Kenyan Gospel music was to become undistinguishable through melody or rhythms from other forms such as Benga, Kapuka, Genge, Chakacha, or Taraab. Singer Emmy Kosgei has even had big Gospel hits using South African elements. Gospel lyrics do make reference to Christianity, but not always overtly. A good case in point is Henri Mutuku's 2001 hit, 'Nakuhitaji' [I need you]. The slow tempo, the passionate crooning and the ambivalent lyrics combined give the song its crossover appeal, enjoyed by secular as well as evangelical teenagers. Another song that enjoyed similar crossover appeal was Esther Wahome's 2005 hit, 'Kuna Dawa' [there's a remedy]. Although Wahome sang about Christian salvation as the *dawa* [medicine] to heal all of one's troubles, her song found great appeal on dance floors where revellers yelled out the chorus as they swayed to and fro, holding bottles of beer.

It is easy to understand why artists struggling for fame should decide to cross over to Gospel – not necessarily because they are believers, but because Gospel music promises a huge fan base. The annual Groove Awards that honour the best Kenyan Gospel talent is now forced to vet its nominees to ensure that only those whose lifestyles conform to the 'Christian way' are honoured. The relocation of Gospel music from churches to alternative spaces, and more specifically to secular entertainment spaces, has created a transformation in the production and consumption of the music and changed the whole meaning of what constitutes dance music in Kenya.

—

Walking through the streets of Nairobi in the 1990s, it was (and still is) not uncommon to hear club music blaring from the speakers in shops or *matatu* mini-bus taxis. As DJs played records in the clubs, a tape would roll in the deck recording as one song segued into the next, with the DJ occasionally providing a running commentary. The master tape would then be 'dubbed' into thousands of copies, to be sold lucratively as cassette tapes. This trend had begun at the height of the Disco era in Kenya in the 1980s when younger commuters, especially school children, would only board the most high-tech *matatus*.

Meanwhile discotheques were all the rage in Nairobi, and there were many to choose from, all with catchy names like Lipps, Visions, Beat House, Dolce, Club Boomerang, Zig Zag, and, of course, the aforementioned Carnivore Simba Saloon. In the mid 1990s the Government made a decision that would greatly alter the social and club culture in Nairobi: prices of alcoholic drinks, which had hitherto been regulated, were now

---

12
From French *secouer* [to shake] – a dance music genre from the Congo Basin derived from Congolese Rumba in the 1960s, having gained popularity in the 1980s in France.

13
Privately owned mini-buses that operate as taxis. Tatu is Kiswahili for three. The name matatu was coined in the 1950s, from the 30 cents fare that was charged from the terminals to any stage on the routes to town.

left open to market forces, and establishments were free to set their own prices for drinks. This decision had a profound effect on club culture. Soon thereafter, Nairobi nightlife was transformed and partygoers shifted their loyalty to clubs and lounges like The Klub House at the Parklands Shade Hotel, which offered music and so much more. No longer was there any reason to pay a cover charge as had been the norm at discos. Of course, not all the discotheques shut their doors. In fact several, like the Florida Club, Dolce, and the Simba Saloon at the Carnivore, remained in business. They survived through a combination of strong branding and an ability to respond to the new challenge in the market by offering unique entertainment menus such as cultural theme nights.

The Carnivore, with its signature Simba Saloon, was a club-cum-restaurant [club/restaurant] boasting a 'beast of a feast' from a variety of meats, including that of wild game. By the late 1990s, the Carnivore ushered in a new era of clubbing in Nairobi by zoning the music scene with different genres on different nights, thereby stretching party days from weekends to weekdays. Hence, for example Bhangra nights on Fridays pulled in a predominantly Indian clientele. While the Sunday evening Soul nights were aimed at a mature crowd, nostalgic for the music of the 1960s and 1970s. A mature and fairly sophisticated racially mixed crowd graced the Jazz night. Other varieties would develop including Rock and Reggae nights. The Carnivore also hosted the National Disco Dancing Competition.

Theme nights in Nairobi, featuring live performances of music from different regions of the country each month, were first witnessed at the Panafric Hotel in 2000. The 'Mugithi Night' was headlined by popular musicians from Central Kenya like Queen Jane and Musaimo. Coastal rhythms would take centre stage on the 'Bango Night' with saxophonist Joseph Ngala. And Benga musicians from Nyanza were the main attraction on a 'Malo Malo Night'. The Carnivore, ever quick to pick up on new trends, started offering a platform for a version of Benga made popular by Okatch Biggy – an artist who was a product of the clubs in Kondele, the area at the heart of the live music scene in the lakeside town of Kisumu. Okatch Biggy had become a national sensation in the late 1990s, and his performances alongside his band, Heka Heka, at the Simba Saloon livened up the normally quiet Thursday nights in Nairobi. Music that preserved tiny pubs was now being embraced by the urban elite. The Carnivore held its first 'Ramogi Night', for music in the Dholuo language in 2003, featuring Musa Juma and his Orchestra Limpopo International, playing Rumba hits like 'Maselina' and 'Hera Mudho' [love is blind]. Juma had moved from the Blaze Club into the city's Eastlands area.

By the 1990s, the live performance scene in Nairobi had not quite returned to the peak it had reached in its heyday, in the 1970s. However, there was a flicker of hope that some significant changes were afoot in the music business. These changes cannot be viewed in isolation from other dramatic shifts in the country, particularly in radio and TV, which up to the early 1990s had firmly been the monopoly of the state. The Government had ceded control of radio and TV, allowing the licensing of private stations, and so now there was a lot more airtime to accommodate the creative arts, especially music.

And just as had happened during the various boom periods in Kenyan music since its Independence, music was again attracting interest from the big corporations. Fans long accustomed to poorly organized, chaotic music concerts were now suddenly getting value for their money with high quality sound, bigger performance stages, and cutting-edge urban music. For example, 'Beats of Season', which had begun in 1995 as an open-air live music festival received sponsorship from Tusker, a beer brand from Kenya Breweries Limited. A record 10,000 fans turned up at Nairobi's 'Carnivore Grounds' for its 1999 edition. The same year, the first 'Benson & Hedges Gold and Tones' concert took place in Kenya at the Impala Grounds where the new generation rappers, Kalamashaka, were the star attraction. The 'Guinness Festival' on the other hand, took musicians like Jah Key Malle, Mercy Myra, Bebe Cool, Zannaziki, Gidi Gidi Maji Maji, and Poxi Presha on tour to perform before crowds in major towns like Mombasa and Kisumu. The satellite radio company Worldspace Corporation introduced the 'Ngoma Nights' [dance nights] every month at the Carnivore, where musicians like Them Mushrooms, D.O. Misiani, and Sukuma bin Ongaro performed. This trend of live music has continued up to today, with Blankets and Wine, run by Muthoni The Drummer Queen, as a defining event. Opportunities were also opening up in advertising as 'Ting Badi Malo' [raise your hands in the air], the hit song by rappers Gidi Gidi Maji Maji, became the soundtrack to a TV commercial.

The growth of the music industry saw the need for self-congratulation, marked by awards ceremonies, although the choice of winners has not always gained unanimous approval. The Kisima Youth Achievement Awards, started in 1994, was the brainchild of producer Tedd Josiah and his associate David Muriithi. From an event that initially celebrated achievements not only in music, but also theatre, journalism, and sports, it eventually became known, just as The Kisima Awards, for honouring the year's best achievements in music. The Hip-Hop group Hardstone, for instance, was a very popular choice for 'Best New Performing Artist' during the 1997 edition, the same year that the Acapella group Five Alive (which featured a young Eric Wainaina who was to rise to fame in the 2000s as a solo artist) won 'Band of the Year'.

A younger generation of musicians was imposing itself with a departure from the established rulebook. In 1997, the trio Kalamshaka got their big break during the 'Star Search' at the Florida 2000 nightclub in Nairobi. Subsequently, they recorded the groundbreaking Hip-Hop track 'Tafsiri Hii' [translate this], about gruesome street life. It was officially released a year later on the compilation *Kenya, The First Chapter*, produced by Tedd Josiah. He was to become Kenya's maestro of Hip-Hop and R'n'B, influenced by traditional Kenyan music. *Kenya, The First Chapter* featured a compilation of songs by rappers. Apart from Kalamashaka, there were Gidi Gidi Maji Maji, Hardstone, and Nazizi Hirji, arguably Kenya's first female Rap artist.

Kalamashaka's single 'Fanya Mambo' [do something], produced by Ken Ring, a Kenyan based in Sweden, became a number one video hit on the Pan African music TV network Channel O, in 2001. It helped spread the fame of the band even further. Some of Kalamashaka's best music was contained in an album titled *Kilio Cha Haki* [truthful cry] in 2004. The album featured a collective of rappers from Nairobi and Mombasa, like Ukoo Flani or Mashifta, with songs on political corruption, police brutality, gun crime, poverty, abortions, rape, and murder. Such was the success of Kalamashaka, that they became the first ever foreign guest artists to perform at the Nigerian edition of the 'Gold and Tones' festival in 1998 before a crowd of 80,000 people.

The aforementioned Hardstone album *Nuttin But De Stone* changed the sound of Kenyan pop music by popularizing an edgy urban sound with lyrics written in Sheng, the hybrid of Swahili, English, and various vernacular spoken widely in urban towns. The remix of its first single 'Uhiki' absolutely tore up both the clubs and radio stations throughout Kenya in 1996 and 1997, playing on the memory of city revelers of the 1980s who had delighted in Marvin Gaye's 'Sexual Healing', whose bass line it had shamelessly lifted. Germany-based Kelele Records released *Nuttin But De Stone* internationally. Multiple Grammy Award winner Lauryn Hill, who was then riding high as a member of the Fugees, appeared as a support act during the launch of Hardstone's CD *Nuttin But De Stone* in Nairobi in 1997. And in 1999, Ndarlin P and his 4-IN-1 introduced a novel rapping style, using rhymes laced with humour, mimicking the various regional accents.

The 2000s: from Ogopa DJs to new media

In this new era of urban Hip-Hop, Nairobi, with its superior recording facilities and top producers, remained a magnet for artists from beyond Kenya's borders. For example, 'Mama Mia', a Dancehall-flavoured pop single and the biggest hit of 2001, came from twenty-three-year-old Ugandan Chameleone (Joseph Manyanja). The song was produced by a team known as Ogopa DJs. They in the years to come would dominate Kenyan club music in a way no other group had done in the past, by developing a hard driving club sound and constantly recruiting new talent. Ogopa DJs produced three compilation CDs containing songs that would virtually dominate the radio and club scene in Kenya for the better part of a decade. Formed in 1999 by two brothers, Francis and Lucas Bikedo, the Ogopa DJs largely avoided the limelight. But their brand gained a powerful presence through the success of artists signed to their label. Their compilation albums *Ogopa 1* to *Ogopa 3* were released between 2002 and 2005. Each album unleashed a string of hits and created new stars.

Ogopa 1: Kenyan Club Classics was packed with dance anthems like 'Ninanoki' [I go crazy], a collaboration between rapper Nameless and female singer Amani. Equally popular was 'Mona Lisa' by Deux Vultures. From this album Mr. Googz and Vinnie Banton reached the finals of the Kora Awards in 2002 with 'Wasee', a song saluting Githurai, one of Nairobi's most populous neighbourhoods. Another seminal artist on the Ogopa DJs label was Redsan, who had launched his career alongside Chameleone. For more than a year, this duo together with another Ugandan artist, Bebe Cool, performed in schools and colleges, and at events like the Miss Kenya beauty pageant and the 'Beats of the Season' festival. They also opened for international Reggae acts performing in Nairobi like Maxi Priest or Chaka Demus and Pliers. After establishing their careers in Kenya, both Chameleone and Bebe Cool returned home and continued to release hits.

Ogopa DJs' second compilation album, *Ogopa 2: Strictly for The Hanye In You*, contained captivating tunes like 'Haree' by Kleptomaniax,

'Baby Don Go' by Kunguru featuring Mr. Lenny and Wahu's 'Liar'. The *Ogopa 3* compilation from 2005 combined the experience of singer Mercy Myra with newcomers like the all-female trio Tatuu and a smooth vocalist called Patonee. Just as their predecessors, the songs had a huge impact nationwide. The Ogopa sound was not just identified by its edgy, House influenced beats, but also lyrically, as this was party music at its very best, with feel-good lyrics in Sheng, celebrating wild revelry, fast cars, and beautiful women.

Perhaps the most mercurial of the Ogopa DJs' musicians was Isah Mmari, better known as E-Sir, who had an effortless ability to deliver catchy rhymes in Sheng, the hybrid of Kiswahili and English. Ogopa DJs released his first single, 'Jo', in 2001. He followed it with a massive club hit titled 'Leo Ni Leo' [today is today]. And then came the party anthem 'Boomba Train' with fellow Ogopa artist, Nameless, in 2003. The latter track became 'Song of the Year' and the corresponding album *Nimefika* [I have arrived!] 'Album of the Year' at the 2003 Kisima Awards.

The massive popularity of this new generation of urban artists meant that there was also a huge demand to see them perform at live venues. Piracy and downloads ate into the sales of records and so the artists relied on performance fees to earn a living from their music. A great crowd-puller was the aforementioned Nameless, who had achieved his big break in 1998 when he won a freestyle battle on radio with his song 'Megarider'—the tale of a guy who cannot drop a girl home because he only has enough money for his own bus ticket. He recorded that first single with producer Tedd Josiah, but later switched to the Ogopa DJs label in 2001, and released hit singles like 'Majitu' [demons] and 'Mannerless'. Nameless' much anticipated solo album, *On Fire*, hit the shelves in 2003.

Some of the new generation of Congolese artists in Kenya started playing music that had very little similarity to the classic style of their forefathers. Twin brothers, Christian and Lovy Longomba, are the sons of Lovy Longomba, a maestro who came to Nairobi with the wave of Congolese Rumba musicians in the late 1970s and played with the group Super Mazembe. They are nephews of another star, Soukous player Awilo Longomba. After initially toying with Gospel music, the younger Longombas turned to the Ogopa DJs, and the result was 'Dondosa' [move your hips], one of the biggest club and radio hits of 2002. Other hits like 'Piga Makofi' [clap your hands] and 'Vuta Pumz' [take a breath] followed in quick succession. The brothers have won many industry honours including a Kora Music Award in 2005 for 'Best East African Group'.

Possible competitors to Ogopa DJs were Homeboyz, founded in 1994 by brothers John and Mike Rabar. What started as a small retail occupation branched out within ten years to become a deejaying school, a rugby-football team, a fully-fledged production house, a merchandiser of bottled water, and a publisher of a monthly entertainment magazine. The creative brain behind the production arm of Homeboyz was Eric Musyoka who started off as a rapper himself. He worked on hits by Prezzo, Tattuu, Ambassada, Mr. Googz, Nonini, and even with artists from other parts of East Africa like T.I.D. From Tanzania and Peter Miles from Uganda.

Reggae has always had a massive following in Kenya. 'Reggae Time', a one hour Thursday morning radio show from the state-run media network, Kenya Broadcasting Corporation (KBC), gained a huge following nationwide. In the late 1990s, Reggae was confined to off-peak afternoon slots on many radio stations. However, radio managers began to notice that there was a significant upsurge in listeners whenever Reggae shows were on air, and in 2005, the managing director of KBC made the astounding decision to turn Metro FM into a twenty-four-hour Reggae station. The impact was immediate. Audience figures leaped up within months, and Reggae went from being 'rebel' to 'cool' music as establishments in uptown Nairobi scrambled to introduce it into their repertoire. Rufftone introduced Dancehall/Reggae into Gospel with 'Mwikhulu' [the Lord] in Luhya language. Produced by Gospel trailblazer Robert Kimanzi in December 2002, it became a big hit on FM stations and in clubs nationwide. Language was obviously no barrier to its popularity.

The newly licensed commercial radio stations may have contributed to the popularity of the emerging urban sound of Kenyan music, but their arrival triggered a whole new debate about their contribution to the music industry. Record dealers feared their sales would be negatively affected by the continuous airplay of music, while some listeners were frustrated by the hit format that rotated a limited number of songs all day long. At the turn of the millennium, debates intensified over the lack of diversity on the new radio stations. It seemed that the stations had very little time for other genres of music made by Kenyans, besides what was broadly classified as Hip-Hop.

Then a certain bureaucrat saw fit to create a genre named 'Traditional Music' – a limiting move which irked acclaimed musicians like Eric Wainaina who in 2002 won a 'Kora All Africa Music Award' for his famous anti-corruption anthem 'Nchi Ya Kitu Kidogo' [land of bribery], whose sound retained elements of African rhythm like Benga. Juma Odemba, lead singer of the successful group Kayamba Africa, also felt aggrieved at being pigeon-hold by the 'Traditional' categorization.

There were a few artists who succeeded in combining contemporary sounds with elements of traditional rhythms, a style that became popularly known as Afro-Fusion. One such notable success came in 2001, when singer and guitarist Suzzana Owiyo recorded 'Kisumu 100' – the official theme song for the centenary of the lakeside city of Kisumu. Its popularity travelled beyond Kenya: Oprah Winfrey and Tom Cruise danced along as Owiyo performed the song during the presentation ceremony for the 2004 Nobel Peace Prize Awards to Kenyan conservationist Wangari Maathai in Oslo, Norway.

Kisumu was later to be gripped by what came to be labelled as Ohangla, the name of a traditional drum played among the Luo people of the region. But this modern day Ohangla was really a product of a synthesized groove. The Ohangla wave was led by Tony Nyadundo: he singlehandedly spread the popularity of the music upcountry, breaking the barriers for a style of music that had largely been restricted to the lake shores. Songs like 'Ngato Ka Ngato Mana Gi Hape' [everyone to his or her own fate] became huge dance floor hits across the country.

The genocide of 1994 forced Burundian musician Kidum to flee, arriving as a twenty-one year old at the Kakuma refugee camp in Kenya from where he made his way to Nairobi. Today, the composer, drummer, and singer and his group The Boda Boda Band commands one of the biggest followings of any live act in Nairobi. Kidum easily charms the ladies, and they sing along to every word of his hits like 'Mapenzi' [love] and 'Haturudi Nyuma' [there is no turning back]. Opting to record in Kiswahili rather than his original language Kirundi won him broader regional appeal and a bigger fan base. Kidum's popularity around the region has been greatly boosted by his collaborations with leading ladies like Uganda's Juliana Kanyomozi and Lady JD from Tanzania's thriving Bongo Flava[14] music scene.

Another refugee from Burundi was Robert Kamanzi, popularly known as R Kay. He became famous in 2001 by producing a funky contemporary Gospel song titled 'Ukiliya Moko' [raise your hands] by the group Shamma, which made the increasingly habitual crossover into the dance charts. Becoming one of the country's top producers came rather fortuitously to R Kay. He eventually set up his own production unit and developed a Zouk[15] influenced dance rhythm working with Deux Vultures and a host of both secular and Gospel acts like Henrie Mutuku, Mr Googz and Vinnie Banton, Esther Wahome, CMB Prezzo, Ambassada, and Rufftone.

Hip-Hop, by its very nature, was always bound to produce artists who court controversy either through their lyrics or through the nature of their personalities and lifestyles. Acts like Kleptomaniax, Mwafrika, Bamboo, Attitude, FBI, or Chiwawa and the Cash Money Brothers conducted constant musical feuds against each other through the release of diss tracks, as each sought the high ground for authenticity among fans. The original bad boy of Kenyan Rap was a former DJ from Mombasa, Poxi Presha (Prechard Pouka Olang), who had moved to Nairobi in the early 1990s and cut his teeth rapping at club competitions. He occasioned a huge cultural shift in Kenyan Hip-Hop when he released the single 'Dhako' [woman], produced by Bruce Odhiambo with lyrics entirely in Dholuo. Famous for his sharp tongue and colourful wardrobe, Poxi did not spare anyone who crossed his path, especially the music producers who, he felt, had short changed him and sections of the entertainment press that he accused of unfair coverage. He released what is considered by some the very first diss track in Kenyan urban music, 'Wape Really' in 2003, directed at all his detractors and those he accused of sabotaging the music business in the country. Poxi galvanized both artists based on River Road, the music hub of the city, and the younger urban musicians in staging a protest march to demand their royalties from the Music Copyright Society of Kenya.

Equally controversial, though for entirely different reasons, was the trend of artists who came to prominence because of the adult content in their music. Calif Records' artist Nonini (Hubert Nakitare) created a huge storm with his first two singles, 'Manzi Wa Nairobi' and 'Wee Kamu' in 2000. Nonini quickly became known for explicit references to sex. The songs received publicity with raunchy videos that somehow still made their way to national TV, before the era of internet video sharing. A new style of urban music had emerged from Calif Records, Genge, named after a slang word for 'the masses'. It was pioneered by a young producer, Clement Rapudo, who as a university student had opened a studio in his

14
A local derivative of Hip-Hop.
15
A musical style from the Caribbean islands of Guadeloupe and Martinique.

parents' flat and started to record emergent acts like Nonini, Jua Cali (Paul Nunda), Pilipili, Circuite, and Jo-El.

Emboldened by Nonini's success, other rappers tackled topics that had hitherto been considered taboo. Rap duo Circuite and Jo-El released 'Juala' [condom] in 2004 which used the analogy of polythene paper to promote condom use. The inside sleeve of their CD showed a semi-nude woman with a pack of condoms tucked in the inside of her underwear. 'Juala' became an instant national hit – but also provoked a huge debate from those who thought the use of explicit language would be interpreted as an encouragement to the youth to indulge in irresponsible sex. Social commentary had been taken to a new generational level.

—

Video became an essential purveyor of popular music. Television opened up to locally produced music videos. By the end of the 1990s, each new, privately owned station had at least two shows to offer, showcasing the latest video releases for both secular and Gospel music. By the mid 2000s, it was not enough for most *matatus* to have a good sound system. They also installed screens, which played music videos. The era of the video disc jockey had arrived, and the mixes were heavily branded with the names of the VDJs, advertising the clubs at which they played.

As technology became more accessible, it became easier to duplicate and distribute music illegally. Gidi Gidi Maji Maji, for instance, sold just 20,000 copies of their 2002 rabble-rousing hit 'Unbwogable' or 'Indestructible', blaming piracy and the lack of a distribution network. The duo – Joseph Ogidi and Julius Owino – made up for the relatively poor sales with tours that took them to every corner of the country and elsewhere. 10,000 fans thronged the Nile Hotel in Kampala, Uganda in January 2003 in the group's first major performance outside the country. After the launch of the song's video in 2003, the doors opened rapidly for Gidi Gidi Maji Maji in 2004 with international tours to the US and the Netherlands. Also in 2004, the duo was named United Nations Habitat Messengers of Truth to raise awareness of the Millennium Development Goals and to support youth development initiatives in slums and inner cities. Gidi Gidi Maji Maji's other big moment was a record deal with Gallo Records of South Africa who released their second album, *Many Faces*. Despite a massive promotional campaign, most fans in Kenya did not take to the group's new musical direction on the album that seemed to have been heavily influenced by the South African Kwaito sound.

The big interest in Kenyan urban music at the beginning of the new millennium coincided with the growth of mobile technology. The very first ringtones were for hits like Nonini's 'Wee Kamu' [you come over (with sexual connotations)], Nameless' 'Deadly', and Redsan's 'Apakatwe' [grab her (with sexual connotations)], which each sold for 60 Kenyan shillings. During the early days, the business of ringtones made hefty profits for companies but the artists themselves were completely cut out of the equation. Producers claimed they were running all over town in an attempt to trace the ringtone creators.

Like elsewhere the digital revolution has brought about a huge transformation in the production of music in Nairobi. One significant outcome was that fewer musicians invested in learning to play an instrument, and many chose, instead, to work with any of a number of producers who were setting up studios complete with softwares like FruityLoops. Technology has been at the heart of breath-taking developments in promotion of and access to music since the first major CD release of a music album by a Kenyan artist in 1997. One of the earliest websites set up to sell Kenyan music was MyMusic.co.ke, and new media like this has stepped into the void left by the distribution networks of old. The physical structures of record companies and record stores have been replaced by the virtual industry of downloads and streaming. Kenya's largest mobile network provider, Safaricom, offers MP3 music tracks and ringtone downloads on its Safaricom Live portal. Other sites like Vuma, run by the Music Copyright Society of Kenya, are dedicated to selling Kenyan music online. A leading provider of mobile phone downloads in East Africa estimates that the business opportunity is worth four million US-Dollars a year. Cellulant, which is a Nairobi based company, says a successful artist can attract anywhere between 200,000 and 300,000 downloads over three months.

The 2010s: from downloads to the future

Today, most artists in Kenya are not releasing their music on physical formats. The big names in the business, many of them rappers, for instance Octopizzo, P-Unit, Mejja, and Juliani are signed to Mdundo—a start-up that allows the artists to sell their music through scratch cards and to keep the money generated from these sales. The company also sells the music on its online platform from which it pays royalties to the artists. Other acts like Sauti Sol or Sarabi have employees who solely manage their individual brands as full-time jobs. Thanks to the popularity of digital platforms, many artists are now able to market themselves directly to the consumers in innovative ways using the online video sharing network YouTube or social media sites like Facebook, Twitter, and Instagram. The first ever downloads awards, the 'Mdundo Awards' show, were held in 2014 with rapper Rabbit's hit 'Ligi Soo Remix' awarded as the most downloaded song on that portal.

    Meanwhile Nairobi's entertainment circuit has spread out from the central business district to the epicentre of Nairobi's nightlife, the so-called Electric Avenue, home to clubs like Rezorus, Bacchus (both closed by now), Molly's, Gipsy's, Black Diamond, Brew Bistro, MUZE, and a number of other lively venues. But even such popular spots are not resting easy as some of their clients are pulled by the attraction of the The VIP lounges in clubs like Galileos and Skylux targeting a niche market. Again, the more offered to complement the music, the more popular the club. From celebrity invitations to Karaoke theme nights, club owners are pulling out all the stops in the battle for business.

At Independence in 1963—where we started—the population of Kenya as a whole was pegged at around three million inhabitants. Fifty odd years later that has increased more than ten-fold. The idyllic vision of the early planners of Nairobi have been largely abandoned to result in a chaotic metropolis where slums and skyscrapers exist incongruously side by side. However, the hallmarks of its popular dance music have remained fairly consistent: imitation, innovation, and socio-political commentary, all spearheaded by changing generations. Homegrown musical styles have fought to hold their own against onslaughts from afar, notably the US, the Congo, and Tanzania. Composers have lent their skills to chronicle both good and bad times, to be lauded or reviled by preceding generations. Young people have always been keen to adopt different crazes. It was an exhilarating heady mix, enough to make a musicologist's delight.

Nairobi, 2018
Mukami Kuria and Sellanga Ochieng' (Blinky Bill)

Blinky Bill, musician, producer, and member of Kenyan electronic music project Just A Band, has an ear that listens and searches for the unfamiliar. He shares his musical curiosity and his discoveries with others, playing and remixing *Zilizopendwa*[16] songs, and playing records he has come across for anyone who visits his studio. On one such occasion, he introduced me to a Kenyan musician with otherworldly sounds. As Bill listened to a DJ set by the US R'n'B singer Erykah Badu, he remembers being struck by one track, comprised of a husky voice crooning words of conviction and love over a Funk-laden musical arrangement. The first minute and twenty seconds feature multiple sounds: a syncopated bassline layered with a funky bass guitar and a lead guitar that follows the tight brass section. Before the one-minute mark, beats and sounds synonymous with the Kenyan coastline and particularly with Chakacha music come in, and the whistles and accented drum rhythms temporarily shift the texture of the song. We move between worlds and genres, from Funk to Chakacha as Ishmael Jingo's voice comes in. Jingo sings with yearning for his lover, telling them of their ability to induce a fever in him:

Love you, love you baby,
You give me fever.
Love you, love you darling,
Cause you give me fever.
I love the way you walk, I love the way you talk,
I love the way you move, I love the way you groove.
Love you, love you baby,
You just give me, give me fever

This song is 'Fever' by Ishmael Jingo from 1974. Jingo's sound is difficult to place, it is a hybrid of many sounds of the time fused together to create what has been termed by some cultural historians and critics as Afro-Rock. Blinky Bill and I wonder who Jingo sang for, who his audience was, and why it is that his sound came to us through a DJ set, while it has been introduced to other Kenyans through the film *The Last King Of Scotland*. The rarity of this sound, Jingo's sound, prompts us to enquire what otherworldly, hybrid sounds are being created in Nairobi today. To what extent the same ethos of Jingo can be found within the creation of music in the Kenyan capital currently?

Blinky Bill's own music is one such example, given the many sources of inspiration he cites. The 'NuNairobi' movement has also gained traction in recent years, embodying the same ethos of ingenuity that the musicians who came before them thrived on. The collective EA Wave, consisting

[16] Literal translation: [they were loved], used to reference songs that were national Kenyan hits in the era after Independence and through to the 1980s.

of producers Ukweli, Nu Fvnk, Jinku, Hiribae, and Muroe is another example. They lay claim to dreamy, cosmic sounds that mirror contemporary music by a range of musicians across the world from Willow Smith (whom they produced) to Kaytranada and Toro Y Moi. Alai K and his project Disco Vumbi and DJ Raph's 2018 album *Sacred Groves* vastly sampling and remixing Kenyan and other African music from the archives are particularly marked by a leakiness between past and present that creates a conversation about continuity and change. KMRU (Joseph Kamaru's grandson) works with ambient and sound collages, as well as field recordings.

These are examples of musicians practising and writing tirelessly, whether or not their music is played by mainstream radio stations. This same ethos drives the contemporary Nairobian musician to produce and perform their music regardless of the audience and public ear, almost collectively stating and affirming their staying-in-power. They play for themselves, whether their music will be played at local radio stations or not. They play for whomever will listen to their unique sounds and the stories that accompany them, often creating their own audiences and followings. The city is infused with a sense of creative ownership, with musicians often arranging series of concerts involving their friends and collaborators.

In August 2016, Blinky Bill posted an image on his Instagram account announcing his forthcoming EP. The image features Blinky's Converse-clad feet, his MiniBrute synthesizer and a sign presumably from one of Nairobi's many sign makers. The sign reads: 'We Cut Keys While You Wait'. The EP title is eponymous, derived from the pictured sign, thus offering a way of thinking about the city, its jua kali [informal, small-scale] craftsmen and Nairobi's musicians. The sign, 'We Cut Keys While You Wait', is symbolic of how quickly craftsmen working informally in Nairobi can produce work for their clients. They can cut spare keys, they can produce signs customized to whatever you require, from the ubiquitous 'Mbwa Kali' [beware of dogs] signs to the infamous barber shop plates featuring the artist's highly unique rendering of rapper Ludacris, to the 'nguvu za kiume' [male strength] signs found across the city, often advertising the services of *mgangas* or witchdoctors offering virility fixes and medicines. With speed and attention they produce whatever the client asks of them: furniture, signs, and keys, with the promise to do so whilst you wait for them.

For Blinky Bill and the city's musicians, this sign is indicative of a Nairobi scene of musicians who, in recent years, are again producing decidedly hybrid sounds, using a wide array of equipment which is often electronic. They do this in unconventional and experimental ways, as Blinky Bill argues, 'figuring out how to express ourselves in a way that makes sense to us'. Within Nairobi, the community created by musicians means that songs, albums, and live shows are often the product of collaboration. This spirit of cooperation seems characteristic of cultural production in Nairobi today.

The ethos of this circle of Nairobi musicians: to perform and play regardless of the audience and public ear, corresponds to conversations amongst Kenyan musicians about whether they are appreciated enough. Conversations by musicians and producers often focus on why it is that clubs and radio stations 'fail to support their own', often playing music from other countries before promoting songs and efforts by Kenyan musicians. In August 2015, it was reported that Kenyan musicians took to the streets of Nairobi to protest the dominance of Nigerians and Tanzanians on the airwaves. In May 2016, Blinky Bill tweeted the following: 'Always amusing to me that you can go out to a club in Nairobi and not hear a single Kenyan song being played.' This was followed by this observation made by Blinky from a nondescript club in Westlands: 'been at some place in Westlands for two hours and they've played not a single Kenyan song.' Following the protest in 2015, musician Eric Wainaina wrote in an article in *Okayafrica*:

> So when a group of Kenyan musicians march the streets of Nairobi saying they want more airplay, what they mean is that they just want more. Of everything. They want more access to great producers, more policies that favour growth not through airplay quotas (who wants to force appreciation?) but through education, more damn money from airplay, more prosecution for content aggregators who don't remit royalties. More space – not protectionism – to be heard.[17]

In his article, Wainana examines the environment in which music is produced, unraveling the similarities between sounds across the continent and within countries. On the other hand, musicians such as Blinky Bill are trying to determine the structure of Nairobi's sonic identity. Blinky Bill cites Cameroonian Manu Dibango and Guinean group Balla et ses Baladins as some of his influences. For him, it is possible to do two things simultaneously: on the one hand, to ask that more space be given to Kenyan musicians to be heard locally, but on the other hand, to also be open to influences from elsewhere across the continent, creating a local modernity and articulation of African identity.

Nairobi has always been a contact zone, a point and metropolis in which many worlds meet, almost with a Glissantian 'world mentality'. It is through these continental exchanges materialising in Nairobi, that the musicians here lay claim to their right to create beautiful sounds and articulate their own versions of freedom. This cultural translation and hybridity continues to influence musicians like Blinky Bill, or the NuNairobi movement. Nairobi then exists in the minds of those who live there and those passing through it as a cosmopolis, laying claim to contemporary sounds from elsewhere and setting up clubs as sites of exchange.

[17] Eric Wainaina, 'Does Kenya Really Have a Naija Music Problem?' Okayafrica, 18 August 2015, <http://www.okayafrica.com/does-kenya-really-have-a-naija-music-problem/> accessed 20 February 2017.

Bibliography

Mwenda, Joe, 'Sweet Success for the Cousins', *Daily Nation*, 14 August 1974.

Nyairo, Joyce, 'The day a coup sneaked up on us', *Daily Nation*, 3 August 2013, <http://www.nation.co.ke/lifestyle/weekend/The-day-acoup-sneaked-up-on-us//1220/1935246/-/8rqagkz/-/index.html> accessed 20 August 2017.

Wainaina, Eric, 'Does Kenya Really Have a Naija Music Problem?' *Okayafrica*, 18 August 2015, <http://www.okayafrica.com/does-kenyareally-have-a-naija-music-problem/> accessed 20 February 2017.

A Matter of Salvation – Politics of Music and Space in Nairobi

Peter Wafula Wekesa, Joyce Nyairo & Mukami Kuria

The 1960s: An Evolving City
Peter Wafula Wekesa

Studies on urbanization in Kenya and elsewhere in Africa are increasingly highlighting the centrality of social history, especially that of the performing arts such as music, dance, and drama in the construction of urban spaces and the experience of leisure.[1] These studies attempt, in a significant way, to draw attention to the nexus between the rural and urban social landscapes and demonstrate how Africans from diverse ethnic and cultural pluralities have, over the years, struggled to make sense, create, contest, and equally exercise choices and control over their existence and identities. The persistent negotiations by the various groups in rural and urban spaces have been mirrored within a complex web that is characterized by intense historical transformations. These involve not only the indigenous players but also foreign entrants. The result of this process has been the creation of a unique heterogeneous socio-cultural environment within the cities. This new socio-cultural environment is unnecessary made up of people from varied cultural, class, racial, and other social backgrounds whose heterogeneous affiliations are distinct from those from rural-traditional backgrounds.

As an evolving pre-independent city, Nairobi's social historiography was already richly endowed and remarkably diverse before 1963, the year Kenya attained its Independence. The city's local entertainment space directly drew from a wide range of styles arising out of the different ethnic and language groups in Kenya. There are over forty-two ethnic groups in Kenya, and critical representations from these groups in the city whether as musicians, workers, or traders, became a key component in redefining its space. The most prominent representatives of Kenya's ethnic groups in Nairobi come from the so-called 'big five' – namely, the Kikuyu, Luhya, Luo, Kamba, and Kalenjin. Members of these groups moved from their diverse rural villages to Nairobi, carrying along their styles, music, and cultural traditions.

In terms of entertainment value, Nairobi's amalgamation of these diverse indigenous styles was however also intertwined with styles from various foreign lands. Kenya and specifically Nairobi has, since colonial times, paid host to people from various parts of the African continent and beyond who came and come as visitors, refugees, workers, or musicians. Though foreigners, these groups form an important part of Nairobi's social and entertainment historiography. Nairobi's urban social spaces, particularly music spaces, offered opportunities for crystallization of both traditional and foreign cultures and styles, where diverse cultures came to express their attitudes to life, their hopes and fears, thoughts and beliefs.[2] As the city evolved from colonialism to independence, its spaces continued to be a hotbed of social, economic, and political activities as well as act as a cultural melting pot.

Originally set up, as a railway station in the 1890s, Nairobi's evolution to prominence largely depended on its role as an economic centre, a capital city of Kenya, and an oasis of peace in the former war-torn broader eastern African region. These characteristics, coupled with the social milieu of music, dance, and drama created a social fabric that was punctuated by ever evolving technology, transmitted by the media (both public and private) to construct individual, group, and national identities. This social fabric generated new realities and forms of living in Nairobi, perhaps crucially, in entertainment spaces, and more so, music spaces. The resultant social vibrancy in the city was obviously intensified by the emerging dance clubs that brought together a rich array of musicians. These spaces have continued to change and expand considerably from live stage shows and radio to include television, the internet, and mobile phones as avenues through which music is attainable.

Colonialism and the post-World War II social space

The evolution of Nairobi and the nature of its social historiography in the 1960s cannot be extricated from the political developments around colonialism and its attendant social, economic, and political policies. Nairobi was essentially a colonial city and its structuring, just like its social mix, reflected metropolitan notions of space and enjoyment whose focal point was external and foreign. The dualism that existed in Nairobi regarding the rural-urban and

---

[1] Cf. Catherine Coquery-Vidrovitch, 'The Process of Urbanization in Africa: From the Origins to the Beginning of Independence, *African Studies Review* 34 (1), 1991, 1–98 cf. Jean Ngoya Kidula, 'Sing and Shine: Religious Popular Music in Kenya', PhD thesis (Los Angeles: University of California, 1998) cf. Eisha Stephen Atieno Odhiambo, 'Kula Raha: Gendered Discourses and the Contours of Leisure in Nairobi, 1946–63', *Azania: Archeological Research In Africa*, 2001, 36–37:1, 254–264 cf. James Ogude and Joyce Nyairo (eds.), *Urban Legends, Colonial Myths: Popular Culture and Literature in East Africa* (Trenton, NJ: New Africa Books, 2007).

[2] To learn more about the diverse musical landscapes of Nairobi please have a look at the first essay in this book.

indigenous-foreign relationships as well as the segregated class structure that evolved in the various key locations in the city largely reflected the manner in which colonialism, running from the 1890s to 1963, came to create boundaries among the three predominant socio-economic groups: Europeans, Asians, and Africans. The city's diversity in social life also came to be manifested in the continuation, assimilation, and experimentation of music that could not have been possible in close knit uniform ethnic and racial society.

Especially after 1945, following the end of World War II, Nairobi became a crucible for a variety of cultures from different Kenyan ethnic communities and beyond. Indigenous Kenyan residents in Nairobi were increasingly exposed to international trends and styles that directly impacted on their indigenous practices and traditions. Thus the indigenous cultures had to accommodate each other, and over time respond to the emerging onslaught and influence from other foreign or international ideologies and philosophies. This ethnic, cultural, and racial conglomeration gave rise to a 'national' if not also 'international' culture represented by a unique kind of cosmopolitanism.

Cosmopolitanism in Nairobi demanded that people from different areas relocate away from their hometowns to the city and be surrounded by neighbours from different ethnicities. Yet, until the outbreak of World War II the colonial government continued to control the African urban population in regard to their mobility, and specifically their social activities. The first colonial urban policies were based on 'separate' development, or more accurately, racial segregation, which to some scholars had all the hallmarks of the apartheid practised in South Africa.[3] In order to serve this purpose, Nairobi was divided into three residential zones. The northern and western (Westlands) zones were reserved for white settlement. The southern zone, part of the eastern zones, and the Indian Bazaar were reserved for Asians. Africans who were authorized to live in town were mainly accommodated in the eastern zone. Those Africans who did not have formal or full-time occupations were regarded as a nuisance and had no business being in Nairobi.

These segregated settlement patterns fed into the social entertainment spaces that emerged in colonial Kenya. How leisure time was spent by Africans was largely controlled and confined to their areas of residence. The rise of community centres and social halls in African areas such as Pumwani, Kaloleni, Makongeni, or Muthurwa was meant to serve this colonial segregation. Their other original purpose was to keep Africans busy during their leisure time, distracting them from engaging in various nationalistic activities that would destabilize the colonial system. However, these community centres and social halls as we shall see below, emerged as vibrant spaces, that not only provided entertainment, but also stirred up political sentiments, African mobilization, and protests.

One major traction for the rural-urban migrations into Nairobi was the opportunity for new jobs and gainful employment. Although Nairobi was officially meant to be home to a 'respectable' working class, increasing industrialization after the 1950s necessitated that an urban labour force be stabilized through various colonial policies.[4] The various shifts in official colonial policy, in the wake of the Mau Mau insurgency[5], significantly impacted the city's population profile as well as the manner in which the various groups immersed themselves and participated in its various social spaces. New jobs demanded new loyalties and alternative placements in terms of ethnic and class hierarchies. For instance Odhiambo has observed that, the various class differentiations that emerged among African residents of Nairobi made a distinction between the educated and the uneducated groups.[6] Most members of the former group had a relatively stabe salary or wage therefore they had time for leisure. Needless to mention, the income patterns dictated the leisure consumption patterns and the cross-cultural life that was quickly sipping into the city.

In terms of spatial manifestations, the earlier formal African settlements in Kariokor, Muthurwa, Land Mawe, and Makongeni began, from the mid-1950s, to be complimented by more 'decent housing' in new estates like the Tobacco village near Shauri Moyo and the Gailey and Roberts apartments near Ofafa Kunguni. The occupants of these residential quarters were conspicuous for their mode of dress (tie and long trousers), as well as for their enthusiasm as urban consumers. The case of the rise of the guitar and how this defined the diversity and vibrancy of the leisure spaces in Nairobi is worth some consideration.

Music and Nairobi's universality

The rise of guitar music in Nairobi became an important aspect in redefining the city's social milieu as much as it was

---

3   Cf. Odhiambo, 'Kula Raha' (see n. 1).
4   Cf. Bethwell A. Ogot, 'The Decisive Years: 1956–1963', Bethwell A. Ogot and William R. Ochieng (eds), *Decolonization and Independence in Kenya* (London: James Currey, 1995).
5   An anti-colonial rebellion of various ethnic groups in Kenya, 1952–1964.
6   Cf. Odhiambo, 'Kula Raha' (see n. 1).
7   Cf. Chrispo Caleb Okumu, 'The Development of Kenyan Popular Guitar Music: A Study of Kiswahili Songs in Nairobi', Unpublished M. A. thesis (Kenyatta University, 1998) cf. Chrispo Caleb Okumu, 'Conceptualizing African Popular Music: A Kenyan Experiment', *Bulletin of the Council for Research in Music Education* (Winter 2000/2001), 145–148.

also central to breaking down the boundaries between various socio-cultural and economic groups. The earliest experience of what could be called club music in Nairobi is linked to the influence of the guitar, thats history goes back to the colonial period.[7] Guitar music can be traced to the military marching bands that emerged in various parts of the country before and after World War I (1914–1918). Especially after the end of World War II a handful of demobilized soldiers, who had been conscripted from various parts of the country, arrived back with a guitar, an instrument that would herald new practices of entertainment in the country for many years to come. The guitar in many respects complimented, but later replaced, a fairly sophisticated accordion that had earlier on also penetrated various parts of rural Kenya. As Awounda has noted, the accordion chords did not quite capture the emotions, popular imaginations and creative impulses of the locals in the ways in which the acoustic guitar did.[8] For this reason, the guitar quickly emerged as a distinctive feature of all the entertainment spaces, whether private or public, across the entire Kenyan ethnic spectrum.

The arrival of the guitar and its instant popularity should, however not be construed to mean that African ethnic areas were devoid of music or entertainment in general before the great European wars and before the arrival of foreign influences. African areas within and outside the city were bubbling in vibrancy with various traditional musical styles long before and after their encounter with colonialism. Indeed, music and dance among most of the African communities was very functional and closely integrated with their specific social organizations, religious behaviours, economic activities, and political organizations. Music and dance in the various African communities, to paraphrase Nketia,[9] was inseparable from life, and was almost everywhere, attached to every activity. It defined the peoples' culture in as much as it was markedly utilitarian. The diverse musical styles in African areas were often accompanied by numerous traditional instruments such as drums, cow horns, gourds, and shakers among other improvised instruments. Music and dance were in most cases learnt informally as part of one's growing up to become a member of the society. Long established cultural norms, ceremonies and activities dictated the nature and performance of these music styles and dances. Thus, the various communities were constantly creating and producing new musical styles.[10] It is not surprising therefore that part of this rich African musical repertoire found its way into the city.

However, it is the arrival of the guitar and other external influences during the colonial period that saw most of the African areas adapt and innovate more vigorously in terms of traditional African music and dance. Ranger has made reference to the first beneficiaries of the new innovation, in the rise of *beni* [from the English word 'band'].[11] *Beni*, whose beginnings can be traced to the coastal towns of Kenya and Tanzania in the 1880s and 1890s, gave birth to a unique *dansi* [dance] by a group of Africans who had been educated and trained in India. This group of Africans, the so-called Bombay Africans, who eventually took up leadership roles as pastors, teachers, and other trades are responsible for subsequently popularizing *dansi* in Mombasa's Freretown area.[12] They initially came to take up leadership roles as pastors, teachers, and other trades. The latter cadre influenced the playing of the new instruments such as the guitar, piano, accordion, and others. Though *beni* quickly spread to inland areas such as Nairobi, they were not overly successful. In Nairobi specifically, *beni* existed until the 1950s.

Again, from the coastal towns of Kenya were two major developments that should be recognized. First, was the continuation of the revolution that started in the early twentieth century by the likes of Siti Binti Saad, who liberated Taarab music from the Sultan's palace in Zanzibar and brought it to the market place.[13] Taarab, with its multiple influences from East African coastal cultures, became an authentic style that impacted the entertainment scene of most urban centres in Kenya including Nairobi. Secondly, coastal communities also developed their own brand of music, based on their native Chakacha and other styles, manipulating the keyboard and the guitar in a way that, for years to come, would be identified with the Kenyan coast, as later exemplified in the coastal Jazz groups such as Mombasa Roots, Them Mushrooms, Bahari Boys, Hodi Boys, and Pressmen Band.[14] The music and performances by these bands no doubt revolutionized the entertainment space in Nairobi among other locations in the 1960s.

Further afield, the emergence of Benga rhythm in Nyanza, western, and central Kenya among other places can be directly related to the arrival of the guitar. Benga's most distinctive feature is its fast-paced rhythmic beat and bouncy

---

8 Cf. Moussa Awounda, 'The History of Benga Music: A Report by Ketebul Music', 2007, <http://www.singingwells.org/stories/the-history-of-benga-music-a-report-by-ketebul-music/> accessed 23 December 2017.
9 Cf. J.H. Kwabena Nketia, *The Music of Africa* (London: Victor Gollancz Limited, 1974).
10 Kidula, 'Sing and Shine', PhD thesis (see n. 1), 1.
11 Cf. Terence Osborn Ranger, *Dance and Society in Eastern Africa 1890–1970: The Beni Ngoma* (Berkeley: University of California Press, 1975), 16.
12 Established in Mombasa for the settlement of freed slaves and named after Sir Bartle Frere who played a significant role in ending slave trade.
13 Cf. Amadi Kwaa Atsiaya, 'Popular Music in Kenya', Music in Africa, 23 August 2015, <https://www.musicinafrica.net/magazine/popular-music-kenya> accessed 23 December 2017.
14 Ibid.

finger-picking guitar technique.[15] Benga beat included a sharp lead guitar overriding the rhythm and bass in a way that the pace of the guitars created a steady rise to a climax or crescendo and a quick refrain. The fact that Benga was basically a fast-paced danceable style made it more amenable to innovation, adaptation, and mass appeal across Kenyan rural and urban centres. Its style was, during the early period of Independence, linked and easily blended with other foreign styles such as Congolese Rumba, West African Highlife, or South African Kwela, as well as the aforementioned Taarab and Chakacha. The key driving force within these styles, especially as they came to impact the urban club music and entertainment space, was the guitar.

Specifically in Nairobi, the guitar, as already noted, became popular during the post-World War II period. Okumu has emphasized that the popularity of guitar music in Nairobi during this period was made possible by the return of the war veterans among other external influences.[16] The returning soldiers did not just bring back new instruments such as violins, guitars, accordions, and piano but also money that they used to buy gramophones and 78 rpm records, which were in vogue in the pre-independence years. With these new instruments, there was a revolution in the new styles such as Cha-cha-chá, Bolero, Samba, Mambo, and Rumba which came from South America, the Congo, and Europe. These styles became popular in all of Nairobi's social neighbourhoods and across various classes. Just before Independence, guitarists such as Fundi Konde, Ally Sykes, and Paul Mwachupa recorded several songs that were played in Nairobi on the broadcasting station. As the period of Independence began, the guitar was emerging as a truly 'urban instrument'. Stapleton and May observe guitarists belonged to urban Africa, playing an instrument whose appeal, like that of cars, records, and films, depended on modernity.[17]

The Nairobi urban space was quickly emerging as the location for the most universal form of interaction. By universal we mean that their socio-cultural composition transcended ethnic barriers, thus allowing their transactions to have a broader global socio-cultural outlook. Nairobi's universality in the 1960s was perhaps well demonstrated by the arrival of external influences especially from Zaire, Tanzania, South Africa, Europe, and elsewhere in the wider world. Examples of bands from these locations deserve special mention because of the way in which they impacted the entertainment space in Nairobi and revolutionized the culture of clubbing in the city.

First was the entry of the Congolese in Nairobi from the 1960s following the civil war in then Republic of the Congo or Congo-Léopoldville (later Zaire, today Democratic Republic of the Congo, DRC). Due to political unrest and chaos, many Congolese, including musicians, were pushed to neighbouring countries like Kenya. In Nairobi, most of the Congolese musicians and bands readily found a receptive audience since popular Congolese recordings by Franco's TPOK Jazz, Dr Nico, or Bavon Marie Marie were frequently played on air. For some of these artists, though refugees, Nairobi provided space for their commercial success away from the dominance of Congolese big bands like Franco's TPOK Jazz, formed in 1956, and Tabu Ley Rochereau's Afrisa L'International.[18] Thus, the musicians came to form an important part of Nairobi's club culture.

In this category one finds Congolese bands such as Les Noir, Bana Ngenge, Orchestra Bwambe Bwambe, Orchestra Makassy, Baba National, Orchestra Les Mangelepa, Zaiko Langa Langa, Orchestra Shama Shama, Orchestra Super Mazembe, Orchestra Virunga, and Orchestra Vundumuna, among others. In Nairobi, these Congolese bands found a large population to absorb, not only their music, but also their new style of dance and dress. By the mid-1960s, Nairobi's nightclubs and other entertainment spots would not have been complete without Congolese music. The Cavacha and Rumba rhythms that were promoted through recordings, played a critical role in popularizing the live bands during this period.[19]

Apart from Congolese bands, there were also numerous musicians from Tanzania and other African countries who made Kenya and specifically Nairobi their home. Tanzanian Rumba became extremely popular and widely accessible through live shows, the radio, and recordings. Paterson has noted that through their Swahili lyrics, most Tanzanian artists managed to connect easily with Kenyan audiences, especially in the themes they explored through their music.[20] The most popular bands from Tanzania included Simba

15 Moussa Awounda, 'The History of Benga Music: A Report by Ketebul Music', 2007, <http://www.singingwells.org/stories/the-history-of-benga-music-a-report-by-ketebul-music/> accessed 23 December 2017.
16 Cf. Chrispo Caleb Okumu, 'Conceptualizing African Popular Music: A Kenyan Experiment', Bulletin of the Council for Research in Music Education, Winter 2000/2001, 145–148.
17 Cf. Chris Stapleton and Chris May, African Rock: The Pop Music of a Continent (New York: Obelisk/Dutton, 1990).
18 Cf. Peter Wafula Wekesa, 'The Politics of Cultural Forms: Popular Music, Cultural Identity and Political Opposition in Kenya', Africa Development, vol. 29, no. 4 (Dakar: CODESRIA, 2004) cf. Doug Paterson, 'Life and Times of Kenyan Pop', in Broughton, Simon, Ellingham, Mark et al. (eds.), World Music Vol 1: Africa, Europe and the Middle East (London: Penguin Books, 2000), 509–522.
19 Cf. Okumu, 'Conceptualizing African Popular Music', (see n. 16), 145–148 cf. Paterson, 'Life and Times of Kenyan Pop' (see n. 18).
20 Cf. Paterson, 'Life and Times of Kenyan Pop' (see n. 18).

Sal Davis, photo: unknown

Just a Band, Africa Salon at Yale University, New Haven, 2015, photo: Joe Were

Orch Virunga in front of Starlight Club, Nairobi, 1982

7-Inch Single *Odero Koduko*, Metric Jazz Band, Sulwe, 1974

7-Inch Single *Nyamwaya J.B.*, Metric Jazz Band, Sulwe, 1974

Wanyika, Les Wanyika, and Super Wanyika Stars. As well as, Dar-es-Salaam Jazz Band, Morogoro and Tabora Jazz bands, Orchestra Safari Sounds, DDC Milimani Park, Baraka Mwinshehe, and Remmy Ongala. Other memorable music stars from the region included Peter Tsotsi and Nashil Pichen from Zambia, who played a critical role in the development of the Equator Sound Band's Twist style, modelled around the South-African Kwela rhythm. Malika Mohammed from Somalia and Uganda's Sammy Kasule were also important.

The early period of Independence also saw the prominence of European and US music in various locations in Nairobi. Apart from the white minority, European and US music leisure activities were popular under the emerging black elite class residing in the city. The presence and popularity of European and US music in Kenya and specifically in Nairobi could be associated mainly with its encouragement as a 'marker of modernity'. For several significant reasons, numerous key, but often uncelebrated Europeans dominated the showbiz music scene in Kenya. Those who seem to stand out are Otto Larsen, Peter Colmore, and Charles Warrod. The trio found themselves drawn to and sucked in by the irresistible allure of Nairobi's pre-independence musical circles as acquainted guitarists, producers, and entertainers. Their feat could be linked to the crystallization of foreign and local styles as well as their formative efforts that entailed the capturing of culturally rooted traditional songs on tape reels and spools.

That European and US music was promoted through the radio and live shows by visiting foreign artists is in no doubt. Calypso, Soul, Jazz, Funk, and later Reggae music, by popular artists from Europe and the Americas, dominated performances in the big hotels in Nairobi and in several clubs. Most of this music was adapted by Kenyan artists with great style and finesse. Perhaps, the biggest influence of Funk came from the late James Brown, America's 'Godfather of Soul', whose style and swagger was imitated by a whole generation of Kenyan artists.[21] It is within the specific spaces where this music was consumed that we turn our attention to.

Early clubbing spaces and an emerging hybrid society

Independence in Kenya brought with it an important transformation of social spaces as sites of entertainment and leisure. As the preceding sections have sought to demonstrate, Nairobi's social spaces by 1963 were becoming highly multicultural and cosmopolitan. The connections between different local and foreign styles ones were being nurtured and negotiated through the creativity around the guitar music and other local and foreign forms. Nairobi was emerging as a city at the centre of innovative ideas because it was also a location for technological development and industrialization. The opportunities offered through popular music in terms of its production and reception, as well the various leisure activities, necessitate that we specifically examine the context that enabled these possibilities. The political transition towards Independence in many respects, enhanced – in as much as it expanded and 'liberated' – the various spaces of leisure within the entire country, and specifically in the city.

Political Independence came with an air of freedom to Africans from both urban and rural contexts in Kenya. For the Nairobi dwellers, just like those in other urban centres elsewhere, Independence similarly ushered in some relative freedom – not only from the colonial trappings but also from the cultural and ethnic ties of the diverse rural settings. This offered social opportunities in the city and allowed for new practices those in the colonial period as well as different from those in the rural settings. For instance, it must be remembered that during the colonial period, the enjoyment of leisure by Africans, both in rural and urban areas, was controlled by the colonial government. As Ranger and Odhiambo observe, a ban had been introduced on African social gatherings both in villages and urban centres.[22] Before the onset of colonialism these gatherings, and indeed other related social activities, had enabled Africans from diverse backgrounds to uniquely congregate for the common purpose to celebrate life, make merry, enjoy music, and share their culture. Thus the ban on African social gatherings undermined and restricted their participation in social activities and in the enjoyment of leisure.

Yet this ban could neither be practically nor realistically enforced given the intricacies of culture as a social practice and given the lean nature of the colonial policy enforcement apparatuses. Especially in Nairobi, the colonial control of leisure spaces proved unpractical since Africans devised alternative methods to beat the system. According to Ranger, Africans who were hard pressed and in need of leisure resorted to forming 'traditional clubs' in which they

---

21 Cf. Bill Odidi, 'Retracing Kenya's Funky Hits', Business Daily Africa, 12 January 2012, <https://www.businessdailyafrica.com/magazines/Retracing-era-of-Kenya-s-funky-hits-era-/1248928-1304586-qnlgpc/index.html> accessed 23 December 2017.

22 Cf. Terence Osborn Ranger, *Dance and Society in Eastern Africa 1890–1970: The Beni Ngoma* (Berkeley: University of California Press, 1975) cf. Odhiambo, 'Kula Raha' (see n. 1).

played and danced to traditional drums and music reminiscent of the life in rural areas.[23] However, this was also later banned in favour of 'modern' community social halls, bars, and nightclubs because the drums and traditional way of enjoying music and leisure caused too much noise for urban white settlers in estates such as Muthaiga. Moreover, the newly introduced 'modern' spaces of leisure provided a clear opportunity for the administrators to monitor and control African activities.

This approach by the colonial powers was born out of the twin reality that leisure cannot be fully controlled and that Africans from diverse categories had become permanent residents of the city as well as permanent consumers of leisure. The most practical way to manage these unprecedented realities was to create formal and closely monitored centres in the city. This saw the construction of social halls that included Kaloleni, Pumwani, Muthurwa, and Embakasi to allow Africans to participate in social activities – but also to keep them busy and distract them from nationalistic activities that would otherwise destabilize the colonial system.

Thus the social and community halls in African areas within the city can be seen as the first officially sanctioned centres where entertainment evolved in colonial Kenya. It is noteworthy however that instead of these social spaces performing their original colonial function of restricting and controlling Africans, they quickly emerged as the hotbed of entertainment and facilitation of other social and even political movements. Most of the prominent African artists found opportunities to entertain their fellow brethren through live music in the evenings and over the weekends. But in the 1960s, these social halls also provided opportunities for political leaders such as Tom Mboya, Jaramogi Oginga Odinga, Charles Rubia, or Milton Obote to address huge political gatherings. It was also here that many trade union meetings were held.

These spaces of leisure continued to be complimented, if not also subverted, by the more 'modern' (meaning western) forms of entertainment from the 1960s onwards. The latter new spaces allowed Africans the opportunity to listen to and enjoy live African and exotic music, as well as dance away the nights, especially in the various clubs and discos. The colonial banning and control of African social spaces and gatherings in the city invariably led to the privileging of western forms of entertainment that were carried over into the early period of Independence and beyond. For instance: bars and night clubs, industrially brewed beer and other alcoholic drinks, soccer or holiday tours – most of which were new to the Africans – were encouraged especially among the working urbanite. These urbanites were, from the 1960s and 1970s, characterized by a sense of smartness: suit and tie, nice outlook, all of which were supposed to be a sign of better living. This characterization does not apply to the majority of the city dwellers, so it largely defined the segregated location of clubs in the city. More often than not most of the clubs during this period had a class hierarchical sieve.

Among the earliest clubs in Nairobi in the 1960s were the Starlight Club off Valley Road, Bonanza Club, Sombrero Club, Gloucester Hall, and Dambusters. These clubs distinguished themselves as entertainment hotspots for Nairobi's emerging elites of government ministers, senior civil servants, pilots, bank clerks, and the like. Their working-class status exposed them to a sizeable income to spend on entertainment. It was this class that sampled the very best of live bands and recorded music that was in vogue. Most of the productions were by both local and foreign artists. The live bands that were invited to these venues played music that mostly reflected the independence-mood and social challenges of the times. Musicians and bands that found success and popularity in playing at these venues included Daudi Kabaka, Bata Shoes Shine Band, Inspector Gideon, Police Band, Scarlet Band, and Tabu Ley Rochereau. These bands were often complimented by live performances from bands outside of Africa that popularized styles such as Calypso, Soul, Jazz, and later Reggae. The latter foreign bands were particularly popular in big hotels such as Brunner's and Panafric.

Thus, these early clubs of the 1960s were clearly multicultural in clientele and they were defined by specific class barriers. Their clientele enjoyed the music in the clubs at night and also during daytime, over the weekends, through the Boogies that became popular from the 1970s. Boogies, though also attracting mainly top local and foreign live bands, had a distinctive character. They provided an occasion, especially for the young people to come to the city, dance to their favourite bands and showcase their newfound sub-culture – haute-couture dress codes and 'erotic' lifestyles – away from parental glare. The fashion sense associated with

23   Cf. Ranger, *Dance and Society in Eastern Africa 1890–1970* (see n. 22).

this new city lifestyle was afro hair, bell-bottom trousers, and platform shoes. But the Boogies soon became a victim to estate gangs, mainly from Eastlands.[24] It was for this reason that they kicked off a controversy within officialdom with the general view being that they were corrupting the morals of the youth. In December 1972 the officials banned the Boogies.

Away from the 'classy' side of the city were equally bubbling clubbing spaces that were characterized by all manner of ethnic and foreign music. Especially with the decline in live shows, discos emerged as the most popular replacements. Through jukeboxes that became a must for nearly all the bars on River Road including Nyanza Bar, Njogu-ini, or Reke Marie, the revellers of different classes and ethnicities congregated after work and over the weekends to enjoy their leisure time. Although the music by Congolese and local Kenyan musicians maintained a strong presence in such bars, the radio, which had become a common feature in every Kenyan household, ensured that music from outside the country also occupied an enviable space.

However, it was Benga, initially regarded as the music of the lower classes, that continued to capture and shape entertainment within and around the city's middle and lower-class residential neighbourhoods. Benga created a unique space for different classes and ethnic groups to negotiate and to break their social barriers. Both local and foreign artists used Benga to assert their prominence on the entertainment scene through the various stylistic and thematic adaptations. They borrowed, repackaged, and readapted Benga into a club circuit affair that came to shape both the private and public leisure spaces in the city. One resultant manifestation of this adaptation came to be demonstrated through the continuous experimentation by various artists to create a distinct Kenyan, yet also cosmopolitan style in Nairobi along secular and religious traditions.

Music for the nation

'Harambee Harambee' was a popular song by Daudi Kabaka in the early 1960s. Kabaka, a composer, guitarist, singer, and performing artist, belonged to a group of successful musicians in Nairobi that included Fadhili Williams, Gabriel Omolo, Paul Mwachupa, and Fundi Konde among others. Their music represented the diverse social space that marked not just the transition from colonialism to Independence, but also between categories like rural-urban, indigenous-foreign, rich-poor, or white-black. 'Harambee' [Kiswahili for 'pulling together'] became a clear call for the then ruling Kenya African National Union (KANU) party in its national development policies and initiatives. Though 'Harambee' was recorded in 1962, a year before Independence, Kabaka captured the nationalistic mood that came to characterize the hopes and aspirations of many Kenyans in the post-independent period. For over three decades the song remained a news signature tune for the national broadcasting station, Voice of Kenya (VOK)[25] with an estimated playing of fifty-three minutes a day for thirty-two years.[26]

Kabaka and his contemporaries redefined the entertainment space in Nairobi by subverting the often narrow ethnic categories with a diverse national repertoire that manifested itself in what came to be known as the *Zilizopendwa*[27] style. These oldies songs fed into the rich urban repertoire. They were inspired by guitar and club music traditions that had surfaced in various contexts in Kenya and the entire African region. A distinctive thematic feature of this music was its attempt at celebrating, not only Independence, but also addressing other social, economic, and political issues affecting of people both in urban and rural areas. Traditional Kenyan styles from the Kikuyu, Luhya, Luo, Kamba, Kalenjin, Maasai, or Samburu among other ethnic groups came to be represented in the *Zilizopendwa* rhythms.

Like these traditional styles, *Zilizopendwa* could be performed within similar social contexts – from ritual ceremonies to recreation, from work songs to praise songs, children songs to love songs, lullabies to popular entertainment.[28] *Zilizopendwa*, though often recorded and sung in Kenya's national language, Kiswahili, equally came to embrace the city's multi-racial and multi-ethnic conglomeration, including more than forty different Kenyan ethnic groups, a sizeable Asian community whose forefathers came to build the railway, and a large number of Europeans who remained after Independence, as well as other foreigners. Thus the *Zilizopendwa* artists came to nourish the entertainment needs of a vibrant and hybrid socio-cultural context that co-existed peacefully by recognizing and respecting each other's cultural inclinations. As the city and its population developed through the challenges and fortunes of the early Independent period, it's socio cultural context continued to flourish through music.

24 Cf. Austin Okande, 'Nairobi's "Mad House"', *The Standard*, 30 January 2014, <https://www.standardmedia.co.ke/business/article/2000103508/nairobi-s-mad-house> accessed 23 December 2017.

25 Later changed renamed Kenya Broadcasting Corporation (KBC).

26 Cf. Donald Otoyo Ondieki, 'An Analysis of Kenyan Popular Music 1945–1975 for the Development of Instructional Materials for Music Education', unpublished PhD. thesis (Nairobi: Kenyatta University, 2010).

27 Literal translation: 'they were loved', used to reference songs that were national Kenyan hits in the era after independence and through to the 1980s.

28 J.H. Kwabena Nketia, *The Music of Africa* (London: Victor Gollancz Limited, 1974).

Religious Music not only reflects the city's racial and ethnic diversity, or its culture; it is more than that as this music fulfills this city's diversity. From the early 1960s and perhaps even before, Nairobi served as an intersection and synthesis of various religious ideologies, views, and artistry. Although home to many religious orientations and worldviews, Christianity, African traditional religions, and Islam dominated the spiritual credoscope in the city. Of the three, Christianity seems to have succeeded on a wider scale in capturing the popular imagination of the Nairobi residents. Chitando argues that this overwhelming popularity of Christianity is due to its earlier association with modernity and the colonial project.[29] A rich Gospel music culture evolved that was shaped by diverse innovations and developments as well as new ideas about its production and consumption. It provided alternative parameters for identity and survival. Yet, the spiritual and aspirational aspects of Gospel music can also be seen in the traditional African songs that became popular before Independence. For instance, Ogot and Kinyatti have demonstrated how religious songs and hymns were actively employed as a mobilizing strategy to raise morale among Africans during the Mau Mau war of liberation.[30] Such hymns sought to forge a common identity between the combatants and the peasant supporters, as well as articulate the goals of the struggle.

Thus, in the 1960s, religious songs and hymns seem to have shifted from the militancy of war to the struggle for peace, unity, and development. As politicians began to exhort the new nation and redefine its national goals and aspirations, artists became an important component of this national building effort. They produced songs through which they urged Nairobians to unite, support their leaders and pull together towards national development. Kidula particularly observed that with the increase in the use of Kiswahili in the city and the country after 1963, more people were being introduced to church choir music through radio broadcasts and much later by television.[31]

The African Inland Church (AIC) in Kijabe and the Anglican Church in Nairobi took the lead in marshalling the Christian congregation into the appreciation and enjoyment of diverse religious songs on the radio and television after 1963. The same period also saw the birth of new African founded Christian movements in Nairobi. With this, new types of music closely related to contemporary African and international popular styles began to be composed, used, and became a focal point. The most prominent of these churches were the Deliverance Church and the Redeemed Gospel Church. Both gave rise to the 'Sing and Shine' programme on television, which sought to nationalise and promote Kenyan music.[32] Through these songs, most churches and religious spaces in Nairobi continued to act as a platform for articulating various socio-economic and political issues concerning the general life, not just in the city but in the entire country.

A time of transition

In the 1960s the emerging social historiography of Nairobi came to be defined in the performing arts, especially in popular music. Though often silenced within mainstream discourses on the evolution and transformation of urban centres, this historiography is especially important in the understanding the dynamics around the construction of urban spaces and the negotiation of forms of life in the Nairobi of the 1960s. The richly endowed and diverse social history represented a significant transition from colonialism to Independence, just as it also marked a negotiation between rural-urban and indigenous-foreign spaces. In an evolving city, Nairobi's entertainment space as characterized in club music and other performances represented a crystallization of different cultural, class, racial, and other categories. This created a clearly heterogeneous environment. The social milieu of music and the spaces in which it was produced and consumed provides an interesting insight into the manner in which social life in the city was negotiated and how the different residence of the city reflected on their individual and collective experiences. Their desires, aspirations, joys, and fears were defined through their new location, and their interaction with a broad multicultural and cosmopolitan reality, away from the rural and culturally close-knit settings.

In this new reality, marked by intense diversities, various new adaptations and continuities became the norm. This norm was perhaps most intensely expressed in music and music spaces. Club music in 1960s Nairobi emerged from a clearly restrictive and controlled colonial arena in which Africans were expected to be passive participants they later seized control. From the diverse forms of live guitar music to discos and other forms, clubbing became a norm and not an exception in the enjoyment of leisure in the city. The complex

---

29 Cf. Ezra Chitando, '"Down with the Devil, Forward with Christ!" A Study of the Interface between Religious and Political Discourses in Zimbabwe', *African Sociological Review*, 6.1 (2002).

30 Cf. Bethwell A. Ogot, 'Politics, Culture and Music in Central Kenya: A Study of Mau Mau Hymns 1951–1956', in William R. Ochieng and Karim K. Janmohamed (eds.), *Some Perspectives on Mau Mau Movement* (Nairobi: E.A.P.H, 1977) cf. Maina Wa Kinyatti, *Thunder from the Mountains: Mau Mau Patriotic Songs* (London: Zed Press, 1980).

31 Kidula, 'Sing and Shine', Ph.D. thesis (see n.1), 45.

32 Ibid., 46.

arena created by this social space and the continued negotiation between local and foreign styles heralded a new space for experimentation. This resulted in the emergence of lifestyles that subverted the narrow ethnic constellations in the city – to engage in pulling together towards national development and to create a truly multicultural society.

The 1970s–1990s: A Mobile City
Joyce Nyairo

Is Molly's a club or is it, as one teenager recently said, 'a gathering of people in a sweaty place'?[33] But to be sure, clubs and sweat have always gone hand in hand. Whether the space is a beach party in Mombasa or a colourful *matatu* [public mini-bus taxi] emitting the loudest *mahewa* [music] right under the nose of the traffic police at 7:30am. Whether it is a make-shift shed, pulsating Rumba sounds beside a petrol station on Dunga Road, or a club out in provincial Eldoret, featuring a mix of academic dons, shop attendants, traders in textiles, farmers, and professionals – no club escapes the pungent smell of perspiration that confirms the patrons are at one with the beat.

While the smell that pervades club life has remained the same for decades, the sounds and sights of night action change all the time. Today, even before one gets to the door of Molly's – and regardless of whether the time is 9pm or 4am – there is an array of tables lined up along the corridor holding a variety of shots. Beside the tables are the sweet male bartenders with a smile and a joke. They announce the brands of drinks with such easy recall amidst all the pushing and shoving. A shot goes for as little as 100 shillings. Inside Molly's there are a equal variety of drinks on offer. Dancing consists of jumping up and down or gyrating twerk movements. Teenage girls in the shortest of skirts and the highest of heels, in all manner of colours, laugh happily next to young men in tight V-neck T-shirts and even tighter skinny jeans. By 2am, a few girls knock off their heels, one of them reaches into her clutch bag for a pair of flats. She wears the flats and places the heels on the table – she is not about to lose sight of them. People have been known to get home from the club with neither heels nor cell phones. Such is the speed with which sketchy patrons relieve others of their valuables inside every club in town. I heard a story about a young man who lost his cell phone to the girl he was dancing with. Alas, gender roles don't seem to mean much inside the club. For their security and peace of mind, many revellers carry a cheap Nokia Asha phone, or some generic brand that no thief worth his name will be interested in, because it has no resale value.

I ask one of the girls who is still in her heels at 3am whether she does not have a pair of flats to change into. Her answer strikes me as extremely sensible in a place so laden with intoxicating things – shisha, alcohol, and things I don't want to list due to their smell. 'The reason I wear heels is that it gives me a responsible time to go home. Once my feet start killing me, it's time to go home. You can't go home when the sun is up. That is just so sketchy.'

So nowadays heels have become timekeepers and no one worth their name dances *mpaka che* [till dawn]? How the times have changed! The *mpaka che* culture has its roots in the old regulated city and its transportation barriers. From its inception in the 1950s, the Kenya Bus Services (KBS), run by the Nairobi City Council, did not provide much public transport after dark. And in the 1960s, *matatus* were few in number and erratic in their movements. According to one Nairobi veteran who made a home in the city in 1953:

> Matatus *first started running on the route from Makadara, Bahati Roundabout, Kaloleni, Muthurwa to town mid-1961. The veterans from the colonial detention camps began the trade by buying the* mariamus *(the vehicles which the colonials were using to carry the Mau Maus to detentions and jails) at 500 shillings. The name* matatu *was coined from the thirty-cents fare charged from the terminals to any stage on the routes to town … later on they spread to other African locations.*[34]

As Mbũgua wa Mũngai explains it, 'by a metonymic process, the price of the fare came to mean the vehicle'.[35] In the mid-1970s, the last bus left the bus station off Temple Road for Kenyatta National Hospital at 11pm. This was the route number seven bus, the most dependable of them all. In the neighbourhoods of Eastlands, Kibera, Dagoretti, and other estates off Ngong Road, buses ran up to about 10pm, but in the formerly white neighbourhoods – Lavington, Karen, Spring Valley, and Kileleshwa – there were no buses after 8pm. There was always a rumour about a number fifty-four bus that took a whole ring around the city, dropping *walevi* [drunkards] off, but who wanted to risk freezing to the bone, waiting for a rumour? Taxis were few and far between,

---

33 Miss Muthoni, in an interview with the author outside Molly's at 5am (2014).

34 Mary Macharia, in an interview with the author (2014).

35 Mbũgua wa Mũngai, *Nairobi's Matatu Men: Portrait of a Subculture* (Nairobi: Contact Zones NRB, 2013), 34.

and their costs were, in any case, prohibitive. Adapting to these transport barriers meant either walking back home after the party or waiting for hours at the bus stop for the very first vehicle at dawn. Party organizers and club owners cut down on the uncertainties associated with either option by running the show until the break of dawn, *mpaka che*. According to Duncan Ogweno, CEO of Go Sheng, an organization dedicated to research and preservation of Kenya's demotic urban dialect, Sheng,[36] the phrase '*mpaka che*' is derived from the Dhuluo language: '*Nyaka piny ru che*' [until the world arises and is clear/daylight].

Going home at dawn may be frowned upon by some of today's youth but it has remained a marker of one's growing independence – or one's desire for independence – ever since people started inhabiting dances in the city. The names Starlight, Club 1900, Sombrero, Hallians, Brilliant Night Club, Zambezi, Small World, Sahara, Dambusters, Cantina, Park Inn, and City Square, which later became Garden Square, are engrained in the cultural memory of Nairobi. These were the spaces of organized nightlife throughout the 1960s and 1970s. There were also informal sites of recreation in the night, in the bars that wind down River Road and its parallel streets, like Tsavo Road, patrons regularly danced around jukeboxes. And then there were those spaces where formal dances would occasionally be hosted: Desai Memorial Hall, Kariokor Social Hall, and Kenyatta Conference Centre. Additionally, the Nairobi mayor threw a huge invite-only ball on New Year's Eve. With live music from either the Kenya Police Band or the Maroon Commandoes from the Kenya Army, the Mayor's Ball was a thing of envy for those who could not be there to hear Habel Kifoto and David Kuria belting out songs like 'Charonyi ni Wasi' [life is hard] and 'Christina'.

Centrality and class differences

In 1979, Les Mangelepas was riding high with 'Embakasi', a farewell song that was to become the emblematic memory of the old Nairobi airport of the same name.[37] Kabila 'Eveni' Kabanze was leading the group with a new dance routine called 'Stage Marshall'. He was trying to recoup the group's fortunes since Bwami Walumona, the lead guitarist, had gone off to form some other band. Mangelepas had moved from the city to play at the far-off venue Bomas of Kenya on Friday and Saturday nights. At Bomas, Mangelepas was aiming for the young, upwardly-mobile professionals. Yet, when they played at the more centrally located Park Inn, right by Haile Selassie Avenue, Uhuru Highway, and Kenyatta Avenue, Nairobi's teenagers had no problem making their way there. Whether they walked, took a bus, or hitched a ride, they could be sure of getting into town by 7pm.

From the Central Business District, the Park Inn was a short and pleasant walk. The culture of pick-pockets and *ng'eta* [muggings] – that incredibly ingenious brand of mugging that involves placing a wooden plank up one's sleeve and using it to knock the air out of an unsuspecting victim – was still a long way off in the bad and fear-filled 1990s. The Park Inn was a rowdy affair full of fast-talking *mtaa* [hood] guys who liked to hang around in gangs with aggressive names like Hatucheki [We don't laugh]. They were a carry-forward from the early 1970s when Nairobi youth became (in)famous for attending afternoon Boogies.[38]

In 1979, bell-bottom pants, wet-look shirts and platform shoes were still trending. The boys in the bands led the way, wearing ridiculously high-waisted trousers often in bright red, stunning yellow or plain black. The buttons ran virtually from the midriff all the way down to the fly. Because this high-waist fashion was so closely associated with the numerous Congolese bands singing *Lingala* songs all over the airwaves and at clubs like Garden Square, they came to be known as '*bolingo* trousers'. For, though the snooty teenagers living west of Tom Mboya Street pretended that they did not listen to *Lingala* music, the one word they seemed to know from the chorus of those songs was '*bolingo*' [love].

Class differences were played out in the type of music one listened to. But to be sure, some local acts did succeed in breaking through these barriers. Take for example, Ishmael or Ismail Jingo. He was, arguably, the greatest Soul singer of his time bar perhaps, Steele Beauttah. It was Jingo who worked some real magic on the international airwaves, and the kids west of Tom Mboya Street were proud to be heard singing along to his massive hit 'Fever'. Jingo was the star attraction at Arcadia. Along with Kelly Brown, Sal Davis, and Slim Ali, he belonged to a crop of Mombasa-born artists who embraced the Funk sound and quickly made their way to Nairobi, where international record labels like Polygram and EMI were based.[39]

When Jingo joined Arcadia's resident band, it soon changed its name to Gloria Africana. Its main rival was the

---

36 Cf. Chege Githiora, 'Sheng: Peer Language, Swahili Dialect or emerging Creole?', *Journal of African Cultural Studies* 15, 2 (2002), 159–81.

37 Opened in March 1958 by the last colonial Governor of Kenya, Sir Evelyn Baring, Embakasi is the precursor of Jomo Kenyatta International Airport, which was completed in March 1978 and renamed in 1979, in honour of the first president.

38 Booklet to the multi-media pack compilation *Retracing Kenya's Funky Hits* (Nairobi: Ketebul Music, 2011), 34.

39 Booklet to the multi-media pack compilation *Retracing Kenya's Funky Hits* (see n. 38), 26.

Starlight-based Air Fiesta Matata featuring the soft crooner Steele Beauttah. The rivalry between Jingo and Beauttah was fierce. Each claimed to be the king of Soul music. Jingo's big moment came in 1972 when Gloria Africana played at the then Embakasi International Airport to welcome James Brown: 'The Godfather of Soul'. Brown, also known as 'the hardest working man in show business', was on transit to Zambia. He was so enamoured by Jingo's rendition of 'Talkin' Loud and Saying Nothin'', that he left his entourage and joined Jingo on the makeshift stage on the runaway.[40]

Clothes and dance anthems

On the west side of town, there were class differences of yet another kind: estate chicks versus the classy babes from the stand-alone homes with treed driveways. In the estates, the girls spent the afternoon borrowing clothes and painting their nails. The shoes had to be platforms of the wedge design. For the few girls who loved to wear jeans, windbreaker jackets were also in vogue. In later years they would swap stories about where to buy the cheapest Gemini heels (imported via Uganda). They would wear plastic Sandak sandals in all colours and they would dye their Bata sneakers in bright blues and pinks. Back in 1979, securing the right wedged platforms was the work of the entire afternoon before a night of revelry. Next came the painting of nails. No one had the money to go to a beauty parlour. All make-up was done at the home of whoever it was who had managed to acquire a make-up kit that, inevitably, held shades that were never intended for black skin. But who cared? Lara 67 and Charming 69 were the nail varnish brands and shades of red trending at the time. You still see those colours now on older women who were once the belle of the ball – a position they hold on to slyly through the colours that once made their nails the talk of the evening.

If 1978 belonged to the Bee Gees and their mighty dance hit 'Stayin' Alive', then 1979 was the year when Donna Summer ruled the radio and disco dance floors. 'Hot Stuff' and 'Bad Girls' seemed to speak directly to Nairobi's frisky teenagers. The more adventurous ones among them would drive all the way to Blue Posts Hotel in Thika and throw themselves into the electric atmosphere of a disco full of psychedelic lights and smoke effects. Those who did not have money and transport to traverse the city and get to the disco at Blue Posts, or the one at Westwood Park in Karen, looked for a house party, or 'groove' as they were known then. A bunch of teenagers would walk from Kileleshwa to Woodley via Valley Arcade, picking up more friends along the way. Grooves sprung up as suddenly as they disappeared. There was rarely ever anything more than four days' notice. Invitation cards were just as rare and gate-crashing was the norm rather than the exception. To this day, I wonder whether those parents who had made a ritual out of travelling to their upcountry *shambas* [farms] every Saturday afternoon have any idea what went on in their living rooms and kitchens between Saturday afternoon and Sunday evening, when they would return to the city ready for office work on Monday.

Let's return to the walking teenagers in search of a party. In those days, before cell phones and GPS, finding a party venue was a hazardous affair negotiated through poorly lit short-cuts and contradicting rumours. Salvation came from whoever had attentive ears. They would pick up on the 'boom-twaff' sound of an amplifier beckoning from a distance. Sometimes, the mobile groove hunters would walk towards the sound of music only to find a lonely watchman nestled next to a transistor radio tuned to Voice of Kenya. Top acts of the day like Anita Ward, the Brothers Johnson, The Commodores, Parliament, Chic, The Manhattans, and Earth Wind and Fire were regularly featured on 'Beat Time', 'Yours for the Asking', and 'Late Date' – the trendy music shows on VOK's General Service.

Once at the groove, as the sound of the Gibbs brothers came over the speakers in the opening bars of 'Stayin' Alive', those who had watched the film *Saturday Night Fever* would quickly strike a John Travolta pose, left hip striking out and right arm raised overhead ready to boogie! (And didn't every groom who wedded in Nairobi in 1978 and 1979 wear a cream suit and red shirt à la Travolta?) No one seemed to worry about the dark side of Donna Summer's lyrics in 'Bad Girls'. Up to that point, few – one exception being Mayula Mayoni in 'Cherie Bondwe' – had sung in sympathetic praise of commercial sex workers. The 'Late Date', or Blues section of the party, was the most painful for the 'floaters'. This was the term for anyone who did not have a partner to hold in a fond embrace of slow dancing. Dancing to Donna Summer's 'Love to Love You, Baby' was a tricky affair. Even for steamy teenagers, there was something way too lurid and X-rated in the moans and groans that endeared that

---

40 Cf. Joyce Nyairo and Bill Odidi 'Fare Thee Well, Nairobi's Home of Song and Sin', *Saturday Nation*, 30 August 2014, <http://www.nation.co.ke/news/Florida-Night-Club-Demolition/-/1056/2434974/-/l4s003z/-/index.html> accessed 20 February 2018.

number to millions across the globe. One had to admire the editing skills of radio presenters who persisted in playing the song despite its explicit content.

Alcohol and celebrities

Cheers to the freakin' weekend,
I drink to that, yeah, yeah.
Oh let the Jameson sink in,
I drink to that, yeah, yeah.

Rihanna's words in her song 'Cheers' (Drink to That) rock the club and everybody sings along – glasses raised high; higher than their hoarse voices. Through the years, alcohol has been a key ingredient of Nairobi's club life. Today at Molly's, the shots draw one in right from the entrance of the building. It wasn't like that just a few years ago. Now, the alcohol wants to find you even before you listen to the first song. These clubs along Nairobi's 'Electric Avenue' employ yet another magnet, the socialite. Once this new breed of 'celebs' rock into the club, people rush up with their smartphones. They plead for a chance to take selfies posing next to the 'celeb'. Next, they quickly post the selfies on Instagram eager to be the first to make the viral announcement about which celebrity is at which club. The selfie provides all the proof that is needed to draw a crowd of keen revellers over to the club, and as Camp Mula booms over the speakers: the 'party don't stop'.

Back in the day, musicians in a live band were the only celebs in the house. Instant cameras were hard to come by so the only photographs of the stars of the day were the few that appeared in the daily newspapers. There was very little alcohol served at Groove parties. Money was in short supply and even after an afternoon of 'Q Club' – the popular term for fundraising – the most that young teenagers could afford was a bottle or two of sherry and a few beers. If a party was well planned, there would be a bowl of punch. Who knew what had gone into the mix? Invariably, it would be empty before midnight. Out at Blue Posts or Westwood Park, there would be alcohol on sale. The brave ones amongst the girls stuck to shandy, a mixture of sprite and beer. But most of the boys tried to drink hard. Somehow, even back then, masculinity was associated with drinking – you were not a man until you had suffered a black-out and your friends had to carry you home.

It's 5am on Friday morning outside Skylux Club in Westlands. The street is choking with cars and pedestrians alike. When did people start clubbing on weeknights? I am watching young men staggering and young girls giggling. Whilst some girls are wrapped up in winter jackets, others are oblivious to the cold, but virtually all of them appear drunk. They have been listening to Rihanna sing about Jameson whiskey. They think Jameson is classy so they have had too much of it. I want to feel outraged that sixteen-year-olds are out clubbing and getting dead drunk from a mix of whiskey, red wine, and vodka that come in blue and red bottles. But the naked truth is that Nairobi kids have been partying like this for decades. Just like the clubs that used to be filled with *Lingala* music or the ones that were dedicated to US R'n'B and Soul in the late 1970s, today the club still is a place of intense self-abandonment. Someone swaying on the pavement is singing, 'So wake me up when it's all over', a line from the hit by the Swedish DJ, Avicii. I wait eagerly. I want to see if he will get to the lines that say:

When I'm wiser and I'm older,
all this time I was finding myself,
and I didn't know I was lost!

The 2000s–2010s: A Multiple City
Mukami Kuria

In the early 2000s, the sonic identity of Nairobi was inextricably linked with the popular genre of *Genge* music. Genge dominated Clubs and was largely attributed to the label Calif Records. In this golden era of both Genge and Calif Records (the two inherently intertwined), these songs were often accompanied by modes of self-fashioning, visible in their accompanying music videos which featured the artists clad in fashionable baggy clothing: Timberland boots, durag head scarves and caps worn backwards. One iconic song is 'Kenyan Girl, Kenyan Boy' by Necessary Noize. The song features call and response, in which band member Wyre sings: 'Kenyan girl, would you come take a walk with me?' to which his fellow band member Nazizi responds, 'Nataki chali wa Nairobi' [I want a guy of Nairobi]. This distinction between the country, Kenya and the city, Nairobi, shows an aspiration to modernity. Rapper Nazizi opens the song with a line of praise and veneration to the inhabitants of Nairobi, 'hii track inaenda kwa wasee wote wa ma3, dere wa ma3, conda wa ma3, pia kama unapanda ma3' [this track goes out to everyone of *matatus*, the drivers, the conductors of *matatus*, even those passengers embarking on *matatus*]. The song ends like this:

Yo mathree za two three Westie,
Two four za Jeri Jerusa na Outer,
46 Hughli, Kile, Ungwaro,
Mogaka piga left hapo na kucheki,
44 Kahawa na Githurai
One all tuko pamoja for life
58 Buru ongeza mahewa man
… Mathreee zote sijataja tuko pamoja kama
Ma ma mabeste haha.

[Yo, matatu number 23 to Westlands,
24 to Jericho, Jerusalem and outer ring,
46 to Hurlingham, Kileleshwa and Kawangware,
Mogaka turn left and see,
44 going to Kahawa and Githurai,
We are all together for life,
58 going to Buru turn up the volume,
… All matatus I have not mentioned, we are still together as friends, haha]

By calling out the *matatu* lines – as *matatus* are also playing the band's songs over their sound systems – the lyrics of Necessary Noize on the Matutus refer to the structure of the city, and its strictly local urban belonging and desire. In this way they offer a way of examining the music's placemaking power, with its pride for local culture which affirms the identity of place.[41]

This identity of place is mirrored in a typical Nairobian way of starting the night. Across the city as the weekend approaches, the urban dwellers of the city receive messages and phone calls – their friends, or even acquaintances ask 'Form ni gani? Uko wapi? Tunaenda wapi leo?' [What's the plan? Where are you? Where are we going to tonight?]. Writer Bethuel Muthee considers the question 'uko wapi?' as a way of entering the psychogeography of Nairobi: '"Uko wapi?" This question is part of daily conversations over mobile devices, to answer is to situate yourself. It does not have to be the truth.'[42] Psychogeography in a city like Nairobi is derived from the culmination of sights, sounds, and textures, and affect from the way in which the inhabitants of the city collectively experience the public space. It is more than the experience of seeing the city's architecture: it is the smell of the butchers' and fishmongers' stalls at City Market, the sound of *matatu* horns at KenCom and Railways, or the inventions in language cap through Sheng, in its new words and phrases and the way it is spoken to capture Nairobians' experience of space and time in the city. Nairobi is a city whose thats, as Ndinda Kioko argues, can be seen even in its absence.[43]

In this text, we will follow two ideas. First, we attempt to go deeper into the sense of belonging and identity of some areas in Nairobi and their soundscapes; trying to read the palimpsest of the city. With this, we aim to look into the psychogeography of the city. Secondly, we delve into political aspects of the locations and soundscapes and reflect on Nairobi as a gendered and oppressive city.

From Westlands to Westie

When night falls across the city it becomes apparent that by day and by night multiple worlds coexist in Nairobi. The city has a way of letting the observant see this, often through quiet encounters. One Friday, driving past the Jacaranda Hotel, one such encounter takes place. An elegantly dressed man appears, walking in the opposite direction. He walks onto Woodvale Grove from Waiyaki Way, the essential artery of the city. Any Nairobi resident with an awareness of the time of day can determine where he is coming from this Friday evening. They would deduce that this man is returning from the evening prayers; the green roofed Mosque located on the other side of Waiyaki Way in the Westlands.[44] A Nairobian would deduce that this man went to the Mosque for evening prayers. He walks with ease past Gypsy's bar.

Gypsy's has an entirely unassuming exterior. The building of the bar melds with the surrounding buildings: Standard Chartered Westlands Branch, Uchumi Supermarket Westlands Square, Mater Hospital Westlands Branch. During the day, Gypsy's hides behind an ornamental gate, with decorative coils once painted in gold, but now coated in layers of thick dirt and exhaust fumes from the nearby road. These gates are common in upmarket residential areas; the grills of the wrought iron-gate are widely spaced often revealing extended driveways, lined with trimmed hedges. A look through the spaces in Gypsy's gate and the façade of the

---

41 The corresponding music video begins with a title asserting: 'This is our culture. Why remove its colour?'
42 Bethuel Muthee, 'Naijographia', *Enkare Review*, 5 July 2017, <https://enkare.org/naijographia/> accessed 10 January 2018.
43 In her essay 'The City is a Photograph', writer Ndinda Kioko explores photographic memory and the contours of Nairobi. She opens with the following: 'A city adopts a certain shape, an arrangement that can be seen even in its absence. Somewhere in my childhood, there is an image of Nairobi, one that I saw whenever I closed my eyes and imagined the city before I immersed myself into it,' Ndinda Kioko, 'The City as a Photograph', *Trans-African*, 16 February 2016, <http://trans-african.com/the-city-as-a-photograph/> accessed 12 January 2018.
44 Westlands is one of Nairobi's neighbourhoods to the West of the city centre, a governmental administrative division, known for its mercantilism.

bar hints at what promise the venue holds when the city reawakens: the pillars are painted chili red, the nightclub lights are fixed to an incongruous metal beam. The exterior aesthetic of Gypsy's is enough to show that clubs in Kenya are not purpose-built but are instead an assemblage of pre-existing structures and Kenyan architectural sensibilities. Only in the daytime does one notice that the dance floor of Gypsy's is covered in ordinary driveway paving blocks – or 'cabro' as it's known there, and only there, a name derived from the now defunct company, Cassman Brown & Co.

Most nights a week, Gypsy's is less unassuming. Heaving with regulars and those passing through the city, the dance floor embellished with jewel-like broken glass, Gypsy's is a microcosm of what is commonly known and affectionately referred to as 'Westi(e)' and its multiple modes of existence, both real and imagined. One cannot be certain of how others define and demarcate this area. This quarter begins on from Woodvale Grove and extends to Mpaka Road and Muthithi Road and the clubs that are found on them. Additionally, there is the world and myth created around this specific part of Westlands. The way in which this vernacular traffics and circulates makes it synonymous with 'Electric Avenue'. Westie? Electric Avenue? Both terms refer to the same notorious part of Westlands.

'Electric Avenue' is feared for the number of nights during which a quick drink has turned into a night in which time is suspended, nights that end as day breaks through the Nairobi skyline. This quarter of the city is equally awe-inspiring for its unparalleled energy. Not only is there the physical, and visible Electric Avenue, but there is the Electric Avenue of the mind. In the minds of Nairobians, there is an imagined cartography of where and what Electric Avenue is. We know what it feels like: street food, lit up signs outside nightclubs, and clubs without boundaries where revelers occupy the spaces inside and outside of the clubs, spilling out onto the pavement; a range of popular music from Nigerian Afrobeats to Tanzanian Bongo Flava and South African House.

Along the strip of clubs on Woodvale Grove one can visit any of the clubs with names that invoke foreign places, languages, and histories – Havana, Privée, Bacchus that is closed now. As well as clubs with more nondescript names such as Molly's, Gipsy's, Skylux Lounge, Brew Bistro and Black Diamond. It is highly unlikely that those visiting Electric Avenue will choose to spend their night in just one club. Henri Matisse's painting, *La Danse* comes to mind as revelers perform a dance of moving from club to club in search of pleasure and music that suits their tastes. They appear inseparable from each other and from the night, prancing from Havana to the precarious open-air vendors with their inevitable *mayai pasua* or *smokie pasua* ['split' egg or 'split' sausage],[45] and from there to Privée arm in arm. As morning arrives unannounced to the club-goers, they exit the buildings and clubs they spent the evening in, in searching for ways to get home.

Westie sounds like a cacophony of thudding basslines and speakers operating beyond their capacity. This is the texture of the sculpted sounds of Westie, a cacophony that Nairobians can still hear of the city in their absence. Not so much a history of lush sounds of Nairobi's rich and complex soundscape spectrum such as the Congolese Rumba, the hard-hitting raw sounds like Genge, blending with sounds of the city. The music can be heard in the streets and vice versa, *matatu* horns can be overheard inside of clubs, such as The Alchemist, located by a *matatu* stop, the horns puncturing the music.

The Alchemist, a relatively new multi-purpose space, has become central to Westie and its bohemian, cosmopolitan, and artsy crowd [The Alchemist was established in December 2015 on the space where, in 2010, one of the pre-Ten Cities parties took place; the editors]. It permanently hosts an array of creative businesses and entrepreneurs, a legendary burger food truck, as well as studios available for jam sessions. In addition to featuring a weekly Reggae night film screenings, live music and gigs played by international acts, this venue offers a space for talks on various aspects of the creative economy and practice for the city's musicians, artists, and filmmakers. The Alchemist is an alternative space enabling independent music to flourish, and creates an environment of subcultures. It has hosted 'Thrift Social', an event held by the 2ManySiblings duo, which has given rise to new forms of sartorial self-fashioning across the city, creating a conversation between music and fashion as modes of expressing and documenting urban belonging.

However, to demarcate the boundaries of 'Westie' would impose limits on the collective imagination of what the city is. Visitors and inhabitants of the city learn that the boundaries of Electric Avenue are indistinctive, yet it is wholly part of what we conceive and imagine as Westie.

---

45 'Split' egg or 'split' sausages are cooked in the day and stored in buckets. On demand the vendor removes the shell of the egg in one stunning uninterrupted motion with a spoon. The state regulates many facets of life, including the licensing of bars and clubs as well as of open-air food vendors. During a recent cholera outbreak in Nairobi, in an attempt to curb the health crisis which had allegedly stemmed from up-market hotels, the government outlawed the selling of open-air food. The neoliberal state externalized blame for a failure in public health policy by punishing the most precarious, cutting off their only income. I join writer and political scientist Nanjala Nyabola in asking: 'why are *vibandas* [huts] being punished for cholera appearing in 5 star hotels?' During this period, I remain unsure as to whether the vendors on Electric Avenue were forced to stop operating.

Just as the area is boundless, nights in Westie can be seamless, and so are the dreams attached to it. Westlands is a theatre of middle-class desire. It is a contact zone, a zone of cultural translation and hybridity, a point at which many worlds meet, 'simultaneously inward-looking and totally open to all influence and receptive to rich dialogues'.[46] This is not only exemplified by Nairobi's contemporary music scene, it is also a metonym of what Nairobi has always been as a city. Nairobi exists in the minds of those who live there and those passing through, as a cosmopolis, laying claim to contemporary sounds from elsewhere and setting up clubs as sites of exchange. No area in Nairobi exemplifies this better than Westie.

From the city centre to the periphery

In this quick paced and fast developing city, where clubs open and close fast and the popular nightlife destinations change in unforeseeable ways, Westie was perhaps the most well-known area in Nairobi in terms of clubs. But we stress the need to navigate nightlife and clubs in different spaces as Westlands does not represent the totality of the city. It might be that Westie is waning. The last developments in 2018 show that, perhaps, Electric Avenue as a continuous contact zone of clubs is no more. In this moment, when Westie might be dying out, it is hard to tell where the nightlife energy will flow to and which areas may become the new entertainment centres.

Perhaps it will move once more towards the Central Business District in the centre of Nairobi, where Friday afternoons arrive gently, and the blistering sun peers through the side-streets as all those who earn a living in the city leave their places of work. The sun, no longer as hot, bathes the streets in a brilliant golden light as office workers, traders, and occupants of the city slow their pace to a gentle lull, unlike the bustle that fills the streets during business hours. A variety of music blares out of shops on Moi Avenue as people stroll along the streets, peering into shops selling everything from mobile phone accessories to underwear and lingerie, as vendors on the sidewalk display textbooks, a variety of self-help books, and the odd political science book on the Greater Lakes Region.

Watching Banda Street on a Friday evening, like Tubman Road and Loita Road, the city appears pedestrianized. Nairobi is known to have numerous pedestrians as well as insufficient or poorly paved sidewalks. The end of the week changes the zoning of the city and whatever the law dictates is pushed aside. Men leaving Jamia Mosque clad in their long white *kanzus* [robes] create a sea of white on Banda street, they passing staff setting up in various bars. The road itself becomes the most popular part of the bar, bar stools and tables are placed in what are ordinarily car parking spaces before people head to proper clubs. This is where Nairobians wind down after work, often drinking cheap beer, at the pub Tribeka for instance, before moving on to pricier venues such as Florida when they are already sufficiently inebriated.[47] A popular practice in Nairobi's club culture is 'parking lot pimping' which involves going to a number of parking lots to meet friends before proceeding on a night out, or at times turning a number of cars into a club by choosing to drink in parked cars, whilst playing music from their heavy-duty systems.

Or perhaps the city's nightlife will once again move towards the Industrial Area to the south-east of the city centre. For instance, Baricho Road, which was an unconventional part of the city by most middle-class standards, in the minds of middle-class residents of Nairobi, hosted one of the most well attended live music nights 'Thursday's Live' at the club Choices. Baricho Road was injected with a bolt of electricity, creating a pulse and environment. Music here shows its power to breathe life and energy into neglected parts of the city, regenerating them and creating new potential (until 'Live' at Choices became 'Live' at J's, moving from the Industrial Area to Westlands).

In any case, the periphery of the city will always hold a special place for any excavation of nightlife in Nairobi. Typically, on the periphery, the bars there are home to the 'one-man guitar' phenomenon, where the music is played by a single man with his guitar, mimicking and transforming US Country music. In the areas of Karen, Ngong, and Kiserian on Kiambu Road and in Ruaka are bars named Mbukaki, a portmanteau of the owners' names. Mbukaki is a bar that is atypical and somehow ordinary at the same time. The waitresses sit with patrons, collectively sizing up newcomers, to see if they are worth their time. Fiston Mwanza Mujila's novel *Tram 83* comes to mind and its refrain: 'Do you have the time?' It is also one typology of bar and scene in Kenya, bars and clubs that exist alongside, parallel, and adjacent to car dealerships.

---

46 In framing the conference 'Other Desires: The African City', held at Columbia's Graduate School of Architecture and Planning on 8 April 2016, convener Mpho Matsipa leaned on the words of Nigerian curator Okwui Enwezor: 'The insistent paradox of all modernities is namely that they are simultaneously inward-looking and totally open to all influence and receptive to rich dialogues.'

47 Aka Madhouse on Koinange Street, demolished in 2014.

Kiambu is undoubtedly the part of the city that identifies with Country music, that sees and hears itself in the voices and songs of US-stars like Kenny Rogers and local *Mugithi* stars like John De Matthew, Mike Rua, and the late Salim Junior. Kiambu is also described as an aspirational part of the city. The city's growing population has pushed the boundaries of what is considered Nairobi to the North and North West of the city: land is cheaper in Kiambu, building regulations less strict, inciting developers to build in the area and to cut corners to minimize costs, in turn putting the lives of tenants at risk. Yet Kiambu is still close enough to the city for residents to commute and to lead a life working and living between the city's core and its periphery. The conditions of Kiambu render it a transitory place, between different juridical regimes, territorial administrations, and a middle place between the rural and the urban. The one-man guitar music is an example of this: it is both rural and urban, it is sung in vernacular but aspires to be US Country music, and it is both outdated and yet very contemporary.

Death and danger

One quickly learns that Nairobi's zoning laws are solely textual rather than prescriptive, with no real effect as they are rarely implemented. This results in frequent contestations between nightclub owners with residents and the police. Every couple of months, on a Sunday morning there is a flurry of statuses on Facebook of people amusing themselves and detailing the interruption of their Saturday nights by unannounced police raids on nightclubs. Perhaps writing in passing about how they managed to escape a police raid at J's or the Alchemist Bar in Westlands, having to run away through back routes often just missing wrongful arrest for having committed no crime. A friend in April 2017 wrote on Facebook: 'Shoutout to J's survivors from last night. What the heck was that. Something out of a 90s hip hop music video.'

Night clubs are not exempt from the excesses of the Kenyan police, who often act extra-judicially, harassing clubbers walking around the Central Business District. In one instance, reported in 2017, a police officer shot a twenty-three-year-old woman in the hand and the thigh as she was leaving a concert by Nigerian star rapper Wizkid at Kenyatta International Convention Centre. Conversely, nightclubs are depicted in Kenyan news stories as occasionally dangerous places: instances of club owners being sentenced to five years in prison for shooting patrons, or the repeated involvement of businessman Chris Obure in nightclub shootings. Another example being at B-Club where one man fell to his death and another two men were electrocuted in the swimming pool.

Clubs are also dangerous spaces for those whose gender and sexuality is incongruous with the masculine domination in public spheres. It is important to point out that the city by night, as it is by day, is hostile towards queer bodies and lives. An article on the website *Pink News* in July 2014 details the arrests of sixty people at what was allegedly a gay bar. Club Envy was raided 'because it was suspected that homosexuals frequented the club'.[48] Conversely, the watchman of the venue argued that it was raided as a matter of licensing, when the infamous Mututho Law came into force, pushed by a former MP and chairman of the National Authority for the Campaign Against Alcohol and Drug Abuse (NACADA). The Mututho Law is actually The Alcoholic Drinks Control Act of 2010, amended in 2012. It was passed in an attempt to regulate the import, sale, production, and consumption of alcohol. The law has been used to justify crackdowns on all kinds of venues, but the confusion over the reason why Club Envy was raided demonstrates the extra-legal nature of queer life and queer joy in Nairobi and the ignorance of the heterosexual Kenyan understanding, confusing queerness and criminality.

Just as queer bodies are rarely ever able to lay claim to leisure, public pleasure, and to occupy space, the freedom of women's bodies is equally limited. While nights in Nairobi are often described as fast-paced and hedonistic, young women are often on the receiving end of cautionary tales and warnings about safety in clubs. The city and its nightlife are therefore gendered, inextricably linked to patriarchy and the way in which it prescribes and restricts the actions of young women. The story of Mercy Keino, a young woman who was killed a few years ago, is relevant. There remains a lot that is unknown and unanswered about the night she died. Writer Keguro Macharia notes that 'of the various narratives circulating about Mercy, only three seem undisputable: she was a student, she went to a party, she was found dead'.[49] What remains notable about Mercy Keino's death is the following observation by Macharia:

> … her proximity to male bodies – the daughter of her father, the woman engaged to a man, the partying student

[48] Nick Duffy, 'Kenya: 60 People reportedly arrested in Gay Bar Raid', Pink News, 7 July 2014, <https://www.pinknews.co.uk/2014/07/07/kenya-60-people-reportedly-arrested-in-gay-bar-raid/> accessed 10 January 2018.

[49] Keguro Macharia, 'On Mercy Keino' *Gukira*, 8 August 2011, <https://gukira.wordpress.com/2011/08/08/on-mercy-keino/> accessed 10 January 2018.

with male friends, the vulnerable university woman under the care of male university officials, the victim of harsh bodyguards (at the party). She incarnates, in all these narratives, an object lesson to young women everywhere: choose your male protectors carefully. Simultaneously, she represents an ongoing lesson in Kenyan modernities: education and urbanization endanger young women. Indeed, living endangers young women.[50]

In a sense the speed of the city renders it and its nightlife ephemeral. If Nairobi at night is fast paced, the city echoes this speed through the continuous changes to clubs, pubs, and bars. Like Muthee, I too observe that clubs here in Nairobi often change names. He writes that Nairobi is a city 'in constant renovation, trying to forget itself while keeping the same structure'.[51] Spaces are appropriated and reappropriated, houses become bars. Sometimes old clubs are demolished or turned into something new, such as the renowned Starlight nightclub that was at its height in the 1970s and 1980s. In its place now sits the Integrity Centre, the building that houses the Ethics and Anti-Corruption Commissions. The zoning laws of the city and their inadequate nature also create a very specific type of Nairobi club: a club or bar at a petrol station. To any ordinary urban planner, to anywhere else in the world, putting a leisure and entertainment facility near a highly hazardous and flammable area would be unthinkable. In Nairobi a number of clubs exist next to or on top of petrol stations: 1824 (formerly known as Rafikiz), Madhouse, and Maggie's. It is surprising that there have not been any fires at any of these special venues.

Wake up and repeat

The image of piety: a man on his way back from the Westlands Mosque, in contrast to Gypsy's on a Friday night, can be a metaphor for our excavation of nightlife in Nairobi today. It stands for the two layers in this palimpsest of the city, its multiple worlds, its ambivalences, contradictions, and often improvised nature. This is what Nairobi is like, we make do with what we have, use what we can, and have a wild time while at it. We drink excessively, to forget or to dance, we drink and dance. Hungover, we wake up and repeat. We fill the clubs across the city and dance until our feet are sore as a matter of salvation. We drink and dance to forget our problems, if only for a night or two. We lose ourselves in the music of musicians from Kenya and across Africa to say we belong here, in the city. As we sing along to the loved hit, 'Bablas' [Hangover] by The Kansoul:

Nataka nilewe waite ambulance
Kesho niamke na mabablas
Nikunywe supu niskie fabulous
Hang'ii ikiisha tena repeat repeat.

[I want to drink until they call
I'll wake up hungover tomorrow,
I'll drink soup, so I feel fabulous
When my hangover is over, I'll repeat it all]

Bibliography

Atsiaya, Amadi Kwaa, 'Popular Music in Kenya', Music in Africa, 31 August 2015, <https://www.musicinafrica.net/magazine/popular-music-kenya> accessed 23 December 2017.

Awounda, Moussa, 'The History of Benga Music: A Report by Ketebul Music', 2007, <http://www.singingwells.org/stories/the-history-of-benga-music-a-report-by-ketebul-music/> accessed 23 December 2017.

Chitando, Ezra, '"Down with the Devil, Forward with Christ!" A Study of the Interface between Religious and Political Discourses in Zimbabwe', *African Sociological Review*, 6.1 (2002).

Coquery-Vidrovitch, Catherine, 'The Process of Urbanization in Africa: From the Origins to the Beginning of Independence', *African Studies Review* 34 (1) (1991), 1–98.

Githiora, Chege, 'Sheng: Peer Language, Swahili Dialect or emerging Creole?', *Journal of African Cultural Studies*, 15, 2 (2002), 159–81.

Duffy, Nick, 'Kenya: 60 People reportedly arrested in Gay Bar Raid', *Pink News*, 7 July 2014, <https://www.pinknews.co.uk/2014/07/07/kenya-60-peoplereportedly-arrested-in-gay-bar-raid/> accessed 10 January 2018.

Kidula Jean Ngoya, 'Sing and Shine: Religious Popular Music in Kenya', PhD thesis (Los Angeles: University of California, 1998).

Kinyatti, Maina Wa, *Thunder from the Mountains: Mau Mau Patriotic Songs* (London: Zed Press, 1980).

Kioko, Ndinda, 'The City as a Photograph', *Trans-African*, 16 February 2016, <http://trans-african.com/the-city-as-a-photograph/> accessed 12 January 2018.

Macharia, Keguro, 'On Mercy Keino', *Gukira*, 8 August 2011, <https://gukira.wordpress.com/2011/08/08/on-mercy-keino/> accessed 10 January 2018.

Muthee, Bethuel, 'Naijographia', *Enkare Review*, 5 July 2017, <https://enkare.org/naijographia/> accessed 10 January 2018.

Nyairo, Joyce and Odidi, Bill Odidi, 'Fare Thee Well, Nairobi's Home of Song and Sin', *Saturday Nation*, 30 August 2014, <http://www.nation.co.ke/news/Florida-Night-Club-Demolition/-/1056/2434974/-/I4s003z/-/index.html> accessed 20 February 2018.

---

50 Ibid.
51 Muthee, 'Naijographia', (see n. 44).

Mūngai, Mbūgua wa, *Nairobi's Matatu Men: Portrait of a Subculture* (Nairobi: Contact Zones NRB, 2013).

Nketia, J.H. Kwabena, *The Music of Africa* (London: Victor Gollancz Limited, 1974).

Odhiambo, Eisha Stephen Atieno, 'Kula Raha: Gendered Discourses and the Contours of Leisure in Nairobi, 1946–63', *Archeological Research in Africa,* 2001, 36–37:1, 254–264.

Odidi, Bill, 'Retracing Kenya's Funky Hits', *Business Daily Africa*, 12 January 2012, <https://www.businessdailyafrica.com/magazines/Retracing-era-of-Kenya-s-funky-hits-era-/1248928-1304586-qnlgpc/index.html> accessed 23 December 2017.

Ogot, Bethwell A., 'Politics, Culture and Music in Central Kenya: A Study of Mau Mau Hymns 1951–1956', in Ochieng, William R. and Janmohamed, Karim K. (eds.), *Some Perspectives on Mau Mau Movement* (Nairobi: E.A.P.H, 1977).

Ogot, Bethwell A., 'The Decisive Years: 1956–1963', Ogot, Bethwell A. and Ochieng, William R. (eds.), *Decolonization and Independence in Kenya* (London: James Currey, 1995).

Ogude, James and Nyairo, Joyce (eds.), *Urban Legends, Colonial Myths: Popular Culture and Literature in East Africa* (Trenton, NJ: New Africa Books, 2007).

Okande, Austin, 'Nairobi's "Mad House"', *The Standard*, January 30 2014, <https://www.standardmedia.co.ke/business/article/2000103508/nairobi-s-mad-house> accessed 23 December 2017.

Okumu, Chrispo Caleb, 'The Development of Kenyan Popular Guitar Music: A Study of Kiswahili Songs in Nairobi', unpublished MA thesis (Nairobi: Kenyatta University, 1998).

Okumu, Chrispo Caleb, 'Conceptualizing African Popular Music: A Kenyan Experiment', *Bulletin of the Council for Research in Music Education* (Winter 2000/2001), 145–148.

Ondieki, Donald Otoyo, *An Analysis of Kenyan Popular Music 1945–1975 for the Development of Instructional Materials for Music Education,* unpublished PhD thesis (Kenyatta University, 2010).

Paterson, Doug, 'Life and Times of Kenyan Pop', in Broughton, Simon, Ellingham, Mark, et al. (eds.), *World Music Vol 1: Africa, Europe and the Middle East* (London: Penguin Books, 2000), 509–522.

Ranger, Terence Osborn, *Dance and Society in Eastern Africa 1890–1970: The Beni Ngoma* (Berkeley: University of California Press, 1975).

Stapleton, Chris and May, Chris, *African Rock: The Pop Music of a Continent* (New York: Obelisk/Dutton, 1990).

Wekesa, Peter Wafula, 'The Politics of Cultural Forms: Popular Music, Cultural Identity and Political Opposition in Kenya', *Africa Development*, vol. 29, no. 4 (Dakar: CODESRIA, 2004).

CAIRO

MUSIC/SPACES

The Cacophony of Cairo

A Battle of Narratives

Maha ElNabawi

▶ **P.87**

SPACES/POLITICS

Clubbing in an Oppressive City

Musical and Social Spheres from Al-Haram Street to Tahrir Square

Ali Abdel Mohsen

▶ **P.113**

The Cacophony of Cairo – A Battle of Narratives

Maha ElNabawi

Mohamed Ashraf never intended to become a driver.[1] Born in 1974, the Cairo native always had his heart set on securing a humble life in making music. By the age of fifteen, Ashraf was self-taught in a range of percussion instruments, most notably the *tabla*, a clay goblet-shaped drum like a bongo, in addition to the Western drum kit. Whispers of Ashraf's 'strong and consistent' drum beat quickly spread through the narrow, dilapidated streets of his neighbourhood, Imababa, in central Cairo. By the time he was eighteen, Ashraf began performing percussions in several Shaabi[2] bands. The gigs consisted of street weddings and festivals within crowded popular-class districts. He explains that the instrumentation of a Shaabi band is typically formed by one to five acoustic pan-Arab melody instruments like the *nay* [reed flute], *oud* [lute], *rababa* [spike-fiddle] and *kamanga* [violin], or also an accordion, in addition to a Western drum kit, keyboards, electric bass, tabla, *daff* [frame drums], *dohola* [larger tabla with a louder sound], the *mazhar* [heavy tambourine with large brass jingles] and the ever-present *sagat* [finger cymbals].

In Egypt, weddings have always been a prominent social gathering and ritual. In popular and middle-class districts, weddings are often boisterous, rowdy events oozing with traditional Shaabi music, belly dancing, and guests celebrating in the streets.[3] By the early 1990s, Ashraf was performing percussions for two weddings a night or four nights a week. He was only making ends meet, but he was thrilled to be playing music rather than falling through the cracks into poverty and immobility known to impoverished neighbourhoods like Imbaba. His performance load soon expanded from weddings and festivals to nightly gigs within the plethora of dingy cabarets, nightclubs, and casinos scattered up and down the Cairo's iconic Al-Haram Street along the outskirts of the city near the Great Pyramids.

As Ali Abdel Mohsen denotes in his essay in this book, the history of Al-Haram Street is rich for its rise and disintegration over the decades. For years, calls from the religious lobby continued to demand that the street's clubs be closed down or moved away due to the lewd behaviour often associated with the intoxicated club clientele and tourists frequenting the area. Many argued that the terrorist attacks by Islamists on Al-Haram Street in the late 1990s, coupled with the burgeoning socio-economic crisis surrounding the area, caused an almost immediate downturn in tourism and activities along the once vibrant road.[4] The result: many of the clubs struggled to endure the lack of tourism and steady patronage, which meant there were less and less gigs for Ashraf and his fellow Shaabi musicians.

As the millennium approached, and the accessibility to music-making technology increased, most notably computers and mixers, the demand for multi-instrumental bands and live singers decreased significantly. Just like that, after twenty years of playing music, Ashraf's dream of becoming a recording artist faded. By 2005 he dropped music entirely due to the increasing financial demands of his growing family; instead he opted for a more reliable income path and began working as a private driver for an upper-class family in Cairo's Giza district.

When speaking to Ashraf, one can find themselves instantly travelling through an intellectual discourse fuelled by his vast understanding of Egyptian politics, religion, culture, and society. But like millions of other talented people in Egypt, as in his case, opportunity is lost as a result of political and economic oppression.

---

1   In interviews with the author (2013). Name changed for sake of privacy.
2   The term *shaabi* literally means 'traditional', 'folk', and 'popular' or 'the masses' in Egyptian colloquial Arabic and often carries connotations of the working class. But as I will explain below, for the context of this book *shaabi* more often refers to Egyptian folk music, and specifically, the urban popular music phenomenon of the same name.
3   Cf. Andrew Hammond, *Popular Culture in the Arab World: Arts, Politics, and the Media* (Cairo: The American University in Cairo Press, 2007).
4   Ibid.

Ashraf never really had the chance to better his position in society. He is part of the status quo, the discarded masses found on the margins of Egyptian society. Due to the corrupt social-political power dynamics reinforced by the State and economic elite, Ashraf has never had more than a few fleeting moments to ensure any financial, mental, or physical security. With a third baby on the way, and no time for politics or art, Ashraf has given up finding drum patterns on his snare and hi-hats, and instead finds them on the steering wheel of his employer's car. He explains:

> You may think it's strange, that I can adapt from being a musician to a driver. But I see my job now as somewhat similar to making music. I still take people from point A to point B – I take them on a journey. I observe every obstacle and opportunity on the way, I hear every horn before it honks; I create spaces, and fill them with motion. At least I tell myself that to keep sane.[5]

Means limited, creativity abound: music during Nasser's Socialism

Led by General Gamal Abdel Nasser, the 1952 revolution broke Egypt free from the shackles of monarchy and colonial occupation, and for the first time since the rule of the Pharaohs, Egyptians would exercise national self-determination.[6] In his article titled 'The 1952 revolution: A legacy of cultural transformation', Egyptian journalist Ahmed Zaki Osman explains that to some extent, Nasser and the Free Officers Movement lacked any concrete idea regarding how to frame the nation's new cultural identity after the ouster of King Farouk I.[7] He also mentions that despite this, the late 1950s and the 1960s witnessed a boom in cultural production. But some critics suggest the output was highly politicised and aimed at serving the revolution's socialist agenda. Egyptian music composer Dr. Khaled Amin describes the Nasser-era as a search for identity defined by 'intense nationalism, uniformity, and a soundtrack sung by Umm Kalthoum, Farid El-Atrash, Abdel Halim Hafez, and Mohammed Abdel Wahab',[8] otherwise known as the 'Great Four' of Egyptian popular music. Amin continues:

> Growing up, my father used to organise this evening at our house here in Cairo called 'Salon al-Fan' [the artists' gathering']. It was the late 1960s and many of the well-known musicians would come like Mohamed al-Mougy, who composed loads of Abdel Halim's songs, also the musician Ali al-Haggar. We were living in a socialist country, so we were kind of limited on instruments and foreign products. But musically, it was fantastic – it was all about al-Musiqa al Arabeya[9] and Tarab[10] like Umm Kalthoum, [Mohamed] Abdel Wahab, Abdel Halim [Hafez]. In fact, Umm Kalthoum used to sing every first Thursday of every month at a publicly broadcasted event, on the regional Sout El Arab station. She would often perform alongside Abdel Wahab who would compose for her in Azbakeya Theatre and then Qasr el Nile Cinema in downtown Cairo. Anyone could attend, but it cost about 2–5 LE[11], and no one really had money at the time – instead we'd have parties and listen to them on the radio.[12]

Nearly three decades after her death in 1975, Umm Kalthoum (b. 1904) is still widely regarded as the greatest Egyptian female singer in modern history. When looking back at her vast body of work, including hundreds of songs and six films, Umm Kalthoum was undeniably prolific. More than that, she was Egypt's first quintessential female popstar, a feat that does not tie her directly to this essay's journey into dance music production and club culture but deserves some mention. That said, it was many

---

5 Mohamed Ashraf, in conversation with the author (2013).
6 Cf. Afaf Lutfi al-Sayyid Marsot, *A History of Egypt: From the Arab Conquest to the Present* (United Kingdom: Cambridge University Press, 2007).
7 Cf. Ahmed Osman Zaki, 'The 1952 revolution: A legacy of cultural transformation', *Egypt Independent*, 27 July 2011, <http://www.egyptindependent.com/news/1952-revolution-legacy-cultural-transformation> accessed 5 July 2013.
8 Dr. Amin Khaled, in an interview with the author (2013).
9 *Al-Musiqa al Arabeya* is characterised by the sophisticated use of melodic and rhythmic modes within vocal and instrumental form cf. Michael Frishkopf (ed.), *Music and Media in the Arab World* (Cairo: The American University Press, 2010).
10 The term *tarab* refers to the state of musical or spiritual ecstasy created by a talented singer, which fills the audience with a great sense of emotion.
11 About the cost of two or three tanks of gas for a small sized car or two bottles of Johnny Walker Black.
12 Dr. Amin Khaled, in an interview with the author (2013).

Club After Eight, Cairo, 2016, photo: Andreas Langfeld

Islam Chipsy Eek at Festival Nuits Sonores Tanger, Tanger, 2015, photo: Manon Duclos

Mahraganat, Cairo, 2013, photo: Mosa'ab Elshamy

Mahraganat Shaabi, Cairo, 2016, photo: René Clement

Young men light a fire during a street wedding with mahragan music in the neighborhood of Salam City, Cairo, 2014, photo: Mosa'ab Elshamy

93 CAIRO PLATES

Alaa Fifty, known as DJ Fifty, in his neighbourhood of Salam City, Cairo, 2013, photo: Mosa'ab Elshamy

DJ Sadat, Salam City, Cairo, 2013, photo: Mosa'ab Elshamy

Salam City, Cairo, 2013, photo: Mosa'ab Elshamy

Movie poster for *Anyab*, directed by Mohamed Shebl, starring Ahmed Adawiya as Amir al-Thoulm [Prince of Darkness], 1981

of her contemporaries who had a deep and lasting effect on the modernization of music production and dance culture in Egypt, chief among them, Mohamed Abdel Wahab (1901–1991), Abdel Halim Hafez (1929–1977) and later Baligh Hamdy (1932–1993) as well as the Algerian singer and dancer Warda (1939–2012).

—

The 1960s was a vibrant decade in the evolution of music production. While the lyrics became increasingly incarcerated within the State narrative of nationalism or love (like almost all of Umm Kalthoum's songs), producers and composers liberalised their music by focusing on innovating the production, instrumentation, and arrangements. But for the most part, throughout Nasser's reign, and the omnipresence of Egypt's form of socialism, musicians had to choose between aligning with the State narrative or disappear from the scene altogether. Suddenly, overnight, to become a famous artist meant holding one of the most precarious professions in Egypt because for Nasser's socialism to thrive, songs had to be sung, movies made, and brains thoroughly washed with nationalist melodies and framed images.

In an interview on the topic, Egyptian culture writer Ahmed Naji explains that while the 1960s were under the iron grip of nationalism, there was a simultaneous surge of cultural opportunity for many artists, particularly those who were cunning enough to play within Nasser's narrative of 'The Great Egyptian Nation' and 'Arab Unity'.[13] Naji goes on to mention that, at the end of the 1950s, Nasser's first trip to the Soviet Union greatly affected his vision of culture, and particularly the need for State control over cultural production. Shortly after his return to Egypt, Nasser and the State brought cultural production under their control, centralising all types of art, music, and dance from pop to Folk, creating mechanisms like the National Band for Dancing and a national folkloric dance troupe.

This is not to say that musicians did not also continue to create Western-inspired music to which the bourgeoisie would dance Waltzes, Salsas, or Rumbas. With new cultural agents mushrooming around Nasser's revolutionary Egypt, the spectrum was bustling with the government's great folkloric revival, seen on the one hand through dance troupes and bands with folkloristic music often largely targeted towards the popular or rural classes, and on the other hand the romantic nationalism reverberated out of Umm Kalthoum and Abdel Halim Hafez. When looking at pop stardom, it was these latter two who reached an almost iconoclastic standing among Egyptian society; rich or poor.

Then there was Abdel Wahab, who was also extremely famous in his own right. He was (and still is) at times accused of either blatant or subliminal classism. He was (and is) also equally criticised and heralded for introducing Western elements into Egyptian music. In a recent interview about the artist, Egyptian film and culture critic Joseph Fahim describes Abdel Wahab as having 'single-handedly transformed … how music was made in Egypt'.[14] Fahim explains:

Abdel Wahab was different – he acted as a bridge between Eastern music and Western pop music. He got rid of the takht,[15] *he shortened the songs and introduced lots of western instruments. He used violins, pianos, later electric guitars. I think Abdel Wahab gave birth to the modern Egyptian pop song as we know it today.*

Fahim goes on to describe the songs as exceedingly modern for their time, eclectic, and significantly more melodic than Umm Kalthoum's work. It was during this period that Abdel Wahab transformed the classical structures of *al-Musiqa al'Arabeya* by manipulating the long song form called *ughniya* [song] into shorter sketches. In the documentary short film about the artist titled *A Growing Symbol*,[16] Lebanese composer and friend, Selim Sehab states that

---

13 Ahmed Naji, in an interview with the author (2014).
14 Joe Fahim, in an interview with the author (2014).
15 The traditional small orchestra in Middle Eastern music.
16 Hashem El Saifi, 'Mohamed Abdel Wahab: A Growing Symbol', YouTube, 10 July 2013, <https://www.youtube.com/watch?v=GYXs-fKhTO4> accessed 10 July 2013.

Abdel Wahab not only introduced new instruments, but new techniques for playing them as well. For example, while the violins have been a longstanding part of Arabic music, Sehab argues that Abdel Wahab enhanced them by adding tremolo to create a more impactful expression, like in the song '*Ma Ahla El Habib*' ['How Beautiful is the One you Love'].

Prior to Abdel Wahab's era, Egyptian music was built upon melody rather than the harmonic patterns found in most Western music of the time. Armbrust argues that while Abdel Wahab's music was resolutely monophonic, a line or two of harmony could occasionally be found in his works, and that his compositions almost always retained the quarter-tone system.[17,18] He also explains that the sophistication of Egyptian music of this kind lay in elements other than harmony, such as *maqam* [modality], *wazn* [meter], or *taqasim* [solo recitals]. While many criticise Abdel Wahab for his western approaches to music, he inarguably impacted the direction of music production that still lingers today. His work in cinema is another example of this: in his film period between the 1930s and the 1940s, he occasionally used tonality in his rhythm section, as in a section of '*Al-Nil Nagashi*' [The Nile is a Revealer]—a song from the movie *The White Rose*, (1933) in which the *qanun* [a string instrument] and the *oud* are strum behind the melody to lyrics that say:

The Nile reveals
Beautiful and dark
The wonder of its colour, gold and onyx
His arghoul[19] *in his hand*
He swims to his master
The life of our country
God make him worthy.[20]

By the end of the 1960s, Abdel Wahab had stopped singing due to the limitations of his aging voice; instead he composed for other singers including Umm Kalthoum and the young Abdel Halim Hafez who he later took under his wing. Some of the clearest examples of Abdel Wahab's prolific genius and ability to modernise with the times can be heard in his compositions '*Enta 'Omri*' [You are My Life], which he composed for Umm Kalthoum in the late 1960s. In the song, Abdel Wahab's incorporation of the nascent electric guitar juxtaposed against the melancholic Arabic timbres adds a burst of youthful colour to the overall tone of the composition as Umm Kalthoum's contralto vocals sing about the pains of love.

While Umm Kalthoum continued her long form song approach, with one song often lasting upwards of fifty minutes, Wahab's modernisation technique instantly attracted a younger generation of listeners and forever changed the way Egyptian music was structured and arranged. In 1988, a few years before his death, Abdel Wahab made a surprise return to the studio, singing a new composition titled '*Min Gheir Leh*' [Without Asking Why]. The accompanying album was a massive hit, selling approximately two million copies.

Another musical figure that defined the post-independence era, and continued the progression of pop music and iconography, was the Wahab-advised Abdel Halim Hafez (1929–1977). While there were several post-independence stars, including Lebanese composer Farid al-Atrash[21] who was based in Cairo with his singing sister Asmahan, it was Abdel Halim Hafez who won over the hearts and minds of Egypt's youth during the Nasser era. Until this day, Abdel Halim Hafez remains an icon in modern Arabic music; he is often considered to be Egypt's first romantic singer and sex icon, most notably for songs like '*Ahwak*' [I Adore You], '*Ebtedi Minen el Hekaya*' [Where Should We Start the Story], and '*Fatet Ganbina*' [She Passed By Us]. Like the great singers before him, Abdel Halim Hafez also worked closely with Egyptian poets including Mohammed Hamza.

Similar to Umm Kalthoum and many other artists of the time, Abdel Halim Hafez publicly

---

17 A quartertone is a pitch halfway between the usual notes of a chromatic *maqam* (scale), an interval about half as wide as a semitone, which is half a whole tone.
18 Walter Armbrust, *Mass Culture and Modernism in Egypt* (Great Britain: University Press, Cambridge, 1996), 91.
19 An *arghoul* is a reed instrument.
20 Walter Armbrust, *Mass Culture and Modernism in Egypt* (see n. 18).
21 Farid al-Atrash is widely known for his thirty hit films that are considered to be classics for their song and dance routine alongside several timeless songs including '*al-Rabei*' [Spring], '*Awwal Hamsa*' [First Whisper], and '*Lahn al-Khulud*' [Eternal Melody].

associated himself with the Arab nationalist regime of Gamal Abdel Nasser, which inspired him to sing numerous uplifting patriotic songs for Egypt and the Arab world such as 'Tahiya li-l-ishtirakiya' [Greetings to Socialism]. Abdel Halim Hafez also made an astonishing number of films in his short life, close to sixteen between the years of 1955–1969. Abdel Halim Hafez attracted a modicum of stars around him, including composers Mohamed Abdel Wahab and Baligh Hamdi,[22] as well as poets Abdel Rahman al-Abnoudi and Salah Jahin.

The above-mentioned artists rose during a revolutionary and capricious time in modern Egyptian history. Their music became the soundtrack to a country struggling for Independence and self-determination, while their songs and collaborations encapsulated Egypt's post-colonial search for a national identity within the Arab world. Until today, their voices continue to reverberate across the country as their songs pour from balconies and taxicabs alike. Oscillating between nationalism and nostalgia, their extensive body of work delineates the foundation of modern Egyptian culture and national identity. In an effort to claim this national identity, these musicians unconsciously helped create major schisms in society by propagating a nationalistic socialist ideology, pushing much of Egyptian society to the margins.

For the young ones and for the masses: Shababi and Shaabi

I don't recall seeing the dance scene prior to the early 1980s–before we used to go to weddings to dance. But that doesn't mean there wasn't a vibrant music environment–in fact traces of the Shababi *or 'youth music' dance scene can certainly be found in the Western-influenced Rock and pop bands from the 1970s. You know, bands like Tiba, 4M, The Friends, Hany Shenouda with Les Petits Chats, and later, al-Masriyeen* ('The Egyptians').[23] *[President] Sadat's* infitah[24] *defined the era–for the first time in years, Egyptians who had the means could travel when they liked, giving the scene in general more access to products from abroad. The music and the fashion were heavily influenced by what was going on in the West–the girls wore miniskirts and the guys' hair grew longer. We listened to whatever cassettes were dominating the global airwaves: the Bee-Gees, Pink Floyd, Grateful Dead, the Rolling Stones, and the Beatles of course. Music was everywhere, it was coming out of the faucets!*[25]

It was the mid-1970s when Egyptian music producer Tarek El Kashef, who recounts the decade in the statement above, opened Cairo's first private multi-track recording studio in the basement of his In-laws' villa. The goal of the studio was to copy and cut popular Western tapes to distribute and sell them at affordable prices, about 2–3 LE (or about 50 Eurocent) a cassette, in addition to squeezing in some recording sessions for local musicians. Times were rapidly changing following the death of Gamal Abdel Nasser in October 1970 and the subsequent succession of Anwar Sadat. Socialism was dead, and Sadat's capitalistic policies, most notably the infitah, were quickly transforming every aspect of the country's socio-economic and cultural life. As Michael Frishkopf writes: 'In the atmosphere of infitah, cassette technology led to the proliferation of localised private-sector production, targeting particular market segments, while fragmenting the broader musical styles associated with Arab nationalism and pan-Arabism.'[26] He continues by stating that cassettes, at the same time, could enable larger circulation due to their relatively inexpensive production and buyers could afford the necessary gadgets, which opened up a new lucrative market for the youth. In his essay titled 'A History of Music and Singing on Egyptian Radio and Television', Zein Nasser explains that

---

22 Baligh Hamdi was one of Egypt's most influential composers who created many hit songs for prominent Arab singers and The Great Four between the 1960s and the 1970s.

23 For more on the 1970s Rock scene in Egypt cf. Angie Batala, 'Reliving the 70's: Egypt's Golden Age of Rock', *Discord Magazine* 4 (2012), 34–43.

24 President Anwar Sadat's economic open door policy.

25 Tarek El Kashef, in an interview with the author (2013).

26 Frishkopf (ed.), *Music and Media in the Arab World* (see n.9), 15.

during the 1970s 'cassettes provided a way around the official song production process, which was monitored by government committees concerned with maintaining social values and high musical standards'.[27]

During this time, the exposure to global sounds led to the rise of a Western influenced musical landscape, which was seen and heard most notably in the burgeoning movement of Egyptian Rock'n'Roll cover bands including The Mass, Les Petits Chats, or Tiba. While these bands had yet to produce any original work, eventually their various musicians such as Les Petits Chats' guitarist Omar Khorchid, the band's keyboardists Hany Shenouda and Ezzat Abou Ouf, or Tiba's Tarek El Kashef went on to make a major breakthrough which has resonated through Egyptian music to this day.

In 1977, Les Petits Chats' Hany Shenouda started his ascent up the industry ladder when he began creating arrangements and compositions for a then little-known Nubian Folk musician named Mohammed Mounir. At the time, Mounir had only released one cassette titled *Alemony Eneeki* [Your Eyes Taught Me]. However, the tape's sound quality was greatly compromised due to the poorly equipped governmental studio where the album was recorded.[28] Alongside Tiba's ex-band member Tarek El Kashef as well as Hany Sabet and Kamal Olama – the latter two being the masterminds behind independent record label and distributor, Sonar Ltd/SLAM – Shenouda began working on Mounir's follow-up album, *Bnetweled* [We are being born], which was later released in 1978 to much accolade by critics and fans alike.

However, it was Mounir's 1981 release of his third album, *Shababeek* [Windows] that would later bring the young Nubian singer into the ranks of stardom. *Shababeek* succeeded in popularizing an entirely new genre of music: *al-Musika al-Shababeya* [youth music] – or *Shababi* [youth] for short, due to the apparent mixture of Arabic and Western influences appealing especially to young Egyptians. This was achieved through utilizing the traditional Arabic singing and instruments such as the *daff*, the *oud* or the *riqq* while underpinning them with a Western beat and harmony. In his essay, 'What's Not on Egyptian Television and Radio', James R. Grippo writes: 'Shenouda helped "popularise" the keyboard, which became a dominant force in Egyptian popular music. In the mid-1980s, this new strain of Egyptian *Bop* [pop] music, eventually labelled Shababi, was marketed to appeal to younger Egyptians by fusing Western popular music styles (Rock, Jazz, or Disco) and instruments (keyboards, drum kit, electric bass, or guitar) with characteristics central to Arabic music (Arabic language, lyrical meanings, or rhythms).'[29] Commentators on the topic often cite *Shababeek* as the seminal album of Shababi music which revolutionised the Egyptian pop music scene.

The album was recorded on a 16-track recorder at the Sonar Ltd/SLAM headquarters in Cairo. Co-producer Tarek El Kashef mentions that he was heavily influenced by Quincy Jones in the recording process, particularly due to Jones' usage of reverb and late 1970s Funk-laced bass lines present on Michael Jackson's *Off the Wall* (1979), which is distinctly heard on 'Ad We Ad', the opening track on Mounir's album. After the success of *Shababeek*, Kahlil and Mounir went on to make several more albums together. Overall, singer Mohamed Mounir has now released more than twenty albums and is one of the most popular Egyptian performers to this day. Meanwhile, Shenouda continued to find success with producing and arranging music, which prompted him to form his own band called al-Masryeen [The Egyptians] in 1977.

—

The musical landscape of the decade was facing a radical shift as a result of a severe economic

---

27 Zein Nasser, 'A History of Music and Singing on Egyptian Radio and Television', in Michael Frishkopf (ed.), *Music and Media in the Arab World* (see n. 9), 67–76.

28 Tarek El Kashef, in an interview with the author (2013).

29 James R. Grippo, 'What's Not on Egyptian Television and Radio! Locating the "Popular" in Egyptian Sha'bi', in Frishkopf (ed.), *Music and Media in the Arab World* Cairo (see n. 9), 143.

decay which was gravely affecting society, in addition to the death of many iconic performers such as Umm Kalthoum (d. 1975), Abdel Halim Hafez (d. 1977), and Farid al-Atrash (d. 1974). The socio-economic gap between rich and poor continued to widen throughout the 1970s. Additionally, the open-door-policy allowed working class Egyptians to travel to the up-and-coming oil towns of Saudi Arabia where they could earn better wages over a period of several years. Upon their return, many of these Egyptian workers brought the conservative Wahabi[30] culture back with them, which had irreparable effects on Egyptian society and culture at large. By the end of the 1970s, the rich were becoming staggeringly richer, the status quo was suffering, and the music began to mirror the entire landscape through the rise of the Shaabi music genre.

Emerging from the dilapidated fringes, in rousing, over-populated working-class neighbourhoods like Imbaba, Shubra al Khayma, Bulaq, Sayyida Zeinub, and many others during the 1970s, Shaabi music was alive with social commentary and realism. According to culture writer, Ahmed Naji, the proliferation and popularization of Shaabi was a sort of revolt against the State's influence on, and ownership of the folkloric scene during the tail end of Nasser's reign. He says, 'It largely started with Zakaria Hagawy, who was a *Mawwal* singer [vocal improvisation sung in colloquial folk poetry] – he's kind of a disaster because he had this idea to go to Tawfik Okasha, the culture minister at the time, with a plan to control the Shaabi music landscape.'[31] The idea was to control folkloric music and keep Shaabi within the framework of Nasser's national vision. Naji continues:

With Okasha's approval, the singer visited various governorates scooping up many of the main Mawwal singers, and placing them within salaried positions in the culture ministry to perform at the whim of the government. They were the State's picture of folkloric or Shaabi culture, they would wear galabayas [traditional dresses] in performance and represent Egypt around their world to reflect a cultural heritage very much controlled by the government – they became a gallery for the state but soon lost their connection with their time and audience.[32]

Then Ahmed Adawiya came into the picture. Though he had already begun performing music in the late 1960s, he would only later become the uncrowned king of Shaabi culture. He rebelled against this infrastructure and image, refusing to adopt the costume and narrow framing of government controlled Shaabi landscape. Instead, he forged a new path – one that reflected his urban reality. Similar to many Shaabi singers, Adawiya's roots are in Mawwal singing. But what separated him from his contemporaries early on was his raucously rebellious sound and image, in addition to the songs' many sardonic double-entendres and social innuendos. His music was full of a certain kind of emblematic punch that spoke directly to a blue-collar worker, to the common man, and to the status quo. He was the fresh face of folklore, with a modern Shaabi twist, singing out the many woes of the people, and for the people, in a vernacular that spoke to those in the margins. For example, in hit songs like 'Zahma ya donya' [Crowded World], Adawiya mulls over how crowded the streets of Cairo are, the infamously bad traffic, the social inequality, and a laundry list of other problems faced by Egyptian society.

Adawiya was specifically influenced by the Algerian singer and dancer, Warda. She is often considered to be the mother of local cabaret culture. Meanwhile, Adawiya himself was largely popularised through the cabarets, in clubs like downtown's Arizona, Sharazade, and Al-Leil. Taking influence from Warda, who was one of the first to break down the wall between performer and audience, Adawiya formed a much

---

30 *Wahabi* or *Wahhabism* refers to Saudi Arabia's particular branch of Sunni Islam, which is a rigidly enforced practice throughout the country. The name derives from Mohammed ibn Abdel Wahhab, an 18th century religious reformer who was a vanguard of the movement.

31 Ahmed Naji, in an interview with the author (2014).

32 Ahmed Naji, in an interview with the author (2014).

more inclusive club and dance culture within the cabarets and weddings. 'Warda is almost like the mother of Adawiya,' says Naji:

> When Warda started to sing, she started in the cabarets in France in the 1950s and 1960s. She continued this way of performance, it's basically dependent on connecting with the audience. For example, if you were listening to Umm Kalthoum or Abdel Wahab in concert, there was a space between the performer and the audience – it was nearly impossible to reach them. But with Warda, and later Adawiya, their songs relied heavily on the interaction between performer and audience – they asked questions to their audience, and engaged them. Adawiya would dance alongside the bellydancer, swooping through the cabaret dancing with the audience, taking sips of their drink, while encouraging them to dance also.[33]

With the introduction of audiocassette tapes as a new recording medium, Adawiya's music spread rapidly due to the medium's low cost and the music's relatable lyrical content. According to Sahar Montassar, the co-owner of the music label Sawt al-Hob, Ahmed Adawiya was the label's largest seller from the late 1970s through to the early 1990s. While high-culture critics, and the elite society blacklisted Adawiya from radio airwaves and television for being 'vulgar' and 'lowbrow', Hany Shenouda asserts that Adawiya's song 'Crowded World' was used in film soundtracks more than any other song in the history of Egyptian cinema.[34] Shenouda also characterises 'Crowded World' as Adawiya's first 'respectable' hit that would appeal beyond his private event circle because like most Shaabi singers, Adawiya often sang at weddings, and in the nightclub scene.[35] His songs were anthems for change in a post-socialist Egypt but his success was met by extreme snobbery from intellectuals on all ends of the cultural spectrum.

Nevertheless, Adawiya has starred in close to thirty films. One example is filmmaker Mohamed Shebl's 1981 cult classic, *Anyab* [Fangs] starring Ahmed Adawiya as Dracula aka Amir al-Thoulm [Prince of Darkness] in a musical horror parody closely resembling *The Rocky Horror Picture Show* (1975). The scene, sounds, and costumes look like the outcome of a haphazard experimentation between Michael Jackson, Adawiya, and David Bowie with no budget, and a 24-hour deadline. Director Mohamed Shebl, who is sometimes referred to as 'the Egyptian Hitchcock', managed to create a debut feature film that embarked on a fleeting albeit enigmatic moment in Egyptian music history: Arabic glam-rock.[36] There's also an epic array of funky, synthesiser-heavy song and dance routines, with choreography so bad it's good. In the film, Adawiya plays the role of a blood sucking Dracula, insinuating that even on screen he would be down casted as the vulgar villain. Despite this, Adawiya still managed to shine as a resounding anti-hero for those who are cult-followers of the film.

Some might consider Shababi singer Mohamed Mounir and Shaabi singer Ahmed Adawiya's fame as two sides of the same coin although their music falls in different genres. With their production teams and lyricists, both artists managed to diverge music from the Great Four's template of nostalgia into a more direct mirror of society, giving a voice and reflection to the realities of Egypt's ever-growing status quo. Producer El Kashef compares Adawiya to Egypt's version of a Rock'n'Roll star; his blue-collar beginnings and the music's content, timbral landscape, and tone reflected the Egyptian society that surrounded him. Adawiya succeeded in not only popularising the genre of Shaabi music, but also in influencing a long line of singers ranging from Hamdy Batchan, known for his 1988 release of '*Fih el Hekawaya*' [What's the Story], to Shaaban Abdel Rahim with his 2000 political anthem, '*Ana bakrah*

---

33 Ibid.
34 Walter Armbrust, *Mass Culture and Modernism in Egypt* (see n. 18), 186.
35 Ibid., 251.
36 For more information cf. Maha ElNabawi, 'Egypt's cinematic gems: Fangs', Mada Masr, 1 November 2014, <https://www.madamasr.com/en/2014/11/01/feature/culture/egypts-cinematic-gems-fangs/> accessed 23 November 2014.

Isra'il' [I Hate Israel].[37] Singer Hamdy Batchan sheds some insight into the struggles of reaching Shaabi music stardom:

> As Shaabi musicians, we often had a hard time getting airtime play on the radio or television during Sadat and Mubarak days. It's because we sang about societal problems, like the way I sing about sexual harassment in 'El Asatok' or Adawiya's 'Zahma ya donya Zahma', which refers to the bad traffic, but more so all the underlying issues like the social equality, economic instability, and all that. They didn't want us on the airwaves singing about reality, they only wanted people to sing about an image that wasn't there – an image of 'habibi' [lover] music. But it didn't matter, because we released cassettes, and everyone, I mean everyone had a cassette player.[38]

Habibi, Hip-Hop, Trance: the impact of the internet

As the success of singers like Ahmed Adawiya, Mohammed Mounir, and Hamdy Batchan continued to grow through the 1980s into the 1990s, the nascent industry surrounding them began to boom as well. Sahar Montasser of the music label Sawt al-Hob explains that during the late 1980s up until the millennium, an offshoot of Shababi called *al-Jeel* [generation] music began rapidly forming and quickly dominating Egypt's musical landscape.[39] This new pop-driven sound was made up of more formulaic, almost scientifically designed music, and it diverged the way music was created and consumed. Montasser continues by listing several key elements that contributed to this transformation of the musical landscape, chief among them were: the advancements in accessible technology (and later the internet), satellite music channels from Egypt and Saudi Arabia (Rotana, Melody, Mazzika), the increased accessibility to modern equipment (i.e. the drum machine and synthesisers), and lastly, the 'genius' of both Atef Montasser and his cultivation of Libyan singer and producer, Hamid al-Shairi.

While al-Shairi certainly had a successful career as a singer, it was his production work with other Shababi artists such as Arab-pop chart-topper, Amr Diab – in addition to Egyptian singers Hisham Abbas and Simone – that utterly transformed Egypt's musical landscape. Al-Shairi is widely regarded as the visionary who, after the rise of Adawiya, was almost solely responsible for creating the Arab-pop genre and soundscape. This al-Shairi brand of Arab-pop later became known as al-Jeel or Habibi music. It is defined by a catchy combination of finger cymbals, rapid handclaps, the traditional three-count drum rhythms and lover's lyrics charged with enough drama and drum machines to push forward the swinging hips of the inner belly dancer found within many Arabic music listeners.

According to Khalid Amin, the success of al-Shairi's music was largely caused by its simplicity: 'It was all drum machines, clapping hands, and finger cymbals.'[40] Basically, Arab-pop was and continues to be driven by rhythm, bass, and cadence coupled with the timbral colours found in the traditional Arabic soundscape. Amin continues by asserting that Arab-pop, and particularly the works created by al-Shairi, are almost entirely apolitical. When listening to most of al-Shairi's successful productions, it becomes exceedingly apparent that the songs have somewhat of a repetitious, mind-numbing quality. At the same time, they are undeniably infectious, and they are most certainly imbued with intent to make the listener dance, or at the least, sing along to. The genre's output is entirely mainstream friendly, inoffensive, and easily consumable by a range of societal factions with cassette tapes sold for 7 LE at the time, or what would now be about 1 euro. Take for example the song *'Nour al-Ain'* [Light of the Eye], which was produced by al-Shairi for Amr Diab and released in 1996. The song opens up with the traditional sounds of finger cymbals, followed by

---

[37] The then still young state of Israel defeated Egypt in the Six-Day War of 1967. Today in Egypt, like elsewhere in the Arab world, wide reaching resentments against Israel are predominant.

[38] Hamdy Batchan, in an interview with the author (2013).

[39] Sahar Montasser, in an interview with the author (2013).

[40] Dr. Amin Khaled, in an interview with the author (2013).

a steady beat of daff drums, Diab's dreamy, pop vocals that repeatedly sing, 'Darling, darling, the light of my eyes' followed by an onset of several harmonious Spanish guitars. The punch line of the track comes in with the accordion and its quartertones, which underpins the rather simplistic, repetitive *Habibi* [love] lyrics with a traditional-sounding Arabic melody.

Amr Diab is arguably still the most famous of Egyptian pop musicians to date largely due to his earlier work like the above mentioned 'Nour al-Ain'. After releasing his first cassette in 1986, titled, *Ya Tariq* [Hey Tarek], Diab continues to secure several hits in the Top 10 Arab-pop charts. Much of Amr Diab's success is also due to his known musical style, which is considered a 'Spanish tinge', made up of Latin grooves and percussions.[41] Until this day, much of Amr Diab's sound, his pop-boy masquerade, and endless love ballads means the singer remains within the ostracised category of Habibi music within the al-Jeel genre.

For nearly ten years al-Shairi's productions dominated the Cairene soundscape – his artists seemingly monopolised the airwaves and satellite music video stations like Melody and MTV Arabia. But unlike Shaabi musicians such as Adawiya, or hybrids like Mounir, and those musicians within their trajectories, this new wave of al-Jeel or Habibi music had almost no relevance to the grim realities and ever-growing polarization within Egyptian society following President Anwar Sadat's assassination in 1980 by Islamist fundamentalists. At the time, religious groups were expressing an absolute rejection of Sadat's open-door policy, the peace deal with Israel, and the subsequent Westernization that has forced Egyptian society to look at everything through a capitalist coloured lens until today. When General Hosni Mubarak became president in 1981, he was quick to not only clamp down on many of Egypt's outward Islamists by jailing or exiling them, but he also tightened the government's grip on media, culture, and almost all forms of expression. As Mubarak's reign continued decade after decade, his manufactured image of Egypt began its rapid descent as the Internet began to aggressively permeate society in the early 2000s.

—

Internet first came into Egyptian households in 1993. A study conducted by the United Nations' specialised agency for information and communication technologies, International Telecommunication Union, showed that, by 2009 the internet in Egypt had penetrated nearly 25% of the population and by 2012 the permeation rate had risen to approximately 44%.[42] As millions of Egyptian musicians, artists, independent publishers, and activists continued to galvanise the Internet, they consciously or unconsciously began challenging and utterly disrupting the state-manufactured discourse and framed images of society. When looking at the YouTube history of Egypt's vast modern musical landscape, it is most certainly Arabic Hip-Hop that defines the early adopters. In June 2007, a local rapper named MC Amin, from the governorate of Mansoura, nearly two hours outside of Cairo, uploaded a raw yet penetrating Arabic freestyle onto his YouTube channel.[43] Sitting in front of his 1990s PC, rapper Ahmad Amin unabashedly recites blatant socio-political rhymes overtop a steady bass heavy breakbeat and a monotonously synthesised melody with a do-it-yourself attitude that kicks forward with every lyrical intonation.

The proliferation of Rap in Egypt first began during the early 2000s with crews such as Asfalt, Zero Boys, and Meya Meya. But it wasn't until 2006 with Rap groups like Arabian Knightz, solo artists like Deeb, and MC Amin that the genre became noticeably popular in Egypt.[44] With the developments in technology, and pirated programmes like ProTools, Ableton Live, and Garageband, anyone with a computer, and the desire to do so, could now make music that

---

41   James R. Grippo, 'What's Not on Egyptian Television and Radio!', (see n. 29), 144.

42   Cf. ICT Eye, 'Country Profile – Arab States – Egypt', 2012, <http://www.itu.int/net4/itu-d/icteye/Country Profile.aspx> accessed July 2013. This is still the latest data since access to these statistics is strictly limited.

43   Cf. MC Amin, YouTube, <http://www.youtube.com/user/mcaminmusic> accessed 5 May 2013.

44   For more information on Egypt's Rap scene cf. Maha ElNabawi, 'Soundtrack of the Egyptian Revolution', in *Community Times* (2011).

45   Long before the proliferation of cheap technology and computers, Egypt's forefather of electronic music is an often overlooked composer by the name of Halim El Dabh. In the early 1940s, while Egypt was still under the monarchy of King Farouk I, the then 23-year-old El Dabh constructed what is often considered the world's first electronic tape piece from the

reflected their conditions, their community, and their attitude. The Rap crews driving this musical rebellion adopted the beats and classic structures of Western Hip-Hop, while also re-appropriating the genre to fit their own ambitions, frustrations, and vernacular.

Meanwhile, on the upper end of the societal spectrum, Mika, an electronic musician and budding Trance DJ, and producer duo Aly & Fila also became early adopters of digital media as a means to release and disseminate their music.[45] On their YouTube channel, which was launched in 2006, the latter Cairo-based producers continue to garner hundreds of thousands of views.[46] After the popularity of their 2003 debut track release, 'Eye of Horus', Aly Amr Fathalah (Aly) and Fadi Wassef Naguib (Fila) caught the attention of Dutch superstar Trance DJ and producer, Armin Van Buuren.[47] The duo went on to release their debut album, *Rising Sun*, in 2006 and their follow up album, *Quiet Storm*, in 2013 under Van Buuren's label, Armada Digital. Their sound fluctuates between Trance, Downtempo, and Progressive Trance, with the occasional embellishments of Arabic characteristics, heard in tracks like 'Laily'.

Aly & Fila continue to hold a large fan-base with over 4,000 people attending their shows in Egypt, in addition to their countless gigs abroad. They rose on the dance floors of Egypt's nascent Techno scene in the mid-1990s, which was later popularised by raves that infiltrated Cairo's upper class with DJs like Judge Jules in the early 2000s. From the time period between the millennium and 2006, Trance, Techno, Progressive House, and the discovery of a little pill called Ecstasy, enveloped even the most unassuming of partygoers who attended the burgeoning rave epidemic that was ploughing through the privileged classes.

As their wealth increased, the rich became almost entirely disconnected from society, consciously or unconsciously. While certain dance music events like Nacelle[48] and ByGanz[49] successfully emerged over the past decade, and continue to push the electronic dance music scene forward in Egypt with local and foreign producers spinning House, Deep House, and Electro, for the most part, the scene was (and is still) only accessible to Egypt's upper class and expat community and does not reflect on the whole of society. Meanwhile, the poor masses, that make up the majority of the country's 90 million people, continued to fall victim to the accelerating rate of corruption that defined the past sixty years of autocracy, military rule, and repression in Egypt. Right there, in between all the power cuts, the gridlocked traffic, and the staggering poverty, lives a musical landscape that so vividly reflects the ever-growing schisms within Egyptian society.

A rebellion: Mahraganat

Tucked away in an inconspicuous alleyway on Kasr El Nil Street, just a few blocks away from Tahrir Square, is After Eight, one of Cairo's most iconic and longstanding nightclubs. In the Spring of 2013, inside the sweltering nucleus of the club's compact dance floor, Egyptian singer, Sadat, begins warming up the meagre stage as rapper Alaa Fifty, Amr Haha, and DJ Figo sound-check in a window framed enclave that holds the mixer, laptop, controls, and some groupies. Together, the crew is known as the al-Sallam Ghosts, after their Cairene neighbourhood, and within moments of kicking off their set, the dance floor fills with swaying, ragging bodies that become instantaneously infected by the cacophony of music, discordant vocal-lines, and the exhilarating cluster of noise that tears through the club's soundscape. It is the type of music that forces you to leap to your feet, regardless of taste – it is loud, rambunctious, teeth chattering and bone shaking music pushed along by speedy rhythms of about 130–140 BPM, Arabic melodies, and absurdly heavy sub-bass lines. The dance floor is made up of mostly twenty-somethings, downtown hipsters and

---

recordings he made of an ancient healing ceremony in Egypt known as *Zar*, a piece titled 'Wire Recorder Piece' cf. Maha ElNabawi, 'Music Permeates Everything', Mada Masr, 15 December 2013, <http://www.madamasr.com/sections/culture/%E2%80%98music-permeates-everything%E2%80%99> accessed 20 December 2013, and Halim El Dabh, 'Wire Recorder Piece', YouTube, <http://www.youtube.com/watch?v=j_kbNSdRvgo> accessed December 2013.

46 Cf. Aly & Fila, YouTube, <http://www.youtube.com/user/alyandfila> accessed 5 May 2013.
47 Aly & Fila, in an interview with the author (2013).
48 Founded by Tito El Kachab in 2009, Nacelle is a regular series of events featuring local electronic dance music DJs/producers like Aly Bahgat and Ali Goede.
49 Launched in 2006 by Ahmed El Ganzoury, ByGanz is the leading event company that specialises in dance music gatherings featuring local DJs and producers like the Toy Boys, and Misty + Hafez.

expats dressed in skinny jeans and flannel while sipping Stella beers and whiskey.

As the set continues, Amr Haha (Amr Mohammed), who produces most of the group's sets along with DJ Figo (Ahmed Farid), rotates between singing through high-pitched, auto-tuned back-up vocals to Sadat's melodically rapped Shaabi lyrics, in addition to occasionally manning the mixer, and dancing in a sort of Tecktonic style; the exalted street dance movements to electronic music. Meanwhile, DJ Figo, is fading the bassline in and out, as mashups of Western Hip-Hop and Arabic melodies float beneath Crunk-toned synth lines that oscillate wildly across the *sharqi* [Eastern] music scale. But the driving force behind their sound is most certainly the ever-looping drum machine that pounds their set along with a timbral palette of Arabic percussions, hand clapping, finger cymbals, and a hypnotizing *nay* line. The lyrics are at times profane; but mostly they are ripe with social commentary, humour, and the unassuming catchiness of Shaabi music. But according to Sadat, the lead vocalist of the group, this effervescent sound is not Shaabi music per se. While elements of Shaabi exist within the composition, this special concoction of electronic music is called Mahraganat [festival music]. It is packed with punch, utter lewdness, and a D.I.Y. attitude that currently has Mahraganat music oozing out of every passing vehicle in Cairo, whether it is a *tok tok*, a microbus, or *falluka* boat on the Nile.

In the middle of the Noughties the musician Ahmed Farid, aka DJ Figo, started to change the alternative and electronic music scenes in Egypt. Alongside a handful of others, DJ Figo helped pioneer one of the most boisterous, aggressive, and danceable musical genres that continues to flourish against all odds with its messy, multitudinous sonic sprawl. DJ Figo's special brand of Mahraganat music – which he sometimes called 'Electro-Shaabi' – was utterly contagious, prolific, and a downright wild musical experience. Born and raised in Sallam City, on the outskirts of Cairo, DJ Figo was one of the first to lay down the foundation of the burgeoning Mahraganat music scene. Producing most of his tracks on FruityLoops, DJ Figo was a testament to the do-it-yourself attitude that fuelled most of Egypt's disenfranchised youth. DJ Figo pioneered the movement with hit after hit. Just a short time after the 25 January revolution in 2011, he released his game changing track, 'Ana Baba, Y'lla' [I'm Daddy, Boy] which featured several other Mahraganat musicians. The track exemplifies DJ Figo's self-contained blend of Shaabi timbres, aggressive MCs, and seamless Techno transitions with each shifting verse and synth-squelch.

Mahraganat music started appearing on YouTube as early as 2007. As Egyptian journalist, Ola El-Saket, writes in her article on the music, 'The story of these music festivals began in the early 2000s with the proliferation of music mixers that spread from the confines of discos to street weddings and other special occasions. The rise of young Shaabi DJs allowed communities to save money on singers and belly dancers, as they provide a complete performance'[50] – and a more modernised means of entertainment. For 1986 born Sadat, the lead vocalist of the al-Sallam Ghosts, it all started when he was about fifteen years old after he took a strong liking to dancing.[51] His repertoire, which is exceedingly entertaining, includes a crossbreed between the in-your-face punch and grind of Hip-Hop, the disjointed motions of the Tecktonic dance trend that galvanised YouTube around 2006, and just the right amount of belly dancer hip-pops and arched backbends. The interchanging Arab, Techno, and Punk attitude of Mahraganat dancing makes it nearly impossible for the audience to resist at least a fleeting attempt replicating the performers' moves.

In an article in *The Fader* magazine titled 'Cairo, something New', writer Jace Clayton explains that, as it happens, Amr Mohammed

---

50   Ola El-Saket, 'The Shaabi music breakthrough', *Egypt Independent*, 22 October 2011, <http://www.egyptindependent.com/news/shaabi-music-breakthrough> accessed 10 July 2013.
51   Sadat, in an interview with the author (2013).

(DJ Haha) was working as a PC repairman and selling personalised ringtones when he first heard Figo's recording of 'Al Sallam Festival'.[52] Clayton continues, 'Suddenly, a world of sonic possibility opened up to him. His facility with software made it easy to splice genres and coax Western synthesisers into the intricate quarter tone tuning of Eastern *maqam* scales.' As Sadat explained in an interview, soon after, they formed al-Sallam Ghosts and began recording out of Figo's studio in al-Sallam City using pirated programs like FruityLoops, a shoddy mixer, and an equaliser.

By 2007, their popularity had begun to soar with their ever-growing exposure on YouTube and through word-of-mouth referrals. They would perform at local weddings, while also driving forward the burgeoning carnivalesque festival movement of Mahraganat music in urban, working-class neighbourhoods. Nearly one half of Cairo's population that is situated in *ashwa'iyyat* [haphazard], unplanned settlements like al-Sallam City.[53] These neighbourhoods are often riddled with poverty, drugs like hashish, Tramadol, and *beesa* [heroin], as well as dilapidated infrastructure, overflowing sewage and utter neglect. Nevertheless just as Shaabi singers like Ahmed Adawiya and more recently, Abdel Basset Hamouda, Hakim or Saad el-Soghayar were rooted deeply within the densely populated working-class neighbourhoods and *ashwa'iyyats*, Sadat's songs are also ripe with the outpours of Cairo's disenfranchised youth and the inarguable marginalization of Egypt's poor.

According to Sadat, his lyrical content is inspired by the Cairo street culture, but it is not always political, in fact he considers his music to be more social commentary than political anthems. But when listening to Sadat's and his companion Alaa Fifty Cent's recently released EP, *Best of Sadat & Alaa Fifty Cent*, it becomes clear that their lyrics are political, socially-inspired, and often times either humorous or downright aggressive. The 14-track compilation ranges between hard-knock political tracks like 'Five Pounds Credit' to the danceable cacophony of Shaabi and electronic noise in 'Enjex'. In the former, the duo's lyrics come with reconstructed protest chants like 'The people want the regime to fall/The people are tired' atop percussive *doff*-beats, hi-hats, and hypnotically synthetic background bleeps. In other more rhythmic and speedy tracks, such as 'Enjex', the duo proves time and again their ability to produce aggressive, Rap-based compositions in addition to dance floor anthems.

—

2014 saw the release of two documentary feature films of the Mahraganat scene, one by Egyptian director, Salma El Tarzi titled *Underground/On the Surface*, the other Hind Meddeb's *Electro-Chaabi*. The latter film chronicles the Mahraganat scene through the lens of Sadat, Alaa Fifty, Figo, in addition to their rival crew, Okka and Ortega. In the film Meddeb shadows several musicians in the Cairo districts of Imbaba, Matareya, and Sallam City. In his neon-graffitied studio in the latter neighbourhood, Sadat sings incredibly poetic, aggressive lines into the microphone, like (translated here):

How many martyrs fell in front of us?
They ran them over with cars.
They tricked us and changed the regime.
They told us life would be good.
It turned out to be an illusion.
He who screams and asks for his rights.
They shoot him like a slave.
Lots of words are being spoken.
And the old regime is still working.
Lots of words are being spoken.
And the old regime is still working.

As Sadat explains it, it was the groups' increasing performances on Emad al-Din Street, in downtown Cairo, that snowballed their ever-growing, local fan-base. Sadat's breakthrough track, which he released on YouTube five years

---

52   Jace Clayton, 'Cairo, Something New', *The Fader*, 16 October 2012, <http://www.thefader.com/2012/10/16/cairo-something-new/> accessed 15 July 2013.
53   Ted Swedenburg, 'Egypt's Music of Protest', *The Arabist*, 20 February 2013, <https://arabist2.squarespace.com/?tag=music> accessed 15 July 2013.

ago, was titled 'Koll A'am' ('Every Year'), but it was the song titled 'Ana Elli e-shty fi Haram' ('My life full of Sins') that solidified their mass popularity as it garnered tens of thousands of views. The collective continues to perform all together on occasion, but it is the sub-pairing of Alaa Fifty and Sadat that have found the greatest success and international recognition. The duo has now begun performing across Egypt and internationally, including France, England, Holland and Lebanon.

A rival Mahraganat crew known as Tamanya Fil Meya (Eight Percent) are often considered to be pioneers of the burgeoning popular class music scene over the past several years. Tamanya Fil Meya is made up of DJ Ortega and his mates Oka and Wezza, all in their late-twenties and mid-thirties. In commercial terms, their financial success was a lot quicker than that al-Sallam Ghosts. For example, in 2012, Oka and Ortega landed a game changing TV commercial deal with Egyptian telecom company, Mobinil. In the aforementioned documentary by Egyptian filmmaker Salma El Tarzi, *Underground/On the Surface*, the director shadows the young singers through their Cairo suburb of Matareya between November 2011 and December 2012, as they rapidly rise to fame to the backdrop of a country spiralling out of control. In an interview about the film, El Tarzi shed some insight on the topic:

I was specifically interested in Oka and Ortega because they had a couple songs that, for me, were very special. Their music sounded better produced, more elaborate – I was instantly hooked to 'Ya Dirixiony' [My Steering Wheel]. The song was very nihilistic; it was 'My steering wheel, my steering wheel', then they start reciting everything they hate in a very monotonous way. They would say things like, 'I'm upset with the world, I'm upset with the traffic, I'm upset with Hamas, I'm upset with…' There was something very interesting about it and I was curious.[54]

When El Tarzi began filming in November 2011, the group Tamanya Fil Meya had already been making rounds in the street festival circuit along with rival crew al-Sallam Ghosts. But it was their song regarding sexual harassment, *'Haty Bosa Ya Bet'* [Give me a Kiss, Girl] that eventually led them to digital stardom.[55] At the same time, they were getting booked two-three gigs a night for weddings and festivals in middle-class neighbourhoods all over Cairo. Tamanya Fil Meya's lyrics are oftentimes less political or socially conscious than the al-Sallam Ghosts'. Director El Tarzi says that Oka and Ortega did not take part in a single protest during the eighteen days that let to Mubarak's ouster in February 2011. When she asked them why they hadn't participated, their reply was that they have always been marginalised and never felt that they were a part of Egypt. In the trailer of the feature film, Oka candidly explains:

We sing about our life, and the things we see. But a mainstream super star like Amr Diab, he comes from a Shaabi neighbourhood, but this was in the past, he doesn't live in Shaabi neighbourhoods. And he knows nothing about our life – the best he can do, is sing about love and heartbreak.[56]

Director El Tarzi thinks that while Oka and Ortega were apolitical at the time, they were entirely revolutionary in their own right. She describes them as being 'underground by definition' because they reflect the status quo – the over spilling masses of Egyptian youth that make up over sixty percent of the country's population.[57] In the filmmaker's words: 'They are not middle-class kids who decide to be underground or not – these guys are underground because they are actually the underdog.'

—

Although many people view Mahraganat music as a passing trend, unsophisticated, and forgettable, there is far more to the burgeoning genre

[54] Salma El Tarzi, in an interview with the author (2013).
[55] The lyrics go, 'Give me a kiss girl / Give me a piece girl', resembling sexualised Rap songs from the 1990s.
[56] Salma El Tarzi, 'Underground/On the Surface Trailer', YouTube, 12 April 2012, <http://www.youtube.com/watch?v=6C1dyAafCnM> accessed April 2012.
[57] Salma El Tarzi, in an interview with the author (2013).

than the sound it produces. With YouTube videos heralding over four million views, a spiralling onset of commercial deals, travelling gigs, and a metastasizing fan base, the pioneers behind Mahragant are potentially redefining the entire concepts of mainstream and commercial music. They are challenging the very boundaries of how music is produced, disseminated, and consumed in Egypt by avoiding the traditional, state-controlled channels of distribution. For decades, the state has used radio, entertainment, and other forms of media as a mechanism to promote what it deems appropriate for the mainstream, often times propagating an overtly nationalistic or unrealistic depiction of Egypt. With their D.I.Y. attitude, the Mahraganat activists defy the state sanctioned mainstream and censorship by releasing their songs directly onto the internet. They make their money through gigs or television commercials and appearances. Like Adawiya and the pirated cassette tape of his time, these musicians only occasionally receive airtime on radio, and it will be some time before their music videos make it to television. For Sadat it doesn't matter whether or not they get a record deal:

> We manage to reach fans through the internet, this is how they find us, it would make no sense to release physical records when all our fans access music online for free. The most important aspect for us is to have total creative freedom in making our music. We already get our own gigs, commercials and ads, so why do we need a label? There's no reason for us to sign exclusive, limiting contracts, simply because we can do it all ourselves.[58]

By releasing track after track onto the internet, these musicians are – consciously or unconsciously – creating an active archive of their work, and subsequently, a more reflective language of the street. In the past, recordings from the pre-1952 revolution era were banned or distorted. Even today, Egyptian public radio only plays about 8 per cent of its archival recordings, while the rest is destroyed or remains unknown.[59] Despite these statistics, by continuing to record and release, while also working through the 100Copies label, Mahraganat musicians of the likes of Sadat, Fifty, Madfageya, and more are continuing to gain traction in Europe with gigs travelling across several cities each year. Meanwhile, in recent years Oka and Ortega have become slightly more irrelevant musically as they head for movie careers.

With women crews illusively emerging online – like Banat Madraset Gamal Abdel Nasser, whose debut video has garnered over 90,000 views on YouTube – the future for Mahraganat music continues to look promising, and far more than a fleeting trend. However, it is still entirely too soon to determine the impact of the genre on society and music in Egypt. It will likely morph into something else in a few years. But, as it seems, the revolutionary/post-revolutionary Mahraganat genre might become one of the more audacious D.I.Y. musical experiments in modern day dance music and dissemination in the Arab world.

—

While Mahraganat music continues to be snubbed by high culture and the Egyptian music industry alike, the independent cultural scene in Cairo has dedicated both time and support to these musicians – regardless of whether they are a passing trend or not. In recent years, both Tamanya Fil Meya and al-Sallam Ghosts participated in the reputable Downtown Contemporary Arts Festival's (D-CAF) music programme, curated by the venerable independent music producer, Mahmoud Refat. Known for his Electro-fusion, Trip-Hop band, Bikya[60], and his independent music label 100Copies, Refat has been one of the leading figures in developing the independent music scene. When asked why he booked Mahraganat music in the D-CAF line-up two-years in a row, he replied, 'We

---

58 Sadat, in an interview with the author (2013).

59 Cf. Lina Attalah, 'The Stories of Sound', *Mada Masr*, 5 May 2014, <https://www.madamasr.com/en/2014/05/05/feature/culture/the-stories-of-sound/> accessed 10 May 2014.

60 Bikya is made up of Mahmoud Waly on bass and electronics, Maurice Louca on keyboard and sampler, and Mahmoud Refat on drums and synthesizer.

wanted to promote direct culture, which is defined by music that represents the street and urban culture, a sound originating from the people without mediation of middle men or large conglomerates.'[61] Refat also believes that the annual festival and his downtown music space and label, 100Copies, could provide a breeding ground for musicians from various countries, social backgrounds, and even genres to learn from one another. In the 2014 edition of D-CAF, an incredible collaboration happened when Sadat and Alaa Fifty were joined by London-based DJ and producer, Faze Miyake, who laid down some deep-hitting, lugubrious grime beats into their set.[62]

Earlier, in December 2013, the bands Wetrobots <3 Bosaina, Sadat, and Refat's Folktronica band Bikya had been invited to participate in the 2013 Worldtronics Music Festival in Berlin, right after the Ten Cities recording in Cairo, where they each performed their own brand of experimental electronic-based music. In their own right, the three performance acts are rather indicative of the current electronic dance music scene in Cairo, particularly when looking at their individual components – Maurice Louca, Mahmoud Refat, Sadat, Bosaina, Ismail Hosny, Figo, Hussein Sherbini – who cross over various subgenres of electronic music including Techno, EDM, Folktronica, and Mahraganat. In his album, *Salute the Parrot*, producer Maurice Louca released one of the most original dance albums of past few years with music that is identifiably Egyptian, but also wildly progressive and artistic.

Meanwhile, Islam Chipsy, a 1986 born avant-garde keyboard virtuoso from Cairo's Imbaba district, is actively and successfully deconstructing the typical Shaabi sonic sphere by morphing it into something that is both familiar and otherworldly. Usually performing with two drummers, his music is heavily percussive and rhythm-based, yet he continues to redefine the possibilities of the holy trinity of dance music: synthesiser, drums, and bass. In 2016, Chipsy performed in over sixty concerts in Europe alone, while continuing to collaborate on Downtempo Shaabi tracks for contemporary icons like Hakim.

—

Cairo is utterly and undeniable cacophonous. In most societies, music is both a reflection of social realities as well as a socialisation device to influence people's perception and behaviour. In Cairo, as elsewhere, the ever-changing musical landscape, and the way in which society consumes it, has always been deeply intertwined with the politics of the time. To discuss dance music is to imagine politics, power dynamics, and cultural production mixed into a record that continues to spin out of control.

In the past, Egyptian music and production mechanisms were incarcerated within the government's framed image of society. With few exceptions like Adawiya and a handful of others, production of music and popularisation of sounds from the margins had little future before the digital age. But now, with the proliferation and emancipation of cheap technology, the accessibility of social media, and the artists' unrelenting will, music is falling back into the hands of the people who listen to it. Now, more than ever before, the musicians hold agency over their music. This in turn has allowed musicians to challenge both the government-constructed narrative of history as well as political events in Egypt. It has given them the power of a counter-narrative.

Epilogue

In June 2014, I caught up with the musician turned driver Mohamed Ashraf at the anniversary event of digital media company, Mada Masr, for whom he was working, and where a group of musicians like Islam Chipsy made appearances. Chipsy was booked to perform the closing set, after a diverse line-up of musicians

---

61   Mahmoud Refat, in an interview with the author (2013).
62   The performance was part of the Cairo Calling collaboration between Rinse FM, 100Copies, and The British Council.

before him including Nadah El Shazly, Meshwar, and Like Jelly. During soundcheck, Islam Chipsy and Mohamed Ashraf hung out in the only shaded area of the garden, waiting for the speakers to be set up on stage. After being briefly introduced, Ashraf and Chipsy spent the next hour talking, animatedly with what seemed to be a lot of laughter and drumming hands – their topic of conversation looked to be percussive. When wrapping up their conversation, Chipsy and Ashraf exchanged numbers. After shaking hands, Ashraf walked back towards where I was standing and said, 'As it seems, we actually know each other from when I used to play drums with [the band] SimSim Shihab. We're all from Imbaba. He's with the new generation – the *deej* (DJ) – with all those electronics and buttons. But something interesting happened though, he asked me if I could help train his drummers in the studio one day.'

'What did you say?' I asked.

'I told him, *yallabina* [let's go]!', he replied, as he walked back towards the parking lot, with his hands drumming along his side.

Bibliography

Armbrust, Walter, *Mass Culture and Modernism in Egypt* (Cambridge University Press, 1996).

Attalah, Lina, 'The Stories of Sound', May 5 2014, *Mada Masr*, <https://www.madamasr.com/en/2014/05/05/feature/culture/the-stories-of-sound/> accessed 10 May 2014.

Batala, Angie, 'Reliving the 70's: Egypt's Golden Age of Rock', *Discord Magazine* 4 (2012), 34–43.

Clayton, Jace, 'Cairo, something New', *The Fader*, October 16, 2012, <http://www.thefader.com/2012/10/16/cairo-something-new/> accessed 15 July 2013.

ElNabawi, Maha, 'Soundtrack of the Egyptian Revolution', *Community Times* (2011).

ElNabawi, Maha, 'Music Permeates Everything', *Mada Masr*, 15 December 2013, <http://www.madamasr.com/sections/culture/%E2%80%98music-permeates-everything%E2%80%99> accessed 20 December 2013.

ElNabawi, Maha, 'Egypt's cinematic gems: Fangs', *Mada Masr*, November 1, 2014. <https://www.madamasr.com/en/2014/11/01/feature/culture/egypts-cinematic-gems-fangs/> accessed 23 November 2014.

El-Saket, Ola 'The Shaabi music breakthrough', *Egypt Independent*, 22 October 2011, <http://www.egyptindependent.com/news/shaabi-music-breakthrough> accessed 10 July 2013.

El Saifi, Hashem, 'Mohamed Abdel Wahab: A Growing Symbol', YouTube, 10 July 2013, <https://www.youtube.com/watch?v=GYXs-fKhTO4> accessed July 2013.

Frishkopf, Michael (ed.), *Music and Media in the Arab World*, (Cairo: The American University Press, 2010).

Grippo, James R., 'What's Not on Egyptian Television and Radio! Locating the "Popular" in Egyptian Sha'bi', in Michael Frishkopf (ed.), *Music and Media in the Arab World* (Cairo: The American University Press, 2010), 137–162.

Hammond, Andrew, *Popular Culture in the Arab World: Arts, Politics, and the Media* (Cairo: The American University in Cairo Press, 2007).

ICT Eye, 'Country Profile – Arab States – Egypt', 2012, <http://www.itu.int/net4/itu-d/icteye/CountryProfile.aspx> accessed July 2013.

Lutfi al-Sayyid Marsot, Afaf, *A History of Egypt: From the Arab Conquest to the Present* (Cambridge University Press, 2007).

Nasser, Zein, 'A History of Music and Singing on Egyptian Radio and Television', in Michael Frishkopf (ed.), *Music and Media in the Arab World* (Cairo: The American University Press, 2010), 67–76.

Osman Zaki, Ahmed, 'The 1952 revolution: A legacy of cultural transformation', *Egypt Independent*, 27 July 2011, <http://www.egyptindependent.com/news/1952-revolution-legacy-cultural-transformation> accessed 5 July 2013.

Swedenburg, Ted, 'Egypt's Music of Protest', *The Arabist*, 20 February 2013, <https://arabist2.squarespace.com/?tag=music> accessed 15 July 2013.

Clubbing in an Oppressive City – Musical and Social Spheres from Al-Haram Street to Tahrir Square

Ali Abdel Mohsen

Monday night, Al-Haram Street. Halfway through her act, Nisma's feet are no longer touching the stage – instead, she dances on a freshly-laid carpet of crisp 5 Egyptian Pound (LE) notes. In the pulsating light, it is impossible to discern the exact colour of her painted toenails, or of the flesh surrounding them. Everything is red, the difference being only in shades and luminosity. The studded embroidery and beaded tassels of her two-piece outfit sparkle like tiny mirrors; her widely smiling lips appear bloodstained. Bracelets and anklets clutter her flailing limbs, but their jangle is drowned by the waves of sound swirling through this tiny, subterranean cave.

Between her and the stairway, marked with a neon exit sign, is a sea of men; some swaying to the beat she keeps, some to their own, and others not at all. Behind her is a quartet of musicians and a red-faced crooner in a crimson tuxedo, and behind them, Fiji, or possibly a Hawaiian island, or some other landscape of paradise, de-scaled and reconstructed in slightly overlapping patches of wallpaper. The beach is bisected by a narrow floor-to-ceiling mirror, and on either side of it, superimposed over the flattened red sky, are spiral strips of decorative aluminium and bouquets of semi-inflated balloons, identical to the ones hanging from the low, stained ceiling. At times, Nisma is joined by one of two younger men in tight-fitting jeans and T-shirts – both employees of the establishment – who shower her with paper money. Eventually, a third, older man – a patron – gets up to do the same. Lifting his traditional *galabeya* dress from around his ankles, he steps onto the stage and, for a few moments, shakes his considerable waist in imitation of the girl in front of him, waving his thick wad around before dispersing it over Nisma – each flick of his wrist sending another note slicing through the air, to be trampled upon by the purple soles of her dancing feet.

The shiny new banknotes come straight from the establishment's vault. For 100 LE, a patron can get ten times the amount in two stacks of 5 LE denominations, on the condition that it be spent entirely and exclusively within the precise confines of the stage, on 'complimenting' whichever girl, or girls, happen to be gracing it. The girls never pick up the money, only come in contact with a bill to secure it in place, should a particularly brash patron – of which there often are – attempt to suggestively slide a handful into her waistband. Some girls flirtingly twirl away; others pause and jut their hip out. The shiny-browed crooner acknowledges each downpour with either a gracious nod, a sly smile, or a repertoire of encouraging hand gestures, while the band members – a bassist, two drummers, and a pounding keyboardist – pay no attention to the falling notes; their stoic, low-gazing stares broken only by the occasional drifting of a hashish cigarette through their line-up, and in the brief interludes between songs.

The stacks of cash are visible, atop entrée-sized dishes, on several tables, mostly ones occupied by pairs or small groups of men and are watched over – only seemingly casually – by the establishment's handful of male employees orbiting the cluster of seated clientele. These men move between three posts: the above ground entrance, the doorway at the bottom of its stairwell, and the bar situated along the inside of that same wall. They are noticeably muscular – being so constitutes the majority of their job's 'requirements' – and their interactions are characterised by two extreme temperaments: the lewd camaraderie and suggestive in-joking shared among the other male, and female employees, respectively; and the no-nonsense nature of their dealings with the patrons – which usually only occur to the misfortune of the latter. At regular intervals, they sweep the bills off the stage with their hands, before dancing back to their posts.

The lines are few but clearly drawn. The girl onstage is for viewing purposes only, and never to be touched – the occasional waistband bonus is always closely scrutinized by the establishment's numerous eyes. Patrons with more vociferous appetites can turn their attention, and their wallets, to the establishment's other female employees, the table girls, who, usually in pairs, will guide the clientele upon arrival from the door to an available table, or appear at its side shortly afterwards. Smiles will be flashed, nicknames will be assigned, some hair might even be tousled as initial exchanges are made; eventually the girls will take their seat at the table – for a price – or respect the clientele's wishes to be left alone – for approximately the same price.

This evening, out of the twelve occupied tables, only three have decided to pay for added company. While the four undesired women mill between the door and the bar, giggling at the bouncers and smacking their lips at the clientele, their four colleagues are flailing around in opposite corners of the cave, asking for drags off of hashish cigarettes which they end up hogging. The table girls might ask for alcohol as well, even though the majority of them are clearly under the legal drinking age. The patrons will almost always acquiesce, leaving the male employees solely responsible for warning, or withholding alcohol from the girls, should they be nearing a level of intoxication non-conducive to business.

In the hands of a few patrons, hashish – rarely ever the cheaper *bango*, or weed, which might be seen as an insult to the establishment – is being rolled in tiny leaves of ungummed Ottoman papers, off of teacup plates or out of palms.

All tables are cluttered with drinks. Yet this accumulation is in no way representative of the variety on display behind the bar where, on glass shelves against a mirrored wall, bottles of all shapes and sizes are lined up, only to be ignored in favour of local beer, Stella, or whiskey. Which leads to a suspicion, later confirmed: the display bottles are for just that – display. The establishment serves only beer, whiskey, and one brand of soda. The bottles on the mirrored shelves behind the bar are filled with a mixture of tap water and food colouring, the latter ingredient for the most part trivial under the staggered rainbow of houselights.

Regulars are allowed to bring in their own bottles for a price calculated according to their degree of familiarity with the establishment's management. On two tables, bottles of Johnnie Walker sit in chilled tin buckets, on a third, Chivas Regal is shared by two men and their table girls. Besides the bucket, their tabletop is cluttered with more glasses than the party needs, surrounding a slightly-less-than-life-size swan sculpted out of aluminium foil. Divided among the depressions along the swan's spine is an assortment of 'snacks': pumpkin seeds, salted peanuts, lupini beans, unsalted peanuts. The swan serves to single out the men's high-rolling status – 'snacks' amount to one of the hidden mandatory costs of the establishment, and are usually only served stingily in tiny bowls or on teacup plates at highly overpriced rates. A box of tissues will also be placed on the table, and immediately opened, in order to add another item to the bill at roughly twenty-five to thirty times its street price. At the swan table, three boxes have already been opened, and barely used.

—

Besides the beer served to the majority of patrons in this establishment, the availability of a second, more expensive option can be seen as less of a response to personal preferences than an investment in a need for further exclusivity; a class distinction, of sorts, within the microcosm of the standard Cairo nightclub. In these establishments, whiskey, for the most part, is consumed not as the end result of some wide-ranging sampling process, but only because history has determined that it is what needs to be consumed at these occasions, in these spaces, if one can afford it. The drink is merely a detail in the larger image of the 'nightclub' – an 'imported concept'[1] – as it was first introduced to Egyptian society; an image subsequently adopted and popularised by a burgeoning film-industry operating at what would become its peak, and later continued ceaselessly by a state-media apparatus desperately clinging to its past relevance in the face of deepening cultural stagnation.

Yet, to conclude that whiskey is served in Cairo's local bars, cabarets, and nightclubs today because of old Egyptian films would be a tremendous over-simplification, and largely inaccurate. Simply put, the spirit celebrated by such venues is predominantly enforced, and further propelled, by the image of a past less plagued by socio-economic restrictions and reduced global standing. The accuracy of the history depicted by this image is irrelevant, as, in a nation of high illiteracy, perceptions of the past are shaped more by song and film than any written documentation. Furthermore, it should be noted that besides its myriad nightclubs, the nightlife area on Al-Haram Street in Cairo's Giza district was also home to the nation's biggest film studios, theatres, and the national film institute, all now existing in varying states of dilapidation. These scenes from a more prestigious era lend dignity to the consumption of an intoxicating drink (and, by association, the intoxication that follows) and elevate the act beyond a mere satisfying of the senses and fulfilment of impulses. It becomes an act of culture, as evidenced by the current national cinematic output; the most recent box office behemoth being, somewhat ironically, *Al-Haram Street* – a sordid, flesh-jiggling extravaganza produced by the butcher-turned-film-producer Sobky dynasty.

It is partially for this reason, that the majority of venues cluttered on the sides and branches of Al-Haram Street differ from most other entertainment-based establishments as they do not need to respond to the latest trends in music, décor or alcoholic beverages in order to retain their clientele, nor do they need to embellish on the essentials. Sahraya, the underground hovel where Nisma puts on her show five nights a week beneath a corner halfway down Al-Haram Street, is a clear example of a philosophy similarly manifested in the house band's setlist which, across such establishments, changes little from night to night, and decade to decade. Except for the occasional instances of history shouldering in – on election eve, for example – the outside world rarely intrudes on such venues.

Despite the activities that take place within, Sahraya and its counterparts are not places of leisure, in the same way that they do not cater to a need to appear fashionable or trendy. Establishments such as Sahraya are responses to a desire for survival – on one end, financially, and on the other therapeutically for their male clientele. They are emergency clinics, of sorts, with services split between two cure-all prescriptions – alcohol and smoke for the mind, and girls for the body. Nothing else is necessary. The band might as well be outdated, and in several similar establishments it is the same; representing rare concessions to evolving technology, but ones made strictly for financial reasons.

Among the establishments of Al-Haram Street, there is little aesthetic difference between the places that haven't redecorated since the 1980s and the ones that have. The freshness of the coat of paint might differ but the general requirements remain the same: a setting to aid the fantasy of escapism – a backdrop of unattainable beauty, be it wallpaper of a tropical beach or a poster gallery of balloon-breasted, single-named 'singers', music to obliterate the senses, and substances to hasten the process lest the sun should come up too early – an unspoken understanding that there is a collective allowance of certain behaviour that, outside the establishment, would be deemed thoroughly deviant.

---

1   Mohamed Abdel Tawab, the establishment's manager in an interview with the author (2016). He attributes the proliferation of Cairo's nightclubs to British colonialism. However, documentation exists suggesting the presence of nightclubs since as early as the beginning of the nineteenth century, when folkloric and *sharqi* dance began to appear on the stages of new, French-style cabarets and music halls.

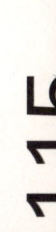

Night club at Al-Ahram Street, Cairo, 2015, photos: Ali Abdel Mohsen

Emad El Din Street, Cairo, 2016, photo: Andreas Langfeld

Sadat and Fifty at After Eight Club, Cairo, photo: Maha ElNabawi

Local wedding with music at Salam City, Cairo, 2014, photo: Mosa'ab Elshamy

Tahrir Square, Cairo, 2016, photo: Andreas Langfeld

Mohammed Ali Street, Cairo, 2016, photo: Andreas Langfeld

Should the advances of a table-girl be turned down, for example, the man risks raising a few eyebrows. Should they further resist, their sexuality will be highly questioned, and they will be made to feel like an outsider. One possibility for the man's resistance may be that he is unable to afford such privileges, and the other guests fear that they may have to financially compensate for him, perhaps paying extra to stop the rebuffed table-girl from involving the other girls, or worse yet, a bouncer. In short, a penalty for having broken the agreement and failing to comply with the rules which the space, by its very existence, deems necessary; for breaking the barrier that separates the outside, or above ground, world. One would be held guilty for devaluing the 'prestige' of drinking whiskey on the beach, and eating grapes out of a swan while having a girl dance just for you, and your shiny new money.

With its chipped-paint walls, scarred tabletops, and sticky seats, the fact that five months prior to the evening described Sahraya didn't exist would be surprising anywhere but on Al-Haram Street, and the fact that three months later it no longer would, most probably wouldn't have surprised its owner at the time, or anyone familiar with the workings of Al-Haram Street.[2] In this particular sea of celebrated hedonism, there is a long-surviving archipelago of big-name establishments, surrounded by a tide of middle-grade venues, and then there are the barnacles, clinging to the bottom of the scene. A quintessential example of the second group, Sahraya's existence was shaped by the ebb and flow of establishments briefly benefiting from the remnants of Al-Haram Street's legacy as a nightlife hotspot – a legacy that has barely been maintained, and only through a few larger establishments that have held on to their names, if not their management, throughout the years, and still manage to attract a roster of well-known belly dancers and singers.

Yet, at an average of 500 LE a table, and upwards on weekends as well as to minor occasions, the more-established venues remain inaccessible to most seeking a taste of Al-Haram Street's offered pleasures. Instead, the majority of patrons turn to the spaces in between, through which flow where the efforts of small-time entrepreneurs can be found in venues like Sahraya, El-Prince, King Time, Lux, and countless others that bleed into one another, as they are bought, sold, taken over, lost, and shut down for their management's failure, or refusal, to come up with whatever sum it takes the authorities that day to turn their eyes away.

—

The song ends, another begins, and to help distinguish it from the previous one, the blue lights of Sahraya's turn a few shades lighter than that of the velvet-like material covering most of the establishment's walls and the entirety of its floor. Immediately, the subterranean nightclub is transported to the bottom of the ocean, and the band begins to spill something appropriately murky; lyrics later revealing it to be a narrative of a broken heart, a tale of misery where each howling confession is accentuated by three descending steps on the keyboard. The crooner wails and hiccups and the belly dancer moves along, the slow contorting of her bruised skin and the sudden jolts in her movements all manifestations of a supposed inner yearning, as is the downward-sloping smile on her face and the lyrics unspooling from the sobbing crooner. For the duration of the lament the scene evokes the inner workings of a machine, albeit one with sand stuck in its gears. It is a stubborn process, the distortion of tragedy into titillation.

Oh world, why the cruelty
Why the torture and blame?
And why has kindness been forgotten
And the eye forsaken sleep?

So the night goes on. Eventually Nisma leaves and is replaced by another girl. More drinks are ordered, more joints are rolled, and the band continues to regurgitate sounds devoured throughout years spent spinning between seedy nightclubs, disreputable 'hotels' and restaurants that serve no food.

Al-Leil and others: legitimacy from history

A more extensive menu can be found up the street, at flagships such as Al-Leil, where the interior décor consists of considerably more than strips of carpeting stapled to the walls. It is establishments like Al-Leil and its contemporaries such as Al-Andalus, Al-Gondola, Tivoli, Parisiana, L'Auberge and a handful of others, that cast a shadow over venues such as Sahraya; representing the earlier, clearer image which is meagrely recreated in Nisma's underground realm. Much of the appeal of, and legitimacy claimed by, these larger establishments lie in their history. Unlike the brief lifespan common among the more modest venues, Al-Leil and the other existing members of its tier are products of the 1960s and 1970s; more specifically, of the nationalization of the cinema industry under Gamal Abdel Nasser. With the resulting shift towards the entertainment aspect of filmmaking, Egyptian cinema, once revolutionary, increasingly became a case of style over stifled, and often censored, substance. It was a style that, escalated by competitive entrepreneurship, was unreservedly manifested by the new wave of Al-Haram Street's nightclubs. Gradually, even the few venues that targeted younger audiences – usually well-to-do teenagers that went from imitating Western dance moves, to form some kind of Beatles tribute band in a non-alcoholic setting – were muscled out of the picture by a growing taste for something flashier.

The nightlife of Al-Haram street, that took off, and lasted throughout two decades, could be seen as a clear evolutionary step from the nightclub scenes of the 1930s to 1950s which flourished in downtown Cairo on Mohamed Ali and

---

2 The venue's former manager, Mohamed Abdel Tawab, is now a 'silent partner' at King Time, the establishment that has appeared in Sahraya's place. He declines to name his other partner who, he claims, is also 'silent'. He cites the reason for Sahraya's closure as 'renewal. We wanted to present a different theme'. With the exception of a new sign, the venue has not redecorated. From the author's interview with the establishment's manager, Mohamed Abdel Tawab, 23 December 2016.

Emad el-Din Streets. This new club life that redefined itself to become the main artery of the national entertainment industry, began to redirect its creative efforts into matters of pure aesthetics.

Progressively, venues became more elaborate, as did the features they offered and their attempts at captivating a star-struck public, resulting in the creation of iconic structures, such as Al-Leil's wavy, blue-tiled mosaic façade: an architectural celebration of the night, complete with a massive neon-lit star in the corner.

Shortly after opening its doors to the public in 1975 – and just as the effects of President Anwar Sadat's open door policy were beginning to be felt[3] – Al-Leil successfully established itself as a hotspot on the entertainment scene, a reputation assisted by the fact that it had been founded by highly-regarded actress and recording artist, Sherifa Fadel. She was known to the public as 'Mother of the Hero' for having lost a son in the 1973 war with Israel – a personal tragedy which formed the basis of one of her most popular songs. Similarly, the establishment took its name from another of Fadel's hits, an anthem of nocturnal yearning.

In its heyday Al-Leil was its own galaxy, attracting as many stars to its entertainment hall as it produced from its stage. Today, the flow of both – particularly the latter – has slowed to a trickle. Yet, on any given night Al-Leil's tables remain occupied by men in suits being waited on by servers in uniforms, while an orchestra of twelve or fifteen tuxedoed musicians motivate a short succession of professional, and sometimes foreign, belly dancers. Then an MC, often a celebrity such as Saad el-Soghayar, who found fame on the smaller stages of Al-Haram Street before starring in the film of the same name, rattles off a series of sexually-charged quips. The parquet stage is surrounded by tables and overlooked by the second-floor balcony, with spotlights swivelling from its railings. There is a kitchen capable of producing multi-coursed meals, and a bar, its surfaces consisting of electrically lit panels, is fully stocked. The main source of light is a golden spiral of a chandelier that stops short of obscuring the balcony's view of the stage, its luminosity synchronized to the band's confidently timed beats.

It is the band, as well as the rest of the performers occupying the stage at various points throughout the evening, where the Cairo distinction between the terms 'nightclub' and 'cabaret' is made clear. Al-Leil belongs to the former category, a classification determined by the calibre of its on-stage talent. In its earlier days, the venue would host bands more akin to orchestras, conducted by accomplished songwriters and proficiently animated through highly-skilled belly dancers – stage acts that were the culmination of years of dedication and considerable financial investment on the part of the performers. As such, a certain sanctity is observed – the stage is not approached as freely and the hashish certainly more concealed – in respect of the artists performing, as well as the establishment prestigious enough to host them.

A 'cabaret' on the other hand, is defined by the absence of these rules. While a deteriorating economy has gradually contributed to the blurring of the line separating the two – it is far less common today, for example, for belly dancers to have their own musicians, not to mention backup dancers, and orchestras have similarly been reduced to house bands – public perception, along with the attitude projected by these spaces, continue to define the larger scene.

Unlike Sahraya, there are no table-girls at Al-Leil. The escorts wait in the wings, or at the bar, leaving it up to the patron to make the first move – unless the patron is a regular with previously-stated preferences. Like Sahraya, money can be exchanged for significantly larger sums to be spent to carpet the stage, although patrons rarely approach the stage, the money instead being handed over to stagehands, who do the showering. Swans make less of an appearance here, instead status is signified by the choices made from wider selections and spreads of elaborately garnished dishes. But there are still countless reminders of the 'privilege' of such exclusivity, or of being able to afford it, even if just for the sake of it. Within the remaining pantheons of Al-Haram Street, it's rare for even the sparsest of bills to amount to any cost less than 1000 to 2000 LE.

—

Today, Al-Leil stands as a rare specimen of a bygone era. By the end of the 1980s, the entertainment industry had shifted its attention to cater to a growing tide of tourists from Gulf nations who gravitated towards burgeoning commercial centres such as Mohandessin and Downtown Cairo, where internationally recognised hotels had sprouted along the Nile. As a result, the spotlight faded from Al-Haram Street and over the following years the once luminous strip became a national symbol of low ambitions, and high despair. It is in this period of neglect that a specific type of establishment flourished – the type of establishment that one might be pointed to by Al-Leil's suited bouncers after failing to measure to their unspoken door policy.

All the way down Al-Haram Street and at the opposite end of the spectrum, lurk the likes of Atoun, a venue long notorious for being a 'nightclub' only because national law prohibits the use of the more accurate description 'bordello'. Located on the corner of an intersection, the three-floor establishment has been shut down numerous times, but, in the chaotic and largely lawless years since the 2011 uprising has, along with its contemporaries, been experiencing a renaissance of sorts. This has in turn informed a new, further deteriorated reiteration of Al-Haram Street history – one depicted in the film of the same name, where rape is worked into the 'plotline' as a source of comedy and titillation.

Should one wander into their radius, the burly, bleary-eyed doormen will insist with a wink that Atoun is a legitimate nightclub, with a live band and proper dancing livening up

---

[3] Following the 1973 war with Israel, and in a reversal of his predecessor's policies, Sadat opened the door to Western capital investment and returned several industries to the private sector. The introduction of this free-market philosophy resulted in a boom in the tourism industry, as well as the proliferation of independent film and music production companies that prioritised profit over substance – both of which contributed to the marginalisation of Al-Haram Street.

its lavish halls. The reality is closer to a boombox on a stool in a sparsely furnished room, where teenaged males shuffle about on a sticky floor in tight-fitting pants, hair either slicked back or hidden under baseball caps, anxiously grabbing each other in anticipation of the next prostitute to push through a barely beaded curtain. Whereas Al-Leil's 'entertainment hall' will be packed with the statesmen of Al-Haram Street clientele, and the occasional group of Western tourists, enjoying performances by top-tier belly dancers and box-office stars. Whilst Sahraya caters to shallower-pocketed twenty- to fifty-years-old looking for a good time, Atoun lures in a younger crowd, recognising the endless profit to be exploited from the wide demographic of sexually-repressed teenage males – young, impulsive, and generally easy to please. As one alleged frequenter enthusiastically describes in an online forum:

> As soon as you step into Atoun, you will be greeted by hostesses with gorgeous bodies and exposed breasts and smooth white thighs; women no less attractive or appealing than Cameron Diaz and Sharon Stone.[4]

The women are middle-aged and do not resemble the mentioned US-American actresses in any way. They first appear as one pays the 50 LE entrance fee, calling out in a less-than-subtle fashion from the steel railing of the staircase that extends from the building's entrance on the first floor to a row of annexed bedrooms. Ceiling fans, mosquito nets and the tops of bedposts are visible through the doorframes. After being led through the first floor entrance and seated at one of the plastic tables lining the stained orange walls of the entertainment hall, a single woman will shuffle over, most likely while drinking from a glass of warm beer included in the entry fee. All of Atoun's drinks are served at room temperature.

In such establishments, there is little pretence. Unlike the table-girls of Sahraya, these women are not dressed for a night out, but rather, the opposite: faded nightgowns over spandex pants and mid-riff revealing (perhaps unintentionally so) tank-tops, little-to-no jewellery, and plastic flip-flops. The conversation will be equally frank, instigated by the woman as she pulls up a seat: 30 LE for a handjob, which will be performed at the table. Acts of further intimacy, however, take place in the bedrooms, and at incrementally higher prices.

Occasionally, a couple will get up to dance, although in Atoun what constitutes the term is little more than stumbled groping; a concession of sorts made by the establishment's female employees for teenagers who might not be able to afford more elaborate attention. The background music has few of the traditional nightlife anthems that have been performed for the past decades in more legitimate establishments; instead, consisting almost entirely of samples of the low-production trend that had been made popular in the past five years – fast-paced, electro-percussion-heavy songs made by generational peers of the adolescent patrons, with lyrics that usually revolve around drugs and the female anatomy. Correspondingly, joints will also be rolled and passed around a table, often *bango* [marijuana] enjoyed by larger parties and in smaller amounts than the hashish circulating in Sahraya.

It should be noted that while Atoun has a stage in a separate room constituting its 'VIP section', it is a space that is only sporadically used, both to celebrate occasions or holidays, and as a contribution to the illusion that the establishment offers legitimate entertainment. The latter purpose has not prevented Atoun from being the target of countless police raids and closures throughout its history, yet the establishment continues to exist today, benefitting from the government's preoccupation with more pressing issues during the turbulent years following the 2011 uprising.

—

Raids and shutdowns have always been a part of Al-Haram Street history, even in periods of relative stability. As much as the area has been shaped by the glamor of show business, to a large extent it has also been defined by the 'scandal' of show business – a detraction that, for many, also summed up the street's appeal. It is for this reason that throughout the 1970s and 1980s venues in various Cairo districts, be they Heliopolis, Zamalek or elsewhere, adopted the tone set by the Al-Haram Street establishments. This adaption led to their performers being booked for weddings and high-society functions, and allowed a new cast of stars; from Shaabi[5] singer Ahmed Adawiya to belly dancer Fifi Abdou, to popstar Amr Diab, to cross over to a broader audience and evolve to appeal to wider tastes, even as tense rivalries and shady politics brewed behind the scenes of the trend-setting nightclubs. Even influential venues have, in their history, been temporarily shut down for reasons as dubious as the promotion of public indecency, and tax evasion; Al-Leil was the subject of a protracted court case, in which founder Sherifa Fadel was forced to hand over ownership of the nightclub to a former employee. Unsurprisingly, the street has also been the frequent subject of ire by Islamists and religious extremists, who occasionally call for across-the-board closures, and raise occasional lawsuits against proprietors.

Ultimately, it was not the interference of the authorities or zealots which robbed Al-Haram Street of its domination of the city's nightlife scene, but rather a combination of factors, namely, the proliferation of televisions, and the 'entertainment tourism' industry appearing in response to increasing numbers of seasonal Gulf Arab tourists, as well as the intrusion of foreign franchises and hotel chains. Options increased, and with them, competition. The party moved on, the street fading in and out of fashion and experiencing occasional periods of loving nostalgia, such as the months following the deposal of Islamist president Mohamed Morsi. But for the most part, the venues of Al-Haram Street have failed to recapture the glory of past decades.

---

4 Kelmety Blogspot, October 2007, <http://kelmety.blogspot.com/2007/10/blog-post_28.html> accessed 14 December 2016.

5 To learn more about Shaabi and other music genres in Cairo please see Maha ElNabawi's text in this book.

While Al-Leil continues to rely on audiences with more traditional tastes as well as the constant stage-to-screen pipeline and its commissions, many of its contemporaries have fallen by the wayside, either shut down or sold off to less-experienced management. There are exceptions such as Gondola, which was recently torn down by its owner; a move that resulted in declarations of victory by Salafi extremists which continue to be repeatedly refuted by the owner's family who cite personal reasons for the venue's destruction. In the end, this more level field has arguably made it easier for venues such as Atoun to stake increasingly larger claims in the landscape of Al-Haram Street culture, and beyond.

Western Disco has arrived: Jackie's

In the summer of 1980, and after much planning, a venue called Jackie's welcomed its first guests – or rather, its first members. In anticipation of the opening night, and the type of patrons it sought to attract, the management had compiled a carefully-selected list of society's elite before sending them each temporary 'memberships' to this new establishment. It was a strategy that proved to be successful. Over the next few months, celebrities, politicians, and the country's leading businessmen all mingled at Cairo's newest, and most exclusive discotheque, in a space that, until recently, had been an underground parking lot at the five-star Nile Hilton hotel.

Unlike other parts of the world, the 1980s in Egypt did not represent a decade of excess, but rather, extremes. On one hand international franchises and world-renowned hotel chains slowly began dominating the downtown landscape; while on the other, the value of the Egyptian pound continued its free-fall, as it had since the late 1960s, alienating increasingly larger segments of the population from the so-called free-market experience. Simultaneously, waves of Gulf Arab tourists had begun to descend on the capital known as 'the Hollywood of the Middle East' in search for the type of entertainment not offered by their more-repressive home nations. Meanwhile the masses of migrating Egyptian workers, who had found work in Saudi Arabia due to Sadat's open door policy, returned to Egypt with extremist ideologies heavily influenced by the Wahhabi interpretation of Islam.[6]

The introduction of such disparate elements resulted in further divisions among social lines. Added pressure was placed on the owners of Al-Haram Street nightclubs – many of which stood adjacent to, or in close proximity of the street's largest mosques – to close down their supposedly immoral establishments. However, nightclub managers had more significant issues to deal with, namely, the migration of their talent towards the more lucrative stages of foreign-owned hotels seeking to market a sampling of local culture to a growing influx of tourists.

Before Jackie's, the Nile Hilton's main entertainment venue was the Belvedere, the sort of establishment ubiquitous among new, 'modern' hotels in its nightly line-up of young local Soft-Rock bands, travelling European entertainment troupes, Egyptian folkloric dance routines, and a belly dancer-and-live-band segment. It was the latter act that proved to be the most popular among audiences of mostly Western tourists and as a result its performers dominated billing and stage time. They were able to command higher fees[7] and allowed to design more elaborate shows.

Then, Disco happened. Having thoroughly permeated its home market, and as its influence was fading from the spaces of its origin, the trend was imported to newer territories unaccustomed to its sounds and aesthetic. In the Nile Hilton's case, an underground garage, given the right renovation, would provide the perfect space to showcase this new Western conception marketed as deviance for the social elite, existing on a deeper level of exclusivity within the already alienating framework of a five-star foreign hotel.

There was always a line at Jackie's, regardless of how full – or not – the actual space was. Inside, an amalgam of styles defined the decor; an indiscriminate hodgepodge of 'Disco' and 'pub' aesthetic, which was how Jackie's presented itself. Unlike the underground discos it sought to emulate, Jackie's also aspired to be a venue for older businessmen, with no interest in dancing, to be seen at. As such, besides a dance floor, the venue was also outfitted with plush, long-benched booths, as well as red leather barstools, many of which were lined along the edge of the dance floor, as opposed to the bar. Additionally, quartets of bamboo armchairs surrounded scattered ceramic-tiled tables, and in one corner stood a bright red London-style phonebooth and in the other, a pool table could be found. Appropriately, the walls displayed a series of overlapping murals collectively depicting an 'around-the-world' theme where the pyramids were bright orange and the Statue of Liberty a large-breasted young woman in a miniskirt.

Besides the illustrations on the walls, actual women, in miniskirts or otherwise, also figured among Jackie's crowd. At this venue there was a higher presence of women then at any other entertainment hall on Al-Haram Street, or other venue in the city, as traditionally women would rarely go out to experience the nightlife; especially not unaccompanied. This was an issue which the management at Jackie's had anticipated: 'It's known that an Egyptian girl doesn't stay out late unless with her family or husband, or unless she has a terrible reputation. So, we offered music, alcohol, in a reliable, high-class setting.'[8] Certain measures were taken by the management, including a close monitoring of the male-to-female ratio of any given night's crowd, as well as a strictly enforced ban on all types of photography. This concern for privacy was also necessary in order to maintain a clientele that ranged from 'members of the (Orascom company conglomerate owning) Sawiris family, and (former president Hosni) Mubarak's kids', to 'older people, rich folks

---

6   This last element posed a particular threat to social harmony as Islamism had been on the rise as a result of the discontent and humiliation of defeat in the 1967 war with Israel – feelings which Nasser's successor Sadat stoked in a ill-conceived attempt to manipulate a spreading ideology to his favour. This strategy ultimately backfired when he was assassinated by militant Islamists in 1981.

7   At the Nile Hilton, for example, local bands such as Ram Jam and Le Petit Chats were paid 750 LE a night, whereas belly dancers and their accompanying singers received approximately 5,000 to 6,000 LE each. Besides these two Egyptian acts, the Belvedere's line-up also included performances by Italian band Torino, and the Luis Principe group from Spain, as well as the Reda Dance Group, a highly regarded local act.

8   Emad Louca, former duty manager at Jackie's, in an interview with the author (2016).

9   Ibid.

who just wanted somewhere where they could have a drink with their mistresses'.[9]

As expected for a 'high-class setting' in a five-star hotel, every aspect of the venue was carefully calculated for maximum appeal among the target clientele, from the wide variety of drinks and cocktails available at the bar, to the type of music provided by the European DJ, who was given one night a week off, during which he would be replaced by an Egyptian understudy.[10] Most nights were segmented according to music. The evening would start off at 9pm, with a selection of slow tunes, broadening out into dance-oriented Arabic pop and Western Disco, peaking, before settling down into House music and ending the night, at around 3am, with another round of slow dance numbers – songs specifically reserved for either end of the evening, so as not to encourage too-close proximity during the midnight hours when the venue would be at its most crowded and patrons at their 'most drunk'.[11]

Recognizing that the desire for exclusivity existed not just among their clients, but their client's children as well, the management at Jackie's reached out to a future generation of patrons. 'Matinee' hours were conceived for the earlier portions of Thursday and Friday evenings, when, for an entrance fee of 15 LE, a well-dressed teenager would be allowed temporary access to a setting of adult fantasy, along with a complimentary slice of cake, and a soft drink. No alcohol was served during matinee hours, and the DJ was forbidden to play slow dance music, lest it should compel the youngsters to touch one another. Despite the restrictions, the concept found success and was soon replicated across similar venues, with varying levels of restriction, or supervision.

Rules were imposed among the older crowds as well, especially at Jackie's, which held itself at a higher standard over similar establishments, as the 'premier discotheque in Egypt at the time'.[12] A strict dress code of jacket and tie was enforced by a team of door selectors that, at one period, included future screen star and son of soccer royalty, Hisham Selim. Meeting the dress code, however, did not guarantee admission. From the management's perspective, being seen standing in line outside of Jackie's was in and of itself a privilege worthy of gratitude, if not boastful claims on the part of those made to wait.

The dress code also imposed a ban on *hijab*, or veils – a rule still practised today, with some degree of controversy. Yet, from the management's perspective the decision followed a simple logic:

The veil is a sacred thing. So why would a veiled woman disrespect that by going to a place that serves plenty of alcohol, where she'd be sitting side by side with a woman in a miniskirt who was getting drunk? We banned it in respect of religion. Besides, we were such an exclusive place, there were women who'd take their veils off just to be allowed in.[13]

National dress, such as the aforementioned *galabeya*, was out of the question as was, perhaps less expectedly, Rap music, which the management determined would 'encourage an inappropriate type of dancing' while also attracting a larger segment of 'black clientele' that would potentially 'make the Western tourists uncomfortable'.[14] Gulf Arab tourists, who, with every summer were appearing in larger numbers, were also turned away or, at the very least, strongly discouraged, for their perceived lack of sophistication and 'belief that money exempts them from having to follow rules'.[15] As wide as the array of privileges it afforded its desired clientele, was the list of pretences with which Jackie's met its unwanted patrons – from common excuses such as 'couples only' and 'fully reserved' to, as the venue soared in popularity, the more straightforward 'go somewhere else'.

—

Go somewhere else they did. By the late 1970s, it had become evident that the much-hyped open door policy had effectively boosted an already affluent minority of the population into a higher sphere of wealth, provided consumer goods and distractions for the relatively small middle-class segment, and relegated the majority of the population to a state of poverty.[16] Despite Sadat's promise that 1980 would be the year in which the Egyptian economy would escape from its bottleneck, the nation tumbled into the new decade with little having been done to address any of the deep-rooted problems threatening any future financial stability. The aim of attracting private capital back to the local market also had a transformative effect on popular culture. Whereas Western investment had largely arrived in the form of hotels and fast-food chains, a considerable amount of Gulf money was poured into the formation of local production companies, and entertainment venues that would regurgitate this new Gulf-financed material, as well as travel agencies to ensure an ongoing turnover of clientele.[17] Furthermore, the emergence of audiocassette tapes as a new recording medium energized the industry and resulted in a spike in production that was not matched in terms of quality. Tapes, or 'albums' so lacking in creativity or substance that the majority of them would be titled according to the year of their release, were rushed in and out of production and

10 Louca admits the management's preference for a foreign DJ 'wasn't so much about skills as opposed to labels. We have the foreigner complex here in Egypt. If you go to a restaurant and find a foreign chef, you'll expect a better meal. We do have good local DJs here, and at the time, many of them would approach us and ask to perform at Jackie's. But a foreign DJ was seen as an indicator of more prestige and more professionalism. It gives the image that the establishment is up-to-date on things.'

11 Emad Louca, former duty manager at Jackie's, in an interview with the author (2016).
12 Ibid.
13 Ibid.
14 Ibid.
15 Ibid.
16 In response to mandates set by the IMF and World Bank, Sadat ended subsidies on flour, rice, and cooking oil, triggering immediate nation-wide rioting on 17 and 18 January 1977.
17 Since its inception in 1987, Rotana Records has steadily grown to dominate the mainstream Arabic music industry; the company itself serving as a subsidiary of Saudi Arabian prince Walid bin Talal's Rotana corporation, which also extends into the tourism and hotel industry. Gulf money also fueled much of the five-star Western hotel scene, an example of which could be found in Jackie's European DJ and the venue's sound system, both of whom were hired under contract by the Qatari company Enova. According to Louca, 'if we ever had a technical issue we'd call Enova and they'd fly someone over to solve it the very next day.'

distributed to the market with the priority of capitalising from the summer tourism boom.

Meanwhile, the unfortunate many who were turned away from Jackie's bronze-and-neon gates often found more acceptance on Gamaat el-Dowal street, where a less exclusive consumerist culture was beginning to thrive. Besides bearing the dubious honour of hosting some of Egypt's first US fast-food franchises, the lengthy strip bisecting the previously calm suburb of Mohandessin was also subjected to a sudden rash of two- and three-star hotels, largely financed by Arab investors, and catering almost completely to Arab tourists. Local businesses followed suit, and establishments formed, or in some cases transformed, themselves to serve the stereotypical Gulf Arab traveller: a deep-pocketed pleasure-seeker whose idea of Egyptian culture wasn't shaped by pyramids and ancient temples, but by the comedians, singers and belly dancers broadcast all throughout the Arab world.[18]

Less-sophisticated versions of the Al-Haram Street standard, offering less-elaborate shows proliferated along Gamaat el-Dowal and its side streets. At these venues, the dress code allowed jeans and *galabeyas*, and embraced the latter when accompanied with traditional *Gulfi* headdress as the attire of a high roller. *Hijab* was less of an issue; it was widely accepted that women who accompanied their men to such establishments were either paid escorts, or had morals of the sort that would place them firmly within the public's broad definition of a 'prostitute'—whether or not she chose to veil herself made little difference.

Until recently, Al-Basha existed as a clear example of this type of space—one that was defined by a defiance that went beyond that which Al-Haram Street displayed towards the authorities and oppression, as well as the attitude that the hotel elite displayed towards the impoverished culture of defeat. The tourists who frequented these new spaces did so in rejection of the notion that privilege could be determined by any factor other than the direct sum of money in your pocket: or that exclusivity meant anything other than pure and immediate financial status. For Egyptians, it was in rejection of an unpleasant truth: that the free market might not have been as free as they had been led to believe. It was a rejection of a government that had failed in socialism as it now had in capitalism, as well as of the rising fundamentalism brewing out of mass discontent.

At Al-Basha, which sat at the bottom of a flight of stairs off the curb of main street Gamaat el-Dowal, the selection of offered beverages consisted of beer, whiskey, and occasionally, gin or vodka—all locally produced and vastly overpriced considering the quality, the setting in which they were consumed, and the likelihood of the glass from which they were being consumed having not been previously washed. One could expect to find a singer on the dance floor, accompanied by a keyboardist, but belly dancers were less of a guarantee, particularly on weeknights. Instead, female entertainment came in the form of the table girls, who would dance if dancing happened to be on one's list of requests. The girls are collectively managed by a single, older female employee working for a percentage of their profits, along with an income from the establishment.

The aesthetics are sloppier than the Al-Haram average, somewhere between the likes of Sahraya and Atoun. The feel of a cavern is well replicated, but the randomness of the furniture, the uneven lighting, and particularly the broom and dustpan leaning against a far corner give the space the feeling of the barely renovated garage that it is. A curly-cornered poster on one wall displays a far-too-close-up image of a heavily-made-up woman.

The disregard for rules that defined Jackie's management's anti-Arab stance was inverted, and fully embraced by these new venues, as long as it was profitable. The same could be said for the tourist police forces patrolling the scene for any violations of public decency laws or other illegalities; the two 'authorities' sharing a common entrepreneurial approach to the Arab tourist that consisted of contact-profit-release.[19] In this nurturing atmosphere it was only a matter of a few short summers before Gamaat el-Dowal street had become a playground for patrons of the 'entertainment tourism' industry.

Besides serving as a vice squad, or rather, the suggestion of one, tourist police largely responded to inevitable flare-ups among clientele of men for whom a night on the town was as defined by competition as it was pleasure-seeking. The fact that an establishment's admission fees, menu items, and prostitutes would be priced according to pre-determined rates was, usually, not enough to prevent the men frequenting these dimly-lit spaces above and below Gamaat el-Dowal from engaging in escalating rivalries with one another, based on the simple arithmetic of money equals power, and power equals pure manliness. As much a testosterone-driven response to the illusion of exclusivity conjured by the establishment as it was a stripped-down re-enactment of the new world's free-market rules, the energy brewing within these spaces would frequently manifest in fights of the 'what-are-you-looking-at-watch-where-you're-going' variety, fuelled by a desire for self-assertion.

This was a trend that, increasingly, became less restricted to the Gamaat el-Dowal scene, as upscale establishments gradually gained larger crowds of hopefuls, in response to the reputation of exclusivity that they had attempted to cultivate. In these hotel discos such confrontations were further fuelled by the more severe selectness that defined the space, as well as cultural sensitivities which may not have been as pertinent within lower-tier establishments. Besides bringing together Egyptians and non-Arabic-speaking tourists in a setting that was the average of their stereotypical 'cultures', these spaces also offered a new context for the rare opportunity to casually intermingle with members of the opposite sex within a society that placed heavy restrictions on such interactions. As a result, a general trepidation, along with the often-problematic trappings of challenged tradition, were both palpable contributions to dance floor dynamics.[20]

18 '[According to] a former director of the Cairo Egyptian Museum… "Arabs were easily the least represented of visitors to the museum" … Arab tourism revolves around nightlife … [they] stay up until daybreak, going to nightclubs, discos, or parties, or just hanging out in the hotel lobby, restaurants, or in the streets. They sleep most of the day, not waking up until the afternoon,' in L.L. Wynn, *Pyramids and Nightclubs: A Travel Ethnography of Arab and Western Imaginations of Egypt* (Austin, TX: University of Texas Press, 2007).

19 The influence of the tourism police was not limited to the middling world of Gamaat el-Dowal: as the former duty manager of Jackie's recalls his venue's enforcement of, and at times exemption from certain rules, was conducted 'with 100 per cent cooperation with the tourism police' in exchange for allowing 'high-ranking officers or their son's occasional visits to the disco'.

During these bustling summer seasons, open, and transitory spaces also became common. Along both Gamaat el-Dowal and the hotel-lined downtown corniche sprouted alternative and significantly tamer options: the in-betweens and, in some cases, the transport. Horse-driven buggies as well as *felucca* sailing boats and their larger, motorized counterparts were given new life by the transformation, becoming attractions through the novelty they provided, the scenery they moved past, and the music they played. They catered for Egyptians out on the weekends and exploring new landscapes, for the mothers, children, and maids abandoned by pre-occupied Gulf men, and for those men themselves, as they moved from one nightclub to the next.

As this scene stretched from the summer to the rest of the year's seasons, reshaping the cultural landscape, the entertainment tourism industry was also echoed, to an even less lustrous effect, downtown. It moved some blocks deeper into the city from where the international hotels dominated, among less-ambitious local establishments that found profit in those who could not afford the five-star privilege offered by the likes of Jackie's, or even the more-accommodating Gamaat el-Dowal strip. Motels and guesthouses that had, until then, largely depended on the regular flow of passengers from the adjacent Ramses train station rebranded and updated their cafés and bars into discos, or their closest approximation of this latest fad. These venues rarely featured Western music, and even the Arabic selections tended to be slightly off of mainstream – production less polished, featuring stars from the edge of the local solar system. They did, however, come with the convenience of rooms to rent, and non-discriminating lobbyists.

Despite their central location, such venues largely existed under the authorities' radar due to a deeply marginalized clientele out of which only the most minimal of profits could be squeezed. As such, patrons were free to revel in an anything-goes atmosphere that would not have been as tolerated had it been attempted in a different context. One lasting example is the Fontana Hotel, which opened in the late 1970s and had, by the middle of the following decade when it converted its top floor space into the Can-Can discotheque, become known among interested circles as a hangout for gay men. On certain nights of the week the dance floor would be mostly occupied by male couples, unbothered by the rest of the patrons, for which there would still be an abundance of female prostitutes to be distraction by. Today, in the midst of a renewed government crackdown on homosexuals and, incredibly enough, atheists[21] the scene has withdrawn somewhat; whereas shortly prior the venue had counted a small number of transsexuals among its unofficial entertainment crew.

As it does now, on Thursday and Friday nights Fontana would host a belly dancer, occasionally with a small backup band, and one who would often reach into the crowd and fish out a dance partner or two. The act would only take a portion of the night, the rest given over to the DJ in the corner, and patrons on the dance floor. In comparison to Gamaat el-Dowal, the menu is narrowed down, the dress code broadened into non-existence, and there is generally less posturing. The girls work in shifts, taking their breaks directly behind the padded swinging doors, where they sit in the stairwell, chat and smoke and play with their children. The patrons are Egyptian, and the rare pair or small group of Arab tourists throwing money onto the dance floor. It is not often that these tourists are seen in this part of town, in this type of space, where anything is offered, no matter how socially 'unacceptable' it may be. These spaces are also found in the brighter-lit neighbourhoods around their hotels, albeit marginally more concealed.

—

In 1988, as the majority of Egyptians struggled under the burdens of unemployment, inflation, and overpopulation, Jackie's renovated and rebranded itself as Jackie's Joint. Competition among high-end establishments over such a small segment of the market had grown fierce and, as a result, compromises had to be made. Gradually, the management at Jackie's Joint was compelled to loosen its dress code and become even more accommodating to previously undesired patrons. While allegedly never compromising to the lengths of other establishments – like the Regina at the Sheraton across the Nile, for example, which was eventually slapped with indecency charges by the authorities, and its owner, Mostafa Abou Eisha, imprisoned – the management at Jackie's Joint still found itself struggling to contain a sudden 'prostitution problem':

They'd come in and stumble at the bar and harass clientele. They'd be brought as 'dates' of a specific sort of hotel guests who themselves would try to market these girls to the patrons of the disco. At first it was easy to spot these girls, but in time and with the deterioration of things, it started to get tricky.[22]

Simultaneously, violent Islamic fundamentalism had drastically increased throughout the decade, with an escalating string of incidents targeting tourists and Christians and, particularly in the Sinai region, Israelis. In the face of such uncertainty tourism figures dropped and the economy took a series of further hits. It was a crisis that would only deepen in the first years of the following decade, and the continued disfigurement of the nation also reshaped the cultural and entertainment spheres. As Louca recalls:

The decline began in the early 1990s. Up until then, our patrons had been foreigners as well as prominent local families and members of high society. But a strange phenomenon started to take place – money began to talk really loudly. Our prestige was of a level where certain sorts of people would be afraid to even walk past our hotel. With the 1990s we started getting guests who weren't up to our standards. Before then if the hotel got an Arab guest

---

20 As Jackie's manager Louca explains: 'The more diverse our clientele became, the more fights we had. Some people couldn't hold their liquor well, men would start hitting on each other's women … fights would erupt over the most insignificant things, misunderstandings and people trying to prove themselves … it got to the point where this was happening almost every night.'

21 Patrick Kingsley, 'Egypt's gay community fears government crackdown', *The Guardian*, 17 April 2014, <http://www.theguardian.com/world/2014/apr/17/egypt-gay-community-fears-government-crackdown> accessed 14 December 2016.

22 Emad Louca, former duty manager at Jackie's, in an interview with the author (2016).

he'd be turned away, even if the hotel had zero occupancy. With the deterioration of the Egyptian pound you no longer had that luxury. So, prestige and image flew out the window. It became strictly about making money, and we had to figure out how to do that. A [venue] of our calibre won't resort to Al-Haram Street tactics – prostitution and botched checks and noqta.[23] We're an upper class establishment. We had to adapt. The most obvious change this resulted in, undoubtedly, was the quality of our clientele. Earlier, people displayed a sense of acceptance, even for the rules. What I'm saying applies to locals as well as Arabs and Europeans… There was an increase in fights and thefts, and Arabs who would try and prove they were above the rules. Obviously, they come with prostitutes and bring in drugs and try to bribe us. We began to plant agents in the crowd. The first time we caught someone distributing drugs in our venue, it turned out she was a European diplomat. Deviance always starts with the rich, not the lower-classes, but with the ones who have money and don't want rules… In the beginning, customers would ask for complicated drinks and cocktails. In time, that became nothing but whiskey, beer, and in some cases, gin. The same difference was seen in the food. We'd have nice elaborate meals, and slowly, according to the requests we got, everything became more limited.*[24]*

While within the world defined by the expensively graffitied walls of Jackie's Joint options might have become limited, outside the opposite was true. The disparity of the past two decades had pushed social divisions to their breaking point, and by the time Jackie's Joint reinvented itself as Latex – a trendy, new, 200-LE-minimum-charge 'club' with themed 'safari', 'oriental' and 'ladies' nights, as well as a black and white rubber aesthetic that extended to its seating, DJ console, and 'island bar' – the cultural scene had itself been segmented into islands; separate spheres in an ocean of insecurity.

Sounds from the unregulated urban sprawl: Mahraganat

The lights start out on the main street; a loose knot of flashing bulbs wrapped around a slanted lamppost at the head of an unpaved road. This is one of the many entrances to the unregulated sprawl that is Dar el-Salam, one of Cairo's largest, and most intricately overlapping slum neighbourhoods, stretching almost parallel to the affluent, expat-friendly suburb of Maadi. The unpaved road is less than five meters wide; the bare-cement buildings on either side of it a minimum of thirty meters high. The lights crisscross between first-floor balconies, beneath them are shops – some so narrow they seem like optical illusions – selling everything from extension cords to individually-wrapped 'universal' remote controls, dead fish to caged rabbits to cow-liver sandwiches, mattresses and kitchen appliances, chains and pulleys, sofas and SpongeBob-patterned pyjamas.

At the end of the road, the light bulbs buzz around another lamppost and trail down an alley to the right. It is at this intersection where the vibrations one could feel from the main street begin to take the distinct form of a bass line; more so, one ubiquitous among the songs of the young genre dubbed *Mahraganat* [festivals] – four evenly-spaced beats, followed a rapid-fire succession of eight, in repetition, like a series of quick heart attacks.

There are vegetable carts strewn about, as well as construction material – piles of sand and pebbles, bundles of steel beams, and bags of cement. Besides existing outside of the government's periphery, Dar el-Salam, like all of Cairo's densely populated slums, also seems to exist outside of time; an impression enforced by a total lack of zoning laws or regulations, and one which has only sped up since the political changes of 2011. Structures are built according to immediate needs, as opposed to any long-term plans. As a result, there are always buildings that need to be hooked up to sewage systems and power grids – both often improvised, or illegally extended from the nearest developed neighbourhood – and homes that need to be expanded.

On either side of all roads the buildings share walls, regardless of their height. There is no space, no alleyways between them, except at intersections, which themselves are more the result of coincidence than urban planning. A building which has stood at three stories for decades can, in less than a month, have its height doubled with additional apartments that either jut out over previously established edges, or pile up at the centre. Except for the first building constructed, the rest of the structures coming up on the block will only have three walls each. Neighbours' windows, regardless of ventilation needs, will be paved over in order to complete someone else's bedroom, or living room wall. The new apartments will be given fresh coats of paint according to their respective owners' tastes or, in all likelihood, left with their red brick exterior or a layer of cement, and allowed to blend into their surroundings, becoming architectural discrepancies, as opposed to merely temporal ones.

A family of farmers that has somehow resisted the city-wide urbanization which, in three decades, saw a fielded landscape yield the redbrick labyrinth that is Dar el-Salam, may finally find their roles transferred from that of agricultural workers to building porters, charged with securing, and maintaining, a new residential premises and tending to its occupants' needs. Similarly, a plot of land that has served as the sole football field, or parking lot for a wide radius of blocks can, overnight, become a construction site without so much as having its sides reinforced or its terrain properly levelled. Often, this will be the result of an unsubstantiated landgrab by one of the area's residents, or, worse yet, one operating at the behest of an outsider. Almost as often, such a move will be met with violent opposition. Construction will then grind to a halt, and, for the years it takes to settle the issue, the resulting architectural skeleton will continue to serve as a parking lot, or football field,

---

23 This is the money an establishment sells to its patrons to be tossed onto the stage and re-collected by the venue as profit.
24 Emad Louca, former duty manager at Jackie's, in an interview with the author (2016).

while attracting various squatters and short-sighted entrepreneurs.

Consequently, words like 'old' and 'new' lose some of their meaning in areas as unregulated as Dar el-Salam, which might be one of the reasons why clear-cut examples – weddings, for instance or funerals – tend to be such communal events.

—

At this point, the lights are almost blinding, the blinking trail culminating in a long spiral down a specially erected pole, at the bottom of which is a bouquet of swivelling spotlights marking the formal entryway into a wedding celebration. The ceremony adopts the shape of the alleyway it occupies, with chairs and tables set in clusters along the sides of the building, leaving a narrow centre aisle for the continuous flow of guests, tray-bearers, and neighbourhood children carrying fistfuls of firecrackers. Many of the latter will be lit and tossed indiscriminately into the seated crowd, and only noticed for the minor injuries and burns they might cause – as the volume blaring from the stacks of speakers at each of the alleyway's corners, overrides that of the firecrackers. At its source, the sounds of the wedding are no clearer than they were half a kilometre away, just considerably louder.

Past the forty or so rows of tables, a stage spans the width of the alley, its surface two metres above ground. The structure is wrapped in sheets of cloth carrying yellow, blue and white geometric designs. Underneath are planks of wood tied together with thick rope. The stage itself is cluttered with six large speakers and thirteen musicians, seemingly piled on top of one another. There are keyboards and a wide range of hand drums, from *tablas* to *duffs* to *riqs*. Between the percussionists is a soundboard and beside it, a narrow DJ console, over which stands a young man shouldering a pair of massive headphones against his ear. At the centre of the onstage crowd, a large, glittering belly dancer twirls in and out of sight, while on the outskirts, another belly dancer watches from her seat, waiting her turn.

Some cheering barely surfaces through the noise as the father of the groom makes his way down the aisle, smiling broadly, one arm waving presidentially, the other receiving newspaper-rolls of *bango*, or cheap marijuana, from the teenaged assistant trailing him, and tossing them, one after the other, into either side of the seated crowd. To his closest friends, the father snaps off pieces of the hashish bars carried in the chest pocket of his *galabeya*. Finer than the darker clouds of cigarette smoke that linger between the guests, the white mist from the scattered joints uncoils in ribbons that reach high above the crowd, disintegrating between the open windows from which the neighbours watch. Directly overhead, a bespectacled elderly man in an undershirt leans over his ledge while next to him a pair of children shift about, the boy waving and screaming soundlessly at the wedding guests below.

There is no alcohol at this wedding, although, on similar occasions in the same neighbourhood, there can be. In this case, however, tabletops are cluttered with ashtrays, tiny tin plates of assorted nuts, beans, and seeds. There are soda bottles and glasses of fruit juice, teacups and cigarette packs and, on one tabletop, a young girl, possibly four or five years old, dancing with a pair of switchblades, the men seated at her feet providing a steady handclapped beat while one, presumably the girl's father, smiles proudly as he films the dance on his camera phone.

Besides the two professionals on stage and the faces peering out of surrounding windows, the young dancer with the switchblades is the oldest girl in sight. There are plenty of women at the wedding, including members of the bride and groom's respective families, all of whom can be found seated in the tented netherworld that constitutes the 'women's section'; out of the sight of the men and tucked behind the stage, where all glimpses of the wedding come courtesy of a screen projecting a live broadcast by the cameraman roaming the other side. The bride will spend much of the night in the women's tent, fawned over by the neighbourhood matriarchs and scrutinized by their daughters, with brief visits by the groom and the fathers who, in turn, will spend most of their night dancing with other men in the main ceremony, often in clusters surrounding the belly dancer onstage.

This is, by Dar el-Salam standards, a big wedding, as one would expect to be thrown for the son of a large supermarket owner and real estate 'developer'. At a humbler celebration, there might be a single belly dancer on stage, if that, and the women in the subsection would likely have to make do without a cameraman and live transmission, or even a tent – often the women will gather in an apartment adjacent to the ceremony. The drugs might not flow as freely, or at all, and the live band might instead take the form of a group of the groom's friends and other neighbourhood youths, passing a less-varied collection of hand-drums among themselves.

The actual music blasting out of the speakers, however, is unlikely to be any different than the usual mix of traditional, working-class Shaabi anthems and the younger, more imposing sonic assaults of Mahraganat music. Across the vast majority of backstreet weddings and alleyway celebrations, the DJ is almost always a younger, often teen-aged, member of the local community, using an assortment of cheaply-rented and outdated no-brand equipment to go through a playlist that includes sounds made by his generational peers or, in some cases, the DJ himself.

—

This has not always been the case. Traditionally, music at these weddings would be provided by a live, if not necessarily professional or renowned band. However, the proliferation of cassette recordings in the 1980s and the growing inclusion of DJs in more prestigious and affluent celebrations paved the way for similar change among the generally more traditional-minded residents of lower-income neighbourhoods. The later introduction of USB ports and memory cards led to another evolution; one that facilitated file-sharing and, crucially, music production.

For the first time, and for a vast majority of young Egyptians, the technology required to make music had become accessible, and the initial response was to compensate for an industry that did not speak to them, but frequently claimed to speak on their behalf. The previous privatisation of the music industry had led to an increase in record companies, but little variety in the sounds being produced. As it does, tradition defined mainstream, and in the period preceding the digital era, the underground scene, with no means of being consistently recorded or documented let alone distributed, had largely been limited to live gatherings so small they could barely be called concerts, often unfolding in a private residence, or a coffee shop, and consisting of little more than a sole performer with a single instrument, recounting familiar verses of yearning or loss, or perhaps some similarly-themed poetry. There were legends among communities, the majority of which existed beyond the city outskirts, bearing little to no influence in the national cultural infrastructure, and only marginally represented, if at all, in the catalogues of 'legitimate' recording companies.

Even the supposed Shaabi sound, which had climbed into public awareness with songs that shied away from the romanticism of mainstream output in favour of grittier, more relatable tales of modern woes and rhyming social commentary, was quickly consolidated by companies that keenly recognized a new niche to market a profit off of. As such, Shaabi singers, including working-class heroes and icons of the marginalized, from Ahmed Adawiya to Hassan el-Asmar to Hakeem, moved from alleyways to stages to cinema and television screens, becoming bonafide superstars while simultaneously redefining the genre to fit the limitations of marketability, and ultimately alienating themselves from the very audiences that had enabled their success. Even the stars that had risen during this period of transition, Shaaban Abdel Rahim being the most prominent among them, were introduced to the wider public through national media outlets as sources of novelty as opposed to legitimate artists – a role which they were lured into by record companies attempting to perpetuate that initial instant of profitability.

In this sense, the Shaabi end of the mainstream spectrum became inwardly competitive, rushing to devour itself in its lowering of standards. The formula set by the sudden popularity of Abdel Rahim determined that the more uneducated a singer came across as and the more outrageous the lyrics that were sung, the more tapes would be bought by an incredulous public, whether for a laugh or an attempt at trend-following, or even, as eventually became the case, as ironic listening by relatively affluent audiences excited by these exotic sounds from another, less-developed world.

Bit by bit, the dissent which had formed the basis of the Shaabi genre was reduced to statements of defiant illiteracy, naïve political pandering, and thinly-veiled innuendos – dissatisfaction and dissent successfully neutered into something more palatable and far less incendiary, or accusatory.

Met with no response other than further generations of worsening conditions, the anger directed towards the state's neglect and society's scorn that had fuelled the Shaabi genre turned in on itself, into a fierce ownership of the outcast stance – or it was redirected towards Israel or a treacherous lover. A definitive sense of rebellion stoked by the government's marginalization had now devolved into a rebellion against the 'taboo' of accepted tastes and social norms. As a result, a slew of novelty records flooded the market with poorly sung innuendos that sexualized everything from fruit to footwear. In the wake of Abdel Rahim waded Abdel Basset Hamouda, Emad Baaroura, and countless others who had gone from singing in the various workshops and apprentice jobs which they occupied, to a world that consisted, almost equally, of alleyway stages and five-star hotel ballrooms.

The other end, or rather three-quarters, of the mainstream spectrum, consisted of higher-production costs and equally vacuous material; mostly bland and inoffensive love songs, ballads of yearning for intimacy or mourning its loss, but rarely ever the celebration of attaining it. Towards the centre of the spectrum is a gradation of Shaabi singers making the transition to a more Western-influenced pop sound, achieved and perfected at the far end by the likes of Amr Diab, a singer whose career evolution can be measured more in degrees of fake tan or tightening shirts rather than any musical innovation.

Open spaces and middle grounds: Sakiet el-Sawy, satellite channels and Western style clubs

It was this general lack of innovation that allowed the introduction of new mediums to make a significant impact, not just in sound but also in space. For the generations that had grown into adolescence against such cultural stagnation, the two-way exposure of the internet and the means to produce and distribute work without having to worry about government permits and censorship, not to mention recording licenses and fees, created a range of new possibilities that demanded outlets that would cater to them.

The most significant of these spaces came in 2003, when Cairo's first privately-owned culture centre opened. Located on the affluent suburban island of Zamalek, and replacing the abandoned junkyard that had previously existed under the 26th of July bridge, Sakiet el-Sawy immediately became the focus of a variety of local, previously pent-up talent, as well as a source of motivation for those who, until then, had never seriously considered developing their skills as performers of an alternative sound, due to the lack of appropriate venues or public platforms. Besides the nightclubs and hotel discos, prior to Sakiet el-Sawy, a small number of spaces that were largely defined by music, usually performed by young, local talent, already existed. However, even the most prominent of these venues, such as the Cairo Jazz Club, which opened in the mid-1990s, were not able, nor did they strive to, expand their clientele beyond a slightly younger version of the Jackie's Joint crowd, due to alienating factors such as their entry fees and high prices, their serving of alcohol, and their emphasis on Western-influenced music, mostly Rock, rarely Jazz, and gradually, House.

Exclusivity was less of a concern at Sakiet el-Sawy where admission fees and ticket prices were intentionally kept low, and where the rules were less about the dress code and more about not engaging in anti-social behaviour, such as cigarette-smoking, even in the space's outdoor areas. This 'openness' extended to the stages as well, which saw the debut of numerous local acts. Whereas venues such as Cairo Jazz Club would host performances by mostly accomplished, if not necessarily mainstream musicians, and publicise them through English-language posters and flyers, Sakiet el-Sawy was far less discriminating in its selection, which would be promoted through weekly newsletters and street advertising, the Arabic text often supported by (slightly flawed) English translations.

The space itself was divided according to the variety of arts its owner, the son of acclaimed Egyptian novelist and former minister of culture, Abdel Moneim el-Sawy, wished to promote. Beyond the entryway corridor, which serves as a gallery for visual arts like painting and photography, lies an indoor stage and seating area used for dramatic performances as well as screenings, lectures, and poetry readings. Running adjacent to these connected spaces is an outdoor area split between a garden and a lower level on the banks of the Nile, leading to a stage situated directly beneath the usually congested 26th of July bridge. It is on this stage that most musical performances, from solo concerts, to festivals, as well as smaller 'battle of the bands'-type events, are held.

Ironically, this last stage is arguably the least appropriate choice for its intended purpose, given the constant and echoing rumbling of traffic overhead, and the poor acoustics offered by the concrete base of the bridge. However, that has not prevented the space from becoming among the most crucial of Cairo's admittedly limited platforms for musicians operating outside the similarly restrictive boundaries of mainstream. While previous decades had seen the cultural scene, and with it most musical venues, shift towards disparate extremes, Sakiet el-Sawy initially appeared as a middle ground of sorts, a venue where converging audiences would include the old and the young, the veiled and the loose-haired, the foreign-educated and the students of national schools; in short, a wide sampling of perceived social 'classes'.

Yet, it wasn't long before that middle ground began to tilt in the direction of traditional conservatism. Being a cultural centre, and not a club, Sakia's imposition of certain rules was to be expected; but the gradual increase of censorship left a growing number of performers cold, many of whom turned their attention to venues that did not ask to preapprove lyrics in case of any 'objectionable' material. Consequently, and despite its initial potential, the space's sound has never broken through the perimeters set by sanitised and non-threatening acts such as Wust el-Balad and Cairokee.

—

Besides a cultural centre, the year 2003 also saw the introduction of a club that came to define the scene, despite not actually existing. During those summer months, American rapper 50 Cent's breakthrough tribute to a lifestyle of excess debauchery was as ubiquitous as the national anthem during wartime. Its popularity was fuelled by the fact that it was among the first of an initially limited line-up of Western songs on the sudden proliferation of free-to-air satellite music channels such as Melody and Mazzika. These channels quickly became new streams of revenue, and competition in the form of television screen sizes, for a massive culture of cafés and coffee-shops catering to a population of youth that, simply, had nowhere else to go on their weekends. In a way, these spaces were defined by the music playing on their televisions – certainly more than the bland menus that were offered, yet the importance of music may be outshined by the tolerance for public displays of affection. In this way the crowds would be determined accordingly.

At cafés where televisions were tuned to the sentimental sounds of Rotana Zaman or any of the many romantic music channels, the clientele would likely consist of young couples, or evenly mixed parties of high-school-to-college-aged males and females. On the other hand, venues more focused on pop sounds supported by glossier foreign videos – not to mention, in many cases, a name and interior aesthetic that bore little association to the local setting – would be frequented by more boisterous crowds of adolescent males, outnumbering the 'date-night' or seemingly-platonic groupings found in quieter venues. Other establishments catered to a clientele of older men, drawn in by any of the Arabic satellite channels which, in an echo of the private recording industry's race to the lowest common denominator, broadcast nothing but belly dancing clips and jiggle-heavy music videos – a visual element which certainly, from the management's perspective was cheaper, more varied, and offered far less of a bureaucratic hassle, than any actual flesh-and-blood performer could.

Outside the cafés, these disparate sounds manifested in a corresponding variety of spaces. Besides the nation's first private cultural centre and the popularisation of subscription-free satellite television, 2003 also saw the founding of Nile FM, the first privately-owned 24-hour radio station devoted to Western music, complete with unnaturally upbeat DJs, global chart countdowns, and a mainstream variety of genre-specific shows. Between the emerging acts and crowding airwaves, which introduced new genres to audiences that previously had little involvement in the Western-recordings market, the city was awash with waves of new sound. Aided by the rush of low-budget production that fed the Shaabi channels, the nightclubs and Gamat el-Dowal scene experienced a rejuvenation, soundtracked by mostly no-name artists and one-hit wonders required to keep an industry of instant gratification running, while the more conservative middle-ground venues, such as Sakiet el-Sawi and, later, the open stages of Azhar Park, continued to soak up the wholesomeness of the remaining mainstream, as well as its identical 'alternative' (i.e. unsigned) acts.

On the more affluent end of the scene, another transformation was taking place, one which bore the first signs of a local 'club culture', according to the Western definition of the phrase. Ignited by both the sudden rise, and by the loss of exclusivity, the 'devaluing' of Western sounds onto the scene as well as the ever-mounting wealth circulating between the privileged minority that served as its clientele, this nascent club phenomenon was a natural evolution of the hotel-disco world. This can be seen in the transformation of Jackie's Joint into the up-to-the-minute-trendy Latex; a move echoed by most of its contemporaries.

Outside the hotels, a similar scene was taking shape, and one in which exclusivity was not as compromised by the commitment hotels held to their guests, even the supposedly undesirable ones. Along the downtown stretch of the Nile and throughout the narrow side-streets of Zamalek, venues began to build their reputations on the ability to throw the wildest parties, as well as the difficulty of being allowed into one. Reservations, dress codes, 'couples-only', and anti-*hijab* policies as well as a whole array of other excuses were used to keep the majority of would-be patrons out. None as effective, however, as exorbitant admission fees at a time when the value of the Egyptian Pound was continuing to wither as it had throughout the previous decade, and the average citizen was living on a weekly salary of less than 200 LE.

What set these clubs apart from the discos of the previous generation was their ability – in some cases, attempts – to set trends rather than just follow them. Whereas the discos provided a set course of contemporary Arabic and foreign hits, the new clubs individually pursued the appropriate subgenres of House, Progressive House, Trance, and Techno, with an attention to music trends and boundary-pushing that went beyond any set precedent. Foreign DJs were flown in as resident performers, Egyptian DJs rose to fame through their opening acts and then, with the exposure afforded by the internet and the demand among an increasing number of clubs, as headline performers with their own crowds of devotees. By the mid 2000's 'rave', 'ecstasy', and 'Tiësto', the Dutch megastar-mainstream DJ's name, had become common phrases for a vast portion of Cairene youths, whether it was those who were exposed to them through the rising number of satellite channels and radio stations, or the privileged few who could afford to experience them firsthand.

It was in response to the popularity of the scene, and the heightened competition within it, that independent event organisers were able to find financial success and notoriety by catering to the escalating demands of a status-driven elite. As such the concept of club space – so obsessed over by venue owners desperate to keep up with the notoriously fickle clientele – underwent a transformation to become a matter not of permanence or convenience, but of open potential. Organisers such as ByGanz and Nacelle became go-to names for those seeking to conjure up the ultimate statement in decadence – at least for that particular weekend. Imported go-go dancers, 'Fuck Me I'm Famous' parties, three-day raves – all features in a microcosm that, by this point, bore no resemblance to the outside world.

As it had since the mid-1970s, the separation continued. The privileged partied harder, and in increasingly transparent privacy, the downtrodden masses were made to find distraction in the slapdash output from a market of cheap thrills while, in the middle ground, culture existed as little more than a broad and toothless smile, the exception being found in the rare spaces that catered to the more offbeat sensibilities of a small niche of artists and art-enthusiasts. It was against this backdrop that a storm began to brew, and continued to until a generation of youths, as much marginalized by the cultural scene as by their own socio-economic status, finally found the means to fend for themselves.

Short-lived convergences: the 2011 revolution and its aftermath

When the 2011 revolution came, it had its own sound. Past the initial eruption of chants, screams, gunshots, and cheers, while there existed a single sustained note of euphoria that, for many, was perfectly encapsulated in songs such as the Cairokee and Wust el-Balad collaboration 'Sout el Horeya' and the entire oeuvre of activist-singer Ramy Essam. He had been detained and tortured by central security officers in the chaotic eighteen days preceding the president's ouster. In that period of time, Tahrir Square itself existed as a club of sorts; a clearly defined area with its own border controls and unifying ideology, and multiple platforms for a wide array of musical acts flourishing on and riffing off of the commonalities that had united the most disparate of audiences. Yet, while glossily produced victory ballads and folksy acoustic narratives might have been the sound of the revolution, Mahraganat music was the sound of the nation that emerged from it, and the turbulence that followed.

Despite the fact that it had begun to creep into public consciousness prior to the revolution, it was through the spirit of a nationally unifying event, as well as the across-the-board absence of regulation that followed, which allowed the Mahraganat genre to explode the way it did. Deemed a new sound for a new nation, not intended for any particular venue, but dominating the ones in which it was played, the Mahraganat phenomenon saw its performers, who had shaped the genre out of their frustration at being marginalised, lifted to the peak of national cultural exposure. From Islam Chipsy performing at the EU Ambassador's residence to an audience of stunned dignitaries in evening wear, to Amr Haha's frequent appearances at house parties hosted by young intellectuals and activists, to the soaring attendance at concerts held in the backstreets of their own fringe neighbourhoods, Mahraganat performers became symbols of a misjudged youth, the no-good kids that proved their worth by ridding the nation of a tyrant. It left little impression on the older generations due to its abrasiveness of sound and the frankness of its content, while younger ones embraced it with all the fervour of a free house for the weekend. Meanwhile, foreigners went crazy over what they interpreted as the sounds of a newly liberated youth.

They were, indeed, a liberated youths; although their role in the liberation process remains questionable, with a majority of the rising Mahraganat performers being the first to admit that they played little to no part in the events of the revolution. Despite the connotation thrust upon it, Mahraganat was the sound of the extreme political apathy felt by an overwhelming segment of the young Egyptian population. A sound that happened to burst through its bubble as the nation's institutions caved in on themselves. The lyrics of this genre were a direct reflection of this, their subjects ranging from sudden loss of one's footwear to weightier topics like the inability to fulfil swelling sexual urges in the face of social restrictions. Bar a few exceptions, most of which appeared as products of a post-revolutionary trend, the lyrics were rarely political in nature. It was this definitive apathy; so deeply seated and comprehensive that it constituted, through its complete lack of interest in, or regard for an equally unresponsive larger society, a form of rebellion in its own right.

The fact that live performances were not held in ambassadors residences or downtown clubs, but in the back alleys and outer, informal neighbourhoods that originally inspired such furious sounds showed this. These concerts were loud and raucous affairs that would feature audiences consisting almost entirely of adolescent males from young teens to young men. They would dance together, in circles around one another or on each other's shoulders, in a craze induced by the deafening, rapid-fire beats and equally erratic flashing lights bursting from a stage crowded by a group of performers—the headlining act, along with other members of their 'crew'. Towards the front of the crowd mobile phones are waved through the air, not much further back, thick clouds of smoke are exhaled into it.

Yet, as is the case in the raves of the upper echelon, the drug of choice in this particular scene comes in the shape of a pill. A cheaper alternative to hashish or even low-quality *bango*, Tramadol is an over-the-counter drug sold as a stimulant that, in the past few years, has spread to a considerable degree among less-privileged classes, where most occupations involve some type of manual labour which demands work in long shifts. With effects such as numbness of body and increased stamina, the drug is also a perfect choice for those wishing to hand themselves over to the relentless force of Mahraganat. Much like the combination of heavy autotune, ear-piercing sirens, distortedly deep bass lines, and synthesized drumrolls sums up a total disregard for any basic rules of musical composition, the concerts in which these sounds were unleashed represented, and celebrated, a total disengagement from the wider cultural, as well as political, scene, and then, a triumph over it—a burst of confidence that was certainly reinforced by the absence of authority that followed the uprising.

By the time the dust of the revolution settled, and the sense of togetherness fostered by it had faded in the face of growing widespread contention, it became apparent that the varying cultural scenes had been soaked back up from Tahrir Square and into their respective bubbles, but not without souvenirs from a short-lived convergence. In some cases, this led to hypocritical results, as seen by top-tier clubs like the recently-inaugurated O Bar, and at events organised by Nacelle. Due to the security vacuum following the revolution they would perform Facebook-profile background checks on patrons before granting admission; with simultaneously playing music or inviting performers from the same neighbourhoods and social 'classes' which they deemed undesirable, or even, 'threatening' to their regular clientele. As a result, the sounds resulting from decades of social divide became new entries on the playlists danced to by members of the one percent.

In other spaces, such as Prince 2 in Giza's Mohandessin district, a different sort of dissonance could be seen. Existing afterhours in an otherwise wholesome commercial shopping mall in the heart of a middle-class suburb, this mirror-walled venue is an example of the profit-friendly anything-goes approach of post-revolutionary Egypt. As made clear by its fifty-two-year-old female manager, Madame Warda, in her proudly-stated observation 'after the revolution, there is nobody to say no anymore', the venue is a recreation of the Al-Haram Street underground, albeit one taken to further extremes. This can be seen in at least two, clearly under aged, androgynously dressed sex workers being present, even under the surveillance of staff.

Occupying store space in a relatively tiny mall, the venue is a small one, its non-elevated 'stage' area extending out between sets of tables and steel, thin cushioned seats. The windows of this second-storey venue, which would otherwise offer a view of a busy intersection and residential balconies—not to mention offering the outside world a peek in—are completely blacked out with sheets of children's stickers; the Mickey Mouse and SpongeBob faces all staring outwards. With the further precaution of thick curtains, as well as a lack of proper ventilation, the abundant smoke from shishas, cigarettes, and joints hangs heavily in the air, and coats all surfaces; an added haze through which to observe a series of galloping, graceless belly dancers as they move to a setlist of all the familiar sounds, along with added elements of the Mahraganat fad as well as post-revolutionary anthems celebrating new, hard-won freedoms.

—

It is in a different type of space, such as downtown Cairo's recently-established Vent, that attempts to forge a new common ground between traditionally disparate elements; a philosophy embodied by the young, long-haired stage manager sitting at the bar during soundcheck, tiredly chewing on a sandwich between sips of her beer. In the background two men move from one amplifier to the next, reconnecting wires and making adjustments while, onstage, a third fiddles with a variety of laptops, producing sporadic bursts of heavily distorted sounds. Tonight's act performs thanks to Dijit, a local music producer who dabbles in experimental genres, and whose promotional material, taped to the outside walls and along the entryway corridor, is strictly in English. The rest of the venue's printed materials and menus are also in English – which list dishes of sticky lemon chicken at 60 LE and arugula and couscous salads for 45 LE, and shots of rum, tequila, vodka, as well as whiskey, for similar prices each.

In the minds of its management, Vent is not strictly a club, but also a culture centre, a hub for creative people to meet and exchange ideas – a place where crowds are not defined by their social class, but by their interest in performing arts. Yet, the notion that this venue is as welcoming to all classes as its management suggests is countered, not just by the English-only menus and wall art including promotional posters for the works of Pedro Almodovar, Günter Grass and Ryszard Kajzer, nor by the 50 LE admission fee or a restrictive maximum capacity of 250, but, rather, by the name which Vent has made for itself despite the initial variety of its programme. Since opening in late 2013 it has been held as one of the city's most tolerant establishments, and one of the few spaces available for those looking for somewhere to party until the mid-morning hours.

A few hours after Dijit's soundcheck, the bare-hanging light-bulbs have dimmed to give the music's accompanying projected visuals more prominence, and the tiny space in front of the stage has become crowded with dozens of well-dressed and fashionably shabby twenty to thirty-year-olds; men and women for whom spending upwards of 100 LE on two drinks and a night's worth of entertainment poses no problem. The turnout is substantial, considering the fact that it is a Tuesday night, and as the evening grinds on, the crowd only thickens. In a past, pre-revolution life, Vent existed as one of downtown Cairo's most prominent nightclubs, Arabesque, and it is that romanticised view of a former era, rather than any forward-looking perspective or attempt at creating a relevant common ground, that seems to have driven the space's current iteration; from its faded, painted floor-tiles, to the chipped-wood surface of the bar, to the simple Shaabi-café style chairs with backs bearing engraved Stella beer logos.

On this evening, the Stella seats remain mostly empty, the majority of attendees crowding the dance floor with moves that seem limited to nodding heads, tapping feet, and some vague swaying – as much of a response as can be expected to experimental noise. On weekend nights, however, when the venue regularly books established names and up-and-comers of the independent scene, or sets by its own resident DJ, things have been known to get significantly wilder, to the extent where the management has had to expel individuals – and in at least one case, enforce a lifetime ban – for reasons such as drug use and alcohol-fuelled belligerence.

All in all, the image cultivated by Vent has not been one that complies more with the aesthetics of venues such as the Cairo Jazz Club, than with traditional notions of a 'culture centre'. The management will be the first to admit that their attempts at creating a space that broke out of the previous model of cultural centres, that were formal and sucked all the fun out of art, while balancing a sense of artistic integrity and making money, had tilted to favour one aspect over the other. In the months after its inception, Vent gradually narrowed its focus so that the theatrical performances it once hosted now only occurred as rare exceptions, and similarly, film screenings were no longer as frequent, for the simple reason that they did not attract a large enough crowd to cover the Venue's costs – which included a staff of servers and kitchen hands that had come from the space's previous identity as a club. Simultaneously, the management struggled to secure consistent funding from most cultural institutions, due to the venue's serving of alcohol – deemed by some potential funders as a source of sufficient profit, and by others as a contradiction to the stated purpose of a cultural centre. The fact that, the bar remains while the promise of a variety of cultural activities has fallen by the wayside, speaks to the management's priorities, not to mention the venue's true identity. As a result, Vent's group of regulars also continues to narrow down to a slightly more artistically inclined version of the exclusive club crowd.

Beyond the (non-)argument of club or culture centre, Vent's management will claim that their role as a space of cultural convergence is still carried out through their stage. While weeknight setlists usually start off with the 'safe', if not exactly progressive Hip-Hop sounds of Tupac, Biggie, and Missy Elliot, before branching out into supposedly more innovative and equally Western-influenced territory, often through live performances by local artists, Monday nights are reserved for homegrown Hip-Hop groups. The night preceding Dijit's act, for example, saw performances by two rival groups from the lower-income neighbourhoods of Shubra and Haram, respectively – or, as the management puts it, from 'a totally different scene … and there weren't any problems with the female patrons or anything like you might expect'. It's an inclusion that seems to have less in common with Sakiet el-Sawy's vision than with the sort of trend-hunting practised by the entertainment-venue industry, bar one significant limitation on Vent's part. Unlike most other local spaces, be they clubs or cultural centres, Vent does not serve as a platform for Mahraganat performers; the venue's management deeming the genre to be 'pretty empty' and deciding 'not to be a part of that trend, or help to spread it … it won't last much longer'.

The same, perhaps, can be said about Vent itself. The venue had been founded as a space to unify the separate worlds comprising the local cultural scene, and as a product of a freer, and more cohesive society. Yet, with that reality refusing to manifest itself, Vent's role has become questionable at best. The real value of the space might be better judged through its role as a summary of a familiar history; from its promising start to a gradual decline, from abandonment to reinvention and a subsequent search for identity; transitions weathered by an increasingly dependent staff faced with little choice but to adapt to the next inevitable shake-up. With the challenges of long-term sustainability once again overpowered by a more immediate need for survival, the future of such a space is by no means guaranteed – or even seems as bleak as Vent's assessment of the Mahragant scene.

Epilogue

In the shifting no-man's-land that is Cairo's curfew hours, a gathering takes place along the side of an otherwise deserted highway. A cool breeze moves through the trees that separate the asphalt from the dark waters of the Nile; on the other side of the road is the beginning of the dirt path leading into Dar el-Salam, from where the members of this party have emerged. The sense of urgency to their nightly proceedings has little to do with the threat of military convoys roaming the streets. Rather, the concern is over the amount of time being wasted.

The boys loiter around a parked vehicle, climbing in and out of it, waiting for its driver, Mohamed, to stop fiddling with the USB-port nailed to the bottom of the handlebars. Minutes later, a member of the group, fed up, crosses the street to where his own 'machine' is parked. He swings onto the front seat, a friend does the same from the passenger side and four more squeeze into the back as, in a burst of sound and light, the tuk-tuk roars to life. With a forward jolt, it begins puttering across the asphalt, trailing smoke and high-pitched synthesizer squeals. The passengers cheer as the driver swerves a tight knot and Mohamed looks up long enough to wag his middle finger at them. It takes him a few more minutes but when he finally gets it started, the stereo belches so loudly it reverberates through asphalt and bone. There is a stammering of blasts as Mohamed skips to his desired track: a thick, sticky beat, like a sack of bricks tumbling down a muddy staircase with increasing speed. A few steps down the staircase is a cyclone of autotune and synths; at the heart of it are eighteen kids spinning around on four tuk-tuks and a Chinese motorcycle. The twelve-year-old gets behind the handlebars of his own tuk-tuk and guides it into the heart of the storm.

It's a quarter to midnight, almost three hours after the start of evening curfew but as far as the boys are concerned, the night has just begun. For a few more hours, these army-patrolled streets belong to them. The boys shout and exchange playful taunts, their voices barely audible over the chaotic sounds of Mahraganat through the speakers, and the nasally growling of tiny engines. They race their tuk-tuks against each other, and then in turns against the motorcycle, they compete over who can make the sharpest swerves – one of the tuk-tuks tumbles onto its side, but there are no injuries and the windshield is easily popped back into place – they make their machines 'dance', snaking across the road in sync with the music's synthesized wails and, eventually, they grab the two panels of steel road-railing which they detached from the sidewalk some previous night to recreate an obstacle course. They act with the joyous impunity of children in a playground, or rather, in tiny, mobile versions of one. Then the machines are parked, and cigarettes lit, and, no longer supported by the excitement of their stunt-driving, the boys' crude humour and heavy-handed horseplay seem to take a sharper edge, but it is all in good fun. Moments later they quiet down at the command of one of their number, who turns up the volume while informing the group that the autotuned rant they're listening to was made by his own cousin Ahmed, also known as Hamada Saba'a, or Hamada Seven. 'Listen to this part,' the child says as the drumbeat speeds up into a furious stumble, like two feet trying to stomp on each other. The group voices its approval.

As the songs bleed into one another and the boys continue to listen, Mohamed climbs back into his tuk-tuk and starts tampering with the tiny equalizer attached to the ceiling, to varying degrees of imperceptibility. It's a new addition to the vehicle and one that has allowed the young driver to serve as the gathering's DJ. Should any of the other boys try to reset the equalizer Mohamed will lash out at them. The tuk-tuk, along with its equalizer, belong to his older brother and his brother's friend – Mohamed is only permitted to drive it during his afternoon shift, for which he receives a small portion of the profit split between the two older teens, and to take it out on the nights where his bosses don't have plans of their own that involve cruising around in the machine.

As tiny as it is, a tuk-tuk is a motorcycle with couches for seats and an overhead cover that can be detached. The machine is typically made to hold a surprising amount of child-sized passengers; eight at a time during various points of the evening, piled onto each other's laps, dangling from the doorless frames. The interior of the vehicle is equally informal, the line between its role as a workspace and a personal space as non-existent as it would be in a bedroom shared by teenaged brothers. There are palm-sized photos and magazine cut-outs, placed under the low laminated ceiling, of Haifa Wahby and Nancy Agram and other silicone-enhanced pop-singers, alongside separate shots of gravity-defying soccer stars – including Mohamed Abu Treika, the former sensation whose role as a poster boy for the Muslim Brotherhood regime during their contentious year in office saw him fall from public grace. On the back of the driver's couch is a sticker of a Nike logo, and there are stickers on the exterior of the vehicle as well – most noticeably one on the back that translates to 'supercool' and another on the front, reading 'God save us'.

Despite existing primarily as sources of revenue, these tuk-tuks have come to represent something else, as seen in the fact that their engines continue to run long after the work day is over, that the boys stay on the street, or return to them, instead of retiring. They have nowhere else to go. Even if they were interested in sitting in cafés, they likely wouldn't be served as it would offend older clientele, if not the establishment's owners, to have children waited on as if they were adults. As well as this, the streets of their neighbourhood are narrow, congested, and unpaved; too claustrophobic for any expression of freedom. The only option, then, lies in the comparatively open roads of the outside world, and the tuk-tuks lend the boys a sense of dominion over them, a rare form of control over an oppressive city. It is this spirit that has shaped their approach to the imposition of curfew hours.

With their tuk-tuks parked haphazardly across the road, the boys continue to talk, smoke, wrestle, and eventually dare one another to write anti-army graffiti on lampposts, laughing as they pass the marker between them. A lack of space seems to be the last of their concerns, and should one be made for them, they would likely approach it with the same sense of distrust held towards any authority that might wish to rein them in. As it is, they remain in control – of their music, of their company, and of their whereabouts. Tonight they may remain on the outskirts of their neighbourhood, with the group having swelled to a number too big to travel in the limited amount of vehicles; on other nights, Mohamed and his friends might trek further into the city, restricted only by how much money they want, or are allowed, to spend on their unlicensed vehicles. In a country of many restrictions but few rules, and a city jagged with structures but little definition, the concept of space takes on a different meaning – particularly spaces traditionally defined by music. When asked about their opinion on a club that would cater to their own musical tastes, the members of the young group collectively dismiss it, with one pointing out, 'we already have wedding halls, but the street weddings are better,' and it should be noted, cheaper.

As the night winds down and the boys prepare to return to the unpaved roads of Dar el-Salam, the notion of the impermanence of the Mahraganat genre is suggested to them, and they dismiss it as outrightly as they did the concept of a 'club'.

'Where's it going to go', one of their number asks, 'when we're all still here?'

Bibliography

Kingsley, Patrick, 'Egypt's gay community fears government crackdown', The Guardian, 17 April 2014, <http://www.theguardian.com/world/2014/apr/17/egypt-gay-community-fears-government-crackdown> accessed 14 December 2016.

Wynn, L.L., *Pyramids and Nightclubs: A Travel Ethnography of Arab and Western Imaginations of Egypt* (Austin, TX: University of Texas Press, 2007).

KYIV

MUSIC/SPACES
It's So Sad I Want to Dance

The Fractions of Kyiv's Club Music

Vitalii Bard Bardetski

▶ P.145

SPACES/POLITICS
Metallists and Neformaly

From Soviet Enculturation to Recent Night Economies

Kateryna Dysa

▶ P.167

Mask, from the series *Maskirovka*, Kyiv, 2017, photo: Tobias Zielony

UFO, from the series *Maskirovka*, Kyiv, 2017, photo: Tobias Zielony

Fire, from the series *Maskirovka*, Kyiv, 2017, photo: Tobias Zielony

Apartment, from the series *Maskirovka*, Kyiv, 2017, photo: Tobias Zielony

Album cover from the band Gruppa Dusppai, 1989

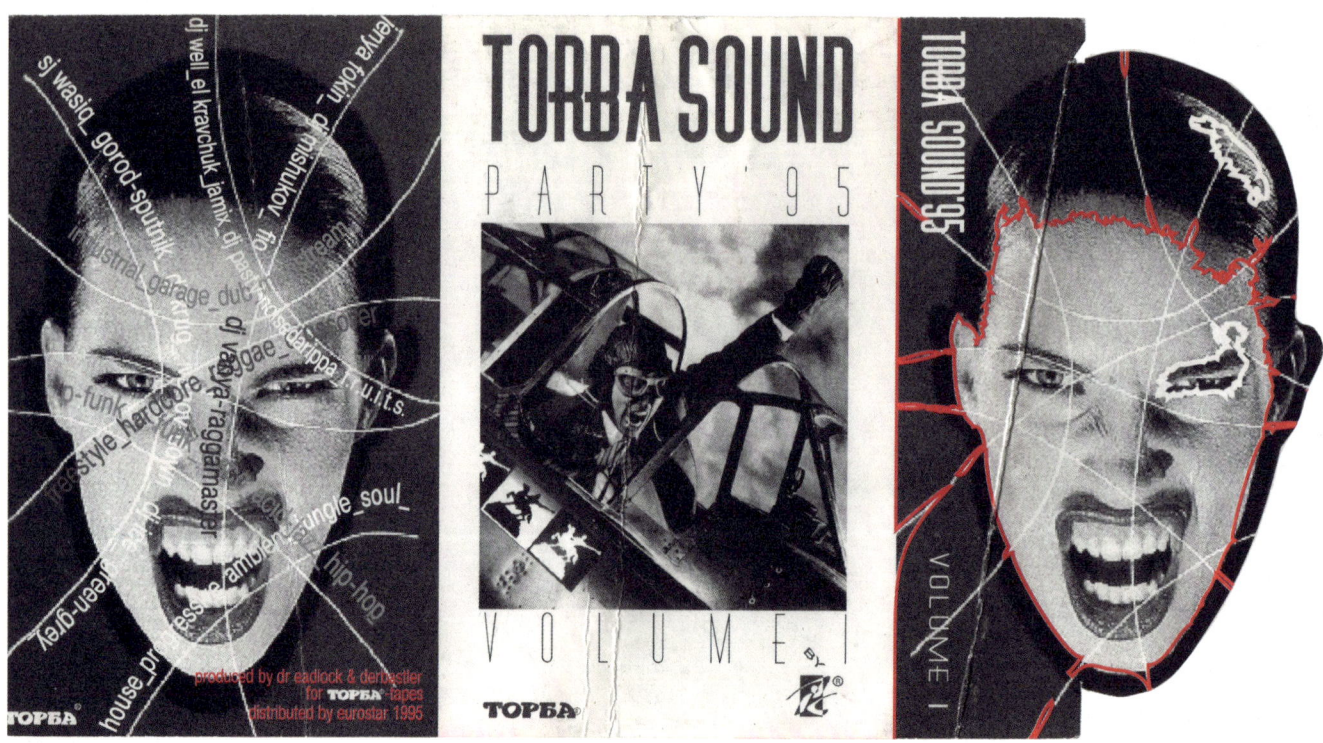

Flyer of Torba Sound Party 95, Volume 1, 1995

Line, from the series *Maskirovka*, Kyiv, 2017, photo: Tobias Zielony

141 KYIV PLATES

Aluminium, from the series *Maskirovka*, Kyiv, 2017, photo: Tobias Zielony

Mandron, first and legendary Kyiv's punk at the very first Rock festival in Kharkiv city, Kharkiv, 1987, photo: Alexej Zaika

143 KYIV PLATES

Plant, from the series *Maskirovka*, Kyiv, 2017, photo: Tobias Zielony

Velvet, from the series *Maskirovka*, Kyiv, 2017, photo: Tobias Zielony

It's So Sad I Want to Dance – The Fractions of Kyiv's Club Music

Vitalii Bard Bardetski

First of all, could you call my city 'Kyiv' from now on, not 'Kiev'? The pronunciation of 'Y' is drawn out, like 'I' in the word 'watching'. This 'Y' sound is like the landscape of the city, with its slopes and its distance, over which Kyiv's club culture extends. An average resident of Kyiv is standing on one of the city's hills, watching people he knows passing by. The posture of the Kyivan is upright, his head is slightly thrown back so he can take a look at the larger area. Kyiv is a big village. In the sense that Kyiv is one of those rather large capitals, where natives and guests get – along with the benefits of the metropolis – all the perks of living in a local community; in the hood. This means that in the big village Kyiv, connections between people are very tightly connected, as everyone knows everyone. If you're new in town, it is likely that, in a couple of days, you will get to know a huge number of new people; you will even be invited to their homes. We don't even do business on phones here, instead we have to meet each other. This socialising is everywhere in Kyiv; you can smell it in the blossom of the chestnut trees.

    I moved to Kyiv in the 1990s after Rave years in Berlin, and within a year or two I knew almost everyone in Kyiv, at least everyone from the nightlife scene. Actually, the mid-1990s could be considered as the beginning of Kyiv's club history, in the common sense of the term 'club', as a place where a DJ or a live band play and the audience is dancing, drinking, and meeting each other. Before that, for example amateur folk dances schools were called 'clubs'. Clubs like these were concentrated in the so-called 'palaces of culture', in the buildings of regional administrations or large enterprises. Meanwhile more affluent people went to restaurants – that were actually clubs, with dances, alcohol, and pop music[1]. Until the mid-1990s it was an exclusive and special event for an average Kyivan to go to a restaurant, mainly for important occasions like birthdays, weddings, dates with a new girl, or because the

[1] Kyiv's pop scene of 1950s, known as *Estrada,* was really cool, but that is a different story.

thirteenth salary had arrived; the yearly premium in the Soviet Union.

The first traces of traditional (in global terms) club culture could be seen in the early 1960s, during the so-called 'thaw' period, after Stalin had kicked the bucket in 1953. Beat music was brought to the city by diplomats and sailors crossing western and eastern borders. With a softer system and approach, quirky *Komsomol*[2] guys started to register *Komsomol Khozraschyot* – self-financed and self-managed clubs. The first of them was probably MK-62 on Leontovycha street, in the café Mriya [dream]. The city festival of proto-Rock'n'Roll was held there, and for, which twelve bands had signed up. The most famous of them should be mentioned: Enej (Aeneas), Second Breath, Red Devils, and Argonauts. There was a lot fuss around this event, and the crowd blocked the whole street.

Back then musicians, their fans and groupies usually gathered at the Maidan [Independence] square, where, in 2013, the Revolution of Dignity took place.[3] They met on the steps of the former monument of the October Revolution or the fountain. From Maidan everyone went to the café Grot or to the aforementioned Mriya. Of course, the repertoire of these bands was controlled by special orders. Musicians avoided bans in several ways: they took Rock'n'Roll standards and wrote songs about *Komsomols* and tireless workers; or they used Folk songs but played them with Rock interpretations. Another method that perhaps spontaneously formed a whole new movement; it combined central and eastern Ukrainian polyphonic singing and Carpathian rhythms. The result sounded quite jazzy and funky, and sometimes even a little bit psychedelic.

Authorities strongly recommended amateur bands to become professionals and to sign contracts with the official concert organisations. Thus, it was planned to integrate fresh cultural trends into the so-called *sharovar* culture.[4] The terms 'group' or 'band' were forbidden for some reason – instead to classify these groups the abbreviation VIA (Vocal and Instrumental Ensemble) was used. Musicians were dressed in weird outfits (Bootsy Collins would have been jealous), and most men had a moustache which

2
Communist youth organisation. Almost all high school pupils were forced to become members. It was a mandatory starting point for careers within communist institutions.
3
Please see Kateryna Dysa's essay in this book for more information about the Maidan events as well as the social spheres of Kyiv.
4
A polished pseudo-national culture. From *sharovars*, the name of loose trousers worn by Ukrainian cossacks.

was probably a sign of their strength and their high testosterone levels. *Moustache Fank* — is perhaps what this movement should have been called. 'Fank' because it was a very peculiar mutated Funk, a Funk that's long journey through the iron curtain and through the damaged communication channels between the East and the West became mixed with the syncopated rhythms of traditional *Hutsul*[5] music.

VIAs were invented by authorities in order to contain the influence of Western culture that, it was believed, was designed to influence the Soviet consciousness. Normally VIA gigs consisted of two parts: one would be the band playing their own music, and the other would be official music with songs about the Communist Party; the unique beauty of nature, friendship, and the happy life of people in the Soviet Union. It was phenomenal, but this plan led to unexpected results, at least in the Ukraine where contemporary Ukrainian songs became the most popular trend in the whole Soviet Union, despite the fact that a large number of musicians migrated to the metropolis, Moscow in Russia. There is still a lot of hype around the Ukrainian 1970s to this day. Dozens of young DJs' shoes were worn down in their search for vinyl from that period at flea markets. For example, the self-titled and only album of the band Vizerunky Shlyakhiv [pattern ways] from 1976 recently became one of the biggest demands from music fans. If you are lucky, you can buy a copy for a whopping hundred euros.

'Music on the bones'

In the 1970s, Kyiv began to grow rapidly, new concrete neighbourhoods were built — so-called 'sleeping' residential areas like Obolon, Kharkivskyi, or Troyeshchyna. The city was flooded with workers from the countryside, who were usually rather religious. But authorities did not build churches for the newcomers in each new neighbourhood. Instead they constructed open-air dance floors or hangars for the same purpose. These venues were called 'discotheques' later on. In addition to official names, these discos had nicknames that are still used today. Perhaps the most famous among them was *Zhaba* [frog] on the slopes of the

[5] An ethnic group living in the Carpathian mountains. Basic knowledge about *Hutsuls* could be taken from the movie *Tini Zabutykh Predkiv / Shadows of Forgotten Ancestors* by Sergej Parajanov, 1965.

Dnipro River.[6] Zhaba got its name from the shape of the canopy over the stage that looked like a frog prepared to jump. A crawling frog. Nearby there was *Kukushka* [cuckoo], a kind of entertainment centre with live gigs, cafés, and barbeque spots. Sometimes you could bring your own alcohol.[7] Near the old town of Podil there was Crocodile; a hidden crocodile.

In the late 1970s, a group of music lovers came together and started to exchange or sell records. Especially vinyls from the west were a kind of currency as US Dollars were strictly forbidden in the Soviet Union. Music was brought to Kyiv from the west (Lviv[8]), south (Odesa), and east (St. Petersburg, at the time called Leningrad), as well as through urban connections and diplomats and families in exile. Collectors usually met once a week near the Botanical Garden and in a couple of other locations. Prices were too high – usually fifty rubles per record, which was slightly less than half of a monthly salary for a Soviet engineer. But there was a low-cost alternative for the masses: Flexi discs that were usually printed on old x-ray photographs and were called 'music on the edges' or 'music on the bones'.

In 1979, the Kyiv factory Mayak [lighthouse] started to produce the legendary reel-to-reel tape player Mayak-205, which became the main device in all discos. It never broke, it did not chew up the tape, and it was not too expensive. Also, at the end of the 1970s, the Kyiv factory, Communist, released a new model of cassette tape recorder, the *Vesna 202* [spring 202]. This device could not exactly be classified as a Soviet boom box – but at least it could work on batteries and thus accompanied small gatherings on park benches. At the same time, dubbing studios where music fans could order reel-to-reel or cassette tapes with their favourite albums of western bands appeared. It was an alternative network of music distribution, and the number of volumes were up to ten times greater than those at Melody records, the formal state network monopoly label.

Smooth-tongued DJs

In 1980, Kyiv hosted some competitions of the Olympic Summer Games that were mainly held in Moscow. These

---

[6] Ukraine's biggest river. It flows into the Black Sea and divides the country into a left and a right side.
[7] For many years the typical Kyiv drink was fortified wine.
[8] A city in the western part of Ukraine.

Olympic Games were boycotted by 66 countries, most of them from western Europe led by the USA because of the Soviet invasion of Afghanistan. Therefore, many participants were from the Soviet-friendly African Union. Not only did this enhance Kyiv's diversity, but it also had a great influence on the musical tastes as well as the dance styles of Kyiv's citizens. As well as this, in the 1980s the show *5 Minutes to Think* appeared on Ukrainian TV. This was an innovative format of an interactive talk show combined with gigs of young Ukrainian bands. This show had a song by German electronic music innovators Kraftwerk[9] in the opening titles and music by the Italian Disco pioneer Giorgio Moroder in the closing titles.

Straight after the Olympics the first almost proper discos with the first disc jockeys started to appear. Among the DJs we should mention Andrii Vasin and Fedir Terpilovskyi. Of course, they were not DJs in the contemporary sense. They were just people who had access to fresh music and who were smooth-tongued. Why smooth-tongued? Well, the DJ was playing with reel-to-reel tape players – so he needed time in order to find the next song. Hence, he had to talk in between songs. There was a blatant lack of information and so stories were invented. Normally, apart from the disk jockey, there was a whole team: a light man, somebody who brought the record, dancers, technician, and fans – all in all, a proper sound system. The venues' music programmes were regulated, as at least half of the repertoire had to be songs of official Soviet pop singers, and most foreign artists were banned; the reasons behind the banning were sometimes ridiculous. For instance, the US Rock star Alice Cooper was banned for promoting violence and vandalism, the Disco and Funk musician Bohannon for eroticism, and Spanish singer Julio Iglesias for neo-fascism. These discos were usually open only until 11pm at the latest – afterwards the working class had to rest.

At the same time, alternative discos such as Enthusiast in Kyiv's Rusanivka district occurred. These were usually spontaneously organised in hastily decorated assembly halls of institutes and student dorms, or in cafés in residential areas. Times were pre-internet era, and what is now called 'promotion' was mainly carried out by word of

[9] 'Die Roboter', 1978. The song contains the line 'Ya tvoi sluga, ya tvoi rabotnik' [I am your slave, I am your worker].

mouth – the so-called 'gypsy post'. One of the most famous DJs and promoters of informal evenings, DJ Soul, remembers:

> We were once very trendy, Donna Summer, Deedee Jackson, Michael… There were three of us – one was putting on the music, the others said a few words. Parties were admission free, we also earned nothing. By the 1990s I did not take fees for the set. We even didn't even have DJ nicknames. There was a constant war with Komsomols.[10]

Despite the lack of any kind of advertising, the improvised discos were regularly visited by people in coats – the feature of the security agency, the KGB. Even from a musical point of view, illegal discos were counterculture to the official ones. In both formats Disco music was played, but at the official parties it was primarily only simulacrum products that mainly came from Germany and France, like Boney M., Ottawan, Eruption, and the indispensable Abba from Sweden as well as songs from the festival of *Italian Song* in San Remo. In contrast, the tracks in the illegal discos were mostly real US Disco as well as New Wave from both sides of the Atlantic.

Another source of the 'western poison'; the cultural influx from the west, were so-called 'currency bars' in the few hotels where foreigners could stay, and bills were issued in US Dollars. These hotels became centres of foreign currency exchange and were surrounded by *fartsovshiki*, sellers of illegal, underground, or scarce goods. The hotel bars where packed with canned beer and cocktails like gin tonic that were unheard for regular Kyivans back then. Among these hotels was Mir [peace], which hosted cultural exchange tourists from capitalist countries, and especially important was Rus, that had a bowling lane, and which could be considered Kyiv's first *almost*-club. It was in Rus where (a first of its kind) a 'capitalist' audience hung out – an enchanting mix of 'golden youth' (kids from the authorities and the official creative elite), the aforementioned *fartsovshiki* dealers, foreigners, artists, and the essential KGB officials. It was impossible for someone from the outside to attend these parties. People had to

[10] DJ Soul, in an interview with the author (2016).

either pay a big bribe to the giant doorman or ask all their circles of acquaintances in order to finally reach someone who could take them inside. Local DJs were trying to mix tracks (although there were no record players or tape recorders with pitch functions) and played pretty trendy stuff for the time, like Giorgio Moroder, Kajagoogoo, or Grandmaster Flash which was especially significant considering that, back then throughout the the great Soviet countrycheesy pop like Modern Talking, CC Catch, and the like, were popular.

By the mid-1980s, you had to make serious decisions in Kyiv. It was a time when music choices said almost everything about you. You had to choose between Disco or Rock. The Rock community was a counterculture to both aforementioned kinds of discos. The Rock scene was quite conservative and was mostly based on the R'n'B tradition—until the unexpected concert in Kyiv of the US avant-garde Rock band, Sonic Youth, in 1989. However, Rock music also had a protest potential, which began to fully develop after Mikhail Gorbachev initiated his *Perestroika* [restructuring] political reforms in the second half of the 1980s. The Rock community had several rehearsal bases, where a few dozen groups gathered. The most famous rehearsal room was located in the auditorium of the Bilshovyk factory. Hundreds of local Punks, Goths, Hippies, Metal lovers, and people from other subcultures spent time in various cafés in the city. With the traditional two-halves of coffee (something like a double espresso) young people spent hours standing around *Kulinarka* [cookery], *Khreshatyi Yar* [cruciform ravine], *Styeklyashka*, *Khreshchatyk*, and countless other Kyiv coffee shops, many of which did not make it to the present, having lost in the capitalist competition. At these coffee shops new bands were created and songs were written, while couples chatted. Perhaps the Kyiv tradition to meet in a café even to negotiate non-serious subjects came from those times. As time is rather relative in cafés, this might be the reason why we never arrive on time.

During the transition of the decades from the 1980s to the 1990s, the situation began to change rapidly. These few years were, perhaps, the most interesting time in the history of modern Ukrainian music. Rock focused less on the R'n'B tradition. Bands like Kolezkyi Asesor [collegiate assessor], Banita Bayda, Rabbota Ho, Kvartyra 50 [apartment 50] and others delivered a unique psychedelic sound of the city. The band VV have produced perhaps the first Rock hit that everyone could dance to – the song 'Tantsi' [dances], was partially inspired by the 1982 song 'Da Da Da' by the German band Trio.[11]

'The union of musical forces'

In the new decade of the 1990s the centre of the creative activity moved to groups of artists who found their locations in squats. First there was the Paris Commune (after the former name of the street where the squat was located) and then BeZhe, an acronym for the actual name of the street. Especially in BeZhe, there were parties where someone just put their favourite music on, and then it developed into a kind of deejaying. At some point the artists realised that you cannot just stare at the patterns of the plaster under hallucinogens from the pharmacy, but you should also begin to move limbs to appropriate music. After the last band performed the concerts at Kosyi Kaponir[12] [oblique caponier] usually turned into dance parties. As in the decade before, musical taste told almost everything about a person – it was an accurate marker dividing people into 'us' and 'them'.

'The key event of the early 1990s should be called "the union of musical forces",' says Eugene Taran, who was at the very centre of developments in Kyiv in the late 1980s and early 1990s.[13] Taran emigrated to Munich, Germany in the mid-1990s. The Munich cult label Compost Records later released his album,[14] which until recently was the first and only Ukrainian breakthrough in the electronic music worldwide. The club-like project he refers to, was a café called *Burevisnyk* [petrel], where anyone who did not fit into the traditional Hippie, Metal, or any other Rock community could find their place. Bands, musicians, and music projects like Medlennyi Rul [slow wheel], Salih, Vadik Yugrinov, or Trio Rytm Gitarystiv [trio of rhythm guitarists] have debuted in Burevisnyk. Taran still has two guitars hanging on the wall, and continues sentimentally:

[11] One of the first live performances of the song from 1988 can be found here: https://youtu.be/L92bXkb-C6U.
[12] A defence building in Kyiv, built in the mid-19th century. It was mainly used as a political prison.
[13] Eugene Taran, in an interview with author (2016).
[14] *Mod and Midi and Space Age*, Compost Records 1996.

Perhaps that is where the Kyiv public first heard Acid House. My and Andrew Salikhov's 8-bit compositions some music critics at that time described as 'Yello', that went down to hell'.[15]

15
Eugene Taran, in an interview with author (2016).
16
Petro: vocals, keyboards; Dima Petishkin: keyboards.
17
With the label Quasi pop Records.

At the beginning of the 1990s a new generation of musicians realised that the sound changed because of new technology. Ivan Samshit was probably the first purely electronic Kyiv band. The group began as a classic pop duo,[16] later joined by keyboardist Ruslan Zhovnirovich. The sound of Samshit was diverse, but overall it was electronic retro-futurism in the vein of British Synthpop band Soft Cell. It was a studio project and for the period that they were active during the late 1980s to the mid-1990s, they recorded about a dozen so-called 'magnitoalbums'. These albums were recorded at a home studio using mostly non-professional and non-multichannel equipment on home tapes known as *magnitophones*. The first proper release by Ivan Samshit was the compilation *Essential Shit*[17] in 2007. The emigration of Petya Kuzmichev (aka Peter Dine, Samshit's main creative force) to Germany in the early 1990s played an important practical role in the development of Kyiv's contemporary music scene. He left his sequencer and keyboards in Kyiv. With this equipment musical loops were created that became the base of the project Shake Hi Fi, which is perhaps the most influential new Rock band from Kyiv. The next one was Gorod Sputnik, named after the Kyiv satellite town, where at the time crazy parties were held. Gorod was the first live dance Rock band from Kyiv, a sort of The Shamen meets Stereo MCs. They even had a permanent stroboscope.

Unfortunately, Gorod Sputnik—as well as the bulk of short-lived groups and collaborations of that time—did not produce any effective physical relics. None of the musicians of the Kyiv underground expected that records could ever be released. So, they preferred to get together and 'slide along the surface of things' instead of spending their time in a studio. Gorod shot two videos and recorded one album, which is still untitled, the original master is probably lost. After Taran's departure to Germany, Andrii Salikhov, half of Gorod Sputnik, continued to sporadically perform solo or with MC Lapot.

Meanwhile, the Soviet Union collapsed, and after three hundred years Ukraine became an independent state again. The Ukrainian reality changed dramatically, as capitalism, with its primary goal of accumulating wealth, came in. But when such a monstrous state like the Soviet Union collapses, it inevitably leads to a breakdown of the national economies. For the first couple of years Ukraine did not even have its own currency. People used a card system to get food. The city sometimes lacked the electricity to light the main streets at night. But at the same time so-called nightclubs, which opened instead of the dance pavilions that the state was no longer able to finance, were shining bright with maximum neon lights.

Former *Komsomol* leaders, who already had experience in economic activities from the *Perestroika* period, and 'bandits' became the new heroes. The latter were not always actual criminals. Often, they were just people who actively and optimistically embraced the new realities of that time, which was later nicknamed the 'crazy 90s'. These first capitalists appreciated all the delights of becoming rich quickly, and they were the first to create real nightclubs in the capital. But in doing so it was also impossible to avoid criminal activity because sooner or later criminal groups always appeared, who took into account the specifics of what doing business, in those days, entailed. Later, this culture was romanticised and remembered in the form of short haircuts, red jackets, and tuned 'devyatka'[18] cars.

In the times of *Perestroika*, Mikhail Gorbachev had tried to fight alcoholism in the Soviet Union. That is why, at the beginning of the decade, the Ukraine was left with little alcohol production of its own. Clubs turned out to be the ideal place to sell alcohol, which was sometimes supposedly imported but, in reality, manufactured in illegal factories. 'Tsar Peter', 'Amaretto', 'Napoleon' – bottles with colourful labels seductively urged visitors to enter the club. But soon alcohol began to lose popularity because speed pills allowed going out all night long.

It is now difficult to argue which club was the first to open. They began to spring up like mushrooms after rain.

18
The ninth model of the Lada car. It was a mark of the middle class among the criminal-business community in the beginning of 1990s.

The owners of the first 'entertainment centres' had been inspired by 1930s USA with the gangster allusions stated above, and concepts of Las Vegas. Almost all of these new clubs' names referred to the US, for example New York, Hollywood, Play Offs, or Flamingo. Nearly all of them were labyrinths of entertainment, consisting of a concert hall with a stage and a dance floor, a restaurant, a strip hall, a casino, VIP rooms, and additional services depending on the imagination of the owners. The entrance fee was around 10 to 20 US Dollars – a crazy amount of money for the time when people could rent an impressive apartment in the city centre for 50 US Dollars per month. The atmosphere was surprisingly enchanting, fun, but sometimes reminiscent of a psychedelic feast in the times of the plague; decadence in the face of turmoil.

In the aforementioned club New York, more or less current dance music started to be played, but it was mostly longer versions of European pop hits by the likes of 2 Unlimited or Dr Alban that were played; mostly from cassettes and CDs. DJ Ice, who came from the Hip-Hop and breakdance community, was probably the first to use vinyl records. He eventually became the protagonist for the establishing of US House music in Kyiv. We met with Vitalik (the name that Ice was given by his parents) in a posh bar in Pechersk,[19] and he has not changed over the last twenty years; he still looks like an old school US DJ, maybe with a few extra kilos.

> *It was a community of several dozen people who considered themselves as progressive youth. We came to a bar or club and offered to play new music. We were mostly treated with scepticism, but the presence of the Klitschkos[20] (both brothers often hung out with us) often helped to solve the problem.*[21]

New music in the form of House or Techno tracks – 'songs that never ended' – was not easily accepted at first, but then occupied almost all the clubs of the capital. DJs like Alex K, Mishukoff, Vell, Ice, Derbastler, and MC Lapot began to define the new night sound of Kyiv. But they mainly played in the unfitting interiors of contemporary clubs that were really not at all like proper clubs. Meanwhile, crowds of teenagers from residential areas visited the downtown and

[19] Governmental area in Kyiv.
[20] Internationally famous Ukrainian boxing champions.
[21] DJ Ice, in an interview with the author (2016).

frightened the public, because social inequality had grown dramatically. Do you have a cigarette? – Boom! No cigarettes? – Boom! Anyway, club music started to become popular among the masses and served as a kind of buffer zone that relaxed social tensions. This club music was simply called 'Rave' or 'Techno', there was no special categorisation in styles. This was absent because people simply had a desire for something new, for something good. In the two years between 1994 to 1996, Ukrainians went a distance in music development that took western countries at least twenty years. Styles, stimulators, people, and locations passed by at the speed of light, leaving no chance to build any consequent chronology of events.

Because of the rapidity of the events, Kyiv's nightclub scene had no time for underground development. Nevertheless, a lot was happening in this field. For example, the six-month short, but very intense, life of the club Stolovka. The name was informal and meant 'canteen', as the club was located in the actual canteen of the closing factory at Kudryavskiy Descent. It was designed by almost all of the coolest artists of the city. The result resembled the location of the movie *The Cook, the Thief, His Wife & Her Lover* by Peter Greenaway (1989). Many pioneers of local electronic music debuted in Stolovka, like the duo Syntezatory (later on: Da Sintezators) or Vasya Tkach. The main music style was Trip-Hop. The first club, which played only real club (i.e. dance) music, was the Cinema club on the left bank of the city. From the visual perspective Cinema was a fairly hidden spot. It had a consequent music policy, and the audience from the city centre, which usually only went to clubs in walking distance, enthusiastically went there. The resident DJs Derbastler and Yoshi played almost the entire spectrum of then-contemporary dance music, from early Trance to Drum'n'Bass. In the morning, visitors went to chill at the water canal and it all looked pretty hip.

Despite all the hype, the whole club community back then was a pretty closed group of several hundred Kyivans, who moved from one club to another. Some Ukrainians (who had enough US Dollars in their pockets and strong nerves in order to survive the queues to visa offices) were able to travel the world. During his first visit to London in the early 1990s, a young businessman from Kyiv named Vitaly Ulitskyy went to the club Ministry of Sound. Ulitskyy, who became the founding father of Torba,[22] perhaps the most famous and influential Kyiv party of all time, recalls:

> I realised that the main thing is the technological organisation of space. I wanted to do something similar in Kyiv. But a fixed spot did not work at all, so we decided to take unusual places and turn them into a party overnight.[23]

Only six Torba parties were held in total. The first Torba took place in the club New York in October 1995 – and turned out to be a real Techno carnival. Everybody was there, from the usual freaks to the city mayor. Torba was a party that many people made for themselves. In addition to generating a fantastic level of enthusiasm, it was also Kiyv's first experience of big brands sponsoring club events, which later became a common practice. Vitaly Ulitskyy stopped Torba at the peak of its success and became a prosperous event organiser. Even to this day many remember his crazy rides in his red BMW through Kyiv's longest street, the Victory Avenue, from the centre to the club Disco 2000, which became the main destination for clubbers in the second half of the 1990s. It was a club big enough for 1,000 visitors, it had a decent sound system and a large dance floor with Trance and a chill zone where Trip-Hop was played. The big hall was run by Kuzya (aka Pubert), the frontman of the Lviv cult band Braty Gadyukiny. After Sergiy (his real name) moved to the capital, the ex-Rock musician got into Trance Techno first. He became a real guru for hundreds of people, and in the year 2000, after a night out, he often gave free morning lectures about the meaning of life on the benches in front of the club.

In 1995, in selected semi-legal bars, including a legendary spot on Barbusse street, a mysterious DJ trio began to seriously light up the dance floors. The trio was called Finski DJs [Finnish DJs] and originally consisted of three former employees of a licensed CD store. After the closing of the store Shura Rachok, Zhenia Belyi and Oleg Sokolov put together a decent collection of music, and for the next couple of years they became the main DJs for the local art

[22] The travel sack that is worn on shoulders. It is used to express either disappointment or excitement, as in: 'Thats torba!'
[23] Vitaly Ulitskyy, in an interview with the author (2016).

bohemia. Their complete mix-up of styles, a total hodge-podge – from United Future Organization's Acid Jazz, to the Stereo MC's UK Hip-Hop, sometimes even up to Punk by the Sex Pistols.

Club culture slowly began to be supported by the media. DJ Tolya (aka Anatoly Veksklyarskyy) launched the show *Misyachni Trambony* on Gala Radio. It was the first show where club music played for the mass audience. Its success was phenomenal, which, in addition to the music's quality, is due to Tolik's unique presenting style. Audiences gathered specifically for common listening from the speakers of a jeep near the Friendship arch.[24] Sometimes it was a real happening and hundreds of people came. Tolik, who was a professional DJ, apparently also had an impact on Kyiv's number one Rock band at that time, Green Grey. This band recorded several albums under the obvious influence of club music. Electronic rhythms made it to national television when one of the channels broadcasted a daily chart show, *Teritoriya A*. This was actually a kind of a talent show, when half of the participants performed tracks in the mood of German Happy Hardcore of the 1990s. Today, from the present point of view, it is possible to listen to it and think it sounds normal. But back then people thought that Armageddon had come. One of the projects of the show *Teritoriya A* was the Eurodance duo Aqua Vita. A few years ago, during the boom of Bastard pop, the postmodern mixture of any possible genres, they experienced a re-birth and their songs could be heard in many fashionable Kyiv clubs.

Later, in early 1997, the station Radioactivity started to air. Kyiv is located at a distance of less than a few dozen kilometres from Chernobyl, the exploded nuclear power station. The radio station broadcast club music only, mostly live DJ sets from vinyl records. Within a year the magazine *New Rock And Roll* was writing about club releases, DJs, parties, and new trends. The *X3M* mag focused on urban culture. New promo groups organised parties from the decoration and promotion, to the first invitations for international guest DJs and negotiations with sponsors. The Graffiti Music team, which also evolved into the first real DJ management, mainly promoted House parties.

[24] Erected originally as a symbol of Ukrainian-Russian friendship.

As well as this, in 1998, the nightclub Ultra opened their doors near Kulyok (literally meaning 'plastic bag', Institute of Culture), where for a couple of years, all of the capital's younger clubbers gathered at the weekend. DJs stood on barrels, spinning almost 24/7. There were almost no alcoholic drinks on sale at the bar, but from the size of the youths' pupils one could say that Ecstasy drugs must have been widely available. Especially in its first year, Ultra was a real living dance hive where many DJs, go-go dancers, and MCs came from.

Once more from scratch

In 2000, the ephemeral one-man label Sale Records released the first collection of Ukrainian electronic music, *Summer Salection*. However, the edge of the new millennium was another difficult period. Even though the economy was very slowly coming to life again after a foregoing currency crisis of 1998, most clubs were shutting down. In 2002, everything began once more from scratch. Experts from a restaurant chain got involved in Kiyv's nightlife with their Opium Dance Club. It was a hookah paradise with the sound of Progressive House, saxophones, and percussions. Generally speaking, the colour gold began to dominate interior designs. Dima Slukin, the capital's nightlife prince of the next five years or so, debuted as a 'face controller'[25] at the Disco House club, Brazil. Later on Slukin opened his own Boogie bar, a tiny bar that functioned almost 24/7, with a dozen seperate toilet cabins including a convenient shelf probably to sniff a line.

In 2003, in a side room of the famous food market Besarabka, the nightclub Tchaikovsky[26] opened. It was the hottest place for two summer seasons. The club was actually cheaply built but looked expensive. Slukin was also the man in charge of Tchaikovsky. Nowadays he picks a local Nicaraguan coffee for Kyiv cafés. Even on Skype his tan looks permanent. He remembers:
> *We just bought a golden cloth and covered the walls with it. Then by chance we found a company that makes chandeliers for churches. Asked them to remove the ecclesiastical symbolism from three of them – and*

[25] A person who stands along with bouncers at the doors of the posh clubs in Ukraine and who decides whether a person could enter or not. The 'face controller' tradition is believed to have appeared in Kyiv after the movie *Studio 54* (1998).

[26] Named after Pyotr Ilyich Tchaikovsky, classical composer (1940–1993), whose family was of Cossack background.

hung them on the ceiling at Tchaikovsky. False crystal looked very cool![27]

[27] Dima Slukin, in an interview with the author (2017).

Chandeliers in general became a fixture of posh clubs in Kyiv for the next few years. But Tchaikovsky itself was emotionally burned within two years. The next generation of clubs in the city centre like PaTiPa, D'Lux, Orangery, or Kaif formed a kind of Bermuda Triangle of mainstream nightlife. To escape from that maelstrom was almost impossible. By the mid-2000s most parties relied on bringing foreign DJs with a well-known name and sponsoring by tobacco or alcohol companies. Visitors had an opportunity to be photographed by a city magazine correspondent, showing their face to the public in pre-social media times. Concert posters were filled with the announcements of international and local mega parties.

Then, in 2007, the Xlib club opened. Your author was its co-owner, so it is hard to stay completely unbiased. The location was a bunker in the basement of a former Soviet bomb shelter. The club was truly innovative and identified current trends for development of the city's club scene. For example, there was no show-off in Xlib. People just came there for the music and to dance. In its best times there was a friendly and fun vibe that resembled the early 1990s and what many people love clubs for. The club Closer, perhaps the most influential Kyiv club in recent years, has developed from Xlib. At the beginning of the Revolution of Dignity in Maidan square in 2013, Xlib opened its massive iron doors for the last time – and this was also a sign. The revolution has changed and is still changing us. It has also affected the club scene of the city.

Socialising, sharing, and a sense of unity

Fundamental social change was a breaking point, it was an opportunity to figure out where we stand, what we are heading towards, and what we had achieved along the way. Was our 'club culture' (I personally don't like this term) able to bring anything really interesting to the world? What does Kyiv sound like at night? Perhaps the problem with Kyiv, in this context, is that we immediately started with large commercial clubs in the early 1990s, almost passing by any underground culture. So now we return to the beginning in the natural evolution of things. At least so it seems after the 2013 revolution, which came with a significant reduction in rent after an economic crisis. This is almost certainly the result of social upheavals, and it had positive sides to it. At the time of writing, almost every week new small DIY bars with music evenings were opening. New clubs like Otel, 56, or Zaal look and sound uncompromising.[28] Slava Lepsheev, promoter of the influential CXEMA parties, agrees:

> *It has become much more interesting over the last two years. Someone opens a bar or a squat, someone organises a party. The city is crowded with enthusiasts, its residents strongly support new projects.*[29]

Parties are now generally held apart from regular clubs in terms of formal buildings. They have moved to the banks of the Dnipro River, to forgotten industrial hangars, to pre-Second World War tunnels. Today, partying in Kyiv has reacquired its original goal: socialising, sharing emotions, and a sense of unity. Due to its extreme roughness and the longitude of the club nights, Kyiv, in recent years, has earned the status of a kind of 'new Berlin'. In addition to the aforementioned CXEMA, a dozen of regular parties by Rhythm Büro, Strichka Festival, Wicked Bass label showcases, LOW, and many others are places where thousands of clubbers from around the world gather. On the other hand, there are producers and DJs who not only define the sound of Kyiv, but also perform regularly in Europe and on other continents. Originating from the Dnipro city Psychedelic and Minimal Techno apologist Stanislav Tolkachev, the Konotop born Deep House prince Vakula, House magicians Cape Cod and Koloah, ethnotronik princess ONUKA, Neo-disco protagonist Pavel Plastikk, and numerous new talents are being raised in this unique city by the Chernobyl nuclear power plant. Kyiv is booming, take a chance to get over here.

We live in controversial times, when a DJ is going to the war front to fight for his country, and during one of his returns he goes back to his main craft and warms up the crowd for UK Rave veterans as The Prodigy. When DJs

[28] For more about Kyiv's current nightlife scene see Chris Giles, 'We Went Post-Revolution Raving in Kiev's Industrial Wastelands', *Vice*, 26 April 2016, <https://thump.vice.com/en_us/article/kiev-cxema-ukraine-raving> accessed 1 May 2016.

[29] Slava Lepsheev, in an interview with the author (2017).

give their records to raise money to help the internally displaced persons. The feeling is that everything is just starting over, at least for club culture. Do we have the right to go to clubs or bars – the right to a relatively normal life? We decided: yes, we do. Whether it is because of this controversy, or in spite of it, as someone recently said, 'sometimes it's so sad that I want to dance'. Kyiv is dancing now as never before.

Translation: Dasha Posrednikova and Pavlo V. Pushkar

Bibliography

Giles, Chris, 'We Went Post-Revolution Raving in Kiev's Industrial Wastelands', *Vice*, 26 April 2016, <https://thump.vice.com/en_us/article/kiev-cxema-ukraine-raving> accessed 1 May 2016.

Cover, from the series *Maskirovka*, Kyiv, 2017, photo: Tobias Zielony

163 KYIV PLATES

Shine, from the series *Maskirovka*, Kyiv, 2017, photo: Tobias Zielony

Make Up, from the series *Maskirovka*, Kyiv, 2017, photo: Tobias Zielony

Yard, from the series *Maskirovka*, Kyiv, 2017, photo: Tobias Zielony

Metallists and Neformaly – From Soviet Enculturation to Recent Night Economies

Kateryna Dysa

In a club in Ukraine's capital city, Kyiv, two girls that had recently arrived greet each other. They exchange news and go to the bar counter while waiting for a special guest DJ. Here they linger for a while: one of them, dressed in jeans and a simple t-shirt, orders an energy drink, another, wearing an elegant top and elaborate necklace, takes a beer. The girl with the beer is a habitué of the club; she always comes with a female friend or other company. She explains her loyalty to this place: 'You know, the most important thing for me is the kind of music they play in the club. There are just two clubs in Kyiv where you can enjoy some *decent* music.' In her case, 'decent' music is Detroit Techno, but in someone else's case it would be other electronic dance music.[1] This attitude to the selection of a club is common among the habitués of Kyiv's clubs; whatever reasons clubbers might provide for their frequenting clubs – either to meet up and socialise with friends, acquaintances, or newcomers, to get drunk and have fun, to listen to music and relax, or the opposite: to get energised or to dance – hardly anyone will agree to go to a club that plays music that is not their cup of tea. Therefore, Sarah Thornton's position may serve as a point of departure for this text. She indicates that:

> Club cultures are taste cultures. Club crowds generally congregate on the basis of their shared taste in music, their consumption of common media and, most importantly, their preference for people with similar tastes to themselves. Taking part in club cultures builds, in turn, further affinities, socializing participants into a knowledge of (and frequently a belief in) the likes and dislikes, meanings and values of the culture.[2]

The millennial youth of Kyiv, en masse, are rather initiative and dynamic. Like their counterparts from other western or many eastern European countries, many of them start working at quite an early age, and those who study combine work with education. Of course, some of them work in offices, but there are many who start their own small and creative businesses. For instance, they open hipster cafés (which are still popular in Kyiv now) or virtual shops retailing hand-made objects through the Internet. In this respect the current young generation is different to the previous one, the young people of the 1990s that were, in a way, rather reactionary and passive. Independent contemporary youth can adjust their time of work and their time of leisure – and thus they happily spend late hours in clubs. So, apparently, there is little difference between habitués of clubs in Kyiv and their counterparts in many other cities of the world.

—

But before we turn to Kyiv's clubs and club cultures, let's imagine a clubber who is not acquainted with the city of Kyiv. Before she or he can make up their mind on where to go in the evening, the clubber needs to orientate themself in the city with basic information that can be obtained

[1] To learn more about the dance and club music genres of Kyiv, please read Vitalii Bard Bardetski's essay in this book.

[2] Sarah Thornton, *Club Cultures: Music, Media and Subcultural Capital* (Middletown: Wesleyan University Press, 1996), 3.

before arrival. For instance, one can find out that, according to the data of the Central Administration Department of Statistics in Kyiv, there were 2,927,227 city residents as of 1 February 2017. This is a considerably smaller population than that of Moscow or London, but nearly the same as that of Berlin, Madrid, or Rome. One can also learn that in recent years Kyiv as well as the whole of Ukraine has witnessed a tendency to population aging. Although the presence of a great number of higher education institutions in the city might imply a large quantity of students, statistical data for 2012 show that the total number of young people aged fifteen to twenty-nine living in Kyiv slightly exceeded 20 per cent. Finally, one can discover that the national profile of Kyiv residents is rather homogeneous: according to the 2001 census, Ukrainians make an absolute majority of 82.23 per cent, whereas Russians constitute 13.14 per cent. Among the five nationalities that top the list one can also find Byelorussians and Poles, amounting to less than 1 per cent each. Obviously, Kyiv is not a city of intensive intercultural communication and exchange. Yet, if one were to get acquainted with the city using this dry data, one would be left wanting.

3
Michel de Certeau, *The Practice of Everyday Life* (Berkeley: University of California Press, 1984), 91–92.

The best way to start an immediate acquaintance with the city is by following the practice of 'voyeurs or walkers', as mentioned by Michel de Certeau.[3] To get familiar with the city one should first have a bird's eye view of it and then blend into it by having paced it on foot. Vast expanse of Kyiv is best seen from its highest point accessible to spectators: the belfry on the territory of the Kyiv-Pechersk Lavra [Monastery of the Caves]. Contemplating the area around, not only can one enjoy the panoramic scenery of Kyiv, but also get an idea of the city's structure: it stretches before the beholder as a multi-coloured and unevenly textured blanket with green patches of parks, a sandy-grey sea of blocks of flats, and a snake-like shape of the river Dnipro in the middle.

The Dnipro divides the city into two parts. On the right bank, wherefrom the clubber beholds the city, lies the historic – and indeed central – part of Kyiv, which is greener and more attractive in terms of architecture, if compared to the sleeping quarters of the left bank. The historic part is relatively compact; it consists of the Upper Town with its architectural monuments dating back to the eleventh century and later. The Lower Town (Podil) which, despite being entirely rebuilt after the great fire of 1811, boasts a well-preserved atmosphere of old times, and Pechersk, a city district with large park areas and a monastery complex which has partly been turned into a museum, the aforementioned Kyiv-Pechersk Lavra. Both the central street of Kyiv, Khreshchatyk, and the central square, Maidan Nezalezhnosti [Independence square], lie in the very heart of the historic part. Having been razed to the ground during the Second World War and then rebuilt in record time after the war, Khreshchatyk is the venue for staging most of the city's public events, including festive celebrations and mass protests.

Behind the centre of the city sprawl sleeping quarters, which, only a century ago, formed the suburbs of Kyiv: Teremky, Obolon, Nyvky, Sviatoshyn. The left bank is covered with yet another series of unvaried sleeping neighbourhoods – the Troieshchyna, Darnytsia, and Kharkivskyi neighbourhoods – linked to the right bank by several bridges.

After indulging in a bird's eye view of Kyiv, the clubber will delve into the vast city; they will measure the urban expanse with their own steps, so that it would feel closer and more relatable. As many other big cities, Kyiv is dependent on its public transport system with its major modes: a metro and the *marshrutka* (privately run bus service). Although the metro is unaffected by traffic congestion, it only has three lines, which means that many city districts remain far from metro stations. Therefore, inhabitants of these districts have to rely on ground transportation. *Marshrutka* is a commercial means of transportation with the ticket prices higher than those of public buses, trolleybuses, or trams; yet *marshrutkas* run more frequently and their routes connect city districts which otherwise have no direct connections. The main problem, with regards to the needs of clubbers, is that all means of transportation stop running at night. Thus, devotees of night entertainment have two options: to get a cab or, using the metro, to arrive with the last train and leave with the first.

Attentive observers can notice that in Kyiv, similarly to the majority of big cities around the world, a seemingly chaotic nightlife is in fact subordinate to certain rules; albeit popular or self-made ones rather than rules designated by the state. For example, an overwhelming majority of participants in nightlife are youngsters. The passengers of the last metro train (running around midnight) are a bright example of this, particularly if contrasted with a crowd on the first morning train (at 5:30am), which mainly consists of senior passengers. The routes of people's night flow also follow certain rules by essentially being concentrated in a few neighbourhoods; enclaves of club life in Kyiv. They affect the routes of cabs, which are the only available means of transport in the city after midnight.

    The public locales of Kyiv, where many general social activities take place, hardly differ from similar places in Western or other major East European cities. These locales are large central streets and squares, gardens, and parks, the hills on the right bank of the Dnipro, quays and compact spots next to metro entrances, as well as central plazas in every district of the city. These very places constitute the favourite walking routes of the Kyivans. Common in the Soviet times was the custom of going from remote neighbourhoods 'for a walk in the city centre' on weekends has remained widespread among the residents ever since. Consequently, during weekends, the central street Khreshchatyk and the Maidan square are crowded with multitudes of urban migrants from peripheral districts; it is in connection with this practice that the central street of the city is completely closed to traffic on weekends.

    What kind of practises can be observed in the public places of Kyiv? Streets, public gardens, transport stops, and underground passages –all of these are the locations of lively street trading, often unregulated, offering all manner of goods, from clothes and toys to cigarettes and sunflower seeds. Hence, there is little space left for other types of activities. A rather peculiar activity, widely practised in public places of Kyiv, is the consumption of alcoholic beverages. There is a specific prohibition stated in Paragraph 178 of the Ukrainian Administrative Violations Code, but many people do not obey this rule. Groups of people get together, sit on benches, stairs, or right on the grass, sipping on beer from bottles or plastic cups.

    For a visitor it is immediately noticeable that creative components constitute a rather insignificant part of urban practices. For instance, street artists can be encountered only at Maidan square and the underground passage next to it. Yet another place in Kyiv where creative practices do occur is Andriyivsky Descent, a street connecting the Upper and Lower Town, where artists and craftsmen put their works on display almost daily. Music as a constituent of creative practices is confined to an even more limited number of varieties. On the one hand, there is a 'sanctioned use' of public space for holding concerts as planned by the city authorities as well as open-air festivals on stages specifically assembled for that purpose. On the other hand, some public places are used by street musicians, though there aren't many of these locations. Besides the central Khreshchatyk street, street musicians often play in underground passages, Kontraktova Square (the central square of Podil), and the aforementioned Andriyivsky Descent. Kontraktova Square is also a spot for frequent improvised jam sessions and a hangout for companies with guitars. Street music in Kyiv is predominantly expressed in the form of live sound, whereas sound systems and dancing on the streets, save for occasional exceptions, are largely missing. Some local observers say that Kyivans are rather reserved by nature and do not easily relax and have fun in public spaces.

The 1960s: 'enculturating the masses' and counter-cultural enclaves

Following the 20th Congress of the Communist Party of the Soviet Union in 1956, when the critique was voiced regarding Stalin's 'cult of personality' and Stalinism was denounced as a 'distortion' of real socialism, in the Soviet Union a short period of mitigation of pressure and control, the period of so-called Khrushchev's 'Thaw', began. The expectations from the country's population were growing when in 1961, at the 22nd Party Congress, a new programme of the Party was announced, according to which, in just twenty years, the Soviet Union would 'have caught up with and overtaken' the USA in all fields. Then, party representatives expected the era of communism would dawn. Whereas the 20th Party Congress destroyed the former ideals held by the Soviet people, the 22nd provided them with a new goal. The 1960s pass under this very banner of utopian expectations, according to Petr Vajl' and Aleksandr Genis.[4]

Yet, already in 1962 and 1963 the boundaries of freedom in political and cultural development were clearly delineated: abstract art was criticised during the exhibition at the Manezh central exhibition hall in Moscow, and works of Boris Pasternak or Viktor Nekrasov, a poet from Kyiv, came under attack. Established in 1960 in Kyiv, the Club of the Creative Youth, whose activists organised creative hobby groups and soirées commemorating active figures of Ukrainian culture, was declared a 'national throng'.[5] Against the backdrop of these developments, music life in Kyiv saw a revival in the 1960s.

To get a better understanding of the situation in the cultural life of the country, it is necessary to recall the idiosyncrasies of the power-versus-state relationship in the Soviet Union. During the entire period that the Soviet Union existed, the authorities maintained a very active position, interfering with cultural processes and speaking on behalf of the people (i.e. the working class). The aim was, in the words of Jim McGuigan, 'cultivating' or 'enculturating the masses'.[6] From the 1920s and onwards, it was necessary to educate the masses in a cultural sense; to inculcate

[4] Petr Vajl' and Aleksandr Genis, *60-e Mir Sovetskogo Cheloveka* [60s World of the Soviet People] (Moscow: NLO, 1998), 12–13.

[5] Yaroslav Hrytsak, *Narys Istoriji Ukrajiny. Formuvannia Modernoji Ukrajins'koji Natsii XIX-XX St.* [Study of the History of Ukraine. Formation of Modern Ukrainian Nation in the 19th to 20th century] (Kyiv: Heneza, 2000), 282.

[6] Jim McGuigan, *Culture and the Public Sphere* (London and New York: Routledge, 1996), 53–59.

them not only with the specimens of 'serious' art, music, and literature, but also with the norms of 'cultural behaviour'. From here stems the constant monitoring and control of the sphere of culture as well as recommendations and censorship; the protection of the public from detrimental influences of 'bourgeois culture' of the 'rotting West'.

In the Soviet Union, referencing a 'club' in the context of music had an association with country clubs. These were the places that functioned, in larger villages throughout the country, with a purpose of 'bringing culture to the masses': this is where films were screened, lectures delivered, and music soirées with dancing took place. If somebody in a city would mention that he or she had been to a club, it implied that this person had just returned from a visit to his grandma or grandpa in the country, where she or he had also visited a local recreation centre. Besides this, there were youth art associations in cities. From here on, this text will mostly speak about club culture in a wide sense as proposed within the framework of the Ten Cities project: places – private and public, open and closed – where music plays and people are likely to dance.

After the 20th Party Congress the political situation became more favourable for youth culture, and overall control seemed to loosen its grip at least a little bit, the first music clubs were founded in Kyiv. One of them was the youth club MK-62 which was created in Kyiv at the beginning of the 1960s. It had eight interest sections, including a couple for music; mainly Jazz and Beat. It goes without saying that the club was controlled and chaired by representatives of the *Komsomol*, the youth organisations of the Party. The club was hosted in the building of the café Mriya [dream], which was located in the centre, opposite the Cathedral of St. Volodymyr. During 1967, nothing short of two Beat festivals were held here, which brought to light a considerable number of Ukrainian bands, including several from Kyiv, and attracted a huge crowd of visitors. Aleksey Kogan, a leading Ukrainian Jazz expert, recalls the café Mriya as the first Jazz club of Kyiv, where the city's Jazz musicians used to play in the 1960s.[7] The All-Union Big Beat Festival of 1968, which was hosted in the assembly hall of the Central Post Office, became a real apotheosis of Kyiv's club life of that time. Thirty Kyivan bands expressed their interest in participating.[8]

However, this seemingly free and active music life in Kyiv, and indeed in the whole country, did not last long. For a short time, the organisation of concerts was in the charge of public institutions of the so-called 'self-accounting' type. But already before the beginning of the 1970s, a state regulation that banned amateur bands was issued. From then on, these bands could only exist as part of certain establishments (philharmonics, theatres, and university houses of culture), or employed by the Ukrainian Concert and Republic Television organisations. According to contemporaries, there were some places where, at the beginning of the 1970s, one could enjoy decent performances by local bands, namely: the Kyiv Art Institute, which organised the best parties for students: the House of Culture at the Polytechnic Institute; and the Kyiv Young Theatre. Simultaneously, here and there emerged pockets of private music parties, where attendees not only listened to music that was officially prohibited in the Soviet Union, but also read and discussed forbidden literature. Yet it would be wrong to presume that all young people who

[7] Aleksey Kogan, in an interview (2013).

[8] Cf. Oleksandr Yevtushenko, *Lehendy Khymernoho Kraiu. Ukrajins'ka Rok-antolohia* [Legends of the Land of Chimera. Ukrainian Rock Anthology] (Kyiv: Aftohraf, 2004).

attended such parties and listened to Western pop music considered themselves anti-Communist or in any way opposing the regime. It was more a matter of taste than politics – they did not like the music that was allowed, it just so happened that the music they liked was branded as 'bourgeois'.

Restaurants were another place in Kyiv where one could experiment with alternative music performances in those times. They were tiny enclaves of countercultures of taste. If the public had not yet arrived but the musicians were already at the restaurant, they would stage an unofficial 'first part', during which they played, for instance, a Jazz programme.[9] This would happen in Kyiv's restaurants Stolychnyi [metropolitan] and Dubky [oaks]. These restaurants, like all others during the Soviet period, were state-owned with an appointed director at the head. The directors and administrators of Stolychnyi and Dubky were Jazz fans and thus did not object to the unofficial 'first part' of the music programme. This was not approved by the authorities, but it did not mean that these directors thereby consciously took an anti-Soviet stance.

The 1970s and 1980s: stagnation and *glasnost*

With the start of the 1970s, the cultural life of Kyiv deteriorated due to general conditions in the country. After the Soviet troops suppressed the protests of 1968 in Czechoslovakia, it became evident that any manifestation of free thinking within the country, even in a limited form as it occurred, would not be tolerated any longer. In the Ukrainian Soviet Socialist Republic, the party leadership changed: the moderate Petro Shelest, who had occupied the post of the First Secretary of the Central Committee of the Communist Party of Ukraine, was replaced by Volodymyr Scherbytsky, who opposed any expression of national idiosyncrasy. From this time onwards, a campaign against dissidence and 'Ukrainian bourgeois nationalism' was launched. It was under this very phrasing that the groups which had Ukrainian songs in their repertoire, like Enei or Berezen, were heavily criticised. Political and cultural life of the country entered the period of so-called 'Stagnation' or 'Neo-Stalinism'. This lasted through to 1985 and was marked by repression, russification, and with regards to music the pervasion of traditional pop music (*Estrada*).

In 1987, a policy of *glasnost* [transparency, and openness] was proclaimed in the country, meaning the mitigation of censorship and the lifting of taboos from some formerly prohibited subjects. Private entrepreneurism, in the form of cooperatives, was allowed. Whereas in political spheres the rhetoric of *perestroika* [restructuring] encountered many problems, in the sphere of culture – and, in particular, youth culture – a real boom came about. A torrent of information about new music tendencies rushed into the country from the West. It was at this very time that numerous supporters of 'non-formal movements' (i.e. subcultures) appeared. All of these developments made it possible for club culture, in a modern sense, to emerge in Kyiv.

Yet, despite the proclamation of *glasnost*, the leadership of the *Komsomol* youth organisation continued to control the city's and the country's music life during the second half of the 1980s. This required bands to get approval of repertoire and authorisation of lyrics from

[9] Aleksey Kogan, in an interview (2013).

a special section of *Komsomol* that was responsible for the youth's education as a condition for obtaining the permission for a public performance.

At the end of the 1980s, University Houses of Culture remained the main venues for the youth to get together and listen to music. The most popular of these locations were the Houses of Culture of the Kyiv Institute of Civil Aviation Engineers, the Institute of Foreign Languages, and the Kyiv Polytechnic Institute. Several music events, that attracted overwhelming numbers of visitors, were staged at the House of Culture of the Darnytsia Plant of Carriage Maintenance. In addition to these events being organised in winter, this plant was located in one of the most industrialised and, in terms of transportation, inconvenient places in the city. Nevertheless, these circumstances did not prevent a huge crowd of enthusiasts from participating in these events.[10] Some researchers believe that any association with Western provenance and culture in the Soviet Union was equal to resistance to the regime.[11] This position is contested by recent research; as Alexei Yurchak demonstrates, some young people of that time could easily accommodate within themselves both Communist ideology and a love for Rock music.[12] Yet again, listening to Rock music and attending Rock concerts at that time were not necessarily signs of outright opposition to the Communist regime.

Since the representatives of subcultures play a significant role in the formation of club culture, it is worthwhile to consider their presence in Kyiv. Up to the 1980s, not many subcultures appeared in the Soviet Union. The first of them, the *stiliagi*, a remote equivalent of teddy boys, emerged in the post-war time and gradually disappeared in the 1960s. For the representatives of this subculture the most distinctive element was an – according to Soviet standards – unusually bright clothing style.[13]

Hippies were another subculture present in the Soviet Union. Soviet hippies date their existence from the year 1967, when a group of Moscow hippies allegedly went out to Pushkin Square to protest against violence. In 1987, Soviet hippies celebrated their twentieth anniversary. But the existence of hippies only became noticeable in the 1980s.[14] The stylistic influences of hippie culture onto Kyiv's youth culture were perceptible in clothes, hairstyles, and the music that they listened to. However, in the Soviet times it was unsafe to be noticeable in a crowd of average conformist citizens, for it was perceived as some sort of protest. In the 1970s–80s, young men with long hair were often detained by the police for violation of public order. There were cases when long hair was cut by force in the police office. Even though Kyiv's hippie movement was not as active and visible as that of the smaller city of Lviv in western Ukraine,[15] there were also places of regular gatherings for groups of local hippies and for those from other towns. In summer, hippies gathered at the so-called Bermuda triangle, a triangle park at Kyiv's Lvivska Square, where they would sit around on benches and might play guitar and sing.

Another popular place for gatherings was (and still is) the so-called 'Tube', an underground passage under Zhovtneva Square (today the Maidan square).[16] Since clubs did not exist at the time, numerous cafés in the city centre continued to host underground get-togethers: café Morozyvo opposite the Besarabskyi Market, BeZhe on Velyka

[10] Tatyana Yezhova, in an interview (2013).

[11] Caroline Humphrey, 'Creating Culture of Disillusionment', in Daniel Miller (ed.), *Words Apart: Modernity Through the Prism of the Local* (London and New York: Routledge, 1995), 57.

[12] Alexei Yurchak, 'Soviet Hegemony of Form: Everything Was Forever, Until It Was No More', *Comparative Studies in Society and History*, vol. 45, no. 3, (July 2003), 480–510.

[13] For more on the *stiliagi* see Juliane Fürst, *Stalin's Last Generation. Soviet Post-War Youth and the Emergence of Mature Socialism* (Oxford: Oxford University Press, 2010), 200–249.

[14] Tatyana Shchepanskaya, *Sistema: Teksty I Struktura Subkul'tury* [The System: texts and structure of the subculture] (Moscow: OGI, 2004), 39–40.

[15] For example, the 'Manifesto of the hippies of the USSR' was initiated and written in Lviv in 1987.

[16] Andrij Manchuk and Nikolaj Polischuk, 'Disidenty Pozavcherashniego Dnia [The Dissidents of the Day Before]', *Gazeta po-kievski*, 4 June 2007.

Zhytomyrska street, Zustrich on Prorizna street, Kava po-skhidnomu, Kobza, Paryzh, and Rosijskyi chai opposite the Lenin Museum. Cafés were the places of more or less regular meetings, where one could not only have a cup of tea or coffee, but also socialise in the circle of like-minded people, and even criticise the regime, which only became possible at the end of the 1980s.

The involvement in the formation of club culture at the end of the 1980s, through the participation in Rock parties organised in various Houses of Culture, provided an opportunity to declare one's aesthetic stance. This often appeared to be rather aggressive, and certainly different from the position upheld by the majority of the population, that was brought up within the confines of Soviet ideology. Speaking about idiosyncrasies of music subcultures, Sarah Thornton emphasises the fact that they are able to destroy many differences such as gender, sex, class, and race – with the exception of one: age difference. Music is possibly a chief defining feature of youth subcultures, whereas clubbing, especially at night time, is a mode of resistance to parental control; a form of liberation from the 'tyranny of home'.[17] It is at the end of the 1980s and the beginning of the 1990s that this element of protest against the ideology and tastes of the parents' generation was most conspicuously manifested. For the first time, young people got an opportunity to openly declare their 'non-formal' music preferences and to display their aesthetic position through their outward appearance; many of them did it on purpose, in order to 'annoy the parents'.[18]

While Rock music can be regarded as the most influential trend for forming a new post-Soviet generation, the end of the 1980s to the beginning of the 1990s can be considered a real turning point in creation of Kyiv's club culture. Writing about clubs, Birgit Beumers, author of the book *Pop Culture Russia!*, points out that in Russia many clubs became a logical continuation of the underground Rock and Jazz movements of the late 1980s.[19] Respectively, the next section will consider the phenomenon of Kyiv's Rock clubs and new subcultures, as well as their oppositional potential at that period in more detail.

The 1990s: rock clubs and a new subculture

Rock music was known to the residents of Kyiv long before the end of the 1980s. There were also some local bands that played music which could be qualified as Rock. Yet it was not until 1986 that Rock music was 'allowed' – though reluctantly – in the country. One of the directives issued at the 27th Congress of the Communist Party entrusted work with the youth to the *Komsomol* organisation. It was also then that Rock music was acknowledged to be an important tool of exercising influence on the youth. Thus, the leadership of the *Komsomol* found itself in an uneasy situation, which is described ironically by Tatyana Yezhova, a notable figure in the popularisation of Rock music in Kyiv in 1980s:

> *On the one hand, they are obliged to give a concert, because they work with the youth, but on the other hand, they are afraid, since nobody knows what can transpire at this concert: the people are seemingly non-Soviet and their songs are non-Soviet, as well as everything looks like non-Soviet. Yet it is necessary to work with the youth, and there is no escape.*[20]

[17]
Cf. Thornton, *Club Cultures: Music, Media and Subcultural Capital* (see n. 2), 15–18.

[18]
Mikhail Dziuba, in an interview (2013).

[19]
Birgit Beumers, *Pop Culture Russia! Media, Art and Lifestyle* (Santa Barbara: ABC-Clio, 2005), 337–338.

[20]
Tatyana Yezhova, in an interview (2013).

It was still implied that a club was a certain art association under control of the *Komsomol* organisation. Belonging to the music organisation named Rock Club allowed musicians to obtain a permit for performance with fewer problems.[21] The Rock Club was an extremely formalised association. A necessary pre-condition for enrolment was filling out an application form, as well as its participants paying a membership fees. Every song, before it could be granted permission to be performed anywhere in public, had to be authorised and receive a censorship permit, which guaranteed that the lyrics of the song had nothing seditious. Regardless of the pronounced Soviet-ness of this organisation, musicians aspired to become part of the Rock Club. Alexanders Kushnir, the author of the book *Golden Underground*, characterised the Rock Club in the following way:

> *Despite a local stir around first actions, they were of little worth: with a rare exception, about fifteen bands drew on dated Hard Rock ... and diluted Glam ... with devastating texts about Perestroika. Kollezhskyi asessor, being the odd one out in the otherwise invariant array, was continuously badmouthed on the pages of Komsomol press and, in this particular context, looked like an outlandish creature.*[22]

The organisation of performances and Rock festivals, followed by the nomination of the 'best band', constituted another direction of the Rock Club activities. Such a festival was staged to celebrate the first anniversary of the Rock Club. An opinion poll was conducted among the spectators and the band VV was acknowledged to be the best. Since VV had only recently joined the Rock Club and became the winner without having given any concert organised by the association – which was against the rules – they shared the first place with the 'veteran' of the Rock Club, a Trash Rock band called Adem.[23]

This association could not have lasted much longer on such heavily formalised grounds. The second year witnessed a rift between participating groups. Some bands left the Rock Club and created a new alliance named Rock-artil. The main venue for music performances, given to the bands belonging to the Rock-artil association in 1988, became the Concert and Dance Hall of Golosiyivsky Park. Taking into consideration the rupture with the Rock Club, this looked virtually symbolic, as the new place was located on the opposite end of Kyiv, with respect to the Rock Club's House of Culture, *Bolshevik*.

The creation of music associations that organised music events in Kyiv was accompanied by some phenomena, which shaped the music community of the young people. Firstly, independent – meaning self-published – music magazines appeared. It seems that *Guchnomovets'*, which was published between 1988 and 1991, was the most interesting project of the time. Apart from overviews of music events taking place in Kyiv, next to achievements of the Rock-artil association as well as interviews, the magazine published satirical sketches and critical articles and reviews. Secondly, the so-called *Balka* gained momentum: a weekly gathering of vendors (back then, called 'speculators') of 'music goods' such as vinyl records, CDs, badges, posters, and so on. At the end of the 1980s the *Balka* gatherings did not have a permanent place and, from time to time, became a target of police raids. Nevertheless, their events were a place

---

[21] Ibid.

[22] Alexander Kushnir, *Zolotoie Podpol'ie. Polnaia Illiustrirovannaia Antologia Rok-samizdata 1967–1994* [Golden Underground. Illustrated Anthology of Rock-samizdat 1967–1994] (Nizhnij Novgorod: Dekom, 1994), 46 [translated].

[23] Tatyana Yezhova, in an interview (2013).

to socialise for Kyivan rockers and representatives of youth subcultures. Here they could not only find sought after 'music goods', but also communicate with those who shared their music interests.

All these processes – the appearance of new spaces where music was played, the creation of music publications, and the establishment of a regular location for weekly gatherings of Kyiv's music community – sparked the emergence of a distinctive public sphere, an open community that gained an opportunity to freely express its critical opinions regarding music, yet not limited to it. By that time state control and censorship got weaker. It became easier for cultural nonconformists to peacefully demonstrate and publicly express their position, without fear of being persecuted or detained by state security or police – though such incidents were not unheard of. It is worth noting that the venues of music events at the end of the 1980s and the beginning of the 1990s were still considered potentially dangerous by the authorities. They sometimes became places of conflict with those whom the *neformaly* [subculture groups] called 'children of proletarians'. The latter attended Rock events with a specific intent of deliberately initiating a fight with 'the hairy'. To stop disorder, the administration of the establishment that hosted the event sometimes, unexpectedly, switched off the lights in the building.[24]

—

At the beginning of the 1990s, when Kyiv became the capital of the now independent Ukraine, the formation of music clubs in a traditional sense was underway. Until then, music events had been organised here and there, without any regularity. The demand for music events was high, contrary to what was offered. It did not really matter to people what band or musician was playing, or where – it sufficed to mention that somewhere they would play Rock music (no matter what kind of Rock) to attract a crowd. Following the high demand, music clubs as places of regular gatherings (concerts, festivals, and parties) started to appear. At the same time, the interested public expressed quite peculiar proposals as to the functioning of Rock clubs in Kyiv. Apparently, in their proposals, people departed from a Soviet vision of club, which was meant to bring 'light of knowledge' to the masses. We can read an example of such a proposal on the pages of the newspaper *Vechirnij Kyiv* [Kyiv by night] from 26 October 1988, authored by a certain V. Ostapenko. He first complains about the general lack of Rock education of the population, being convinced of this by the festival Zirky roku-88 [Stars of Rock 1988], which was held at a football stadium:

> *I went there in the hope to hear Rock, but it turned out that it was a festival of Soviet Punk Rock, moreover, not of the best quality. If it would have been possible to find out from posters beforehand that there would be Punk Rock bands on tour, I would not have gone there. I do not like Punk Rock… To improve the music culture of the youth, it is necessary to provide a highly professional level of enlightenment and provision of information, so that rockers would distinguish the very 'Hard Rock' from 'Punk Rock', or 'Heavy Metal' from 'Baroque Rock' and 'Latin Rock'.*[25]

[24] Tatyana Yezhova, in an interview (2013).

[25] V. Ostapenko, 'Vospityvat' Muzykal'nuiu Kul'turu [To Educate in Music Culture]', *Vechirnij Kyiv* [Kyiv by night]', 26 October 1988 [translated].

After these complaints, Mr. Ostapenko suggests organising a Rock club, where members would meet up on a weekly or fortnightly basis. Only 'true lovers and admirers of Rock music' would be allowed to join as members, their applications scrutinised through 'exclusively music and moral' questions to help single out 'real rockers'. Suggestions concerning the underpinnings of club operations sounded very Soviet-like:

At every meeting, a lector (club member) who has a deep knowledge of a particular area of Rock delivers a lecture about music of a certain band or about some music trend, which is accompanied by a demonstration of video clips, slides, and playing records of songs. At the end of his lecture, club members make their contributions to the topic … After the discussion, lovers of Rock music socialize, exchange cassettes, badges, posters, photographs – all of which lasts for an hour to an hour and a half. The council of the club maintains a liaison with the Komsomol, commerce, warehouses. Club members in turn according to the order of their tickets are provided with recordable cassettes, rare vinyl records, photographs, and posters.[26]

As we can see, the Soviet vision of clubs still remained deeply rooted in the heads of some people, who could not imagine them without a link to the *Komsomol* or devoid of any association with enlightenment, morality, as well as fair distribution of scarce material benefits. It becomes clear from this passage that all cultural processes, including clubs, were thought of in the framework of the aforementioned discourse of 'enculturating the masses'.

Against the backdrop of these concepts regarding the places where 'real rockers' could socialise, there were clubs in Kyiv that started functioning on a permanent basis – they were no longer associations of musicians, but places open to the general public. For instance, at the House of Culture, Burevisnyk, on the left bank of the river Dnipro, a small rehearsal hall was transformed into a place for weekly performances of young bands and a hangout for Rock music get-togethers. Visitors had to pay an entrance fee. Another innovation was the setting up of tables, with the possibility of having a cup of coffee. There was no permission to sell alcohol in these places yet. Intonatsii [intonations] became the first Rock club, according to traditional concepts of such a venue. It developed out of a rehearsal spot at one of the dormitories of the Kyiv Polytechnic Institute. After some time, the club was renamed and became known as Barvy [colours].[27] In spite of the building's limited size and capacity, and its bad acoustics, music events have regularly been held there since the beginning of the 1990s. To give a music performance in Barvy was an aspiration of many new bands. Thus, from the beginning of the 1990s, Rock clubs found their niche in Kyiv's nightlife, and, already during the 1990s, a row of rock clubs with daily programmes and their own public sprung up. In the same period, Rock music in independent Ukraine ceased to be associated with counterculture and the expression of opposition, and Rock clubs were increasingly marginalised.

Generally speaking, during the second half of the 1980s, a rather unusual process could be observed in the Soviet Union: youth subcultures from different countries created a kind of superstructure, a so-called 'system',

[26] Ibid., emphasis by Kateryna Dysa.
[27] Mikhail Dziuba, in an interview (2013).

with common worldviews, slang, attributes, forms of communication, organisation of spaces, lifestyles, etc.[28] Most significant were the subcultures and music styles of such as Hippies, Punk, Heavy Metal, Indie Rock, and Reggae. Kyiv's metallists [Heavy Metal fans] were one of the most active subculture groups present both at concert venues and in the public sphere. In the same period of the 1980s and beginning of the 1990s, Heavy Metal generally flourished not only in the former Soviet Union, but also in other parts of the world. Heavy Metal fans were quite prominent in the history of Kyiv's club culture development; they were most likely to be the most active participants in music events of Kyiv in this period. To be a metallist meant to challenge social norms. The music they listened to was a challenge to order; moreover, metallists raised attention by their appearance: men with long hair, men and women in black shabby clothes with demonic or even satanic symbols, the latter hand in hand with their interest in magic and occultism. At the end of the 1980s, some occult books, which had been banned before, were re-published. A metallist could now become proud owner of three-volume *Practical Magic* by Papus.[29]

Since there were almost no regular music clubs at the beginning of the 1990s, metallists organised their club life in several ways. Beginners could stage a performance at smaller venues (e.g. school concerts, regional clubs), whereas groups that were already known had the possibility to play on the city's bigger stages, for example the above-mentioned Houses of Culture of various universities. A permanent hangout of Trash Metal fans at the Botanical Gardens next to the Universytet metro station was a more informal way to organise club life. These get-togethers were regularly attended by five to fifty people.[30] At these gatherings, alcohol facilitated socialising—even though at that time, as already mentioned, alcohol was not sold at music events or the few existing clubs, and one was not allowed to bring it to concerts. The attending Metal fans drank primarily beer; strong alcohol was avoided. Sometimes, representatives of other subcultures, for instance Punks, who smashed empty bottles, came to these gatherings. The Trash Metal fans were offended by this, since bottles could be returned, and more beer could be bought for the return fee. As with any other informal group, metallists could get into trouble: occasionally they became the target of assaults by so-called *gopnyky* (comparable to rednecks or lads), who were triggered by the outward appearance of metal fans.

The 2000s: night economics and a rising entertainment industry

Since the end of the 1990s, the urban space of Kyiv, which until then had had small enclaves of entertainment, has been undergoing a re-branding. The former, mostly improvised enclaves of entertainment started to shift towards the promotion of professional night economics. The development of night economics has been perceived, in many cities, as part of the respective city's revival process, connected with profits as well as the creation of an individual marketing image; nevertheless, the development of places of night entertainment has often been accompanied by problems and scandals, which are also reflected in the construction of the city's image.[31]

[28] Cf. Shchepanskaya, *Sistema* (see n. 14).

[29] Mikhail Dziuba, in an interview (2013).

[30] Ibid.

[31] Paul Chatterton and Robert Hollands, *Urban Nightscapes* (London: Routledge, 2003), 2–3.

Readers should bear in mind that the development of a real nightlife in Kyiv, similar to other cities of the former Soviet Union, was a fairly new phenomenon. It was not until after the disintegration of the Soviet Union, at the beginning of the 1990s, that the societies of those states which were newly formed on its ruins started adopting the so-called 'consumer culture'. Interestingly, this happened at the same time that the consumerist society in the West was beginning to crack and acknowledge negative consequences of consumerism.[32] It was precisely around this time during the 1990s in Kyiv as well as in other large cities of the former Soviet Union, that a series of social and economic mechanisms began to unfold that heralded the creation of a new night regime of city life. In an article about the industry of nightlife in the cities of Russia, Aleksej Penzin identifies these processes: the introduction of night lighting that included, among others, shop windows, advertisements, street illumination; the establishment of businesses providing continuous services, such as nonstop supermarkets, and switching television channels to the mode of around-the-clock broadcasting; and finally, the formation of fashionable young clientele that embraced nightlife styles.[33]

Since the end of 1990s the music club industry in Kyiv started to develop quite dynamically. By the mid-2010s the number of clubs in Kyiv could be estimated between seventy and slightly more than one hundred – which is not a significant figure for a big city. Clubs were dispersed almost all over the city. However, the highest concentration was (and still is) in the central part. This is quite understandable, as it is by far easiest to get to the centre from any other part of Kyiv. In the period of the 1990s and early 2000s dozens of both smaller clubs, mostly located in basements, and large high-status clubs covering extensive areas sprouted in the city centre and near the central area of Podil. Due to their limited space, the smaller clubs were not able to host large parties. They were mostly located in underground places with narrow, elongated rooms that could hardly accommodate the clientele that was in the mood for dancing. Apart from this, nearly all of these smaller clubs also functioned as restaurants and pubs – hence, the major part of their space, or at least half of it, was allocated to tables and chairs for visitors. Consequently, more often than not, the music that was played in these clubs was meant for listening rather than dancing. The prime examples for this were 44 and Divan.

In contrast to these underground venues, huge, fashionable, and ostentatious clubs for nouveau riches began to appear in the late-1990s to early-2000s. They did not have any spatial problems, besides large dance floors, they also had lounges, restaurants, and summer terraces. The epitome of such a club was the D'Lux. This posh kind of club attracted (and many of them, still do) a wealthy audience, especially members of the so called 'gilded youth'. They did so, not so much by playing specific music genres or running quality parties, but by simply maintaining a status of 'not for everyone', for 'the chosen few'. As one of my respondents mentioned in her interview: 'Some of my acquaintances wouldn't agree to go to any other place in the city, accept for this, because it's not that prestigious, even though they play some Russian pop music in that "prestigious" club!'[34]

Next to the city centre, the top location for night clubs include two more districts in the city, where by the mid-2010s the concentration of clubs

[32] For more on consumer culture see: Mike Featherstone, *Consumer Culture and Postmodernism* (Los Angeles: Sage Publications, 2007).
[33] Aleksej Penzin, 'Industria Nochi [Industry of the night]', '*Kriticheskaia massa* [Critical Mass]', no. 2, 2004, <http://magazines.russ.ru/km/2004/2/pen14-pr.html> accessed 19 June 2013.
[34] Yulia Nazarenko and Maria Chorna, in an interview with the author (2017).

was similarly high: first the neighbourhood near the Polytechnic Institute and the Shuliavska metro stations, and second, the city quarter around the Lybidska and Holosiyivska metro stations. This is where dormitories of the Polytechnic Institute and the Taras Shevchenko University, Kyiv's two major universities, are located. These areas became home to large clubs with fair prices that attracted students from other institutions as well. Saxon and Forsage were the most popular among students. Habitués of these clubs described the central clubs as 'glamorous' and 'ostentatious', explaining that their favourite clubs had everything necessary for hanging out—several dance floors, a cheerful atmosphere, good music, and all at affordable prices. Experienced clubbers of Kyiv recount that, while they were students, they got into clubbing by visiting nothing else than these large students' clubs—yet since then they have outgrown them.[35]

Experienced clubbers recall that some of the most interesting and fanciful parties of the late 1990s took place in the Al Capone club which was located in the cinema theatre Zhovten. There, party organisers invited some of the most interesting DJs of that time, and organised unusual theme events. For some time in the 2000s, the Sound Planet was considered, by experts, to be the club with the best sound and the most interesting events.[36] Somewhat apart from the rest were two underground clubs of Kyiv: Xlib and Cinema Club. Many clubbers recall these places as 'legendary', with Xlib they relate the birth of the Kyiv underground culture in 2008–2009; people said that it was important for them to attend most of the music events going on there and get their friends involved.[37] Kyiv's club life was roaring, smaller and bigger clubs in all parts of the city flourished, people with all kinds of taste in music could find something of their liking, and it seemed that it would go on like this, if not forever, then for a very long time indeed. Then came the uneasy fall of 2013.

2013 until the present: the rupture of *Maidan* and its aftermath

The first part of this text was finished in the Summer of 2013 when most of the clubs mentioned in the previous subchapter, were still happily functioning and Kyiv clubbers lived carelessly and light-heartedly. Then, by the end of that year, the situation in the country and especially in Kyiv changed dramatically. At the end of November 2013, the president of Ukraine, Viktor Yanukovych, was to sign an Association Agreement between Ukraine and the European Union. However, along with his government, he suspended this decision at the very last moment for then unclear reasons (as it came out later, the suspension was due to political and economic pressure from the Russian president). The Ukrainian civil society immediately responded to this by initiating protest demonstrations on the night of 21 November 2013. The central square of Kyiv, Maidan Nezalezhnosti, became the main site for the civil protests and opposition gatherings for the next three months—that is why the whole event was ultimately nicknamed *Maidan*. Up until 30 November, the protest was peaceful. In the last couple of days students from several leading universities of Kyiv became the main moving force behind the *Maidan* protests. This later turned out to be the most optimistic and cheerful time of the

35
Kateryna Sosnina, in an interview (2013).
36
N.N., 'Klubnaia Zhizn' Kieva: Art-Direktor Stas Tvi o Tusovkakh [Club Life of Kyiv: the Art-Director Stas Tvi About Hangouts]', *BZh*, 26 December 2016, <http://bzh.life/posts/lyudi-stas-tvi> accessed 25 March 2017.
37
N.N., 'Klubnaia Zhizn' Kieva–Istorii o Klubnoj Zhizni: Zhurnalist Mark Pollok o Tusovkakh Kieva [Club Life of Kyiv–Stories About Club Life: Journalist Mark Pollok About Kyiv Hangouts]', *BZh*, 12 December 2016, <http://bzh.life/posts/lyudi-pollok> accessed 25 March 2017.

whole series of events. Right from the start, music was an integral part of the protests. Various groups and individual performers were playing and singing, while the crowds were responding by singing along, dancing, and jumping.

The mood of the whole event changed radically after police forces had severely beaten on young people who had stayed on *Maidan* on the night of 29–30 November 2013. From then on, the protests grew in numbers (sometimes up to 400,000–800,000 protesters in Kyiv); the demands of the protestors also changed. Now the demonstrations were not just pro-European, they became anti-governmental and anti-corruption, demanding that the president and his government resign and to punish those who were guilty of the violence that had occurred. Music did not disappear from the *Maidan*. From that time on it became a necessary part of the protests. Several stages were constructed upon which politicians, civil activists, and musicians were addressing the protesters. Music was vital for several reasons. First, with the temperature being below zero, it was music that charged protesters with energy, especially at night-time. Second, another essential function was to cheer up and unite people when they were overwhelmed and tired after days of confrontation with governmental forces at the time of violent escalation.

You could hear music in many locations and in many forms. Two stages (big and small) provided opportunities for renowned performers, as well as for beginners, to join in and share their music and singing with the protesters. They all performed for free. The biggest and most memorable music event was the concert of the famous Ukrainian group Okean El'zy on 14 December, which brought around 100,000 people to Maidan. It was a powerful and beautiful scene when all those people sang with their cell-phones' flashlights on.

Young performers were mostly invited to play at night. One of them was Lesyk Yakymchuk, then a student of the National University of Kyiv-Mohyla Academy and a musician just starting out. He recalled that there was a need for music for the whole period of Maidan. Even in the darkest days of late January and through to February, when people were killed, protesters needed music to help them move through this ordeal. He stated that during those performances it was senseless to play your original music; people wanted something recognisable, something they all knew and could join in sing along to. The musician was both surprised and inspired by how easily people reacted to music – as a practising performer he was sure that Kyiv's public was not easy to shake up.[38]

People recalled that you could hear music in various locations all over Maidan: some people brought guitars with them; others were just singing in groups. Already in December of that year, several pianos appeared on the central streets of Kyiv near Maidan. At least one of them (located in front of the house of Kyiv city administration) was used most of the time and many people gathered around it. Another piano was further away from the protest location and closer to the site of governmental forces base, on Bankova street. If you decided to play there it was less about being heard by people but rather to demonstrate your political position.[39] There was one more type of rhythmic sound that people could hear on the central streets of Kyiv in those days: the monotonous and loud sound of stone paving being picked out from the ground and knocked; it was probably very similar to the sounds one can hear in a

[38] Lesyk Yakymchuk, in an interview (2017).
[39] Ibid.

quarry. These stone cubes were used as weapons by protesters at the times of violent escalation.

Needless to say, during those months Kyiv's club life became very languid if there was any. Although sometimes you could get the illusion, especially if you moved away from the centre of the city, that Kyiv lived a normal life: most of the people went to work, children attended school, and some people relaxed in bars, restaurants, and clubs, as if nothing was going on. Some clubs that were directly on the Maidan square or nearby had to shut down temporarily, some of them, like the gay club Pomada [Lipstick], ultimately had to change their location.

After the mass killings of Maidan protesters on 20–21 February 2014, the regime collapsed, and Viktor Yanukovych secretly ran away from the country. But the problems for Ukraine and its people did not end with that. From late-February through to April, Russia annexed and occupied the Crimea peninsula. Russia sent out its forces to destabilise the situation and start a war in Ukraine's Donetsk and Luhansk regions. It is easy to conceive that, under such circumstances, most of the people in Ukraine were not in the mood for hanging out. In addition to all these disasters, in 2014 an economic crisis struck the country. This was more than some of the clubs – and even the whole capital city – could stand. In the next few years some of the clubbers' favourite sites shut down, among them the legendary Xlib, as well as one of the oldest Rock clubs, 44, and the Rock and Jazz favourite, Divan.

However, by early 2017, the situation for Kyiv's clubs was not altogether that sad anymore. Huge luxury clubs such as the aforementioned D'Lux, as well as Arena, Crystal Hall, and others fully recovered and now organise parties and performances almost daily. Kyiv Podil area became home for the clubbers' new favourite sites for underground parties, the club Closer, which is not actually situated that far from the former Xlib location. At the time of writing, Closer and its open-air site Lesnoy prichal bring the most interesting foreign DJs and performers to Kyiv.[40] In the last couple of years these and some other initiatives such as Skhema witnessed the revival of underground Rave culture in Kyiv.[41] Here, young people hang out, relax from the still rather depressing reality, experiment with drugs, and even try to reconceptualise the meaning of these drugs.[42]

Summary

To sum up, music clubs constitute a rather new phenomenon for Kyiv. Clubs, in a conventional sense, only appeared in the city at the beginning of the 1990s. Yet, with a closer study of this phenomenon, it becomes clear that club culture existed in the city well before the 1990s, evolving around music events that had been organised since the 1960s, in public places such as Houses of Culture of educational institutions, factories, and other establishments. The end of the 1980s became a turning point – along with a change in political course, the experience of music gatherings in the life of the youth, in particular youth subcultures, became more intense. Rock clubs used to be most successful and widespread in Kyiv. During the 1990s, following development of a professional night industry, a great number of music clubs emerged in the city

[40] N.N., 'Klubnaia Zhizn' Kieva [Club Life of Kyiv]', (see n. 37).
[41] For more information about the rebirth of underground Rave, see: Tom Ivin, 'Exploring Ukraine's Underground Rave Revolution', *YouTube*, 31 May 2016, <https://youtu.be/P4G1r2u8m9g> accessed on 27 March 2017.
[42] Yulia Nazarenko and Maria Chorna, in an interview with the author (2017).

which satisfied nearly every musical taste. The Maidan events of 2013 and 2014 became the hallmarks of club cultures and the music life of Kyiv that turned public and politically essential. Although the post-Maidan crisis struck some of the clubs rather painfully, the situation now gradually improves.

Bibliography

Beumers, Birgit, *Pop Culture Russia! Media, Art and Lifestyle* (Santa Barbara: ABC-Clio, 2005).
Chatterton, Paul, and Hollands, Robert, *Urban Nightscapes* (London: Routledge, 2003).
De Certeau, Michel, *The Practice of Everyday Life* (Berkeley: University of California Press, 1984).
Fürst, Juliane, *Stalin's Last Generation. Soviet Post-War Youth and the Emergence of Mature Socialism* (Oxford: Oxford University Press, 2010).
Hrytsak, Yaroslav, *Narys Istoriji Ukrajiny. Formuvannia Modernoji Ukrajins'koji Natsii XIX-XX St.* [Study of the History of Ukraine. Formation of Modern Ukrainian Nation in the 19th to 20th century] (Kyiv: Heneza, 2000).
Humphrey, Caroline, 'Creating Culture of Disillusionment', in Daniel Miller (ed.), *Words Apart: Modernity Through The Prism Of The Local* (London and New York: Routledge, 1995).
Kushnir, Alexander, *Zolotoie Podpol'ie. Polnaia Illiustrirovannaia Antologia Rok-samizdata 1967–1994* [Golden Underground. Illustrated Anthology of Rock-samizdat 1967–1994] (Nizhnij Novgorod: Dekom, 1994).
McGuigan, Jim, *Culture and the Public Sphere* (London and New York: Routledge, 1996).
N.N., 'Klubnaia Zhizn' Kieva: Art-Direktor Stas Tvi o Tusovkakh [Club Life of Kyiv: the Art-Director Stas Tvi About Hangouts]', *BZh*, 26 December 2016, <http://bzh.life/posts/lyudi-stas-tvi> accessed 25 March 2017.
N.N., 'Klubnaia Zhizn' Kieva–Istorii o Klubnoj Zhizni: Zhurnalist Mark Pollok o Tusovkakh Kieva [Club Life of Kyiv–Stories About Club Life: Journalist Mark Pollok About Kyiv Hangouts]', *BZh*, 12 December 2016, <http://bzh.life/posts/lyudi-pollok> accessed 25 March 2017.
Shchepanskaya, Tatyana, *Sistema: Teksty I Struktura Subkul'tury* [The System: Texts and Structure of the Subculture] (Moscow: OGI, 2004).
Thornton, Sarah, *Club Cultures: Music, Media and Subcultural Capital* (Middletown, CT: Wesleyan University Press, 1996).
Vajl', Petr and Genis, Aleksandr: *60-e Mir Sovetskogo Cheloveka* [60s World of the Soviet People] (Moscow: New Literary Observer, 1998).
Yevtushenko, Oleksandr, *Lehendy Khymernoho Kraiu. Ukrajins'ka Rok-antolohia* [Legends of the Land of Chimera. Ukrainian Rock anthology] (Kyiv: Aftohraf, 2004).
Yurchak, Alexei, 'Soviet Hegemony of Form: Everything Was Forever, Until It Was No More', *Comparative Studies in Society and History*, vol. 45, no. 3, (July 2003).

JOHANNESBURG

MUSIC/SPACES
Dangerous Combinations and Skeem Sam Foundations
The Most Beautiful Black City in Africa?
Rangoato Hlasane
▶ P.193

SPACES/POLITICS
Imaginary Republics
Dancing after Dark in Johannesburg
Sean O'Toole
▶ P.215

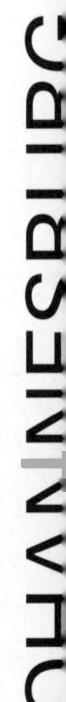

The Jazzolomos: Jacob 'Mzala' Lepers (bass), Sol 'Beegeepee' Klaaste (piano) and Benni 'Gwigwi' Mrwebi (alto sax), Johannesburg, 1953, photo: Jürgen Schadeberg

DRUM Magazine, Johannesburg, February 1955, photo: Jürgen Schadeberg

Sol Rachilo, actor, Johannesburg, 1958, photo: Jürgen Schadeberg

Todd Matshikiza, *Drum* journalist, composer and jazz piano player, Johannesburg, c. 1955, photo: Jürgen Schadeberg

DRUM Magazine, Johannesburg, May 1955, photo: Jürgen Schadeberg

Sophiatown Street, Johannesburg, 1950's, photo: Jürgen Schadeberg

Township Shuffle, Sophiatown, Johannesburg, 1955, photo: Jürgen Schadeberg

Miriam Makeba, Johannesburg, 1955, photo: Jürgen Schadeberg

Graffiti in Sophiatown, Johannesburg, 1955, photo: Jürgen Schadeberg

Sophiatown demolished, Johannesburg, 1959, photo: Jürgen Schadeberg

Dangerous Combinations and Skeem Sam Foundations – The Most Beautiful Black City in Africa?

Rangoato Hlasane

Almost a decade after South Africa's transition to democratic governance, the music trio Mafikizolo monumentalised their country's historical Kwela music genre in a song titled 'Kwela' (2003). As in the song, the accompanying music video features veteran trumpeter Hugh Masekela. He is shown entering a fictional prison cell, where he encounters the original three members of Mafikizolo.[1] The video is a feast of archival material alongside a site-specific intergenerational dialogue. Shot at Constitution Hill, the clip presents a historical re-enactment of random arrests for 'dompas' violations – the infamous reference book used to regulate and control movement of 'black' people within urban centres of South Africa. In Mafikizolo's video we experience it all: the sonic textures of the time, anecdotes of encounters with security police, the city under construction, protests in front of the Great Hall at Wits University, burning tyres on the street, and soldier drills in symmetrical formation.

In this video we see the subversive role, place, and agency for song and dance in South African society. Throughout the re-enactment of mug shots and questioning, all the poses and moves point to the *Pantsula* dance practise. Not that of gangsterism, evident in narratives such as in the film *Mapantsula* (1988), but that of dance, dress, and determination. In a single moment of intergenerational dialogue and dance between the band and Masekela, power is suspended when the police on duty opens the cell door to his bewilderment, being faced with a challenging song and dance, and closing it behind him to the sounds of 'Ek is die Baas' [I am the boss].

In this essay I follow the songs people dance/d to in Johannesburg, responding to where they go, have been, and take me. I treat them as living spirits to listen to and speak to.[2] I use the idea of place with the subjectivity of having been there physically, or through memories of other people. Given that the development of the music industry in Johannesburg mirrors migration across South Africa, the region and the continent, this text follows these routes, pushing and pulling, closing and opening like fragments of stories that follow people's movement across the dispossessed land. As writing about music is always late – due to the rapid changes as well as the anti-chronological character of the subject of music – the fragmented and cyclic nature of this text attempts to generatively counter this inevitable catch 22. In a sense, it befits the transient nature that defines the instability of the dispossessed and the landless who use song to monumentalise erased landscapes.

The earliest recording of South African music took place in London in 1931, organised by Brunswick Gramophone House.[3] South Africa's first record company was established in 1933 by Eric Gallo.[4] Before then, songs were a social, political, and spiritual accompaniment to work, weddings, initiation, spiritual rituals, and funerals – like a shadow that is always there, a reflection of one's spirit. Music is uncontainable. But in 1960 apartheid, authorities placed a ban on Jazz bands – particularly those that were racially mixed, but most definitely black Jazz bands as well – from playing at inner city clubs of Johannesburg. A decade earlier, the film *The Pennywhistle Blues/The Magic Garden* (1951) showed a black boy playing a pennywhistle in the street for the

---

1   Tebogo Madingoane, Nhlanhla Nciza, and Theo Kgosinkwe.
2   If you can, have your South African music catalogue/playlist on hand, or open up your tab for *YouTube*. This is a long-play essay: repetitious and anti-chronological.
3   Cf. Christopher Ballantine, *Marabi Nights – Jazz, 'Race' and Society in early Apartheid South Africa* (Scottsville: University of KwaZulu Natal Press, 2012).
4   Cf. Sello Galane, *The Music of Philip Tabane – An Historical Analytical Study of Malombo Music of South Africa* (Tshwane: University of Pretoria, 2009).

very first time on screen. This cinematic experience marks a period of transition through two genres, a relay between Kwela and its predecessor, Marabi.

When Marabi began its recession at the end of the 1930s, a new pennywhistle offshoot developed in Alexandra, a black township in the north-east of Johannesburg. A song by Aaron Lerole, a whistler known for the hit song 'Tom Hark', popularised the Zulu term *khwela-khwela*, [get up, get up], in reference to police vans frequenting Johannesburg townships to arrest black people. The Kwela style became popular very quickly after record companies witnessed its success among both black and white audiences. Artists such as Spokes Mashiyane and Elias Lerole sold more than 50,000 copies. Needless to mention, their returns were devilishly disproportionate to the profits made by the owners of white, racist, patriarchal, and sexist record labels.

Kwela was succeeded by *simanje manje* [now-now] or Mbaqanga [Zulu for an everyday cornmeal porridge] as it was named by the record companies, the name connoting cheap, fast, and temporal product. It was defined by a roaring, melodious bass supported by electric guitars. Largely promoted by Rupert Bopape, the chief exponent of this style was Simon 'Mahlathini' Nkabinde with The Mahotella Queens. These styles, which I will write about later in further depth, illuminate primordial South African club culture. A walk around the eastern part of central Johannesburg, specifically Jeppestown, evokes a street bash of Kwaito meets Maskandi[5] meets Mbaqanga; from the shop window displays to the evolving silkscreen banners along Main Street, that advertise Iscathamiya[6] and Maskandi performances at the hostels nearby.

Marabi is a sense of place

Christopher Ballantine, in his important book *Marabi Nights*, points to the irresponsibility of the South African Broadcasting Commission (SABC) and recording companies, particularly Gallo Records, in their minimal preservation of South African music before the 1950s. Marabi, lauded as the first urban genre in South Africa, has largely been unrecorded in its earliest form, believed to have emerged c. 1920. Marabi is speculated to have got its name from Marabastad, a mixed-race neighbourhood in central Pretoria. While celebrated, it was also known to be the dance and music of lowlifes and drunks. The shebeen[7] has, for largely simplistic and colonial reasons, been denounced to nothing more than a place of thought. *Chimurenga Magazine* launched the edition 'The Curriculum is Everything' (2010) about the shebeen as a platform for political intervention and resistance and declared: 'The Shebeen as a College of Music'.

The Marabi music that drew people into the shebeens is characterised by keyboard and organ-driven cyclic melodies based on songs that migrated from the rural homelands to the city. These songs were imbued with a new spirit of urban African people, pulled out of a perceived glorious and atrocious ancestry and compelled by the forces of capitalism to dig gold as migrant labourers. Marabi went mostly unrecorded, but 1930s and 1940s popular Jazz ensembles such as the Jazz Maniacs and The Jazz Revellers would rise to fame borrowing reluctantly from the Marabi idiom. The so-called respectable members of black society did not favour Marabi, preferring jazzier and more 'sophisticated' US-influenced music.

What is the place of the anthem in a country without a name?

While Marabi disappeared around 1939, its impact on black music has endured. Kippie Moeketsi, whose alto sax invoked the ghosts of the Marabi scene, is known as the biggest exponent of the

---

5   Electro-vocal music style focusing on Nguni idioms and lived experiences.
6   An a cappella, male dominated musical dance practise rooted in indigenous music practises, Christian hymnody, and migrant stories.
7   An unlicensed bar.

style. It was re-activated time and again, effectively through the Jazz of Abdullah Ibrahim's album *Mannenberg – 'Is Where It's Happening'* (1974). *Mannenberg* was successful due to its fusion of South African musical idioms and US Jazz, especially proving the enduring strength of the Marabi sound. John Edwin Mason recalls the power of *Mannenberg* with grace:

> In the 1980s, Mannenberg *had a second life as an anthem of the struggle against apartheid. Some called it South Africa's 'unofficial national anthem'. Once again, the song acquired a new meaning, this time through the efforts of musicians, especially Basil Coetzee and Robbie Jansen, who made it the musical centrepiece of countless anti-apartheid rallies and concerts.*[8]

Apartheid legislation like the Immorality Amendment Act of 1950, promoted forms of exile. The act made it illegal for people to mix racially, through residence or work. Ibrahim, like many other musicians, left the country in the 1960s, due to such oppressive systems. Generally, South Africa saw a mass exodus of the best popular talent in the 1960s such as Miriam Makeba or Louis Moholo. Makeba, for instance, decided to stay in the US while other musicians followed their own leads to escape the intense apartheid laws in South Africa. Cape Town's group, Blue Notes, a Jazz sextet founded in the early 1960s, being a multiracial musical group was in itself a provocation and invitation of danger.

Ons phola hier – we won't move!

Marabi is echoed by the musical compositions of Sophiatown, a mixed-race township on the outskirts of Johannesburg. A Jazz mecca in the 1950s, Sophiatown is often romanticised, despite its lack of public basic necessities such as running water. Some people see a sophisticated cultural space reflected through art, food, family, and growth while others see US influences in Sophiatown through dress, music, film, and literature. It was a free hold land, sold to people of different races and different ethnic groups enabled by poor urban planning.[9]

Sophiatown was demolished by apartheid authorities in 1955.[10] Its black residents were forcibly moved to a new township called Soweto (a portmanteau name for 'South Western Township' – a town made of many ships, shipped). Traces of Sophiatown still linger today, most noticeably in the cultural space called the Afrikan Freedom Station located 'at the foot of memory' in Westdene, in the former Sophiatown area.

The loss of Sophiatown reverberates. From the early to mid-2000s, fashion designer Nkhensani Manganyi monumentalised *Drum* magazine prints on T-shirts sold at a pan-African boutique store, Stoned Cherrie, at the trendy The Zone@Rosebank mall. A decade later, Zakes Bantwini fills the relatively new Soweto Theatre to the limit for a Sophiatown tribute concert, with an orchestra, and a showcase. Notably, the Afrikan Freedom Station's festival 'Beyond the Mind of the Oppressed' ran for two editions in 2014 and 2015 at the Soweto Theatre, featuring artists who have graced its walls in Westdene (Sophiatown), thus retracing, destroying, rebuilding, and rewriting history.

Ndofaya and Meadowlands, my love

Meadowlands, a township in Soweto, was one of those new homes where people were forcibly moved to at the height of apartheid. This new home was adopted (and adapted, as a form of defiance) in song – a passive resistance. Many of the first-generation residents of 'Ndofaya', as Meadowlands is widely referred to ever so lovingly, were reported to have been descendant from

---

[8] John Edwin Mason, '"Mannenberg": Notes on the Making of an Icon and Anthem', *African Studies Quarterly*, vol. 9, issue 4 (Fall 2007), 25.

[9] Cf. Luli Callinicos, *Who Built Jozi? Discovering Memory at Wits Junction* (Johannesburg: Wits University Press, 2012).

[10] Cf. N.N., 'The Destruction of Sophiatown', *South African History Online*, (27 January 2011), <http://www.sahistory.org.za/topic/destruction-sophiatown> accessed 10 July 2013.

Sophiatown. The African Jazz Pioneers, with Dolly Rathebe, offer an atmospheric rendition of the song 'Meadowlands' (written in 1956 by Strike Vilakazi and originally sung by Nancy Jacobs And Her Sisters), reflecting on the reluctant move:

Otla utlwa makgowa are / Are yeng ko Meadowlands / Meadowland Meadowlands / Meadowlands sithandwa sam.

Otlwa utlwa botsotsi bare / Ons dak nie, ons phola hier / Phola hier, phola hier / Phola hier, sithandwa sam.[11]

An evocative beauty in the hideous story that serves as a tense link between Sophiatown and Meadowlands, 'Meadowlands' is as much a protest song as it is a ballad, an ode to a new lover. While Meadowlands is divided by ethnic difference, its residents relive the Sophiatown era of mixed existence. Ushering new energy into a township that would give birth to one of the country's foremost music producers, Mandla 'Spikiri' Mofokeng. Meadowlands is well marked in one of his songs; 'Ndofaya' (2001) is named after the pet name for Meadowlands. Ndofaya's post-apartheid spatial planning in its different zones according to Spikiri goes like this:

Zone 1 asi funi amawaza [we don't take bullshit].
Zone 2 sithi two for joy.
Zone 3 s'push'i e passion [we are passionate].
Zone 4 ziwa more [it rocks].
Zone 5 fak isiqiniso [we tell the truth].
Zone 6 abagata e mova [watch out for the police].
Zone 7 up!
Zone 8 zithi ola! Heita [we greet]*!*
Zone 9 ga Ratau / go jewa mogodu moo [Ratau's, where we indulge in tripe]
Zone 10 ten times guluva [we are street wise].[12]

Contrary to the apartheid-state design of the township, Meadowlands was 'where something is always happening 24/7… where people get along'.[13]

Malombo: melodi ya Mamelodi

During this time of exile and distant vibrations, the home front enjoyed continuous development by those musicians who decided to stay behind for a variety of reasons. Galane considers some music styles such as Mbube, Kiba, Indlamu, Mushongolo, Mantshegele, Kgantla, Iscathamiya, Domba, Tshikona, Mqhentso, Amaelubo, Ishameni, and Malombo as those that remained largely uncorrupted.[14] While 'uncorrupted' may suggest a rigidity that would undermine any cultural practise, the allusion is that of a sustained lineage that overcomes external factors through resistance.

In Mamelodi, in the east of Pretoria, Dr. Philip Nchipi Tabane grew up soaking up the Sepedi/Northern Sotho music of Kiba/Dinaka, along with music could be found in a township such as Mamelodi, which included Jazz. His interest in the spiritual practises and music of the Venda people would see Tabane experiment in phases with a sound known as Malombo. In 1969, Tabane was observed as apolitical, despite his manipulations of US immigration restrictions and Apartheid South Africa repression, moving back and forth over the Atlantic in a complex yet regular pattern to deliver the development of Malombo music.[15]

11 'You'll hear the whites say / let's move to Meadowlands / Meadowlands Meadowlands / Meadowlands, my love. / You'll hear the tsotsis [a Sesotho slang word for a "thug" or "robber"] say / we're not moving, we're staying here / staying here, staying here / staying here, in our beloved place.'
12 Mandla 'Spikiri' Mofokeng, 'Ndofay', *Habashwe*, 2007.
13 Ibid.
14 Cf. Galane, *The Music of Philip Tabane* (see n. 4).
15 Cf. Galane, *The Music of Philip Tabane* (see n. 4).

Malombo, according to Raymond Mphunye Motau in the introduction to Tabane's album *Ke A Bereka* [I am working] (1996), means 'the spirits (of ancestors)' in TshiVenda language.[16] The politics of Tabane's kind evokes land, landlessness, landscapes, and language. The music of Malombo is a sprawling field laced with forces of nature of the physical (rivers, caves, mountains, hills, valleys, and all its vegetation, animals, and human beings), and the spiritual (God, spirits, vocal evocations). Malombo is a cyclic revamp of before-after, death has nothing on Malombo, it is its own most singular sound. Malombo is both permanent and endangered.

Looking at the record industry's hold over the production and distribution of music, it is important to observe what a monument Malombo music is. Of all the genres Galane lists (and by no means exhaustive of the large number of styles practised in Southern Africa), Malombo is one of the few genres that have developed to a mainstream level – coyly noted by Galane, as old as the African Union, both having been officially formed in 1963.[17] While Marabi, as noted, had managed to incorporate many genres including those listed by Galane, Malombo rather developed itself as an aesthetic that both defies mainstream packages as well as the notion of music as a product.

The effect of the political climate on dance music

By 1970, Soweto's population approached one million, as Coplan notes,[18] composed of South Africa's various ethnic groups. A classic 'divide and rule' apartheid strategy – but the lyrics of popular music would subvert this reality with celebration of 'livin' in harmony' as expressed in 'Sweet Soweto' (1975) by The Minerals,[19] and by Spikiri's aforementioned 'Ndofaya'. Despite the municipal's legal drinking holes, social spaces such as *stokvels*[20] and hostels would continue to be the important social spheres for music, dance, and politics. Indeed, the shebeen culture, advocated by Marabi, continued to define the place of socialisation, not without the consistent disruption by the security police.

What is telling about the rural/urban experience and what could be described as the sentiments of the music itself, are the rural sonic idioms infused with Western instruments and US Jazz sensibility, with lyrics that consist of rural songs of praise songs for heroism interlaced with stories about migration hardships. Even more telling is the strategy for the production and recording of this kind of music, which, by the 1970s, had evolved into Mbaqanga. It was in Soweto where Rupert Bopape (an important recorder and talent scout for Mbaqanga musicians working for the record company Gallo-Mavuthela) would dig through the hostels and mines, discovering talent, while the late West Nkosi would similarly travel the rural areas searching for new artists.[21]

The effect of the harsh political climate would be the source of unity in music, as Coplan observes: 'Groups tended to be multi-ethnic, reflecting and blending of various local African musical traditions … as well as producers' efforts to find musical "common denominators" among the heterogeneous urban audience.'[22]

After the 1976 youth uprisings these songs would begin to employ a more political edge. A new sound was emerging as US music was gaining ground. The rise of the Black Consciousness Movement intensified. A popular musical exponent of this political sensibility would be the group Harari, originally formed in 1968 by Selby Ntuli, Sipho Mabuse, and Alec Khaoli. Not only was Harari successful in amassing a following of both working and middle-class black people, but they also attracted a multi-racial fan base.

---

16 Mphunye Raymond Motau, 'Linernotes', in Philip Tabane, *Ke A Bereka* (Johannesburg: Kariba Records, 1996).

17 Cf. Galane, *The Music of Philip Tabane* (see n. 4).

18 Cf. David B. Coplan, *In Township Tonight! – South Africa's Black City Music and Theatre* (Chicago: University of Chicago Press, 2008).

19 The Minerals, 'Sweet Soweto', *Sweet Soweto*, 1975.

20 To learn more about *stokvels* please see Sean O'Toole's essay in this book.

21 Coplan, *In Township Tonight!* (see n. 18), 228.

22 Coplan, *In Township Tonight!* (see n. 18), 236.

Harari is credited as a precursor to the South African black music of the 1980s. The groups' synthesis of Hard Rock, US Funk, *Maskandi* guitar, and political sensibility opened doors for the music of Blondie Makhene, Yvonne Chaka Chaka, Brenda Fassie, and especially that of Chicco Twala, who would later become the go-to producer with a serious political agenda throughout the 1980s. Like elsewhere, the emergence of synthesizers, craftily incorporated in Harari's self-titled hit album from 1980, would influence and dominate the 1980s scene.

State of emergency

The 1980s enjoyed a staggering number of hits, but these were not the people's hits, as singer Blondie Makhene notes:

In 1983 the South African music was going through a dry spell. South African music was in abundance, but American hits had a strong hold on us. We performed and recorded American cover versions while we were trying to find our musical identity in the pop arena.[23]

While US music wreaked havoc on South Africa's dance floors, in 1983 Makhene embarked on a national tour as part of Blondie & Pappa – with backing vocalists including the star to-be, Brenda Fassie. After the tour, the international classic 'Weekend Special' (which strangely enough was not an instant classic)[24] was recorded. Makhene had taken Brenda Fassie to every imaginable township to convince the people that their own music was the future, when, in 1983, the song finally entered the public sphere. The single sold more than 200,000 copies, announcing the arrival of the so-called 'Township Pop', soon to be illegitimately christened 'Bubblegum'.

'Weekend Special' was such a unique experiment that the producer Melvyn Mathews had yet to unleash a monster of a similar breed, leaving a 'bitter-sweet'[25] sense of achievement in his creative life. This is not to say that black urban music could not surpass the success of 'Weekend Special', for the song fits the game changer role. 'Weekend Special' opened the proverbial doors for iconic songs that ruled cultural spaces, broke boundaries and instilled a fiery spirit in the masses for decades to come. Indeed, its signature bass and the cheeky harmonious vocals served as a baton connecting the roots of Mbaqanga right up to the bass culture of today as propagated by independent record label Kalawa Jazmee and others. As Coplan noted, in 2007: 'Over two decades later, there is hardly a local Kwaito or pop music diva who does not cite Fassie's inspiration.'[26] Ken Haylock, managing director of the record company CCP, adlibs in the sleeve notes of Brenda Fassie's greatest hits collection *The Queen of African Pop – Brenda Fassie 1964–2004*: 'The 1980s saw an unbelievable run of local hits.'[27]

Fassie, who tasted the height of artistic practise, succumbed to the pressures of a celebrity, as a woman in an exploitative industry. She rose back to dizzying heights with producer Chicco Twala and the 1998 national bestseller album, *Memeza*. But who is Chicco Twala?

Twala created songs that expressed the anguish of exile, laced soundscapes adorned with the continent, himself being a scholar of music from across Africa, especially of Fela Kuti. Following this success, acts entered the scene with experiments in synthesizers and elements of Disco, laced with pre-democracy urgency messages. Nelson Mandela was called from his holding cell as Twala, one of the country's most successful hit producers, delivered the message that the people wanted him back home in 'We Miss You Manelo' (1989). The harmonious accordion, melodious

---

23 Sam Mathe, 'Special team behind the MaBrr magic', *Mail & Guardian*, (2 August 2013), <http://mg.co.za/article/2013-08-02-00-special-team-behind-the-mabrr-magic> accessed 29 August 2013.
24 Ibid.
25 Ibid.
26 Coplan, *In Township Tonight!* (see n. 18), 295.
27 On the physical album sleeve of *The Queen of African Pop – Brenda Fassie 1964–2004* (Sandton: CCP Record Company, 2001).

bass, and hi-hats carried a candid open letter to the detained prisoner in English – and it was not really a secret who this 'Manelo' was. The song became a mouthpiece that reached the rural enclaves all the way from Johannesburg. Twala also teamed up with protest poet, Mzwakhe Mbuli, to record 'Papa Stop the War' (1990), another direct song speaking to power, urging the oppressors to 'listen to the voice of reason'.

In the 1970s Twala played for bands including Umoja and Harari, as well as his own group, Image. While his political music did not go unnoticed by the audience, it was only in the 1980s that Twala made it, producing hits for the likes of Yvonne Chaka Chaka, Brenda Fassie, and the Big Dudes. In the late 1980s, he gave a platform for people like Spikiri Mofokeng and M'du Masilela, among many others. Besides making Brenda Fassie a household name again in 1998, with the earth-shattering *Memeza* album, Twala was also involved in the hugely successful DJ Walker project with another 1980s star, Senyaka, producing the massive radio and dance floor Kwaito hit 'Chisa Mpama' [Whiplash] (1999).

Rivalry with other players in the tumultuous 'Bubblegum' game matched the 1980s in South Africa, a decade marked by two states of emergency. The potency of this subject matter, formed within new expressions can be felt at its best in Harari's aforementioned self-titled album from 1980. Hidden messages in songs came in even cleverer fashion. One seemingly unlikely place of the political discourse is none other than the shebeen. Yes, the watering hole is as political as the grooves of a protest song. Where does the black body return to life after 365 days of migrant labour? Take the miner who asks the master-brewer where the traditional beer is. He knows that when he gets home, he will find his *Umqombothi* waiting. Not surprisingly, Yvonne Chaka Chaka's song 'Umqombothi' [Name for a traditional South African beer] (1986) enjoyed success across the continent.

Songs that travel will adopt new meanings

Chaka Chaka's 'Umqombothi' crossed borders, gaining currency from each shifting meaning to, what on the surface is a drinking song, a fire-starter. In South Africa, the 1980s represented an urgent time with high anxiety. Men left their families in Southern African homelands for mines in Johannesburg. Many returned, many did not. So, when people in Lagos changed Yvonne Chaka Chaka's 'We MaDlameni / uphi umqombothi' [Hey traditional beer brewer / Where is the traditional beer?] to 'Women are many / looking for husbands', the message clearer when it returned to Johannesburg. The message sears closer to home, speaking of the vicious socioeconomic cycle for many women. In the shebeens and bar lounges across Johannesburg, the song was the Friday release from the shackles of the nine to five. In retrospect, there is nothing jovial about 'Umqombothi' – it is about the destruction of the black family structure.

Interlude

A roll call of songs about drinking in South African music that people danced to, then and now:

CNDO ft. Big Nuz, DJ Tira, DJ Cleo, Professor, '6 Pack'
Yvonne Chaka Chaka, 'Umqombothi'
Trompies, 'Sweety Lavo'
Brothers of Peace, 'Egoli'

The Brother Moves On, 'Dagiwe'
The Brother Moves On, 'Babalaas'
Makhendlas, 'Shwela Jwaleng'
Thebe, 'Jolas'
Vetkuk vs. Mahoota, 'Via Orlando'
Mafikizolo, 'U Dakwa Njalo'
Amaswazi Emvelo And Mahlathini, 'Utshwala Begazati' [Shared Beer]
Philip Tabane, 'Tlabalala' [Home Brewed Beer]
Boom Shaka, 'Madlamini'
Mob Club Masters, 'Zamalek'
Spikiri, 'Follow Me'
Thath'I Cover Okestra Vol. 5, 'Siya 'bshaya'
Kwesta, 'Ngud'

Around 1993, when the star of the 1980s, Senyaka enjoyed the success of his album *Ma-Gents*, artists like Brenda Fassie were feeling the crunch of change. The energy of the 1980s was replaced by a new sound, ironically this was evident in Senyaka's offering, itself produced by Chicco Twala's protégé, Mandla Mofokeng. It introduced a well-refined bending bass that would define Kwaito. Senyaka, who was well respected as the 'Godfather of African Rap', is credited as the first Kwaito artist. Already his inimitable 'Go Away'[28] (1987) was a feast, with the panning and stereo-sound experimentations, and the stretching of digital effects in minimal fashion are highly effective, but there is also the whistle, the human effect of note in South African music and social dance spaces. Well arranged in turns, taking turns from accordion and deep melodic bass, the whistle is a wonderful gimmick to each verse before the towering hook, laced with handclaps comes around, a true precursor to the soundtrack of the streets throughout the 1990s.

So, the mid-1990s saw Fassie wrestle with every imaginable Kwaito sound. But, sadly, the schizophrenia of her efforts either proved that Kwaito was not her forte, or that Fassie was simply ahead of her time. Indeed, by the time of her death in 2004, the late Brenda Fassie had collected the least Kwaito royalties of her entire career.

The rhetoric of celebration

At the South African Music Awards 2015, the 'Record of the Year' was the 2014 Kwaito revised song 'Caracara' by K.O., a rapper who was also part of the group Teargas. 'Caracara' is a history class in the truest sense about the relationship between Kwaito and Hip-Hop. There could be no better addition to a text on the history of dance music in South Africa than the line from 'Caracara':

Mina ukujaivangak' qala ngi mngaka, manje se ngi mngaka.[29]

There are many points of entry into the story of Kwaito. Let us start with the confrontational, yet subliminal 1994 song 'Traffic Cop – Ibiz e'Moyeni' by Brothers of Peace, which infected a new form of political sensibility in the dancing masses. It starts with an intro, a dialogue between an obviously black car driver and a white male speaking Afrikaans, acting as a traffic cop. His existence in the scene is to question the young black male behind the 'whip' [car] and unjustifiably challenge his ownership status of the automobile. In the song, band member Oscar Mdlongwa

---

28 From his debut album *Fuquza Dance* (Johannesburg: Eric Frisch Productions, 1987).

29 Loosely translated as: 'I have been dancing since I was a toddler, I am still dancing now'. This line is borrowed from Trompies' 'Bengim'ngaka' from the 2004 album *Respect (Toasted Gona Ganati)*. It is a real dance-circle starter.

and Bruce Sebitlo repeatedly set the record straight to all those who cannot bear the sight of a young black and gifted driving whips that advance their mobility.

'Traffic Cop' took a dive to save itself, as it was contested by a banger from Trompies titled 'Sigiya Ngengoma' (1994). It was noted that the two songs shared the line 'Ibiz' eMoyeni'.[30] Instead of waging a copyright war, Brothers of Peace and Trompies teamed up on the Kalawa Jazmee Records label. Together in the mid-1990s they formed a producer dream team from then on known as the Dangerous Combination Crew: Mandla 'Spikiri' Mofokeng, Oscar 'Oskido' Mdlongwa, Bruce 'Dope' Sebitlo, Don Laka, and Chris 'Christos' Katsaitis.

This dream team would grow to spark life into the diverse sound of the Kalawa staple. For years since the advent of Kwaito, in the 1990s alone the label has launched exciting sounds from acts such as Bongo Maffin, Boom Shaka, Trompies, Thebe, Chakaroski, Alaska, Crowded Crew, Skizo, and Baphixile. Hit after hit, year after year, across the broadest palettes of sound within one genre then provisionally christened Kwaito. One label provided some of the most consistent musicians in the dance genre before the whirlwind success of Mafikizolo. Indeed, Mafikizolo only remained an under the radar Kalawa band until the new millennium, waiting for the radical shift in Kwaito, one that would place Kwaito in between Afropop and House.

The year is 1996 and Kwaito has a name. We still hear of Gong, notably through the album *Introducing Gong!–Moving On* from 1996, a seminal work by Makhosini Henry Xaba with Lindelani Mkhize. At the time when colleagues from other multinational record companies were sneering, Gong was one of the projects searching for a name to package this energy that ran through the streets of townships and rural settlements of Southern Africa. Mkhize's work as an executive was met with Xaba's Jazz sensibility (under the name Joe Nina, for the uninitiated), himself already destroying dance floors, with one of the 1990s most sensual masterpieces, the LP *Ding Dong* (1994), a collection of standard mid-tempo Kwaito with deep bass, hi-hats, and twitters. The title song 'Ding Dong' would be a game-changer as a Kwaito love song–not because there were few romantic songs in the highly masculine Kwaito repertoire, but because Joe Nina's vocals were on the money in terms of vernacular speech. This would also concretise its status as an evergreen Kwaito hit.

Before that, Joe Nina produced two albums under the name LA Beat with Mduduzi 'M'du' Masilela, dropping the track 'Boss of The Road' (circa 1992), a recording that is hard to find.[31] Masilela himself made a grand entrance with the crawly 'YU4Me' (1995) that cemented the role of bass in Kwaito. Give the people a tight bass at the centre of any element, and you have a Kwaito anthem. 'YU4Me' is held together by a drum and bass-like staccato drum programming and earnest lyrics relating to backstabbing and meddling in other people's business. The lyrics to 'YU4Me' are ambiguous because they hinted at M'du Masilela's notorious tensions with his ex-band, the four-piece group Mashamplani, over royalties. In this track, M'du confronts Mashamplani to 'mind their own business'. Nonetheless, people would dance to both M'du and Mashamplani, the beef stayed in the recording booths, not on the streets.

Together Mashamplani and M'du had given us the now classic 'Hey Kop' (1995). As Mashamplani 2 the band offered the exciting LP *Kunjalo Kunjalo* (1996) followed by the below average releases *Neva Neva* (1998) and *4Ever* (1999). The group had no chance in the changing soundscape of the new millennium.

M'du as a solo artist enjoyed a banger album with *YU4Me* in 1995, with the title track as one of the soundtracks to the 1990s. The album was followed by *Ipompe* (1996). M'du is one of the

---

30 'Call it out in the public', as in 'to broadcast'.
31 Although its baseline can be unmistakably heard in Arthur Mafokate's 'Vuvuzela' (1995) and TKZee's 'Mambotjie' (1999).

few solo Kwaito artists who created remix albums of his own music and of the artists at his label, M'du Records: his two volume *Shwabana Ghost Mixes* from 1996 and 1997 offered exciting sounds very different from the Kwaito of the mid-1990s, heavily influenced by Jazz and Drum' n'bass. But perhaps his best remix album is a largely unknown side project called LMJ (Let M'du Jam), released in 1998 and featuring instrumental tracks laced with a Jazz sensibility. The album came out the same year as the hit-heavy album *M'du Or Die* (1998). This, the Mashamplani projects, and other releases by M'du Records make the period from 1995 to 1999 the most successful time in M'du's life, a true contender to the title 'Godfather of Kwaito'.

Truth and Reconciliation Commission

The Truth and Reconciliation Commission and the Human Rights Violations Committee investigated human rights abuses that occurred between 1960 and 1994 in Apartheid South Africa. In 1995, the then ruling king of Kwaito, Arthur (Mafokate), would not have it. He would say it straight to the 'baas' [boss]:
   Baas, neeee, baas / unga bizi iKaffir.[32]

Sonically, except perhaps for the propelling drum kick, the song offers little production value. As a song, it welcomes one to the party as a messenger of great news – in this case, the unspoken. Mafokate's enterprising methods saw an opportunity for enhanced visibility through assembling albums by new talent, first with AbaShante (a twist of Raggamuffin style sound with Kwaito drum kicks and melodies), then with a group called New School. 'Kaffir' may very well have been ahead of its time, but Kwaito wanted to speak with a liberated voice to power, and to life as it unfolds in front of its eyes. It was too much to handle amidst the 'Rainbow Nation' celebration after the end of Apartheid.

At the time when Boom Shaka's 1995 'Kwere Kwere' (a derogatory term for black non-South Africans) and 'Kaffir' transmitted messages through limited mainstream media and its instruments, there was no social media or smartphones to speak of. Conditions rendered the experience of music a personal social affair. In practical terms, when Kwaito emerged and did not have much radio airplay nor distribution acumen as an independent genre, it was the medium of cassette that offered it mobility across the regions of Southern Africa, following the routes as if searching for the radicle.

'Sigiya Ngengoma', Trompies' first 1994 hit, suggested that 'we strike with a song'. Music is the weapon, and people were celebrating, because the year was 1994, and Apartheid had ended. When the Pantsula super group Trompies dropped 'Sigiya Ngengoma', word on the street was of a war between Brothers of Peace and Trompies. However, Trompies had a different position to declare on 'Sigiya Ngengoma': 'You find me on a different style.' This statement completed the biography of the members, whose careers date back to the 1980s alongside top musicians of the genre with the highly contested name 'Bubblegum'. After deciding to do a side project, Mandla 'Spikiri' Mofokeng produced this ground-breaking album with Eugene 'Donald Duck' Mthethwa, Zynne 'Mahoota' Sibika, Emmanuel 'Copperhead' Matsane, and Jairus 'Jakarumba' Nkwe. After soaking themselves with the politically charged music of their older peers, it made sense for Trompies to announce their 'different style'. This style, contrary to the seemingly stripped-down lyrics, could not be any less political, for the new playground had to come with its own rules and

---

[32] 'Boss, noooo, boss / don't call me kaffir' – a derogatory Afrikaans term used by apartheid whites to refer to black people. From Arthur Mafokate, 'Kaffir', *Kaffir*, 1995.

conflicts. Mandla Mofokeng relates the story: 'This song caused lots of conflict. It had created problems at some stage'.[33] His band colleague Sibika triangulates:

There was this one track we shared with Oskido and them, 'Ibiz' eMoyeni'. The Trompies rhythm of the song at the time was on Bailo's beat. So Spikiri didn't like the song. I suggested that we change it. And we decided to add vocals and so forth, just started throwing in 'Ibiz eMoyeni'.[34]

As previously mentioned, 'Ibiz' eMoyini' translates to 'call it out in the public', as in 'to broadcast'. It is to be free, to open it up, as in freedom of speech. For the song it is for you to request it at parties, on radio, to speak about it, sing it and spread it. Thus, within a week there were these two similar tracks out on the radio and foremost Kwaito platform, YFM, a fertile ground for tabloids to speculate who came up with the song first. The effect ironically mimicked the Apartheid strategies of division, as Trompies band member, Sibika, recalls: '[it] made things worse because when we read BOP articles, we'd be angry and vice versa'.[35]

Indeed, the driving factor behind Trompies' 'Sigiya Ngengoma' – that sturdy, banging and bending bass – was quite at first. This bass made this style different. Brothers of Peace would lock their producer, Don Laka, in the studio all day and night trying to recreate this bass with a keyboard. In fact, the bass came straight off the Mbaqanga catalogue, something that Kalawa Jazmee would grow to specialise in and bend all possible rules. That Trompies' band member, Nkwe, delivered it to his crew, goes to show how singularly historical Kwaito is. Sibika sums it up: 'Because of that song, hence today we have Kalawa Jazmee.'[36] Indeed, 'J.A.Z.M.E.E.' is Jairus, Zynne, Mandla, Eugene, and Emmanuel. But the real formation of Kalawa was rooted in the occasional encounters between Oskido and Don Laka, inside a lift in a Hillbrow tenement, a series of encounters that went unnoticed for a while.

Don Laka had his first album in 1972. His career blossomed further by producing and performing with artists such as Ray Phiri and Sipho Mabuse. He is now regarded as one of South Africa's premier producers, having produced for Mango Groove, Sharon Dee, and Johnny Clegg among others. However, it is perhaps his involvement in Kalawa Jazmee that made the greatest impact in the industry as a whole. Not only did Don Laka produce one of the first Kwaito super-groups, Boom Shaka, but he also enabled creativity and integrity to govern at a label started by young black males on the eve of so-called 'freedom'. Oscar, Don, and DJ Christos went on to form the original Kalawa Records: Katsaitis, Laka and Mdlongwa.

According to Bongo Maffin's member, Stoan Seate:

Trompies, BOP, and Don Laka started it all. Trompies put a rubber stamp on the Pantsula identity, while BOP on the other hand pushed the boundaries of what was known as Kwaito music. And of course, Don Laka brought the jazzy touch to the music. These guys lead the Kalawa Jazmee revolution and were on the cutting edge of Kwaito evolution.[37]

The culture of Brothers of Peace was brilliant. It was about coming up with concepts, a project that would invite other musicians to feature, to give them an opportunity to grow. It did, from Dr. Mageu to Bafixile, to just about every player in the scene and straight to the South African Music Awards (SAMAs). Meanwhile, Trompies' Eugene Mthethwa reminds us that no award ever came their way.[38] He demands to know, how could a producer like Mandla 'Spikiri' Mofokeng not receive a national recognition award, let alone a lifetime achievement award? In a sense, Spikiri's album *The King Don Father 2.5* (2011) will go down in history with a self-award. With this album,

33 *VUMA: A Music Revolution*, (dirs.), Vincent Moloi and Norman Maake (Glowstars/SABC, 2009). Vincent Moloi, and Norman Maake (dirs.), *Vuma: A Music Revolution* (Glowstars: SABC, 2009)
34 Ibid.
35 Ibid.
36 Ibid.
37 *VUMA: A Music Revolution*, dirs. Moloi and Maake (see n. 33).
38 Cf. Ibid.

Spikiri immortalised his then twenty-five years in the nationwide game that, included a list of artists ranging from Teargas to Crowded Crew and DJ Mgiftana on a double CD album. Regrettably, there are no women on this list. While the double album is solid, it is perhaps the song 'Skeem Sam' [a *tsotsitaal*[39] term for my right-hand compatriot] that serves Kwaito most. Nevertheless, the song also refers to one of Kwaito's pioneering groups of the 1990s, Skeem. Thus, the naming of the song is an ode to Kwaito and its pioneers. This pioneer nod is further reinforced by the invitation to General (of Chiskop), Junior Mabhokodo (of Boom Shaka), and Ishmael (of Skeem) to perform on 'Skeem Sam'. A further reading along these lines finds the presence of DJ Tira and Professor, formidable forces in urban dance music since the early 2000s, representing the Durban-based record label Afrotainment, which is considered as the first significant dance music label formed outside of Johannesburg. Considering ongoing debates on the Durban sound being House and the cheesier version of 1990s Kwaito, 'Skeem Sam' can be listened to as a community of *Sghubu* [drum] solidarity. 'Skeem Sam' cleverly counters the countless Kwaito obituaries of the 2000s. The repeated use of the line 'gangsta, gangsta, gangsta' pays hommage to US Hip-Hop in more complex terms than the lazy formula of Kwaito being 'slowed down House with raps'.[40]

House on fire

The relationship between Kwaito and House has been inseparable, starting with the fact that one of Kwaito's most important exponents, Oscar 'Oskido' Mdlongwa, started out as a House DJ. The height of this relationship is marked by the year 1998, when Bongo Maffin and Boom Shaka's albums indicated the power of House music towards the new millennium. From 1998 on, DJ Fresh's mix series *Fresh House Flava* became one of the bestselling serial compilations of House music, followed by Vinny Da Vinci's *Deep House Sounds*. By the early 2000s original House productions with a distinct South African flavour began to circulate, which was made by many artists associated with Kwaito, not the least Oskido's *Church Grooves* series, as well as a noticeable change in his duo Brothers of Peace (with master producer and Kalawa co-director Bruce Sebitlo). Parallel to this growth, far out of Johannesburg, new approaches to dance music developed, notably in Tshwane and Durban. From this point on, this text will go in and out of Johannesburg, as well as back and forth in time, to reflect the interchangeability of Kwaito and House.

In Mafikizolo's 2013 song 'Vimba Kanjani', band members Nonhlanhla Sibongile Mafu and Theodore Tate Kgosinkwe want to know what makes 'that song', the kind that 'invades the entire place', the sound that fills the belly of the club, pulls the senses off the skull of every gyrating body on the dance floor. A song that is heard at every place, is loved by everybody, played through earphones, played at every radio station and on all YouTube channels, at every *stokvel* and *shisa nyama* [barbecue party], a song for weddings and street bashes, from the night vigil to the house on the hill, to the cemetery. A song that wakes you up at five o'clock in the morning.

Could it be the song to erase the space between Brenda Fassie's classic *Weekend Special* (1983) and her other game-changer, *Memeza* (1998)? Or the song that meets Arthur Mafokate's confrontational 'Kaffir' (1994) and the across-the-borders transfiguring 'Umqombothi' (1985) by Yvonne Chaka Chaka? Something between Abdullah Ibrahim's unofficial liberation national anthem fpr the liberation struggle, 'Mannenberg' (1974), and 'Madibuseng' by Trompies (1996)? Is it a nation-building song like a crossover of 'Nkalakatha' by Mandoza (2000) and the FIFA World Cup 1998 unofficial national anthem 'Shibobo' by TKZee & Benni? Could it be the spiritual chant

---

39 Street vernacular consisting of a variety of mixed languages.
40 Cf. 'Sghubu Solidarities: Sonic Family Trees as Kwaito Writing for Itself', a contribution to *Meditations on Thath'i Cover Okestra and Kwaito* (Keleketla! Library; Hebbel am Ufer [HAU]: Berlin; and the 10th Berlin Biennale of Contemporary Art, 2018).

of Revolution's 'VhaVenda' (2001) with Dr. Philip Tabane meeting the child-friendly Balobedu[41] history class of 'Tsa Mandebele', the 2013 song of the year contender by Oskido & Candy?

One song invades all spaces releasing endless Pan-Africanist sentiments with more than ten million plays on YouTube: 'Khona' (2013) by Mafikizolo. It wreaks havoc. 'Khona' has well refined vocals and super-smooth melodies and grooves held together tightly by banging drum patterns. It makes for a Mafikizolo classic, placing the duo as one of the most enduring acts in the South African music scene, dance or not, Joburg or not.

Woz' eDurban: The deeper side of call and response

Durban Kwaito Music, which has been provisionally (and reluctantly) labelled 'DKM', is one of the most important game changers in the South African dance music scene. What appeared to be a pain in the neck to some, was in fact a well needed catalyst. Pioneers sounded ambivalent on the direction Kwaito seemed to have been pushed into, the direction being that of House music. It threatened Kwaito's very essence, particularly with Kwaito being the bastard child of a 'slowed down House' narrative. But what the Durban crew presented was a healthy distance – from Joburg, Kwaito's hometown, from Kalawa Jazmee, Kwaito's home. With no strings attached, they were able to build on what had been established a decade earlier. Johannesburg embraced the sound, and you are bound to hear statements alluding to both Joburg and Kalawa in the DKM songs. Yet hardcore Kwaito cats are unhappy with Durban and its impact on Kwaito.

But growth is healthy because it means that Kwaito will never die. It is also important because it provokes Kwaito pioneers and amateurs alike; it asks people to remain innovative and relevant. For former member of the TKZee family, Kagiso 'Gwyza' Diseko, it is:

> ... the evolution of sound, it's cool because it means that the sound is growing and people are embracing new things 'cause right now if I'm gonna hate on the Durban sound it means I'm hating on my own development and my own challenges. It's like being a soccer player and beefing at skills of my opponent. There was a time, before we [TKZee Family] made it when Kalawa sound was the in thing. You know what I mean? We came through with our own different flavour, and until they began to embrace it. At the time when we came, it was Vibe Lezinto, boMdu, boKalawa, Arthur... We came in and we did that and until they appreciated that and gave it its dues and started liking it, only then could they start liking their own growth. Me saying my beats are 120, 100 it doesn't mean I've lost Gwyza. It just means, age happened, genres grow, life in general.[42]

One of the golden children of House is the producer and superstar DJ Black Coffee, who grew up in Durban. He upped his career with a remix to Hugh Masekela's hit 'Stimela' (originally from 1980), opening doors for House music influenced by ethnic, urban sounds. An innovator, his 2012 double album and DVD *Africa Rising* features a 24-piece orchestra at Durban's Moses Mabhida Stadium.

Like Brenda Fassie put a stamp on dance and the albeit short-lived Afropop with the 1998 album *Memeza*, Culoe De Song's debut album *A Giant Leap* (2009) cemented that deep, back to the roots House, oozing with spiritual tenets.[43] On *A Giant Leap* the vocal chants by the late Busi Mhlongo infested the country and its borders through 'Webaba'. And on the second number, 'Gwebindlala', Thandiswa Mazwai sings with deeper delivery than most vocal House around town since the late Lebo Mathosa's experiments.

---

41   An ethnic group of the Northern Sotho group in South Africa.
42   Gwyza' Diseko Kagiso, in an interview with the author (2013).
43   Culolethu Zulu aka Culoe de Song was born in the province KwaZulu-Natal, some 150 kilometres from Durban. His first name is an IsiZulu name meaning 'our song'.

But the real devastation of sounds comes from DJ Tira's House music label Afrotainment. DJ Tira breaks it down to Kwanele Sosibo (2013): 'I think we brought some colour into these cloudy days of South Africa. Livelihood, my man, speed up the tempo. You know that before we arrived the tempo was slow, neh?'[44] Smug as it sounds, Durban Kwaito sways between 'Ufuna uk'groova? Woz' eDurban!' [You want to have a good time? Come to Durban!] and 'Kalawa Jazmee / Egroova Durban' [Kalawa Jazmee / is partying in Durban] in rapid tempos.

Interlude: All roads lead to Johannesburg

Mafikizolo's 2002 album, *Sibongile*, with its very Afropop sound opens with a tribute to Marabi music, the song itself accordingly titled 'Marabi'.

Namhlanje u ya hamba
O bekele eGoli o bekela eGoli mntanami
O ba bone ba tsotsi ba Jozi
Qapela mtwanami
O ye eGooooooooli
Mina ngihamba ngi sbekeli eGoli
Mina ngihamba ngi sbekeli eGoli.[45]

'Marabi' is shaped along lost landscapes scattered in the shadow of memory, it sounds like a dirt road soundtrack headed for the national road N1, in the back of a taxi carrying dreams of family in a dual life, urban and rural. 'Marabi' evokes yearning and heartache, longing and nostalgia; it evokes a feeling of distance and far away love, of landscape and attachment. This ambience is created particularly through the songs opening, with its finger claps, saxophones, vocals, lyrics, driving bassline, and penny whistles.

It is not driven by a bass drum or bass kick; the essential instruments in most dance songs and overused by the music industry. Instead, its pulse is propelled by vocal harmony of a time in the faraway place of childhood choirs from the village, with eyes on the city of gold. It is a perfect entry into an Afropop album, as it pays allegiance to other people's memories before exploiting them for their cultural value. Mafikizolo was the Afropop poster group of the 2000s, deeply focused on a study of Johannesburg, connecting Doornfontein to Sophiatown and elsewhere, not only through their sound, but also the carefully researched CD covers, stylings, and video locations.

Before 'Marabi' and the sound of Afropop

On the 1998 album *Final Entry*, Bongo Maffin evocates Miriam Makeba through the hit 'maye-Makeba', named in honour of the people's fearlessly graceful 'Mama Africa'. A tribute to Makeba's 1967 classic, 'Pata Pata' (originally written by Dorothy Masuka). Bongo Maffin announced their arrival on the scene as a formidable Kwaito group with a Pan African consciousness, a cross-referential group that places the dance floor bass alongside clever lyrics. But 'Makeba' was merely a sign of things to come.

Bongo Maffin, formed in Johannesburg in 1996, combined elements of Soul, Hip-Hop, Ragga, R'n'B, African spiritual chants, and of course, House. For example, the song 'Thath'isighubu'

44 Kwanele Sosibo, 'Kwaito 2.0: The House that Durban Built', *The Con*, (10 July 2013), <http://www.theconmag.co.za/2013/07/10/kwaito-2-0-the-house-that-durban-built/> accessed 9 December 2013.

45 'Today you depart / departing for Johannesburg, my child / watch out for the criminals of Johannesburg / watch out my child / go to Johannesburg / I'm leaving for Johannesburg / I'm leaving for Johannesburg'.

[untranslatable word for a drum and the pleasure to play it], from their debut album *The Concerto* (1998), brought Bongo Maffin intergenerational success in the late 1990s. It opens with a bass rhythm so melodious you salivate over the rest of the song's element with absolutely no idea what genre this song will end up as. There was no name for it. Bongo Maffin stood out as that Africanist Kwaito group that tried to stretch their genre. They repeatedly called their musical style 'Gong' in their songs. Indeed, *The Concerto* reads: 'Kalawa Jazmee Records, A Bad News Production, D Gong music'. Bongo Maffin remains in the heart of many as one of the finest politically and spiritually charged bands of Kwaito. It was with Bongo Maffin that House music emerged in Kwaito.

The significance of the late Lebo Mathosa

After the 1998–99 hit music, dust settled. The new millennium brought with it a great deal of discomfort for Kwaito heads, as the genre had to take a break from the public. 1999's *YMag* cover declaration of 'House music all night long' began to ring true, as 120 per minute House beats reverberated from every street corner. They came even from traditionally Kwaito artists such as Lebo Mathosa, who used to be a member of the Kwaito band Boom Shaka and who denounced the genre.[46] Mathosa opened the floodgates for the lucrative House vocalist business. In fact, one of her hottest House-y tunes was 'Ngiyakuthanda' [I love you] (2000), featuring Shana, Black Coffee's trio.

However, one of the best manifestations of urban music in South Africa was Lebo Mathosa's unofficial 'Siyaziwisa' [We are partying] video. In this video, shot DIY style on a fringe to a big outdoor festival east of Pretoria (now Tshwane) at Moretela Park, Mathosa momentarily turns a street into a stage. It is a stage where individuals share their own responses to 'Siyaziwisa', a song is about getting the party started. A video shoot becomes a display of power. Here, everything is a prop: cars, rocks, people, and the street. The video flows into the actual scene, with snippets of sounds and voices from the set/street permeating into the video. Mathosa reverses a standard in Kwaito, Hip-Hop and R'n'B video representation of power: she is in the driver's seat of a car, with another woman in the passenger's seat, singing her own verses. Yet, the verses to the song speak to deeper issues of self-determination, vision and the concept of hard work instead of mere playfulness and male braggadocio. Other scenes include Mathosa and her group of dancers performing in unison, intercepted by revellers and residents showing off individual styles.

The set is a public space, a street. When Kwaito hit the country in the early 1990s, township streets would turn into ephemeral spaces for music performances, deejaying, and dance. This video, with its variety of dance styles, represents dance culture in the country; improvisational, every day, and always new.

In Lebo Mathosa, we see the rise of women in music, in leading verses. She not only fought for ownership of her music in financial terms, but for the very writing and singing in her own voice. Her investment in not only the very formation of Kwaito, but also in the development of Soul, R'n'B, Ragga/Dancehall and her ultimate specialty, 'African spirituals', Mathosa provided models for musical artistry for many musicians. She was an iconic role model for non-musicians. Finally, she worked hard, shifting labels to define what she does, negotiating a brutal task in the music sector historically controlled by racist, patriarchal, sexist, unjust, and often white, businessmen.

---

46 Cf. Aryan Kaganof, 'The Kwaito Story–Lebo Mathosa interviewed by Aryan Kaganof', *Kaganof.com*, 2006, <http://kaganof.com/kagablog/2006/09/24/the-kwaito-story-lebo-mathosa-interviewed-by-aryan-kaganof/> accessed 2 August 2013.

Songs that keep saving Kwaito and other death stories

In the middle of this sped-up dance music, there have been interesting saviours of Kwaito throughout the decade. Innovation was the only prerequisite. Take for example Mzekezeke, a creation of the then hugely popular YFM presenter, DJ Sbu. Speculated to be DJ Sbu himself, Mzekezeke was a masked monster. He started as a comic character on DJ Sbu's radio show, making prank calls to VIPs ranging from Kwaito stars to politicians. The character became the mouthpiece of the people, able to ask difficult questions with regards to power. His broken English and politically incorrect questions fitted the changing nature of national socioeconomic discourse.

Thus, the next natural, financially sound step was to release music: *S'Guqa Ngamadolo* (2003), Mzekezeke's first album, sold more than 100,000 copies and got the 2003 South African Music Award for Song of the Year. It was followed by the equally (if not more) successful *Izinyoka* (2004) and *Storotoro* (2005). The year 2006 brought the last album, *Ama B.E.E.*, forcefully criticising the new middle-class benefiting from the government's Black Economic Empowerment (B.E.E.) programme. Mzekezeke's masked identity and voice-of-the-people lyrics gave the country that humble heroic non-celebrity, devoid of naked women, fast cars, expensive clothes, and all pop things.

Another explosive game changer was Bonginkosi Dlamini alias, Zola, whose musical name is derived from an area of Soweto. Zola career blew up as an actor on the controversial TV series, *Yizo Yizo*, featuring on its soundtrack and he went on to release a string of hit albums with street anthems. The best of Zola's talent shone through on his debut album *Umdlwembe*, which was released in 2000 and included the KayBee produced 'Ghetto Scandalous', featuring the then golden child, rapper Amu. To date 'Ghetto Scandalous' remains one of the most successful syntheses of Kwaito and Rap, a precursor for the kasi-rapper[47] extraordinaire, Pro Kid, in the mid-2000s. If there is any song that deepens the glorification of the township it is also 'Ghetto Fabulous'. It does so in the most complex, spectacular, and profound of ways. The level of sophistication in Zola's 2000 masterpiece is clear, in the way a song is a mantra; a prayer; a lament; a reason for living.

But perhaps the greatest saviours of Kwaito would be two musicians who have heavily influenced each other and who represent the most important Kwaito bands of the 1990s. Next to the aforementioned Lebo Mathosa from Boom Shaka, this is Kabelo Mabalane from TKZee. Under his first name Kabelo he went solo from his group in 2000, teaming up with the crème de la crème of producers and creators. He released his debut *Everybody Watching* in 2000. A fresh offering in terms of lyrics, the album came with custom-made hits including 'Pantsula 4 Life', 'Amasheleni' [Money], 'I'm Going Crazy', and 'Meketeng' [Weddings]. The latter featured Ali Katt, former member of late 1970s band The Minerals and 1980s disco player, the song itself was a return to Katt's 1986 hit, 'Let the Good Times Roll'. Kabelo's follow-up album *Rebel With A Cause* (2002), did not disappoint, offering the swirling bass of the M'du engineered 'Ayeye' next to 'For As Long Ngisaphefumula' and 'Jazz Lover, Undercover'.

Kabelo's delivery and choice of producers added some colour to the tough times as of Kwaito's went through its transition. In fact, he took it back to the days of lyrics, of beautifully constructed *kasi* idioms on dance music, and can thus claim the status of being one of the last vanguards of classic Kwaito slow jams as the doctor ordered them – with socially engaged lyrics and clever wordplay. One of the most enduring Kwaito players, Kabelo is still active in the scene, collaborating with both the old and new school players from South Africa and the continent.

47 *Kasi* is a slang word for townships, with roots in the English term 'location' and the Afrikaans approximate 'lokasie'.

In Kabelo's work, along with that of the likes of the late Brown Dash and Professor, Kwaito creates a lyrical density with great vigour. This tradition is kept alive by exponents of the 'New Age Kwaito', among them Okmalumkoolkat, Duncan, Ma-E, Moonchild, Sho Madjozi, Dear Ribane, KiD-X, Cassper Nyovest, and the SAMA 2015 record of the year winner, the aforementioned K.O. with his 'Caracara'. Hip-Hop is a significant thread between the Kwaito made in the classical period from 1994 to 2004 and the 'New Age Kwaito', at the time of writing this text, in the mid-to-late-2010s. The difference is the point of reference. While Kwaito made in the period between 1994 to 2004 referenced Hip-Hop and Soul of the US, the current 'New Age Kwaito' is Hip-Hop that itself references old school Kwaito.

The growth of House and Hip-Hop in South Africa owes its success to the social, political, and economic foundation laid by Kwaito between 1994 and 2004. This is evident in the House and Hip-Hop produced since the early 2000's. The musical activities of Kabelo Mabalane and Lebo Mathosa inspired the type of Hip-Hop and House that came out of this region: musical, lyrical, danceable, thought-provoking, and contextually in place.

Because history repeats itself

The manner in which Africans engage with music today remains a metaphor for dispossession and destruction. What Africans had to sacrifice in handing over their indigenous knowledge to pressing machines across the globe is directly linked to land theft and colonisation. In engaging with the music of the people from c.1960 to now, a sense of place guides the reader through black music repertoire, in fragments and anecdotes delivered through cycles and repetition. Is it possible for the truest music to live on wax, plastic, magnetic tape, or computer chips, let alone in text?

Bibliography

Ballantine, Christopher, *Marabi Nights – Jazz, 'Race' and Society in early Apartheid South Africa* (Scottsville: University of KwaZulu Natal Press, 2012).

Callinicos, Luli, *Who Built Jozi? Discovering Memory at Wits Junction* (Johannesburg: Wits University Press, 2012).

Coplan, David B., *In Township Tonight! – South Africa's Black City Music and Theatre* (Chicago: University of Chicago Press, 2008).

Galane, Sello, *The Music of Philip Tabane – An Historical Analytical Study of Malombo Music of South Africa* (Tshwane: University of Pretoria, 2009).

Kaganof, Aryan, 'The Kwaito Story – Lebo Mathosa interviewed by Aryan Kaganof', *Kaganof.com*, 2006, <http://kaganof.com/kagablog/2006/09/24/the-kwaito-story-lebo-mathosa-interviewed-by-aryan-kaganof/> accessed 2 August 2013.

Mason, John Edwin, '"Mannenberg": Notes on the Making of an Icon and Anthem', *African Studies Quarterly*, vol.9, issue 4 (Fall 2007).

Mathe, Sam, 'Special team behind the MaBrr magic', *Mail & Guardian*, (2 August 2013) <http://mg.co.za/article/2013-08-02-00-special-team-behind-the-mabrr-magic> accessed 29 August 2013.

Mojapelo, Max, *Beyond Memory – Recording the History, Moments and Memories of South African Music* (Somerset West: African Minds, 2008).

Monaheng, Tseliso, 'Jacked by Nostalgia', *Mahala.co.za*, (22 February 2013), <http://www.mahala.co.za/culture/jacked-by-nostalgia/> accessed 29 August 2013.

Motau, Mphunye Raymond, 'Linernotes', in Philip Tabane, *Ke A Bereka* (Johannesburg: Kariba Records, 1996).

Mpe, Phaswane, *Welcome to Our Hillbrow – A Novel of Postapartheid South Africa* (Scottsville: University of KwaZulu-Natal Press, 2001).

N.N., 'The Destruction of Sophiatown', *South African History Online,* 27 January 2011, <http://www.sahistory.org.za/topic/destruction-sophiatown> accessed 10 July 2013.

Sosibo, Kwanele, 'Kwaito 2.0: The House that Durban Built', *The Con*, (10 July 2013), <http://www.theconmag.co.za/2013/07/10/kwaito-2-0-the-house-that-durban-built/> accessed 9 December 2013.

Stapleton, Chris, and May, Chris, *African All-Stars – The Pop Music of a Continent* (London: Paladin, 1989).

Dirty Paraffin, 2011, photo: Paul Shiakallis

Mongezi Feza, Louis Moholo, Dudu Pukwana & Sammy Maritz (from left to right) at Downbeat Club, Johannesburg, 1963, photo: Basil Breakey

Kippie Morolong Moeketsi, Dorkay House, Johannesburg, c. 1963, photo: Basil Breakey

Free Style Pantsula, Soweto Township, Johannesburg, 2016, photo: Chris Saunders

Sihle Khambule, from the series *Alternative Kidz Series*, 2009, photo: Musa N. Nxumalo

Moonchild Sanelly, Anthology of Youth, 2016, photo: Musa N. Nxumalo

Toyi-toyi, 2017, photo: Musa N. Nxumalo

Imaginary Republics – Dancing after Dark in Johannesburg

Sean O'Toole

In 1956, Lewis Nkosi, a 20-year-old journalist who had just quit his job at the Durban-based Zulu-language newspaper *Ilanga Lase Natal* [The Natal Sun], arrived in Johannesburg to begin work at *Drum*, a new Anglophone African current affairs magazine. Nkosi, whose name still looms large in South African arts and letters, even after his death in 2010, immediately became part of the city's Jazz-infused high life. He made friends and socialised with the cosmopolitan intellectuals that staffed *Drum*, among them Ezekiel 'Eskia' Mphahlele, Todd Matshikiza, Bessie Head, and Can Themba. It was Themba, a gifted short story writer, who Nkosi later remembered for his 'detachment', 'wit', and 'romanticism', who introduced the transplanted Durban writer to author Nadine Gordimer. In a 1986 interview, Gordimer recalled Themba arriving at her home one day with 'a rather snooty-looking young man': Nkosi. He cultivated an indifferent air in Gordimer's home. 'Any music in this place?' he asked Gordimer at length. 'Yes,' she said, gesturing to some vinyl records. 'This is not music,' responded Nkosi. 'It's all classical!'

Nkosi was a man apart. At the time of his visit, he lived in Themba's one-roomed house – dubbed the 'House of Truth' – in Johannesburg's Sophiatown. Recalling Sophiatown in a 1972 essay, Nkosi described the mixed-race residential neighbourhood north-west of the central city, demolished by the Apartheid government in the late 1950s as a 'folk institution'. It was, Nkosi elaborated, a place composed of 'extravagant folk heroes and heroines, *shebeens*[1] and shebeen queens, singers, nice-time girls'. Nkosi only bunked with Themba for three months though. A developing friendship with a white woman, saw him move into her home in the white suburb of Parkview. 'He didn't care a damn and would simply come out of that house in the morning always looking extremely well-dressed,' recalled Gordimer. 'And nothing happened to him. He had a way of staring at people … if whites started any nonsense, it just fell away.'

Nkosi arrived in Johannesburg during a remarkable flare of black urban culture at the end of the 1950s and the beginning of the 1960s, a time of the 'the new African cut adrift from the tribal reserve – urbanized, eager, fast-talking and brash', as he would later write. Music and dance – and, in its own way, alcohol too – were central to the character of this cultural renaissance. Sophiatown, with its 'swarming, cacophonous, strutting, brawling, vibrating life', as Themba described it, was the epicentre of this

[1] Unlicensed watering hole.

scene. 'There weren't really any clubs,' recalls Jürgen Schadeberg, a Berlin-born photographer who extensively photographed Sophiatown during its heyday. The dance venues, he says, were very makeshift, informality being a persistent feature of Johannesburg's dance halls and drinking establishments, not all but a fair many.

Schadeberg remembers: 'there was this place, which was originally an old corner shop. The windows were covered with cardboard. They made a little stage with old pieces of wood. This is where people went and danced.' One night in 1955 Schadeberg walked into this Sophiatown dancehall with his Rolleiflex camera. He was twenty-four and had a head full of Jazz. Amid the melee of bodies moving around the room that night, he spotted one particular couple dancing. The photograph he took offers a valuable clue on the character of dance and revelry during the formative years of high Apartheid between 1948 and 1990. The woman wears a beret and twinset, the man a flat-cap and beige boiler suit. Their manner distantly echoes the smartly dressed couple dancing barefoot in one of Malian photographer Malick Sidibé's many photos of Bamako's post-independence *joie de vivre*. But in Schadeberg's photo the couple's expressions are less joyous, more concentrated; the two dancers' eyes pinched shut. I read it not singularly as a gesture of rapture but refusal: they are rejecting the political savagery disassembling their neighbourhood, a brutality happening more or less in tandem with the experimental modernism unfolding elsewhere on the continent.

—

Photography is important to this essay, which attempts to write a history of the many dance venues, formal and informal, that have been a part of Johannesburg's urban fabric since 1955, which marks the start of mass evictions from Sophiatown. Photography offers an important means to visualise, as much as imagine, the topsy-turvy world Nkosi arrived upon in 1956. On the one hand, the late 1950s was a period of intense civic agitation. News photos from the period show men and women of all races gathered in huddles conversing, often amiably. The locus of struggle was typically the formal city, in particular its courtrooms, more often than not the great staircases and public areas that typify these places of the law. The 1960 Sharpeville massacre and jailing of the country's anti-apartheid political leadership four years later, both well-known events, however marked a shift towards a more physically segregated and repressive society. But, and this is important to recognise, for all the repression and violence that marked the Apartheid years, there was also lightness and dance. Joburg was, as it still is, a city infected by music, dance and alcohol. These three phenomena – music, dance and alcohol – have been central pillars of Johannesburg's social and economic culture since its hasty formation in 1886, following the discovery of gold.

Set against the backdrop of Johannesburg's emergence as an economically prosperous, musically vibrant and politically volatile post-war metropolis, this essay selectively surveys the club histories and dance venues that were a feature of the city's nightlife from 1955 onwards. Johannesburg is a dispersed and atomised metropolis: its micro-histories are diverse; they do not always intersect. It is impossible to write a complete history that encompasses every club and social space. Furthermore, this essay does not attempt to exhaustively survey every dance style or explore the on-going role of alcohol in consolidating Johannesburg's white capitalist culture, an area of research better covered by historian Charles van Onselen and geographer Chris Rogerson. While interested in lending visibility to Johannesburg's racially diverse population, the principal focus of this essay is on black and white dance venues, in particular those spaces that operated as contact zones between these two prominent Johannesburg race groups.

While South African writers, across a range of disciplines, are actively digging in the muck of history to write new stories about the country's racially divisive past, there is no definitive history of Johannesburg's nightclubs and dance venues, nor for that matter a defining study of the habits of this city's contradictory moods after dark. This essay is a contribution towards this still nascent area of study. Embedded in the narrative is a secondary focus, my research drawing attention to those few spaces, some only loosely identified as dance venues, that challenged an increasingly hard-line white racism after 1948.

Often without explicit political agenda, these spaces – many of them short-lived and forgotten, some more musically experimental than others – offer a way to read Johannesburg's history at its most convivial and joyous, as well as its most embittered and unstable. Much of what is chronicled happened at night, or at least gained its form and meaning when Johannesburg was at leisure, relaxing, and dancing after dark. The night is a time of diversionary pleasures, a time of respite – pause, but no release – from the city's acquisitive and mercantile logic. Yet, behind this filigree of pleasure offered by music, dance, and alcohol there remains the sobriety of a city characterised by exploitation, oppression, alienation, violence, and enforced strangeness.

Finding light in the dark city

An amalgam of vanquished Boer republics and English colonial outposts that unified under a single flag in 1910, South Africa's modern history – political, economic, social, musical, right down to the basics of finding pleasure after dark in clubs and dance halls – is defined by an overarching narrative of racial antagonism. This narrative was decisively shaped by the 1948 election victory of DF Malan's majority Afrikaans-speaking National Party. The outcome of this whites-only poll, which gave the National Party (operating in an alliance with NC Havenga's Afrikaner Party) a slender parliamentary majority, initiated a new chapter in an already sullied history of white colonial conquest and racial subjugation. Very quickly, the National Party instituted a technocratic programme of racial discrimination and forced separation, summarised by the term 'Apartheid'. Among the various aims of this pernicious ideology and system of social engineering was the extradition of the black body from the white city, to peripheral ghetto locations and ethnic Bantustan republics propped by the Apartheid state.

However, despite increasing state oppression and social engineering, notably through mechanisms like the new Immorality Act of 1957, which criminalised sex (or even the verbal suggestion thereof) between white and black people, there was significant mingling across the social and physical divides that marked where and how Johannesburg's residents socialised. Author Nadine Gordimer, for instance, accompanied *Drum* magazine's proprietor, Jim Bailey, to various mixed-race venues in Doornfontein, an important inner-city neighbourhood for socialising in the post-war narrative of clubs and dancing in Johannesburg, as well as in Sophiatown.

'It was a time of tremendous, memorable parties I'll never forget for the rest of my life,' said Gordimer. 'We danced *Kwela*[2] solidly. There was a great crowd of musicians and that's how I met Todd Matshikiza.' In addition to his journalism, Matshikiza was also a composer and Jazz pianist. 'If there was a piano, Todd would play like a dervish all night. Todd was the first black man I ever danced with. He had the distinction of being even smaller than I am. We were quite a midget couple.' Gordimer's anecdote is revealing. This hedonism and mutuality which endures, was less of an expression of political resistance than of shared interests and common values. Music and dance drew people together, as it still does, however fleetingly. In Johannesburg, this togetherness has long served as a means to escape the city's mercenary and oftentimes arid mercantile culture.

A city founded on and sustained by a faith in quick wealth, Johannesburg is an unromantic setting for bohemian excess. For Nkosi, Johannesburg was a desert, a far-flung metropolis cut off from the western cultures it desperately aped. Underlying the habits and routines of post-war Johannesburg's inhabitants, Nkosi intuited 'an appalling loneliness and desolation'. Writing in his 1965 essay 'Home and Exile', he adds that these very reasons 'made it so desperately important and frightfully necessary for its citizens to move fast, to live very intensely, to live harshly and vividly, for this was the sole reason for their being there: to make money, to spend it and make more'. His insight chimes with an earlier statement by one of the city's original get-rich rabble. 'We are none of us here for the benefit of our health,' wrote a miner in a letter to a Johannesburg newspaper in 1893. 'Money making and money grabbing is the alpha and omega of those resident on these fields.'

[2] After the Zulu expression for 'get-up!' A pennywhistle-based street music with jazzy underpinnings and a skiffle-like beat. To learn more about the history of dance music in South Africa please see Rangoato Hlasane's essay in this book.

These boisterous descriptions are fundamental to understanding Johannesburg, a city of fraught natural environments and baroque thunderstorms, of tremulous first arrivals and wistful exits, of trade, plunder, theft and sudden death, of love, heartbreak, friendship, and brittle mutuality. The grim years of high Apartheid, which spatially reinforced existing segregation and saw the rollout of an institutionalised Protestantism, added a further layer of complexity to the character of Johannesburg. An escape from the city and its complexities took one of two forms: literally leaving the city, which meant defeat or freedom, or, as most inhabitants did and continue to do, retreat – to the shebeens and nightclubs, haunts and hangouts.

Requiem for Sophiatown

Sometimes referred to as 'Little Harlem', Sophiatown occupies an important symbolic place in the club history of Johannesburg. Described as a 'bastion of nontribal urbanity' by music historian Gwen Ansell, and an 'exciting cultural Bohemia' by Nkosi, its terraced Edwardian homesteads recall an earlier urban formation of the city. Sophiatown was founded in 1904 as a rental-only living space for black residents forcibly evicted from the mixed-race neighbourhood of Brickfields following a reported outbreak of the plague. By the 1950s, when its dance scene was in full swing, it was a congested mixed-race suburb pressing up against its white working-class neighbours. While its energy radiated outwards, Sophiatown was also a centripetal force, the centre of an experimental and syncretic form of modernity.

In the late 1950s, dancers in Johannesburg's numerous temporal and imaginary republics were actively shunning the manners and graces of Imperial England in favour of the optimism and jauntiness of the United States. For people like Nkosi and his cohorts, Sophiatown – with its Jazz-infused *tsaba-tsaba* dance scene and two big cinema complexes, Balansky's and Odin – functioned as a kind of ground zero for this new urban sensibility. Notwithstanding its slum-like qualities and thriving criminal underclass, Sophiatown offered residents a community and an infrastructure, the latter generally lacking in the new black settlements formalised by city officials on the southwestern periphery of the city.

'We listened to Ella Fitzgerald, Louis Armstrong, Stardust, Frank Sinatra, and lots of others,' recalled singer Dolly Rathebe in 1997. Rathebe, along with Dorothy Masuku and Miriam Makeba, forged her reputation in Sophiatown's dance halls, including the white-owned Odin. 'Sophiatown was like the sunny side of the street.' Rathebe's music checklist is useful in highlighting a new orientation among black Johannesburgers, who were less inspired by the confidant polyphony emitted by newly independent black African states in comparison to the United States and its cool modernist sounds. 'America had a huge influence on black South Africa, mainly through the movies and music, which had developed into a kind of subculture,' remarked Jazz writer Don Albert, in 2007. As a young man Albert frequented the Jazz scene. 'I was fascinated by these hip black people dressed in their peg-bottom trousers, snap-brimmed hats and American-style raincoats jitterbugging or dancing almost in slow motion, at half tempo that was almost suggestive.'

Sophiatown and its particular brand of high life represented the culmination of four decades of musical innovation, one in which US Ragtime and Swing merged with indigenous sounds to create an authentic local idiom – Jazz for short. This sound would deeply figure and influence the dance scenes that followed, the culture it spawned still an important reference point for contemporary musicians, fashion designers, and photographers. However, it is important to recognise, though, that the adoption of US-American attitudes and sounds was never a wholesale process: it was 'never a one-way traffic', as music historian, Ansell, wrote in 2012. Still, the love affair with the US was, in a sense, monogamous.

Another historical anecdote underscores this point. Shortly after the launch of *Drum* magazine in 1951, editor Anthony Sampson met a man at the Bantu Men's Social Centre (BMSC), the influential social club in central Johannesburg. 'Tribal music!' spat the man in a floppy US-American suit. 'Tribal history! Chiefs! We don't care about chiefs!' He was responding to the patronising scope of the first few issues of *Drum*. 'Give us Jazz and film stars, man! We want Duke Ellington, Satchmo and hot dames! Yes, brother, anything American. You can cut out this junk about *kraals* and folk tales and *Basutos* in blankets – forget it. You're just trying to keep us backward, that's what.' No doubt embellished for the purposes of Sampson's 1983 biography, however this story does vest a broader insight as urban Johannesburg was literate and impertinent, and also interested and knowledgeable about the world – especially the US; that faraway place with a sound and image that resonated in Sophiatown.

But, concurrent with this new optimism, and compelled by its own internal energy, was the Apartheid juggernaut. In 1955, a battalion of armed policemen entered Sophiatown and forcefully expelled residents defying eviction orders issued under the Group Areas Act of 1950, a key apartheid law. Indian residents were despatched to the new suburb of Lenasia, mixed-race coloured people to Eldorado Park, Chinese inhabitants to central Johannesburg, and the majority black population to Meadowlands, a new settlement forming, part of a jigsaw puzzle of exclusionist urbanism established in 1904 at the former Klipspruit sewage dump. In 1963, three years after Sophiatown was entirely demolished and its 65,000 inhabitants relocated, this new urban formation on the southwest edge of the city was collectively renamed Soweto. Johannesburg was entering a new phase of its history.

Exile and improvisation

In 1964, eight senior African National Congress (ANC) leaders were found guilty of treason and sentenced to life in prison. The increasingly oppressive political regime of Hendrik Verwoerd, the hard-line nationalist elected prime minister in 1958, also prompted a mass exodus of artistic talent from the country. Nkosi, who would graduate to chief reporter at *Drum*'s Sunday newspaper, the *Golden City Post*, accepted a fellowship to study journalism at Harvard University in 1961; Bessie Head moved to Botswana; and Themba moved to Swaziland, where he died a drunk in 1968. By the mid-1960s, many Jazz musicians had left the country. Those who opted to stay found it difficult to improvise in the new government–planned townships, essentially labour compounds serviced by the bare minimum civic necessities.

The material impoverishment of Johannesburg's townships nonetheless contributed to distinctive forms of night-time entertainment, the provisional and ephemeral character of which cultivated 'specific orientations toward, knowledge of, and practices for, dealing with urban life', to repurpose a quote by urban theorist AbdouMaliq Simone. In other words, people found new ways of negotiating privation. As has so often been the case in Johannesburg's history, music and dance played a key role in negotiating the new, the strange, and the unknown.

An example of this improvisational practice, that emerged in mid-twentieth century township culture, was the 'concert-and-dance' phenomenon. Drawing on the institution of tea meetings, polite community events devoted to song, township residents repurposed schools and church halls for all-night entertainment. Starting at 8pm and continuing until the early hours, concert-and-dance events began with a seated vaudeville concert before the hall was transformed into a dance area. 'Concert-and-dance employed large ensembles, modelled on American swing bands, whose sound, unlike *Marabi*[3], was big enough to fill the communal halls newly built in the townships,' writes Ansell in her pungent story of urban black music, *Soweto Blues*.

Predating the demolition of Sophiatown, similar events were also staged as more upmarket versions, in city venues like the aforementioned Bantu Men's Social Centre (BMSC) and Inchcape Hall, both in the CBD. Notwithstanding the forced removal of black citizens to its margins, Johannesburg relied on black labour to function. Although largely fashioned to serve as a white urban centre, Johannesburg's CBD nonetheless included after-hours entertainment venues catering to the city's black working men, many employed in clerical and physical labour jobs.

Where trade unionist Naboth Mokgatle danced at Inchcape Hall, BMSC was equally convivial. Founded in 1924, by Reverend Ray E. Phillips and a group of white liberals and black professionals, BMSC's members included ANC-activists Nelson Mandela and Walter Sisulu. It offered a

[3] Township shebeen music was originally based on pedal organs and with links to US-Jazz, Ragtime, and Blues.

library and recreation (billiards, chess) facilities, its main hall used as meeting venue for political organisers and dance venue by night owls. Walter and Albertina Sisulu held their wedding reception at BMSC in 1944; Mandela was best man and the Merry Blackbirds, Johannesburg's 'most polished' black Jazz ensemble, provided music. Todd Matshikiza and his wife Esme were also regulars. 'In a way the BMSC was quite formal then, although you did have the jitterbug and music from America post-1945,' Esme recalled in a 2006 interview. 'We had very formal dances with the Merry Blackbirds band with their bow ties. Solomon "Zuluboy" Cele's Jazz Maniacs were less formal, more like people's music – and then came the cheeky college boys of the Harlem Swingsters.'

In 1958, playwright Athol Fugard staged his first full-length play, *No-Good Friday*, at BMSC. It was not an isolated instance. In Johannesburg, politics, theatre, and musical performance have long coexisted, often in the same space. A good example of this overlapping occurred next door to BMSC, at Dorkay House, a new training venue and administrative centre established in 1958 for Union Artists, an all-black drama group. Dorkay House staged talent contests and small shows. One aim was to develop large touring concerts. Todd Matshikiza's 1959 Jazz musical, *King Kong*, which launched the international singing career of Miriam Makeba, was its most celebrated creation. *King Kong* was initially performed in the Great Hall at the University of the Witwatersrand (Wits). Being a private institution, the university was able to circumvent the race laws of the time and offer the show to multi-racial audiences. This tactical victory over Apartheid saw this liberal English-speaking university emerge as a key venue for musical experimentation and cross-cultural contact in the decades to come.

Negotiating the White Republic

In 1961, The Jazz Epistles, a short-lived bebop band that included Dollar Brand (later known as Abdullah Ibrahim), Kippie Moeketsi, Jonas Gwangwa, and Hugh Masekela, won first prize at the Cold Castle Jazz Festival, held in the Johannesburg City Hall. Phillip Tabane, an extraordinary guitar virtuoso and in later years accomplished musical experimenter, was awarded a prize in the solo category. Founded in 1958, the itinerant Jazz festival was the next year staged in Soweto's Moroka-Jabavu Stadium. By then Masekela, Gwangwa, and Brand were already in exile. But a new vanguard was emerging. Chris McGregor and his Septet – a precursor group to the influential Blue Notes – performed to 4,000 Soweto Jazz fans, including 'tight-panted girls twisting on the football pitch'.

Jazz in Soweto was not simply a key modernist musical form; it was also enraptured dance music. The 1964 Cold Castle Jazz Festival confirmed the popularity of Jazz in Soweto when 40,000 punters packed into the Orlando Stadium, a football ground. The Malombo Jazzmen (which included Tabane) shared first prize with the Early Mabuza Quartet. The festival's success was however marred by violence. Six men were killed outside the festival gates as rival gangs fought, prompting the withdrawal of the title sponsor. It would be the last of these influential, era-defining Jazz concerts.

North from Soweto, over the sulphurous yellow mine dumps that still separate the former township from the CBD, Jazz culture was also taking hold, particularly in the residential neighbourhood of Hillbrow. Built on a northern ridge overlooking the city, by the 1960s Hillbrow was likened to the Latin Quarter in Paris and New York's West Village. Its vibrant Jazz underground was ambiguously greeted by mainstream culture. 'Hillbrow and Berea, which were once fashionable residential suburbs, have now become a favourite field of activity for bebop addicts, brazen Jazz hounds and bar-smashing youths,' wrote psychiatrist Louis Franklin Freed, in his book *Crime in South Africa* (1963).

Jazz photographer Basil Breakey, who offered members of the mixed-race Blue Notes Jazz sextet a floor to crash on in his Hillbrow flat after gigs, recalled the neighbourhood's Jazz years very differently. The Verwoerd government, which was spearheading a policy of separate development, was actively policing pass violations. For the Blue Notes, this complicated the practicalities of their 1963 residency at the Downbeat, a Jazz venue near the Chelsea Hotel in Catherine Street. 'We had to be secretive, because they [black Jazzmen] were not allowed to be in the white area, as they didn't have a pass to work,' said Breakey in 1993. 'They were meant to be in the location.' Despite the mythology that has grown up around the Blue Notes, who transformed into a Free Jazz group in Europe after they went into exile in 1964, their stay in Hillbrow was unremarkable. Downbeat drew a predominantly white audience, although black patrons were not unheard of. 'It was never really full, and was struggling to survive, with the guys playing there about three times a week,' recalled Breakey. 'Downbeat never really made money. The music was very avant-garde … It was not just entertaining stuff, it was very expressive, very expressionistic, reflected the society at the time.' The venue lasted six months.

—

As the 1960s progressed, Hillbrow's Bebop addicts and Johannesburg's white Rockers, who in a 1959 Schadeberg photo are shown lethargically dancing at the Rand Easter Show during the city's first brush with Rock'n'Roll, were updated by a new generation of night crawlers. This new generation looked to England, not the US, for inspiration. In his autobiography *Boy From Bethulie* (2004), well-known actor, Patrick Mynhardt, describes visiting a club called Marrakech at the then upmarket Summit Club in Hillbrow, where he found himself 'mesmerized by a go-go girl in a mini-skirt dancing in front of a mirror'. Her name was Zaza Zimmerman; there was also a Felicity Fouché, and the DJ was named Neville Peacock.

'There were psychedelic and ultra-violet lights and if you stood under the latter, all your *klein goed* [small things] shone like a beacon for all to see,' photographer Anne Lapedus Brest remembered, a former patron. Flashing lights, like smoke machines, lasers, and video projections, were a hallmark of 'upmarket' entertainment features, and in Johannesburg keys into a history of formalised dance venues with liquor licenses. For much of the city's history, these formalised economies catered to principally white patrons.

Other Hillbrow clubs cashing in on the youth culture boom of the 1960s were Club-a-Go-Go, Yellow Submarine, and Purple Marmalade, which also featured Soul acts like Francis 'Zorro' Kekana and The Miracles, both from Pretoria. There were also discotheques at the Ambassador Hotel (Friday and Saturday) and Chelsea Hotel (nightly). Hillbrow's white heterosexual nightlife may have been boisterous, sometimes even prone to spill over into violence as class differences led to brawling, but in the main, it did not represent a significant destabilising threat to the prevailing social order. By distinction, Johannesburg's gay party scene did.

Roman Dutch common law, which was imported to the country by Dutch colonisers in 1652, criminalised sodomy. In 1966, police raided a private home in the wealthy northern suburb of Forest Town. Nine men 'masquerading as women' were arrested. The raid was discussed in parliament, prompting a threat to extend anti-homosexual legislation.
'The result, in opposition to this threat, was the instigation of the Homosexual Law Reform movement, whose sole aim was to prevent the proposed anti-gay bill from becoming law,' write Mark Gevisser and Edwin Cameron in *Defiant Desire* (1995), an important study of gay culture during Apartheid. By the mid-1960s, they write, there were several gay-owned men-only dance clubs. The Farmhouse, north of Johannesburg on the road to Pretoria, was the most popular. Closer to the CBD, there was the Hideaway in Berea and 'hippie-ish' Midniter in the central city.

The submersed but convivial nature of the white gay scene existed in marked distinction to that in Soweto, where the outlets for gay socialising – let alone dancing – were limited. One documented form of socialising for gay men, this in a society where the traditions of patriarchy endure, were the Monday night *stokvel* parties. A long-established alternative way of pooling wealth among black South Africans either denied or unable to access formal banking, *stokvels* remain a vibrant part of township life. Lenders contribute to a shared pool that intermittently pays out the collection to each member. *Stokvel* meetings, which mix the earnest business of money with the sale and consumption of alcohol, are hospitable affairs, albeit closed to outsiders. It is this aspect, their essential privacy, which has long made them gay-friendly socialising spaces. Although poorly documented, the decades-old existence of *stokvels* as gay socialising venues complicates the flippant white narrative of hetero- and homosexual dancing during the Apartheid years.

Resistance and Avant-Gardism

[4] Rand is the South African currency.

The legacy of the 1960s in the west, in particular its millennial ideology, had a marked impact on white South Africa. White prosperity, the product of an extended post-war economic boom, saw white middle-class youths begin to experiment with alternative identities sponsored by the proliferation of western musical subcultures. In the 1970s, the city's underground scene took shape around Jazz, Folk, and Blues groups, with 'acid-astral rockers' Freedom's Children playing to enraptured Hillbrow audiences at Club 505 and the Ambassador Hotel. The Out of Town Club, a dance venue north of Johannesburg, hosted open-air music festivals in the mould of Woodstock. These concerts were sometimes marred by hooliganism. 'Most of those doing the fighting, or at least starting the brawls we were later to find out, were policemen,' said Dave Marks, whose Third Ear sound rig became a feature of the segregated outdoor festivals of the 1970s.

Inspired by his encounter at Woodstock, Marks approached the event's legendary sound engineer, Bill Hanley, to donate some of the Woodstock speakers to his fledgling sound company. Hanley agreed, on the proviso the speakers were not used at segregated festivals. The condition was not always honoured, as white promoters offered lucrative usage fees. Nonetheless, Marks largely honoured the spirit of the original transaction, his Third Ear rig providing the sound for the Free People's concerts, an annual music festival produced by Wits University throughout the 1970s and 1980s, as well as in Soweto. 'Unlike city festivals, township shows were a pleasure in the 1960s and 1970s,' Marx has stated. 'There were no fights inside the playing field. People squeezed every last drop of enjoyment out of their hard earned rands.'[4]

The 1970s not only marked the blossoming of Johannesburg's white bohemia, there was also a 'renaissance of black opposition', to quote political historian William Beinart. With a population approaching one million in the 1970s, Soweto remained an oppressive labour dormitory. It had one hotel, one cinema, and only one established nightclub. The newly upgraded Jabulani Amphitheatre, a 15,000-seater outdoor cultural and sporting venue built in the suburb of Moroka in 1952, became a key site of political congress and after-hours carousing. Currently disused, it hosted concerts by African American performers such as The Staple Singers and Dobbie Gray, as well as the four-day long 1974 Soweto National Jazz Festival. The latter event, which featured the Third Ear rig, included a performance by Malombo, Phillip Tabane's genre-defying Jazz-fusion trio.

In 1976, television was introduced to white South Africans. In the same year Soweto students revolted against the state-led implementation of Afrikaans as the language of instruction. The revolt, which keyed into a far deeper disaffection with the status quo, saw numerous state-owned properties destroyed. Tellingly, the Jabulani Amphitheatre was left untouched.

Ironically, students affiliated to the ANC's underground network in Soweto bombed its only nightclub. Founded near the Orlando railway station in 1972 by Lucky Michaels, Pelican was a meeting place of 'clevers, socialites, wannabes and hangers-on', according to journalist ZB Molefe. Its iconic status was reinforced by its visual prominence. 'Until the 1980s no building could be built higher than one story; for a long time, only the unlicensed Pelican nightclub had a second floor,' writes Bill Nasson in *All, Here, and Now* (1992). Routinely packed, the Pelican offered food, music, and dancing. 'For a few hours, from 10pm until 6am, the sea of swirling bodies on the dance floor and the tables would forget Apartheid,' wrote Molefe.

Dancing bodies late at night express a different solidarity to bodies tightly packed in a political march. The bombing of the Pelican reinforces this difference. According to veteran journalist Harry Mashabela, the Pelican, along with another shebeen on Mapetla Street, was bombed when owners overlooked students appeals not to sell liquor. 'Students wanted shebeens to identify themselves with the struggle by abstaining from selling drinks,' writes Mashabela in *A People on the Boil* (2006). A somewhat obscure historical footnote, the Pelican bombing highlights the submerged tensions between South Africa's struggle culture and the pursuit of individual pleasure. In white Johannesburg, the complicated relationship between dance and political dissidence became a facet of Johannesburg's increasingly hedonistic gay club scene.

In contrast the Dungeon, an enduring icon of the gay club scene, 'funkier clubs with more guys, more adventurous music and more camping' emerged, write Gevisser and Cameron. They included the Anaconda, Mandy's, Blood, and Zipps, venues whose 'dark Disco' was 'blatantly sexual' and 'throbbed with sensuality and defiance', as one regular has put it. Journalist Matthew Krouse, a regular patron as a teen, says there was a definite political edge to attending these clubs. Artist Steven Cohen agrees, although carefully calibrates the nature of the political edge: 'Emerging into the radical (not quite non but less racist) gay fuck clubs of the 1980s, and the wild cruising world of shops, clubs, toilets, parks and bushes was an education in exploring the limits of civil liberties and the delicate aptitude of downright law breaking which has become so useful in my work.'

The low rent nature of the venues, adds Krouse, also allied them to the tradition of prohibition-era speakeasies in the US, where entrance was strictly regulated. While many of the gay clubs enforced a 'no blacks' policy, Mandy's didn't. Rechristened New Mandy's when it relocated to 96 End Street, the venue was raided by police during the bustling summer Christmas holidays in 1979. Homosexuality, while tolerated, was still illegal. White patrons were manhandled, photographed, and verbally abused, while a still harsher treatment was meted out against the few black gay men present at the club. The event, which heralded a period of renewed police harassment, galvanised the gay community. 'Many South African gay people refer to the 1979 Mandy's Raid—and not the 1966 Forest Town Raid—as South Africa's Stonewall,' write Gevisser and Cameron. After the closure of Mandy's in the mid-1980s, this End Street address became a fashionable New Wave club, Idols, and later still, in the late 1990s, the up-for-it white Rave club ESP.

End days, and new beginnings

In 1986 Shifty Records, an independent record label founded by musicians Lloyd Ross and Ivan Kadey, released *Live At Jameson's*. A live recording of the Cherry Faced Lurchers performing a year earlier during their residency at Jameson's, a Jazz and Rock venue in the CBD, the set included 'Do the Lurch'. The song humorously describes the growing alienation of Johannesburg's white underground through the jaunty narrative of one of its key protagonists, James Phillips, formerly the vocalist with Punk band Corporal Punishment. The song is a masterpiece of vernacular Punk. In the song Phillips tells of his attempt to enter Q's Supper Club, one of a handful of upmarket white Disco and High-Energy clubs that thrived in the CBD (and also included Xanadu, Caesars Palace, and Raffles). The doorman points to Phillips' cheap sport shoes. Phillips responds by name checking a well-known white music producer and is instantly welcomed into a world of 'flashing lights' and 'DJ in misery'.

None of Shifty's diverse catalogue, which included white rabblerousing Rock and Afro-Jazz fusion, received airplay on the two white-owned independent radio stations, Capitol Radio 604 and Radio 702, established to challenge the state broadcaster's ruthlessly segregated and musically dour radio programming. Jameson's, which possessed an archaic, albeit still-valid, Boer republic liquor license allowing it to serve mixed-race audiences freely, functioned as one of a handful of redoubts against segregated pleasure. Managed by Herbert Scheubmayr, a gay former Olympic swimmer from Austria who previously ran a club in the Chelsea Hotel with Dave Marks, Jameson's shared Shifty's freeform musical tastes. With its diverse line-up of acts, it represented an idealised republic in a segregated society. Another key venue in the central city was DV8, based in the Dawson's Hotel in Hillbrow, which provided a platform to musical acts éVoid and Via Afrika, whose brand of ethnic New Wave briefly found favour with New York club DJs. 'We wanted our music to be a visual experience of textures, cultures, and language—a celebration of the wonders of being African and the realisation of this privilege,' said René Veldsman of Via Afrika in 2000.

This suturing together of musical forms, fashion idioms, and dance styles remain a character of Johannesburg's fringe clubs. But in the 1970s and 1980s, musical syncretism and cultural cross-pollination was disapprovingly reviewed by the state. In Soweto, shebeens and informal club spaces faced routine harassment, not only from the authorities but also from the Makabasas, a police-armed gang based in Orlando who targeted political activists. The harassment sometimes extended to white musicians and venues. Folk singer Roger Lucey's career was famously sabotaged. 'It was a time when *jolling* [Dancing and carousing] was dangerous, where police tear-gassed clubs and right-wingers slashed tyres at Rhythm Against Detention gigs,' says music promoter Deon Maas. Music and dancing, rather than being spontaneous expressions of culture, were eyed with suspicion by the state. 'The police and the state security apparatus seemed to generally view musical preferences as a political rather than a personal choice,' wrote music historian Anne Schumann in 2008.

—

State power, while notionally omnipresent, is markedly sedentary and reactive. This is a strategic weakness. In February 1990, the African National Congress was unbanned, and its leadership released from prison. A tense and protracted negotiation between black and white politicians ensued over the next four years. This interregnum, which witnessed a great deal of violence in the townships and the rapid repurposing of Johannesburg's ailing CBD, was also the source of flourishing new dance scenes. Echoes of the electronic dance music revolution that was sweeping across Europe were already a part of the DJ mixes at clubs like Idols and Thunderdome in Johannesburg. At Kippies, the small Jazz nightclub built next door to the Market Theatre, and run by legendary 1980s popstar Sipho 'Hotstix' Mabuse, exiles mingled with old friends in a venue named after the Sophiatown saxophonist, Kippie Moeketsi.

Established in 1976 and located in the city's former Indian fruit market, the Market Theatre hosted Johannesburg's earliest rave, 'Luna-Sea', in a disused retail annex. Held in February 1992, its organisers, the Activ8 DJ crew, played a mix of European Trance Techno and British Hardcore/Breakbeat. Key members of the largely Pretoria-based collective included Graeme 'G-Force' Hector and Christos 'DJ Christos' Katsaitis. In 1992, Activ8 DJs provided the music at key early warehouse raves held inside the disused Piccadilly Theatre in Yeoville, the vacant Wembley Arena in Turfontein, and an empty light-industrial tower block on End Street.

This informal and itinerant scene rapidly formalised. In 1993, the club Fourth World opened in Doornfontein. It was the first Johannesburg dance venue to focus entirely on 'machine-made, Acid-laced, and 4/4-propelled grooves', to quote music critic Greg Bowes. Jointly founded by Eric Kirsten and Preston van Wyk, who had recently returned from London where he worked as a fashion designer with dance music pioneer Jazzie B of Soul II Soul, Fourth World initially ploughed a lonely furrow. Its ethos was millennial, druggy, and optimistically non-racial, even though it attracted few black ravers.

The fast-paced tempo of Fourth World's club scene, demanded in part by the ecstasy and LSD-fuelled drug culture, was, by 1995, being copied and commercialised by rival promoters. Peter White's large corporatized Mother events typified the endgame of a commercialised white rave scene and recalled the shrewd niche programming of Clive Calder's white Folk Rock events north of Johannesburg in the early 1970s. Many of Fourth World's original DJs retreated from the increasingly cynical white rave scene, some preferring to focus on black audiences. Christos Katsaitis, dubbed the 'godfather' of South African House, was involved in cofounding the record labels Kalawa, House Afrika, and Phat Kat in the early 1990s and is an established hit-maker.

In the early 1990s, as new black dance music was being honed by Arthur Mafokate and M'du Masilela, Katsaitis entered the emerging black electronic dance music scene. In its earliest manifestations, Kwaito was formulated and defined at informal parties and record label sponsored events in the townships that satellite Johannesburg, Pretoria, and Rustenburg. According to one account, a community hall in Tembisa, a township northeast of Johannesburg, hosted the first version of a township rave. In the central city, which since the mid-1980s had witnessed an exodus of white corporations to increasingly far-flung new premises north of the city, formerly white neighbourhoods like Hillbrow, Berea, and Yeoville were transforming – both aurally and demographically. Solly Rametsi's Razzmatazz in Hillbrow and Tandoor in Yeoville both became closely associated with the Kwaito sound.

Established in 1991, Razzmatazz launched the career of Oscar 'Oskido' Mdlongwa (aka Oscar Warona). Cofounder of Kalawa Records, with Don Laka and Christos, and an early mentor to current Afro-House sensation DJ Black Coffee (Nathi Maphumulo), Mdlongwa's biography is a typical Johannesburg story of rags to riches. After ditching a job as a technician at a car dealership, Mdlongwa set up a food stand on the pavement outside Razzmatazz, largely because of his interest in music. He was invited to play in the club a week later when the resident DJ failed to arrive. During his early residency at the club, Brenda Fassie, the queen of 1980s Bubblegum pop and an early adopter of the Kwaito sound, frequented Razzmatazz.

Highs, lows, and in-betweens

Like Hillbrow, which rapidly transformed into a predominantly black neighbourhood by the end of the 1990s, Yeoville, a bucolic white bohemia formerly populated by lower-income Hasidic Jews, also changed complexion. House of Tandoor on Rockey Street became a key venue, both for Kwaito and Ragga/Dancehall. Formerly an Indian-themed restaurant neighbouring a popular neighbourhood bar, by the late 1990s it had transformed into a multi-space live music venue. Bongo Maffin's Adrian

'Appleseed' Muphemhi played here. Kwaito's quick succession from underground sound to mainstream soundtrack was not without its problems. 'What Kwaito lacks thus far is an underground of the underground,' observed journalist Themba ka Maathe in 2003. He contrasted its poetics and generative potential with Hip-Hop, which was founded on a kind of literacy. 'If you look at most of the Kwaito stars like Mandoza, he was a carjacker. Kwaito helped those guys to get out of the traps of the township, the crime, and the drugs. If it had not been for the excitement that the people had about the new democracy, Kwaito would never have happened. The music was, and even now still is, a celebration.'

The celebration was capped, at least musically, by the establishment in 1997 of the youth radio station, YFM. Based in the inner-city suburb of Bertrams, within one month of its first broadcast 600,000 predominantly young black listeners in the greater Johannesburg and Pretoria metropolitan area had tuned into YFM. Originally managed by Dirk Hartford, a former labour activist who has since returned to his trade union roots, YFM, in its early incarnation at least, was an important beacon for a kind of music-inspired intellectualism. S'busiso 'The General' Nxumalo, who together with Sifiso Ntuli in 1996 founded the Politburo Sessions, an itinerant nightclub project, was the first editor of the radio station's print publication, *Ymag*.

YFM also provided a valuable platform for Hip-Hop through its 'Rap Activity Jam' sessions, which pitted rival MCs live on air. New talent discovered on this live show included Pitch Black Afro (Thulani Ngcobo), a classically trained musician who switched to Hip-Hop in 2000. Audiences for Hip-Hop were always smaller than those for Kwaito, which despite its lyrical paucity and rudimentary musical structure came to define the postliberation moment. At early 'Rap Activity Jams' young MCs delivered rhymes that rehearsed gestures, themes, and phraseology from US Hip-Hop culture. Bands like Skwatta Kamp, formed in 1996, helped create a more indigenous sound. Their 2003 hit, 'Feel Like Dancing', drew heavily on Kwaito style, offering a rudimentary bass and uncomplicated lyrics with unpretentious styling (T-shirts and jeans). Despite the uptake of Hip-Hop, in the early 2000s Johannesburg only had one Hip-Hop club, Rippingtons, which hosted open mic sessions on Saturdays. By the mid-2000s, Soweto's Orlando West neighbourhood claimed a small Hip-Hop scene, with the Slaghuis [butchery] operating as a live venue in Diepkloof. In 2007, Skwatta Kamp's Nkululeko 'Flabba' Habedi acknowledged: 'Hip-Hop is still young, cats are still learning and people are still trying to get into the groove of local Hip-Hop.'

The informal, hard-to-track nature of the Soweto Hip-Hop scene is matched by the even smaller Indie Rock scene, which for a time in the late 2000s flourished at a private home in Pimville, Soweto. It is safe to say that by the early 2000s, the rigid typologies of Apartheid life, that had determined who could like what kind of music and dance in what locality, were being upended. Anything was possible. Smiso 'Okmalumkoolkat' Zwane, one half of the Electro-pop outfit Dirty Paraffin, whose sounds blend UK Bass music genres and French electronic style with Zulu musical idioms, summarised the unpredictable, open-to-change spirit underlying young Johannesburg in a 2012 interview. 'The local music scene is trying to find itself,' said Zwane, whose band has played at the Alexander Theatre, part of a network of hipster dance venues that include Kitchener's and SubLevel, both in Braamfontein. 'Gatekeepers are old and they want the same damn song. Gatekeepers are not in touch with what the youth is currently fond of and up to. We are not competing locally; we are competing internationally.'

Right now, right here

In 2007, the Maponya Mall, a private development named after Soweto entrepreneur Richard Maponya, opened along a main axis road through Soweto. The mall's aim was not philanthropic: it aimed to tap into Soweto's estimated 4.3-billion R[5] consumer market. There are many markers of Soweto's transformation, ranging from bus stations to the newly opened Soweto Theatre, a venue with three performance spaces seating 430, 180 and 90 patrons. While many in Johannesburg mourn the closures of the Bassline in Melville (2003) and Kippies (2005), two key Jazz venues, the legacy of Johannesburg's Jazz scene still figures prominently in the manners of Johannesburg's nightlife. Sophiatown continues to loom large in the imagination of Johannesburg, partly because it represents a brief-lived black urban renaissance that is now a realisable long-term possibility.

In June 2012, a month after the opening of the Soweto Theatre, Zakes Bantwini, a big second-generation Kwaito star, hosted a one-night only musical at the venue. Titled 'Upfront', it was billed as 'a tribute to Sophiatown' and followed a familiar concert-and-dance format. 'It was one of the most extraordinary nights in my theatre career, in the sense that he sold the place out, online, in two days, gone,' said Carl Johnson, the theatre's general manager. 'He filled the 430-seater main venue with tickets priced at R300[6] a head.' For a young generation of upwardly mobile professionals the price was the equivalent of a modest meal for two at any city eatery. Bantwini's show included a 13-piece band, dancers, a string section, styled VJ'ing on a video wall, and a roster of guest performers, including superstar DJ Black Coffee. The audience came dressed in suits and ball gowns, as if headed for the Bantu Men's Social Centre or Odin Cinema, back in the day. 'Growing up', stated Bantwini in a pre-concert statement, 'I was told about the great musical stories of Sophiatown, and as a musician I want to bring this culturally-rich era to life. This was a time in our nation's history that was brimming with musical talent and where legends were born.'

Navigating contemporary Johannesburg, a city of fitful moods and glaring income disparities, requires something between unbridled optimism and

[5] At the time around 430 million Euro.
[6] At the time around 30 Euro.

calculated scepticism. This place is also a city of sudden endings and unexpected death. In 2008, a wave of anti-immigrant violence took shape and spread out from a township on Johannesburg's eastern outskirts. As has always been the case, locals retreated to their preferred haunts. There was a diverse array to choose from. Privileged white youths could seek out the bland corporatized leisure entertainment offered by Tiger Tiger, an imported brand concept of British nightclubs. Hipsters could lurch at The Woods or Kitchener's. Thesis, then a newly launched fashion retailer in Soweto, was about to host its first Social Jam Sessions, a monthly live music platform echoing the concert-and-dance formula. In Hillbrow, young women prepared for another night's reveal at the Summit Club, now a strip club. Different names, different sounds, similar patterns: that's Joburg for you. But this city leaves no room for complacency. Onwards.

In 2006, planners in the city of Johannesburg published the city's first long-term strategy document. It set out to offer a 'coherent story' of Johannesburg's future development path. Responding to recent developmental shifts, including South Africa's incorporation into the BRICS bloc of developing economies, the city's forward-looking strategy reconceptualised Johannesburg as a 'world class African city of the future', which it qualified to mean 'a vibrant, economically inclusive and multi-cultural African city'. Two years later, a thirty-five-year-old Mozambican man, Ernesto Alfabeto Nhamuave, was cruelly burned alive during the early days of the xenophobic violence that spread across South Africa. That violence continues to flare up, in Johannesburg as elsewhere. Africa is an imaginary ideal as much as it is a geographical reality for Johannesburg.

Perhaps a clue to resolving the unstable influence of Africa, an idea that has always been held at bay in Johannesburg due to its transatlantic love affair, lies in the call to dance issued in a 2012 invite to one of S'busiso Nxumalo's Politburo Sessions. 'The General on the dex and a whole lot of speshal guests,' read the invitation, naming a venue in the far-flung northern suburb of Rivonia. 'LIVE performance by Les Fantastiques Guys … Kinshasa in Jozi.' A new conversation was being proposed. Audiences are responding. People are dancing to the new sounds, and in the process learning, and changing the city, a habit music and dance has always sponsored in this physically diffuse city. This evolving moment represents the next chapter in the story of Johannesburg, in particular the story about its enraptured moods and changeable character after dark, when there is less talk and more dancing, and everything is possible.

Bibliography

Ansell, Gwen, *Soweto Blues – Jazz, Popular Music & Politics in South Africa* (London: Continuum, 2004).

Freed, Louis Franklin, *Crime in South Africa – An Integralist Approach* (Cape Town: Juta, 1963).

Gevisser, Mark, and Cameron, Edwin, *Defiant Desire – Gay and Lesbian Lives in South Africa* (London: Routledge, 1995).

Lodge, Tom, and Nasson, Bill (eds.), *All, Here and Now – Black Politics in South Africa in the 1980s* (Cape Town: David Philip Publishers, 1992).

Mashabela, Harry, *A People on the Boil – Reflections on 1976 and Beyond* (Johannesburg: Jacana Media, 2006).

Mynhardt, Patrick, *Boy from Bethulie* (Johannesburg: Witwatersrand University Press, 2004).

Seven, Alexandra Township, Johannesburg, 2016, photo: Chris Saunders & Impilo Mapantsula

DJ Invizable, Orange Farm Township, Johannesburg, 2015, photo: Chris Saunders

Vilacoster Pantsula Crew, Swaneville, Johannesburg, 2016, photo: Chris Saunders & Impilo Mapantsula

NAPLES

MUSIC / SPACES
Under the Volcano

From Caruso to Neapolitan Power and Vesuwave to Techno

Danilo Capasso

▶ P.241

SPACES / POLITICS
Neapolitan Nights

From Vesuvian Blues to Planetary Vibes

Vincenzo Cavallo and Iain Chambers

▶ P.263

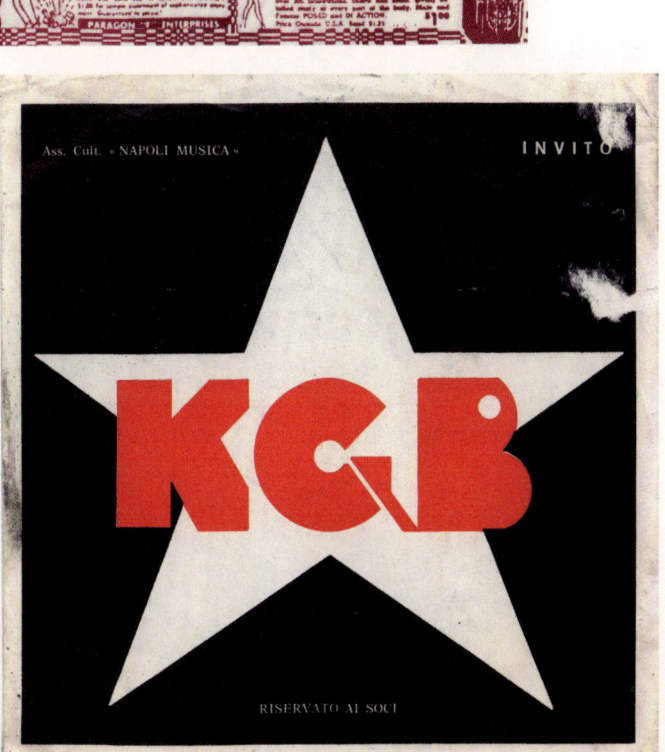

Flyer for a live concert with different bands at Diamond Dogs, Naples, 1987

KGB club flyer, Naples, 1989

237 PLATES NAPLES

Flyer for Contropotere record release CP01, Tien'a Ment, Naples, 1995

Contropotere, Stella Headquarters, Naples, 1992, photo: Oliviero Toscani

Tien'a Ment squatters at work, Naples, 1992, photo: Giovanni Calemma

Under the Volcano – From Caruso to Neapolitan Power and Vesuwave to Techno

Danilo Capasso

When it comes to club culture in Naples,[1] one cannot help but begin with the tightly packed urban form produced in the diverse areas of the Gulf of Naples. Its temperate climate makes the streets and squares here a privileged meeting place. A stream of impulses runs through a porous urban backdrop, continuously re-elaborating and re-mixing contents and aesthetic outbursts with music being the most powerful means of expression. It is a city that is apparently on the edge of Europe, culturally hybrid, dialectically caught between Mediterranean and Central-European identities with influences and exchanges from the Atlantic. It defines a geography of togetherness and a soundscape with planetary resonances. Enrico Caruso,[2] the first worldwide popstar sailed to the US and carried the Neapolitan tradition with him, thus opening the way for the success of Neapolitan music as the Gospel of the populations who emigrated from southern Italy. Just as it was the case with other important port cities, from these same ships, rhythms and sounds have also returned for most of the century. They have hybridised the musical veins of the city.[3]

From 'nait clubs' to 'Neapolitan Power': the 1950 to 1970s

At the end of the Second World War in 1945, Renato Carosone was the most famous artist to interpret the city's cultural milieu. In the early 1950s, he, along with his small orchestra, opened the season of Neapolitan night clubbing, playing at the Shaker Club; a club reserved for the newly rich and the US military. From 1943 onwards, Americans were a regular presence in Naples, where their main naval base in the Mediterranean was located. Their presence, apart from significantly influencing the sounds of the city, kick-started the emergence of nightclubs as a new form of entertainment, both in Naples and in all of Italy. During the early years of the post-war economic boom until around the mid-1960s, Italian night clubbing was mainly for an elite, rich bourgeoisie. However, it also offered a unique training ground for many Italian musicians, some of whom would become famous during the 1960s; the era of singer-songwriters that became the cornerstone of the Italian pop scene for the next twenty years.

The sound of Carosone and his band was a blend of Jazz and Swing featuring Latin American rhythms and Neapolitan song. The attitude was ironic, the concerts were hilarious performances at the very limits of pure comedy within the domain of parody, but the rhythm was addictive and his songs became particularly famous. In 1957, the single 'Torero' topped the US charts for two weeks. In the same year, after having played in Caracas, Cuba, and Rio de Janeiro, Carosone arrived in New York to perform at Carnegie Hall. Back home, the Naples of the 1960s was still largely tied to tradition and vernacular cultures, represented by classic Neapolitan songs and events like the *Festa di Piedigrotta* and the *Festival della Canzone Napoletana* that had already reached the peak of their notoriety during the 1950s. This was the socio-cultural context in which the elite attended the exclusive 'nait clubs', meaning nightclubs that were located not only in the city centre but also in prestigious tourist areas near Naples such as Capri, Ischia, or Positano.

But to go dancing? In the post-war period Il Giardino degli Aranci in Via Manzoni next to the cable car station was successful, it was a 'dinner-dancing' place, which was followed by the Lloyd in Via Partenope and the Shaker Club in Via Nazario Sauro. In these clubs, many small bands of that time performed, such as Carosone, followed later by Peppino

---

[1] This narrative was constructed by consulting a variety of sources: the internet, publications, record covers, memories, and personal experiences, and last but not least a number of interviews that were undertaken in order to explore certain periods of time that I considered the most relevant; those of the 1980s and 1990s. It is definitely not an exhaustive work, so I apologise if I have failed to mention anyone.

[2] Enrico Caruso was born in Naples on 25 February 1873 and died in Naples on 2 August 1921. He was the first artist in history to sell more than one million records.

[3] To learn more about the social strata of this sound legacy, please see Iain Chambers' and Vincenzo Cavallo's essay in this book.

di Capri, The Showmen, the Alunni del Sole and many others.[4]

In 1959, Italian singer Domenico Modugno won the Sanremo Festival with his song 'Nel Blu Dipinto Di Blu (Volare)' [In blue painted in blue (flying)], the first musical signal of the forthcoming years of rebellion, uprising and new bohemianism all over the West. But Naples seemed unable to produce any artists or movements of relevance. However, in the city's underground scene a new generation of artists, born after the war and intent on creating an original style of 'metro-Mediterranean' Blues, was already preparing to emerge. Their music, which would fully unfold in the early 1970s, would become better known as 'Neapolitan Power'. Their references and ingredients reflect the ambivalence of the city in its relationship to music. On the one hand, there was the influence of 'white' British and transatlantic Rock and Beat, on the other, the intake of 'black' African-American R'n'B and Jazz – and all of this grafted onto Mediterranean musical roots.

With this mixture, the Neapolitan scene revamped itself in the second half of the 1960s, when, in addition to the already hugely popular band The Showmen, there was a new wave of bands such as Battitori Selvaggi, Volti di Pietra, Città Frontale, and the outstanding Balletto di Bronzo. The latter was a cult band of the Italian Progressive Rock scene of the time. While Balletto di Bronzo's debut album from 1970, *Sirio 2222*, was still rooted in the Beat and pop music of the Anglophone scene, their second album *YS* (1972) was, and is, considered a cornerstone of Italian Progressive Rock. In 1971 it was Osanna's turn, a band created as a spin-off of the aforementioned Città Frontale. Osanna's sound evolved from a Rock setting into articulate complex layers that embraced various stylistic nuances, mixing old and modern sounds with Jazz improvisation and Blues scores together with the rediscovery of Neapolitan popular music. Their first album, released in 1971, was titled *L'Uomo*. In 1972, after having recorded the soundtrack to the film *Milano Calibro 9*, a classic Italian crime drama, they released their second album *Palepoli*, filled with new creativity and which led to the rediscovery of local popular music.

It was time to redefine Naples' sound identity. The artists linked to Neapolitan Power were warmly accepted by both the public and the recording industry. The cultural dynamics that defined the birth of this music scene marked the gradual return of Naples to the core of Italy's musical mainstream. Especially the work of the group Nuova Compagnia di Canto Popolare (NCPP) during the early 1970s helped the city regain its aesthetic uniqueness. The NCPP emerged in 1971 with a self-titled album, and they became internationally known by performing at the Spoleto Festival in 1972. Then, Edoardo Bennato, a prolific and unconventional songwriter (and architect) as well as the brother of NCPP's Eugenio Bennato, released several albums before attaining success with his album *Sono Solo Canzonette* in 1980.

Tony Esposito was the inventor of unique percussion instruments with a peculiar sound. An example for this is the Tamborder played on his 1985 hit 'Kalimba De Luna' which sold five million copies worldwide. His first album, *Rosso Napoletano* (1975), was an instrumental work clearly oriented towards ethnic world music. Meanwhile, the drummer Tullio De Piscopo, a percussion acrobat, became known for his breathtaking technique and funky Soul sound. He grew up playing in the American nightclubs near the NATO base in Naples. De Piscopo released his first record in 1974. His single 'Stop Bajon' from 1984 is still a dance floor classic in some international DJs' sets. Finally, the youngest of the artists to be connected with Neapolitan Power is the remarkable Enzo Avitabile. Like many of his peers he also has deep roots in Funk and Jazz, and his remix of the single 'Black Out'[5] fortuitously became a Balearic hit at the Amnesia club in Ibiza.

---

4   Arecata, 'Napoli che se n'è andata', *Le Stronzate di Pucinella*, 11 May 2013, <http://pulcinella291.forumfree.it/?t=65852153&st=15> accessed 1 May 2014.

5   The 'father of Balearic Beat', Amnesia's DJ Alfredo, lists 'Black Out' in the top twenty-five of Balearic Classics with this note: 'An Italian musician from Naples that got this Funk House music track that I found in a warehouse in Milan and made a big splash in Amnesia.' www.alfredoibiza.com/chart, accessed 1 May 2014.

In 1988, Hip-Hop innovator Afrika Bambaataa collaborated with him on the album *Street Happiness*.

We will meet some of these artists by focusing on two events, these are relevant heterotopic moments of the local urban culture as it emerged from the confused magma of the internet and from the evidence gathered during this research. These events are the Be-in Festival of 1973, organised by the aforementioned band Osanna, and the Festival of Licola of 1975. These years were characterised by Progressive and Psychedelic Rock. The aftermath of large hippie gatherings such as the Isle of Wight and Woodstock was still in the air. The Be-in Festival can be considered the Neapolitan Woodstock, albeit a little anachronistic. It was attended by more than 25,000 people, and it was the first event of alternative music on this scale in Naples. The location was a Go-Kart-track on the Camaldoli hill at a place called the Kennedy Sports Centre. The bands and solo musicians on stage were Biglietto per l'Inferno, Franco Battiato, Living Music, Era d'Acquario, Pholas Dactylus, Atomic Rooster, and of course the organisers, Osanna.

The second event was the Festival of Licola in 1975. More than simply a music festival, the event, lasting four days from the 18–21 September of that year, was a 360-degree cultural event with strong political connotations. Nearly 50,000 people attended with approximately 4,000 attendees in the temporary campsite. The event was organised by left-wing students, with support from political forces and countercultural collectives. The slogan of the festival was: 'from the student movement to the whole proletariat youth'. It was a culmination of political activism with performances of music, film and theatre at a large campsite by the sea. Among the many invited artists were Italian and Neapolitan groups and songwriters such as Banco del Mutuo Soccorso, Alan Sorrenti, the Nuova Compagnia di Canto Popolare, Franco Battiato, Francesco De Gregori, Napoli Centrale, Tony Esposito, Canzoniere del Lazio, and several other political Folk songwriters.

The arrival of Punk and 'Vesuwave': the 1980s

The 1980s could be regarded as a decade of transition projected towards the technological revolution in communications and the accompaniment of globalisation. In Naples, Punk had arrived in town a few years late, taking its lead from the sound of the Sex Pistols channelling the refusal of social and cultural homogenisation. In the specific case of Naples, there were also political and aesthetic polarisations between left-wing culture, catholicism, and latent fascism. To speak of the 1980s in Naples is also to speak of the earthquake on 23 November 1980 and the damage it inflicted upon the city and the surrounding regions. It was Italy's worst natural disaster after the Second World War.

A few months after the earthquake had shaken the city, the City Hall, a club mainly oriented to Jazz, hosted a historic event that brought Naples to international attention in the contemporary art world. At this party, organised by the gallery owner Lucio Amelio, Joseph Beuys met Andy Warhol. The City Hall, located halfway between the new districts and the historic centre, was a key place in the history of clubbing in Naples. It was a club that for more than twenty years after the end of the 1970s hosted major events that marked the city's cultural life.

One of the leading characters of this period was Salvatore Magnoni. Today he produces excellent red wine and olive oil from his property in the heart of Cilento, about a one and a half hour drive south of Naples. For about twenty years, Magnoni was an active member of the music scene in the city, creating some of the events and promoting clubs that marked Naples' nightlife. He was always busy behind the counter of one or another record store[6] or in the

---

6 From Tattoo Records store to Flying Records store and, moreover, he founded Fonoteca, one of the first Italian CD-rent shops in 1991.

centre of a club playing and organising music events. Back in 1982, Salvatore and his friend, Salvio Cusano, debuted with a show titled *Speed of Life* at the new independent station, Radio Marte. Their music program attempted to counterbalance the dominating presence of artists and music associated with Neapolitan Power, the mixture of Rock, Funk, Jazz, and Blues framed in a Mediterranean matrix that was re-working the popular music tradition. At the same time, the radio show was also an attempt to move away from a commercial drift towards Disco and pop.

In general, the relationship between Neapolitan artists and the city runs cyclically between attempts to re-elaborate the centrality of Neapolitan-ness, and the need to escape from this identity which is considered a burden that blocks the de-territorialisation of sonic identity. In this context, there are cultural currents that seek to (re)connect the city to a cosmopolitan flow. These are not bound to a local identity and move away from immediate political influences, finding a space of creative evolution in music; a meeting point beyond ideologies and social barriers. Such impulses were favoured and accompanied by Punk culture, a trend that would often lead Naples to maintain direct contact with the principal central cities of this movement, particularly with London, through importing its music, artists, records, and trends. In this period, the city was listening to Italian pop and Disco music in the clubs. There were still also the purists of 1970s Progressive Rock, the orphans of the post-hippie Psychedelic scene, and Jazz that the city has always loved and played.

Magnoni's and Cusano's radio show was the first attempt to suggest new and different sounds, broadcasting music by the likes of Wall of Voodoo, Echo & Bunnymen, The Clash, Psychedelic Furs, or Iggy Pop. At the beginning of the 1980s, the city started to see the first Punk clubs such as ZX in Via Atri in the historical centre, Trilogy on the Vomero hill (where we find Gigi D'Aria, the first alternative DJ at the decks), Pulsar in Via Costantinopoli, and Caffè della Luna in the Chiaia district. At the same time, Magnoni, Cusano and some friends were looking for a club to offer new kinds of music open to spontaneity. On 11 June 1984, Diamond Dogs opened its doors. The club's organisers were young people who came from different social backgrounds and from different parts of the city such as Vomero, Piscinola, Soccavo, as well as from certain provincial areas. Magnoni recalls:

There were arguments between us. There was the more radical wing of extreme choices, and there was the urge of pop, just as there were the Wednesdays of Nicola Catalano, Atrocity Exhibition, Industrial noises to some, and Saturdays with the dance music of Patrizio Squeglia. Between us, there was the late sixty-eight and the after-effect of seventy-seven. There was the working class, the petty bourgeoisie, the artisans of the province, the middle class of Vomero and the jet-set of Chiaia. The cultural references traced a large map in the moody geography of the left in the early eighties. On one side were the purists, celebrating the unity of Italy, of songwriters and of Progressive Rock; on the other the political incorrectness of New Wave, where magazines like Il Male *and* Frigidaire *mingled. Within the boiler-room of The Diamond Dogs these tendencies co-existed, the Lennon style glasses of Luca and the black combat boots of Tonino 'Piccolone', the long blond hair of Stefania and the short, chiselled cut of Sandra.*[7]

Diamond Dogs was the classic kind of downtown club that can still be found in areas of the historic centre today, housed in underground spaces typically consisting of a number of small rooms and cellars in old buildings. In the case of Diamond Dogs, it was a creative

7   Salvatore Magnoni, in an interview with the author (June 2013).

misappropriation of disused cisterns of the ancient Greek and Roman aqueduct. These are hidden spaces, rarely visible from the street and often hidden in courtyards where passing through a small door and down a flight of stairs you can access such hidden worlds. Magnoni recounts:

> The DJ booth was initially on the mezzanine, and then a year later it was below, behind the front of a van. The whole place was carved out of a porous tuff rock. Under the DJ booth we put the bar, which was actually a refrigerator that failed to cool drinks, not that there were even many drinks and those finished right away, and some paper bags for food, to stuff with hundreds of sandwiches. There was no running water, no electricity, no cocktails, no glasses. Cans and bottles of beer, a deadly slicer for cheese and ham. The hygiene of a pirate ship. The walls were not plastered. We covered them with lime which was cheaper, but soon the high rate of humidity in the caves mixed with the warmth of the bodies liquefied the lime and got onto the clothes of anyone who touched the walls. Walls on which every one of us drew things, dancing bodies, shooting stars. They were primitive frescoes, narrating our wishes, the desire to meet. Even these drawings would not last long, time slipped away, like dreams in the morning.[8]

Magnoni recalls a certain difficulty that the left (the Communist Party) faced when reading the contemporary situation and when encoding the styles and genres in their cultural context. This led some of the young left-wingers, both in the 1980s and the early 1990s, to regard the revolutions of Punk and New Wave with suspicion and to distance themselves from Techno music. This not only happened for aesthetic reasons, but also due to political stances. For the left, music had to be a direct protest with an explicit social commitment – it was not expected to speak of love, it could not simply be instrumental, disengaged, overly hedonistic, or, even worse, nihilistic. It was this latter cultural constellation that configured the creation of spaces such as Diamond Dogs. This certainly created a breaking point in the history of Neapolitan clubbing and caused a lot of tension for sound. Diamond Dogs was, from a classical left-wing point of view, a disturbing space. It was a topographically anomalous space, uncodified, and a heterotopia that questioned the traditional references of social conflict, at least in the Italian context.

Diamond Dogs lasted until 1988, but before its closure it collaborated with one of the first squats at the time, Segnali di Accelerazione, located in the province of Acerra. This collaboration brought about a very fruitful exchange between the suburban and metropolitan areas, leading to a flow of ideas and relationships that marked the way for future occupations, and new suburban clubs. Unfortunately, in this magma of creativity and confusion, heroin reared its ugly head. The drug undermined the creative push from the inside and the possible evolution of what was taking place as it gained the upper hand in these years, becoming a very serious social problem. In the early 1980s heroin was much more widespread in the suburbs, and organised crime groups had distribution centres located primarily in Ercolano, an area in the shadow of Mt. Vesuvius. As well as being the centre of the largest flea market in the region, where generations of alternative people invented their sartorial style, Ercolano was, for a long time, an important drug marketplace. Before the influx of heroin, the most common drugs were hashish, grass, amphetamines, and acid. Ecstasy appeared in the city at the end of the 1980s with the arrival of House music and contemporary clubbing.

At Diamond Dogs Neapolitan bands that were part of a new local aesthetic trend called 'Vesuwave', the New Wave of the Vesuvius, were to be found. These were artists who looked for music from the UK in order to emancipate

---

8 Ibid.

the Neapolitan sound, the now stagnating Neapolitan Power. Among the groups of the Vesuwave who performed at Diamond Dogs were Bisca, Les Bandards Foux, Rhythmotion, Almamegretta, Cibo, Terrapin, or Contropotere. From other parts of Italy came Detonazione, Diaframma, Liquid Eyes, and Not Moving. Several London bands played in the club, for example, Christian Death, Jazzbutcher, Living in Texas, and Playn Jayn. In November 1984, the team running Diamond Dogs organised a Nick Cave concert at the Ausonia theatre in Naples.

Aside: Disco music in Naples

Disco music in Naples was the brainchild of the Niespolo family, entrepreneurs who inaugurated Kiss Kiss, the first Disco oriented club in the city in 1972. In 1976, the owner of Kiss Kiss had the idea of broadcasting the rhythms of Disco live on air. So, on 12 September at 6:30pm DJ Sasà Capobianco opened the show on 89.0 FM with the single 'Ramaya' by Mozambican singer and composer Afric Simone. The programme, which would last ten years, was called *Discolive*. On the back of the success of this programme Radio Kiss Kiss was born. It was one of the first independent radio stations in Naples to broadcast live from a club. Today Radio Kiss, to which the name was shortened, has become a large commercial radio network that broadcasts all over Italy.

In Naples, Disco clubs were mainly located in the newer districts of Vomero, Chiaia, and Posillipo. Here discotheques like The Galapagos, Papillon, Piccadilly, or La Mela opened their doors. These clubs were mostly located in upper-class parts of the city, the so-called 'wealthy Naples'. In some of these clubs during the 1980s, ambitious DJs began to dismantle the boundaries between commercial Disco music and Funk and Soul music. They moved easily from 'Rapper's Delight' by Sugarhill Gang to 'Because the Night' by Patti Smith. Clubgoers did not meet in clubs to listen to a certain type of music; rather they met there because of class and political orientation. It was, therefore, often possible to see young people on the dance floor making the fascist salute while dancing to alternative proto-Punk singer Smith's 'Because the Night'. This was one of the results of the aforementioned social and political polarisation that split the city's cultural life, and it showed in many contradictions and aesthetic de-contextualisation.

A phase of transition: towards the 1990s

In September 1986, John 'Johnny Rotten' Lydon (former member of the Sex Pistols) played at the Teatro Tenda Partenope with his band P.I.L. The concert took place immediately after the success of P.I.L.'s 1985 album titled *Album*. Ivan Maria Vele, who we will meet again later in this story, was in the audience. He remembers the impact that this concert had on his life:

> *P.I.L.'s live performance immediately and indelibly marked the fate of a small but persistent generation of Neapolitan post-punks. We were teenagers with Punk hairstyles, full of studs, and Doc Martens shoes. At that time I was sixteen, and I came from the modern district of Vomero. For me, the concert was almost a mystical event. I was struck by the electrifying performance of the Punk icon par excellence, Johnny Rotten. For the first time in Naples we did the pogo and spat to the remaking of the Sex Pistols and at the same time to the experimental sound of P.I.L.: a mixture of ethnic tribalism, funeral ceremonials and psychedelic Dub. This vision would guide me – seven years later – to the full revolution of Progressive House that I personally contributed to with United Tribes, a cell of militant urban tribalism that we had formed to just say NO to the commercial flattening of the House music scene and the politicized alternative of the social centres.*[9]

9   Ivan Maria Vele, in an interview with the author (July 2013).

In the late 1980s, the geography of Naples' nightlife was divided into two main categories. On the one hand were the clubs where you could listen to pop or commercial music, attended mainly by the young people of the affluent classes and positioned in the richest areas of the city. On the other, there were an unspecified number of small 'alternative' clubs that sought to offer up more underground genres of music, linked to the scenes of Post-Punk, Gothic, Indie Rock, Industrial, and New Wave. These clubs were in the historic downtown urban clusters in the heart of the city, which, in the years after the earthquake of the 1980's, were downtrodden and deeply infiltrated by crime. At the same time, they were places of alternative cultural practices and underground realities, in deep resonance with the aesthetic decadence and existential spleen of the time. This was a real phase of transition, a moment of expectation and even of boredom in the context of a weary aesthetic mood where everything presaged the need for a new revolution. The active ingredients of this historic transition were already in progress, and they would arrive in town with echoes of the British Summer of Love from 1988 that was based on Acid House and, before that, through the 'Balearic' sound that excited the nightlife of Ibiza and Rimini. Here, around 1989, in a phase of apparent stagnation, the cards for the history of contemporary clubbing in Naples were shuffled.

In Naples, the first attempt to open a House music club occurred at the My Way club, a small historic venue in the wealthy district of Chiaia. It was the first Sunday House music club organised by the promoter and DJ-team Funk Machine. It quickly became a uniquely bizarre evening, something of a well-kept secret of the few who had the chance to enter. It was where the first generation of ecstasy users in the city met, dancing to Acid House until dawn. Clothing was colourful, gays and straights mixed, whistles and smiley faces appeared on t-shirts, but there were also new and sophisticated mixtures of style.

In 1989, even Kiss Kiss, the largest nightclub in the city with a capacity of more than one thousand people, opened its doors to House music. The years of DJ Sasà Capobianco and Disco music came to an end. Now it was the turn of DJs from the Funk Machine to set the standard. Even at Kiss Kiss, there were many colourful young people with bandanas and whistles, wacky glasses and T-shirts adorned with smiley faces; the aesthetic identities of the 1980s were dissolving, the 1990s began. The Friday night House music at Kiss Kiss included classic American and British anthems of House and Acid of the day. The track list included 'Jack Your Body' by Marshall Jefferson or 'Strings Of Life' by Derrick May, plus tracks by Coldcut, Leftfield, or Inner City. The Funk Machine crew, having introduced the city to House, were precursors. An avant-garde dance crowd was already in touch with a new idea of clubbing, later to be developed by other promoters.

Between 1989 and 1991 there were still some alternative clubs within the city centre, such as the Rookery Nook and the KGB spinning Indie Rock, Industrial Electronica and the classics of New Wave and Punk. These clubs tried to continue on from the experience and success of Diamond Dogs. Meanwhile, two new clubs opened in the city centre. These venues, Velvet Garage and Notting Hill, would go on to play an important role during the following years.

Aside: Tien'a Ment, a new generation of occupied spaces

On 29 July 1989, a group of young Punk anarchists occupied an abandoned public building in the district of Soccavo. They called it 'Tien'a Ment' [do not forget, or keep in mind] in Neapolitan dialect – and was also a reminder of the tragic events that had occurred in Tiananmen Square in Beijing in the same year. This was the first of a new generation of occupied spaces in Naples, although this particular space immediately defined itself as independent from any political stance. During its seven-year existence, Tien'a Ment became a landmark for the most anarchistic and libertarian souls of the city's underground scene. It was a space open to a variety of aesthetic shades ranging from Punk to Trash, from Industrial electronic music to illegal raves. In line with the Punk DIY attitude, Tien'a Ment was keen on self-production as a principle, providing space and resources to create independent music, theatre, and counter-information. However, it was also active within the social sphere of the district through workshops for children and free food programme initiatives. Some keywords of the movement were: anti-militarism, vegetarianism, and self-production. Over a big wall, at the entrance of the building, there towered the statement 'Neither heroin nor police'. They called this place Tien'a Ment. Giovanni Calemma, today a photographer and DJ in London, was one of the very first squatters and recalls the Tien'a Ment experience:

> There are three very important moments that I remember about Tien'a Ment. There was a special energy among the people in the first days of the occupation. It had a special dynamic and constructive quality to it. Day after day, the abandoned site was taking shape: a bar and a concert venue were built. In December 1990 Napalm Death [British Grindcore and Death Metal band, ed.] came to play at Tien'a Ment. The concert was a fundraising event for a friend who had been arrested during the Poll Tax protests in London. The energy during the event was unbelievable. In 1991, there was the unforgettable concert by Death In June, with spoken words by David Tibet and the drums of Douglas P. that hypnotized the crowd. The Neo-Folk band ruled that night, unifying hardcore Punks and new Techno heads under one roof.[10]

Tien'a Ment provided a hub for the city's music underground. Many Neapolitan groups elected it as the place for their performances, but it was also a popular destination for several touring bands of the most extreme musical genres to come from Europe and Italy. Tien'a Ment was part of a network of similar spaces with which its tribe of members kept in touch and promoted cultural exchanges.

Central to the creation of Tien'a Ment was a group of artists and musicians based in Naples' Stella district. They lived in a large apartment, which included a lab and a rehearsal room called La Stella. This kind of commune, devoted to millennium mutations and aesthetics, was also the home of Contropotere, a nomadic band that settled in the city seeking a creative base. Two of the founders of Contropotere were Neapolitan: Lucia Vitrone and Adriano 'Bostik' Casale. They are described by Helena Velena, a legendary figure of Italian Punk[11], in the book *Lumi Di Punk*, a collection of memories from the Italian Punk scene from 1977 to 1989:

> Among other things, as Attack Punk Records (independent Punk label) we produced a record by a band from Naples called Contropotere.[12] I loved that group so much. They were a group of travellers, 'nomads', let's say. … Contropotere lived and travelled in a van with dogs, then already the prototype of gutter punks, and there was this wonderful singer, Lucia, with very short miniskirts, long hair, and perpetually torn fishnet stockings, with her suspender belt always unfastened and always shorter than the miniskirt … their concept of countervailing power was fundamental … Aside from the wonderful records of Mediterranean Punk-Jazz, they fucked off music, tucking everything that passed through their minds into it, from their Neapolitan-ness to Jazz, to experimentation. Then they made electronic stuff, wonderful … Lucia was really fantastic, once again a woman with incredible subversive energy, who claimed a strong sexuality, 'mimicking

---

10 Giovanni Calemma, in an interview with the author (September 2014).

11 Cf. www.helenavelena.com.

12 This was the first album by Contropotere: *Nessuna Speranza, Nessuna Paura* (Attack Punk Records, 1988).

and undermining' the erotic imagination ... deconstructing it, the sexy doll image ... it was beautiful.[13]

In the final years before its closure, Tien'a Ment also became a location for electronic music and Techno rave events, attracting the caravans of the Techno nomads Spiral Tribe to the city. These were travellers armed with great sound systems that were literally war machines. The Spiral Tribe resided for a few weeks at Tien'a Ment, heedless of the urban context in which they found themselves. They promoted rave parties in Tien'a Ment at an unsustainable rate and duration for the local residents. At this point, the local press started to publish stories about satanic rituals, a fact that gave off negative vibes and provided an excuse for the authorities to organise a forced eviction. This occurred shortly after the departure of the Spiral Tribe in January 1996. Today, in place of Tien'a Ment there is a nightclub named Accademia.

House music and the Centri Sociali: the early 1990s

Walking down the streets of Naples in 1990, one could see a very different street poster than the usual standard. The poster showed a man with his arms wide open towards a sky made of water. It was the manifesto of a rave party titled 'Humanity'. This rave was organised by a group of new promoters, the Angels of Love. One of these promoters was Francesco Furiello who had recently returned to the city after having spent a period amid the buzz of the British Summer of Love in 1988. In previous years, he had been a member of Skizo, one of the many Punk bands of the city.

The Angels of Love were determined to bring clubbing and House music to Naples. For the occasion they chose a very large space: the Teatro Tenda Partenope, a big tent dedicated to live music which had opened in 1977 in the western part of the city. This was the same location where a few years earlier P.I.L. had also played. Apparently, this was the first rave party organised in Naples. The sound was most certainly UK-oriented. On the decks were some London-based DJs such as Charlie Hall, Mr. Monday, and Eren Abdullah. The sound was a kind of primitive Progressive House music. From 1991, Angels of Love organised their House music parties at clubs like the KGB, Havana, Vertigo, and Ciao Club. The city's interest in House music at that time was growing quickly, although it was still a largely underground phenomenon and the available venues were not always well suited for this new type of entertainment. It needed space, powerful sound systems, the license to be open to and after 6am, and to be suitably located for accessing after-hour parties in homes or improvised clubs. A few months later the Angels of Love launched the legendary Hipe club.

However, this new wave of music and clubbing was not the only emerging trend. Parallel to the arrival of contemporary club culture Naples had also become an integral part of new Italian music and cultural scene: the so-called Centri Sociali or occupied social centres and politically motivated squats. From the early 1990s onwards, the Centri Sociali would once again become important places of aggregation and cultural production. This emerging scene was tied to the radical left. Despite the contradictions, the new generations were able to create a synthesis of style and political communication drawn from African American and Caribbean culture: Hip-Hop, Reggae, Ragamuffin, and Dub were the genres that would flood the peninsula from now on, transforming the entire panorama of Italian pop thereafter.

In this context, Naples, which with a few notable exceptions had not produced any kind of new music trends of late, saw the formation of a new generation of bands that would achieve success, both in terms of audience and sales. Among them were 99 Posse, Almamegretta,

---

13 Marco Philopat, *Lumi Di Punk* (Milan: Agenzia X, 2006), 36.

or Bisca, and later on A'67 or Co'Sang, along with a myriad of others. This new cultural movement began in the late 1980s, after more than a decade of yuppieism, growth without development, the catastrophic consequences provoked by heroin, and the political terrorism of *anni di piombo*[14]. The new movement emerged from within the student movement in 1989 when a new generation found a peaceful relief valve of their political struggle in music and in Centri Sociali. The social conflict and the protests remained but they had now acquired a different form. The Centri Sociali of the 1990s could generally be considered as the clubs of the radical left.

On 1 May 1991, a group of young people occupied an abandoned industrial building in the industrial suburbs of Eastern Naples, which they baptised Officina 99. It would become one of the most popular and longstanding Italian Centri Sociali. Not only was it a place of aggregation for the movements of organised political dissent, it was also the home of important musical events and the cradle of a generation of musicians, including the band 99 Posse[15], which was named after the centre. This was the time of the Rap/Ragamuffin inflected sound of the 99 Posse with their debut single 'Dì Original Trappavasciamuffin Stailì' (1992) and of the Neapolitan Dub Reggae of Almamegretta[16] with their EP 'Figli Di Annibale' (1993). The former release is the manifesto of a generation of youngsters who had grown up in the galaxy of the Italian Centri Sociali. Between 1992 and 1995, 99 Posse were committed to an artistic and productive collaboration with Bisca, a band that had been a long-term fixture in the musical history of the city. Their biggest hit came in 1996 with the album *Cerco Tiempo*. In this period 99 Posse began an independent label, distributed by Naples' Flying Records, which, between 1995 and 1998, launched other artists such as Radio Gladio, Speaker Cenzou, and Bala Perdida. With the successful third record of 99 Posse, *Corto Circuito*, released in 1998 and selling 160,000 copies, the music of the Centri Sociali had fully arrived in the mainstream of Italian culture.

The aforementioned Almamegretta would chart a similar course, but with an attitude more directed to the cultivation of a universal Dub sound deeply rooted in Mediterranean music. They released their debut *Animamigrante* in 1993 as well, and then reached commercial and artistic success with *Sanacore*, mixed by well-known UK producer Adrian Sherwood in 1995. This album defined the style and the sound that would distinguish the band in the years to come. The sound of Almamegretta was also appreciated in the UK as Bristol's Trip-Hop band Massive Attack commissioned them to remix one of the songs from their second album *Protection* (1994). The result was the dubby 'Karmacoma' (The Napoli Trip), including raps in Italian, which was released in 1995 on Massive Attack's 'Karmacoma' EP alongside remixes by Bristol's Portishead and UK project U.N.K.L.E. After *Sanacore* Almamegretta became a renowned band with a wide audience. But by 2001, both 99 Posse and Almamegretta had depleted their initial charge, and they were either splitting or radically changing direction.

Aside: Flying Records

In the late 1980s, Naples had become home to a new independent music label, Flying Records, that held a significant position in the Italian and international music scene throughout the 1990s. In addition to being a production label, it was also involved in record distribution and retail in Naples with stores in the main districts of the city. Flying Records imported many genres of music and contributed to the divulgation of music scarcely available elsewhere in the city's traditional stores. Furthermore, qualified people were working in the shops; often DJs or promoters from the local scene. Flying Records was not only a shop, but a real independent label achieving fame and notoriety, especially in

---

14 Literally translates as 'the leaden years', meaning years of armed struggle and terrorism by both the left wing underground organization Brigate Rosse, the red brigades, as well as neo-fascist groups.
15 Cf. www.novenove.it.
16 Cf. www.almamegretta.net.

the world of House music, commercial dance music, and Hip-Hop.

In Neapolitan studios, American and British productions were recorded or remixed, and dance music tracks produced by Flying Records achieved excellent results in European charts in the late 1980s. But Flying Records' lucky break came through those artists who began to perform in the Centri Sociali, a genre which had become integral to the new Italian pop scene. Flying Records' studios contributed to the success of Neapolitan and Italian bands such as 99 Posse, Articolo 31, Prozac +, and, later on, Valerio Jovine – until the late 1990s when the label had to close its doors due to an accumulation of debts and mistaken artistic choices. The work of a new generation of musicians from Naples was produced in Flying Records' studios. Not since the outburst of Neapolitan Power, the artists of which had become popstars in the Italian music mainstream by then, had there been such fertility of production, records, and buzz surrounding them.

Hipe, space, ciao: the early and mid-1990s

The arrival of House music had redefined the culture of clubbing in Naples, but also of the communities formed by music. By 1991 the clubbing scene in its various forms was buzzing, though interest was principally centred on the new House music clubs. Despite the initial influence of British Progressive House, the city synchronised with the sounds that had been more successful in Italy and that were to be found more easily in DJs' record-stores. They mostly consisted of American House on labels like Strictly Rhythm or Nervous. The towns of Rimini and Riccione, with venues like Cocoricò, Club dei 99, Vae Victis, Ethos Mama Club, became hot spots on the map of Italian clubbing. In Naples, the aforementioned Angels of Love were moving in the same direction, promoting DJ Claudio Coccoluto as well as big names of American House music such as David Morales or Todd Terry.

In mid-1992, Post-Punk anarchist Ivan Maria Vele and Susy Luciano, a regular clubber in Riccione, formed a non-aligned group which aimed to differentiate itself from the Angels of Love. Ivan & Susy, along with their resident DJs Danylo (me, Danilo Capasso, author of this text) and Jg Bros (the Generale brothers, Massimo and Paolo) launched their first night at the My Way club titled 'Deep Inside The City'. This was the same club to which the Funk Machine team brought House music a few years earlier. Within a few months, My Way hosted Italian DJs like Ralf, Leo Mas, Luca Colombo, Flavio Vecchi, and Gabry Fasano. This would culminate with a one-off party, which saw the US DJs Frankie Knuckles together with Dave Morales for the first time in Naples.

The situation would acquire shape with the opening of a new club named Hipe, just outside the city in Caserta. Hipe, which had a capacity of at least 1,000 people, was the first venue in the history of the metropolitan area of Naples mainly devoted to House. It was a typical postmodern style discotheque, a glittering dancehall with many mirrors and a sound system with a crunchy wooden sound. The large ballroom was circular with a large pillar in the centre. Hipe attracted crowds from all social and cultural backgrounds, and the dance floor was a true contact zone between diversities. Hipe's story changed at the end of 1992, when it moved to a much larger space in the city of Caserta. This was the period in which House music exploded as a phenomenon, dominating local clubbing. The new Hipe club was a concrete warehouse, with more than 1,500 people on its dance floor every Saturday. Naples was now recognised as a key destination for many Italian and international DJs.

After the time at My Way, Ivan & Susy were involved in running the new Hipe club where I also became resident DJ. We went to see the new place during the construction process; it was a giant underground space, a large deposit of concrete with two very wide naves. Before becoming a club, it had been a food storage warehouse. It did not have any decoration, just grey concrete, a large counter with the bar, and a kind of stage for the DJ booth. This new venue could hold up to almost 2,000 people, and it was always packed. Together with the Jg Bros, I played every Saturday, sometimes at the opening, sometimes at the closing. What I liked most about this situation was the power to wipe out the social and ideological conflict between people through empathy and the aggregating energy of the sound. The DJs were important, but the people were interested in the music and dancing; they were the show. All in all, it was a complete jump from everyday life.

In my perception, it was also a form of 'the politics of no politics', an absolute novelty, something entirely different from what was happening at the Centri Sociali such as Officina 99. House music erased political backgrounds, dogmas, as well as previous aesthetics. The club was a liminal space, a space of transition and transformation. Music was the main ingredient of this new attitude of being together which, combined with the effects of ecstasy, would end the nihilism of the past decade with a fast stroke of sound. The new Hipe club reopened in November 1992 as a premiere national event. The guests were renowned US House DJ team Masters at Work. During this season, the Hipe club hosted several DJs with whom I had the pleasure to share the decks, above all, one of the fathers of House music, Robert Owens, a great vocalist with a deeply tribal sound. We finally had our Paradise Garage.

House clubs in those years were all located in the provinces of Naples. Clubbers travelled by car, and early in the morning they drove back to town or went to some after-hours party. It was not unusual to see large groups of clubbers having breakfast at motorway service stations, like Martians, slumped back into everyday life having just emerged from an extra-temporal sonic tunnel. In Naples, as in other cities, some people went out from Friday to Sunday evening, if not longer. It was like a space-time continuum, where the music laid a metronomic base which measured a stretched time lapse unfolding towards infinity. An intensive socialisation supported by MDMA and 4/4 bass drum pulsations. Catharsis and redemption, the happy unconsciousness and the psychedelic trip. This new scene brought with it a positive and progressive attitude and the new music was also a new project of togetherness.

Meanwhile, the Angels of Love project had certainly not ended. Actually, their audience had increased. In 1993, their new venue was Cube which had a capacity of 3,000 people. Guest DJs were renowned US stars like Tony Humphries or Roger Sanchez. London's newly opened, huge club Ministry of Sound invited them to organise a one-off party in their venue. Naples had now entered the privileged circles of European clubbing. In 1994, the American DJ Little Louie Vega was a guest of the Angels of Love for the entire season at Cube. From here on, House music in Naples would be associated with the Angels of Love, which grew unabated from Cube to bigger clubs like Ennenci and Metropolis where up to 10,000 people danced.

—

Between 1993 and 1994 the clubbing scene in Naples experienced a second evolutionary spin-off. While the Angels of Love continued along the path of House music, there was the emergence of a Progressive Techno scene in the city. There was a buzz that could be felt in the air. It manifested itself around groups of clubbers who wished to look beyond the House sound, now considered an almost commercial mainstream phenomenon. They wanted to reconnect with their Punk roots and looked to the UK's Progressive Techno scene and its offerings like the project Sabres of Paradise or releases on the label Rising high, which were finally available in local shops. Inspired by psychedelic Techno tribalism, several people, among them Ivan Maria Vele, Lulu Kennedy, the DJ team 3 Imaginary Boys, and myself, the author of this text, founded the United Tribes[17] (of underground and progressive people).

It was an almost militant and self-referential organisation that, overnight, ended the domination of House music and opened the doors towards a new musical landscape. Bored by Soul voice samples and A capella, tired of piano House riffs and funky guitars, we went back to the basics. Solid beats with deep kick-drums and penetrating basslines, the music of this period laid the basis for different genres that would emerge from these roots, above all, Trance Techno. UK Progressive House was filled with the debris of Punk and Dub Reggae, but everything was reconsidered in a landscape of electronic sounds and beats. It was not yet a globalised sound, de-territorialised like Techno, where it is often impossible to define a geographical origin. The first events organised by United Tribes were a glimpse of a journey into the future, commencing from the past. This starting point in the past was the reopening of Diamond Dogs, for three unforgettable nights before the police busted it. Co-founder Ivan Maria Vele recalls:

> There were clubbers dancing and pogoing to the tribal-progressive rhythm of Underworld, Sabres of Paradise, Leftfield. Punk and Disco music finally lived together, and the revolution of United Tribes occurred – albeit episodically – in the historical Diamond Dogs and especially at the rave where we announced 'The end of the industrial age! Ecchereccà 3',[18] an event that in the spring of 1994 showcased the symbiosis of Electronic Dub and Progressive House with gigs and DJ sets from Ziontrain, Almamegretta and Paul Daley from Leftfield. United Tribes would disappear after this event.[19]

The event Ecchereccà 3 can be considered as an aesthetic and historic turning point for local club culture where Progressive House, Dub, and Techno met in front of about 3,000 people. It helped to connect the musical experimentations that flourished around (and not necessarily in) the Centri Sociali with the electronic sound of the underground dance music world. The UK Dub/dance band Zion Train would continue to perform in the city on several occasions over the years. One of their members, Neil Perch, cooperated with the Reggae/Dub music scene of Neapolitan Centri Sociali and ended up collaborating years later with both the singer Luca Zulu of 99 Posse and with Almamegretta.

Parallel to United Tribes, other aesthetic and transitional spaces were emerging in 1993. There were other Progressive tribes in the city that did not want to surrender to the House homogeneity dominated by Angels of Love. One of these clubs was the Space, a 1980s-like dancehall dispersed in the countryside of Pompeii, surrounded by orchards and vegetable fields. The Space was organized by Space Race, another group of promoters active in this new Neapolitan Progressive Techno scene. Among its members were Paolo Traverso, who was already an active promoter in the Post-Punk scene in the 1980s, and Lino Monaco, now a member of the experimental electronic project Retina.it.[20] Monaco, at the time nicknamed 'Skinny Puppy', remembers the times of Space:

> The Space was one of the first after-hours clubs in the region, certainly a new way of living club culture, which was no longer made up of sleepless nights but rather sunny, musical mornings. The first DJs not aligned with the classic Disco music that raged on the radio or in the clubs in those years, were the 3 Imaginary Boys, Francesco Monetti, Danilo Capasso, Random Noize, and numerous others. They alternated at the console on those mornings, often along with guests from different European places.[21]

---

17 United Tribes of Underground and Progressive People founders are: Giovanni Calemma, Danilo Capasso, Katia Fiorentino, Lucio Luongo, Lulu Kennedy, Francesco Quarto, Massimo Smaldone, Ivan Maria Vele, 3 Imaginary Boys (D. Vigorito, R. Biccari, M. Simeone).

18 Surprise exclamation which translates as 'What's up here!?'

19 Ivan Maria Vele, in an interview with the author (July 2013).

20 Cf. www.retinait.com.

21 Lino Monaco, in an interview with the author (October 2014).

The Space was very popular. It opened early on Sunday morning and went on until late at night. The audience also came from other regions, attracted by the stories that circulated around it. A new generation of local DJs shared decks. One could breathe an air of novelty here, as DJ Francesco Monetti recalls:

> Many stopped attending parties at night to go dancing directly in the morning at Space in Pompeii. It is not an exaggeration to say that the atmosphere was revolutionary. Everyone felt as though they were living a kind of collective dream that could change the world at any moment. A great sense of freedom pervaded the club. Moreover, the location was a sports centre free from any canonical reference to a disco, and the dance floor was a large, empty, completely dark room in which there were darts of a small laser and a few lights, along with the sound system that, week after week, became more powerful.[22]

After a succession of parties the police came, as usual, and closed the venue thus ending this extraordinary experience. Shortly after the experience of Space Race, a group of promoters called Totally Cool launched the Ciao Club just outside the city. At the height of its success, the Ciao Club began to attract too much attention because of overcrowding, and in September 1994, once again, the police closed it. This is how the intertwined stories of United Tribes and Space Race defined a phase full of turning points, producing heterotopic dynamics which caused numerous ramifications and experiences. Between 1994 and 1996 the scene continued to grow, but the first generation of music promoters and clubs tended to withdraw.

Aside: the 'Neapolitan Renaissance' of the city centre

From 1993, in addition to the electronic dance music scene, there were new and important political changes to the city's habits and nightlife spaces. A minor local political revolution, often referred to as the 'Neapolitan Renaissance' kicked off with the election of a new, centre-left mayor, Antonio Bassolino. The early years of this administration were presented as a real change that seemed to involve civil society and a new kind of urban consciousness that was also reflected within the public sphere. Culturally, Bassolino's administration was not that far away from the political stance of the Centri Sociali, though obviously much less radical. Furthermore, he was also interested in the regeneration of degraded districts of the historical centre. In the long run, this revolution would not change things substantially but it would be enough to reanimate the streets of the centre which led to them no longer being a marginal meeting place. After years of neglect and disinterest, these areas started to improve. The small downtown streets became an important hub of the city's nightlife, like a large atomised club, a dispersed and dotted meeting point, in which courtyards of universities and small squares were often turned into locations for concerts and cultural activities. This was part of a general process of renewed attention to the historical heritage that would lead UNESCO to declare the historic centre of Naples a World Heritage site.

Young people met in the streets and squares of Bellini, Cisterna Dell'olio, Via Nilo, and Gesù. In this constellation of spaces, venues like Notting Hill on Piazza Dante or Velvet Garage and bars like Kinky and Superfly were the preferred spots on the city's night map. Velvet Garage opened in 1991. One of the protagonists of this new club was Salvatore Magnoni, who had formerly run Diamond Dogs. The Velvet was a small club, which held up to 250 people, a tuff cellar consisting of numerous rooms with crossed vaulted ceilings. In these years, the city centre was not generally an area where one could find House or electronic music venues. With some mid-week exceptions like the

---

22   Giovanni Calemma, Danilo Capasso, Lucio Luongo, Francesco Maria Quarto, and Ivan Maria Vele, *United Tribes. La Storia*, (Naples: MAO Media & Arts Office, 2015), 15.

chill-out music evenings on Wednesday at the Velvet, electronic music tribes mainly danced in the clubs of the Neapolitan hinterland. In the historical centre, the sound was more catered to Reggae, Trip-Hop, and Acid Jazz, all in all towards the leftist musical streams close to the Centri Sociali.

Contrary to Velvet, Notting Hill was a large venue, suitable for live music, with one single, long, narrow room with the stage at the end, again extracted from the large cellars of a historic building, which held up to 500 people when fully packed. During these years, Notting Hill became one of the principal stages for a generation of artists from the local and national scene. Here too, we found bands like Bisca, Almamegretta, Daniele Sepe, 24 Grana, as well as Subsonica from Turin, Lele Gaudì, Roi Paci, and many other bands that performed both in political demonstrations and in urban clubs. There were DJs like Dub Professor (also manager of the club), Salvatore Magnoni, or Enzo Casella who alternated between Indie Rock, Hip-Hop, Funk, Reggae, and Dub. Notting Hill closed its doors around the year 2000.

Techno takes over: the late 1990s and early 2000s

By 1996, the entire electronic music scene had changed direction, the core of the market and production had moved to Germany. It was time for Techno. The undisputed pioneer of the internationalisation of Neapolitan Techno within the planetary circuits of dance music was Marco Carola[23]. He was the forerunner of a generation of DJs and producers from Naples to rise on the global electronic music scene. The new continental Techno music went on to build a definitive bridge between the sound of Detroit and the Kraftwerk-style German electronic music tradition. This was a new cosmopolitan Dub that abandoned any reference to genre or melody and entered into a more atonal and concrete dimension. It reflected, above all, the explosion of the Berlin clubbing scene.[24] From the mid-1990s to the end of the decade the Techno market was booming and Marco Carola found his style in this new ambit, starting a prolific career as a DJ and producer, becoming one of the most popular DJs in the world.

Today, the panorama of the international electronic dance music scene includes many artists who grew up on this local breeding ground. Marco Carola and most of the DJs of the new scene have a different cultural background from those of the previous generations. Due to the difference in age, they are less influenced by the underground culture of the 1980s, with a sound with fewer references to African American or Caribbean cultures. After some small commercial dance productions in Italy, Marco Carola moved on to Minimal Techno. He produced his first set of vinyl records independently, which were published and distributed directly from Germany very soon thereafter. His productions immediately caught public attention, for the simplicity of the composition and for the fact that they so perfectly lent themselves to being mixed. His first own label was Design Music, followed by Zenit. These labels marked a turning point in the Neapolitan scene, hosting the first productions of many local DJs. Marco Carola's name was connected with a new generation of promoters and clubs, like *Orbeat*, which was also one of the first Neapolitan magazines dedicated to the Techno scene. In 1998, in the wake of *Orbeat*, another group of promoters founded the team International Talent. Elena, an active clubber in those years, remembers the period of 1996–2003:

From 1996 on, the number of people who followed Techno parties doubled. The parties were open-minded. However, the years from 1996 to 1998 were years of panic, loads of parties, no alcohol, only on Sunday afternoons during the after-hour parties. These were often organized in the parking lots of the clubs, with music coming from the stereos of open cars. We were all friends,

---

23 Cf. www.marcocarola.com.

24 To learn more about Berlin's spaces, crowds, and music please see Tobias Rapp's and Florian Sievers' essays in this book.

no criminals, and no cocaine. Techno headz, compared to those of the Angels of Love (House music), were fewer, but there was also some collaboration.[25]

Next to Marco Carola, Gaetano 'Gaetek' Parisio, was the second pioneer of this new wave of DJ producers. He had attended the city's clubs in the early 1990s and, having met Marco Carola, began deejaying and went on to release his first own music production in 1996. In 1997, Parisio founded his first label, Conform. In the following year, he co-founded ART Records with Carola and finally launched the Southsoul label in 2000. Parisio's style still retains an old-school flavour without following or trying to anticipate trends. He sticks to the ideas of original underground Techno which refuse to seek success at all costs. Moreover, Parisio is also one of the few DJs in electronic dance music to have promoted humanitarian projects through their music. In 1999, inspired by the tragic events of the war in Kosovo, he released the compilation *Techcommunity 4 Kosovo*, which included tracks by Marco Carola, German Sven Väth, Swedish Cari Lekebusch, French Laurent Garnier, and British Surgeon and James Ruskin. The proceeds were donated to the Red Cross to help refugees of the Kosovo War.

Danilo Vigorito was another DJ and producer on this new scene. After having started with the aforementioned DJ teams United Tribes and 3 Imaginary Boys, he worked for Flying Records studios as a sound engineer and producer between 1995 and 2000. Within a brief period, he was promoted from assistant director to chief sound engineer and also worked with 99 Posse during the production of two of their most important albums. Different aesthetic trajectories met almost by accident, and Vigorito would greatly benefit from these experiences. His first EP was released in 1999. On his second album, *Homegrown Tears* (2012), he introduced elements and classical melodies of Neapolitan music in a very moderate way. Among the recent exponents is producer Davide Squillace, whose label and art project, This And That Lab, is lively and inflected with colourful pop accents. Finally, Carola Pisaturo and Chiara 'Miz Kiara' Graziani are, to date, the only women to represent Naples on the international DJ scene. Pisaturo has an eclectic style, ranging from House to Techno, with a hint of melody and warm contributions from a Mediterranean matrix. Miz Kiara, a vinyl addict since the 1990s, has a sophisticated crossover sound between all shades of electronic, House and Techno music. Techno and Tech House are now no longer niche genres in Naples – they have replaced House as the mainstream of electronic dance music.

'Sintesi' and current fragmentation: the 2000s until the present

By the year 2000, in many cities of the Northern hemisphere club culture and electronic dance music had become a recognised phenomena and entered the mainstream. With the diffusion of laptops and the emergence of a new generation of digital audio-visual synthesis software, music production would change radically, marking the final passage from analogue to digital. This had an immediate impact on experimental electronic music and the more intellectual and conceptual fringes of dance music. This often hybridised sound and digital media. In Naples, in 2002, 'The Sintesi Festival of Electronic Arts' was launched. 'Sintesi'[26] was a cultural project designed to produce a dialogue between Naples and this new international network of contemporary culture. At the same time, a lot of attention was paid to the promotion of artists and productions from the local scene. Between 2002 and 2005 several editions of the festival took place.

The importance of 'Sintesi' could be seen by the spaces in which it was realised: Renaissance churches and historic buildings of the city centre, underused and particularly spectacular as

---

25 Elena, in an interview with the author (July 2013).

26 The festival was curated and organised by Danilo Capasso, Giuseppe di Gangi, Sasi Maglia, Mario Masullo, and Francesco Quarto.

gathering places for music. It was a parallel and complementary scene to that of the clubs and electronic dance music. It leant towards a more mature and minimal sound, which rediscovered the historical avant-gardes of Concrete and Minimal music while seeking to redefine the position of the new electronic arts in a contemporary context. It attracted an adult audience of clubbers, though not exclusively. It was looking for new content, variations, and a new intellectual dimension of the scene. The 'Sintesi' festival became a space of convergence and contact among different musical cultures, a period of healthy, aesthetic hybridisation driven by the new possibilities offered up by the development of digital sound synthesis.

—

At present, clubbing under Vesuvius is driven by artists and organisations that cover a wide range of music in a variety of locations. The aforementioned Almamegretta, for example, have, despite having changed their members over time, never stopped making music. Their lead singer, Raiz, has produced several solo albums. Meanwhile, 99 Posse, after working on individual projects for several years,[27] have recently reunited and are said to be producing a new album soon. Marco Messina, one of the founders of the group, is among the producer-musicians involved in the Ten Cities project – along with Lucio Aquilina[28], another still relatively new Neapolitan DJ/producer. In the last few years, the city has also seen the growth of a Psy-Trance[29] scene linked to Sonica,[30] a festival that has taken root in a forest of the regional hinterland. Gaetano Parisio, Marco Carola, and Davide Squillace have now all relocated to Barcelona and they come to the city, from time to time, to play as guests. Especially Carola, who regularly deejays at Amnesia in Ibiza, is now a popstar. At the same time, there is a new generation returning to pure Techno, who have even played at Berlin's famous club, Berghain. Among them

Domenico Crisci, who purely produces with analogue instruments and only publishes on vinyl.

There is also a solid team of local DJs in operation, among them me (Danylo), Roberto Biccari, Giovanni Calemma, Giancarlo Lanza, Francesco Monetti, Aldoina Filangieri, DJ Deaf, JD, Dez, and the flawless Jg Bros. Some are young, others we have already encountered in this story. This is by far no exhaustive list. So, at the time of writing, there are also other realities in the city, other parties, and other crews that I may well be unaware of. Among the many new venues and events, Woo parties are worth a special mention. They are the brainchild of Augusto Penna, a passionate clubber and music-listener with an eclectic taste. He organises an annual electronic music festival called *Don't Touch Naples*, as well as summer parties in extraordinary locations such as the ancient thermal pools of Agnano, where the audience can end the night with a dip in the sulphurous waters. Woo parties can also be found in clubs of the historic centre, or by the sea in the western part of the city at the edge of one of Italy's largest industrial wastelands, Arenile di Bagnoli.

Generally speaking, the electronic music scene of the city is now mainly active internationally and no longer seems interested in reworking the local sense of Neapolitan-ness. Nowadays, the landscape of Neapolitan clubbing resembles a white sheet on which more and more dots have fused together, creating a map on which it is difficult to distinguish individual elements. The references are various, music has created different niches, different families, different shades that blend into a rhythmic magma, bouncing back and forth in time without a rational progression or linearity. The breaking, processing, and turning points condense from time to time at some particular event where the right artistic and emotional trajectories converge in a chaotic and serendipitous manner. In this urban sphere, musical and

27 Luca 'O Zulù' Persico, and Maria 'Meg' di Donna continued their careers as soloists or in other formations.
28 Cf. www.lucioaquilina.com.
29 Psychedelic Trance Techno music.
30 Cf. www.sonica-dance-festival.eu/it.

aggregative cultures arrive and depart as aesthetic and social micro-utopias, provoking lines of flight as heterotopias and zones of experimentation. Then to disappear or evolve into something else.

Bibliography

Arecata, 'Napoli che se n'è andata', *Le Stronzate di Pucinella*, 11 May 2013, <http://pulcinella291.forumfree.it/?t=65852153&st=15> accessed 1 May 2014.
Bainbridge, Luke, *The True Story of Acid House: Britain's Last Youth Culture Revolution* (London: Omnibus Press, 2013).
Calemma, Giovanni; Capasso, Danilo; Luongo, Lucio; Quarto, Francesco Maria; Vele, Ivan Maria, *United Tribes. La Storia* (Naples: MAO Media & Arts Office, 2015).
Fabbri, Franco and Plastino, Goffredo (eds.), *Made in Italy: Studies in Popular Music* (New York: Routledge, 2013).
Philopat, Marco, *Lumi Di Punk* (Milan: Agenzia X, 2006).

Tien'a Ment squatters at work, Naples, 1992, photo: Giovanni Calemma

DJ Danylo playing at Hipe club, Caserta, 1992, photo: Lucio Luongo

Dave Morales playing at My Way club, Naples, 1992, photo: Giovanni Calemma

Album cover Almamegretta, *Sanacore*, Naples, 1995, design: Angela Maione

United Tribes' friend Giacomo enjoying an afterhour on the city rooftop, Naples, 1994, photo: Giovanni Calemma

Neapolitan Nights – From Vesuvian Blues to Planetary Vibes

Vincenzo Cavallo and Iain Chambers

Culturally speaking Naples can be considered to be in a space that extends both from southern Europe and from North Africa. This is not simply a geographical location but also a political and cultural premise. Here one can view Naples in a Mediterranean-centred perspective where the city appears as a strategic hub located in the mids of many commercial, cultural, and historical routes. This is rather obvious but when considered in musical terms it provokes a suggestive counter-narrative. At this point, a local political and cultural consensus that considers itself in exclusively Occidental and European terms falls apart. Historical evidence and contemporary cultural arrangements actually propose a city that co-exists in a multiplicity of circuits orbiting around diverse nuclei, not all of them either local or European in their constitution. Against the prevailing narrative of modernity that has consistently located Naples in the European periphery, Neapolitan sounds and visual culture propose a diverse space, a form of heterotopia in which the city re-composes its centrality through the rhythms and reasoning of musical rituals. This is a crucial element in understanding the centrality of music in shaping Neapolitan cultural identity and its affective public economy.

Alongside this, it is important to register the particular historical and cultural context of post-1945 Italy in which the music we discuss profoundly shifted the sonorial and cultural landscapes of the city. To the foreign observer, Italy is a country soaked in Catholicism. This is profoundly marked in the south with shrines on every street corner, in the niches of walls: talismanic icons drawing upon even older, pagan, sentiments. Italy is also a country that had the biggest Communist Party in Western Europe. As a mass party, often close to taking political power, despite the opposition of the United States and the orchestrated politics of tension sustained by public bombings and terrorism, the Partito Comunista Italiano (PCI) pursued a series of historical compromises with 'family values' and Catholicism leading to profound political caution over the civil rights involved in divorce, abortion, and the public funding of private, religious schools.

The profanity of secular sounds and irreverent bodies has had to insist on their presence in this milieu, where the desire for local and national continuities, rather than breaks and confrontation, have characterised modern Italy. Punk, for example, could never have been invented in Italy. In the same vein, one of the authors vividly remembers comrades in the far-left extra-parliamentary organisation Lotta Continua who, after hours of heated debate, marches, and occupations, would expect the pasta to be ready on the table once they returned from the 'struggle'. Structures and their accompanying sentiments run deep. This is also the context characterised by popular music that sought to maintain both the tradition of traditional *bel canto* [beautiful song] and the institutionalised sentimentality of family values that were reaffirmed each year on public television in the Sanremo Music Festival.

The 1960s and 1970s, as elsewhere in the world, were moments of rebellion and revolt in both form and content. It was probably one of the most significant periods of Italian pop music. In 1958, Domenico Modugno won the Sanremo Music Festival with 'Nel Blu Dipinto Di Blu (Volare)' [In blue painted blue (flying)]. From that moment everything changed. It was during this period that the *Cantautori* [singer-songwriters writing and performing their own material] became the voice of political and cultural transformation. These singers linked their identities to stylistic schools, usually associated with a city. The Cantautori were urban storytellers, and most of them quickly became political activists, with their words and music representing a specific historical and cultural space. Among the most famous schools were those of Genoa, Milan, Bologna, and Rome. In the 1960s Naples was famous for artists such as Peppino di Capri and his Rockers, nothing comparable to the main scene of such singer-songwriters as De Andrè, Jannacci, Guccini, and De Gregori.

Another significant dimension was that of more pop-oriented music proposed by Lucio Dalla and the markedly original Lucio Battisti, later followed by the altogether more explicitly Rock sound of Vasco Rosso. It is only later, towards the end of that decade and the beginning of the 1970s, that artists such as Edoardo Bennato started to open up a unique path towards the Neapolitan Folk Revival. Here artists revitalised the traditional Neapolitan sounds from the fourteenth and fifteenth centuries through the addition of contemporary and provocative verses. They also opened up the space for the subsequent Mediterranean Blues of artists such as Pino Daniele and the subsequent Neapolitan Power scene.[1] These are the first real Neapolitan Cantautori, with their musical style and sentiments deeply connected to the city, unique in their radical manner of re-framing Naples as a new site of meanings.

Objectives and methodologies

This article explores the reformulation of the public sphere under the impact of local subcultures and musical affiliations commencing in the 1960s and continuing down to the present. We have decided to adopt an interdisciplinary or 'cultural studies' approach in order to focus on the political dynamics of contemporary Neapolitan club culture and its historical foundations, conflicts, and defining traits. We are interested in understanding how the forms and contents of the sounds contributed to shaping political ideologies, cultural formations, social class structures, and urban, ethnic, gender, and sexual identities.

We consider club cultures – their spatialities, practices, and proposals – in terms of what Foucault once referred to as heterotopias.[2] Parallel to the institutional organisation of consensual understandings, the heterotopic provides a parallel counter-space. It promotes a time out from institutional rhythms, even an interruption, certainly an interrogation, of the hegemonic framing of bodies held in a uniform and unilateral time.

Lived space can be defined in terms of both relations and dislocations. Here, we encounter particular relations of proximity and distance, of interactions and separation. Such relations contribute to the creation of both transitional places and established ones designed to host institutions with specific functions (schools, offices, prisons, churches, etc.). They also lead to the production of 'counter-spaces'. The latter are real places

---

[1] To learn more about Neapolitan Power and other genres of Neapolitan pop music, please see Danilo Capasso's essay in this book.

[2] Cf. Michel Foucault, 'Of Other Spaces: Utopias and Heterotopias', trans. Jay Miskowiec, *Diacritics*, 16, no. 1 (Spring 1986), 22–27. First published in *Architecture/Mouvement/Continuité*, no. 5 (October 1984), 46–49.

in which culture is represented, contested, and subverted at the same time.[3] In precisely this manner we consider clubs as heterotopias. They provide spaces in which the culture that sustains them is both legitimated and subverted. In our opinion, it is music that creates the processes that sustain such heterotopic spaces.

So, we are arguing that cultural formations cannot exist that are not at the same time sites of heterotopias with their specific functional and dysfunctional structures and dynamics. This suggests that in order to understand the reshaping of the public sphere under the impact of subcultures and musical affiliations we need to understand the structures and dynamics of Neapolitan club heterotopias. Our intention, then, is to explore these heterotopias in order to re-map the archive of musical memories imbricated in the history of Naples and to understand how such memories impact the understanding of the present. This then draws us into modernity that is not simply doubled by subaltern actors and forces seeking to contest the hegemonic version of a history that insists on a unique telling. Recognising the intersecting and planetary distribution of difference, location, and singularity there emerges an understanding of the constellation of modernity that is disseminated in shifting rhythms along multiple scales and within the combinations of heterogeneous powers and practices.

Against the empty dream of an utopian alternative promoting withdrawal from the seemingly unavoidable impositions of actuality, the instance of heterotopia proposes that we step out of an existing version of time to drop deeper into the folds of the contemporary world; there to assay and acquire its potentialities. Here, time is split from itself to permit the registration of other temporalities; an imposed and seemingly inevitable future is marked by the return of other, unacknowledged times. No longer the victim of a rigid archive, confined to the predictable rhythms of a numbing tradition, here the past becomes a vibrant tissue that interpellates and interrupts the present. The authorised combination of materials fall apart, the archive is unlocked and its documents, voices, objects, and silences are scattered over altogether more contingent maps. Set to diverse patterns and imperatives, the past comes to be configured by present urgencies in an emergent critical space. In this sense, the past, present, and future are still emerging, still in the making; understandings have not yet docked; they are still underway, open to contestation, redirection, and reformulation.

To step sideways and remove oneself from the implacable logic of a single-minded modernity is to step out of the cage of an abstract temporality. As a conscious cut, an alternate take, a blue note, and deliberate dissonance, this idea of heterotopic thought and practices seeks to burrow below both the topographical logic of Foucault's disciplined spatialities and the eternal dialectic of narratives and counter-narratives. If we could consider remix as a method, just like Jazz improvisations on the musical 'standards', or the unhomely melody of the Blues or the DJ's timely 'cut', then we can confront the sedimented and striated composition of a modernity that does not move to a single beat or uniform pulse. In this form of historical and cultural mix, we are encouraged to think more in terms of subjective forces, shifting combinations and unplanned vibrations, rather than remain locked in the power of established positions

[3] Ibid.

contesting and dividing the singularity of sense. The historical conjuncture is ultimately a performative space elaborated along multiple planes, diverse trajectories, and unpredictable depths. The ratio is neither linear nor transparent. At this point, it is instructive to return to Foucault's noted radio talk on heterotopia and consider this statement:

> *Heterotopias are most linked to slices in time – which is to say that they open onto what might be termed, for the sake of symmetry, heterochromies. The heterotopia begins to function at full capacity when men arrive at a sort of absolute break with their traditional time.*[4]

These are slices in time, intervals in the narratives, interruptions in the machinery of truth. Foucault's arguments suggest far more than simply registering the question of spatiality and acknowledging the unregistered volume of the contemporary world. To cut space up into a heterogamous assemblage is also to multiply time in diverse rhythms and temporal insistences. Neither is homogeneous. The desire to represent modernity as the perfect match of linear time and homogeneous space is thwarted. This teaches us that critical labour is not simply about contesting the imposed temporalities of hegemonic rationalities. Rather, critical labour is also about constructing a space beside ourselves; here the reconfiguration of actualities releases another set of spatio-temporal coordinates and another manner of reasoning. What now returns to the map is what was excluded by the premises of the previous cartography of power, of knowledge. This operation, like a Deleuzian 'fold', creases and deepens spatiality while rendering diverse temporalities proximate. It produces the interleaving of heterogeneous dimensions that resonate with the circulation of bodies, histories, cultures, and capital in what we come to understand as a manifold modernity.

In this sense, as Foucault insisted in his Preface to the 1966 volume *The Order of Things*,[5] the heterotopic breaks through and beyond the homogeneous order of discourse. The heterotopic proposes the elision of the imposed. Language and space no longer match as the former is unable to contain and control the latter. The map is no longer reality, merely a limited representation. At this point, the epistemological device – the map, the discipline, and institutional knowledge – promotes an ontological rift. For if utopias are the product of language, heterotopias are manufactured and maintained in the mutable materialities of space and exceed the attempts of language seeking to impose its order.

If utopias by their very nature do not exist, they are nevertheless cultivated and cared for in language. Heterotopias, on the contrary, even if unregistered and unrecognised, do exist. They, too, require language and are therefore not without their utopic drive. But they sustain diverse experiences of inhabiting history and culture, different practices of time and space. Alternative, subaltern, and subordinated to the rules that occlude their presence, heterotopias exist and persist as counter-spaces beside and outside the dominant syntax of sense. Their presence uproots the premises of the linguistic and discursive order, proposing a flight and freedom from its imposition. They propose a disturbance, an intimation of the unhomely. If space is produced[6] and never simply given, it is not only produced by our language. It is construed, constructed, crossed, and signified by many different bodies, pulses, and rhythms.

[4] Ibid., 25.
[5] Cf. Michel Foucault, *The Order of Things* (London & New York: Routledge, 2002).
[6] Cf. Henri Lefebvre, *The Production of Space* (Oxford: Wiley-Blackwell, 1991).

Sounding out the city

Francesco Rosi's famous films presented post-war Naples as gripped by the 'hands on the city' of the ruling Christian Democrat party, the cultural censorship of the Catholic church and the sharp practices of property development and political corruption in the post-war boom. Beneath this conservative veneer, older, almost pagan, popular rites of street culture and associated beliefs have constantly threatened to break through the brittle barrier of institutional rhetoric. It was in this space that the subtle disorientation of the Blues—proposed by James Senese, Napoli Centrale, Pino Daniele, or Edoardo Bennato—crossed the street from the post-war port clubs for US servicemen into the urban stronghold of Neapolitan song.

The latter sound, notwithstanding all the claims of autochthonous autonomy, was itself the hybrid composition of a mobile Mediterranean musicality.[7] Hints of melisma, microtonalities, Arabic *maqam* scales,[8] and the torn and twisted vocals that mark Rebetiko, Fado, Flamenco, and Arabic songs orbited in its vicinity. If the official culture—deeply mired in a historicism that considered continuity and the 'passive revolution' of timeless cultural stasis as the unique guarantee of its veracity—then seemingly 'imported' sounds that became increasingly strident from the 1970s onwards proposed a detour, even a deviation, from the predictable score. Punk, Reggae, the New Romantics, Dub music, and Hip-Hop found an audience and clubs, followers and fans, proposing a series of shifting sound communities that inhabited and cut up the inherited spaces of the city.

Neapolitans seem to be unable to embrace the new without re-calling and re-framing the past. In order to justify a legitimate desire for freedom, they have constantly connected it to the assumed autonomy of what we will later define as Napoletanità [the Neapolitan-ness]. In Naples, it is always a matter of roots as everything has to be appropriated and authenticated as Neapolitan in order to gain entry to the institutional story of the city and be accepted by its intelligentsia. Meanwhile, sounds from elsewhere—North America, the Caribbean, North Africa, and Northern Europe—and from other port cities (New York, Kingston, Liverpool, and London) had already entered the Neapolitan soundscape. They left their traces while simultaneously being transformed into local topographies of sense. Sounds, youth, and subcultures emerged that were not simply the poor copy of an 'original' template located in Kingston or London. By the Mediterranean Sea and under Vesuvius, Dub and Punk have both connected to such 'sources', while at the same time translating and transforming such signs and sounds into life in the bay. The line 'Dark was the night' simultaneously recalls the bottleneck Blues lament on Blind Willie Johnson's guitar from 1927 and the volcanic paving stones of the dimly-lit baroque streets of this Mediterranean metropolis. Drawing both from afar and the ambiguous insistence of the uncertain present, music reconfigures the cultural and historical score. It proposes another mix, another chance, and even a new ontology. It is in this manner that it becomes possible to consider a further political economy of meaning suspended and sustained in sound.

Of course, this is also where the abstract and academic understanding of the public sphere is taken for a ride, and eventually gets lost. The presumption that the modern *agora* of public democracy emerges in

[7] Cf. Iain Chambers, *Mediterraneo Blues. Musiche, Malinconia Postcoloniali, Pensieri Marittimi* (Turin: Bollati Boringhieri, 2012).

[8] To learn more about Arab maqam scales, please see Maha ElNabawi's essay about music in Cairo in this book.

transparent communication between rational individuals à la Habermas becomes altogether more confused once caught, slowed down, and decomposed between the bass and the fumes of marijuana or else seized in electric treble and amphetamine fast-forward. The modification of time and space in a mix of sounds pushes the categories of public and private out of their formal distinctions. In the flux, the city acquires psychic contours in a trip that is ultimately impossible to reduce to a common tale. Communities of sound provide a very different soundtrack to the more predictable routines of urban life. A cultural and historical inheritance, despite the identitarian self-referentiality of Napoletanità, can be cut up, remixed, and reassembled. Gaps are exposed, jumps occur. Nothing is cancelled, but everything is rearranged. Tradition becomes translation. Youth and musical cultures provoke a counter-space. In providing a Foucauldian heterotopia, there is no utopic alternative, but rather a set of parallel spaces and practices sustained in sound. These refute and subvert the rationality of a public sphere, which believes the world can be represented and reasoned in transparent exchange and conventional order.

Perhaps, as Jacques Derrida once suggested, it is the embedded, lived-in, place of the city, rather than the abstract space of the nation or the trans-national space called Europe, which provides the laboratory for the more extensive and constantly negotiated becoming of democracy.[9] This hypothesis is confirmed by our investigation on how Neapolitan heterotopias change according to the needs of embedded lives rather than those of an abstract Europe, which is increasingly losing its economic and cultural appeal. In the city, the blocking mechanisms of state and European legislation often come to be blunted and diverted in the textures and issues of daily urban life. If the law exercises the unilateral procedures of power, the realities of street life and cultural proximities often lead to gaps, negotiations, and compromise.

It is precisely here that the capitalist organisation and disarticulation of the 'social' is most effectively challenged. It is here that the structural and structuring logic of the neo-liberal political economy, seeking to colonise not simply the present but also the future and the past, is most sharply exposed in its quotidian details and dangers. It is also here that alternative counter-narratives, refusals, revolts, and deviations acquire substance, a life, and flesh. Finally, it is here that the historical and cultural interruption proposed by what official culture has chosen to refuse, to expel, and negate – the urban underclass, the 'illegal' migrant, youth revolt, gender and racial discrimination – acquires critical force, reminding us of a mutable and multivalent modernity that is never merely 'ours' to administer and define. In this cultivation of social space, where the public and private are increasingly entangled in emerging and unsuspected configurations, the subordinate cultures of the city propose a more extensive and significant historical and cultural perspective than the narrow prospects offered by the existing political machine. In the interstices of this framework, the city makes space for the re-thinking of the existing political order and its public sphere.

From the club to the squat

Between the 1980s and the end of the 1990s, a set of heterotopic situations emerged in Naples that can be mapped in our cartography of

9
Jacques Derrida, *Of Hospitality* (Stanford: Stanford University Press, 2000).

broken histories. Music created new spatialities, that are fundamental to identify. These spatialities were not a place of counterculture. They were not necessarily political spaces consciously questioning the status quo. Rather, they proposed alternative spaces in alternative registers of time and place. As such, they broke with existing understandings of Neapolitan club culture by creating new categories and genres in which emerging values were consciously and unconsciously translated and transmitted.

This transmission took place within a corporeal and non-verbal dimension; the only way of stopping or interfering with it was, and is, to shut it down; to make it illegal and to persecute the believers by attacking their places of worship. At this stage, it is the sites of transmission, the physical places themselves that become the real protagonist of the scene. It was the new cultural leaders of the club culture who wanted the community itself, its codes and aesthetics to be the principal star. This emerging cyberculture had its own spiritual leaders and gurus, but very few superstars. The network, that is the new relationship between humans, machines, new sexual identities, and the interaction of this shifting assemblage within a specific space became the real mobile subject. The 1980s destroyed the pre-existing public spheres to open up new possibilities for the 1990s. During these two decades, the wilder reasoning of the new public sphere, and its interrogation by official public spaces and practices, generated the current discussion about contemporary Neapolitan club culture and its links with the historical past of the city.

At the beginning of the 1980s, the Neapolitan scene was identified with the aforementioned Neapolitan Power, an extremely popular genre that mixed Blues, Jazz, and local music: James Senses, Pino Daniele, Rino Zurzolo, Tullio De Piscopo. This sound was the result of a historical process in which Naples experienced an important transition from the end of the Second World War to the conclusion of the so-called *anni di piombo* [years of lead or years of the bullet] of terrorism. During the 1970s and into the early 1980s, the country was sucked into an intense and violent conflict between the Italian state and extra-parliamentary organisations such as the Red Brigades and other armed political groups. In 1980, a bomb exploded in Piazza Fontana in Bologna killing 125 people and this further amplified the 'politics of tension'. The government of the day approved a series of laws giving more power to the police. Within a few years, these armed left-wing organisations were dismantled, and youth culture initiated a path towards other horizons.

It was in this period that the Punk movement arrived in Naples and brought with its music the creation of new spaces, new values, and new perspectives. In this historical moment, previous ideologies began to lose their capacity to attract youth and avant-garde initiatives. A new place in downtown Naples was opened by a group of young people who wanted to break with the local Neapolitan Power tradition: Diamond Dogs club. This space, and the way people clubbed there, had all the characteristics of a heterotopic situation in which an emerging sense of cultural identity was being built. Diamond Dogs opened in 1984, and its explicit manifesto was to distance itself from local politics and to exit from the *anni di piombo* and associated insurrectionary values. Here, underground culture separated itself from its immediate past and connected to what was happening elsewhere abroad. It was a place in which novel encounters between different scenes could occur.

Before Diamond Dogs there were basically three scenes: Italian pop and Disco, native singer-songwriters, and the Blues, Rock, Jazz constellation from the 1970s. Now, a space existed where Neapolitan youth could listen to new sounds and trace in them innovative scenarios that were not necessarily tied into an immediate political and cultural past. Here, the aesthetic and cultural boundary between this internal space and an external Napoletanità was what really counted. The organisation of events was altogether more spontaneous than in the consolidated and institutionalised music scene. Within the organisation of the club's programme there was much debate and discussion. Some people were coming from the pop scene and were advocating a more pop-like programme. Others were proposing more extreme reasons and rhythms. Left-wing intellectuals, middle-class kids, and Punks co-existed. They met to dance and debate a different future, a new trajectory, outside the existing scenarios promoted by the previous generation.

Diamond Dogs was an alternative rather than a counter-space as political and ideological values were not necessarily questioned or rendered explicit. The real rationale behind the creation of Diamond Dogs lay in the necessity to create a space able to accommodate a wide spectrum of new musical tendencies, largely coming from the UK, together with a local emergent New Wave scene known as Vesuwave. It was a place in which a DJ could play Wall of Voodoo, Echo & the Bunnymen, The Clash, Psychedelic Furs, or Iggy Pop along with the first live artists using synthesizers, and even dance music on Saturday nights. This multifarious musical mix produced new sonorial spatialities where corporeal configurations and non-verbal extensions through sound and dance, and simply being in those space, produced a diverse sense of cultural possibilities that did not exist in the already established pop clubs, or in the Rock, Blues, and Jazz circuit.

—

There were also other places in which such musical and cultural mixes were being experimented. There were the squats or Centri Sociali [social centres]. The process in which a new wave of music became part of Neapolitan squat culture takes us into another heterotopic moment. The squatting movement emerged at the end of the 1980s and the beginning of the 1990s, and it left an irrevocable signature on the subsequent soundscape. In particular, it was in two squats in Naples in this period that emerging rhythms were translated into physical and conceptual spaces leading to the production of two very different heterotopic formations.

The first is Tien'a Ment [don't forget in Neapolitan] occupied in 1989. It clearly alludes to what was happening in China on Tiananmen Square in this period where the state had massacred protesting students. The squat was located in the northern part of the metropolitan periphery. It was occupied by a group of people who declared that they had no political affiliation and were largely related to the Punk and squat scene in London. It emerged that the first Tien'a Ment concert had been a fundraising event organised to collect money for the release of 'Collega': a friend who had been arrested during the xPoll Tax protests in London.

This place, and the community of people involved, totally broke with the previous scene. The Tien'a Ment community publicly declared that it did not want to be politically affiliated. This clearly led to a re-shuffling of inherited ideological positions and the earlier rigid identification of specific sounds with precise political attitudes. Significantly, the community was organised around music rather than political ideologies. It was not politics choosing the music, but rather sound proposing a very different understanding of what constituted the 'political'. It was a different space in which diverse groups came together under one roof: from hard-core Punk to the new Techno heads. Here Punk became Post-Punk, and groups such as Contropotere and others experimented at the Punk extremes and its various mutations into Cyberpunk, Hardcore, Noise, and Trash, pioneering an abrasive path towards electronic music.

The other squat was Officina 99. It was occupied in 1991. This squat has a clear left-wing orientation. There is a group – 99 Posse – that takes its name from the squat which it popularised by creating a song about it. The track became a hit and an integral part of the soundtrack of a specific historical period characterised by a series of massive anti-globalisation protests that took place in different parts of the Western world, from Seattle to Genoa. Squats were no longer marginalised places but focal points for the reshaping of urban areas and culture. Naples symbolically led this urban and political phenomenon through the songs and music from Officina 99. Here, in the squat, the new musicalities that had emerged elsewhere were embedded in the left-wing discourse. Officina 99 was the antagonistic and profoundly anti-institutional response of the left-wing movement to what was happening elsewhere in places such as Tien'a Ment.

In this sense, Officina 99 did not break with existing politics but rather with its cultural order. The music of the Neapolitan left no longer remained the same. New sounds were approved and popularised: Dub, Hip-Hop, and on some occasions even Techno began to be played. This opening had a huge influence on the manner in which white Neapolitan youth began to relate to African, African American, and Caribbean music, especially Reggae, Raggamuffin, and Rap. It was in this period that illegal African immigration became a political issue as part of the wider anti-globalisation movement. In the squat, African immigrants were hosted and supported. The squats played, and in some cases are still playing, an important role in providing legal, educational, and health services to illegal immigrants. Once again, there was the emergence of different contact zones in which Neapolitan culture commences an engagement with creolisation.

It was out of this process that the sounds of the group Almamegretta emerged. The band was founded in 1988. It was also during this period that the student protest movement known as the *Pantera* [Panther] began. The latter commenced with the occupation of the University of Palermo in 1989, immediately followed by occupations in Naples. Southern Italy was not only guiding a youth rebellion with its university students but also regarding sounds. Almamegretta and 99 Posse instantly became the soundtrack of the political wave that subsequently flowed into the anti-globalisation movement in Europe. Naples, and Italy in general, acquired a new centrality.

The networks of sound that rendered the Caribbean proximate to the Mediterranean, or London to Naples also transformed a peripheral European city into an unsuspected centre. Moving from the cultural and historical edge of southern Europe, Naples opted for a new centrality. The Dub sound of Almamegretta, for example, reopens the local archive of repressed memories and negated histories, to set in play other coordinates and other maps. Southern European history of subordination and oppression is connected to the contemporary injustice of neo-liberal globalisation. African ancestry is evoked in redemptive rhythms, sounds, and sentiments in order to denounce the hypocrisies of the present in which goods and capital, but not human beings, freely circulate. This was one of the principal arguments of the anti-globalisation movement. This is a new narrative that emerges in the sounds and sentiments of diverse musical genres.

In the song 'Figli Di Annibale' (1993) Gennaro 'Raiz' Della Volpe, the singer of Almamegretta, recounts the story of Hannibal coming from Africa with elephants via Spain and France, crossing the Alps and conquering Italy. As Raiz sings: 'This is why many Italians have dark skin / This is why many Italians have dark eyes'. This is a fragmentary remembering of the past which is symbolically reconstituted within a contemporary context to query the present. It provokes an interrogation and proposes other identities and ontologies. It induces a cultural crisis. The present is interrupted, cut-up, and reassembled in the light of the histories and possibilities it has structurally repressed and studiously avoided. These musicians are self-consciously at work here, remixing historical provocations, crossing them with transformed sounds to promote other spaces, narratives, and identities.

An emerging and heterogeneous modernity that does not merely mirror an imagined life in New York or Berlin allows for the return of ghosts and their proposal to creolise both the past and the present. Over a heavy bass riddim, Hannibal once again conquers Italy – 'Africa… Africa… Africa…' – and a negated *Black Athena* reverberates in the south of Italy and Europe where once we were all wops and without papers.[10] This is obviously not simply about records, recordings, and commercial success. It is, above all, about the elaboration of an effective cartography, a new and diverse mapping of the city that cuts into the earlier corpus of understanding. It leaves a wound, it bleeds, it festers, and it is incurable. In the same key, the periphery of the city's official culture sends a message downtown to the administrative and commercial centre. Like the graffiti-covered subway coaches rattling out of the Bronx into Manhattan, the sounds of the bands Co'sang and A67 from the ghettoised housing estate of Scampia (rendered notorious in the novel and film *Gomorrah* (2008)) rework a trans-national metropolitan mix of sounds and subcultures into a precise semantics. They give shape to another cultural horizon, one that lies far beyond the provincial gaze of local power.

—

If the heterotopic moment generated during the Tien'a Ment period was able to question the cultural ontologies of the Left, Officina 99 developed a new cultural style organized around music rather than traditional political activities. Despite radical differences in terms of ideologies, common

[10] Raiz, *W.O.P.* (Italy: Phoenix Entertainment, 2004).

practices emerged. It was music that defined the spaces. These two principal squats continued to co-exist until Tien'a Ment was forcibly cleared and has never since been re-occupied. Unlike Officina 99, the Post-Punk Tien'a Ment movement never had a clear political plan or organised structure. At the same time, diverse singularities that formed part of a multitude, wrongly defined by some as a movement, were subsequently to transform sounds and lives into Techno and other electronic fragments. Eventually the Tien'a Ment scene came under the influence of Techno and other electronic music and a new generation of clubbers developing elsewhere in Naples during the first half of the 1990s.

A new ontology had now emerged from Neapolitan club culture. It led to the rise of new forms of social, cultural, and political existence. In this conjunction, Tien'a Ment and Officina 99 were undoubtedly the local protagonists in the formation of new and significant heterotopic situations. In the same period, further cultural forces were also coming into play. The general rise of club culture worldwide from the late 1980s onwards had promoted a completely new scene in Naples by the early 1990s. Left-wing political movements were no longer the unique point of reference for alternative perspectives. Earlier oppositional rhetoric and aesthetics were now questioned by the existence of these emerging spaces and their practices. Many walls were coming down and something new was happening in town.

By the early 1990s, in the wake of the heterotopic fallout that had cancelled an earlier musical and cultural order, the Neapolitan club scene, based on electronic dance music in the form of House, Progressive, and Techno was producing a series of fragmented and temporary autonomous zones.[11] Condensed in diverse spaces – from nightclubs and private villas to camping sites and warehouses – sounds came together in a radical dance floor reconfiguration of cultural and musical semantics. Here middle-class youth would mingle with others from different social classes. House music was erasing politics while transforming the dance floor into an unadulterated contact zone. This emerging configuration transformed a mix of musicalities into a new physical and conceptual space destined to irreversibly alter the Neapolitan club scene, its ecosystem, and its associated public sphere.

Among these sounds and spaces, influences were neither discussed nor celebrated. There was no apparent need to establish genealogies. Earlier developments were now decanted into new scenes and sounds. It was an emergent third space. It promoted encounters without the baggage of too much prejudice. It was precisely here, in 1994, that Post-Punk, Dub, and Reggae were able to meet House music and propel the Neapolitan club scene into its golden age. The new and the old were remixed in a manner to accommodate the emerging sounds of the city. It was in this period that the United Tribes were organising parties in which Almamegretta, Zion Train, and Paul Daley from the famous UK project Leftfield were sharing the same stage.

White Neapolitan youth began to listen and play with Afro sounds, transforming and transmitting them through their own codes and spaces. While the Post-Punk movement was bringing Dub music into House and Techno sounds, the Posse scene from Officina 99 was promoting Reggae, Raggamuffin, and Hip-Hop as the sound of the anti-globalisation

[11] Cf. Hakim Bey, *T.A.Z. The Temporary Autonomous Zone, Ontological Anarchy, Poetic Terrorism* (New York: Autonomedia, 1991).

movement. At the close of the 1990s and the beginning of the new century, Reggae became extremely popular. The Kinky Bar, a bar and club in the old town, proposed African American, Caribbean, and African music genres, the so-called 'black music', outside the squats. The place became a contact zone between white middle-class kids and illegal immigrants who wanted to socialise. Reggae was everywhere. Southern Italian youth began to renegotiate their own identity by relating to Africa and the sounds of the black diaspora. From Lecce, another southern Italian city in Puglia, Sud Sound System became the first Reggae group to sing in a local dialect. In Naples, artists such as Marcello Coleman were singing Raggamuffin style in Neapolitan. Southern roots now stretched rhizomatically out of Italy, across the Mediterranean into Africa and along the routes traced all around the Black Atlantic. This, in turn, becomes a counter-cultural narrative against current European immigration policies and the neo-liberal global order.

New aesthetics required new spaces, producing another heterotopic situation. A multitude of diverse singularities (white middle-class and left-wingers, creole kids and illegal immigrants, white Rastas, and non-politicised youth) gathered at massive beach parties to listen to Reggae, Dancehall, and Raggamuffin. These beach parties were not organised by squats such as Officina 99. They were now commercial events. You bought a ticket to hear the music and have fun. It was also a place where it was possible to meet African youth and where an emerging creole generation could proudly display the colour of their skin. To be dark became an advantage, not because of paternalistic political slogans defending African immigrants, but because it is cool to be African, and even cooler to be a black Neapolitan. Once again, something has changed in town; a new ontology is under construction. The Neapolitan public sphere is passing into a further phase of creolisation. The Afro sound has left the squats to be played in the clubs and on the beach. Mario Balotelli, the black Italian soccer player born in Palermo, is listening to R'n'B. 'Black music' is no longer exclusively the sound of the anti-globalisation movement. Reggae, Raggamuffin, Reggaeton, and R'n'B are now part of a new cultural formation and soundscape.

Clubbing culture nostalgia and creolisation

In this context, the spaces of club culture reveal themselves as heterotopias. According to Foucault, parallel to the spatial and institutional organisation of consensual understandings, heterotopic spaces provide a counter-space. They promote a time-out from institutional rhythms. If the prevailing social organisation of the public sphere is here sometimes deepened and confirmed, it is simultaneously also contested and subverted. In the continual crossings between authorised and heterotopic variations of cultural and social life that mix and confute simple distinctions between public and private, temporary communities emerge that are sustained by citizenship in sound. This possibility acquires further pertinence when it accommodates the recent ingression of music and cultures, of bodies and histories that have literally migrated from elsewhere to take up residence in the city's soundscape and its daily life. It marks a profound historical shift, exposing the cultural concerns of Naples to radically more extensive coordinates, as the local and the global are increasingly intertwined in each other's trajectories. Here, music promotes an emergent and differentiated commons.

It is the end of the 1990s and the beginning of a new century; the cyberculture revolution has accomplished its mission. There is no longer the need to preach about the power of the internet anymore. The internet is a mass media, and no longer a frontier. Youth is now discussing its political beliefs online, flash mobs are becoming the paradigm of the new protests, dating and sex have expanded into hybrid relationships that involve the use of social networks and online porn communities, DJs have begun to create their own pages to advertise their production and communicate with their fans, and suddenly the star system is back again. The network itself, the club, is no longer the main protagonist, it has become merely the infrastructure for the building of a new industry. Facebook, Instagram, and Reddit have taken the place of the 1996 'Declaration of the Independence of Cyberspace'.[12]

Such shifts have been interpreted as a form of decadence by a disenchanted generation. This includes part of the Neapolitan electronic club scene, mainly populated by white Neapolitans. They feel that Naples is losing something in this moment, while for the Creole and black Neapolitans, no obvious need to connect musically with the Neapolitan past emerges: their roots are elsewhere, their contemporary symbolical and cultural routes are different. While a part of the city buys into the general feeling of the decline of the West and considers the present and the future to be darker than the past, another part, peopled by migrants and black people, is developing a different scenario. For this latter group, the present and the future become critical horizons in the Neapolitan public sphere where there is no need to embrace a local Napoletanità and its melancholy aesthetics of 'full decadence'.

Between these two poles there is also another discourse, developed mostly by white middle-class Neapolitans, and in general southern Italians, who feel closer to African, African American, and Caribbean music, the so-called 'black music', and its cultures. They seek to connect contemporary 'black music' to their local music past and believe that southern Italy has played a major role in developing such forms of cultural appropriation due to its historical and cultural proximity to Africa. However, they also believe that such processes are part of a global trend and that many other European cities are also developing their own styles and scenes in a similar manner. Their vision is far closer to the politics of creolisation, altogether more focused on the present and the future and less on the centrality of Neapolitan tradition as providing the premises of musical identification and belonging.

—

These differences also emerged in a series of interviews we undertook in order to understand the meaning of local Napoletanità when connected to different music scenes. One of these is related to the so-called electronic scene that includes House and Techno, and the other to 'black music' including Reggae, Drum'n'Bass, Hip-Hop, R'n'B, and Reggaeton. The idea here was to understand how different Neapolitans use diverse musical genres and how club scenes create distinct spaces and heterotopias. We interviewed people who are all in their thirties to compare their

[12] Cf. John Perry Barlow, *A Declaration Of The Independence Of Cyberspace*. Electronic Frontier Foundation, 1996, <https://www.eff.org/de/cyberspace-independence> accessed 1 July 2014.

perspective on a shared time frame that runs from the end of the last century until the present.

According to Diana,[13] a Neapolitan party organiser since the 1990s, Neapolitans have been the precursors of House and Techno music, first with the famous party organisers Angels of Love, then with DJs such as Marco Carola, Gaetano Parisio, Rino Cerrone, Markantonio, Davide Squillace, and Danilo Vigorito. Diana suggests that at the time there was no need for special guests to come from abroad because these DJs were all internationally recognised. During this period the scene was extremely vibrant, while today Diana thinks that her club followers are considered outsiders. Diana belongs to a scene that emerged after the Post-Punk encounter with House when Techno was becoming increasingly white and European and losing its connotations of creolisation.

According to Diana, despite the lack of infrastructure and the absence of institutional support, Naples remains among the most significant House, Techno, and Electro scenes in the world – '*arrivare a Napoli voleva dire e vuol dire ancora oggi aver raggiunto un traguardo*' – [to be invited to play in Naples was and remains a goal]. Diana also suggests that the House and Techno scenes are now merging and becoming more commercial; not necessarily a bad thing in her opinion. She continues to believe that Naples still plays a major role in the club scene: '*sanno che arrivare qui significa avere una vetrina importante*' – [they know that this is an important place to be showcased]. Diana also told us that when she was partying during the golden period at the end of the 1990s the audiences were 'incredible': everybody knew the tracks that the DJs were playing even before the internet revolution; everyone was savvy about the technical equipment. The people who attended these parties were experts in the music genres they listened to. She concluded by saying in English that this was 'real club culture'.

Augusto, another famous promoter of the electronic music scene in Naples, makes a similar argument.[14] In his opinion, Naples played a key role in the Italian and European club scene. Augusto talked of the glorious past of the House music scene that brought to Naples, prior to any other Italian city, artists such as the US DJs Frankie Knuckles, David Morales, or Louie Vega. He also stressed that international artists at the end of the 1980s and the beginning of the following decade sought to play in Naples, and cited the Techno scene at the beginning of the 1990s when famous artists such as Jeff Mills, Richie Hawtin, or Darren Emerson were in town.

However, Augusto also thought that the avant-garde scene began to decline at the end of the 1990s when Barcelona, London, and Berlin took over. It is interesting that Augusto compares the club scene of Naples with other club scenes such as London and Berlin. Naples is not a capital and of course, does not have the same economic or political role in Europe as these other cities. Through making such comparisons, he elevates Naples to their level through the powers ascribed to the music made available by the club scene.

Mattia is a Neapolitan creole.[15] His mother is from Cabo Verde, and his father is from Naples. He told us that Cape Verdeans are totally integrated into Neapolitan society, however in terms of music and social gathering

[13] Diana, in an interview with the authors (November 2014).

[14] Augusto, in an interview with the authors (November 2014).

[15] Mattia, in an interview with the authors (November 2014).

they have very different habits. When they go out they choose the 'black music' scene, very few of them are into the House, Techno, or Electro scene, most of them like to go to the Arenile, a beach club in the ex-industrial part of the city where they play mostly R'n'B, Drum'n'Bass, and Reggaeton or the Kinky Bar, a place in old historical centre where they play Reggae.

According to Mattia, the fact that Naples is considered an important place for House, Techno, and other electronic music does not interest the Creole population. They do not share the same heterotopia: they are not interested in connecting Naples to the glories of a previous local club scene. They are altogether more focused on the present scene that is quite active but very fragmented. Talking of his personal experiences, Mattia looks to possible future scenarios rather than the past. He is aware of the cultural and musical past of Naples but thinks that in the future the 'black' scene will add even more energy to the city, especially with the beach parties that are taking over the Arenile beach club. Finally, he told us that Naples does not have such a strong identity as Salento (an area in Puglia in southern Italy) because, in Naples, you can listen to a bit of everything in 'black music', while Salento has become exclusively famous for its Reggae music scene.

Stefano is a Neapolitan who moved to Salento about eight years ago.[16] In Naples, he was into the Reggae music scene when the Kinky Bar was at its very peak of popularity at the end of the 1990s. During this period 'black music' in Naples, especially Reggae, attracted much of its audience from those who did not identify with the House or Techno scene. During this transitional period, the so-called 'black music' world was not a totally separate scene. Often the same people were listening to Rock and other types of music while they were also into Reggae. This was when Stefano, originally from a middle-class neighbourhood in Naples, began to identify with the Rastafarian movement. When the 'black' musical scene in the city began to evolve into something else he decided to move to Salento.

In Stefano's opinion, the Neapolitan musical past is profoundly connected to an African one. He spoke of traditional Trance music, practised in southern rural communities and investigated by the famous anthropologist Ernesto De Martino, such as the Tammurriata and the Tarantella. He made the connection between these phenomena and the popularity of the contemporary 'black music' scene in southern Italy. He believes that this is the reason why both Naples and Lecce (the capital of Salento) have played a major role in the development of the Italian 'black music' scene. However, he thinks that they are no longer central, as 'black music' is now highly popular all over Italy. He cited the case of Sir Oliver Skardy, a Venetian artist who plays and sings Reggae in a local Venetian dialect.

Charting the configurations of these heterotopic moments it becomes possible to understand how existing cultural (and political) meanings have been consistently challenged by the irruption of new sounds: from Diamond Dogs to Tien'a Ment and Officina 99 arriving at the Kinky Bar and the beach parties. In all of these places previous ontologies were challenged, and new categories emerged without fully cancelling or

[16] Stefano, in an interview with the authors (November 2014).

destroying what previously existed. In this fashion, a new complexity began to characterise the city's fragmented public sphere.

Today, a nostalgic vision of the city is like a white flag waving an unconditional surrender to a historicist perspective rooted in the memory of the 1990s. Locked in the past, it is unable to create a dialogue with the present, it is destined for melancholy. Elsewhere, collective memories routed through Euro-Mediterranean cultures have emerged to interrupt (and interrogate) Eurocentric nostalgia and to project futures on another cartography. Meanwhile, those of African and non-European descent, their children and offspring, are in Europe to stay. Now this is also their place. This is where they were born. They are neither simply African nor European. Their existence radically questions existing understandings of citizenship, the public sphere, and national culture and identity.

Moving from here and learning from the south

From the 1980s up to the present, there is a common thread that unites the different heterotopias produced by white Neapolitan artists, clubbers, and event organisers. This is a shared 'Neapolitan-centric' counter-narrative that is not necessarily shared by other ethnic groups who are now contributing to the fragmentary disassembling and reassembling of the musical and cultural landscapes of new heterotopias. The latter are adding novel layers of planetary impulses and interpretations to the city.

If we have heterotopias and counter-discourses that seek to re-centre the city in an inherited historical and cultural tradition, we also have other heterotopic practices that take the city on a journey towards altogether wider coordinates. In the latter case, the musical journeys are simultaneously de-provincializing and relocating narratives of the city in a planetary cartography. Here both the home-grown and seemingly 'foreign' are constantly being negotiated and reworked. While the counter-narratives of Neapolitan-centrism continuously re-produced themselves in different historical moments and music styles, we are now involved in a new scenario. The musical and cultural citizens of non-European descent, and even parts of the white middle-class are attentive to 'black' sounds and are fragmenting and reworking such heterotopias into new public and private spaces. This phenomenon can be linked to the rise of new modalities of subjectification and identifications, ranging from Napoletanità to Italianità [Italian-ness], and their continual reconfiguration in the contemporary historical scenario.

This is to argue that the music does not represent an isolated object of study or attention but is rather the instigator of processes that involve the production of cultural and historical identifications. Such processes involve multiple dynamics and powers in which narratives are produced and disseminated to affirm specific discourses and counter-discourses. In this sense, the cultural appropriation that is occurring today is both deeper and more extensive than previously. We are assisting in the rise of a so-called multicultural society in which the historical past is no longer located in a unique historical temporality or cultural location. If Europe is in Africa, Africa is also in Europe. The south of the planet is not simply 'down there'; it is significantly also in here, in a colonial past and post-colonial present, in the everyday life of citizens, rather than in the abstract procedures of institutions. Europe is consistently being remade and reworked along networks that connect diverse cities, cultures, and continents that come together in sounds and club cultures.

Blue veins running through an urban body and these could be the tracks laid down by the Neapolitan Dub band Almamegretta and its singer Raiz, just as they had been traced earlier in the extended saxophone soul of James Senese and Napoli Centrale. Today this inheritance – simultaneously local and planetary – reverberates in the hybridising sounds and sentiments that spiral across the beach in the ex-industrial area of the Arenile. Visceral intensities have been folded into the dark recesses of the bass-bearing doubling, dubbing, deepening, and dissemination of subaltern sounds. Born in the Caribbean and on Atlantic shores, subordinate sensibilities have led to unplanned sonorial routes subsequently folded into the concentrated 'dread' of the city under the volcano.

Between the black Atlantic and the blue sonorities of the Mediterranean it becomes possible to chart an ecology of rhythms, beats, and tonalities that produced sonic cartographies where, as Kodwo Eshun and Steve Goodman put it, 'sound comes to the rescue of thought'.[16] Drawn from a dissonant archive, a musical inheritance emerges in which traditions of Arab music making and African American Blues criss-cross, explore, and deepen the spaces between the official measures of modernity. Today, Africa returns to the diaspora. A repertoire drawn from the margins and the marginalised – from the subaltern south and urban underclass – bends, repeats, and replays the notes of modernity. It gives form to unsuspected sounds and sentiments that cross and creolise the landscape: in the Caribbean, in the Mediterranean … in the contemporary world. These musical cartographies provoke forms of interference that render hidden histories and negated genealogies audible, sounding them out and rendering them sensible. Not only do such sounds come to matter, they also propose and extend critical matters. They become a narrative force that draws us towards what survives and lives on as a cultural and historical resource able to resist, disturb, interrogate, and fracture the presumed 'unity' of the present.[17]

To think of the Neapolitan music scene in its extended Mediterranean tonalities in terms of the sonorial suspension and the unsuspected deepening and dispersal of the empirical present is to embrace what Gilles Deleuze and Félix Guattari would have called a 'minor' history.[18] Here sonorial cartographies provoke an interruption, or slash, in the existing, official map. Returning us to what has been overlooked, negated, and denied, such indicators permit another story and an unsuspected landscape to emerge. If established powers refuse to listen, as they inevitably do, then these sounds trace another, largely unrecognised and undisciplined, projection that shadows and potentially interrupts the seamless surface of public and consensual understanding.

The effects of such sounds push the premises of historical and sociological analysis beyond their explanatory frames. What fails to be represented in such disciplinary terms nevertheless exists and persists as an interrogation, a potential interruption. Here, considering the Mediterranean as 'an infinity of traces without … an inventory'[19] and Naples as one of its reverberatory chambers, sonic histories propose a persistent 'noise' that disrupts the institutional silence of the historical register. Such sounds become a source of critical disturbance and the musical archive

17
Steve Goodman, *Sonic Warfare. Sound, Affect and the Ecology of Fear* (Cambridge: MIT Press, 2010), 82.
18
Cf. Georges Didi-Huberman, *Devant Le Temps. Histoire De l'Art Et Anachronisme Des Images* (Paris: Minuit, 2000).
19
Gilles Deleuze and Félix Guattari, *Kafka. Towards a Minor Literature* (Minneapolis: University of Minnesota Press, 1986).
20
Antonio Gramsci, *Selections From The Prison Notebooks* (London: Lawrence & Wisehart, 1971), 324.

they sustain 'a question of the future itself, the question of a response, of a promise, and of responsibility, for tomorrow'.[20] Like the sea, that once facilitated their passage, sonic processes resist representation and propose an affective economy, 'stripped of consolation and security'.[21] Opposed to the stasis secured in officialdom and its version of the public sphere, such sounds are destined to disturb existing configurations of time, space, and belonging in sounding out communities to join.

So, while white Neapolitan are listening to House, Techno, and Electro, contemplating the local past and are occupied with trying to halt what they perceive as a contemporary decadence, elsewhere creolised cultures are proposing new horizons. The latter is altogether less concerned with recovering the city and rather more in re-directing it towards other non-European spaces directly connected to their lives. These processes have significant political implications on the city's public sphere. Counter-discourses embedded in these creolised cultures and lives have the potential to delegitimize the existing shaping of space and power, unbundling their temporalities and narratives. If not always able to withdraw from being captured from the places the city allots them, they are nevertheless able to create liminal spaces in which hegemonic arrangements are consistently contested, confuted, and alternatives proposed.

It is precisely here, we would argue, that the musical formation of the public sphere, largely hidden and unobserved by the formal mechanisms of the politics, sustains the heterotopic promise and potential of redrawing the sense imposed by a control culture. Sounding out the edges of everyday life, temporarily transforming the ordinary into the extraordinary, the musical reconfiguration of urban space leaves a trace, disseminates an interrogation, and seeds a discontinuity with the predictable. Ultimately, it is the postcolonial register of these sonorities, as we have seen in the distinct dislocation of local Neapolitan heterotopias from exclusively autochthonous coordinates to creolised planetary horizons that usher in a new critical cultural cut with the promise of a world yet to come.

[21] Jacques Derrida, *Archive Fever. A Freudian Impression* (Chicago: University of Chicago Press, 1998), 36.
[22] Kodwo Eshun, 'Drawing the Forms of Things Unknown', in Kodwo Eshun and Anjalika Sagar (eds.), *The Ghosts of Songs. The Film Art of the Black Audio Film Collective* (Liverpool: Liverpool University Press, 2007), 78.

Bibliography

Bey, Hakim, *T.A.Z. The Temporary Autonomous Zone, Ontological Anarchy, Poetic Terrorism* (New York: Autonomedia, 1991).

Barlow, John Perry, *A Declaration Of The Independence Of Cyberspace*. Electronic Frontier Foundation, 1996, <https://www.eff.org/de/cyberspace-independence> accessed 1 July 2014.

Chambers, Iain, *Mediterraneo Blues. Musiche, Malinconia Postcoloniali, Pensieri Marittimi* (Turin: Bollati Boringhieri, 2012).

Deleuze, Gilles and Félix Guattari, *Kafka. Towards a Minor Literature* (Minneapolis: University of Minnesota Press, 1986).

Derrida, Jacques, *Archive Fever. A Freudian Impression* (Chicago: University of Chicago Press, 1998).

Derrida, Jacques, *Of Hospitality* (Stanford: Stanford University Press, 2000).

Didi-Huberman, Georges, *Devant Le Temps. Histoire De l'Art Et Anachronisme Des Images* (Paris: Minuit, 2000).

Foucault, Michel, 'Of Other Spaces: Utopias and Heterotopias', trans. Jay Miskowiec, *Diacritics*, 16, no. 1 (Spring 1986), 22–27. First published in *Architecture/Mouvement/Continuité*, no. 5 (October 1984), 46–49.

Foucault, Michel, *The Order of Things* (London & New York: Routledge, 2002).

Eshun, Kodwo, 'Drawing the Forms of Things Unknown', in Kodwo Eshun and Anjalika Sagar (eds.), *The Ghosts of Songs. The Film Art of the Black Audio Film Collective* (Liverpool: Liverpool University Press, 2007).

Goodman, Steve, *Sonic Warfare. Sound, Affect and the Ecology of Fear* (Cambridge: MIT Press, 2010).

Gramsci, Antonio, *Selections from the Prison Notebooks* (London: Lawrence & Wisehart, 1971).

Lefebvre, Henri, *The Production of Space* (Oxford: Wiley-Blackwell, 1991).

NAPOLI

A Napoli impazzano le **Ivan & Susan Promotion**, che ci regalano le serate dell'**HIPE** regolarmente tutti i sabati, nella nuova sede della via Nazionale Appia 24 di Caserta. Djs fissi sono **Danilo JJ Bros** e la new entry **Emiliano**. L'idea è quella di aprire una vetrina sul mondo, con addirittura videoart di **Luisa Ferrari** e altri. Moda e spettacolo. **Ralf** (ancora lui?! - n.d.r.) è l'ospite fisso una volta al mese, con **Flavio** e **Ricky** dell'**ECHOES** in alternanza. Di tanto in tanto non mancano i guests stranieri, quali **Jonathan Moore** e **Robert Owens**.

★ Milo Gualano

Naples' clubbing scene on *InTown Magazine*, Naples, 1993

First issue of *Orbeat Magazine*, Naples, 1999

Flyer for Richie Hawtin DJ set at CUBE, Naples, 1996

DJ Carola Pisaturo, 2016, photo: Erica Cevro-Vukovic

DJ Marco Carola on the decks, Naples, 1995, photo: Alessandro David

Protest against the forced eviction of the Tien'a Ment squat, Naples, 1996, photos: Danilo Capasso

BERLIN

MUSIC/SPACES
Dancing in the Niches

How the City's Free Spaces Nurtured Avant-Garde Music

Florian Sievers

P.289 ▶

SPACES/POLITICS
Do it Yourself

Looking for Freedom in Constant Collapse

Tobias Rapp

P.311 ▶

Mufti (FM Einheit) and Blixa Bargeld (Einstürzende Neubauten), Berlin, 1984, photo: Eva Maria Ocherbauer

Showcase Dancer at E-Werk, Berlin, 1995, photo: Tilman Brembs

Ratten-Jenny at Blockschock, Berlin, 1987, photo: Jürgen Gässler

Dancing in the Niches – How the City's Free Spaces Nurtured Avant-Garde Music

Florian Sievers

The opening was small. A dark hole, maybe half a meter wide, hidden behind thick bushes. To get in you had to squeeze your way between concrete walls and then duck down, because in the next room it wasn't possible for a full-grown adult to stand up straight. They cowered into a narrow chamber where the rumbling waxed and waned but never ceased – the sound of cars and trucks passing overhead. Since his childhood, Christian Emmerich knew of this secret; the oddly shaped cavern in the pillar of a highway bridge in the city of Berlin. He grew up nearby in the district of Schöneberg, and sometimes hid out here as a boy.

Years later, on 1 June 1980, he scrambled into this niche together with Andrew Chudy. Both were twenty-one years old. Emmerich now called himself Blixa Bargeld [*Bargeld* means 'cash'] and Chudy had christened himself Andrew Unruh [*Unruh* means 'unrest']. Together at this point, they made up the industrial band Einstürzende Neubauten. The two had come to this claustrophobia-inducing cavern with cars rushing unceasingly overhead to record some of their first music – with instruments that included a few metal parts from an old washing machine, tin cups, rusty lids, and iron rods. Plus, a battery-operated radio amplifier and some flashlights so they could see. Bargeld and Unruh lit a candle to find out if there was enough oxygen in the cavern. Then they set to work, pounding on their instruments and screaming out lyrics such as: 'Tanze, tanze, für euren Untergang, meine Energie wird es sein!' [Dance, dance, for your extinction, the energy will be mine!] They recorded the material with a tape recorder and later released it as one of the first demo cassettes of the band called Einstürzende Neubauten.[1]

Places like this early recording studio, where Einstürzende Neubauten hammered on metal parts, were to be found everywhere in Berlin. Indeed, these hideouts, shelters, and protected zones where the most absurd, crazy, self-made music could find a home still exist today. In the course of Second World War and the final battle for Berlin that lasted until April 1945 every second house in the German capital was levelled. In the decades that followed, Berlin was only partially reconstructed. Ruins were left behind and it stayed that way – blank spaces in the urban fabric that could be filled with something new. 'Looking at those ruins makes people think "What if we…?" or "We should try…" – sensations that would never be inspired by the rest of West Germany pedestrian friendly zones,' wrote the journalist Klaus Hartung back then; 'The utopia of ruins is much more than an aesthetic.'[2]

After the erection of the Berlin Wall in 1961 – which not only separated East from West Germany but ran straight through the city of Berlin – until its destruction in 1989, anyone in West Germany who felt out of place amid the country's sudden economic prosperity came to West Berlin: artists, slackers, or young men trying to avoid their military service.[3] The western side of the city formed an island that was entirely surrounded by East German territory. Still partly destroyed by the war and now surrounded by electric fences, watchtowers, and barbed wire, West Berlin was inhabited by a multitude of outsiders – people fleeing from the restrictions of West German society. 'The people in the West [of Berlin] grew into a real, to put it ironically, village community, with no hinterlands and no outside influences. The young population was an unusual mix that you couldn't find anywhere else in the world,' recalls Alexander Hacke from Einstürzende Neubauten.[4] Their energetic, for the most part nocturnal, excursions and experimentations were fuelled by the absence of a night curfew, which was abolished back in 1948 when the border between the Eastern and Western sides of the city was still open, and the two competed for guests and visitors. This (non-)regulation is still in effect.

Because the people were happy with the little that they had, not only did they sometimes built their own instruments (like the

---

1
Cf. Klaus Laufer, 'Eingeschlossene Bergleute machen sich zum Beispiel durch Klopfzeichen bemerkbar', in Wolfgang Müller (ed.), *Geniale Dilletanten* (Berlin: Merve, 1982), 23.
2
Cf. Théo Lessour, *Berlin Sampler* (Berlin: Ollendorff, 2012), 199.
3
Due to the city's special status within West Germany, residents were not required to perform mandatory military service.
4
Alexander Hacke in Max Dax and Robert Defcon, *Nur was nicht ist ist möglich – Die Geschichte der Einstürzenden Neubauten* (Berlin: Bosworth, 2006), 16.

Einstürzende Neubauten, who often stole their percussion instruments from construction sites) but also pieced together their lives and art. Life in Berlin, with all its niches, was cheaper than anywhere else and most people active in the different scenes lived on public welfare. Many took the opportunity to completely immerse themselves in musical experiments without any consideration for the possibility of commercial exploitation, record deals, or chart success. 'Within the narrow confines of this island it was possible to cross boundaries in ways that were totally unthinkable anywhere else.'[5] Self-made and self-empowered, Berlin became a city of niches and do-it-yourself culture – which it still is.

In this urban island's gaps and empty spaces – some of which were short-lived and some of which became institutions – a lot of music was created, especially electronic music,[6] which was often also club music. As early as the 1930s, avant-garde composer Oskar Sala co-developed the Trautonium, one of the first electronic musical instruments. By the 1970s, Berlin was already considered 'the home of people who cut up cassette tapes, played music backwards, hooked up sound systems in strange configurations, and tried to rile their audiences up in any conceivable manner'.[7] Many different subcultures were able to develop without getting in each other's way, and at the same time also without influencing, inspiring, or helping each other out when needed.

—

All this must be qualified by two observations. First, of course in Berlin – as in virtually every big city – there is not and never was just one type of music that people danced to in clubs or listened to when they wanted to escape the world. The so-called 'guest workers' who were lured to West Germany from countries like Italy or Turkey to fuel the economy starting in the early 1960s, certainly brought their own (dance) music with them. This music, however, was almost never heard in the city's major clubs or dominant subcultures – until, that is, the 1990s when the second or third generations began to record Turkish or Arabic Hip-Hop and make it onto the charts. Even before this, the empirical reality was different from the impression that this text might otherwise create. In the 1960s and 1970s, most residents of Berlin preferred to dance to so-called *Schlager* (a kind of antiquated German-language pop with often highly clichéd lyrics) or to Blues Rock, Jazz, and Beat. Only a minority opened themselves to the new worlds and states of consciousness of so-called *Krautrock* and Cosmic music. And in the 1980s Heavy Metal and those catchy modern German-language pop groups marketed as 'Neue Deutsche Welle' [New German Wave] were far more successful and popular among the general population than the experimental noise made by formations such as Einstürzende Neubauten, which only appealed to a small subculture in the divided city.

The most remarkable music of the postwar period to come out of Berlin and the music that, in retrospect, has had the most enduring influence was almost always produced electronically – with synthesizers and rhythm machines, later with drum computers and software. This text will examine these forms of music created in the context of minor sub-subcultures. It wasn't until the 1990s, when House and Techno enjoyed great popularity for an entire decade, that (avant-garde) electronic music and the popular taste of the masses crossed paths. Now electronic music, generally referred to as either 'House' or 'Techno', shapes Berlin's image more than any other musical form. These genres' roots, however, stretch far back into the city's history, with the most important figures emerging time and time again.

The second observation is that virtually all the important figures discussed here came from the western side of the long-divided city. In fact, virtually the entire story of Berlin's electronic (club) music scene unfolded in the West, as for many years East Berlin stagnated almost completely under the socialist regime, at least in terms of relevant subcultural musical experiments. The main reason for this was the eleventh assembly of the Central Commission of the East German government in December 1965. In the course of a debate later dubbed the 'Kahlschlag Discussion' [*Kahlschlag* means 'clear cutting'], politicians claimed that Western pop culture was a vehicle of vices such as 'nihilism' and 'pornography' and officially declared it the culture of the

5
Wolfgang Müller, *Subkultur Westberlin 1979–1989* (Hamburg: Philo Fine Arts, 2013), 44.

6
This expression refers to the original method of producing music with synthesizers and drum computers, which differed greatly from the conventional production of music in band formations. Later, when virtually every form of music production was more or less 'electronic', it referred to those genres that placed conscious emphasis on the electronic production methods as an aesthetic element.

7
Julian Cope, *Krautrocksampler* (London: Head Heritage, 1995), 34.

imperialistic enemy. State financial support for such music was put to an end, musicians were forbidden from performing, and bands stopped making music. While there was somewhat more acceptance from the government of Rock music at the start of 1969, it was still very carefully monitored. And monitoring by government authorities doesn't exactly foster experimentation and excess. As a result, in terms of avant-garde music, East Berlin limped far behind West Berlin – with the single exception of the intrepid East German Free Jazz scene.[8]

It is true that in the early 1980s Punk and Hip-Hop also emerged in East Berlin, and in 1984 the first unofficial East German breakdance championship was held.[9] But these scenes were extremely small and musically quite basic, as they mostly copied Western models.[10] On 31 January 1980, the band Tangerine Dream performed at the Palace of the Republic – the first time a West German band played in East Germany. The band inspired a small scene of imitative synthesizer groups and such musicians as Pond, Key, or Hans-Hasso Stamer, who up until the collapse of East Germany released a few Synthpop albums on the state label Amiga.[11] This music was accepted by the government because it was primarily instrumental and thus free of ideology.

For a few years Tangerine Dream, being allowed to play in East Berlin by the government, was one of the most important representatives of electronic music in Berlin. But it wasn't until the late 1980s, shortly before the state's collapse, that the cultural policies of East Germany would relax somewhat once again. At that time, a few Post-Punk and experimental Rock groups with some electronic elements appeared in East Germany (officially they were referred to as 'other bands'), including Feeling B and Ornament & Verbrechen [*Verbrechen* meaning crime] from Berlin.

1960–1979: All back to zero

The East German government's leadership wasn't entirely wrong when they discerned 'nihilism' (that is, a rejection of the established societal order) in aspects of Western culture in the late 1960s and early 1970s. At that time many young West Germans realised that so-called de-Nazification – the removal of Nazi functionaries from politics, culture, the business world, and administration – hadn't been particularly successful. In many places the same people held the same positions of power as they did under the Nazi regime – and these people were often the youth's own parents and grandparents. For this reason, a part of the younger population rejected the West German value system completely. Many revolted against earlier generations, became involved in leftist and radical leftist groups, and experimented with new forms of communal living. They longed for a new beginning, free of the gruesome past. And this found expression in their music.

Many German musicians were looking for alternatives to capitalist mainstream music, as embodied by Blues and Rock from the US. They came to create, for the most part without entirely being aware of it, the first genuinely German forms of pop music: 'a music that grew out of the cultural "nothingness" that young Germans felt in light of Germany's role in World War II.'[12] Due to Germany's connection to the West and the US, British, and French soldiers stationed in the country, musicians wavered between an emotional link to such genres as Jazz or Beat, and radical rejection of this music because they opposed the ongoing war in Vietnam or capitalism in general. Some wanted to destroy all the old rules and structures, do away with old traditions and conventions. Whether it be the division of songs into verse and refrain, the idea that in every band a percussionist must play the same standard Jazz drum kit – or the obligatory hierarchy of singer, guitarist, bassist, drummer, each fulfilling a specific role.

Instead, some German musicians began to use all their instruments without any clear distinctions to create rhythm. They experimented with raw, basic anti-musical ideas. Fascinated by the powerful, expressive potential of sound, people without any training began playing instruments – as would be the case a decade later with Punk. Some began using the compact synthesizers that suddenly appeared on the market relatively inexpensively, not as extra ornaments for the fixed structures of Rock music, as was the case in the 1960s, but in order to invent adequate new forms. Not everyone in this scene was a non-musician. Some came upon experimental approaches by way of their conventional musical training, studying for

8
Cf. Lessour, *Berlin Sampler* (see n. 2), 159–161.
9
Cf. Felix Denk and Sven von Thülen, *Der Klang der Familie – Berlin, Techno und die Wende* (Berlin: Suhrkamp, 2012), 26.
10
Cf. Bert Papenfuss et al., 'Remember Prenzlauer Berg', in Wolfgang Farkas, Stefanie Seidl, and Heiko Zwirner (eds.), *Nachtleben Berlin. 1974 bis heute* (Berlin: Metrolit, 2013), 87.
11
Cf. the compilation edited by the author of this text, *Mandarinenträume – Electronic Escapes from the Deutsche Demokratische Republik 1981–1989* (Munich: Permanent Vacation, 2010). The liner notes include an account of how, with their synthesizer compositions these musicians dreamed their way from the narrow confines of East Germany into outer space.
12
Stuart Baker and Adrian Self, liner notes to the compilation *Deutsche Elektronische Musik* (London: SoulJazz, 2010), 4.

example under the composer Karlheinz Stockhausen or attending the workshops for improvised electronic music held by the contemporary composer Thomas Kessler in Berlin.[13] The result was that in the late 1960s and early 1970s an avant-garde, non-Blues-based, structurally open form of Psychedelic Rock emerged in Germany. This form was called by the British press, at first disparagingly, 'Krautrock', a term derived from the pejorative term used for Germans in Second World War: 'Kraut'. Some people involved in the scene embraced this label, others spoke of 'Cosmic music', as, above all, they desired to project themselves into outer space with their synthesizers. Moreover, the general term 'Psychedelic Rock' was used when drug-induced psychedelic elements were added to more traditional Rock forms.

These experiments flourished above all in illegally occupied houses and alternative art and living projects in Berlin, where many artists and outsiders came to escape the consumption craze and pressure to perform of the booming post-war economy. Ton Steine Scherben may have provided the soundtrack of the occupied house scene, but the more stylistically conservative brand of Rock, that this band began to play in 1970, is not aesthetically relevant for the developments described here. Those involved in illegal house occupations didn't just listen to such conventional Rock. In 1969, for instance, a band that called itself Agitation, later Agitation Free, played at the model alternative project Kommune 1. The jam band-like formation produced a free-spirited, flowing ethnic Space Rock. Among its members was the musician Christopher Franke, who named contemporary composers such as György Ligeti and Karlheinz Stockhausen as his influences, and who would soon leave the band to join the considerably more successful synthesizer pioneers, Tangerine Dream.

From a contemporary perspective, the most musically interesting apparition from this early closely interknit Berlin scene is Conrad Schnitzler, who was born in 1937. He had studied under Joseph Beuys and internalised this artist's famous doctrine 'everyone is an artist'. In Berlin's free cultural spaces, he saw his chance to finally convert the phrase into musical practice. Not only was Schnitzler the founder of the underground club Zodiak Free Arts Lab (thus creating a breeding ground for the entire Berlin Krautrock and Cosmic music scene), but also, at a very early stage, he began to play improvised synthesizer concerts. Among the instruments he used was a self-built 'cassette organ', which could play a kind of proto samples on eight different cassette players. Schnitzler recorded sounds from Berlin to use as samples, integrating the city itself into his music. Beginning in the early 1970s he released hundreds of albums in limited editions on different labels. Released as an EP in 1980 by the major label RCA, the Synthpop piece 'Auf dem schwarzen Kanal' [On the Black Channel] was the most notable of these recordings. Monotone dissonances and Kraftwerk-like synthesizers flash and flicker over a stoically steadfast computer rhythm, while an electronically distorted voice recites Dadaist poetry. Over thirty years later the cold, alienated machine aesthetic of this three minute and thirteen-second piece still fascinates listeners.

Schnitzler was also involved, in a less prominent capacity, in several other influential projects. Together with the musicians Hans-Joachim Roedelius and Dieter Moebius he founded the Krautrock band Kluster, which after Schnitzler's prompt departure renamed itself Cluster. In Schnitzler's club Zodiak Free Arts Lab the hippie Jazz collective Eruption came together, which included three musicians—Klaus Schulze, Manuel Göttsching, and Edgar Froese—who would later all re-emerge in other contexts. In general, almost all the bands and music projects in this small, experimental scene in Berlin were interrelated, as in the cramped island city they were continually exchanging members, while churning out one record after the next.

With Schnitzler's involvement, Eruption would evolve into Tangerine Dream, the most well-known and successful of Berlin's first electronic music groups. Despite its title, *Electronic Meditation*, the band's first album from 1970 was made without synthesizers or drum machines and with an unorthodox line-up that included the former Blues rocker and Beat guitarist Edgar Froese on guitar and organ, Conrad Schnitzler on cello and violin, and former Eruption drummer Klaus Schulze on percussion. With stationary

13
Cf. Lessour, *Berlin Sampler* (see n. 2), 194.

organ chords, liberated yapping guitars, monotonously rumbling drums and Schnitzler's plaintive cello, *Electronic Meditation* now sounds as much like Jazz and contemporary Classical music as it does a form of Rock freed from all conventions.

Soon thereafter Tangerine Dream would, under Edgar Froese's guidance, place increasing emphasis on synthesizers – until ultimately hardly anything else was left but their ebbing and flowing waves, generating soundscapes of endless dimensions. It is as if Tangerine Dream had dreamed itself beyond the limits of the island city into outer space – or into different realms of reality entirely. The enormous equipment towers that the band set up for their performances were like the tools used to free themselves. In any case, state-of-the-art sound technology – Moog or Farfisa synthesizers, rhythm computers, quadrophonic sound systems – increasingly became the band's acoustic and optical focus.

This can also be both heard and seen on Klaus Schulze's solo debut album *Irrlicht*, which he released in 1972 on the Psychedelic Rock label Ohr [ear] after he left Tangerine Dream. An insert that came with the album contains a diagram entitled 'Quadrophonische Symphonie für Syn. Orchester + E-Maschinen' [Quadrophonic Symphony for Syn.Orchester + E-Machines] that illustrates the conscious and unconscious effects of structured and unstructured sounds. In the centre is a circle labelled 'New Music' (by which Schulze presumably meant his own) which influences 'Traditions' and 'New Functions'. This all funnels into a circuit diagram – apparently the focal point of Schulze's theoretical reflections. Photos from this time show, appropriately enough, the musician sitting on the floor wearing an astronaut-like helmet, completely surrounded by music machines, while a monstrous modular synthesizer looms behind him.

For all its rambling instrumental jams and endless sound surfaces, the music of Agitation Free, Tangerine Dream, Klaus Schulze, Cluster/Kluster and (for the most part) Conrad Schnitzler is rhythmically generally quite reserved – this is not dance music. Ultimately this group of Berlin-based musicians preferred to travel to alternative realities while sitting cross-legged than to stimulate the body to dance. Their effusive pieces extend for the full twenty minutes of one side of an album, so that the space journey is never interrupted, with no real climax, as unremitting as a trip to the furthest reaches of the inner self. This is also presumably why there are virtually no vocals on these recordings; the human element would only have irritated listeners.

This is one of several similarities between this and contemporary forms of electronic dance music like House and Techno, which for its part almost does nothing but appeal to the body: the free combination of sounds and sound textures; long, rhythmically repetitive and thus hypnotic pieces without the standard verse-refrain structure; electronic instruments – all elements of today's electronic club music in Berlin. The abandonment and rejection of conventional music patterns and self-empowerment through new technologies are also motifs of both scenes. One used machines to descend into inner realms, the other lost itself in the external world, the world of dance clubs.[14]

'This new Berlin idealism rejected the cheap Carnaby Street capitalism on which much of the American and British scenes thrived,' Welsh musician and author Julian Cope would exclaim enthusiastically a few decades later.[15] Krautrock and Cosmic music also attracted globally successful and aesthetically more conservative pop stars to Berlin from, of all places, the US and Great Britain. They hoped to find new inspiration here and booked the Hansa Studios for their recording sessions. 'Recorded at Hansa by the Wall' can be read on several releases from this period. This is where Lou Reed, for example, recorded his album *Berlin* in 1974, which celebrated the morbidity and gloomy niches of the half-ruined city. David Bowie recorded his Berlin trilogy (*Low*, *Heroes*, *Lodger*) here. Under the influence of producer Brian Eno, *Low* (1977) in particular, makes use of the rhythmic repetition and electronic elements of Krautrock. Eno had already worked together with Cluster and the Krautrock band Harmonia. Finally, Iggy Pop recorded *The Idiot* (1977) in Berlin, experimenting with Industrial music references and drum machines. In the song 'Nightclubbing', which Grace Jones would later cover, he sings about time spent with Bowie in Berlin: 'We walk like a ghost / We learn dances

14
This assessment of Krautrock differs from that of Tobias Rapp in his text on Berlin in this book. According to Rapp 'the musical influence on later dance music [was] minimal'.
15
Cope, *Krautrocksampler* (see n. 7), 36.

brand new dances / Like the nuclear bomb / When we're nightclubbing'.

1980–1989: They like decay

When on 12 December 1981 Manuel Göttsching returned to his home studio after a long tour with Klaus Schulze he was in the mood to make more music. In such cases he always made sure a synthesizer, rhythm computer, and tape machine were turned on – so he could get right to work when the inspiration struck him. The guitarist was once a member of Eruption, which emerged from the Zodiak Free Arts Lab circle. He then founded the band Ash Ra Tempel, which released its debut album of the same name in 1971. On this album Göttsching's guitar outbursts, sparkling synthesizer cascades and Klaus Schulze's drums yielded an overwhelming 'Prog Krautrock'. Now he was doing his own thing.

Which is why on that evening of 12 December 1981, Göttsching put on a solo concert just for himself. Besides his guitar, the only instruments he used were keyboards, a sequencer, and a drum computer. He played a single long uninterrupted piece, an almost classically improvised jam, though his only improvisation partners were machines. 'I luckily had the reflex to press the red "record" button on the tape machine,' he recalled twenty-five years later.[16] In 1984 he released what he found on that recording device on Klaus Schulze's label Inteam under the title *E2-E4*. He edited none of the material, merely dividing it onto the album's two sides. The title of the album refers to a classical chess opening, but he also cited the hexadecimal system that he had just learned while programming his Apple II computer and the robot R2-D2 from the *Star Wars* films as sources of inspiration.[17]

Whatever lurks behind the ambiguous title, the music is captivatingly beautiful: almost a full hour of guitars flowing and wavering in two chords, melancholic synthesizers and a pulsating computer drumbeat. Harmonic monotony. This curious piece of music initially garnered little attention, but it would soon unleash a wave of adulation that continues through to the present. In 1989 the Italian Disco producers Sueño Latino made a remix of it, and it served as inspiration for the many African American producers in Detroit who at that same time were in the process of creating Techno from African American Funk and European Synthpop. Even the legendary Detroit Techno artists Carl Craig and Derrick May sampled it in 1992. *E2-E4* is both a late echo of the Cosmic music of the 1970s and a premonition of the happiness-hormone-inducing Ambient Techno of the 1990s.

The old Krautrock hero Göttsching, who has devoted his entire music career to free-flowing space music, proved to be astonishingly attuned to the approaching 1980s. In the decade's early years, he programmed and produced the pulsating dance Rock of the female band Die Dominas as well as the dissonantly squeaky Electro-pop of the Berlin duo Geile Tiere. These bands were part of a new scene that would later be called 'Post-Punk' – at the time energetic and intensely avant-garde. To their members the Cosmic music and Krautrock excursions of Göttsching and his colleagues must have seemed like the stoned strumming of over-the-hill hippies. These new bands found entirely new niches in the city where they challenged conventions in new ways. Once again, as previously in Berlin's musical history, they wanted to do everything themselves, from building their own instruments to releasing their own albums. And they invented new forms of electronic music. Though they distanced themselves from the old Krautrockers, they used the same old synthesizers and rhythm computers, albeit with an entirely different intention. They were no longer interested in meditative self-reflection but wanted to charge their music with energy and a jagged machine drive.

Of course, in the late 1970s and early 1980s, a lot of classic three-chord Punk could be heard in Berlin. From an objective perspective, however, this style must be seen as a reversion to old Rock conventions: vocals-guitar-bass-drum, verse-bridge-refrain, Blues structures, and strutting around like a star. 'We saw Punk as really fast Rock'n'Roll, nothing special,' comments the musician Gudrun Gut, one of the most important figures of 1980s Berlin.[18]

At that time the city was getting more and more rundown. The first buildings built in the 1950s as part of the post-war reconstruction

16
Manuel Göttsching, liner notes to the album *E2-E4 – 25th Anniversary* (Berlin: MG Art, 2006).
17
Ibid.
18
Gudrun Gut in Dax and Defcon, *Nur was nicht ist ist möglich – Die Geschichte der Einstürzenden Neubauten* (see n. 4), 48.

were showing initial signs of decay. In many districts ruins from Second World War were still slowly crumbling, while other houses stood empty. For the avant-garde scene this was a blessing, as these houses offered the opportunity and space to experiment. As a reflection of and reaction to this environment, these experiments increasingly revolved around decay and destruction. Around noise as music. Around destructive discord. Another radical gesture to signal a new beginning: the old objects, meanings and musical styles were to be smashed in favour of new ones. Completely in keeping with what Walter Benjamin, himself born and raised in Berlin decades earlier, had written about creative destruction: 'The destructive nature only knows one motto: make space.'[19]

—

On 4 September 1981, a festival entitled 'Die große Untergangsshow – Festival Genialer Dilletanten' [The Great Perdition Show – Festival Ingenuous Dilletantes] was held in the Tempodrom concert hall in Berlin. Here the city's new scene came together for the first time: Post-Punk bands, Noise groups, Experimental Rock formations with names like Sprung aus den Wolken [Jump from the Clouds], DIN A Testbild [Standard Test Pattern], or Die Tödliche Doris [Deadly Doris]. And then there was Kriegsschauplatz Tempodrom [Battlefield Tempodrom], a band created especially for the event that featured a certain Maximilian Lenz (Frank Xerox), who would go on to become one of the most famous Techno DJs in all of Berlin under the name Westbam in the early 1990s. In the audience was his future collaborator Matthias Roeingh (Dr. Motte), as a beer can throwing Punk. In the 1990s he would organise the giant Berlin Techno parade: the so-called Loveparade.

Originally a typographic mistake, the misspelling of the festival's name 'Geniale Dilletanten' (the correct spelling is 'Dilettanten') was soon employed intentionally. These Berlin musicians used errors, incompetence, and negligence to dispose of conventions and find new forms – which in reality were to be non-forms, incapable of becoming standard cultural practices or rigid genres with recognisable traits. More important than any idea of progress was individuality. The main thing was to make music that had little or no precedent. The weapon of choice in this endeavour was ear-splitting discord. 'Ingenious Dilletantes want and need no control and certainly no mastery over their instrument,' wrote Wolfgang Müller, one of the festival's two organisers in the festival's manifesto.[20] He goes on (albeit somewhat convolutedly): 'The miss-playing, the misspelling is to be seen as a positive attribute, the opportunity to discover yet unknown forms of expression.'[21] Here Müller is explicitly referring to Beuys' well-known phrase: 'Everyone is an artist.'[22]

—

One of the bands that appeared at the Geniale Dilletanten festival had officially launched a year and a half earlier with a concert in the Berlin club Moon: Einstürzende Neubauten. A group of tried-and-true non-musicians with the kind of odd aliases fashionable at the time. Singer and frontman Blixa Bargeld spent, as he once said, the 1970s listening above all to Krautrock and bands like Can, Kraftwerk, and Neu!.[23] And like the Krautrockers and synthesizer musicians of their age, he wanted to stretch the concept of music to the breaking point. Neubauten recorded one of their first cassettes using cast away household objects in that small cavern inside a bridge support and built all their instruments by hand: pipes, T-bars, steel springs, chains, canisters, bathtubs, jackhammers, and welders. They collected these materials from Berlin's countless wastelands – at junkyards and in collapsing buildings. Or they simply stole them from construction sites. In this way Neubauten turned what other people had discarded or the city had left to decay into music.

Einstürzende Neubauten even used the city itself as a source of material, just as Conrad Schnitzler had once done, as they didn't just record music inside bridge columns, water towers, parking garages, and abandoned metro stations but also used real sounds from city life on their records, for example, the clattering of relay boxes and ticket machines or the cries of Berlin demonstrators. Their music was crowned by the expressive, artful, and passionate vocals

19
Walter Benjamin, 'Der destruktive Charakter', in *Gesammelte Schriften* (Frankfurt am Main: Suhrkamp, 1991), 396ff.
20
Wolfgang Müller, 'Die Instrumente stimmen', in Müller (ed.), *Geniale Dilletanten* (see n.1), 49.
21
Wolfgang Müller, 'Die wahren Dilletanten', in Müller (ed.), *Geniale Dilletanten* (see n.1), 10.
22
Ibid., 14.
23
Cf. Dax and Defcon, *Nur was nicht ist ist möglich* (see n.4), 33, 238.

of Blixa Bargeld, who in fragmented lyrics, that might have been fuelled by cocaine, sang in praise of sickness and destruction. In the song 'Steh auf Berlin' [Digging Berlin] from their first full-length album *Kollaps* (1981), Bargeld calls out: 'I like decay, I like sickness, I like downfall, I like the end.' In an interview, clearly influenced by the city crumbling around him, he prophesised: 'There is a war raging in the cities, and that's a good thing … It won't be long before everything collapses. Our odysseys are destroying the cities, nocturnal forays are levelling them to the ground. … For me this is the time when things collapse, the end, once and for all. Three, four more years, then it'll all be over.'[24] Strangely enough, at this time the Kongresshalle conference centre in Berlin caved in, as did an administration building and then a bus station. Soon thereafter the Deutschlandhalle, built in 1935 in the Westend district of Berlin, was closed due to the risk of collapse. Looking back now it seems as if the bone-jarring music of Einstürzende Neubauten and their glorification of destruction and decay brought a self-fulfilling prophecy upon the city.

When they recorded their beats using scrap metal parts, Einstürzende Neubauten often worked with loops – a basic technique of electronic dance music. However, they made sure that their recordings and concerts offered absolutely no party potential. 'Whenever a kind of danceable music developed from an improvisation at a Neubauten concert we immediately stopped playing,' recalls the band member FM Einheit.[25] But even if Einstürzende Neubauten themselves refused to see any relation between their music and Techno,[26] by consecrating rhythmic cacophony as music and by redrawing the border between what is noise and what can be music, they laid one of several conceptual foundations for what would later become Techno in Berlin.

In fact, the majority of the different types of music being made at that period in Berlin was equally not danceable in the sense of club music as we know it now. In the 1980s avant-garde, to some extent grooving Post-Punk was to be heard from bands like DIN A Testbild (whose debut album *Programm 1* was released in 1980 on Klaus Schulze's label Innovative Communication) or Malaria!, with jagged guitars, deep female voices, and strict rhythms that would with time develop into a kind of proto-Techno. But in the social segment of 1980s Berlin that believed it was fated to witness the inevitable downfall of itself and the city, dancing was generally looked down upon as a frivolous amusement.

Of course, in Berlin's New Wave and Post-Punk clubs, for example Linientreu or Dschungel, people nevertheless danced to the latest releases. Above all, there were a few select border-crossers who originally came from this scene but had been experimenting with danceable electronic music for quite some time. One of them was Maximilian Lenz, who, with his band Kriegsschauplatz Tempodrom, had already appeared at the Geniale Dilletanten Festival but in the mid-1980s had transitioned from Punk and Post-Punk to club music styles such as Disco, early Hip-Hop, and Hi-NRG, and who, in the course of this transition, christened himself 'DJ Westbam'. In 1985, Lenz (at the time just twenty-years-old) released the song '17 (This Is Not A Boris Becker Song)' as part of the project Cowboy Temple – a raw fragment of Belgian New-Beat Disco with a clattering, stomping computer rhythm upon which an enormous number of samples were unleashed.

This piece (as is the case with many of Westbam's more serious later productions) features the same sample aesthetic as the Hip-Hop of their time. But Westbam also points out that electronic dance music originally emerged from those (Post-)Punk releases, on which bands played electronic instruments as an avant-garde gesture.[27] In his opinion Techno/House, like certain forms of Punk, attacked conventions and virtually never made use of standard instruments – for which reason they are ideologically and aesthetically related. 'We got ourselves an 808 and the first House records and wanted to get down and dirty, like the Geniale Dilletanten. Because we felt that's where music belongs,' recalls Westbam.[28] In 1989, he wrote in the liner notes to his debut album *The Cabinet*: 'What Punk was for the 1970s, that's what DJ music is for the 1980s. The only difference is that Punk marked the end of an era, while DJ music, though a lot of traditionalists don't want to hear this, marks the start of a new one.'[29]

24
Klaus Maeck, *Hör mit Schmerzen* (Bonn: EME 1989), 32. Maeck cites an interview from *Spex* 9/1981.

25
FM Einheit in Dax and Defcon, *Nur was nicht ist ist möglich* (see n. 4), 81.

26
Cf. Dax and Defcon, *Nur was nicht ist ist möglich* (see n. 4), 191–193.

27
Cf. Westbam, 'Alle zusammen – und nach vorne', in Farkas, Seidl, and Zwirner (eds.), *Nachtleben Berlin* (see n. 10), 116.

28
Westbam in Denk and Thülen, *Der Klang der Familie* (see n. 9), 55. '808' refers to a drum computer of that name created by Japanese gear producer Roland.

29
Westbam, liner notes to the vinyl LP *The Cabinet* (Berlin: Low Spirit, 1989).

It was not only because of his optimistic attitude that Westbam was a solitary figure in the city at the time. Otherwise in the late 1980s in Berlin tedium, self-disgust, boredom, and lethargy spread out – the so-called 'Berlin disease'. Surrounded by the Wall, subsidized by and yet disconnected from the Bonn Republic, Berlin had become an island of decadence. The cool self-destruction and apocalyptic flair of the city's residents had become a hollow pose. 'There was no fire left,' recalls label owner and producer Mark Reeder, who came to Berlin in the early 1980s and founded the Trance-Techno label MfS in the early 1990s. 'The freshness and spontaneity were all gone.'[30]

Just as the Berlin syndrome was starting to get unbearable, a new noise crashed down on top of all the boredom: Acid. This hard, raw, hypnotic, usually entirely instrumental type of Techno and House, characterised by squealing modulated synthesizer lines originated from Chicago, where it had emerged in the mid-1980s. It first became big in London and didn't wash up on the shores of Berlin until the late 1980s. There the new sound, which was created above all from the improper use of the TB-303 bass synthesizer made by the Japanese company Roland, found enthusiastic audiences. Its endlessly morphing structures are reminiscent of Krautrock but place much greater emphasis on the body. At the same time Acid was also received in Berlin as jarring, avant-garde Noise music – very much suited to the stagnating city's more open-minded Post-Punks who, by now, were bored stiff. Things began to happen again: for many of those dying of tedium from the Berlin syndrome the official permission to dance to avant-garde music was a kind of salvation. Then the Berlin Wall came down.

1990–1999: From the basement all the way to the top

In the late 1980s it once again became necessary to keep your head low if you wanted to enter the niches where the most fascinating self-made music of the age was being heard. From a kitchen in a wing of a dilapidated historical building, people climbed through a small hole into a basement. Down there was a space for maybe one hundred people. You couldn't really jump, as the ceiling was only 1.90 meters high and dust came showering down. Having opened its doors in 1988, it was at the Ufo club that Acid really took off, just before the fall of the Berlin Wall.

The greatest multi-talent in the history of Berlin's electronic music scene ran this illegal mini club: Dietmar-Maria Hegemann, born in 1954. A chatterbox, impresario, and catalyst who came to West Berlin in 1978. Between 1982 and 1990 Dimitri (as everyone called him) organised the annual Berlin Atonal, a festival for non-conformist music that more or less followed in the footsteps of the Geniale Dilletanten.[31] Not only did bands like Einstürzende Neubauten and Malaria! play at Berlin Atonal, but Hegemann also connected with avant-garde electronic musicians from all over the world, including Detroit, where producers Juan Atkins, Derrick May, Jeff Mills, Mike Banks, or Robert Hood were in the process of putting Techno in its final form – a purist, post-industrial, machine-made music that (in contrast to House, which had developed from Disco and often included vocals as well as naturalistic instrumental sounds) consists primarily of entirely abstract, entirely electronically generated sounds and which was influenced by such European genres as Industrial and Synthesizer pop. Just before or after the invention of Techno, which together with House is still the most important electronic club music worldwide, a few of its African American inventors performed at Hegemann's festival.

In this way Hegemann forged a connection that would influence Berlin's club music for decades to come and that turned the city into a global epicentre for Techno – a distinction it still owns to this day. After the closing of Ufo in 1991 he opened Tresor, which was considered one of the most important underground Techno clubs in the city for almost a decade, featuring regular appearances from Detroit DJs. What's more, artists from the US frequently released music on the associated label Tresor Records. Hegemann was thus able to create a close tie between the Techno city Berlin and the city where the music originated, Detroit, initiating a long reciprocal partnership that not only helped releases and DJs from both cities find audiences and interest worldwide, but also had a great impact on Berlin itself, where after the fall of the Wall Techno spread like wildfire.

30
Mark Reeder in Denk and Thülen, *Der Klang der Familie* (see n. 9), 21.
31
Since 2013 'Berlin Atonal' has been held annually in Hegemann's current club, the new Tresor.

In the early 1990s the city's size suddenly doubled. Once the Berlin Wall came down, East Berlin – with its endless rows of pot-holed streets lined by crumbling old buildings and squares framed by grandiose socialist architecture – and West Berlin were united. When the Detroit musicians came here for the first time in the early 1990s they felt right at home, as they saw a de-industrialised city full of ruins just like their own hometown – dark, cold, grey – where subcultural niches were able to flourish. The same was true for producers from Berlin when they travelled to the US city or simply heard the dystopian, futuristic, and often melancholic Techno from Detroit. This music celebrated a decaying future, rusty robots, factories in ruins, and the use of technology in unintended ways inside buildings once built for completely different purposes. The stoic, wordless Techno tracks from Berlin and Detroit filled these spaces. In somewhat mixed metaphors, journalist Anton Waldt claims, 'The roaring and creaking of Detroit's failing heavy industry became the Techno big bang of the German wastelands.'[32]

At the time, of course, Funk and Disco and the genres that followed in their wake were also heard in the clubs of Berlin, as they were in Frankfurt am Main and Munich. Centres for such music were the clubs frequented by US soldiers stationed in Germany. For this reason, the line of development that led from Funk and Disco to House or Hip-Hop also took root in the city. But with Techno it was different. More dramatic. On the one side stood the African American pioneers with their reverence for European noise and technology experiments; on the other, the Berlin fraction, which, thanks to the city's long history, had open ears for electronic music and experimental discord. The two sides recognized each other as kindred spirits. The African American Detroit-based producer Chaos (Marc Floyd) described this special relationship with a fitting yet ludicrous term: 'Afrogermanic'. 'Wir haben eine neue Musik' [We have a new music] sings a voice in German on the Electro track that was released by the Detroit label Underground Resistance.

Along with the very first Berlin producers like 3 Phase feat. Dr. Motte, almost all the important protagonists of the first two generations of Detroit Techno released music on Dimitri Hegemann's Tresor label: musicians like Jeff Mills, Juan Atkins, Eddie Flashin' Fowlkes, Blake Baxter, and Robert Hood. Hegemann dedicated numerous albums to the partnership between Detroit and Berlin. In 1993, for example, he gave Tresor release number 14 the title *Detroit Techno Soul*. That same year the compilation *Tresor II – Berlin Detroit – A Techno Alliance* appeared in collaboration with the British label NovaMute. In 1996, Tresor release number 43 was named after the area code for Detroit: *313*.

At the same time, Tresor Records was also forging ties to Berlin's own past. One of its first albums from 1992 was a compilation of works by various Berlin-based producers – *Auferstanden aus Ruinen* [Rising Up from the Ruins], a reference to the city's historical and current state. The compilation *Tresor II – Berlin Detroit – A Techno Alliance* included work by the long-time Berlin resident Thomas Fehlmann, who was part of the 3MB project. Not only did he release one of the very first German Techno albums *Uro Breaks* in 1990, under the project name Readymade, but back in 1986 he made the first basic forays in the direction of electronic dance music with the sample-based piece 'Fehlmann's Ready Made'.[33] 3MB (3 Men in Berlin) titled one of their tracks (recorded together with one of the fathers of Techno, Juan Atkins) 'Die Kosmischen Kuriere' [The Cosmic Couriers] – a reference to a Berlin label for Cosmic music in the 1970s. Playing alongside Fehlmann and an alternating cast of band members was the other permanent member of the trio 3MB, Moritz von Oswald. He had a similar Post-Punk background as his friend, and, in the mid-1990s, began to release extremely deep, highly Dub-influenced Techno productions on different labels.

But at first, the Techno that Tresor released sounded anything but deep. Jeff Mills, Mike Banks, and Robert Hood (X-101) called one piece on the first Tresor release 'Sonic Destroyer'.[34] The title was their manifesto, as they put out nerve-wrenching, churning, roaring, and fast and brutal Techno. Tresor printed the phrase 'True Spirit' on its records because they saw themselves as the representatives of the real – hard, grim – spirit of Techno. All over the world record labels occupied an extremely important position in the Techno scene as

32
Anton Waldt, 'Trockeneis und Tränengas', in Farkas, Seidl, and Zwirner (eds.), *Nachtleben Berlin* (see n. 10), 130.
33
Not only did FM Einheit, from Einstürzende Neubauten, contribute to the piece but it was also recorded in the exact same studio in Berlin-Kreuzberg where one year earlier the band had put together a tremendously rhythmic album – *Halber Mensch*.
34
Hegemann and his friends created the label to release this album.

independent protagonists, each putting forth its own aesthetic. In fact, for the most part Tresor Records only released pure Techno – monotonous and hypnotic, as raw and concrete-hard as the Tresor club itself. The sound was fast and quite often dissonant, unrelenting and full of references to the Industrial music made by groups like Einstürzende Neubauten, even if this band rejected Techno. The wistfulness and melodies of the first Detroit tracks lay buried underneath the tempo and density.

The hard sound wasn't, of course, the only one in Berlin; a city of countless niches. In early 1993, after a long night in the Techno club Bunker, which was also known for a very heavy sound, Berlin-based producers Marcos López and Mijk van Dijk (Michael van den Nieuwendijk) went back to the studio. They weren't tired but rather pumped up, in the mood to make some music of their own. So, they programmed a rattling House beat with razor-sharp hi-hats, and unconventionally layered epic melodies on top. Several times the piece caves in to make room for synthesizer carpets. At one point the rush of the ocean washes out all other movement. Together the two producers called themselves Marmion. 'Schöneberg', the piece named after their native Berlin district, was released in 1993 as part of the 'Berlin' EP on the Hamburg Trance label Superstition.[35]

'Schöneberg' would become, along with 'Café Del Mar' – also released in 2003 by the Berlin-based producers Paul Schmitz-Moormann (Kid Paul) and Harald Blüchel (Cosmic Baby) who called themselves Energy 52 – one of the biggest Trance Techno hits. Trance Techno was a rhythmic, melodic form that utilised original melodies from Detroit Techno and epic synthesizer sounds, reminiscent of Tangerine Dream and Klaus Schulze, to create auditory spaces as expansive and dramatic as the big room clubs in which the music was played. The Trance label MfS specialised in this form of music offered by producers like Cosmic Baby and Paul van Dyk.[36] In an ironic gesture, the label went by the same name as the official abbreviation for the Ministry of State Security of the collapsed East German government ('Ministerium für Staatssicherheit'), which, in German, is better known as the national intelligence service 'Stasi'. The label's founder Mark Reeder insists, however, that the name actually stands for 'Masterminded for Success'. Another example was Low Spirit, the label of the pioneering figure DJ Westbam, which put out the trivial, incessantly successful pop Techno made by the radio moderator Marusha. It was music for the masses throwing their arms up in exultation.

And in 1990s Berlin, Techno, especially in its quite accessible Trance form, appealed to these masses. Thus, with Techno a Western subculture made an inclusive gesture for the very first time. Punk, for example, was always against something, against the system, against the prevailing structures. This opposition froze over the decades into mere obligatory rituals. In the 1990s Techno, on the other hand, was open to anyone who wanted to join in – everyone could feel personally invited to listen to Techno at that time. This was especially appealing in a city that had just been reunified. Here Techno proved, perhaps also because it is almost completely instrumental, capable of captivating a wide range of people from both sides of the city. People who, after the fall of the Berlin Wall, believed they had reached the end of history and saw themselves as the initiators of a completely new societal and aesthetic order. The Technomania of the 1990s reached its climax with the Loveparade: Berlin's annual outdoor Techno event, which between the years 1989 and 1997 swelled from an underground event of 150 participants to one of the largest mass gatherings in Berlin since the Nazi era. A million people danced to Techno in the streets – with its peaceful, inclusive gesture it was the complete opposite of Nazi demonstrations.

For the first time in the history of electronic music in Berlin, mainstream taste and the avant-garde crossed paths, just as at early Techno parties, avant-garde forms were played alongside those with more mass appeal. In this sense, early Techno possessed an entirely new kind of political self-awareness. This type of music exists beyond the realm of language and thus does not communicate a political discourse through lyrics, but with its universally comprehensible non-stop 4/4-time bass drum, Techno creates very concrete utopias, something like Temporary Autonomous Zones[37] for people who want to dance. The 'ravers', Techno dancers, found their fulfilment in the

---

[35] Marc Chung, one of the original founders of the Superstition label, was a member of Einstürzende Neubauten for many years.

[36] Paul van Dyk now releases globally appealing radio pop based on Trance and enjoys international success.

[37] Cf. Hakim Bey, *T.A.Z.: The Temporary Autonomous Zone* (New York: Autonomedia, 1991).

masses. It was a hippie-like togetherness in which it was not subjective sensations but collective experiences that matter. No more stars – at least this was the intention early on, and on the dance floors men and women, homosexuals and heterosexuals, people with white and dark skin were supposed to be equal.

In this way Techno and House clubs, at least in theory, also became protected areas for minorities. At the time, some called this utopia 'raving society' – with the sound of Techno everyone should and could love everyone and everything else. Of course, not every raver understood Techno as a nonverbal political form. Many clubbers just wanted to have a good time without having to think about anything. But many had this political consciousness – even if it was sometimes only indirectly present in the form of unwritten rules regarding equality and equal rights on the Techno dance floor. At any rate, the cynicism and irony so characteristic of the 1980s were suddenly completely irrelevant.

No wonder the 1980s generation, which was so accustomed to discourse, borders, and political confrontations, rejected this development. It felt like selling out, like betrayal. Thus, in 2013 the otherwise so progressive Wolfgang Müller, who in the 1980s was one of the co-organisers of the Geniale Dilletanten festival, still railed against the massive Techno parades of the 1990s: 'The hedonistic Loveparade with its affinity for ecstasy and alcohol offers the opportunity to make what is, in essence, a very political vision attractive – a neo-individualistic, liberal ideology. It gave birth to the vision of a society freed from the chains of the state, a society that through the commitment and efforts, so to speak, of its individuals is completely self-regulating.'[38] He criticized Techno as 'unideological' and 'always ready to give in to the pressure to perform'. This testifies to a fundamental lack of comprehension. But to some extent Müller is also right. Some subforms of Techno, especially Trance, did develop very quickly into easily consumable, superficially commercial radio music – as if designed to give a lift to the workers inside the capitalistic production machine or to provide them with some relaxation at the end of the day so as to restore their productive energy.

When Techno originally emerged in Berlin, appealing Trance was still part of the subculture and could be heard at parties alongside hard Tresor Techno and other variants. Soon, however, the aesthetic, artistic programme and attitude of commercially successful labels like Low Spirit or MfS elicited a backlash. Due to the abundance, mass-appeal, and melodiousness of such music, other electronic music producers got more serious, more severe. The most extreme sound came from the trio Atari Teenage Riot and their dedicated label Digital Hardcore, which released leftist radical Punk Techno, for example, the absurdly distorted metal Punk Gabber piece 'Raver Bashing' (sic!) from 1994.

—

Next to becoming unbelievably big and successful like Trance or unbelievably radical and hardcore a third option was to strive for greater depth. This was demonstrated from 1993 onwards by two Berlin natives who are still among the most fascinating electronic music producers of Berlin. One of them was Moritz von Oswald, who has already been mentioned as a member of 3MB. Oswald is a classically trained percussionist and timpanist who played in Post-Punk bands before he began releasing electronic club music in 1989 under names such as Marathon, Time Unlimited, or His Name Is Dime. In the Hard Wax record shop that opened in 1989 in Berlin, and which still exists today, he quickly met shop founder and owner, Mark Ernestus, who had studied art and had later run an artists' bar.

The two became studio partners and began trying something completely new: They fused the 4/4 bass drums characteristic of Techno with the reverberation effects and echoes of classic Jamaican Dub and Reggae. In this way they reconnected Berlin Techno with African American and African Caribbean musical forms that circulated back and forth over the 'Black Atlantic'[39] between Africa, Europe, and the New World. In the ensuing years the two producers would drift further and further away from standard Techno forms, ending in a certain sense somewhere between Dub/Reggae and Techno, as their music could be described either as highly Dub-influenced Techno or Techno-driven Dub. The two released their work on a series

38
Müller, *Subkultur Westberlin 1979–1989* (see n. 5), 239.
39
Cf. Paul Gilroy, *The Black Atlantic – Modernity and Double-Consciousness* (Cambridge: Harvard University Press, 1993).

of labels, each of which pursued its own, clearly defined stylistic program, among them were: Rhythm & Sound/Burial Mix for Techno-driven Reggae, M-Series/Maurizio for minimalist Techno, Main Street for House, and Chain Reaction for the productions of befriended musicians.

The most successful of these was the project Basic Channel, which served as both a band/project name and the name of the associated label. Basic Channel got started with Techno and was in terms of its sound not that distant from M-Series/Maurizio, before it turned increasingly away from the dance floor through systematic reduction. Sometimes all that remained was rhythmically swirling Dub clouds, with a bass drum that was only present in the distant background or even vanished entirely, with countless noises and instruments buried in the mix. The result was, to some degree, a washed-out Techno that sounded as if one was hearing it while waiting in line outside the club. Yet sometimes it was merely a free flow of textures and layers, static noise and endless echo chambers developing ever onwards in the subtlest nuances. In this way, Ernestus/von Oswald reconnected Techno as a form of sound research to the Cosmic music of the 1970s[40] and to the 'noise-is-music' attitude of the 1980s. At the same time they helped build a bridge from club music to contemporary electronic and electro-acoustic avant-garde works. With great meticulousness they completed every stage of the production process themselves, from mixing to cutting the records.

In the 1990s Ernestus/von Oswald's various labels were, alongside Tresor, the most successful of a long list of subculture Techno labels in Berlin. Interestingly, very few of these attracted any real attention outside the city's confines. Among the exceptions were Elektro Musik Department, which, in terms of its creative orientation and the background of the musicians, was allied to visual art and released rigid, slow, ultra-serious, ultra-reduced Drone Techno. Or the label Bpitch Control, which, with releases ranging from girly vocals to soft beats to a merciless Techno buzz, was extremely multi-faceted. Shortly after the turn of the millennium the founder and director of Bpitch Control, Ellen Allien, sang on her first solo album *Stadtkind* [City Kid]: 'Berlin / du gibst mir die Kraft / bin ein Teil von dir / Stadtkind" [Berlin / you give me power / I'm part of you / city kid]. She also titled her second album *Berlinette*; sounds like true love.

Ultimately, in the late 1990s and early 2000s, club music and electronic dance music from Berlin suffered a series of aesthetic setbacks. Musicians such as Peaches, Gonzales, and T.Raumschmiere and the label Kitty-Yo combined Electro beats with synthesizers and creaking guitars to create so-called Electroclash – a music style originating in New York that incorporated show effects and that perished in a flurry of Rock clichés which had long since been believed dead (star poses on stage, glamour, and arrogant self-importance). DJ-producers like Kaos mixed danceable Post-Punk with House, thus emulating the cocaine-driven New York Disco chic of the 1970s and 1980s – a new phenomenon in a city whose most interesting forms of club music had always revolved around an underground attitude, anti-elegance, and an uncompromised rejection of commercial exploitation. These were the last convulsions before Berlin underwent a long-term downturn in nationally and internationally relevant avant-garde music.

2000–2009: Recovery in the underground

At first it sounded as if a drummer had withdrawn inside himself and begun laying down a stripped-down yet ambitious beat. Then came a Jazz-like bass line. These elements were finally joined by more and more percussion and effects before the music was suddenly interrupted. A women's choir sighed a few indiscriminate syllables and by the time the piece had regained momentum it was so full that it sounded like a complete Jazz combo were playing in a smoky club, interrupted time and again by a Brazilian Samba drum group. The piece of music described above is called 'Fedime's Flight' – and it cannot be compared to any music ever made by means of machines in Berlin and pressed onto albums to dance to: lush, sparkling and smooth yet refined, embracing the entire history of Jazz, of all things, which in the history of Berlin dance music had never played an important role.

At the turn of the millennium an aimlessness lay over the city, at least as far as

40
In 1994 Ernestus/von Oswald even released a remix of Manuel Göttsching's *E2-E4* titled 'Remake (Basic Reshape)' on the Detroit label Planet E.

experimental, intrepid electronic club music was concerned. At the time no one noticed this, as some remarkably fine sounding, successful and well-known labels and projects were spreading an entirely new Berlin sound across the globe. Among them was the producer collective Jazzanova. The group's various members first encountered one another in the late 1990s in clubs and backyard bars in the Eastern part of the reunified city, where they resisted Techno's dominance with a fusion of danceable Jazz albums from the US, low-key Hip-Hop, or Brazilian Bossanova. In 1997, the collective finally completed its first *Jazzanova* EP. It was released by the label Jazzanova Compost Records, a collaboration with the Munich-based record company Compost, which had been active for some time. It wasn't long, though, before they launched their own platform under the name Sonar Kollektiv. In addition to a piece named after a major street in East Berlin 'Allee der Kosmonauten' [Cosmonaut Avenue], *Jazzanova* EP contained 'Fedime's Flight'.

Jazzanova and their associated record labels also released Reggae from New Zealand, Folk with acoustic guitars, and Deep House with softer beats and supple chord progressions, but their focus was so-called Nu Jazz – an electronic revival of danceable Jazz with some complex programmed beats, as can be distinctly heard in 'Fedime's Flight'. The pieces often sounded as if they were made by instruments although they were usually completely computer generated. The sound was appealing, could be used as background music, and enjoyed considerable international success as a lifestyle accessory. Nu Jazz developed into a general term for a wide range of stylistic nuances. What the pieces all had in common was that they were conventionally orchestrated and heavily influenced by various forms of Jazz.

Except for the stoic repetition of beats which were more or less in the foreground, Nu Jazz was not aesthetically related to any of the strands or movements that had, up until then, prevailed in Berlin's underground clubs. The focus here was not intentional discord as a means of self-empowerment. There were no pointed breaks with conventions. The music machines weren't seen as a liberation from anything. Nu Jazz was not a niche experiment without thought for commercial exploitation. This break with all the breaks was perhaps one reason for its extraordinary long-term success around the turn of the millennium. In a city that seemed to be completely dominated by the once underground genres of House and, to an even greater extent, Techno, reaching all the way into the mainstream scenes, accessible, danceable Jazz was itself a kind of anti-niche.

Somewhat more experimental were the electronic labels Scape, Morr Music, and City Centre Offices, which were active at the same time and also garnered intense international attention. At the turn of the millennium they primarily released music which, in contrast to Jazzanova and Nu Jazz, placed emphasis on its electronic production methods. This music wasn't really danceable, and for the most part also turned its back on Berlin's prevailing electronic music traditions. Instead of noise and breaks it employed soft Dub static, child-like music box melodies, faint sounds, and careful beats, which, all together, yielded a kind of campfire music for computer users and early internet surfers. It was a new introspection and cuddliness – which perhaps was so well received because after the crash of the so-called 'new economy' many people in the West working in service agencies and creative professions experienced, for the first time, exactly how cruel the world of digital capitalism can be. In early 2000, just as the new millennium was getting underway, the first so-called 'dotcom' bubble burst. Stocks for internet companies were grotesquely overvalued, share prices quickly bottomed out all over the world. Many people, among them professionals from the 'creative' industries, lost their invested capital – and with it their laid-back faith in the future.

—

At the same time, the Techno insanity of the 1990s was winding down. At the end of the millennium DJs and party organisers were still able to make a lot of money with Techno, as were music producers with new releases. This led to ever more bombastic parties, over-inflated egos – and in some cases to equally bombastic and over-inflated tracks. Then many big brands started cutting back their excessive sponsoring of Techno parties. Musicians lost their source of income

– in part also because music started to be distributed, on a larger scale, illegally online. Next the mainstream media turned its back on Techno, as Berlin's once dominant club music now seemed worn out, exhausted, over and done with. Electronic dance music had come from the underground and made it all the way to the top, but now it was, with the exception of a few short-lived token riotous subgenres like Electroclash, on its way back down again.

Astonishingly, this did the music itself no harm. On the contrary, it gave Techno the chance to shrink back down to a healthy size. Now, when no one could afford excesses any longer, only those who were really serious kept at this culture. What's more, in the midst of its downfall niches where new experiments were possible emerged once again, as there were no longer any expectations of chart success or profit. In the new millennium a new kind of purism took hold that culminated in a genre that would shape the following decade: Minimal Techno. This stripped-down form harked back to, among other predecessors, the early Berlin pioneers, Basic Channel. Like the work of the producers Ernestus/von Oswald in the 1990s, this music was reduced to its essential elements – a bass drum, a hi-hat, and one other sound that changed imperceptibly. This was charged with an earnestness and stoicism diametrically opposed to the gaudy Techno of the years before, while also drawing on the hypnotic monotony of certain types of Krautrock from the 1970s. Minimal Techno was the sound of the recession – but also of a newly discovered joy in experimentation. The question often appeared to be: How little does a piece of music need in order to work in the club and get people to dance?[41]

The new reduced sound of the city soon linked up with aesthetically similar efforts in other Western metropolises. For the first time the Berlin club music scene began – this was also due to the low rents in many city districts at the time – to attract large numbers of activists from other Western cities: DJs and producers, label owners and party organizers from German cities like Cologne and Hamburg, as well as from Great Britain, Spain, the US, and Canada. In 2004, the famous producer and DJ Richie Hawtin (Plastikman) relocated from Ontario, Canada to Berlin and brought his label Minus with him. It wasn't long before the Canadian and his clique were reaching audiences as large as Trance did in the 1990s, with a Minimal Techno that was highly technical (and often seemed soulless).

Along with well-respected German platforms for Minimal Techno and House – including Kanzleramt from the small town of Bad Nauheim or Pokerflat from Hamburg – the label Perlon moved from Frankfurt am Main to Berlin. In its wake the Chilean-German DJ and producer Ricardo Villalobos also relocated to the capital. Villalobos would soon acquire notoriety for his over-the-top DJ performances, where a single Minimal Techno piece seemed to develop over hours, with very few clearly identifiable and rather veiled climaxes, hypnotic, and in a kind of sleepy way excessive. Many of the pieces that Villalobos released on records had a similar sound. For example, his EP 'Fizheuer Zieheuer', on which he lets a sample from a brass orchestra wander, waft, and wind its way over a simple beat for forty minutes, with only slight modifications by means of echoes and percussion samples. Listeners and dancers could lose themselves in this piece of new mental absence, which can quite easily be grasped as a return to the endless Krautrock jams of the 1970s. In the 2000s hypnotically meandering Minimal Techno like 'Fizheuer Zieheuer' was played at so-called 'after hours' – events that were held in clubs, private apartments, or parks after the party itself was over. Already exhausted from dancing, people were docile and open to experiments such as Villalobos' many productions and DJ sets.

This sloppy, sluggish after hour aesthetic with unconventional sounds and laid-back beats was one focus of the club Bar25, which opened in 2004, and of the label of the same name founded two years later. Bar25 wasn't much more than a wood cabin in the middle of an amusement park on the shores of the Spree (the river that flows through Berlin). The label was launched with the producer Matt John's meaningfully titled 'Kommt Was Nach Montag' [What Comes After Monday], which refers to the fact that parties in the city usually extended beyond the weekend. This was a work of minimalistic dicking around Techno, with countless psychedelic and playful samples stumbling

41
Some of the Techno pioneers from Detroit had already worked on this same idea in the mid-1990s. One of the first and most interesting was Robert Hood with his album *Minimal Nation* (1994).

in and out. The club's sound system tended to be low-powered and had almost no bass. As a result, the label's releases were not anywhere near as hammering as, for example, Tresor Techno of the 1990s. Bar25's label also released bizarre Folk pop and signed oddball Rock bands. It was less about sound experiments than it was the social component. Thus, at the sprawling parties at Bar25 the hippie-ish ideas of 1990s Techno[42] were also revived, as was the communal life of the Cosmic musicians of the 1970s.

The diametric opposite of this was the other important club of the 2000s, which opened, likewise, in 2004 and also had an associated record label which stood for the club's aesthetic: Berghain and its label Ostgut Ton. If Bar25 (now closed) stood for Dionysian excesses, Berghain – housed in a former heating and power facility – embodied the return to the Spartan, serious, sombre, concrete and industry style of the 1990s. The club's sound system is one of the best in the world, powerful and bass-heavy, and the high-power releases of Ostgut Ton sound as if they were made for it. Launched in 2005, the label's first single 'Dawning/ Dead Man Watches The Clock' (serial number 'o-ton01'), from two Berghain DJs Marcel Dettmann and Ben Klock, was no-nonsense Techno: mighty, massive, and majestic, with its emphasis on drums and only a trace of melody on its edges, raw, gloomy, and glowering. From the very beginning, Berghain and Ostgut Ton occupied the position in Berlin once held by the Tresor club and its label: locations for the city's serious, avant-garde Techno sound.

After the first wave of club music activists (musicians, DJs, and party organisers) had moved to Berlin early on in the decade, with the opening of Bar 25 and Berghain in 2004 a massive wave of party tourists and newcomers came to the city from every imaginable country, at least in the global north. Inexpensive flights sold by discount airlines from international locations boosted party tourism[43] and made a form of life possible, especially in the creative industry, in which place of employment, place of residence, and private and professional relationships were scattered across various (mostly European) cities. This influx was bolstered by the 2006 football World Cup in Germany, which brought many people to Berlin for the first time. The 2008 film *Berlin Calling* enjoyed success across Europe, adding to this effect. Objectively speaking, the film told the tragic story of a Berlin Techno DJ who, after a drug-induced psychosis, never really gets back on his feet. Yet people all over the world preferred to see it as an ode to Berlin's never-ending parties.

On the soundtrack to the movie, released in 2009 on Ellen Allien's above-mentioned label Bpitch Control, was a piece called 'Sky & Sand' by the East Berlin native Paul Kalkbrenner. It begins with a gently clattering beat but quickly develops into an epic hymn that borrows from Trance melodies, augmented by the laconic vocals of Kalkbrenner's brother Fritz praising the club as a joyful place: 'In the nighttime / when the world is at its rest / you will find me / in the place I know the best / dancin', shoutin' / flyin' to the moon'. The video clip features romantic shots of Berlin, and ecstatic party scenes from the city's clubs, as well as material from the film itself. The song became a massive hit in many Western countries. After its low point earlier on in the decade, by the late 2000s electronic music had once again assumed its lofty position.

No End: World market at last

The traveller might come from Nigeria, France, the US, or South Africa. In the late evening, he or she climbs into a taxi outside one of Berlin's airports or the train station and says to the driver: 'Take me to a club. I wanna dance.' The driver will, in all likelihood, turn around and cast a dumbfounded look at the passenger. As through the night and into the early morning, when the lights of Berlin are turned on and then off again, there are any number of clubs, parties, events, and scenes to choose from. These range from Brazilian Baile Funk to Hip-Hop from the US, to mainstream pop, to Darkwave/Gothic, and even to Jazz and Blues. That's one side of the story. On the other hand, this taxi driver will, if nothing else is said, ultimately steer the traveller to one of the many clubs in Berlin where DJs play House and/or Techno. For now, in the late 2010s, these forms of club music still reign supreme over the city's nightlife. To such an extent that the Berlin municipal authorities refer to the club scene in their

---

42
Equality, freedom, love, etc.

43
Cf. Tobias Rapp, *Lost and Sound: Berlin, Techno und der Easyjetset* (Berlin: Suhrkamp, 2009).

marketing materials to attract tourists and new residents.

These new residents are coming in great numbers. Berlin is now considered, at least in the global north, a paradise for musicians and especially for electronic musicians, who rave about the sense of freedom in the city where artists have been filling niches for five decades. They go on about the do-it-yourself ethos, which took hold all the way back in the 1960s, and about the easy-going creativity without the pressure of commercial exploitation. That is, in any case, the ideal, though the reality is generally much more boring and less free to boot. Be that as it may, the influx of people revives the city's club music long after the Minimal Techno of the 2000s had devolved to monotony and clichés.

It is through immigration, which was partially triggered by club culture, that a new phenomenon comes into the city's history – for the first time the ideas of immigrants are making their way into the most prevalent club music, House and Techno. But it isn't marginalised economic refugees from emerging or developing countries that are leaving their traces in the city's clubs. The children, for example, of Turkish guest workers, or the Syrian refugees, or the Somali asylum seekers have hardly had any impact on Berlin's electronic dance music until now. Almost all the non-native producers and DJs making names for themselves come from globalised industrial nations like Spain, Great Britain, the US, or France.[44] In comparison to previous decades, these newcomers have created a relatively great deal of cultural variety. Which is presumably also the reason why Berlin no longer has its own distinctive electronic club music. What's heard in clubs can, in a general sense, still be called 'House' and 'Techno'. But if you listen more carefully you will catch elements of Footwork from the US, as well as that ugly rockish Techno that the French apparently love so much. Then there is the British influenced big room sound, as well as the Minimal Techno of the 2000s, which large fractions of Spaniards and Italians are untiringly tweaking.

If one had to identify a sound characteristic of Berlin in the mid- to late 2010s then it would be a potent Berghain-like Bass Techno, influenced by British genres such as Dubstep – slower and deeper than, for example, the Tresor Techno of the 1990s but just as raw and sombre. This is joined, for the first time in the city's history, by a second important form of dance music – House, as it can be heard, for example, on the records of the Innervisions label, which emerged from the Jazzanova label Sonar Kollektiv in 2005. This label releases a technical energetic House sound that has replaced Minimal Techno as Berlin's most successful club music. And recently a gender-crossing, free-flowing, yet hard and edgy electronica can be heard from an international LGBTQ community that is exploring the city's as well as musical freedom.

All things considered, people in the late 2010s no longer come to Berlin because of a certain sound. They bring their own music with them instead and send it out from here to the rest of the world. Thanks to modern telecommunication and inexpensive flights, club music producers who have moved to Berlin can continue to develop their aesthetic projects unaffected by their location. As a result, there is no genuine Berlin club music anymore. Only a few long-standing institutions and producers, who primarily congregate around Berghain and the Hard Wax record shop, continue to release new music in accordance with their old purist values, exploring niches, doing it themselves, trying new things out with little interest in commercial success.

Despite this aesthetic transformation, club music as a whole – once again, like in the 1990s, though this time totally different – has found a place in the centre of society. Not just the city marketing department, but even the public transportation operator, BVG, use House and Techno to tout Berlin's image as a contemporary, cosmopolitan city. There are also things like Rave restaurants with very good food, some of which have been around for over ten years now, and party-exhibition fusions that are well accepted. Many of the expat artist communities are known in the city for their parties. There are also parties and clubs with explicitly leftist alternative political agendas. There might soon be clubs with nurseries for the somewhat older ravers of the first and second generations – or posh raves geared especially for well-off upper-middle-class kids. We do not know what kind of music

44
In the 2010s a great many people came to Germany from countries like Spain or Portugal as economic refugees because the economies in their native countries were hit hard by the global financial crisis.

will fill these novel niches of night culture. It will presumably be repetitive, electronically produced, and pieced together according to its own criteria. Hopefully, it will continue to explore and inhabit niches and hopefully it will question, attack, and finally dispose of conventions. For only those who continually push the boundaries of the freedoms that this city has to offer will be able to hold onto it.

Bibliography

Baker, Stuart, and Self, Adrian, liner notes to the CD compilation *Deutsche Elektronische Musik* (London: SoulJazz, 2010).
Benjamin, Walter, 'Der destruktive Charakter', in: *Gesammelte Schriften* (Frankfurt am Main: Suhrkamp, 1991).
Bey, Hakim, *T.A.Z.: The Temporary Autonomous Zone* (New York: Autonomedia, 1991).
Cope, Julian, *Krautrocksampler: One Head's Guide to the Grosse Kosmische Musik* (London: Head Heritage, 1995).
Dax, Max, and Defcon, Robert, *Nur was nicht ist ist möglich – Die Geschichte der Einstürzenden Neubauten* (Berlin: Bosworth, 2006).
Denk, Felix, and von Thülen, Sven, *Der Klang der Familie – Berlin, Techno und die Wende* (Berlin: Suhrkamp, 2012).
Farkas, Wolfgang; Seidl, Stefanie; Zwirner, Heiko (eds.), *Nachtleben Berlin. 1974 bis Heute* (Berlin: Metrolit, 2013).
Gilroy, Paul, *The Black Atlantic – Modernity and Double-Consciousness* (Cambridge: Harvard University Press, 1993).
Göttsching, Manuel, liner notes to album *E2-E4 – 25th Anniversary* (Berlin: MG.Art, 2006).
Lessour, Théo, *Berlin Sampler: From Cabaret to Techno: 1904–2012, A Century Of Berlin Music* (Berlin: Ollendorff, 2012).
Maeck, Klaus, *Hör mit Schmerzen. Einstürzende Neubauten* (Bonn: EME, 1989).
Müller, Wolfgang (ed.), *Geniale Dilletanten* (Berlin: Merve, 1982).
Müller, Wolfgang, *Subkultur Westberlin 1979–1989* (Hamburg: Philo Fine Arts, 2013).
Rapp, Tobias, *Lost and Sound: Berlin, Techno und der Easyjetset* (Berlin: Suhrkamp, 2009).
Westbam, liner notes to vinyl LP *The Cabinet* (Berlin: Low Spirit, 1989).

Love Parade, Kurfürstendamm, Berlin, 1991, photo: Tilman Brembs

E-Werk, Berlin, 1995, photo: Tilman Brembs

Love Parade, Großer Stern, Berlin, 2003, photo: Tilman Brembs

Love Parade, Kurfürstendamm, Berlin, 1994, photo: Tilman Brembs

PLATES

Drum and Bass DJ Goldie at WMF, Berlin, 1996, photo: Tilman Brembs

A girl wearing an outfit from fashion designer Frank Schütte, Berlin, 1995, photo: Tilman Brembs

Clubber at E-Werk, Berlin, 1996, photo: Tilman Brembs

Do it Yourself – Looking for Freedom in Constant Collapse

Tobias Rapp

[1] Thomas Pynchon, *Die Enden der Parabel* (Reinbek: Rowohlt, 1981), 576–577.

The first modern Berlin-based club never really existed. What we have instead is a description. It can be found in *Gravity's Rainbow*, a novel published in 1973 by American writer, Thomas Pynchon. The story is set at the end of the Second World War, in a country that once was Germany and would soon be Germany again. It is the short interim between the last months of war and the beginning of the post-war period, in which there is only the 'Zone': an area with no laws and only a few rules.

The ruins of Berlin are at the centre of the Zone and Pynchon's protagonist, the confused US secret service agent Slothrop, ends up staying there for a few days. He has long forgotten about the mission that sent him there: he just drifts. Along the way, somewhere in the ruins of the Tiergarten park, he meets 'Säure' Brummer, a Berlin backyard criminal and black market dealer, and his two female companions. Together, they make their way to the Chicago Bar, past the burnt ruins of the Reichstag, past singing Russian soldiers and past slogan-bearing walls and body bags, the latter containing the dug-up bodies of those who were killed and buried under the rubble in the battle for Berlin. Slothrop is dressed up as a rocketeer; the two women are wearing costumes from Wagner operas, which they found in the prop store of an opera house.

> *Slothrop, Säure, Trudi and Magda come in a back entrance, out of a great massif of ruins and darkness lit only here and there, like the open country. Inside, M.O.s and corpsmen run hither and thither clutching bottles of fluffy white crystalline substances, small pink pills, clear ampoules the size of pureys. Occupation and Reichsmarks ruffle and flap across the room. Some dealers are all chemical enthusiasm, others all business. Oversize photos of John Dillinger, alone or posed with his mother, his pals, his tommygun, decorate the walls. Lights and arguing are kept low, should the military police happen by. On a wire-backed chair, blunt hair hands picking quietly at a guitar, sits an American sailor with an orang-utan look to him.*[1]

Almost everything that made Berlin nightlife so special and exciting over the last forty years can be found in Pynchon's description of the Chicago Bar. It was by no means easy to visit these bars – anyone from out of town not only needed someone who knew where to go, but also where to find the place. The path often led through piles of rubble and backyards. Lots of drugs were being consumed, with acid (*Säure* is German for acid) playing a predominant role; be it as a drug in the 1970s or as a music style in the 1980s and 1990s. The people at the clubs were sometimes eccentric, but most of all they aimed for excess. The interior design wasn't hung up on glamour; rather it had something of a do-it-yourself (DIY) feel. The main point, however, that it was a temporary space that had opened up in some backyard, cellar, or in an abandoned factory. That was what made it charming. Next week or next month, the party would go on elsewhere. When one space was exhausted, you looked for a new one – after all, there were enough of them. These spaces were opened by history. They weren't conceived of as party locations. The parties took place in the ruins left behind by the great European war; whose destructive force was so massive that some of the ruins are still there in the twenty-first century and are only now slowly beginning to disappear. This is the basis from which the international appeal of Berlin's present-day club life evolved. This was where it all started.

In the immediate aftermath of the war, places like the Chicago Bar might have actually existed in Berlin. There has been little research into the subcultural life of that period, and this is unlikely to change. Back then, nobody would have thought that one day their nightlife would be of interest to others. On the contrary, with the end of the Third Reich and its murderous policing authorities only dating back a little while, the less information that was communicated, the more secure people would have felt. What is certain, however, is that from the 1960s to the present day, there have been countless places similar to Pynchon's Chicago Bar. One thing, however, is different: In the Chicago Bar, a guitarist was strumming his instrument. In contrast, if we want to recount the history of Berlin's nightlife and its clubs today, we will almost automatically resort to the history of electronic dance music, meaning House and Techno in the broadest sense, because this music and its culture are two major factors defining the city today.

Berlin, the capital of Europe's most powerful economy, has been a coveted place for Europe's youth since the turn of the millennium, if not earlier. Different from London or New York, however, the reputation of Germany's capital does not derive from fantastic job opportunities, or from the dream of rapidly becoming rich and famous. Berlin's appeal is almost solely based on its image of being the capital of the underground and of subcultures. In this context, the city's clubs and dance music play an important role. The new Berlin was invented on its dance floors.

Berlin's nightlife, as it represents itself today, is made up of many sources; in countless places. In terms of music, these places often have little or nothing to do with contemporary electronic dance music. The thread running through almost all of Berlin's subcultures is often connected to music, while at the same time entirely unmusical; Berlin is a city of social experiments, of the niche, of finding oneself, and of DIY culture. This started in the 1960s, when, after the construction of the Wall, many well-off citizens left and the first communes developed in the huge empty bourgeois flats. During the 1970s, new forms of living together were tried out during the first squatters' movement. The same is true for the 1980s, when the alternative culture of the city's Kreuzberg district was experiencing its heyday, and for the 1990s when, after the fall of the Wall, empty buildings in the Eastern parts of the city enabled similar experiences.

Music is and has always been part of these developments – and the music has always been defined by a similar attitude: by an ethos of DIY and experimental culture. This is true for the first electronic musicians at the end of the 1960s, for the 1970s Punk bands, for the Post-Punk and Noise bands of the 1980s, and the Techno acts of the 1990s to late 2010s. Social experiments need protected spaces. Hence, the history of Berlin's dance music is also a history of these spaces: the clubs.

Although this history only began in the late 1960s – interestingly enough at roughly the same time Thomas Pynchon penned *Gravity's Rainbow* – its roots can be found earlier, in post-war Berlin. The widespread destruction of the city, the division that followed soon after, the feeling among the older generation of West Berliners of being surrounded by the hostile state of the socialist GDR, which was strengthened by the socialist state crushing the uprising of 17 June 1953 and the 1961 construction of the Wall, the four-power status which institutionally separated West Berlin from the Federal Republic of Germany – all these aspects unintentionally created a situation that resulted in Berlin becoming the capital of underground culture. Those who were living in West Berlin at this time then might have felt as if they were living in a frontline city defending the liberties of the Western world. In retrospect, a different picture emerges, what was being created was the first niche city in the world – an ex-metropolis that had to make to do without an established middle-class bourgeoisie and without the headquarters of large corporations. A city where cultural production was not driven by prosperity. Rather it represented the city's actual wealth.

It is by no means easy to describe this history categorically. Over the course of time, the term 'subculture' has, in the global North, taken on all sorts of different meanings. In the 1970s, the protagonists of subculture predominantly saw themselves as members of an anti-culture, also in a political sense. This changed when, from the 1980s through to the end of the 1990s, subcultural activities were seen as part of a parallel society. The situation changed again in the 2000s and 2010s. While the subcultures in Europe and the US might still feel they belong to a small and uncompromising cultural avant-garde, they have, in fact, often become part of the marketing and branding of their respective cities for which tourism is an important source of revenue.

Clay, stones, numerous shards

The history of Berlin as a place for electronic music began in 1967, in a basement club called Zodiak Free Arts Lab or the Zodiak Club. It was located in the basement of the Schaubühne, a leftist, avant-garde theatre. The Schaubühne was a theatre collective, working on overcoming bourgeois theatre, with equal rights for all its members, from lighting technicians to actors, writers to costume designers. It was located in a multipurpose hall belonging to the Arbeiterwohlfahrt (Workers' Welfare Federal Association) on the Landwehr canal, in Berlin's Kreuzberg neighbourhood.

The Schaubühne was a source of frequent scandal: In 1970, the government accused the theatre of communist agitation and threatened to withdraw funding. It was around this time that director Peter Stein joined the theatre. He was to become one of the most influential protagonists of German *Regietheater* (director's theatre) – the most important development of German city theatre since the Second World War. In 1982, the Schaubühne moved out of the building. Today, another theatre is housed there: one of the sites of Hebbel am Ufer (HAU), which is of similar importance as the Schaubühne during its heydays. It experiments with what a globalised world might look like on stage. Interestingly enough, the HAU features an advanced, experimental music programme. However, these days the music programme takes place on the theatre's main stage, not on an auxiliary stage or in a basement.

In contrast to this, the Zodiak Arts Free Arts Lab was nothing more than a dark basement room. Entrance fees were cheap or free, the gigs usually started late at night to avoid interfering with the theatre performances, and all of the gigs were experimental. One part of the room was painted white, the other was painted black, equipment was scattered around and often damaged during performances. The shows wanted to be everything but concerts in a conventional sense: sound research, performances, or happenings. Here, something new was to be invented while the old had to be conquered and destroyed.

In terms of music history, this was one of the places where Krautrock was born, the first independent and genuinely German brand of Rock music. Important bands such as Ash Ra Tempel performed there, The Agitation who were later called Agitation Free, and Klaus Schulze and Tangerine Dream played their first gigs there. Zodiak was run by Conrad Schnitzler and Hans-Joachim Roedelius, themselves legendary Krautrock personalities. Together with Dieter Möbius, they founded Cluster, one of the genre's most important bands.

The influence of Krautrock on contemporary dance music is often overestimated.[2] Sure, some of the bands worked with the first synthesizers, but this music was not dance music and never wanted to be. Rather, it wanted to break with traditional conventions of listening, it wanted to annoy the establishment, to destroy the bourgeois society, to change the world. In other words: it followed the same programme as the classical avant-garde. None of the Berlin bands were particularly interested in rhythm. It was more about noise, from which this kind of music derived its intensity, and the joy of turning what used to be noise into music. The Krautrock movement was driven by a deep mistrust of anything traditional: tradition was the enemy; parents and their culture were highly suspect. The Second World War and the Holocaust had taken place only one generation earlier. A cultural tradition that had not been capable of preventing these crimes was to be rejected. This music translated the civil unrest that shook West Germany since the mid-1960s into sound.

Although its musical influence on future dance music is debatable, the Zodiak Free Arts Lab was an important place in the development of Berlin's club culture over the next few decades. It started something that has defined Berlin's subculture to the present day. It was music with a radical belief in DIY, experimentation, and trying out new things. Furthermore, the club was the first to experiment with something that would be repeated countless times: how to seize a space, how to fill that space with music for a time, how to avoid being squelched by others, how this space is going to enable new and exciting connections – and how to shut down such a venue again.

The Zodiak existed for a little longer than a year before it closed at the beginning of 1969. Today, it is hard to determine exactly why. Was it the noise pollution? Did the contract expire? According to Hans-Joachim Roedelius, the Schaubühne management was simply fed up with dope-smoking hippies hanging out on the lawn in front of the theatre and making fun of the theatre audience.[3]

[2] To learn more about the history of dance music in Berlin, please have a look at Florian Sievers' essay in this book. With regards to Krautrock both contributors on Berlin have differing opinions.
[3] Hans-Joachim Roedelius, in an interview with the author (2006).

In 1968, West Berlin was in upheaval. The bisected city was itself divided by protesting students on the one side, and long-established Berliners on the other. But it was not only the student protests that shook the city – other cities experienced similar events. More than anywhere else, West Berlin was a place of experimentation, where new forms of living were put to the test. Many of the huge flats in formerly well-off western neighbourhoods were empty, with their former inhabitants having moved to West Germany. While the bourgeoisie left the city, many young conscientious objectors moved in. If you were a citizen of West Berlin, you were exempt from compulsory military service. This was part of the city's four-power status under which the winners of the Second World War (the US, Soviet Union, the UK, and France) ruled Berlin.

Consequently, students and other young people looking for a different kind of life started to set up flat shares, to share the large apartments in pairs, threes, fours, or even more. This was something totally new and radical. Until then, they either had to live in student dormitories, where they were required to adhere to the house rules, or they had to rent flats where they would live under the direct social control of their landlords. That was over now. At the end of the 1960s, some flat shares declared themselves communes in which everything was shared – from meals to sometimes even sexual partners. There were not many of them. But the ones that existed were influential. Living together was declared a political act. The political militancy of the late 1960s, which would permanently alter German politics, society and culture through demonstrations and assassinations, would not have been possible without the communes. These were the places where things were discussed, prepared, and organised.

In fact, new radical artistic and new radical political forms of life in the late 1960s and early 1970s were closely linked for a time. Both were concerned with a general liberation from prevailing norms. For a time, artists and activists saw themselves fighting for the same cause. Members of the band Agitation Free, for example, lived in the so-called Kommune 1. Mani Neumeier, the head of Agitation Free, later said that music itself became a 'political statement'.[4] The alliance between the student movement and Rock music was also due to the simple fact that there was not yet a club scene; instead, the universities provided options for gigs. The Berlin newspaper *Tagesspiegel* wrote about a legendary gig at the Technical University of Berlin (TU):

> *In a concert at the TU, the bands Agitation Free, Tangerine Dream, and Amon Düül performed expansive sound processes spreading over several hours, which, with their compulsive repetitiveness, were reminiscent of the ritual models of exotic tribes. ... The repertoire of thumping and throbbing musical gestures, of bands of noise, the total absence of any formal musical concept, have a strictly barbaric feel.*[5]

This was intentional. What the Krautrock bands were looking for in the beginning was exactly this seemingly 'primitive' DIY sound. Freeing oneself from the burden of one's ancestry, leaving one's socialisation behind, and starting anew was part of the programme.

[4] Theo Lessour, *Berlin Sampler* (Berlin: Ohlendorff Verlag, 2012), 182.

[5] Cf. Wolfgang Burdl, 'Rausch, Aggression und Laissez Faire', *Tagesspiegel*, 1968 cf. 'Lutz Ludwig Kramer', Wikipedia, Die freie Enzyklopädie, <https://de.wikipedia.org/wiki/Lutz_Ludwig_Kramer> accessed 13 September 2013.

The most important band during the formative years of the alternative Berlin scene was not a Krautrock band, but the Rock group Ton Steine Scherben (Clay Stone Shards). Named after a statement by German archaeologist Heinrich Schliemann when he was talking about his excavation of Trojan treasure: 'What I found was clay, stones, shards.' No other band displayed such an innate connection between political militancy and aesthetic dissidence as Ton Steine Scherben. For example, the song 'Der Kampf geht weiter' [The Fight Goes On] became the soundtrack to a video, demanding that Horst Mahler, a radical left-wing lawyer, be released from prison. Whether 'Macht kaputt, was euch kaputt macht' [Destroy What Destroys You] was actually commissioned by a member of the RAF, as a persistent rumour would have it, has never been confirmed (neither has the RAF's opinion that the song was 'politically unusable'[6]). What is a fact, however, is that the band published a manifesto with the title 'Musik als Waffe' [Music as a Weapon][7] in the anarchist magazine, *Agit 883*, and they produced their first single 'Keine Macht für Niemand' [No Power for Anyone] themselves and distributed it via anarchist bookshops. This was, in itself, a revolutionary act; the first truly independent German labels would only appear at the end of the 1970s.

The greatest achievement of Ton Steine Scherben, however, is likely to be the invention of 'Kreuzberg'. Today, this Berlin quarter is probably one of the most widely known neighbourhoods in Germany, if not in Europe. A quarter with a distinct local identity: resistant, colourful, multi-cultural, and alternative. When Ton Steine Scherben was founded in 1967, the previously blue-collar neighbourhood of Kreuzberg was a no-name area. The subcultural life took place around the Freie Universität in Dahlem, and Savignyplatz in Charlottenburg, where the huge and cheap bourgeois apartments were located. Rio Reiser, the band's lead singer, later wrote in his memoirs that he ended up in Kreuzberg largely by coincidence. The factory floors you could rent there were the cheapest way to live, and 'rumour had it that there was still a true young proletariat, the kind you know from brochures'.[8] Cheap, and potentially this was where the revolution was going to take place: it was this image that would make Kreuzberg renowned worldwide.

Back then, the area was not only enclosed by the Wall on three sides. It very much looked as if it was doomed in other respects as well. The Berlin senate's redevelopment policy envisaged the demolition of the old housing, which was to be replaced by modern high-rise estates. However, in order to be able to demolish buildings street by street, the tenants had to be evicted through a lengthy, time-consuming process. This left many buildings vacant for quite some time, which outraged many who were looking for a place to live. It was the beginning of the squatters' movement that would keep West Berlin on edge until the early 1980s. Their fight was not just about housing. It also addressed the question: who owns the city? And: how do we want to live? This was the birthplace of the civil society in Berlin as we know it today. The residents of the inner city areas said: our vision of Berlin is different from that of the authorities. We won't go. We will fight back, and we will stay.

---

[6] Lessour, *Berlin Sampler*, (see n. 4), 188ff.

[7] Interestingly, Fela Kuti had a similar idea at the time in Lagos/Nigeria.

[8] Thomas Groß, *Berliner Barock* (Frankfurt am Main: Suhrkamp Verlag, 2000), 16.

The fact that such questions made their way into songs and that pop culture began to directly interfere in urban space was new – and nobody could do it better than Ton Steine Scherben. With lines such as 'the buildings belong to us', 'we'll win the final battle', or 'this is our house', they not only provided squatters with powerful slogans, they also introduced urban space as a subject of popular culture.

They did so most successfully with the 'Rauch-Haus-Song' [Rauch House Song]: 'Mariannenplatz was blue, there were so many cops there, / and Mensch Meier had to cry, probably from the tear gas. / And he asked somebody: "Tell me, is there a party here today?" / "Something like that," said someone else, "Bethanien is being occupied."'[9] The 'Bethanien' was the nurses' dormitory of a former hospital that now stood empty, and Georg von Rauch was an urban guerrilla killed in a shootout with the police in December 1971. Ton Steine Scherben not only sang about the occupation of the building, they were on the front lines of the action. The building was occupied only a few days after Rauch's death on 8 December 1971. The police tried to prevent this, and a street fight ensued, in which the squatters successfully defended the building – and, surprisingly, soon afterwards, they were offered a lease agreement.

What was new was not only that the seizing of urban space became a subject of pop culture, as mentioned before, but also that, in so doing, pop culture claimed to be more than just entertainment: it started to interfere with urban processes and to change the city. The reclaimed spaces were understood as an alternative world. As connected islands of a counterculture. It started here.

In fact, similar conflicts were taking place in all major West German cities. Urban planners were working on concepts of the car friendly city everywhere, they wanted to replace the old, run-down buildings with new apartment houses – all in the name of progress. The idea was met with resistance everywhere. There was nowhere, where this demolition plan could be fully carried out. The fact that much of the old housing has remained – and today these areas are the most sought-after quarters – is the result of a struggle that sometimes turned bloody.

In Berlin, a comparatively undercapitalised metropolis, these battles would have deeper, longer, and more complex effects than in other cities, because, in Berlin, it was no longer possible to imagine urban planning without the city's subculture. It was the sand in the gears of urban redevelopment. Sometimes, however, it also became the unintentional drive behind real estate prices, as an argument for the attractiveness of a location. In some lucky instances, subculture even became a site's developer.

—

As much as Berlin was, and is, the capital of the underground, there is another historical thread that cannot be ignored. Even though it hardly ever intersects with the history of alternative culture, it has played an important role in the development of Berlin's club culture: the history of the GI discos – the clubs for US soldiers who had been stationed in Berlin since the Second World War. This history started immediately after the war. The 298th US Army Band (with Chet Baker on trumpet) was one of the first units to enter Berlin. However, 'GI disco' is a fuzzy term, and at

[9] German original: 'Der Mariannenplatz war blau, so viele Bullen waren da / und Mensch Meier musste heulen, das war wohl das Tränengas. / Und er fragt irgendeinen: "Sag mal, ist hier heut 'n Fest?" / "So was Ähnliches", sacht einer, "das Bethanien wird besetzt."'

the beginning these clubs, usually officers clubs, were only located on barrack grounds.

Germans could go there too, if they exchanged Deutschmarks for US dollars. But everything was organised by the army and the bouncers were military policemen. It all changed quickly when the Germans realised there was a great deal of money to be made with US soldiers as clientele. Clubs predominantly aimed at US soldiers sprung up everywhere, and, for the first time in Germany, the music of black America was played: Jazz, Soul, Funk, Disco, and later, Hip-Hop and House. This music was one of the origins of today's club music, and it has a long tradition in Berlin: as the music of the GIs.

However, these clubs are interesting for more reasons than just their music: in a city with a predominantly German population, they were the first truly multi-cultural clubs. Not only because they were mainly oriented towards an African American clientele, but African Germans also liked to go there because the GI clubs were among the few places that they did not feel like a minority, where they did not stand out. Likewise, the children of the guest workers from Turkey, Spain, then Yugoslavia, Greece, and elsewhere, as well as the migrant children of the first generation, frequented the GI discos: African American music captured their feeling of belonging to a minority that is neither acknowledged nor respected by the majority. What Kreuzberg likes to claim for itself – being part of the colourful Republic of Germany, being tolerant and open to other cultures – was not just a claim in these clubs for the US occupation soldiers who were often insultingly labelled as 'imperialists' by the political left. It was a reality.

The 1986 bombing of West Berlin's La Belle disco put an end to all this. Three people were killed and the Libyan government under Muammar al-Gaddafi was suspected of carrying out the attack. Of course, there were other GI discos, until, in the early 1990s, large parts of the US army were withdrawn. But, after the La Belle bombing the clubs had lost their innocence, and the ease that had defined the interaction of different cultural groups vanished. Security measures were stepped up everywhere and many GIs stopped publicly mixing with Germans.

Anti-heroes in the walled-in city

When David Bowie moved to Berlin early in the summer of 1976, he was hoping to go into hiding. He was heavily addicted to drugs and had arrived from the blazing lights of Los Angeles, at the time probably the brightest city in the world for a popstar. He was looking for a gloomy place to regenerate. Today, it is hard to imagine that a superstar could rent a normal flat in Berlin and would be more or less left alone, for almost two years, to find the peace he was seeking. But that was what happened. Back then, Berlin was left behind in the global development of internationally successful pop, there was no notable scene to speak of. The city was still marked by the Second World War, even though the first glass and concrete high-rise buildings had been erected next to bomb sites.

Later, in an interview, Bowie would say that it had at times been difficult to differentiate 'between ghosts and the living'[10] in West Berlin. But he also went out: to Kreuzberg's artists' pubs, to the gay bars in Schöneberg, to Dschungel, a club he referenced in his melancholic 2013

[10] Tobias Rüther, *Helden: David Bowie und Berlin* (Berlin: Rogner & Bernhardt, 2008), 51.

Berlin song 'Where Are We Now?' But most of all, he rode around on his bicycle, went to museums, and painted. Berlin was not cool. At the end of the 1970s, it was by no means obvious whether the city had a pop-cultural presence at all. Bowie was hardly interested in the Berlin music scene. What mattered to him was the city's past: the Berlin Expressionists, 1920s subcultures, the megalomaniac delusions of the Nazis, and finding his peace.

At the end of the 1970s, West Berlin was a black hole into which you could vanish. The great ideological-political battles between the original Berliners and the mostly immigrated radical left were over. Nobody won, everybody lost. In February 1975, terrorists from the 2 June Movement kidnapped Peter Lorenz, the chairman of the Berlin branch of the party Christian Democratic Union (CDU). They wanted their comrades to be freed from prison. Lorenz was held captive in a Kreuzberg basement, and the police were unable to find him. Surprisingly, the kidnap was successful: five militants were flown to Yemen, and Lorenz was freed. However, in the fall of 1977, the confrontation between the Federal Republic of Germany and the Red Army Faction (RAF) ended tragically: banker Jürgen Ponto was shot and killed, as was industrialist Hanns Martin Schleyer. Three RAF terrorists presumably committed suicide in prison.

It was the beginning of the end of one of the greatest narratives in German politics. Yet, for West Berlin's alternative culture, the failure of their ideology of fundamentally changing the world paradoxically marked the beginning of a unique cultural boom. The aim was no longer to challenge and attack the political system; instead, from then onwards, people began searching for happiness by consciously carving out a niche.

The Tunix[11] convention, at the Technical University in January 1978, marked the beginning. Tunix was an immediate response to the dreary months of the so-called German Autumn with its RAF killings and killed: 'We've had enough!' read the call for the event. 'We're all taking off! … to the beach of Tunix'.[12] It was the beginning of the 'new social movements', between 5,000 to 20,000 people came, among them French philosopher and social theorist Michel Foucault who, during the congress, also went to Dschungel club – where he found himself, if only for a moment, standing next to David Bowie at the bar.[13]

No other place would have offered more favourable conditions for the Tunix ethos than the divided city of West Berlin. In 1971, the government had introduced the 'Berlin allowance', an additional tax-free eight per cent on top of people's gross salary for everyone working in Berlin. Additionally, West Berlin's economy was propped by both generous bank guarantees and compensation for reduced VAT. The abundant flow of money resulted in several huge corruption scandals. Like the city itself, Berlin's subculture was a swamp flower, as those who came to live there could do so without having to work much.

'West Berlin was "time off", a free space,' as Wolfgang Müller put it when looking back on the early 1980s.[14] As founder of the Punk band/art project Die Tödliche Doris, Müller was himself a part of the era. 'Freedom' and 'creative development' were the central values of those years. Most of the people who were a part of the scene lived in cheap backyard apartments with coal stoves, worked as little as possible, and mainly concerned themselves with exploring the free spaces the city had to offer;

[11] A colloquial translation would be the 'Do Nothing' conference.
[12] Cf: 'Treffen in Tunix', Wikipedia, Die freie Enzyklopädie, <https://de.wikipedia.org/wiki/Treffen_in_Tunix> accessed 13 September 2013.
[13] Rüther, *Helden: David Bowie und Berlin* (see n. 10), 116.
[14] Wolfgang Müller, *Subkultur Westberlin 1979–1989* (Hamburg: Philo Fine Arts, 2013), 45.

if you don't have any economic pressure, you have a great deal of time. A typical day went like this:

> *At some point, you left your flat and walked around from one place to the next. It wasn't uncommon, for one reason or another, to hang out in someone else's flat for six hours. From there, you would move on to the club, which would have just opened or was still open. Then you would move on again. Perhaps you would sleep for a while, either at your place or at someone else's who you'd just met. And it kept on like this all the time.*[15]

[15] Ibid.

The band Einstürzende Neubauten, whose guitarist Alexander von Borsig aka Alex Hacke told this story, were the most widely known band in this scene, the only one that would attain international fame. They are unique and, at the same time, deeply rooted in the history of Berlin's subcultures. Still today, lead singer Blixa Bargeld emphasises, in interviews, how important Ton Steine Scherben had been for him. With their uncompromising gesture of starting from scratch, with pure sounds, the Einstürzende Neubauten were clearly related to a band like Cluster. What makes them unique, however, is their radical and dark individualism, their rejection of any form of representation, even if it was these features that articulated the self-image of the whole scene.

Everywhere in the western world, subculture activists sought to become independent of the mainstream. 'Independence' was indeed the most important subcultural idea of the decade. More often than not, the term was used in connection to the question of how you could escape the power of large record companies and how you could maintain your artistic and individual integrity. This created the so-called 'indie scene', a network of independent record companies, distributors, booking agencies, and concert organisers. Much of that which characterises Berlin's subcultures today was organised in the West Berlin of the 1980s. Many of the then protagonists would also be influential personalities in the 1990s and 2000s. The whole idea of sustaining oneself with subcultural activities arose during those years. Mainly because people needed so little to make a living.

Mark Ernestus, founder of the record shop Hard Wax in the 1990s and part of the pioneering Techno project Basic Channel, designed Kumpelnest 3000 in 1987 as the graduation project for his art degree: a bar located in a former brothel; it still exists today. Dimitri Hegemann, who, after the Wall came down, opened Tresor, one of Europe's most important Techno clubs, organised the first Berlin Atonal Festival in 1982 which would become the major stylistic influence for the Industrial and Noise scene. The festival took place in SO 36, a club co-founded by painter Martin Kippenberger, who died in 1997 and is still one of the best-known German art stars.

However, the seemingly limitless freedom of Kreuzberg's parallel society also had a dark side: brutal lethargy. 'Berlin Sickness' is the term coined by some musicians, among them the Einstürzende Neubauten, who used the phrase for a 1981 German tour. The term referred to a particular attitude towards life: 'The essence of this attitude was that you would be completely unable to sort out your life. You would hang about somewhere with dirty fingernails and no money, hoping that someone would come along with a joint'[16], Techno club owner Johnnie Stieler later criticised. Stieler grew up in East Berlin and was only confronted with the habits of West Berlin's scene after the Wall had come down.

The film version of the 1981 book, *Christiane F. – Wir Kinder vom Bahnhof Zoo* [Christiane F. – We Children from Bahnhof Zoo], narrates the story of a young girl who is addicted to drugs and prostitutes herself in the streets around the Zoologischer Garten to finance her addiction. The film drew a mass audience and quickly acquired cult status with its iconic representation of the image of Berlin. Interestingly enough, 'Helden', the German version of David Bowie's world hit 'Heroes', which he had penned a few years earlier in Berlin, became the film's signature song. The song is actually about a couple that kiss in front of the Berlin Wall. The film transformed the song's meaning: teetering on the brink of the abyss became the great heroic Berlin act.[17]

Kreuzberg of the 1980s was also a village in the shadow of the Wall, much like the rest of the city. When the US president Ronald Reagan visited the city in 1987, the fear of protests was so huge that the area was completely fenced off and separated from the rest of the city by a police cordon. The then mayor called the protesters 'anti-Berliners'. Being provincial in a different way, the city's petit bourgeois quarters entrenched themselves in their identity as frontline fighters against the socialist GDR surrounding their city. 'There was no exchange between the literary-academic circles, the bourgeois audience, and the different political parts of the public during the times of West Berlin,' states the philosopher Martin Bauer in retrospect.[18] 'The West-Berlin milieus were spared the civilising imposition to discuss aesthetic judgments of taste, political opinions and differences in lifestyle via the medium of argument.' Therefore, 'the narcissisms of the smallest differences were able to develop freely. Twisted perceptions of reality were the products of such neglect. Not cosmopolitan tolerance but petit bourgeois indifference was what organised the neighbourhoods.'

Interestingly enough, the development in the eastern part of the city was quite similar. Until late into the 1970s, each and every subcultural expression was relentlessly prosecuted. The GDR saw pop culture as a powerful agent of US imperialism. This started to change from the end of the 1970s. Although East Berlin's subculture was entirely infiltrated by Stasi agents who knew about almost all meetings, the feeling within the scene was a different one: they shut themselves off from the GDR society, they believed to be among themselves and tried to ignore the state. Punk bands formed, breakdance groups were set up, the artists' and poets' scene in Berlin's Prenzlauer Berg area developed.

Here too, civil society was formed in the fight against the demolition of housing stock. Here too, entire streets were left to fall into disrepair because the plan was to demolish the buildings and replace them with large modern structures. Here too, this created problems, which the authorities were not able to control, just like in Kreuzberg fifteen years earlier. Here too, squatting was the answer. Initially, only flats were squatted, but after the end of the GDR, entire blocks of buildings became squats too. Moreover, there was something else that united the subcultures in West and East Berlin: dance music – seen as flat, commercial entertainment – was unwelcome.

[16] Alexander Hacke, in Max Dax and Robert Defcon, *Nur was nicht ist ist möglich – Die Geschichte der Einstürzenden Neubauten* (Berlin: Bosworth, 2006), 49.
[17] Felix Denk and Sven von Thülen, *Der Klang der Familie – Berlin, Techno und die Wende* (Berlin: Suhrkamp, 2012), 136.
[18] Martin Bauer, 'Durchgangsstation, endgültig', *Berliner Zeitung*, 16 March 2001.

However, the explosion of Techno music after the fall of the Wall only appeared to come from nowhere. The protagonists were there when the Wall was standing, even if there were only a few of them and they were almost invisible. The exception: DJ Westbam. During his club nights at Metropol, a large club near Nollendorfplatz in Schöneberg, starting in the mid-1980s, he began to mix Italo Disco with the American Hi-NRG records – and a short time later, took on music production himself. Interestingly enough, his first parties took place at the Ex'n'Pop, a bar where Blixa Bargeld, singer of Einstürzende Neubauten, had once worked.

But the true breeding ground of the Techno scene was elsewhere: Ufo. A small basement hole where the DJs and producers who would soon define the sound of Berlin partied together. There were not many of them. When, in 1989, the first procession with Techno, the Loveparade, marched along Ku'damm, only a few dozen people joined in. It must have been an unsettling sight: gaudy maniacs dancing in the street, following a van. The slogan 'Friede, Freude, Eierkuchen' [Peace, Joy, Pancakes] was meant to provoke both the well-off West Berlin audience and the guardians of Kreuzberg's subculture. Nothing could have been further removed from their dark neo-existentialist stance than this horde of colourful nutters.

Four and a half months later, the Wall came down.

Once again, music activist Dimitri Hegemann responded with typical Kreuzberg lethargy. His office, a messy storefront, was located in a former shop on Köpenicker Straße, not far from the checkpoint at Heinrich-Heine-Straße. When the first East-German Trabbie cars rolled into the western part of town with honking horns and hundreds of East Berliners jubilantly flocked into Kreuzberg, he briefly went out into the street, rubbed his eyes, went back into his office, and laid down on the sofa to sleep. The idea that a historical event would take place in the present, not in the past, and that this event would affect everybody's life was not part of the worldview of a 1980s Kreuzberg hipster.

Berlin, open city

Nobody anticipated the fall of the Wall. Neither the GDR regime, nor the Soviet leaders, neither the Americans, nor the West German government. It was one of the twentieth century's major strokes of good fortune; without any bloodshed, the GDR simply collapsed. Since no one anticipated it, there were no plans as to how to deal with the new situation. People had to improvise, and that is one thing subculture activists have always been better at than the authorities. Just as East Berliners flocked into West Berlin to marvel at the glittering shops, there was a similar movement in the other direction. Hundreds of artists, squatters, students, and other people headed to East Berlin where they found inner-city neighbourhoods with entire streets that were abandoned – and East Berliners who had already begun to squat in flats and buildings.

When, shortly before the official reunification, the GDR introduced the West German D-Mark, East German industry began to collapse – mostly because it had been subsidized by the state for years and, with production costs that were too high and often out of date technology, produced only a few competitive products. This meant that there were now not only abandoned houses but also abandoned factory buildings. What made the situation even more complicated was that many of the plots of land originally belonged to Jewish citizens who had been expropriated by the Nazis. During the GDR era ownership had changed yet again. The reunification treaty included the principle of 'return overcompensation', and the heirs of the former Jewish owners were to be given back their property. This was complicated and took a long time. It was an exceptional situation in world history where a major city of a leading industrial nation had to make do with a total and complex stopgap solution. For the Berlin subculture, this was a dream come true.

From the fall of the Wall until the mid-1990s, East Berlin was one large adventurous playground – at least for those who took advantage of the situation. There are many reasons for the fact that, in retrospect, Techno seemed to have been the soundtrack of those years, even if the real nightlife of that era was different. Yes, Techno and House were played everywhere. But there was also Reggae, Hip-Hop, Ska, Punk, and Easy Listening. If there was a predominant aesthetic, then it had at least as much to do with the flea market eclecticism of many DJs as with the 'machines in ruins' aesthetic of Techno.

But the reason why the music with the straight four-to-the-floor beat has remained and become a feature of Berlin's identity, while all the other styles disappeared after a short while, is likely to be the power with which this predominantly lyrics-free genre lent itself as the sound of a new beginning. In the years after the Wall had come down, this music seemed to be just as unmarked as the city itself. In retrospect, we could trace back many different lines that point to the time before the fall of the Wall. However, back then, everything felt exciting and new.

For a Berliner, it is almost impossible to imagine the peculiar life of East Berlin's bohemia at the beginning of the 1990s. Renting a flat was extremely cheap, there were – in the middle of the industrial nation Germany – no telephones, next to each door there was a little roll of paper where you could leave messages if you wanted to meet up with others. Most flats were still at a post-war standard with coal ovens for heating and single glazed windows, despite the very cold Berlin winters. Most of the furniture was found on the streets, as East German neighbours bought new furniture and threw the old stuff away. Many buildings were empty and inspected by squatters. It was not unusual to break into those buildings, change the locks, and open an improvised bar in the rooms you liked. Those bars were really everywhere, and each weekend hundreds of people would wander through the streets and backyards in search of new venues. Often, these bars would only exist for a few weeks. If those who ran those places got bored, they went looking for another place.

Both E-Werk and Tresor, the two most important Techno clubs in the 1990s, came about in this way. E-Werk was a former power station; Tresor was located in the vault rooms of the former Wertheim department store, the building itself having been erased by Second World War bombs. The club WMF, named after the building of the Württembergische Metallwarenfabrik, changed location eight times within fifteen years. However, the large clubs were only the most visible ones. The whole city centre, an area of Berlin which had once been vibrant during the 1920s, but had become a gigantic building site, was more alive during the night than during daytime. All the city's hedonists got their chance; nobody asked for a permit or for approval by the building inspection authorities. You only had to seize the space (and maybe found an association for the support of the arts and then declare each party to be an event organised by the association).

It was a party that stood in strange contrast to reunification in the rest of Germany, which was predominantly a triumph of the West German capitalist system over the socialist East, as well as a sell-out of the East to the West. A different lifestyle characterised Berlin's inner-city areas. 'The state that has established itself in the interim period between the two systems is close to what utopians in the nineteenth century described as anarchism,' stated journalist Ulrich Gutmair, 'an order that seems to function almost without governance'.[19] Temporary autonomous zones were created in everyday life. These spaces opened up for a while, new situations unfolded and were soon gone again. Nothing remained as it was, everything was transient, and that's what defined the beauty of those years.

It soon became clear that the fleeting nature of the moment was not all advantages. 'While some slept until the next party started, the very person you had just danced all night with might be buying the building in which the party had taken place' remembers Natascha Sadr Haghighian.[20] After the fall of the Wall, driven by the hope that Berlin would soon play a part in the big concert of the world's metropolises, many property developers were keen to grab East Berlin land. Driven by tax write-offs and the decision to reinstate Berlin as Germany's capital, prices began to soar. However, redeveloping the city took longer than originally thought. The property situation was so complicated that it often took authorities years to find out which part of land belonged to whom. Fifty years after the war, it was difficult to track down heirs who were often spread over several continents.

In retrospect, it seems almost inevitable that the concept of interim use [Zwischennutzung] emerged. This meant the temporary letting of unused rooms to interested parties, often from the cultural sector. In reality, however, the emergence of this idea was rather a happy coincidence: The right woman held the right chair at the housing association in Mitte, which managed most of the property. Her name is Jutta Weitz, she was one of the officials in charge of commercial property – and one of the central figures in the East Berlin of the 1990s. Weitz liked the hedonists with their often strange ideas, and she started to rent them spaces on a temporary basis. The consequence of this was that even when squatting was no longer possible, it was still possible to get spaces in East Berlin without being able to provide a detailed business plan. Galleries, clubs, bars, studios, and all sorts of strange mixtures of these forms sprang up. It was a time of great cultural boom that took place, without much attention in the media.

However, East Berlin's subculture was not invisible, and the rise and fall of Rave and Techno as the first unified German pop-cultural movement got a large public response. On a very superficial level, this response can be seen in the visitor numbers of the Loveparade. About 150 people

[19] Ulrich Gutmair, *Die ersten Tage von Berlin: Der Sound der Wende* (Stuttgart: Tropen, 2014), 17.

[20] Ulrich Gutmair, *Die ersten Tage von Berlin: Der Sound der Wende* (see n. 19), 181.

came to the first parade in 1989. In 1990, this number rose to 2,000. From then on, the numbers more than doubled each year until it was said to have reached over one million in 1997. This figure is probably too high, as were the figures given for the following years, which were, again and again, said to be over a million. From 2001, the numbers decreased, and in 2003, the Parade took place in Berlin for the last time. It is the almost classic story of youth culture: from the darkness of a basement into the limelight of the charts – and then down into the dust of oblivion.

For a while, those who wanted to, were able to earn a lot of money with electronic music. The movement grew, and many believed that it would go on like this forever, that this music would know no boundaries. Friendships fell apart over the question of whether you wanted to remain in the underground or whether you wanted to enter the charts. For the first time in Berlin, these questions were no longer theoretical; there was a way out of the Berlin clubs and into the charts. Westbam and Marusha became popstars. Yet, the growth wasn't sustainable. In pop culture, the same laws of social movements applied as everywhere else, and for those who have profited from growth for years, who live on the beauty of growing, stagnation is death. Techno, it seemed, was over at the end of the 1990s.

The Rave bubble burst at roughly the same time as the property bubble. The German government indeed moved to Berlin as planned; the city became a major German city again. But instead of a big boom, a depression set in. When Berlin subsidies were cancelled, the city's remaining industry collapsed and no new companies came to fill the gap, at least not in sufficient numbers. At the end of the 1990s, the city was left with tremendous debts, a decreasing population and grave social problems. The buzzword *Clubsterben* [the death of clubs] appeared for the first time. It had become more difficult to find new venues. Many subculture activists began to realise that their actions had taken place in an utterly exceptional situation in world history – and the fear of conditions becoming normal, took hold.

Decreasingly poor, still sexy

If you walk through the streets of Berlin Mitte today, you will be surprised at how little has remained from the exciting subculture after the fall of the Wall. Basically nothing. Subcultures are always temporary. However, the fact that hardly a gallery, no clubs, and no bars have survived is quite surprising indeed. Gone are the no-name, open-air bars in backyards, often simply named after the days of the week on which they were open: Monday bar, Tuesday bar, Wednesday bar. Gone are all the basements, barracks, factory halls, and other venues where you would sit together at night, drinking, talking, and dancing. Many of the buildings are still there, but nothing about them is reminiscent of those wild years, which are nothing but an episode in the long life of those buildings – just like the Kaiserreich, the war, and socialism. However, what is even more surprising is that this disappearance has not done any damage to the city's attractiveness. Berlin is still the European capital of subculture and dance music, even more so than in the 1990s. The streets are full of young people who have come to Berlin because of this reputation. What has happened here?

In fact, the economic collapse of the post-reunification boom at the end of the 1990s was a godsend for the subcultures. The fact that investors ran out of money also meant that the remaining inner-city wastelands – of which there were many at the time – were not built over. The fact that the population was still decreasing, although there was a flood of redeveloped flats coming onto the market, meant that, for some years, rental fees and property prices not only stagnated but actually went down. The city became cheaper at the turn of the millennium and the fact that Techno, as mainstream spectacle, had disappeared meant that music could retreat into the darkness of the niche in order to renew itself – only that all the protagonists had become a little cleverer through the experiences of the 1990s.

Berlin's rise to become the hipster capital would not have been possible without the deep crisis the city went through around the turn of the millennium. At the beginning of the 2000s, Berlin was the metropolis of bankruptcy, a city in which nothing worked, at least nothing which was initiated by politicians and investors. When, in 2006, the Bayer group bought the Berlin-based Schering AG, the city lost its only company listed in Germany's main share index, DAX. Berlin remains to be neither a financial centre nor a centre of mechanical engineering; no automotive brand has its headquarters in Berlin, no computer company, and no chemical company. At the beginning of the 2000s, it very much looked as if this would never change.

Two developments that are completely unrelated to Berlin would mark the beginning of the city's renaissance. First of all, the liberalisation of the European flight sector, which from the end of the 1990s allowed cheap city trips. It would take some time until Europe's dance-crazed youth noticed what possibilities this entailed. This changed at the beginning of the 2000s when increasingly greater numbers of ravers started to come flying into Berlin. All of a sudden, you could hear all sorts of languages being spoken in the queues in front of the city's clubs. The 'Easyjetset' was created, named after the low-cost airline.

Furthermore, the subcultures networked over the internet, again something new. No scene was quicker in doing so than the electronic music scene. Soon people in Italy's Bologna or Toronto, Canada would be better informed about the programmes of Berlin's clubs than those living in the German capital. You only had to want to know. How important this internationalisation would be for the scene became obvious in March 2010 when the Icelandic volcano Eyjafjallajökull erupted and paralysed the whole European air travel. On that weekend, all of Berlin's clubs were only half full at best. People simply couldn't come.

In the 1990s, it was the alliance of East German ravers from Berlin's suburbs, the gay community, and the creative scenes that shaped Berlin's nightlife. In the 2000s, the tourists joined them as a fourth group on an equal footing. Additionally, around the river Spree, at the border between the neighbourhoods of Kreuzberg and Friedrichshain, a new club mile was forming. In the 1990s, the clubs were located in the city centre, which was no longer possible, all free spaces there had been taken by companies, institutions and newly arrived state agencies. Hence clubs moved to the Spree area. Interestingly enough, this was also an area the Senate had earmarked for building offices. A plan that would be met with resistance. This culminated in summer 2008, in a regional referendum, in which the majority of the population decided against the plans for the so-called 'Media Spree', the senate's large-scale development programme.

This referendum marked the beginning of a significant cross-milieu debate, which the city of Berlin has been having ever since, and in which the big questions are being discussed: How do we want to live? Who owns the city? Which role does culture play? Which role does money play? Can we avoid displacing the poor? The Berlin clubs and the corresponding subcultures play a central and contradictory role in this debate. On the one hand, the operators of clubs themselves are investors who upgrade the district in question. On the other hand, they stand for a different form of urban development, for the promise of emancipation that forms the core of all subcultures.

The discussions have become more urgent because, since 2008, in the wake of the worldwide credit crunch, property prices in Berlin have soared. A lot of money was moved at the time, on the hunt for investment opportunities. The cheap and obviously undervalued Berlin property market seemed, and still seems, to be a lucrative target. This was a new development, unfolding with the relentlessness of a threat. The impression was that Berlin, the subcultural paradise, seemed to want to oust the very hedonists who had turned it into a sought-after place in the first place and get them to move to the suburbs.

But this was, and is, mainly just a fear. In fact, cultural life in Berlin is as dynamic and vital as it has always been. There are more clubs than ever before, more artists and musicians live in the city today, with more arriving constantly. Furthermore, club owners and party organisers have learned their lessons from the 1990s and are now focusing on sustainability. The era of temporary clubs that would move from one location to the next is over. Berghain and Bar25, the two trendsetting clubs of the last ten years, operate in different ways and have become permanent institutions. Berghain operators have bought the building, and although the Bar25 operators had to vacate the area because the soil was contaminated and had to be cleaned up, they were successful in finding investors for a risky project to build a new neighbourhood on the site, which enabled them to buy the property. Tresor has redeveloped a huge old power plant, and other clubs have secured long-term leases.

This is something new: a subculture that understands itself as a player in urban development. Of course, this has to do with the self-confidence resulting from the economic success of this former sub-culture. Where there is money, there is power. However, this is also the preliminary end of a particular Berlin model of subculture, whose strengths has always been a certain kind of tunnel vision. The truly interesting artistic developments were created in the dark and felt most at home there too. A darkness in which one preferred to remain, among like-minded people. After all, the city was big enough to avoid each other, unlike other German cities where, like it or not, you would find yourself confronting each other in the same bars at night.

Now the subcultures are beginning to account for themselves. It is also their activists who drive the discussions on what kind of city Berlin actually is and wants to become. The fact that the Senate has abandoned its practice of selling land simply to those who offer the most money, and, since 2012, has also been taking into account social and cultural aspects, is the first positive result from this development. How far subcultures will actually remain subcultures in these situations, remains to be seen.

Bibliography

Dax, Max, and Defcon, Robert, *Nur was nicht ist ist möglich – Die Geschichte der Einstürzenden Neubauten* (Berlin: Bosworth, 2006).

Denk, Felix, and von Thülen, Sven, *Der Klang Der Familie – Berlin, Techno und die Wende* (Berlin: Suhrkamp, 2012).

Groß, Thomas, *Berliner Barock* (Frankfurt am Main: Suhrkamp Verlag, 2000).

Gutmair, Ulrich, *Die ersten Tage von Berlin: Der Sound der Wende* (Stuttgart: Tropen, 2014).

Lessour, Théo, *Berlin Sampler* (Berlin: Ohlendorff Verlag, 2012).

Müller, Wolfgang, *Subkultur Westberlin 1979–1989* (Hamburg: Philo Fine Arts, 2013).

Pynchon, Thomas, *Die Enden der Parabel* (Reinbek: Rowohlt, 1981).

Rüther, Tobias, *Helden: David Bowie und Berlin* (Berlin: Rogner & Bernhardt, 2008).

MacScene de la Gucci performing at E-Werk, Berlin, 1996, photo: Tilman Brembs

Last evening at galerie berlintokyo, from the series *Temporary Spaces*, Berlin, 1999, photo: Martin Eberle

Tresor, from the series *Temporary Spaces*, Berlin, 1996, photo: Martin Eberle

E-Werk, from the series *Temporary Spaces*, Berlin, 1996, photo: Martin Eberle

Kunst + Technik, Berlin Mitte, from the series *Phantom Clubs Berlin*, Berlin, 1997, photo: Nina Fischer & Maroan el Sani

berlintokyo, Berlin Mitte, from the series *Phantom Clubs Berlin*, Berlin, 1997, photo: Nina Fischer & Maroan el Sani

Sniper, Berlin Mitte, from the series *Phantom Clubs Berlin*, Berlin, 1998, photo: Nina Fischer & Maroan el Sani

Sexyland, Berlin Mitte, from the series *Phantom Clubs Berlin*, Berlin, 1997, photo: Nina Fischer & Maroan el Sani

Jeans Team, concert at Sniper, from the series *Temporary Spaces*, Berlin, 1997, photo: Martin Eberle

LUANDA

MUSIC/POLITICS
Hums and Buzzes
From Semba to Kuduro
Marissa J. Moorman

▶ P.337

SPACES/POLITICS
Movements on a Map of Sounds
Luanda's Dual Urban Matrix
Ângela Mingas

▶ P.359

Hums and Buzzes – From Semba to Kuduro
Marissa J. Moorman

Luanda today hums and buzzes with tractors and construction cranes, the zip of motorbikes punctuating the pulsations of stop-and-go traffic, and the call of the cobrador [collector] on the candongueiros, the ubiquitous blue and white collective taxis that ply the city's streets: 'Mutamba! Mutamba! Mutamba!' for those candongueiros heading to the old city's transport hub, Mutamba Square, and 'São Paulo! São Paulo! São Paulo!' for those heading back to the musseques [Luanda's informal neighbourhoods][1] from downtown. Transport, sound, space, and circulation intimately linked. Issued on foot, the sometimes shrill cry of 'peixe espaaaaaaaaadah!' by the peixeira, Luanda's ambulant female fish vendors, slices the morning air and competes with the familiar voices of the morning news speaking formal Portuguese on car radios and on the transistors of security guards, arrayed outside the homes of the wealthy and local businesses. A Chinese street vendor approaches from the distance and the sound of a battery-operated loudspeaker announces his wares well ahead of him: 'Mata barata! Mata barata! Mata barata!', the recorded drone of a roach poison for sale. Out of this contemporary soundscape, the local Hip-Hop breakbeat variation, Kuduro, blasts from the candongueiros, spontaneously combusting in street side dance-offs, mimicking the frenetic vertical growth of the city and challenging horizontal civic camaraderie of its inhabitants.

Kuduro put Angolan music on the international stage and on the global music map, where it circulates as 'ghetto tech'. Its propulsive beat, deconstructive choreography, and playful sartorial style grabs the audience's attention anywhere it travels. Music videos showcase Luanda, Angola's capital, with both its musseques and its shiny new downtown. Artist, Cabo Snoop, with his sweet smile, skinny candy-coloured jeans, cartoon-emblazoned T-shirts, and

---

[1] Musseques have been a part of the city since at least the eighteenth century. The word comes from the Kimbundu word 'mu-seke' meaning in the 'sandy places'. It referred, at first, to areas of the city that the asphalt did not reach. Musseques have existed in the heart of the city since the eighteenth century. Until the mid-1940s musseques continued to be enmeshed with downtown neighborhoods but by the 1960s only a handful of African elites lived in the baixa neighborhoods of Ingombotas, Bungo, and Coqueiros and the musseques were pushed out to the urban periphery. Thus, by the mid-twentieth century a series of oppositions shaped local discourse and urban geography: asphalt/sand; baixa (downtown)/musseque; white city/black city. Musseques described the socio-economic, racial, and cultural divisions of the city.

rubber band legs won the Best Lusophone artist award at the MTV Africa Music Awards with the hit 'Windeck' in 2010. Titica, Angola's, and perhaps Africa's, first transgender star, became a hit in 2011 with her long locks, breast-lifting moves, and come-hither gaze. Both globetrotted with the show Os Kuduristas, promoted by one of the Angolan President's sons, Coréon Dú, himself a musician.[2] This is music by and for the young.

Even as it travels the world, Kuduro is indelibly Luandan. Twenty-seven years of civil war, following fourteen years of an anti-colonial war, produced urban decline in, and mass migration to, Luanda. A city built for little more than a quarter million suddenly held an estimated four to five million residents. Infrastructure maintenance lagged behind. Extensions to water, electricity, and education? Simply out of the question. Kuduro emerged out of this and often provided alternative structures – psychic and material – of managing urban life. Kuduro means 'in a hard place' or 'hard ass'. It takes a locative ku [in, or at] from the local language Kimbundu and adds it to the Portuguese word for 'hard'. Or it gives an alternative spelling to the Portuguese word cu [ass] and squeezes out the hyphen, occupies the space, just like immigrants to the city have built homes on what used to be rooftop terraces and turned custodial closets into sleeping spaces.

When the civil war ended in 2002, Luanda entered a boom of construction as windfall profits from the oil industry hit the ground in bricks and mortar. High-speed growth channelled to elites marginalised the bulk of the urban population. Kuduro once represented the voice of the dispossessed (in the civil war years). Even though it grew out of downtown discotheques in the late 1990s, it took hold in the musseques. Today, the biggest artists no longer produce in musseque studios but with downtown production companies tied to the political elite.

The sound of Kuduro is still relatively new. Largely produced on computers

---

2   See their website Os Kuduristas <www.oskuduristas.com> accessed 24 March 2014.

with the FruityLoops programme in home-based studios in the musseques, this music could not have been produced thirty years ago. But much about this music is not so new. The roots of Cabo Snoop's and Titica's styles – cutting edge dress and dance, crossing borders (to the Congo, and beyond, for inspiration), and even Titica's transgender play – reach back into Luanda's musical past. So does the development from this musical genre as a political outsider to a political insider. The cross-class appeal of the music and its provision of social mobility echo musical genres of earlier periods. The links between transport, space, sound, and circulation have always been the dynamic kernel at the centre of Angola's urban music.[3] To trace this movement, let's hit the streets of the musseques and baixa [downtown], places not far from Mutamba Square (where the nineteenth century City Hall presides from a hill across from the 1960s glass block of the Ministry of Finance, separated by a busy vein of transport), between the 1960s and the 2000s.

Semba in the colonial city

If we wandered through the late colonial city (the first Portuguese arrived in the late 1400s and Angola had been under erratic Portuguese occupation since the early 1500s) what would it look and sound like? The baixa had all the trappings of a European, colonial coastal enclave with new high-rises that shot up along the palm-lined seaside promenade of the Marginal, thanks to the coffee boom of the 1950s. Portuguese settlers dominated this space and Africans worked here mainly in a service capacity, even if that had not always been the case in Luanda's history. Sidewalk cafés served bicas [espressos] and fancy pastries to the employees of downtown businesses at the end of the day and children leaving school. Passing by the offices of the newspaper *Diário de Luanda* [Luanda Daily] the smell of ink wafted from the printing presses. At night, neon signs set the zone aglow.

[3] To find out more about the movements and circulations in the urban space of Luanda please read Ângela Mingas' text in this book.

Pushed out to the city's margins, the musseques housed the city's African residents: those newly arrived from the country's central and urban denizens, which have a longer, multi-generational tenure. In the musseques, the cry of roosters, children playing, cheers from pick-up football games in the streets, and the sounds of daily life emanated from quintals [enclosed backyard space]: washing, brooms sweeping fallen leaves or ash from the night's fire, the scratch of uncooked beans being sorted in metal pans, and women singing to themselves as they worked. Occasionally, a car would trundle by. Or police trucks would thunder through raising dust and spreading fear. By the 1960s, at the end of the workday, the sound of the radio could be heard slipping out an open window or over a quintal wall. Listeners preferred the programme *Tondoya Mukina ó Kizomba* [There's a Party in Our House], broadcasted by Sebastião Coelho, the son of Portuguese settlers and an emigrant from Nova Lisboa (today Huambo) in the south, a champion of the local, popular urban music, Semba.[4]

Luandans celebrated yearly carnaval, carnivals according to the Lenten calendar (a 300-year tradition by the 1960s).[5] Amid the clamour of the anti-colonial war, the Portuguese, nervous about large gatherings and boisterousness, banned carnaval in 1961 for seven years. But carnaval dance groups and the musical groups that support them, are derived from broad social and cultural networks that outlast the whims of state policy. In fact, the Semba bands of the 1960s emerged from groups called turmas. When young men would return from work – and work opportunities increased with the reforms after 1961 as international investment in the Angolan economy spiked – they would gather in small groups in musseque quintals to play music together. Neighbours or relatives (cousins, or uncles) would appear, and sometimes friends from more distant musseques would show up too. At times, these informal groups coalesced into or out of the percussion sections of carnaval groups, outlasting that

[4] Sebastião Coelho, *História da Comunicação em Angola* (Luanda: Executive Center, 1999), 196–198, 203; Marissa Moorman, *Intonations – A Social History of Music and Nation in Luanda, Angola, from 1945 to Recent Times* (Athens: Ohio University Press, 2008), 157.

[5] David Birmingham, 'Carnival at Luanda', *Journal of African History* 29 (1), (1988), 93–103. The typical dances and music of carnival are: Varina/Semba (not the same as the popular urban music but an influence on it), Kazacuta, and Cidrália.

annual event. In these sessions and spaces, at night and on weekends, younger men would learn from older men, picking up a guitar, a drum, or a dikanza [a scratcher, like the Brazilian reco-reco]. They played at family gatherings – birthdays, baptisms, and the odd anniversary.

One or another band existed in the 1940s and 1950s. No one could forget the legendary Ngola Ritmos, the band by Aniceto 'Liceu' Vieira Dias and the others. They were nearly booed off the stage of the Cine Restauração in the baixa when they performed in folkloric dress and sung in Kimbundu for a Portuguese audience. Hard to imagine a greater irony since all of them spoke fluent Portuguese and worked as civil servants in various colonial offices and ministries in the downtown. But as soon as they started singing the Portuguese classic 'Maria Vai a Fonte', even in their African beads and fabrics, the audience loved them. Ah, colonial arrogance and small-mindedness (and they deemed Africans provincialized children). But underneath that quaint exterior, a few members of the band became involved in nationalist organisations. Sung in Kimbundu that music had a message and the message was 'wake up!'

The band combined European instruments like guitars with the Angolan dikanza, hungu [a gourd resonator, the berimbau in Brazil], and hand drums. Band leader, Liceu, had travelled the country with his father, a civil servant, collecting local rhythms and transferred their notation to guitar chords, creating the base of Semba. Being an avid listener of Brazilian Samba, he imagined a similar transposition: producing the alchemy between the urban and the rural, the African and the European. This did not simply mean the reproduction or borrowing of the sounds of Samba but it entailed a transatlantic feedback loop. Samba is, itself, imbued with rhythms, melodies, and movements re-imagined in South America by African and Afro-descended people enslaved and forcibly taken across the South Atlantic from West Central Africa (especially Angola's interior) and West Africa (namely, the Bight of Benin).[6]

6   See the Transatlantic Slave Trade: database, www.slavevoyages.org, accessed 24 March 2014.

Liceu and some other band members campaigned for Angolan Independence in small, underground cells that distributed pamphlets with anti-colonial messages. Informants exposed the activities and members of these groups which led to the imprisonment of Liceu and another band member in 1959 in the infamous case of the 'Processo de 50', where the state arrested, tried, and jailed fifty individuals, Angolan and Portuguese. Another sweep led to the arrest and imprisonment of yet another band member in 1960. State repression made political organising and expression unwelcome. Discontent percolated.

—

In 1961 three rebellions exploded in Angola. The Portuguese responded with extreme violence. The war was on. Nationalist organisations, inside and outside of the country, took on a formal character in two exiled nationalist movements: the Popular Movement for the Liberation of Angola (MPLA) and the National Front for the Liberation of Angola (FNLA), located in the neighbouring Congos.[7] Inside Angola, the reformist mode of war infiltrated urban life and the music scene. More money circulated; a consequence of reforms instituted by the colonial government. Young musicians, not wealthy by any means, could afford to purchase instruments on layaway in downtown shops. Reforms promoted 'bread and circuses'. Far from being booed off the stage, the state radio, small private radio stations, and local businesses encouraged local forms of music, and Semba flourished. Local entrepreneurs opened recreational clubs throughout the musseques so that turmas transformed into more permanent bands, and the quintals and backyard parties departed and were replaced by gigs at clubs.

In the early 1960s, electric guitars and guitar solos, inspired by the Congo's legendary Franco and his band OK Jazz (and other stars of Congo's music hall like Wendo Kolosoy and Dr. Nico), began to be featured in bands. Eduardo

[7] A third movement, National Union for the Total Independence of Angola (UNITA), joined the struggle in 1966.

'Dúia' Garcia Adolfo, guitarist of the band Os Gingas, is credited for introducing the guitar solo to Angola.[8] However, Dúia introduced much more than an imitation of Congolese guitar solos. He left his imprint and a legacy on the Semba bands that emerged during this period and after. Drawing deeply from a cosmopolitan set of sounds that included the music of Ngola Ritmos, Cape Verdean Coladeiras (a dance for pairs) and Mornas (slower, mournful songs; quite a few Cape Verdeans worked in Angola and lived or partied in the musseques and some musicians remember learning guitar from them), American Soul, Brazilian Sambas, Latin American Merengues and Plenas, and Congolese Rumba.

Local DJs, like Manuel Faria, who later opened the club Kudissanga Kwa Makamba [Meeting of Friends], spun this sort of music on vinyl at quintal parties in the musseques in the 1950s. As long as the car battery hooked up to the record player kept running, these sounds saturated musseque nights.[9] Dúia took the noises that circulated throughout the musseque and mixed them with locally produced sounds. He further spiced the mix Ngola Ritmos had made. The Gingas did not last but Dúia's mark did. Mário 'Marito' Arcanjo liked Dúia's sound and studied with him. Marito's guitar was the glue for Os Kiezos. Zé Keno of Jovens do Prenda studied at Marito's knee, although Zé Keno insists that his style is all his own.[10] Carlitos Vieira Dias (Liceu's son) joined the Gingas before they disbanded. To this day, he is one of the most respected, and most humble Angolan guitar masters.

What did Semba sound like? The genre includes the music of Ngola Ritmos and that of Jovens do Prenda and more recently Paulo Flores. The embracing of a half-century causes elasticity in a genre. Angolans deploy the term as a catchall phrase to describe the urban popular music that developed in the 1960s and 1970s – unleashed by Ngola Ritmos, electrified by Dúia, and consolidated by Jovens do Prenda and Os Kiezos. It draws on the musical practices

---

8 José Weza, *O Percurso Histórico da Música Urbana Luandense: Subsídios par a história da música angolana* (Luanda: Ensaio, 2007), 61–2.
9 Moorman, *Intonations* (see n. 4), 120, 161.
10 From interview by Samy Ben Redjeb with Zé Keno, in the booklet of the compilation: *Angola Soundtrack: The Unique Sound of Luanda 1968–1976*, Analog Africa no. 9, liner notes, 14 (Analog Africa 2010).

of rural areas with Kimbundu lyrics and the inclusion of local instruments as well as their transposition to European practices. The Semba rhythm anchors music, although it can be played faster or slower. With an ineluctable tropical lilt, a cross rhythm builds a productive tension that sets couples twirling on dance floors and in quintals.

Musseques housed urban nightlife. The band Os Kiezos [The Brooms] took its name from an occurrence where, at one party they played in the Rangel musseque, they made people dance so vigorously that it raised the dust in the quintal. By the 1970s, no longer dismissive of the new urban sounds, Portuguese immigrants and official state visitors headed to the musseques for a night of entertainment. In the musseques, musicians stood out as trendsetters in their dress, new forms of masculinity, and urban culture.

The musseque clubs – places like Salão dos Anjos [Salon of the Angels], Giro-Giro [Turn-Turn], Club de Maxinde, and Kudissanga Kwa Makamba – functioned on the basis of membership but opened their doors for the price of a ticket. If the dashing singer Urbano de Castro performed (supported by Os Kiezos or Jovens do Prenda), a line would form outside the club and wind along the street. Well-dressed young men and their nattily clad female dates chattered in anticipation. Resplendent in the latest fashion commissioned from his tailor, Urbano 'Urbanito' de Castro, embodied the cosmopolitan city. He would jump on stage with his bell-bottoms swishing, grab his guitar, a big medallion settling on his chest, and he would break into song. Inspired by Latin American rhythms, Urbano's trademark Rumbas and Merengues, like 'Rosa Maria', lamented a lost love to an upbeat, danceable rhythm: 'Choro, choro, até meio dia / procurando Rosa Maria / quem desapareu / eu andei noite e dia procurand o / a mulher que mais amei / Rosa Maria!'[11] The song 'Semba Lekalo' criticised drunk young women but had audiences swaying their hips rather than wagging their fingers in disapproval. This music entertained in order to educate.

11   I cry, cry, until noon / looking for Rosa Maria / who has disappeared / looking night and day / for the woman I have most loved / Rosa Maria!

Sung primarily in Kimbundu, Semba brought the sounds of the rural world into the heart of the city, while giving the music an urban beat – faster paced, danceable, and electrified with wah-wah guitar sounds alongside dikanza scratchers and hand drums. Young men and women sang and danced to tales of romances gone sour, jobs lost, friends disappeared, and bad behaviour (short skirts, cheating boyfriends, witchcraft, etc.) among friends, family, and neighbours, much of it elliptical critique of daily life in the colony.

Most of the time indirect criticism kept musicians out of the interrogation units of the much-feared International Police for State Defense (PIDE – Portuguese dictator António Salazar's force of secret police). But everyone knew that they sent bufos [informers] to the clubs, into musseque bars, and to night-time haunts so that no precaution by club-owners and audiences was too little. Musicians typically composed and sang in Kimbundu, the language from this region of Angola, even if most of them no longer spoke it at home. The interpretation of lyrics left space for multiple readings. At the same time, the clubs and the music produced a sense of something much larger. They produced a sense of Angolanidade [Angolanness]. They also spawned a sense of cultural autonomy, a feeling that Angolans could do things for themselves. This nurtured nationalism. Clubs provided spaces where Angolans could organise themselves. They required leadership, meetings, and internal democracy on a small but meaningful scale.[12]

A nascent recording industry, with names drawn from local words like ngoma [drum] and rebita [a nineteenth century elite Luandan dance], fuelled the growing scene and mobilised the sound of Semba. Radio broadcasted the sound in and to other Angolan cities. People with disposable incomes purchased singles that were released weekly with hip, young Angolan musicians on their covers – this week Jovens do Prenda's 'Lamento da Mãe' [Mother's Lament], next week Belita Palma's 'Astronauta' [astronaut]. A street festival known as Kutonoca brought bands from one musseque to another

---

12 Moorman, *Intonations* (see n. 4), 90–93.

every Saturday, circulating musicians and music throughout the urban space, offering performances for novice bands, and creating name recognition for more seasoned musicians and groups.

—

By April 1974, when a military coup in Portugal (by generals tired of fighting intractable wars that they could not win in Angola, Guinea-Bissau, Cape Verde, and Mozambique), hastened decolonisation, some high-profile musicians enjoyed greater name recognition than the heads of the independence movements. More visible and more popular, their notoriety could lend incoming politicians a flashy sheen they lacked. For some, it became a liability.

Independence arrived on 11 November 1975 under peculiar conditions. Civil war broke out instantly. Cleavages had developed over decades, along political and social lines drawn deeply during the colonial period and entrenched during the fourteen years of anti-colonial war in different neighbouring states of exile. The protracted and poorly managed decolonisation transition from April 1974 to November 1975 failed to create stability. As musicians tell it, the music stopped. Full stop. Clubs closed. Political propaganda took over the airwaves. Musicians mobilised behind political banners – Urbanito toured with the MPLA President Agostinho Neto, and Teta Lando distributed pamphlets for the FNLA. A very young António 'Santocas' Sebastião Vicente quickly recorded a song, all in minor chords, lauding the heroism of the MPLA soldier Valódia. Musicians put their lungs and windpipes at the service of politics. The Angolan Civil War entangled itself in the Cold War. And the Cold War entwined itself in the civil war.

Music lost its autonomy. But it received state support. The Merengues – headed by Semba guitar master Carlitos Vieira Dias – travelled internationally, presenting Semba to the world (particularly the Eastern Bloc) and backed many musicians on locally recorded singles. The newly formed Ministries of Culture and Youth held music festivals throughout the country, promoting various musical styles. So did the military. But the vibrancy of the musseque music scene faded. The old clubs were converted into recreation centres for 'the people' so that the revolution could be made with 'happy faces', as the slogan of the second president, José Eduardo dos Santos declared in the early 1980s.[13] Still, something was missing.

Kizomba – there's a party!

Music still mattered. But its cadences differed. The main nerve centre of musical production and broadcasting after Independence, Rádio Nacional de Angola (RNA, Angolan National Radio), sat along Rua Ho Chi Minh, just down the street from the MPLA party headquarters and across the street from the Ministry of Culture and the Ministry of Education, next door to Televisão Popular de Angola (TPA, Angolan Popular Television). This part of the city between the Military Hospital, Lucrécia Paim maternity ward, and the big, modernist Catholic Church, Sagrada Família, is a node of ministerial and party power. RNA and its employees became a tight, high-functioning operation after the attempted coup on 27 May 1977.

One of Angola's darkest periods ensued. Much respected MPLA ministers like Saydi Mingas, among others, were killed on the day of the attack. The coup plotters – or supposed coup plotters, as the meaning of this event remains disputed[14] – targeted the radio station, not uncommon in events of this sort. As a result, President Agostinho Neto bolstered radio's role in the new state. Deep factions within the ruling party in the midst of civil war could not be tolerated. News and information spoke in one voice. The wide-scale repression that followed the events of 27 May 1977, silenced a once vibrant debate over the party's – and the nation's – future.

13 Weza, *O Percurso Histórico* (see n. 8), 151.
14 For literature on 27 May 1977 see: David Birmingham, 'The twenty-seventh of May: an historical note on the abortive 1977 *coup* in Angola', in *African Affairs* LXXVII (1978), 554–564; Américo Cardoso Botelho, *Holocausto em Angola* (Lisbon: Vega Editora, 2007); Miguel Francisco, *Nuvem Negra: o Drama do 27 de Maio de 1977* (Porto: Clássica Editora, 2007); Jean-Michel Mabeko-Tali, *Dissidências e poder de estado: o MPLA perante si próprio*, vol. 2 (Luanda: Nzila, 2002); Dalila Cabrita Mateus and Álvaro Mateus, *Purga em Angola* (Lisbon: Edições Asa, 2007); and Lara Pawson, *In the Name of the People: Angola's Forgotten Massacre* (London: IB Tauris, 2014).

The three highest record producing stars of the late colonial period, Urbano de Castro, David Zé, and Artur Nunes, were killed in the massacres that attended the attempted coup. LPs and singles of their music suddenly disappeared from the shelves of the RNA's music library and slashes eradicated their songs from compilations on vinyl.[15] Despite the limitations on what could be said and played on the radio station, it possessed a sizeable budget and employees went about their work with professionalism and dedication. Not only did RNA play music but the station employees travelled the country – even as the civil war raged – recording local musical practices. Back in Luanda, programming focused on a new children's show, on building and opening the new recording studio CT-1 (the only place that musicians had to record for over twenty years), and on putting on big street shows to keep people entertained as the war and economy only generated grim statistics.

From the basement of the RNA and the camaraderie of Makarenko high school close to the radio station, where officials recruited students to work at the station, the group S.O.S. emerged in the mid-1980s. In its first iteration it was known as Os Puros [The Pure Ones]). Band members Eduardo Paim, Bruno Lara, and Levy Marcelino, Nelson Nascimento, and, later, Simons Manssini played and sang while Carlos 'Cassé' Ferreira served as the key lyricist and radio professional.[16] While other bands were still active – Os Kiezos still played, the Merengues recorded with artists more than any other band, and Jovens do Prenda hung on – the only other band of young musicians was Afra Sound Stars, from whom S.O.S. borrowed instruments and inspiration. By the mid-1980s like variety in food and footwear, these too were scarce. Once employed at the radio station in studio CT-1, Paim and Lara had much greater access to a wide variety of instruments, synthesizers, amplifiers, and a suite of recording equipment.

Parties on weekends continued even though local music lost some of its lustre. After all, people still celebrated birthdays, anniversaries, and baptisms.

15 Weza, *O Percurso*, (see n. 8), 140; Moorman, *Intonations*, (see n. 9), 187.
16 Carlos Ferreira, in an interview with Marissa Moorman (2011); Eduardo Paim, in an interview with Moorman (2011).

The war, however, transformed the night. The military subjected young men between the ages of eighteen and thirty-five to compulsory recruitment. Rusgas [random sweeps] filled the gaps in the military. The recolher obrigatório [curfew] meant that no one could be on the streets between midnight and 5am. Rumours of what happened when caught without the papers that proved you had completed service or that showed your status as exempt – namely waking up in a distant land in a uniform and with a gun in your hands – kept young men off the streets at night. But parties did not end. Literally. They just went on all night long. Luandan DJs, ever cosmopolitan in their taste, spun music from the Antilles, Latin America, and Europe. The Caribbean music style Zouk took hold and did not let go, particularly after the band Kassav' from Guadeloupe performed to a packed house at the Cine Karl Marx in the mid-1980s.

S.O.S.'s song 'Carnaval', cut from Zouk cloth at an Angolan angle, got the crowds dancing. The song marked the beginning of what would become known as Kizomba.[17] Rationing, shortages at state stores, compulsory military service, interminable lines at the bread shops, and requests from neighbours ('Oh, vizinha, só um copo de açúcar!' [Oh, neighbour, just one cup of sugar!]) structured daily life. Young people danced to music as they always had. But dance evolves. Listening to music from Guadeloupe, Martinique, and from bands like Kassav' and the Guadeloupean Zouk/Compas band Experience 7, young men and women began to change the older Semba moves.

When Angolan groups and musicians started mixing Zouk with elements of Angolan Semba, Merengue, and the Latin American music they had already imbibed deeply, a novel musical/dance genre resulted.[18] This was happening in Lisbon too, where Paulo Flores, heir to both his father's DJ collection and ear, and who visited Angola on vacations, began playing similar sounds. In the late-1980s he returned to Luanda to record with S.O.S.'s Eduardo Paim. Many accord his hit 'Cherry' status as the first Kizomba (on the LP *Kapuete*

---

17 Paim, in an interview with Moorman (2011).
18 Vladimir Prata, Grande Entrevista: Eduardo Paim 'Sou o Precursor do Kizomba', *O País*, 22 June 2012.

Kamundanda, 1989).[19] Ruca Van-Dunem and Ricardo Abreu composed, and played synthesizers with Flores, Paim, and others, building the genre.

This music encapsulated the moment. It is synthed up, but its smooth, tropical sound made it danceable and possible to play when acoustic and electric instruments were few and far between. The older generation of musicians dismissed it as overly influenced by Zouk, but they danced to it nonetheless. 'Kizomba' is a Kimbundu word. It means 'party', 'entertainment' (remember Coelho's radio show 'Tondonya Mukina ó Kizomba'?). Luís Esteves, a DJ, and the owner of the Luanda record store and distributor RMS which opened in 1994, remembers that the new form of dance that developed to accompany Zouk, and other Antillean music spun at the time, as well as the new sound produced by Angolan bands that had adapted those sounds with local rhythms, lyrics in Portuguese, and stories of quotidian life, wanted for a name. 'Kizomba' worked. All night parties at homes and discotheques gave the name resonance, even though some older musicians insist that it is a misnomer because it did not describe anything essential about the musical genre.[20]

Kizomba had legs. Some Angolans left during the 1980s and 1990s, looking for better lives abroad. Kizomba knit Lisbon closer to Luanda and pulled Houston to Benguela. In the Portuguese-speaking African diaspora in Lisbon, it sunk in deep. Lisbon's African discos like Mussulo and Luanda (both Angolan-owned) and African ones like B-Leza featured Kizomba stars and DJs that spun their music. Cape Verdean and Guinean musicians released similar sounds. By the late 1990s, one could purchase cassettes on Luanda's streets of the Kizombas played in Luanda's clubs by Cabo Love (Cape Verde), Roger (Guinea Bissau), and the Lisbon-based Angolan group Irmãos Verdades. If you were unsure of the titles young street sellers would sometimes break into tune. Walking home from the archives one day, I crossed paths with some zungeiras [ambulant street vendors], cases of Coca-Cola piled high on their heads,

19 CD compilation *Angola 80's 1978–1990*, liner notes, (Buda Musique 2000), 21.
20 Weza, *O Percurso*, (see n. 8), 174.

belting out the hit song 'Yolanda' as they trudged up the hill to the hospital, Josina Machel. Kizomba played on radios in barbershops, in cars, in quintals, and in nightclubs. In the tradition of Semba musicians, Kizomba songs, at their best, riffed on daily life.

Paulo Flores, with rare sensibility, humour, and poetic grace, captured the struggles and delights of life in 1990s Angola in 'Cabelos de Moda' [Stylish Hair]. In this song, Flores indirectly criticises the tendency of young women to date what they think are older men of means. Mocking the practice, he counsels young men to play the game in reverse: dye their hair white, put on a wedding band and a tie in order to attract the attention of young women.

Other genres vied to be heard by the 1990s when, as S.O.S. band member Paim puts it, 'prices replaced values' as the state opened the economy to the market. Gabi Moy's song 'Vizinha Zongola' re-energised Semba, criticising nosy neighbours with lyrics in a mix of Portuguese and Kimbundu. Os Versáteis brought fast-paced Kilapanga rhythms from northern Angola to Kizomba and Semba. Their hit 'Casamento' [Marriage] highlighted the pressure on urban space caused by the war and its impact on romance: 'Casamento, casamento, não! Seria uma loucura! / casamento, casamento, não! Seria uma aventura! / Não tenho uma casa / nem sei onde morar!'[21]

Kuduro and urban durability

New nightclubs opened: Pandemónio in the downtown neighbourhood of Cazuno, Matié off Mutamba Square, Paralelo and Horizonte 2000 in Vila Alice, Animatógrafo and Contencioso near the Marginal sea promenade, and Navi-Hotel on the Ilha (Luanda's peninsula). Young Angolans, among them DJs, who had travelled abroad, came back with CDs from Europe, including Techno music that soon got played in Luanda's clubs. Rappers like Big Nelo got their start in the early 1990s and by the mid-1990s the Rap groups

21 Marriage, marriage, no! It would be crazy!/ Marriage, marriage, no! It would be an adventure!/ I don't have a house or even know where to live!

S.S.P. and N' Sex Love hit the music scene rapping in Portuguese with thick Luandan slang.

At the same time, often singing in the same spaces, a new set of night-time 'animators' appeared, chanting skeletal lyrics over Techno-inspired sounds. New dances already began exploding from this music with particular moves like gato preto [black cat] and açúcar [sugar]. At the Banca Recreation Center, also in the neighbourhood of Cazuno, Sébem and Tony Amado threw lyrics over instrumental recordings like Bruno de Castro's 'No Fear' (recorded by the Angolan-owned and operated RMS label – associated with the Luanda distributor – based in Lisbon and recorded in Madrid in 1994). Amado sang 'Dança, dança, Van Damme, dança!' [Dance, dance, Van Damme, dance!] while imitating the Belgian action movie star's stiff posterior swing from the film *Kickboxer* in his dance moves. This was just the latest iteration of transnational conversation ramifying in Angola music.

Woven around failed elections in 1992 and the return to war, as well as an unbridled head-on rush into capitalism, this new music and dance transmuted exhaustion with the war, the violence done to male bodies in the process, and the decay of urban infrastructure into a 130–140 beats per minute, aggressive, bumping sound. Unlike Semba and Kizomba, Kuduro is not a partner dance. Danced alone, in desafios [challenges] on street corners or in musseque streets where a circle often forms, Kuduro dance and sartorial panache reclaim urban space and the young male body. Dancers finesse control over the most minute muscle contractions transforming them into waves, sweeps, and acrobatic drops to the ground.[22] Bodies mutilated by the war – by mines, fighting, and the indignities of life lived under its duress – are put back together in Kuduro dance.[23]

Virgilio Fire's successful 2001 song 'Kazacuta Dança', with its refrain 'estamos sempre a subir!' [we are always on the up!], succinctly captured the unstinting hope, despite the desperate conditions, with which most Angolans lived as the war ground on. The song hit its zenith when the Luena Peace

22 The journalist and author Jomo Fortunato refers to this as a 'deconstructionist choreography'. Jomo Fortunato, 'Origem, formação e contextualização histórica do kuduro', *Semanário Angolense*, no. 378, Ano VII, 31 July 2010.
23 Nadine Siegert and Stefanie Alisch, 'Angolanidade Revisited – Kuduro', Norient: Network for Local and Global Sounds and Media Culture, 2010, <http://norient.com/academic/kuduro/> accessed 24 March 2014, and 'Grooving on Broken: Dancing War Trauma in Angolan Kuduro', *Art and Trauma in Africa: Representations of Reconciliation in Music, Visual Arts, Literature and Film*, Lizelle Bisschoff and Stefanie Van de Peer (eds.), (Berlin: I.B. Tauris, 2012); Marissa Moorman, 'Anatomy of Kuduro: Articulating the Angolan Body Politic after the War', *African Studies Review* 57 (3), December 2014, 21–40.

Accords finally ended the civil war in April 2002, and reason was pushed aside by delirium in the refrain's resonance. Using the computer programme FruityLoops and recording in small, musseque studios, Kuduro, which got its start in downtown clubs, took off in the musseques. Aspiring Kuduristas [Kuduro artists] recorded the hits of other artists and one or two originals and burned a hundred CDs for a fee. They distributed these for free to candongueiro taxi drivers to promote their music.

Older musicians dismissed it as a short-term trend, describing it as música descartavel [throw away music]. Critics applauded acts like Puto Português who moved from Kuduro to Semba, prompting one prominent commentator to call Kuduro 'children's music'.[24] Musseque acts, full of menace, thick with rivalries, sometimes strung up with drug charges, like Os Lambas, received lashings in the press but a huge following among musseque youth. In the meantime, a tiny group of Kuduristas with a political edge have adopted the sobriquet Kuduro consciente [conscious Kuduro].

In the second decade of the twenty-first century, Kuduro garnered one powerful champion while most of the intelligentsia dissed or ignored it. Coreon Dú, the artistic name of José Eduardo Paulino dos Santos, one of the sons of Angolan Ex-President dos Santos, claims membership in the Kuduro generation and allegiance to the genre. He started the 'I Love Kuduro' campaign and festival. Employing a US consulting company, they turned it into 'Os Kuduristas', an international festival of Kuduro 'dance, music, and lifestyle' that travelled to Berlin, Paris, Amsterdam, New York, and Washington DC in 2012. Like Semba before it, Kuduro underwent the transition from political outsider to political insider, helping to re-brand Angola. It was not just about war anymore but becoming a new Dubai on the Atlantic – sun soaked, insouciant, and hip.

Like all urban dance music, Kuduro constitutes a cultural dynamic that draws from diverse sources, be they internal or external, rural or urban,

---

24   Ismael Mateus, 'Uma estranha obsessão official pelo kuduro', *Semanário Angolense*, no. 373, Ano VII, 26 June 2010.

international or national, baixa or musseque. They cross social and class boundaries. The music thrives on mobility: moving in and around the city, from one city to another, first on radios and vinyl, on foot or in cars, and today via Bluetooth and MP3, but still on foot and in vehicles. If Semba helped create new political realities by crafting a sense of Angolanidade through the airwaves and on dance floors, Kizomba forged a spirit of 'can-do-ness' creativity during the fracturing years of the civil war, and Kuduro has bridged the late war years to the petro boom, mediating capitalism and Angolanness again. Young DJs are producing Afro-house and tweaking Kuduro, pulling sounds from across borders both inside and outside Angola. Luanda's dance floors will continue to vibrate with a diversity of music because Luanda's DJs travel, even if they never physically leave the city.

Bibliography

Birmingham, David, 'The Twenty-Seventh of May: An Historical Note on the Abortive 1977 Coup in Angola', in *African Affairs* LXXVII (1978), 554–564.

Birmingham, David, 'Carnival at Luanda', *Journal of African History* 29 (1), (1988), 93–103.

Botelho, Américo Cardoso, *Holocausto em Angola* (Lisbon: Vega Editora, 2007).

Coelho, Sebastião, *História da Comunicação em Angola* (Luanda: Executive Center, 1999).

Fortunato, Jomo, 'Origem, Formação e Contextualização Histórica do Kuduro', *Semanário Angolense*, no. 378, Ano VII, 31 July 2010.

Francisco, Miguel, *Nuvem Negra: o Drama do 27 de Maio de 1977* (Porto: Clássica Editora, 2007).

Mabeko-Tali, Jean-Michel, *Dissidências e Poder de Estado: o MPLA Perante Si Próprio*, vol. 2 (Luanda: Nzila, 2002).

Mateus, Dalila Cabrita and Álvaro Mateus, *Purga em Angola* (Lisbon: Edições Asa, 2007).

Mateus, Ismael, 'Uma Estranha Obsessão Official Pelo Kuduro', *Semanário Angolense*, no. 373, Ano VII, 26 June 2010.

Moorman, Marissa, *Intonations – A Social History of Music and Nation in Luanda, Angola, from 1945 to Recent Times* (Athens: Ohio University Press, 2008).

Moorman, Marissa, 'Anatomy of Kuduro: Articulating the Angolan Body Politic after the War', *African Studies Review* 57 (3), December 2014, 21–40.

Pawson, Lara, *In the Name of the People: Angola's Forgotten Massacre* (London: IB Tauris, 2014).

Prata, Vladimir, Grande Entrevista: Eduardo Paim 'Sou o Precursor do Kizomba', *O País*, 22 June 2012.

Siegert, Nadine and Stefanie Alisch, 'Grooving on broken. Dancing War Trauma in Angolan Kuduro', in: Lizelle Bisschoff and Stefanie Van de Peer (eds.) *Art and Trauma in Africa: Representations of Reconciliation in Music, Visual Arts, Literature and Film*, (Berlin: IB Tauris, 2013).

Weza, José, *O Percurso Histórico da Música Urbana Luandense: Subsídios par a História da Música Angolana* (Luanda: Ensaio, 2007).

Kuduro performers on a rooftop in Sambizanga, Luanda, 2015, photo: Anita Baumann

Local Kuduro event in the neighbourhood of Sambizanga, Luanda, 2015, photo: Anita Baumann

Kuduro performers in their neighbourhood of Sambizanga, Luanda, 2015, photo: Anita Baumann

Sebem, from the film *Kuduro–Fogo no Museke*, Luanda, 2007, photo: Jorge António

Titica, photo: unknown

Movements on a Map of Sounds – Luanda's Dual Urban Matrix

Ângela Mingas

In 2013, when the global oil price was at an all-time high, Luanda was one of the most vibrant cities in Africa, fuelled by an economic growth predominantly driven by Angola's crude oil production which is one of the highest on the continent. Consequently, the city was a pole of attraction for immigrants of different cultures. Four or five years later, the situation was different – low oil prices had slowed economic growth. Nevertheless, the city is still one of the continent's most vibrant, it is still attracting immigrants in large quantities, and it is as culturally abuzz as ever. This buzz was, and still is, partly because for the last few decades the city has been a battleground between two cultural and musical phenomena. On one side the traditional urban culture of Semba,[1] on the other the local gone global genre Kuduro.[2] In both cases, the city's musical scenes are, above all, supported by a certain type of community originally named turma. These groups came into existence in colonial times as a form of acculturation of the black indigenous population. Today, they are, by and large, no longer called turma – instead the terms used have changed to 'staff' or other English expressions such as 'gang'. But they maintain the same structure whatever the artistic forms of expression may be.

This essay combines field surveys directed by the Scientific Research Centre of Architecture of the Lusíada University of Angola during 2013 and 2014 with bibliographic and other documental retrieval. The analysis basis consists of three different partitions. The first partition is the city with its morphological idiosyncrasies and its two primordial cultures, the Portuguese and the Ambundu.[3] The second partition is the music culture in the city and its collective protagonists. This state of collectivity is not only a constant throughout the chronological period of analysis but it is also fundamental and motivational for Luanda's music scenes. The third partition of our research basis is formed by the diverse architectural typologies, which make up the network of clubs in the city, from public to private, and their respective variations. Throughout this essay, we will browse through the city and its musseques[4] in order to understand which places the personages of the respective musical scenes belong to. It is interesting to note that the social life of the African community, which begins confined to the musseque of the colonial era and is now spreading to the entire urban area, remains very similar throughout the historical period that we have reviewed.[5]

The segregated urban sphere

The city of Luanda in Angola and its specificities can only be perceived comprehensively when realising that this is the most ancient Euro-African capital city of the whole Africa Bantu[6] culture. While it currently enters the third phase of the Republican period in Angola,[7] its morphological

---

1   An urban music genre. Its classical instrumentation includes a five-string guitar, traditional drums and dikanza scrapers, although nowadays other instruments have been introduced. The lyrics vary from romance to political awareness. The genre is of Luandan origin created by Liceu Vieira Dias in the 1950s. For more information about these and other music genres please see Marissa Moorman's essay about music in Luanda in this book.

2   A dance style invented by Tony Amado in the late 1980s; an urban musical genre from Luanda from the 1990s, electronically produced with repetitive structures and rapped lyrics about everyday life.

3   Ethno-linguistic group and Luanda's original population. Their language is Kimbundu.

4   From Kimbundu: museke; red, ferrous soil, characteristic of the Luanda region; settlements for enslaved men, located beyond the city's border. Later districts where the indigenous population was confined during the colonial period. Today they are degraded districts, often with a lack of infrastructure support. Neighbourhoods of spontaneous occupation during the post-independence period and during Angola's long-lasting civil war.

5   Two authors from different historical moments, like José de Sousa Bettencourt and Pepetela, have very similar descriptions of everyday life in the musseques, although with an interval of twenty-five years separating each other, the first being in a colonialist perspective and the second in a republican cf. José de Sousa Bettencourt, *Subsídio para o Estudo Sociológico da População de Luanda* (Luanda: Instituto de Investigação Científica de Angola, 1965). And Pepetela, *Luandando* (Luanda: Elf Aquitaine Angola, 1990).

6   Bantu is a designation for the 300 up to 600 ethnic groups in Africa who speak Bantu languages. Those ethnic groups inhabit a geographical area stretching east and southward from Central Africa across the African Great Lakes region down to Southern Africa. On the continent, twenty-two countries are mostly, if not entirely, Bantu which represents nearly 40 per cent of the African nations.

7   During the timeframe of this project, the social reality in Luanda and, on a wider scope, the whole country went through two historical periods: colonial, ▶

characteristics stem from slavery and colonial heritages. These characteristics have created, and still create, social exclusion. The strongest evidence of this is a prevalent differentiation between the formal and informal city and its organic variations. This differentiation since the city's foundation promotes separated urban behaviours. Of course, the dual character of the city does not imply an even split. This is easily perceptible by the asymmetry between the official city and the musseques, which cover respectively two thirds of Luanda's area. Since the musseques are the city's most important urban expression, the impact of their social and anthropological reality is prevalent. This is reflected in all facets of society, from environment to culture, from social to economic. The musseques in Luanda are frequently interpreted with one of two very different perspectives. They are either seen as a place from where Luandans came from and therefore the source of urban culture, or they are seen as a degraded place of crime and poverty which should be eradicated.

Luanda represents nearly a quarter of Angola's national population.[8] Mainly by means of immigration, this population has exploded in the course of the last thirty-five years, with people coming from different origins. Up to the last decade of the twentieth century the majority of its population were Mbundu people.[9] Today, the mosaic is far more complex. From African to Asian, many communities have their cultural expression in the city, manifesting in restaurants and nightclubs, for example. This diversity also has its own territories. Some neighbourhoods are even identified nominally by its major population, such as the Congolenses [Congolese] area, while others are only connoted with a particular immigrant community, for example the Martires de Kifangondo neighbourhood with immigrants from Mali.

The urbanisation process has been intense with a brutal impact on the city's natural structure, creating a state of irreversible imbalance in the morphological characteristics. Mainly, the city has lost the visual impact of its hills and woods. At the same time the urban development of the city has shown a tendency for the desertification of the centre. Musseques feature on almost all levels of the city. Only the oldest part of Luanda, the historical centre of Ingombota, may soon become the only district without musseques due to a political-administrative renewal process for the capital. But still the city centre is the destination for two connected people's behavioural phenomena: commuting migration as the daily mobility between the periphery and the centre and transhumance (the seasonal movement of people and their livestock between fixed summer and winter residences). While the commuting mainly affects the national and African foreign population, transhumance affects mostly the European/Western foreign population, also known as expats. Many, or maybe even most, of these expats have or had working contracts including a premise of a ticket per year to 'go home' during vacations. This even affects the city's occupational density as many people move towards their homelands during Christmas, Easter, or Northern hemisphere summer.

Recently Luanda has been designated both a county as well as a city, with the aggregation of former municipalities now designated as districts.[10] This has two consequences: first, it is possible to manage its territory and second, the city finally has a physical frontier. But the dual landscape does not have a single border. Instead, it has to be imagined as the result of an urban implosion, which caused the collapse of the urban space with a permanent effect at all scales of one's perception. To take a walk through the city of Luanda involves being in permanent contact with the formal and informal.

Take, for example, the contrast between two end-to-end neighbourhoods: Maianga[11] and Catambor.[12] The first is the result of an urban revitalisation in the 1960s, with Modernist architecture in an orthogonal layout and drawn

ending 1975 which was characterised by the Fascism of the Portuguese government and the war for Independence; Republican, which can itself be divided into three phases. Phase 1 (1975–1992) characterised by Independence, the Cold War and the dictatorial socialist system; phase 2 (1992–2002) characterised by the transition to the capitalist and democratic parliamentary system and the Civil War; and phase 3 (2002–2012). The first post-war decade, characterised by the Civil War and the end of capitalist and democratic presidential system.

8   According to the 2014 National Census, Angola has a population of 24,383,301 people, the province of Luanda, a population of 6,542,944 and the city of Luanda 2,107,648. The population density is the highest in Angola, with 2067.8 inhabitants/km². Luanda has an occupational density 143 times that of the country (14 people/km²) while it covers only 0.2 per cent of its territory. The Census of Population from 1973 and 2013 put the population of the province of Luanda at 800,000 and 6,500,000 inhabitants

according to the canons of Le Corbusier.[13] Marien Ngouabi, a long avenue in the historic district of Maianga, is still referred to by its colonial name, 'António Barroso'. It is flanked by large buildings with eight or ten floors and a second category of organisation: spacious yards villas and public parks with gardens that support a Western lifestyle inherited by the assimilated population of the colonial era. The boundary to Catambor is defined by a hill which confined the native population to this place. Over the centuries, its population adopted a special way of life, mainly due to the spontaneous occupation of the space by immigrants from Cape Verde. The special characteristics of Maianga and the hill to Catambor have been immortalised by the Angolan poet, Mário António, and his poem, 'Noites de Luar no Morro da Maianga' [Moonlight Nights on Maianga's Hill]. These lyrics were later sung by Ruy Mingas,[14] the resulting song became one of the most popular Angolan songs of the last century.

> Girls dating in timber made backyards / Old women chatting over old issues / Seating on the mat / Men getting drunk in the taverns / And emigrants from the islands / With sea salt in their hair / The emigrants from the islands / That speak of witchcraft and sirens / And play guitar / And pull out knives during fights.[15]

The city of Luanda is designed with contrasts, and most of the musseques are associated with songs that are registered in the citizen's memory. Those songs are part of the people's identity with lyrics describing their habits and customs. Though music is, of course, not exclusively defining the city – it has a strong commercial vocation, from the trafficking of enslaved men to candongas [from Kimbundu: 'ka ndonga' – to trade, to sell at higher prices]. This trend has carved the characters of the city and these are connoted with the sounds of the city.

From the zungueira[16] to the candongueiro[17], the city centre is like a magnet, attracting the population of the musseques outskirts daily. This phenomenon of convergence to the city centre is not limited to citizens on the periphery, it extends to other provinces as well. Luanda has had historically transoceanic connections to Portugal and Brazil since the era of slavery. All of this turns the city, a centenarian capital at both province and country level, into a neuralgic centre of the country. This centre, like all urban centres created in the country from the sixteenth century to the eighteenth century, follows a morphological structure of Uptown and Downtown with the indigenous population being marginalised, located beyond the city boundaries. The city was segregated from its foundation on.

—

respectively. cf. José Teixeira Lopes Ribeiro, 'Características Gerais da População de Angola', ONU – UNFPDA – Fundo das Nações Unidas para População, 2005, <http://membres.multimania.fr/redeluso/ao/cadernos/vol07-1/Parte5.doc> accessed 16 November 2011.

9   Although the designation Ambundu is a Portuguese confusion of the term 'Kikongo Mbundo' to designate the region of Luanda. Some argue that the designation applies to a broader ethno-linguistic structure, including the provinces of Luanda, Bengo, Kwanza Norte and South, and Malanji cf. Linda M. Heywood, *Central Africans and Cultural Transformations in the American Diaspora* (Cambridge: Cambridge University Press, 2002).
10 N.N., 'Lei de Alteração da Divisão Político-administrativa das províncias de Luanda e Bengo', *Diário da República*, Lei no. 29/11, 15 November 2011.
11 Originally the Kimbundu name for the wells that supply the city of Luanda. There were two main wells, the Maianga of the People and the Maianga of the King. These two places are classified as being Assets of National Cultural Interest. Today Maianga is the name of the integrated neighbourhood in the district of the same name.
12 Considering that the 'Ka/Ca' prefix in Kimbundu means 'little' or 'belonging to', and Tambor means drum, the word Catambor could mean 'small drum', or 'the place for the drum'.
13 The Corbusian canons refer to the five characteristics of the Modernist architecture movement (free plan, free facade, stilts, patio, and horizontal ribbon windows) described by Swiss-French architect Le Corbusier (Charles-Edouard Jeanneret-Gris) in his book *Vers Une Architecture* [Toward an Architecture] (1923).
14 Ruy Mingas: musician, politician, and Angolan athlete. A member of a group of influential musicians in the urban culture of Luanda, next to Liceu Vieira Dias, Carlitos Vieira Dias, and André Mingas. He developed his career as a political intervention singer (from the late 1950s to the early years after Independence) 'musicking' the great nationalist poets of his time, among them Mário António, António Agostinho Neto, António Jacinto, Manuel Rui, Mário Pinto de Andrade, and Eugenio Lara Filho. He is also the father of the author.
15 Portuguese original: 'Moças namorando nos quintais de madeira / Velhas falando conversas antigas / Sentadas na esteira / Homens embebedando-se nas tabernas / E os emigrados das ilhas / Com o sal do mar nos cabelos / Os emigrados das ilhas / Que falam de bruxedos e sereias / E tocam violão / E puxam faca nas brigas,' cf. Francisco Soares, 'Mário António: Lírica Completa', 2010, <http://www.adelinotorres.com/literatura/> accessed 7 August 2012.
16 From Kimbundu: 'ku zunga' – to walk. Luanda's street hawkers, female street vendors.
17 Individual that practises 'candonga' [trading].

This urban morphology, like in many other African cities, is perfectly captured in the term 'Euro-Africanism', with an urban centre layout formatted for a Western experience and based on European cultural values, and with a periphery for the indigenous population. This segregation of the urban sphere maintains a dual heritage of socio-cultural values between the formal and informal city. In this duality lies the genesis of Luanda's urban culture including music and its related manifestations such as dance. Although it seems reductive to work with contradictions such as asphalt-earth, conservative-transgressive, European-African, wealthy-poor, these physical contrasts are still the background of the urban culture of Luanda, whatever the focus of analysis might be.

The DNA of the Euro-African city, which is a product of classical gentrification as well as varied migratory phenomena, has its own mutation dynamics, endowing these two realities of formal and informal with very distinguished features while establishing unique urban spaces as points of coalition. These might be, for example, a formal building in an informal settlement, or an informal market in a formal neighbourhood. If we perceive the dual urban spaces metaphorically as white and black, we could imagine grey zones as a transitional phenomenon. These grey zones, usually caused by urban implosion causing disruption in the urban space homogeneity, may be called 'contact zones'.

These contact zones might assume different shapes, depending on different situations. In the formal city it may be a spontaneous market that kitandeiras[18] create outside a formal market or the occupation of open leisure spaces in the city by street boys, or even the occupation of urban voids or unutilised spaces. In the informal city the interventions of urban rehabilitation – a government programme with the title 'National Reconstruction', implemented after the end of the Civil War in 2002 and commonly understood as 'micro-planning' – generate alien social and urban bodies such as mediatheques, cultural and recreational centres, or youth houses, among others. These are generating new forms of use and appropriation of the places. This process might initiate a vicious cycle, which starts the separation between formal and informal and the implosion of this duality into contact zones, which are then rehabilitated and reinterpreted through urban and/or architectural interventions – an upgrading which may result again in the exclusion of citizens.

However, the city is also a place of multiple subjective and intangible territories, created by circumstantial appropriation of the citizens in their use of the urban space. As a place, the city is constantly transmuted, acquiring different features and adapting to each functional aesthetic. It is appealing to build in someone's mind the city through its characters (zungueiras, candongueiros, kitandeiras, calcinhas[19]), and observe the layers in which it is structured in the minds of the citizens. Each city's character claims Luanda in different formats. In a similar way being Axilwanda,[20] Kalwanda,[21] or Luandan[22] implies that the same city represents different perspectives for its population. The first two of these have the notion of their cultural roots having been built over hundreds of years, while the third is still a developing body with a collective memory still under construction, and also changing towards a reality no longer local but essential and irreversibly globalised.

These circumstances are responsible for the social environment of Luanda which can be seen both as transcultural[23] and conservative[24] at the same time. This general duality of character is not restricted to the difference between formal and informal. It is all encompassing. As a society, the city's population is clearly dominated by the intangible force of a vibrant and mostly youthful population with strong links to the native culture. Here, 'native' means that, nowadays, as an independent country, people no longer feel the need to hide their African roots. At the same time, as the Kalwanda maintain

18 Women that sell in the kitanda [a designated market area].
19 Term used during the colonial period to describe African citizens of Luanda.
20 The indigenous population of Luanda's peninsula who claim the origin of the cultural identity of Luanda for themselves, as the possessors of the oldest traditions of the city. In Portuguese, it is spelled 'Axiluanda'.
21 Kimbundu: 'from Luanda'. Mixed population between white Portuguese and black Ambundu with origins in the eighteenth century, clearly urban and the source of the urban culture of the city. 'There is no denying that there is a Kalwanda culture, urban, based on the culture from Ambundu and a strong European influence, via Portugal and Brazil.' Pepetela, *Luandando* (see n. 5), 163.

their assimilated influences, imposed Westernisation is still very strong in Luanda – even though it is losing ground as time goes by. This condition makes the city the national absorber as well as a potent coloniser of the Angolan cultural universe. In short, what happens in Luanda happens throughout the country.

Music between public and private spaces

Music and the spaces where it is played are undoubtedly one of the most important elements for the understanding of the city. Interpreting the architectural and urban typologies of (music) clubs may contribute to a general understanding of the city. Apart from the two architectural categories of urban areas, formal and informal, we can find two new categories of urban spaces here: public and private, including all nuances between the two.[25] When we analyse these categories we can determine the way the people from Luanda listen to music, and therefore peek into the origins of their social behaviour.

Here, public space primarily means non-built urban voids that are appropriated by citizens affected by poverty to perform mainly business and/or leisure activities. Public spaces are also places for roaming and urban transhumance for music, expressed in its most exuberant way through the Candongueiro taxis,[26] which will be addressed later. There are two variations of private spaces. On the one side, we find the ones for private use; mainly places like backyards or patios. On the other, are private spaces for public or semi-public use such as nightclubs, bars, or cultural and recreational centres,[27] some of which are managed by associations.[28]

While clubs in private spaces of any variety, from music clubs to cultural clubs, appear both in formal and informal contexts regardless of the patrons' living standard, clubs in public spaces exist predominantly in contact zones. Those are mostly itinerant, due to the transhumant characteristic of their definers and users, for example Candongueiro taxis and also roulottes[29] that sell fast food. These subjective space appropriations have mainly occurred during the democratic opening period, because their existence is unconditionally linked to the mobility and freedom of the citizens in the city. Both post-colonial as well as a democratic development are presuppositions for the spontaneous manifestation of a group of citizens to gather in a public context.

Assuming that music is an existential phenomenon, we can treat the spaces where it is performed and listened to as anthropological places.[30] Some of these are a result of architectural design such as bars and nightclubs, or ephemeral events such as festivals or rallies. Others are more short-lived, for example spontaneous parties in public spaces like taxi parking lots.

The social spheres of music scenes: first contact

Hearing Luanda's noisy symphony of machines and crowds is a mental exercise that requires a slow heartbeat to be able to hear the silence in between the noises. That silence is the heir of the

---

22 A person born in Luanda; a Luanda resident of multiple origins, races and creeds. Migratory population of the twentieth century and also post-independence, encompassing multiple sources both domestic and foreign. A cosmopolitan and multicultural population.

23 Transcultural (cross-cultural) means a musseque space, because it absorbs the immigrant population (domestic and / or foreign) and for that reason all that comes from it is the result of multiple influences.

24 This is referring to the Kalwanda people, a transcultural (cross-cultural) product themselves, but settled in Luanda since the city's founding, winning particular feature from the nineteenth century on, when the social affirmation of mixed race families extended after the exodus of the Portuguese in the course of the abolition of slavery.

25 Between these are intermediate categories like semi-public or semi-private. A space might be characterised by two viewpoints: the legislative that defines the urban principle *latu sensu* and the architectural principle which defines the functional occupation principle *stritu sensu*.

26 Collective transport in the form of mini-bus vehicles, almost exclusively Toyota Hiace model.

27 Although in the current Angolan law the definition is 'Cultural and Social Interaction Center' the term in everyday language has become the 'Cultural and Recreational Center' cf. N.N. (2014), 'Regulamento Geral dos Planos Territoriais, Urbanísticos e Rurais. Decreto n.º 2/06 de 23 de Janeiro', *Diário da República*.

28 The term 'association' means all voluntary unions of Angolan or foreign citizens with long-lasting character aimed at the pursuit of a common purpose and non-profit purposes cf. N.N. (1991): 'Lei das Associações. Lei no. 14/91 de 11 de Maio', *Diário da República*.

29 Caravans. Even though a caravan is not only for commercial purposes, in Angola the word 'roulette' means a caravan that sells food.

30 According to Marc Augé places are all spaces with which man develops his social activities and consequently builds an emotional, relational memory cf. Marc Augé, *Não-lugares. Introdução a uma antropologia da sobremodernidade* (Venda-Nova: Bertrand Editora, 1994).

kakulo[31] and the dipanda[32] celebration sounds, celebrating the goddess of the sea and Angola's freedom. That silence is the successor of the lamentation of thousands of enslaved men with hung voices by the sidewalks. That silence calls for Rebita,[33] the aristocratic Kalwanda's Polka. It is the silence of refugees from wars far and near.

When listening more closely, the sounds can be distinguished from each other. The morning trade of the zungueiras, the disguised appeal of the bisneiros[34] at the office door, the rushed rumbling of the cupapatas,[35] the announcement of the taxi drivers' routes, or the insolent dictatorship of a gate security guard. At night, the ambience changes pace. The female street vendors now prepare pinchos [barbecue, skewered meats], the shady man offers liamba [Kimbundu: cannabis] at a night club's door, the beggar returns home, the security guard turns on the television, and whores whisper their skills to the distracted walker in the old and centennial neighbourhood of Coqueiros, disguised by their collective laughter at the yard doors. Beer is sold and excuses the chitchat over everything in the streets. These are the 'Moonlight Nights on Maianga's Hill'.

Everything is a moving contrast. Light and dark, night and day, shout and whisper, speed and wander, pain and joy, fear and bravery. No, it is not 'Sábado no Musseque'[36], as the poem by António Agostinho Neto from 1948 goes, which reflects the segregation between blacks and whites. Indeed, this is no longer confined to the imagined borders that separate the musseques from other parts of the city. The musseques today form a mental geography, belonging to everyone, a driving force and a generator, ancient, multicultural by excellence and Angolan by name. Here, music thrives.

Music and identities

In the musseques and elsewhere, Luandan people – although there is music from abroad – mainly consume music produced in the country. No international singer is more hummed than the new icons of Semba or Kizomba,[37] and more modern, Kuduro and Afro House music scenes such as Matias Damásio, Ary, Yuri da Cunha, or Yola Semedo. These are new faces that bear no resemblance with the kotas[38], such as Liceu Vieira Dias, Bonga, or Lilly Tchiumba. But the younger musicians are legitimate heirs of a long and difficult social process of claims and affirmations. This process began with anti-colonial nationalism in the middle of the twentieth century, forged by Pan-African movements, when people began to claim their cultural heritage. One of the results was the affirmation of Luanda's popular music, the Semba.

The kotas say that Luanda has always been a city of sounds, where one listened to music in every corner of the musseque. It is still so, only other sounds. Guitars and drums have been replaced with large columns of DJs, and their sounds, irreverent and new, are the actors of the irreversible change on the face of a 'new man' as it is foretold in the verses of the national anthem.[39] During the first years of socialist post-independence officials used music as a means for disseminating political propaganda, mostly to form an identity for the newborn country and for all the concepts associated with the idea of a 'nation'. Interestingly, most of the musicians of post-colonial Angola, the 'First Republic'[40], had started their career during the colonial era. Today, would-be kotas like Paulo Flores, who, despite being a worthy representative of post-independence Semba, sings nostalgia with an unmistakable touch of Portuguese Fado tone, with his cry of 'país que nasceu meu pai' [my father's country] longing for a time that stood irreversibly behind.

The majority of music today is about subjects such as sex and religion, and especially love. In Luanda people have not always sung about this feeling of affection. But the topics have changed throughout the years. Today, Yuri da Cunha sings 'Tu és o amor da minha vida' [You are the love of my life] or the corny Matias

31 Kimbundu: celebration held by the Axilwanda as a tribute to Kyanda, the mystical entity of the waters. It takes place each year in November during high waves season.

32 Kimbundu: freedom. The expression was assimilated into the colloquial language of Angolans, referring to the celebrations on 11 November, the day when national independence is commemorated.

33 Urban music genre played with accordion and the scraper dikanza, associated with the celebrations of the most noble mixed families of Luanda and later of those assimilated, having its origin in the late nineteenth century. Lyrics are about everyday life. A dance with differentiated structure of Luandense origin belongs to the genre and is mainly danced in ballrooms. Couples dance choreographies coordinated by the head of the circle, perform synchronised gestures marking the time with strong beats of the foot on the

Damásio's romanticised 'Como eu te amo, como eu te quero' [How I love you, how I want you]. Even the 1986-born transsexual singer Titica claims 'Sou mais fofa que a tua garina' [I am cuter than your girlfriend]. All these are achievements by an irreverent youth.[41]

Nevertheless, nowadays Kuduro and Hip-Hop are the predominant weapons of social and political intervention. When claiming, for example, women's rights or the right for living a good, healthy, and safe life, these musical genres work as relievers of social tensions. These are not only about the city but about the whole country. There are claimants like Dog Murras who imagines his music as a letter from a servant or an Angolan citizen, or MC Kappa who exults people's rights in the musseques, in particular in Catambor. And Nagrelha, the real anti-hero with his criminal and irreverent posture, is even defying the system and taking localism to the extreme when proclaiming a local district as the 'Independent Republic of Sambizanga'. These are voices that rise against a system that has not yet been able to eradicate segregation, and that, in the eyes of many, accentuates it. But even if the lyrics speak of juvenile prostitution, of the gap between rich and poor, alcoholism, or male chauvinism, straightforward political criticism is rarely heard.

Angola is experiencing a wave of positivism marked by strong political propaganda emphasising the country's political and economic stability, at least according to the current government. Musicians are increasingly at the service of the system. In fact, the most expressive musicians serve the ruling party. Some of the most famous ones are even promoting the president and appear in rallies and other governmental activities during election season. Over the past few years, a process of cleansing of the sung content has been carried out. Some musicians used music to protest against the government. Now, some musicians are still protesting – not against the government, but against their colleagues who are against the government.

Transforming spaces

Night life in Luanda is slowly starting to express the right to be lived freely. DJs exhibit the ability to produce sound at deafening levels. They 'warm up the drums'[42] hours before the parties begin so as to prepare everything for the night. But the city still hides behind walls. Then only sound is a transgressor, an invader of others territory. Carnaval is the only celebration that differs: a street parade with music and costumes with European carnival roots and a history almost as old as the city's, one that has allowed the euphoria of enjoying the street since colonial times. During the colonial period, public demonstrations were forbidden to blacks, except during carnaval. Over the course of the last decades carnaval was the most politically targeted and as such it has transformed its social impact according to what the circumstances dictate – from exaltation to socially important achievements, to manifestations of traditional identity. It acquired different contours in the early days of Independence with a whole symbolism associated with an independent country's new social culture in formation. This post-independence carnaval did not happen all over town, instead it was reduced to Luanda's Marginal, the main coastal avenue bordering

---

34 An individual who makes a bisno – from the English 'business': a deal but with an air of illegality.
35 'Motorised'. A word originating from the Angola's central Benguela province applied to an individual taxi service with motorbikes.
36 'Saturday in the Musseque'. In this poem, the musseque is where Laundan culture is born.
37 Kimbundu: festivity; a term adapted to designate the fusion of Semba and Zouk music genres, starting in Angola in the 1980s.
38 Kimbundu: The eldest among the rest. In colloquial language it is a general term of respect.
39 The first stanza of the national anthem of Angola says: 'We honour the past and our history / Creating through our work the new man.' This metaphor of the 'new man' is commonly used with some disdain by the elders when referring to the new post-independence generations, while they consider themselves as fighters for an independent country in which they have created this new Angolan citizen.
40 Primeira República [the First Republic] began on 11 November 1975, the date on which the first Constitutional Law in the history of Angola came into force. It lasted until 1992 when the second Constitutional Law was approved. It was characterised by a socialist system and a single party rule.
41 'Juventude Transviada': The title of the song of Luiz Melodia, a Brazilian singer and author, who composed it during the military dictatorship in Brazil in 1975. The title of the song refers to the movie *Rebel without a Cause* with actor James Dean, and means the dreams of the young ones.
42 A colloquial expression meaning preparing a party. The expression comes from the fact that traditional drums like Ngomas are made from wood with the end coated in tanned leather. These skins must be heated close to a low heat source for a few hours before being played to sound well.

floor. The dance involves certain complicity between the couples as gestures imply frontal contact between the bodies which can lead to an exchange of glances and smiles. It is thought to have a strong influence of Polka, a folk dance from Central Europe.

Luanda's bay which is also one of the city's main sights and landmarks.

The Angolan Government and MPLA, the ruling party, suffer, as most states and government parties in Africa do, of a chronic weakness. Carnaval therefore represented an ideal way to try to mobilize popular support. Those involved are more than two hundred carnaval groups, distributed throughout numerous neighbourhoods, musseques, parishes, slums, fishing villages, suburbs and dilapidated buildings of the metropolis. Each community is characterized by a group of clearly differentiated social attributes and reflects its identity with an ostentatious carnaval image. The most successful groups participate in the grand parade, in which thirty-three finalists compete to achieve the prize and the champion status. The Government's Political party decided in 1977 that from that year on, the parade would be held on March 27. It was on that date that South Africa withdrew from Angola after the 'second war of liberation' in 1975–1976. The date was chosen with some care from among the possible anniversary dates. May 1, particularly, was considered and rejected for it was not sufficiently linked to local political achievements, and for not allowing, that easily, the popular manifestation to combine to the political message. The expulsion of South Africans (although they continue to invade the territory from time to time) was chosen as the only purely patriotic achievement that could be linked to the growing charivari of a traditional carnaval.[43]

Today Luanda's carnaval is not only linked to all of the most significant music styles of the city. It has also spread over the entire country. But everywhere the symbolic structure remains the same: the King and his Queen followed by their court, in a clear allusion to the monarchic structure of the Portuguese nobility.

The carnaval and similar party days have always represented a flexible reaction to the traumas of change, a firm attachment to the values of the past and an ironic representation of the exorcism directed at the contemporary demons.[44]

The street, being the most common place of expression for carnaval dances or Kuduro turmas [a social group of young musicians. See chapter 'Turmas and danças'], is often transformed into a space of exhibition and debate through a physical language that defines action and reaction. Apart from carnaval's exceptional circumstances in Luanda's streets as public spaces and in the backyards as private spaces, people usually dance in one of two different ways. In one, there are musicians, bands, or DJs who must be able to interpret the dynamics of the audience – and then attendants form a group that reacts together, not leaving any possibility for individual behaviour. At the same time single people challenge each other in an arena to Kazukuta[45] and its rhythmical variations like Kuduro. In the other, we find couples for whom the music is secondary because what is valid is the mastery of the dance performers. They show off by their mastery of ballroom dancing to older musical genres like Semba. These participants – musicians and dancers – create their own rules of coexistence in defiance of regulatory action from higher entities, be they spiritual or profane. In general, dancing in Luanda encourages dialogue with others. The importance of dance for socialising is fundamental, either for the recognition of spaces, for guiding behaviour, or for enabling communication. All social actions are in some way linked to music, dance, or movement. From joy to sadness, movement is a common ground without a scheduled time or place.

Certain music genres such as Kazukuta or Kuduro implicate the structuring of a dance circle. The idea of dancing as part of, or within, a circle is as ancient as mankind and culture. Made up of everyone, the urban format no longer requires that men remain on one side and women on the other, as was tradition. But the

---

43 David Birmingham, 'O Carnaval em Luanda', *Análise Social*, vol. XXVI, 111, 2nd ed. (1991), 417–429 (translated from Portuguese by the author).

44 Birmingham, 'O Carnaval', (see n. 43); Portuguese original: 'O Carnaval e outros dias de festa semelhantes representaram sempre uma reacção flexível aos traumas da mudança, um apego firme aos valores do passado e uma representação irónica da exorcização dos demónios contemporâneos'.

45 A folk dance music genre based on repetitive percussion with lyrics about everyday life, associated with the festivity for Kalwanda.

46 Kimbundu for 'swing'. A dance step where there is an intentional front body clash between a man and woman.

behaviours and symbols have been inherited. The public – as part of the soul force of who performs – forms a circle that closes around those that are dancing while clapping hands, singing, and encouraging the dancers. The latter, in the centre, are trying to exhibit the best possible performance, with the aim to engage a pair or a disputer. Usually, no one remains alone in this spontaneous arena, but when it happens it is a sign that the gathering failed to captivate and convince.

When a participant has the courage to step in the circle to face another dancer, there are two approaches. If of the opposite sex, the pair in the ring tries to dance until they find a common rhythm that might culminate in the body clash of the massemba[46] dance step – otherwise one of the two turns back to the circle giving room for another to try their luck. If a dancer of the same sex enters the circle, a competition will follow, where each contestant tries to get more applause than the other. Excitements often happen when a kota enters the dance, when children reveal to be good dancers, or when uninhibited foreigners adventure an attempt without prejudices. The applauses and whistles reflect joy and excitement, as it is described in Agostinho Neto's poem, 'O Bailarico':

Come on Maria Rosa / Light up those chairs / Music boys / Burst me with that Samba of the other day. / Joy! / Jig, cheer up! / Everybody dance / My people. / Dance until eight o'clock in the morning / To the rhythm of our drumming beat / 'Cause today is the day of joy / Joy / Joy / Only joy.[47]

The round dance is used to gather people and create cohesion in communities. So, the most important aspect is the comradeship that it creates. This type of dance, which in its ancestry was among other dances part of traditional enthroning celebrations, is transported to the urban scene as the most democratic moment of the party in which everyone participates. To join the dance is to join the community. To become part of it is to dance with it; to sing its refrains. Thus, membership is completed. Dancing and singing bring about a movement where the individual ceases to exist alone and instead becomes a consequence of other individuals.

This social integration of groups through music goes back to the seventeenth century with the carnaval. However, it is important to note that during the colonial period local authorities encouraged associations oriented to music and sport, proliferating in the 1960s in more than a hundred sport clubs, turmas musician groups, and danças [a social group of young dancers. See chapter 'Turmas and danças'] in Luanda. The associative movement was encouraged by the colonial rulers, and 'tapped as a magnificent vehicle of acculturation'.[48] The public, in the musseque, fused the European and African cultural components like musical rhythms or dances, turning them into cultural products of Luanda's visible miscegenation. So, the musseques as urban manifestations of transculturality were used and manipulated for an acculturation process. However, during this process they also helped create the greatest phenomenon of national urban music, the Semba, and all its rhythmic derivations.

Turmas and danças

Created in the 1950s, turmas and danças are cultural associations for music bands and dance groups authorised by the colonial government. In contrast to sports clubs, which were mainly for soccer, then only a men's game, turmas and danças allowed women to join. Both types of groups create musical spaces through appropriation, whether in public or private. Occasions for this are: carnaval (once a year), the 'Muzongués[49] da Tradição'[50] (weekly), taxi stops (daily), or bars and clubs (weekly from Thursdays to Sundays). The emotional bonds between group members of turmas and danças as well as the disputes between groups show similarity to Western concepts of 'subculture'. Originally the turmas were

47 Original version in Portuguese: 'Vamos Maria Rosa / remexe-me essas cadeiras / rapazes da música / rebentem-me com aquele Samba do outro dia. / Alegria! / Rapaziada, animar! / Tudo dança / Minha gente. / Dançar até as oito horas da manhã / Ao ritmo do nosso batuque / que hoje é o dia da alegria / alegria / alegria / só alegria' – Please note that it is Samba here, the name of the Brazilian music genre, not Angolan Semba.

48 Bettencourt, *Subsídio*, (see n. 5). Original version in Portuguese: 'aproveitado como veículo magnífico de aculturação.'

49 Axilwandan soup of fresh and dried fish cooked with palm oil, sweet potatoes, manioc, and seasoned with hot pepper.

50 Sunday programme of the Kilamba Cultural and Recreational Center. See chapter 'Farras, festas and bodas'.

social groups with strong bonds, either through consanguinity or because they belong to the same community. Young people whose image is associated with leisure, who use their artistic skills as a primary form of expression. Their core interest was music, which they used as their main form of expression and for different purposes, from entertainment to political intervention. Starting with the Ngola Ritmos[51] – who were a turma as well as a successful music band – the phenomenon became more relevant from the 1960s onwards. Nowadays the most expressive equivalent is the Kuduro band Os Lambas, the 'demons of Sambizanga'.[52]

In the twenty-first century the turmas still provide a strong dash of Luandan urban cultural personality. But of course, the turma format has changed over time. While traditional turmas used acoustic instrumentation – from traditional instruments such as ngoma drums[53] and dikanza scratchers[54] to Western instruments like the guitar introduced by Liceu Vieira Dias – the contemporary turmas use mostly electronic instrumentation. The folkloric music version has the greatest visibility during carnaval, an occasion that traditionally stirs up rivalry between the groups, when the fighting weapons are rhythms and toques.[55] It is very common nowadays to find the turma idea reflected in DJ groups or in taxistas [groups of taxi drivers].

While a turma can perform without a dança the opposite is not possible. Like the turmas, the danças were also specified movements that first appeared after the mid-twentieth century. Each of these groups literally invented 'beats' and 'steps'. These ways of interpreting the rhythms of those days characterised these groups when performing at parties or spearheading the carnaval. The most famous dança ever was the group Cidralha, which started in 1950s. Even though the group no longer exists, the dance moves they created prevail to the present day and are still danced during Luanda's carnaval by other associations. Nowadays, dance moves can also be created by singers, for instance 'Do Milindro' was invented by the Kuduro singer Agre G. These dance steps are then reproduced in nightclubs and even by international artists like Brazil's Xuxa.[56]

Historically the danças specialised in specific musical genres, from the most folkloristic to foreign ones. One of the more folkloristic ones was the music genre Kazukuta which also enabled the emergence of Kabocomeu.[57] This is a Carnaval group founded in 1952 – and also the name of a specific cultural phenomenon which has three characteristic elements: the Kazukuta as a party rhythm with a reasonable strong percussion, participants accurately dressed in black Western suits, pants, jackets, coats, and hats, and a mandatory accessory: the umbrella.[58] What started as the group leader's personal style emerged into a scene defining an iconic dress code when it reappeared after Independence at the 'Carnaval da Vitória'[59], where it was awarded. While foreign musical influences for danças at the beginning were mainly from Brazil, from the 1980s onwards they included North American Hip-Hop as well as Caribbean Zouk. These genres were assimilated into Angolan genres like Kazukuta and Semba, producing variations in its expressions. For example, Semba and Zouk fused into Kizomba. Kazukuta absorbed the rhymes from Hip-Hop, establishing a path to Kuduro.

Originally, Kuduro started as a dance style which later evolved into a musical genre. The whole phenomenon is deeply linked to the musseques, and consequently it has the negative connotation of poverty and crime. In the musseques it always served as a key vehicle against social exclusion, poverty, and discrimination. The transformation of the dance into its own musical style is directly linked to electronic music and marks the first time an Angolan sound arrives on the world stage. It comes at the same time as other global music genres produced on computers by poor people in irregular settlements, a cultural

---

51   Ngola Ritmos [Angola Rhythms]: Angolan musical group. 'Ngola Ritmos emerged in 1947 by the initiative of guitarist Liceu Vieira Dias and Nino N'Dongo. The group's goal was to preserve the Angolan culture and to affirm national identity in an attempt to react to colonialist imposition, which rejected all indigenous cultural manifestations. Thus, they sang songs mostly in the native language Kimbundu, with the intention of raising the culture of their ancestors and to establish a relationship between the countryside and the city, whose differences were quite pronounced. Given the difficulty in imposing and transmitting their music through the radio or television (through restricted communication, only accessible to selected citizens), the group worked for friends on birthdays, parties, from time to time in shows, and in the Bairro Operário (place of transition between the slums – peripheral areas – and urbanization), where they incited the fight for independence.' Porto Editora, 'Ngola Ritmos', Infopédia, 2013, <http://www.infopedia.pt/$ngola-

phenomenon of the twenty-first century, from South African Gqom to Ivorian Coupé-Décalé. Or Brazil's Tecnobrega, about which we read:

> Tecnobrega – which literally means 'cheesy techno' – is a musical genre that was born in Belém, in the state of Pará, in the North of Brazil, and stems from a cottage musical industry and the local communities that have supported this musical genre. We could argue that tecnobrega constitutes an example of a bigger cultural phenomenon that has been branded 'global periphery' in which we can find many different styles of music, such as Kuduro in Angola, Kwaito in South Africa, Bubblin in Suriname, Sonideros in Mexico or Funk Carioca and Tecnobrega in Brazil.[60]

Today, Kuduro in Angola is an extraordinary phenomenon supported by mass media which marvels about the genre's unique sound, social posture, or apparel aesthetics. But from a symbolic point of view, the contours of the Kuduristas' behaviour are not yet defined. They are admittedly a distinct class of musicians who affirm themselves through irreverence and the cult of personality. Of all the musical styles in the Angolan culture, Kuduro has created a community different from that of others, because the Kuduristas present themselves as daring with specific marketing of their music, with thematic festivals such as 'I Love Kuduro', social networking including specific pages on the music, fashion design for Kuduristas with a particular interest for an eclectic look. The phenomenon has built a complex aesthetic that incorporates clothing, music, dance, and language at lightning speed. But in our perception, it missed the opportunity to be a social movement, because, so far, it lacks a common ideology that aggregates all the factors in an assembly line of principles and of integration in culture.

Nevertheless, we identify three very different approaches within the scene: the conservatives that preserve the line of social criticism which began with singers like Rey Webba, Dog Murras, and Sebem in the 1990s; the bullies with an aggressive attitude about sexuality such as the transsexual Titica or the female Kuduro rapper Noite e Dia [Night and Day]; and the parochialists, using their songs to defend their places which on countless occasions appear as aggressive attacks against other neighbourhoods. The latter creates a chain of conflicts, the most famous of which was the feud between Kudurista Nagrelha from the musseque Sambizanga, the typical anti-hero and recognised criminal, and Puto Lilas from Rangel, who is regarded as well-behaved, and even associated with the Pentecostal Church of Luanda. These representatives of Sambizanga and Rangel, both neighbourhoods characterised as problematic due to high population density, have created memorable songs like Puto Lilas' 'Me Dá Só Sangue' [Please, Give Me Blood] – in a musical representation of the eternal struggle of good against evil.

Music on the move: taxis

In Luanda, like in many other African cities, 'taxis' are a form of collective transport – mini-buses that go half-flexible routes, depending on what you pay, crammed with people, travelling at breakneck speed. But what is more, as in many other African cities, these mini-buses form a social phenomenon that goes beyond mere

---

ritmos> accessed 10 May 2015. For more information about Ngola Ritmos, please see Marissa Moorman's essay about music in Luanda in this book.

52 They are one of the Angolan groups of the moment, named after the musseque Sambizanga. The duo, formed by Nagrelha and Bruno King, is specialist in polemics.

53 The ngoma is made of wood covered with cow skin pegged on both ends, and it can be played with sticks or with the hands.

54 A percussion instrument. Traditionally, the dikanza was made from a sawtooth notched cylindrical body made of bamboo or wood and is played with a wooden stick. The instrument is used in many styles of Angolan traditional music. Also known as reco-reco.

55 A dance step. It is initially associated with a specific song and may expand to others according to the community's acceptance.

56 Stage name of Maria da Graça Meneghel, a Brazilian actress, businesswoman, and pop singer, double winner of the prestigious Grammy award.

57 The name comes from the Portuguese 'acabou, comeu' meaning 'stop it and eat'. This expression comes from the fact that after finishing the carnaval routes around the city the groups gathered at their starting points to eat. Even though the Portuguese is 'acabou, comeu', nowadays the word Kabocomeu is frequently spelled with a 'k'.

58 The steps that characterise the Kabocomeu closely resemble that of the Brazilian carnival dance style Frevo, even the umbrella is common to both, although Frevo is more acrobatic.

59 Victory's carnaval cf. Birmingham, 'O Carnaval', (see n. 43).

60 Jaron Rowan in *The creative industries and the cultural commons: transformations in labour, value and production* (London: University of Goldsmiths Doctoral Thesis, 2012), <http://research.gold.ac.uk/8022/1/CS_thesis_Rowan.pdf> accessed on 22 July 2014.

public transport. Most of the vehicles are marked with the names of 'staffs', meaning the groups of people to whose fleet the respective vehicles belong.[61] These 'staffs' have given themselves creative names like: 'Negro que brilha' [Negro who glows] or 'Ninguém fica' [No one is left behind]. Three additional elements belong to taxis: the stops, the routes, and the messages. The use of these elements creates a unique language not only of transhumance in the city, but also of music places. Taxi drivers play loud music non-stop, mostly Kuduro, Kizomba, or Hip-Hop, using this as a form of advertising for themselves as well as entertainment for their passengers. Due to their movements, driving the same routes back and forth all day, the taxis define specific territories which are networks rather than places if compared to more conventional clubs. Nevertheless, taxis are an important music as well as clubbing phenomenon in Luanda.

The bus stops are often car parks that represent central points on the taxis' routes. They are changing points or resting occasions. At bus stops, taxis are hired to advertise a product. And they serve as promotion or marketplaces for the music produced by the turmas, which are often associated with a particular 'staff'. At the bus stops, music fills the atmosphere creating sound waves that can be felt properly when in one of the vehicles. The car with the best equipment, and therefore the greatest sound range, benefits by attracting the most customers. It is a constant parking party. The most popular sites during the weekdays are the Congolenses square, which is halfway to the outer suburbs, and the central Praça da Independência where it is common for artists to launch their music with sales and autograph sessions.

On weekends (especially Sundays, as Saturdays are working days for the taxi drivers), the locals change to the beach areas. It used to be Luanda's peninsula,[62] but lately, since the population has been removed from downtown by the government due to an urban requalification project, taxi drivers often head for the southern city beaches. On these days the sidewalks there are invaded by high-potency sound systems that are connected using wires crossing the streets from the shops located on the other side of the road. With a table, some chairs, and serving beer, groups of teenagers and young adults spend hours drinking and dancing. All this happens under the eyes of policemen who interfere only in the case of temper exaltation caused by too much drinking.

When not resting at the bus stops or taking a break at the beaches on weekends, the taxi drivers are constantly moving. Their fleets form a universe separated and hidden from the majority of citizens. They have their own rankings according to criterias like 'staff' influence, quality of the vehicles, or skills of the drivers. The highest ranking will be handed the most lucrative routes – which is once again considered the best for marketing and promotion for political parties or for musicians.

As all taxis have to be of the same brand, model, and colour by law[63], what sets them apart are sprayed stencil writings on their exterior. Written messages are an identification factor of fleets and 'staffs'. They are symbolic because they are mostly placed on the rear panel of the vehicle – which means that when being able to read it, one is slower than the vehicle. This leads to rivalry between 'staffs'. It is common to observe taxis in city traffic which are dangerously trying to overtake each other in order to get to the client first.

When a taxi leaves another one behind or gets in front of a regular driver, the one behind sees a slogan that references a state of mind, a 'staff', or a creed. For example, '20 Buscar' [I came to pick you up][64] is addressing the client, but 'Os Metralhas' [The bad guys][65] is a representation of the 'staff'. There are also religious slogans such as 'Jesus era de grupo e era de bem' [Jesus was part of a group and was a good guy] which the drivers use to distance

---

61 According to unconfirmed sources, some taxi fleets are owned by individuals with contacts extending to the National Police and some of them are said to be connected to drugs and sex traders.

62 Portuguese: Ilha de Luanda, a peninsula in the sea directly in front of Luanda's downtown forming a lagoon. In administrative terms, the peninsula belongs to the municipality of Luanda.

63 A blue and white Toyota Hiace mini-bus model.

64 A play between the sound of the Portuguese number 'vinte' [twenty] and the phrase 'vim-te' [I came for you].

65 The equivalent to the cartoon characters The Daltons from the Belgian comic strip 'Lucky Luke'.

themselves from the widespread image of taxi 'staffs' being criminal gangs. Nowadays, some taxis are using their rear panels for advertisement (of products or events such as parties or concerts) and political propaganda (rare, mostly during elections season).

Farras, festas and ambientes

Back in the times of wars – anti-colonial and later civil – music lived hidden in private circuits. From 1977 to 1990 a curfew, which prohibited the average citizen from moving in the city between midnight and five o'clock in the morning,[66] created a new phenomenon in Luanda's nightlife. One was that of farras [backyard binge drinking], where people met in backyards to stay off the streets when the curfew was on. At that time and even today, these backyard binges had, and have, two varieties: family celebrations like birthdays, and associative which was organised by bohemian groups whose unique purpose was to entertain, using occasions of all kinds from national holidays such as the dipanda celebrations to the carnaval. One of the most famous examples of Luanda's associative backyard encounters was the Sociedade Produtora de Festas Tetracoloridas e Highlightadas (SPROFTH). After the lift of the curfew in 1990, some of their members became club owners, running venues like the Paralelo 2000 or the Mathie in the early 1990s. Their activities even stretched to the Luandan diaspora in Lisbon in the form of Mussulo Club, which was the biggest music club during the 1990s and considered the best African club in the capital of Portugal.

Another curfew-induced phenomenon were the patos [unauthorised participants or uninvited guests]. These people invented tricks to get into events and venues, often becoming the entertainers of the parties themselves. The patos were knowledgeable of the city's ins and outs and defiant of authority. It often became a game of police-and-robber, and usually there were young rebels spending the night in police stations, because they were caught without the pass that was required to circulate in the city. Later, all the partygoers that made it through the night would head for Luanda's peninsula to take the traditional muzongué soup with jindungo [pepper] to prevent hangovers. Some of them, the most bohemian, once on the beach ended up sleeping there, later mistaken for one of the beach swimmers.

Nowadays, the format of festas [parties] has been established as a more public forum. This is addressed with merchandising connected, in most cases, to sexuality. It is common to see taxi drivers announcing parties with the most incredible and prosaic names like: 'Xuxuado's Party'[67] or 'Wet T-Shirt Binge'. The DJ at festas is always the poster figure, along with a possible Kudurista or dance groups. But posters also clearly list the turmas that support the event. Next to the turmas, parties are also run by bars, discos, or cultural associations that occasionally use them to promote their establishments. All of them define specific communities. One example is '80's: Disco Fever', a party hosted annually by the restaurant/bar Coconuts, located on the seafront on Luanda's peninsula. It is clearly dedicated to the expatriate community of Luanda consisting of European, mostly Portuguese, attendants – businessmen, oil-rig workers, technicians, and managers. They are attracted by foreign beverages, global food like sushi, and mainly the music that is played: European and North American pop like Madonna, Boy George, Bananarama, or George Michael. The DJs who play this are mostly Angolan from the diaspora in Portugal, but also Portuguese whose migration to Angola has risen in recent years due to economic factors. These festivals are sponsored by big companies such as the Banco Fomento de Angola, or the phone provider Unitel. As one flyer reads:

For five years living the Disco Fever and each edition is looking for the next. Be the

---

[66] Implemented by the Communist rulers after the attempted coup d'état from 1977 and set aside with the implementation of the Second Republic in 1990.

[67] From the rude slang word xuxuta [vagina]. It also means 'tight apparel' and applies to the Lycra clothing which reveals female private parts.

production involved, the guest singers, the desire to relive a time or the desire to know what it was, the truth is that there are few who do not regret having stayed out and there are many that guarantee without any hesitation that it is the 'party of the year'.[68]

Many festas and other nocturnal activities are concentrated in the charismatic neighbourhood Coqueiros in the historic centre of the city. This neighbourhood, built in the seventeenth century, hosts some of the most visited places in the city –from the extinct Kaus, a Hip-Hop bar, to the Taverna, neighbour of the Royal, a former house of prostitutes, and next to the Majestic Grande Hotel de Luanda from the early twentieth century. However, the most famous venue was undoubtedly the Palos bar, located on the Largo do Pelourinho.

Outside, it is an unassuming building with a small sign that says 'Palos'. Once inside, the dark corridor opens up to reveal an outdoors garden courtyard complete with a menagerie of animal sculptures that surrounds the dance floor. There is even a mezzanine upstairs which overlooks the ground below. Palos is sort of an institution in Luanda, as it has been in existence even during the later days of the civil war. The music is decidedly discobeat and funky. Most of its regulars are Portuguese speaking expats from Portugal, Brazil and even Cabo Verde, so expect the occasional Samba music played too! Palos sometimes has private parties, so only the in-crowds are allowed in by the bouncers. Like clubs of this ilk in Luanda, it is pricey.[69]

This place has always been surrounded by controversy. Its owner is the charismatic Paulo von Haff.[70] The place itself was in the focus of local media companies with recurrent accusations of racism. One of the reasons for this were alleged denials of entry to black individuals, who later claimed that the reasons they were given would not have applied to white individuals in equal circumstances. Although accusations of racism are questionable, the same does not apply to the drug issue:

The police conducted a drug search operation in Palos' nightclub employing search dogs, found drugs and, subsequently, arrested some people. This was not the first operation of its kind in the disco. Police say, moreover, that these 'routine operations' have been carried out at various night amusement houses Luanda. It was as a result of these operations that ended the Eden Club on Luanda Island and other houses of the capital. More in another operation police had arrested two people in Palo's who were in possession of cocaine.[71]

However, this bar became famous for its theme parties like the owner's birthday party, which gained an unmatched importance and where the elite of the night would go. Themes like 'The Pharaohs', in which Paulo von Haff performed as Ramses II, remained in the city's memory as one of its most talked of parties on social networks and local media.

A more private side of clubbing and socialising in Luanda is represented by the ambientes [leisure environments]. This refers to family gatherings such as wedding celebrations, christenings, or Saturday lunches where family and friends are in the backyards, eating, drinking, and dancing. An interesting exception are the Sunday dance and music sessions 'Muzongué da Tradição' which take place at the Kilamba Cultural and Recreational Centre, a small, one storey colonial building.[72] Since their first edition in February 2007 they have become a place of tribute to the ancestors of Angolan popular music of the 1960s and 1970s.

These events have transformed the cultural centre into a compulsory place to go for lovers of Semba in its most original form. This music or other genres that are considered traditional are played live recreating a similar environment

---

68 Sapo, '80's @Coconuts–5ªedição', 2012, <http://banda.sapo.ao/festas/disco-fever-80s-coconuts-5edicao#> accessed 22 January 2015. Portuguese original: 'Há cinco anos que vive o Disco Fever e a cada edição se anseia pela próxima. Seja pela produção envolvida, pelos cantores convidados, pelo desejo de reviver uma época ou pela vontade de saber como era, a verdade é que são poucos os que não lamentam terem ficado de fora e são muitos os que garantem, sem quaisquer hesitações que é a "festa do ano".'

69 Virtual Tourist, 'Nightlife Luanda', 2010, <http://www.virtualtourist.com/travel/Africa/Angola/Provincia_de_Luanda/Luanda-1922982/Nightlife-Luanda-TG-C-1.html> accessed on 22 January 2015.

70 Native Angolans with European names are common. There are two reasons for this: either these are families of European descent or they were named by their former slave owners as part of their registration as slaves.

to that of the backyard. The events are mainly attended by families of the Kalwandas, the mixed population between white Portuguese and black Ambundu. Originally, the muzongué meant a specific moment at a party, usually at the end; at dawn. But what was a night closing ritual has now become an associative backyard encounter, starting at the end of the morning and running until sunset. Today, it is common for Sundays to start with a muzongué.

Behind closed doors

Walking through the streets of the city's historic centre, we can pass by the legendary Palos or the famous Zorba, a club that is said to be the property of the President of the National Assembly of Angola, without noticing that in the evening these places are pillars of Luanda's nightlife. The same happens in the distinguished neighbourhood of Cruzeiro on the city plateau at the fringe of Luanda's Bay, where the employees of the National Treasury used to live in the 1950s. Today, an emblematic skyscraper with some of the most luxurious shops of the city towers here. Nothing would make us realise that on its third floor the vibrant Doo.Bahr is hidden. This bar is the property of Isabel dos Santos, daughter of Angola's Ex-President and one of the wealthiest businesswomen in Africa, according to *Forbes Magazine*. Therefore, it mainly attracts the city's upper class, because only the wealthiest Luandans can afford this: sons and daughters of government officials, upper middle class, rich tycoons, the military elite, as well as foreign professionals.

> *It's a highly social place – where people go to see and be seen rather than to actually dance, although the place is more of a lounge rather than a club from Monday to Wednesday. We went on a Thursday, when they begin the party nights, yet not many people were dancing. The music was good, and we heard a little of everything: hip-hop, R&B, afro-beat and afro-house. As for the drinks, one can find the best cocktails of Luanda. Here cocktails are made in the true sense of the word. They do not make gin-tonic and then call it cocktail as it happens in other places of the city – no, here, there is a really dedicated team of barmen who know the art of making a good cocktail.*[73]

With all this status one would expect a greater visibility for the site. However, like almost all clubs in the city it is not visible from the street. At night, the whole city is quiet. Some of the few places filled with life are sidewalks crowded with parked cars where street boys are trying desperately to keep an eye on parked cars or to sell marijuana. A barbeque grill is set up the whole night making hamburgers and hot dogs for the night owls. It is also an entertainment spot with background music to attract customers. These are the only open places in the city where nightlife happens. Apart from that, the streets often appear empty. This disguise of the urban vibe is heir of the curfew and, for years, the illegality of private property. In the 1990s, when times changed, venues catered mostly to expats or the military community who settled in the city which was still in a embryonic stage of the democratic society. Thus, nightclubs in Luanda became connected with prostitution and drugs – an image that still prevails among a significant part of the population.

As sneaky and hidden as nightclubs appear in the city it is very different on the peninsula. This is a leisure spot where nights are competitive, from the neon panels with club, bar, or restaurant names to the loud and extravagant advertising of parties outside. However, the peninsula nights have been the target of criticism for being too close to a Western lifestyle. The audience of bars/restaurants like, for example, Chill Out, Lookal, and Shogun is largely white and male, with easy-made access to prostitutes who are black or of black descendants. The food and music is Western. Most significantly, these spaces are located on the coastline with private

---

71 Angonotícias, 'Discoteca Palo´s ... Cocaína na noite', 2009 <http://www.angonoticias.com/Artigos/item/21970/discoteca-palos-cocaina-na-noite> accessed 22 January 2015 (translated from Portuguese by the author).

72 Founded in the colonial times of the 1960s, the Centro Social Maria das Crequenhas, as it was known then, is located in a former 'indigenous neighbourhood' in the Rangel district. After it was reopened by the second president José Eduardo dos Santos in 2001 it was renamed 'Centro Cultural e Recreativo Kilamba', and the neighbourhood's name was changed to Bês (Bs), because the streets here are named B1, B2, B3, and so on.

73 Luanda Night Life, 'Doo.Bahr', 2012, <http://www.luanda-nightlife.com/por-tipo-by-type/bars/doo-bahr/> accessed 22 January 2015.

beaches or protected by security guards for the peace of clients. But these manifestations of segregation have diminished because, on several occasions, the local population has spoken out against it, criticising luxury immigrants who are protected by local authorities.

But of course, luxury clubs in the city or on the peninsula are not everything. Scattered throughout the city's districts, Luanda has more than a hundred official nightclubs, bars, and recreational centres aimed at less wealthy people. One example would be King's which is located in the geographical centre of the city. This club is not a common destination for the Luandan population since it primarily promotes live Alternative Rock concerts. King's Club has been promoting contemporary Rock music bands like the founder of contemporary Angolan Rock, the band Black Coffee, or the Hardrock band Mvula that won the All Africa Music Awards 2015 in Nigeria. But other communities visit King's as well. For example, it organises alternative poetry shows. Another example is the W disco, which has a place for local music such as Kizomba, Kuduro, and Afro-House. It attracts a fairly young population, national rather than foreign. It is common for turmas to promote their parties or presentations here.

And then there is the Elinga Teatro. It is the headquarter of one of the oldest national theatre companies, founded on 21 May 1988, named after the Umbundu word for 'action', and a place of worship for intellectuals and artists of all kinds. Starting off with its location, the building and the ambient, everything in this place is transgressive. For example, there are nights where you can hear music from multiple sources from Reggae to House. Here marijuana can be consumed and nobody is bothered. Because both a national and foreign population is in attendance, it encourages a free and uncompromised spirit, expressed by the graffiti on the walls of a nineteenth century townhouse. It should have been gone a long time ago. But it is, at least at the moment of writing, still there.

The end? A phenomenon named Elinga

The press is on a rampage. Newspapers and blogs publish headlines like: 'Elinga, an affective heritage', 'Why is it that Elinga is important?', 'Elinga Teatro – from cultural heritage to car parking', or 'We need to save Elinga Teatro'. Never has so much been written about a building in Luanda. The chronicle of a foretold death is rewritten every day and the demands are always the same: let Elinga stay. But what is this Elinga?

The Elinga Teatro is located in the Carmo neighbourhood in the historic centre of the city. It occupies a sobrado house from the nineteenth century.[74] It is one of those rare cases of urban transmutation, which, more than a building of Luanda's downtown, becomes a symbol of the urban culture of the city. The two-storey building has the compact and austere appearance of houses built during slave times, following the plain architectural style rules. Even though robust, the interior is rather fragile. The stairs are made of Brazilian timber from slave ships, and one can still feel the metal balusters of the balconies while resting in the main lounge on the first floor. The manifestation of the Elinga phenomenon started in the 1980s, during the Civil War, when a shutdown space downtown was conceded to the Elinga Teatro group. This group was the inheritor of generations of artists and intellectuals, and for over twenty years they manufactured the symbols that transformed a house into a place full of social meanings. In a society that was not used to open criticism, it emerges today as one with the greatest claimants of civil rights movements that the city has ever witnessed, resorting only to art as an argument.

Like the stones in a game of dominos, Luanda's old buildings fell one after the other to the violence of the devastating cranes, all on behalf of a progressive Luanda. Many of them were far more imposing than Elinga's building, for

---

[74] 'The sobrado houses are residential buildings with unique features in the architecture of the ancient city of Luanda. ... The ground floor, with very thick walls made of rammed earth (an earth architecture technology) or in rough masonry, ... is the physical support of the wood structure that supports the upper floor that will be then called the townhouse. ... Wooden floor: they were mainly produced in wood coming from Brazil on slave ships. These logs served to make weight and thus prevent vessels from sinking as their tare weight was not sufficient. As soon as the ships reached the port, these logs were replaced by slaves and abandoned and converted to construction. Their dimensions determined the dimensions.' Ângela Mingas in *O Centro Histórico de Luanda. Dissertação de Mestrado*. (Porto: Universidade Lusíada do Porto, 2008).

example the City Central Market, that housed thousands of citizens, or the centennial palace of Dona Ana Joaquina, the most emblematic house in the city of Luanda, residence of the famed slave owner, after whom it was named in the nineteenth century. There were no farewell parties, awareness campaigns, reports, signed petitions, or other manifestations of indignation for any of them. But they were before the brink of the demolition of the Elinga building, which was supposed to be demolished as well, but represents more than one stone upon another. Indeed, it represents a way of being. As journalist Marta Lança has written in an article for the online news channel *Rede Angola*:

> That informality and availability towards the other, without money commanding the nature of relations, representing a certain downtown of Luanda, of socio-cultural mix of experimentation and modernity, between the local and the global, with Angolan and foreign, it is practically only here that such happens. The coexistence of two types of architecture[75] is a milestone in the history of the city, the traces of other times side by side with the fast pace of a bustling city, are also there well represented. We are not lacking justifications for the preservation and enhancement of the Elinga.[76]

Many believe that Elinga will really disappear:

> This centre of the Angolan culture, birthplace of protestor artists, will soon disappear, with its coloured pink walls reduced to rubble, crushed by bulldozers and experience thus the same fate as that of so many old houses in the centre of the Angolan capital handed over to property developers attracted by the fragrances of black gold of the second oil producer in sub-Saharan Africa. And yet, the theatre had all the conditions to escape this evil fate.[77]

In such a scenario it is easy to understand the outrage around the disappearance of a place like this. In the twenty-first century, the planned demolition of a building in Luanda is no longer news. What was, in fact, very displeasing was that the exchange turned into an insult, because instead of the theatre a car park was planned, as well as offices, a hotel, and so on – a myriad of uses, all of them mercantilist, none of them cultural.

At a certain point, the idea of cultural heritage appeared to be the building's salvation. A law-decree appeared that would have classified the building as a 'monument' decades ago. Destroying patrimony is illegal. Thus, this is the direction the movement took, referring to the time of enslaved men who covered walls with slogans like 'This is the place to where I belong and no one can take me away from here,' written by an anonymous person who, after all, represents so many. But it did not last long. After a vigorous social awareness campaign, mobilising thousands of people, the government, through the Ministry of Culture, silently disqualified the building without ceremony.

It looked like the end of the pro-Elinga movement. The voices slowly quieted. But then a post on Facebook reactivated the movement by asking for another breath. E-mails began to circulate inviting 'former combatants' for a conversation about Elinga. On one very hot Luandan Saturday, at lunchtime, people gathered for a traditional mufete[78] in order to chat. Actors, architects, sociologists, rappers, writers, Rastafarians, social activists, rich people, and poor people spoke of informal democracy and of culture, of the need to enforce the right to belong to a place. On that day, the Elinga, which had been living house, and empty building and a theatre, was once again transformed. It was back in the media, it became a field of debate, put the intellectuals on fire. It surprised everyone, this time for something so different that even though accidental, it was predictable. A movement was generated.

In 2016, at the moment of finishing this essay, the Elinga is still there. The theatre

---

[75] The nineteenth century style of the Elinga building marks a sharp contrast to the 1960s International Style of its surroundings.

[76] Marta Lança, 'Elinga um Património Afectivo', *Rede Angola*, 2004, <http://www.redeangola.info/especiais/elinga-um-patrimonio-afectivo/> accessed on 29 March 2014 (translated from Portuguese by the author).

[77] Christophe Châtelot, 'Mort d'un theatre à Luanda, victime des promoteurs', *Le Monde*, 2012, <http://mobile.lemonde.fr/international/article/2012/09/25/mort-d-un-theatre-a-luanda-victime-des-promoteurs_1765361_3210_html> accessed 29 March 2014 (translated from Portuguese by the author).

[78] Kalwandan grilled fish with beans cooked in palm oil, roasted manioc flour, and onion sauce with hot pepper.

company was evicted by the current owners, a private company that works on the development and management of real estate projects. After that, all of the other communities that used the place – artists that rented studios, DJs that had their regular performance days, small dance companies – slowly said goodbye. It is still possible to go to the Elinga to see a theatre play, or to listen to alternative music. Still, even though the core community is no longer there, as one enters the place, one can feel the vibration that is all over the building. As you walk up to the first floor, in the stairway you can read, 'No to homophobia' or 'No to racism'. Words, which serve as a kind of antidote to prejudice. In fact, as one reaches the main hall, one is overwhelmed by words, colours, and sounds.

For a decade this building had been the scene of a controversial feud. It has faced an utterly silent power machine, which was confronted with the only thing for which it was not prepared… an idea.

Bibliography:

Angonotícias, 'Discoteca Palo´s … Cocaína na noite', 2009, <http://www.angonoticias.com/Artigos/item/21970/discoteca-palos-cocaina-na-noite> accessed on 22 January 2015.

Augé, Marc, Não–lugares. Introdução a uma antropologia da sobremodernidade (Venda-Nova: Bertrand Editora, 1994).

Bettencourt, José de Sousa, Subsídio para o Estudo Sociológico da População de Luanda (Luanda: Instituto de Investigação Científica de Angola, 1965).

Birmingham, David, 'O Carnaval em Luanda', Análise Social, vol. XXVI, 111, 2nd ed. (1991), 417–429.

Châtelot, Christophe, 'Mort d'un theatre à Luanda, victime des promoteurs', Le Monde, 2012, <http://mobile.lemonde.fr/international/article/2012/09/25/mort-d-un-theatre-a-luanda-victime-des-promoteurs_1765361_3210_html> accessed 29 March 2014.

Heywood, Linda M., Central Africans and Cultural Transformations in the American Diaspora (Cambridge: Cambridge University Press, 2002).

Lança, Marta, 'Elinga um Património Afectivo', Rede Angola, 2014, <http://www.redeangola.info/especiais/elinga-um-patrimonio-afectivo/> accessed on 29 March 2014.

Luanda Night Life, 'Doo.Bahr', 2012, <http://www.luanda-nightlife.com/por-tipo-by-type/bars/doo-bahr/> accessed 22 January 2015.

Mingas, Ângela, O Centro Histórico de Luanda. Dissertação de Mestrado (Porto: Universidade Lusíada do Porto, 2008).

N.N., 'Lei das Associações', Diário da República, Lei no. 14/91, 11 May 1991.

N.N., 'Lei de Alteração da Divisão Político-administrativa das províncias de Luanda e Bengo', Diário da República, Lei no. 29/11, 15 November 2011.

N.N. (2014): 'Regulamento Geral dos Planos Territoriais, Urbanísticos e Rurais. Decreto n.º 2/06 de 23 de Janeiro'. In: Diário da República, 2014.

Pepetela (1990): Luandando. Porto: Elf Aquitaine Angola.

Porto Editora (2013): 'Ngola Ritmos'. In: Infopédia, <http://www.infopedia.pt/$ngola-ritmos> accessed 10 May 2015.

Ribeiro, José Teixeira Lopes (2005): 'Características Gerais da População de Angola', ONU – UNFPDA – Fundo das Nações Unidas para População, <http://membres.multimania.fr/redeluso/ao/cadernos/vol07-1/Parte5.doc> accessed 16 November 2011.

Rowan, Jaron (2012): The creative industries and the cultural commons: transformations in labour, value and production, <http://research.gold.ac.uk/8022/1/CS_thesis_Rowan.pdf> accessed 22 July 2014.

Sapo (2012): '80's @Coconuts – 5ªedição', <http://banda.sapo.ao/festas/disco-fever-80s-coconuts-5edicao#> accessed 22 January 2015.

Soares, Francisco (2010): 'Mário António: Lírica Completa', <http://www.adelinotorres.com/literatura/> accessed 7 August 2012.

Virtual Tourist (2010): 'Nightlife Luanda', <http://www.virtualtourist.com/travel/Africa/Angola/Provincia_de_Luanda/Luanda-1922982/Nightlife-Luanda-TG-C-1.html> accessed 22 January 2015.

Members of the Kuduro dancing and theatre group performing in a neighbourhood in the outskirts of Luanda city, Luanda, 2015, photo: Anita Baumann

Luanda Carnival series, Luanda, 2015, photo: Max Fonseca

378 | LUANDA | PLATES

Luanda Carnival series, Luanda, 2015, photo: Max Fonseca

Luanda Carnival series, Luanda, 2015, photo: Max Fonseca

Kuduro fans performing in the neighbourhood of Sambizanga, Luanda, 2015, photo: Anita Baumann

Ngola Bar, Luanda Pop, Luanda, 2005, photo: Kiluanji Kia Henda

Ngola Bar, Luanda Pop, Luanda, 2005, photo: Kiluanji Kia Henda

Ngola Bar, Luanda Pop, Luanda, 2005, photo: Kiluanji Kia Henda

LAGOS

MUSIC/SPACES
Throw to Me and I Throw Back to You

From Jùjú and Fuji to Afrobeat and 9ja Lamba

Mallam Mudi Yahaya

P.387 ▶

SPACES/POLITICS
Circadian Rhythms

The Many Layers of Lagos

Mallam Mudi Yahaya

P.409 ▶

Throw to Me and I Throw Back to You – From Jùjú and Fuji to Afrobeat and 9ja Lamba

Mallam Mudi Yahaya

When it still existed, Rehab nightclub in Lagos regularly saw DJ Debby, the venue's in-house DJ, priming the sound system for the crowd that was expected for a club night. Here, all the Nigerian contemporary music royalty came to hang out and to be seen. With a dance area meant to accommodate fifty to a hundred people, the club opened up from the minimal furnished dance floor to a courtyard that showcased a swimming pool and a pool house. Rehab was located on a banking and business street in the highbrow Victoria Island district, and from its entrance, complete with muscular and edgy bouncers, it betrayed nothing of its ambitions. The lighting at the bar was not too bright and not too dark, with an international selection of cocktails, local lager, and foreign beers. Grilled fish, lamb, and baked pastries with savoury fillings were available. Later that night everything would have been as usual, jam-packed with over quadruple the number of its intended capacity – a rather significant statistic for this part of Lagos that is upmarket and exclusive in nature. The music blasted, and the celebrity stars took over.

Lagos' nightlife has recently awakened from a decade long slumber, caused by an economic downturn of foregoing structural adjustment years. These days there are new lounge bars, strip clubs, gay bars, and prostitution on the street corners. The sound in most of the venues – with a dash of House and Hip-Hop – is strictly *Naija* [for Nigeria or Nigerian]. The Naija sound is a mix of indigenous African rhythms in an incestuous relationship with US style pop, Hip-Hop, and R'n'B. The seemingly insatiable thirst for the Naija sound in the club scene – made up largely of a combination of successful corporate professionals and the hip Nigerian university crowd – follows in the DJ tradition of less upmarket clubs that played popular indigenous Jùjú or Fuji music beats during the course of the night to ignite the dance floor, mixed with foreign popular music. This tradition came up in 2014 following the release of the hit 'Happy' by Timaya featuring Jùjú legend Sir Shina Peters, and its modernised Jùjú, which had the popular chorus 'Dance, dance, dance and forget your sorrow'. Nightclubs like Rehab, which has now shut down, were a good example of how indigenous and yet global the club scene in Lagos had become.

Lagos: the old centre

Lagos is a predominantly Yorùbá speaking, cosmopolitan city and the former capital of Nigeria from the amalgamation of Nigeria in 1914, through to Independence in 1960, until the Nigerian capital was relocated to Abuja in 1991.[1] The colonial era established Lagos as a coastal port that has always been a multi cultural contact zone, offering access to resources, technology, and an enabling atmosphere for creativity, patronage, and reputation building. These, and many other factors, make Lagos the undisputed commercial seat of the Nigerian popular music industry. As the predominant culture and language around Lagos is Yorùbá, it has become the Nigerian commercial musical language of choice for lyrical output.

The Yorùbá language is widely spoken in this West African sub-region and has cultural connections to countries like Brazil and Cuba. The Yorùbá are one of the three major ethnic groups in Nigeria, which also include the Hausa-Fulani and the Igbo. In total, Nigeria has more than 250 ethnic groups. Yorùbá holds a special position in influencing lyrical output in Nigeria, due to the ability of the language to reach a wider audience – especially when code switched in music, which has made the Yorùbá language universally adapted by other Nigerian languages. Code switching is a creative way of fusing ethnic Nigerian languages with English or more commonly Pidgin English. The latter is the whole region's informal *lingua franca* – an English based hybrid of linguistic influences that is spoken among the Nigerian urban populace, which evolved through the spread of imperialism and from urban migration. As most Nigerians are bilingual and many

[1] Cf. Takiu Folami, *A History of Lagos, Nigeria: The Shaping of an African City* (Florida: Exposition Press, 1981).

even speak three languages or more, code switching has become a signature technique employed by most Nigerian music artistes to skilfully use language alternation as an identity marker. By increasing the participation of a diverse, multilingual audience, code switching enhances the aesthetic and rhetorical qualities of Naija popular music.

The tradition of code switching between imported and indigenous elements can be found again in the emergence of the contemporary hybrid popular Nigerian music phenomena. The colonial, and Christian mission educated, Lagos elite separated their 'cultured' Christian church music from the seemingly 'pagan' native (Yorùbá) music – to the effect that Yorùbá music, while flourishing and blossoming among the uneducated indigenous folk, was for a long time left almost completely untouched by Western music and instrumentation.[2] Among the indigenous, traditional music with almost no Western stylistic affinities and mostly ignored by the Western educated elite were Jùjú, Sakara, and Apala music. These genres were created entirely from traditional instruments and encompassed instrumental and vocal music, a combination of drumming, singing, and dance. But it is important to note that Jùjú music evolved rapidly from its traditional Yorùbá percussion roots with the *Iya Ilu* [talking drum] to include electric guitars – which then became its signature sound.

This musical dichotomy between Western music and 'traditional' music was very pervasive; to the effect that efforts where made by composer Fela Sowande to adapt African sound to Western classical instrumentation and form.[3] The resulting genre was called 'Nigerian Art Music', and Sowande's classical piece in this genre, *African Suite*, was recorded and released by Decca Records in the UK in 1955. Sowande, who was born in 1905, performed his own compositions on the BBC Africa Service, and later served as Music Director of the Colonial Film Unit. Ironically, despite working in a 'Western' musical style, Sowande considered himself a cultural nationalist and composed his last major opus, *Nigerian Folk Symphony*, to mark Nigeria's independence from Britain in 1960.

Classical music in the form of Christian choral music also had an unexpected effect. It was here that female musicians could comfortably exist. The traditional cultural attitude of the time discouraged female secular musicians. The conventional suggestion was that secular music performed by any female was a damning commentary on her moral suitability. With this logic the only secular music that women could be found performing was traditional genres like Waka music that was linked to Islam and by extension had a moral undertone. Not all the Western educated Lagos Yorùbá elite were convinced that this was the right cultural path to follow for a people that had a deep secular cultural relationship with music, irrespective of gender. Herbert Macaulay, the front-line Nigerian colonial independence nationalist, quickly recognised the connection, use, and impact traditional music had on the indigenous uneducated, not to mention the potential political power the music wielded.[4] He rallied up support from his fellow Lagos elite for more inclusion of Yorùbá traditional music in church practices.[5]

By the 1920s it was established in the minds of Lagos' educated elite that a racial divide existed, which allowed ascendancy to church leadership exclusively to the British missionaries. The agitation for the adoption of Yorùbá culture into the rituals of worship, especially choral music, grew. As the cry for Nigerian national Independence advanced, the church increasingly became a battleground to fight European hegemony, using music as an artistic symbol that challenged the status quo. Faced with the challenge of more inclusiveness, the British missionaries slowly accepted sections of the hymns to be sang in native (Yorùbá) tongue, which was previously considered 'offensive' and not worthy for use in holy worship. The practice of using European musical frameworks with the adaptation of African elements continued until political and economic forces eventually made Nigerian music go beyond code switching and find its way into the church and the concert halls unaltered.

Highlife and Jùjú: culture contests

The battle of cultural dominance between Western/European sound and African beats continued, and in 1960 it reached a peak. As part of the Independence day celebrations on 1 October, the Nigerian government intended to invite Edmundo Ros as the main dance band – as opposed to a Victor Olaiya's

[2] Cf. Bode Omojola, *Yorùbá Music in the Twentieth Century: Identity, Agency, and Performance Practice* (Suffolk, England: Boydell & Brewer, 2012).

[3] Cf. Bode Omojola, *The Music of Fela Sowande. Encounters, African Identity and Creative Ethnomusicology* (Music Research Institute: MRI Press, 2009).

[4] Cf. Isaac B. Thomas, *Life History of Herbert Macaulay, C.E* (Tika-To[r]e Press, 1946).

[5] Odejobi Cecilia Omobola, 'Influence of Yorùbá Culture in Christian Religious Worship', *International Journal of Social Sciences & Education*, vol. 4 (2014), 587–589.

band which was only given the slot of the second dance band.[6] Edmundo Ros was a Trinidadian musician living in the UK and ran one of London's leading nightclubs at that time. He was selected with the understanding that Princess Margaret, the British Queen's younger sister, who was coming for the Independence celebrations, liked his music. A 'union' of Nigerian musicians organised an eight to nine hundred men strong protest demonstration, petitioning the Prime minister, Alhaji Tafawa Balewa, against the invitation of a foreign band as first choice.[7] The prime minister gave in, and at the Independence dance the musicians' union and Nigerian Victor Olaiya's band performed.

'Dr. Victor Olaiya', as Olaiya was popularly referred to, was born in 1930. He played with the Sammy Akpabot band and was the bandleader of the Old Lagos City Orchestra before joining Bobby Benson's Jam Session Orchestra. The trio of Olaiya, Akpabot, and Benson represented the best of Big Band music coming out of Nigeria in the 1960s. Olaiya's musical style was greatly influenced by James Brown, and it is considered an early precursor to what would be known as Afrobeat. Afrobeat stars Tony Allen and Fela Kuti played with Sir Victor Olaiya before they went on to achieve individual musical success.

Olaiya was considered 'The evil genius of Highlife'. The designation Highlife is a somewhat conventional phrase, used to refer to different forms and genres of popular music in Anglophone West Africa that includes guitar bands, dance bands, and various Palm-wine sounds. Hundreds of Highlife bands played across West Africa, and the music was imported into Nigeria from Ghana. The 'golden age' of Highlife spanned from the 1950s through the 1970s. It was music that was characterised by rhythmic guitar melodies and soulful singing. Highlife was a music form that was perceived as being at the intersection of 'modern' Western sound and traditonal indigenous African music styles. The Pan-African decolonising movement did little to encourage its popularity as it was commonly seen as Western derived music.

Notable among the huge Highlife hits of the 1960s that had embraced singing in Pidgin English and indigenous language was Sir Victor Uwaifo's 1966 song 'Guitar Boy & Mamywater'. Apparently, it was inspired by an encounter with a *mami wata* [mermaid] which spiritually connected very well with the decolonisation mode of indigenous Africa of the time. Sir Victor Uwaifo was born in 1941. He trained as a graphic artist and sculptor and was a member of the Bobby Benson Highlife band. Uwaifo made history in Nigeria when he won the first Golden record in Nigeria, West Africa and Africa for his song 'Joromi'. To date, 'Joromi' enjoys exalted standing ovations among Uwaifo fans, and his legendary skills of playing the guitar with his tongue and both feet are still mentioned in popular conversation. In 1983, in appreciation of his talents and contributions to Nigerian music, the Nigerian Federal government honoured Sir Victor Uwaifo with National Honours. Uwaifo was the first professional musician in Nigeria to receive such an award.

—

After Nigeria's Independence in 1960, the public was attracted to any sound that was 'progressively' postcolonial. The Pan-African post-independence sound from Congo —Congo Rumba—was the popular rave. It was the sound identified as the music of the new progressive Africa, despite its obvious mixed hybrid constituents. 'Black' music of any form (including African American music) was also popular, Nigeria was already known in the Jazz world through Babatunde Olatunji.[8] Louis Armstrong, who had visited Nigeria in 1959, visited it again in 1961. On the Lagos scene, Fela Ransome-Kuti played Jazz music with his Koola Lobitos band. As the popular music taste favoured a more authentic African sound, Jùjú music began to emerge as the sound of choice of the people over the Highlife band sound by musicians like Bobby Benson, Eddy Okonta, Rex Lawson, Osita Osadebe, Victor Olaiya, or Roy Chicago.

Ironically, it was Jùjú music that the imperial colonial authorities had turned to for Second World War propaganda in the Nigerian southwest.[9] At that time the southwest of Nigeria was the most educated part of the country that provided the most political resistance to the imperial authorities' policies. The adaptation of Jùjú music was a calculated strategy to woo the common man over to the imperial war propaganda. Jùjú

6
Olushola Ricketts, 'Victor Olaiya was against a national band for independence', *New Telegraph Newspaper*, 3 October 2015, <http://newtelegraphonline.com/victor-olaiya-was-against-a-national-band-for-independence/> accessed 17 November 2015.
7
Sola Balogun, 'Independence Concert: Tafawa Balewa Inisisted That I Must Play on That Day–Victor Olaiya', Nigeriafilms.com, 7 September 2010, <http://www.nigeriafilms.com/news/8674/3/independence-concert-tafawa-balewa-inisisted-that-.html> accessed 17 November 2015.
8
Cf. Jon Pareles, 'Babatunde Olatunji, Nigerian Drummer, Dies at 76', *The New York Times*, 9 April 2003, <http://www.nytimes.com/2003/04/09/obituaries/09OLAT.html> accessed 17 November 2015.
9
T. Ajayi Thomas, *History of Jùjú Music: A History of African Popular Music from Nigeria* (Jamaica, NY: Thomas Organization, 1992).

music, from its talking drum roots, derived its modern pitch and quality from the 1920s Palm-wine sound. This was originally based on a diverse set of string based musical styles that included guitars, banjos, hand drums, and shakers and was frequently played in bars in Sierra Leone and Liberia. The Lagos-born version of the Palm-wine sound was a composite that had integrated brass instrumentation, written notation, Islamic percussion, and acquired Brazilian musical routines.

Apparently Jùjú music got its name from the tambourine, an instrument that was popular with the early Jùjú bands. The influential musician Fatai Rolling Dollar's (1927–2013) account of the origination of the name describes a process where the tambourine was thrown between members of a Jùjú band during music sessions while maintaining the tempo of the beat. It was this process of throwing the tambourine that gave rise to the name Jùjú from the Yoruba phrase '*Ju si mi, kin ju si e*' ['Throw to me and I throw back to you']. Shortened to 'Ju Ju' ['throw throw'].

By the mid-1960s, Jùjú was mainstream music, and I.K. Dairo was its big king. Jùjú music was seen as more authentically African than Highlife, which echoed a lot of the colonial experience. Isaiah Kehinde Dairo was born 6 January 1931. He was the son of a carpenter, he worked odd jobs while building a musical reputation on the Jùjú music scene. His first Jùjú band was called the Morning Star Orchestra, which he formed in 1954. By the early 1960s he had changed the band's name to the Blue Spots and had many popular hit songs to his name. The Blue Spots played at working class nightclubs rather than middle class joints, and this increased their appeal and popularity. I.K. Dairo was attributed with many innovations in Jùjú music, he expanded the Jùjú band from trios and quartets to full dance bands, he pioneered the use of the accordion in the music and is credited for introducing Latin American and Christian choral influences that to this day remain established attributes of the style.

Fuji, Apala, and Waka: new hybrids

With the wave of Independence came a resurgence of the fervour of ethnic nationality. With ethnicity came the politics of religion. It is during the mid-1960s that the Islamic-inspired music, Fuji, started to evolve. It is important to note that many traditional Yorùbá drummers at that time, and until this day, are Muslims, and a good majority of the biggest patrons of popular music at the time were also Muslim entrepreneurs. The Nigerian civil war (1967–1970) broke out after the secession of eastern Nigeria to form the republic of Biafra.[10] The Nigerian civil war was a catalyst for the evolution of new music styles. The army bands provided creative space for musical experimentation and innovation. The army initially supported musical groups, as every brigade desired a music group to be attached to it. The army started poaching musicians from civilian bands, and quite a number of popular Nigerian musicians enlisted into the Nigerian army. The Nigerian army music directorate was well kitted with musical instruments, and the musicians had quite a bit of time to practice and experiment between war front concerts.

The civil war was also probably the final nail in Highlife's coffin as most of the Christian Highlife musicians came from the secessionist eastern part of Nigeria and had gone back to Biafra. There was a dearth of musical entertainers in Lagos, so the vacuum was quickly filled by Jùjú and Fuji musicians. Fuji music can be described as Jùjú music without guitars (although present versions of Fuji music employ the guitar sound). Sikiru Ayinde Barrister (1948–2010), one of Nigeria's best-known singer-songwriters, introduced Fuji music. Alhaji 'Chief Doctor' Sikiru Ayinde Barrister, as Ayinde was popularly called, named his sound after the Japanese Mount Fuji, the mountain of love, largely because the name in its abstraction resonated meaning to him. Sikiru Ayinde Barrister worked as a stenographer and served in the Nigerian army during the civil war where he developed the genre. Fuji music is an exciting, amplified dance music based on a rhythmic combination of an Ajisari/Were beat (an Islamic type of music, commonly played by Muslim children during the month of Ramadan), talking drums, a drum set, *Sekere* (a gourd rattle), bells, claves, bells set to vocals in form of poetry. While Jùjú music was favoured by Christians, Fuji was understandably favoured by Muslims. Jùjú music was seen as more

10
Cf. Alfred Obiora Uzokwe, *Surviving in Biafra: The Story of the Nigerian Civil War* (Bloomington, IN: iUniverse, 2003).

gentrified, while Fuji was seen as more 'common'.

At the end of the civil war another underground yet pioneering genre of Yorùbá music came into circulation – Apala. A typical Apala combo consists of only three instruments: the gourd rattle Sekere, an Akuba (a set of three small, stick-hit Yorùbá congas) and an Agidigbo (a four or five key thumb piano with a rectangular box resonator). Sometimes a Gangan (talking drum) is also employed. Leading drum and percussive instruments in combination with vocal mastery of proverbial folklore distinguishes the Apala music sound. The music was traditionally used for entertaining people during social events and festivals and is considered, like Fuji music, to be a sound derived from Islamic culture. Apala, like Fuji music, is said to have begun as a creative musical intervention during the Muslim fasting month of Ramadan. It was created in the tradition of Ajisari/Were, to wake people up for the early morning pre-fasting meal. It is believed to have no particular date of origin and is said to have been in existence in a form called 'Ere f'owo b'eti' [cover your ears]. Stylistically, the largely acoustic Apala sound differed in tonality and content from the more syncretic Fuji sound. Apala is older and more difficult to master than Fuji music and is said to have been in existence even before its early exponents, like Ligali Alade Adebayo, made the sound mainstream.

Apala music was brought to the contemporary music limelight by the legendary musicians Haruna Ishola and Ayinla Omowura. The latter, also referred to as 'The Egunmogaji of Egbaland' [The Royal leader of the masquerade of Egba land], trained under his father as a blacksmith and is believed to have worked as a taxi driver before venturing into Apala music. He reinvented and upscaled the music with a new twist of social change and political satire that was energised by the glamorising of marijuana. The established belief on the street, then, was that marijuana was issued to soldiers during the civil war to numb the senses of the troops against the challenges and the trauma of war. Naturally marijuana was also linked to the creative prowess of musicians that enlisted into the army. Ironically, this glamorising of marijuana is not compliant to Muslim faith, separate from the fact that many interpretations of Islam do not encourage indulgence in music. But this trend witnessed in Ayinla Omowura's music – in combination with his preaching for social change and political rethinking – would be further promoted by Fela Anikulapo Kuti. Even today Ayinla Omowura enjoys a cult following among public transport drivers, mechanics, and traders. Omowura died on 6 May 1980 at the age of forty-seven. He has recorded more than twenty LPs, all of them selling a minimum of 50,000 copies on the first day of release.[11]

His contemporary, Haruna Ishola, started out by recording for multi-national recording companies like Philips and Decca who were pioneering the recording business in Nigeria. At the end of the 1960s, Ishola started his own record company, Star Records, in partnership with Jùjú music legend I.K. Dairo. He was the first indigenous African to establish a properly equipped recording company with mastering, mixing, and recording facilities and recorded hit songs like 'Ododun larorogbo' [every year we receive news].

Parallel to Apala's evolution, another style exclusively for female lead singers emerged: Waka. This music, like Apala, is an Islamic influenced traditional Yorùbá sound and, like Apala, is much older than Jùjú or Fuji music. It is believed to have been adapted from the Northern Nigerian Hausa tribe in the 1800s and was traditionally performed only accompanied by hand clapping. The Waka sound then evolved to introduce accompaniment in the form of Seli or Pereseke [tin cymbals and jingles], and eventually drums as well as other percussion instruments followed. Although the roots of Waka music are in Islamic culture, its lyrics often deal with secular interests. This further broadened its appeal to attract Christian patrons as well. Even though Waka groups later comprised a combination of five to six male and female musicians, the main proponents of the sound have always been female musicians like Majaro Acagba (popular in the 1920s and 1930s) or Salawa Abeni, the Waka Queen. The latter, who eventually married the famous Fuji musician Alhaji Kollington Ayinla, released her debut album, *Late General Murtala Ramat Mohammed*, in 1976. It became the first recording by a Nigerian female artist to sell over a million copies. For her efforts Salawa Abeni was crowned

11
Cf. Festus Adedayo, 'Ayinla Omowura: 35 years after', *Nigerian Tribune,* 2 August 2015, <http://tribuneonlineng.com/ayinla-omowura-35-years-after> accessed 17 November 2015.

'Queen of Waka' in 1992 by Oba Lamidi Adeyemi, the traditional ruler of the Yorùbá state of Oyo.

Records and rivalries: a golden era

Critical to the mass consumption of all these new hybrid sounds were the shellac and vinyl discs because they were relatively affordable and easily available. The Decca West African series for single play (SP) on 78 rpm shellac discs was introduced in 1947 with WA 101 (the first Decca release).[12] Decca's West African series was originally manufactured in the UK. But as a result of rising record sales Decca built a recording studio in the late 1950s at Winneba, near Ghana's future capital Accra. Decca also bi-annually sent recording engineers to Yaba in Lagos to record music on portable equipment.

In the 1960s, Decca West Africa was producing one quarter of a million records a year – mostly singles that were suitable for Highlife recordings and choral music. During this period the ten-inch 78 RPM shellac discs began to disappear and were replaced by the more economical and durable seven-inch 45 RPM discs – the perfect format for Western pop music singles aimed at the mass market. In 1963, Nigeria finally got its own pressing plant by Phonogram, the second one to be built by the company in Africa after one in South Africa. It was originally established as part of Philips West African Records. Phonogram later built a new studio in Onitsha, a commercial town in South-Eastern Nigeria, which was destroyed during the Nigerian Civil War. EMI also built its second African factory in Jos, Nigeria, after its first in South Africa. Decca, unlike its UK rival EMI, believed in the West African music market and stayed on when Independence came for the British colonies. Decca presided over the transition from colonial era to post independence. Unlike EMI, who closed all its shellac operation around Africa with the exception of distribution outlets in South Africa and Nigeria, Decca saw the transition from shellac to vinyl, from 45 RPM formats to the 12-inch 33 RPM long-playing album, and from colonies to independent states.

Indeed the long-playing (LP) vinyl album was the unsung hero of the golden era of Nigerian music. The post civil war oil boom had created a very strong Nigerian recording industry. Its success was also a fallout of the indigenisation excitement that was sweeping throughout Africa. Newly independent African countries, including Nigeria, quickly realised that true and real political Independence came with economic Independence as a prerequisite. Nigeria, like other African countries, embarked on policies that were aimed at strengthening control of specific economies by reserving exclusive rights to indigenes. One of these economies was the music recording industry. The oil boom turned Nigerian record labels into big business empires. The LP emerged as a creative canvas on which Nigerian musicians could express themselves like never before. The LP was essentially ideal for soundtracks, Classical music, and Jazz recordings, which suited the format for Jùjú and Fuji music with its long song suites. Jùjú and Fuji music recordings in the 1970s were very experimental, instruments like the wahwah guitar effect or the saxophone were introduced into the genres. The musicians developed a spontaneous taste for dropping into the mix anything that caught their fancy, from Broadway show soundtracks to Western pop tunes.

Expectedly, musical experimentation of this diversity resulted in innovative compositions that generated rivalries between the musicians. The most famous rivalries of this era were those between King Sunny Ade and Ebenezer Obey in Jùjú music and Alhaji 'Chief Doctor' Sikiru Ayinde Barrister versus Kollington Ayinla in Fuji music. The supposed contention between Ade and Obey in the 1970s enthralled public enthusiasm into a mania which enthroned Jùjú music as the musical centrepiece in Lagos and the Yorùbá speaking states of Western Nigeria. But the Sunny Ade versus Ebenezer Obey rivalry was not the type of feud that incited enmity. Rather it encouraged competition. The situation forced both musicians to introduce more creativity to their instrumentation and lyrical delivery, resulting in an exceptional series of evergreen hits. For example, King Sunny Ade challenged Ebenezer Obey with hits like 'Esu Biri Biri' [Gather Around Me Quickly]. In reply Obey delivered tunes like 'Iwa Ika Kope' [Wickedness Is Not Profitable]. And although both of them re-introduced multiple guitars into Jùjú music, which had already been used in the 1940s by the Jolly Boys Orchestra, Ebenezer Obey claimed

12
Cf. John Collins, *Music Makers of West Africa* (Passeggiata Pr: 1985).

innovative responsibility for modernising Jùjú music from a traditional musical expression to a sophisticated urban sound which he called his 'miliki system' [enjoyment system].

Behind the scenes both musicians were friends – but they saw the commercial opportunity in manipulating and stoking the situation to both their advantages. The perception of a rivalry boosted the sales of records, which were produced and distributed in quick succession. Tactfully, both made claims and pronouncements that tended to depict musical superiority over the other. A stimulating angle to this situation was that the two musicians had very distinct musical styles, philosophical leanings, and artistic approaches: King Sunny Ade's style was seen as very entertaining and popular for dancing while Ebenezer Obey's style was perceived as philosophical, reflective, and appealing to the 'mature' mind. Both musicians drew patrons from the upper classes that could afford their big band setups. It was typical for both musicians to play at the same venues at different times of the day that reflected the tone of their music and lyrics.

—

Meanwhile the Fuji musicians Alhaji 'Chief Doctor' Sikiru Ayinde Barrister and Alhaji Kollington took their own rivalry to another level. The constructed feud between King Sunny Ade and Ebenezer Obey was child's play in comparison as it bore no viciousness and was not abusive. But the two competitors also known as 'Kebe n Kwara' ('Praise for the one from Kwara' – Kollington) and 'Alhaji Agba' ('Senior Alhaji', Alhaji signifying a man that has performed the holy pilgrimage to Mecca – Barrister) took no prisoners. Their quarrel was fuelled by tendentious recordings, rumours, verbal tussles, and partisan fans. Although names were never mentioned in the lyrics of the Fuji strife, it was very obvious who was being referred to when each sang about the other. Similar to Ade's and Obey's differing styles, Barrister's blend of Fuji music was regarded as lyrically conscious and philosophical in focus while the more aggressive Kollington sang with vibrant and vulgar expressions, delivering a more danceable and more entertaining brand of music.

Kollington and Barrister competed over everything: who deserved to carry which title and to use which alias? Who went on tour first? Who slept with whom first? Who travelled to the United States of America first? On one occasion when Barrister had visited Disney World in Florida, he released an album about the fantasy and advancement he saw in the US (*America Special*, 1986). Legend has it that his album spurred an invasion of Nigerian tourists to the theme park that eventually led to a university in Orlando, Florida, honouring Barrister with an honorary doctorate degree in Music. Thus 'Dr.' Sikiru Ayinde Barrister. Upbraided by this development, Kollington assumed the sobriquet 'Professor Master' after a trip to the US. To date it is unknown how he got the title. The biggest rivalry between the two, however, was on the issue of who actually invented Fuji music. This is a battle that outlived Barrister who died on 16 December 2010. There are those who believe Barrister founded Fuji music and others who claim he merely evolved and modernised an existing sound he called 'Fuji'.

Despite or as a result of these rivalries, the demand for Jùjú and Fuji live bands at the so-called Owambe parties has not waned until this day. Owambe are marathon parties that were standard social entertainment in Lagos by the late 1970s – and Jùjú music was their beat of choice. These parties began mid-afternoon and typically lasted till daybreak, featuring a combination of dancing with long stretches of sitting down; ideal for listening to music. The term 'Owambe' derives from an old party tradition from the early days of Jùjú music. In those days it was popular for women to wear waist beads with their undergarments. These beads were worn to accentuate the waist and bottoms of women and usually rattled when dancing. As most Nigerian traditional dances require some dexterity of the waist and bottom, the ability to move these body parts is also an essential skill to dance to Jùjú and Fuji music. To add a spark to a party and to encourage dancing it was typical for musicians to be cheeky by inquiring about waist beads of the females on the dance floor. Musicians would often call out 'S'owambe?' [Is it there?], to which the dance floor would shout in reply 'Owambe!' [It's there!]. Owambe parties typically take place from Friday afternoons until Sunday night in different permutations. Ideally, Owambes would be organised in a hall, outside on a field, or traditionally at the house of the celebrant, in which case it is not unusual for the party to occupy the whole street and at times the adjoining streets as well. Due to the size of these events, they are usually sponsored by the rich and able.

Western influences: the 'Afro'-prefix

By the 1970s, Western influences on Nigerian contemporary music arrived on a broader scale and was beginning to be audible. So, the 1970s became the golden period of the 'Afro'-prefix, which hints at the influence and experimentation African music was undergoing. Now there was an emerging concept of the new Nigerian music producer, which had been virtually non-existent in the 1950s and 1960s Nigerian music scene. In came producers like Odion Iruoje, Lemmy Jackson, Laolu Akins, Emma Ogosi, Tony Okoroji, and Jake Sollo. These producers were at the forefront of musical experimentation that gave birth to Afro-Rock, Afro-Funk, or Afro-Soul bands like Ofege, The Funkees, Monomono, and BLO, or Afro-pop bands like The Clusters, The Cyclops, The Juleps, and The Centipedes.

Notable among the new producers were Odion Iruoje and Jake Sollo. Iruoje had worked with Fela and brought Apala musician Ayinla Omowura into the limelight by producing his first hit album. He was also the producer of Eppi Fanio who created an Afro-Folksy music sound that hoped to be as unconventional as Fela Anikulapo-Kuti's Afrobeat. Iruoje also produced one of the most successful Nigerian albums of the 1980s, Kris Okotie's *I Need Someone* (1980). Jake Sollo (Nkem Okonkwo) was a member of the Afro-Rock/Afro-Funk bands The Hykkers, The Funkees, and Osibisa in 1976. He went on to become the most sought after and prolific Nigerian Afro-Rock/Afro-Funk producer with his signature Prophet-5 synthesizer.

Another notable musician at that time was William Onyeabor who is believed to have studied cinematography in Russia, returning to Nigeria in the mid-1970s to start his own music label and to set up a music and film production studio. He recorded a number of hit songs in Nigeria during the 1970s, the biggest of which were 'Atomic Bomb' and 'Better Change Your Mind' in 1978. Onyeabor's music was made with analogue synthesizers, which was not typical for African pop musicians who at the time preferred guitars and drums. William later left music for Christianity after nine self-released albums.

Meanwhile, musicians like Joni Haastrup, known as Nigeria's 'Soul Brother Number One', or Segun Bucknor sought to introduce their version and admiration of Afro-Soul music to the Lagos scene. Afro-Soul bands like The Strangers, the aforementioned Hykkers, and 'Nigeria's James Brown', Geraldo Pino (originally from Sierra Leone), were already active. Joni Haastrup's main inspiration was James Brown, and he went on to work with Ginger Baker, touring Europe with a collection of Lagos musicians before settling with Monomono. Segun Bucknor was influenced by the music of Ray Charles which he had heard during his three-year sojourn at New York's Columbia University where he studied liberal arts and ethnomusicology. He cultivated an exuberant aesthetic style to accompany his Afro-Soul sound in sympathy with the popular new Pan-African identity. Refraining from Western style attire that distinguished popular musicians of the day, he and his band, The Revolution, went shirtless with wreaths of cowrie shells. Bucknor appeared in dramatic fashion with his hair shaved into a half-mohawk, adding to his performance a trio of psychotic-looking, body-gyrating seductive young ladies named 'The Sweet Things'. Overall, Segun Bucknor, whose cousin Wole Bucknor had tutored Fela Kuti on the piano, was a trailblazer in terms of visual stage dynamics.

By 1976, the Afro-Rock/Afro-Funk/Afro-Soul experiment had run its course and Disco music was becoming popular in the Lagos club underground. The queen of Nigerian Disco, Christy Essien Igbokwe, released the first Nigerian Afro-Disco album, *Freedom* (1977). She cut this first album when she was sixteen. Essien-Igbokwe, known as Nigeria's Lady of Songs, was among a force of female singers who made an impression in Nigeria in the 1970s like Martha Ulaeto, Onyeka Onwenu, or Patty Boulaye. But despite all the experimentation, the biggest hit of 1976 was an album that attempted to recall the heydays of Highlife music: the herculean *Sweet Mother* by Prince Nico Mbarga and his band Rocafil Jazz. The song took the Congo guitar style that was thrilling francophone West African dance floors and blended it with Anglophone Highlife – producing a massive staggering title song that instantly became an international Anglophone West African anthem. Sadly, even 'Sweet Mother' was not enough to bring Highlife back to the music and dance scene.

Fela Kuti and Afrobeat: a musical firebrand

Many musicians in Lagos made use of the new LP format's potential in various forms. However, no Lagos musician explored the creative possibilities of the LP like Fela Anikulapo-Kuti.[13] The typical three-minute song allocation for a 45 RPM single was inadequate for him to express his artistic ambitions. Typical Fela songs were long, many lasting more than 20 minutes, with the short songs at least 10–15 minutes in length, and they could go up to 45 minutes each when performed live. Traditionally, his tracks opened with an instrumental introduction jam part, which would be 10 to 15 minutes long, before Fela commenced the main vocal part.

These details hint that Fela was a complex man. Indeed, Fela Anikulapo-Kuti (1938–1997) was one of the most critical musical and political firebrands in post-independence Nigeria. He was at once an entertainer extraordinaire, a shaman (he was also called 'Abami Eda' [chief priest]), a politician (he floated a political party, and ran for President), and to some, a subversive character. He was an exalted freedom fighter and agent provocateur that pioneered Afrobeat, a stimulating blend of Jazz, Funk, Highlife, and traditional West African rhythms. Fela's first commercial Afrobeat song was the 1971 hit 'Jeun K'Oku' [Chop & Quench] – a vibrant track, which reportedly sold 200,000 copies. To many this song marked the birth of Nigerian Afrobeat, although the mature authentic sound of Afrobeat, as we know it today, was better observed with his 1972 two-song LP *Shakara*. He followed this with the 1973 track 'Gentleman', which was one of Fela's first of many statements decrying his countrymen's colonial mindset. In this song Fela declares in Pidgin English that he is an 'Africa man original', rather than a contrived British 'gentleman'.

Fela's tracks were designed to reveal more detail and subtext as one listened to them over and over again. From his 1969 stint in Los Angeles, during the Civil War, Fela had learnt the relationship between LP album culture and higher states of mental consciousness, based on the provision of a musical experience that induced long meditative periods, which ideally would not be interrupted by having to change the record side. Based on his US experience, Fela also openly advocated the smoking of marijuana because, as he frequently said, 'the God of Africa created this herb to enlighten his people'. On his album *Expensive Shit* (1975), the title track alludes to a scandalous incident, in which Fela swallowed a marijuana stash during a search of his home, only to have his faeces searched for evidence. In 1974, Fela's proclamations on the benefits of marijuana had already caused trouble with the Nigerian authorities, and in retaliation he released his album *Kalakuta Show* (1976). It was Fela's spectacular rejoinder to two infamous police raids that saw Fela charged with 'possession of dangerous drugs' and 'abduction of minors'.

In a career that spanned four decades, Fela recorded over fifty albums. The notion of the album as a revolutionary musical force appealed to Fela, and he was an early Lagos pioneer in producing concept albums. For Fela, the album was a complete product, and every detail, right down to the album cover art, was part of the musical experience. The album sleeve became a symbol of Fela's identity. His albums were based on a theme on social commentary, with strong statements delivered with attitude and urban Lagos style. Fela's music instituted strong messages that spoke about race politics, culture, economics, and the return to traditional African belief systems.

With all these ingredients, it was little wonder that Afrobeat was a colossal success in Lagos and young people assembled from all over Nigeria to hear Fela's music. Despite its popularity, the music was not well suited for Lagos radio station programming. In the 1970s all Nigerian radio stations were government run. Not only because of the fact that Fela's tracks were way too long for radio broadcasting slots, but also based on his

[13] Cf. Michael Veal, *Fela: The Life and Times of an African Musical Icon* (Philadelphia: Temple University Press, 2000).

anti-military lyrics and songs that, at times, extolled sexual liberation next to his praising of marijuana, radio stations censored his music. Fela's Afrobeat fan base had to rely on albums to enjoy the sound. Fela refused to play songs at The Shrine (the name of his night club where he gigged on a regular basis) once they were widely available for sale. This worked brilliantly as a marketing strategy to sell his LPs and to encourage his fans to visit The Shrine for new and fresh music.

It was not only Fela's Lagos fans that visited The Shrine but musicians from all over the world. With FESTAC '77, the Fela fascination grew, and James Brown and Gilberto Gil among others visited the club. FESTAC '77 was the Second World Black and African Festival of Arts and Culture that took place in Lagos in 1977. It was the largest cultural event ever held on the African continent and more than 17,000 participants from more than fifty countries attended. The FESTAC festivals were proposed as Pan-African commemorations and ranged from performance and theatre to debate and symposiums. Lagos was now a Mecca for creativity, and with the influence and new interest in Nigerian sound from the swinging 1960s, Western musicians trooped to Lagos. For example, British musician Ginger Baker of the famous Rock band Cream lived in the city from 1970 to 1976. He set up a recording studio where he (together with Jide Alawiye) produced, among others, Bongos Ikwue's 1973 debut, the heavily psychedelic *You Can't Hurry the Sunrise*. Paul McCartney of the Beatles recorded an album in Lagos with Nigerian musicians like Remi Kabaka. Fela himself worked on the *Stratavarious* album by Ginger Baker (1972) and collaborated with Roy Ayers on the album *Music of Many Colours* (1980).

Sonny Okosun: message music

The 1970s were also a period of African liberation struggle and coup d'états. This spawned the emergence of a socio-political protest sound which manifested itself not only in Afrobeat but also in Ozzidism.[14] This was a kind of political message music named after Ozzidi, a renowed river God of the Ijaw indigenous group of people. The musician Sonny Okosun was the founder of Ozzidism and was known as the high priest of Ozzidism. He believed that genuine development could only begin after political Independence. His musical style included Reggae, Afro-Funk, Highlife, and Gospel. In his music he sang in Edo, Igbo, Yorùbá, and English. In 1969 Okosun started his career by joining Sir Victor Uwaifo's band Melody Maestros. Later he organised and played with several local bands before starting his own record company in 1972. Sonny Okosun was probably the only Nigerian musician whose stature within Africa in the 1970s competed and often even surpassed that of Fela Kuti's.

In 1977 Sonny Okosun released his album *Papa's Land* where he sang about imperial manipulation of leadership and control. In the lyrics of the title song 'Papa's Land' he emphasised that 'Africa must be ruled by Africans.' Okosun saw no reason why Africans should not be capable or allowed to rule Africa. The focus of Okosun's songs included African unity, Apartheid in Southern Africa, and political Independence for African countries that were still under colonial subjugation. Based on the strength of the lyrics, 'Papa's Land' was eventually adopted as the official anthem of the freedom fighters in Zimbabwe. The repressive Apartheid policy in South Africa was the prime target of Okosun's lyrical attacks. Okosun's 1977 song, 'Fire In Soweto', even became a major international hit. Its original record company, EMI, did not do much to promote it, but it was sub-licensed to the London-based label Oti, which promoted it successfully to become a Pan-African chartbuster. In 1978, the South African government officially banned 'Fire in Soweto'. In 1980, the song was the soundtrack for Samuel K. Doe's coup d'état in Liberia. That same year, Sonny Okosun was the first musician to come on stage at Zimbabwe's Independence celebration, where Bob Marley also performed.

Sonny Okosun relentlessly opposed the Nigerian military government's annulment of the 1993 Nigerian Presidential election. This first truly democratic election in Nigeria was declared to be won by Chief MKO Abiola before being annulled by the army general Ibrahim Babangida. Despite Okosun's record of opposition to undemocratic Nigerian governments, he was accused by the Nigeria press of never indicting any of Nigeria's abominable military dictators or civilian

14
Cf. Sonny Oti, *Highlife Music in West Africa: Down Memory Lane* (Nigeria: Malthouse Press, 2009).

cleptocrats in his music. Regardless of this accusation, Okosun's music undeniably raised the political consciousness among the common man in Africa.

Okosun performed in so many West African countries that he earned the epithet of 'the most ECOWAS oriented performer', after the Economic Community of West-African States. In the late 1970s music piracy was already rife across Africa, yet Okosun was releasing up to four albums a year, selling more than 100,000 copies of each of them. So, Sonny Okosun was the first Nigerian musician to win the EMI gold awards in 1974. All in all, he won fifteen gold discs and five platinum discs from record sales. In the 1970s and 1980s, he toured the United States and toured through Nigeria with the Reggae stars Jimmy Cliff as well as Toots & the Maytals. Sonny Okosun was also a friend of Eddy Grant, with whom he collaborated in 1979 on reworking his hits 'Fire in Soweto' and 'Papa's Land'. Even Peter Tosh spent three weeks in Okosun's home in Lagos where he completed songs for his classic album, *Mama Africa* (1983). Sonny Okosun persistently claimed that Bob Marley had corresponded with him in a letter, expressing his desire to record his song 'Holy Wars'. In 1982 and in 1985, he joined musicians Bob Dylan, Run-D.M.C., Bruce Springsteen, Miles Davis, and Ruben Blades on *Sun City*, a benefit record against Apartheid. In 1986, Okosun's song 'Highlife' was in the soundtrack of Jonathan Demme's 1986 film *Something Wild*.

Sonny Okosun died in 2008. A *New York Times* obituary on his death quoted him as saying that he believed that the elements from elsewhere were simply returning to Africa, where they had originated. The result in its time was a zestful, funky strand of what later came to be called 'World Music'.

Decline and female liberation: the 1980s

At the end of the 1970s, the policy of the indigenisation of recording company ownership in Nigeria discouraged foreign ownership of business. In retrospect this policy was counter-productive as foreign record labels had offered well established distribution networks and better economies of scale that would have benefitted Nigerian music's international reach. The policy of indigenisation severed the link from Nigerian music to international music markets. To make matters worse, in 1980 Sony revolutionised how music was listened to and consumed with the Sony Walkman, the first low cost portable cassette player, selling millions of units worldwide.[15] The rise of cassette popularity and the attendant high rate of piracy, facilitated by the importation of hi-tech duplication machines from the Far East, precipitated a decline in fortunes and forced the main record pressing plants and record labels in Nigeria to close down.

Nevertheless, the influence of foreign culture was still being felt – and in 1981 'The Way I Feel' was released, the first Nigerian Rap by Ron 'Ronnie' Ekundayo, a popular nightclub DJ and TV presenter. Michael Jackson's 1982 album *Thriller* had spawned a wave of derivative music productions from Chris Mba, Moses Jackson, Emma Dorgu, and a host of other Nigerian Michael Jacksons. The Afro-pop music scene was also gaining momentum and Felix Lebarty was the undisputed star of Afro-pop in Nigeria. His smash hit 'Ngozi' cemented his reputation as Nigeria's 'Lover Boy', which was also the title of one of his albums. In a different direction, Charles 'Charlie Boy' Oputa, a Nigerian singer/songwriter and one of Nigeria's most controversial musicians, attained success with his 1985 hit 'Nwata Miss'. Oputa, who was also popularly referred to as 'Area Fada and His Royal Punkness', based on his alternative lifestyle and biker aesthetics, experimented with electronic sound. He also collaborated with his Swedish-Nigerian cousin Alban Nwapa, the successful pop singer Dr. Alban, on songs like 'Wok Wok Africa', 'Commercial Waste', and 'Carolina' (sung in Nigerian Pidgin English). Dr. Alban later went on to international success to an estimated sixteen million records selling worldwide with hits like 'It's My Life' or 'Hello Afrika'.

—

While some music scenes suffered from the demise of the major record labels, the traditional music scene saw a lot of innovation. The historical dichotomy between Western music and traditional indigenous music had played out in interesting ways with the younger generation of Nigerians. They were

[15] Cf. Ben Marx, 'How the Sony Walkman Changed the Way We Listen to Music Forever', Allday.com, <http://allday.com/post/4587-how-the-sony-walkman-changed-the-way-we-listen-to-music-forever/pages/2/> accessed 17 November 2015.

bombarded with Western culture through television and other sources of popular culture. As a result, many of them regarded Western music as modern, hip, and sophisticated. At the same time, they had a suspicious if not contemptuous relationship with more traditional indigenous music like Jùjú and Fuji, which they viewed as music for the old folk. But the dearth of Western music also created a vacuum that renewed interest in experimentation with traditional indigenous sound. So Jùjú music went international with King Sunny Ade who signed with Island Records in 1982 and subsequently getting nominated for a Grammy award in 1983. The biggest hit on this new Jùjú scene was Sir Shina Peters' hit album *Ace* in 1989.

While these general changes took place in the early 1980s, a lot also changed especially for female musicians. Prior to the 1980s, it was rare to hear female voices in the mainstream popular Nigerian music scene, except for traditional genres like Waka.[16] This misogynist phenomenon was based largely on the Nigerian cultural gaze of appropriateness as music was deemed an unworthy career path to follow for a 'decent woman'. Female musicians were seen only as a few rungs up the ladder from a prostitute.

In the early 1970s, female singers Nelly Uchendu and Joy Nwosu had managed this delicate balancing act well. The escape trick was categorisation: once a female musician was categorised as a 'Folk singer'—as opposed to a liberal 'pop' or 'Rock singer'—everything was fine. The identical twin act the Lijadu Sisters, who had started out packaged as 'Folk singers' but switched to a blend of Afro-Rock, Soul, and Afrobeat after having met the British drummer Ginger Baker, suffered from being perceived as 'easy' ladies. This was further complicated by the fact that they were said to be second cousins to radical Fela Kuti and Nobel laureate Wole Soyinka. They prematurely retired from the music scene and languished into obscurity—until a renewed interest in classic Nigerian Soul and Funk recently put them back in the spotlight.

Another route to a music career for women was through a respectable position in television. This was the route that female musicians like Patti Boulaye, Julie Coker, Theadora Ifudu, and the aforementioned Christy Essien Igbokwe took. Boulaye (born Patricia Ngozi Ebigwe) was an inspiration to many Nigerian women. She was brought up a strict Roman Catholic and initially wanted to become a nun. But then she fled Nigeria at the age of sixteen for the UK after the Civil War and went on to become the UK's Diana Ross. Boulaye became successful and had her own TV show, 'The Patti Boulaye Show'. She was known in Nigeria as the lady in the Lux beauty soap commercials. She starred in one of the first Nigerian feature films, Ladi Ladebo's *Bisi, Daughter of the River* (1977). But women like Boulaye were exceptions to the strict rule of appropriateness.

The 1980s changed this—and the new liberated Nigerian woman launched herself on the Lagos music scene, complete with trousers and lipstick. Singers like Uche Ibeto, Funmi Adams, Onyeka Onwenu, Martha Ulaeto, Ima Valentine, and Julie Pip were at the forefront of radically changing the cultural gender status quo. Oby Onyioha, for example, persuaded women to seek better options in her song 'Enjoy Your Life' (1981). This emancipation process was also going on in other genres of Nigerian popular music. Salawa Abeni, the Waka queen and ex-wife of Fuji star Alhaji Kollington, released a series of abusive hits albums after she was accused of waywardness and unfaithfulness by her bitter ex-husband Kollington in his hit record *Tani O Jo* [Who does it resemble] (1981), a reference to Abeni's first child. All this was because Salawa Abeni had the 'audacity' to leave him and marry someone else. By the 2000s, female musicians like Asa, Seyi Shay, Yemi Alade, or Cynthia Morgan were mainstream and out there.

Gospel and Galala: come to Jesus!

By 1983, the Nigerian economy was in recession, and the newly elected civilian government had instituted austerity measures. This belt tightening period saw the decline of the ostentatious Owambe marathon party in Lagos, and the public taste for music was leaning more towards spiritually conscious music. With the Owambe parties becoming unpopular, Jùjú music's appeal also started to wane. Ebenezer Obey took to Gospel music, and even freedom fighting Sonny Okosun reinvented himself as Gospel performer 'Evangelist Sonny Okosun'. The born again train also moved into Afro-Pop, and

[16] Cf. N.N., 'Highlife Piccadilly – African Music on 45 rpm records in the UK, 1954–1981', Musical Traditions, <http://www.mustrad.org.uk/articles/african.htm> accessed 17 November 2015.

musicians like Kris Okotie, Felix Liberty, or Dizzy K. Falola became pastors and evangelists. This evasion of secular musicians into the gospel music scene created new categories of Gospel music: Sacred Pop (popular commercial Gospel music) emerged. The church as the new venue for popular music production in form of 'praise worship' – including crossover collaborations with secular musicians – was a commercial success. At the peak of Sacred Pop, Evangelist Sunny Okosun's 1994 album *Songs of Praise* sold almost a million copies. Nigerian Gospel music split into secular inspired sub-genres like Gospel-Reggae, Gospel-Afrobeat, Gospel-Jùjú, Gospel-HipHop, and – with regards to its Islamic roots, the most ironic sub-genre – Gospel-Fuji, with musicians like Dekunle Fuji and Midnight Crew.

With this spiritual awakening came the rise of Nigerian brewed political conscious Reggae music. Sonny Okosun was the first Nigerian artist to fully encapsulate the opportunities of Reggae in his music. He had deconstructed the Reggae beat and re-constructed it in his own sonic impression, rather than just copying Caribbean drum and bass. The first Nigerian Reggae album was 1984's *Lamentation For Sodom* by Tera Kota (Femi Gboyega).

Nigerian Reggae has its roots in the 1970s and 1980s Reggae revolution in Great Britain. Nigerians in the UK diaspora were drawn to the music and introduced it to the Nigerian homelands by sending home records. The official stand of the Nigerian government was to fight colonialism and Apartheid, so the government-controlled radio stations were encouraged to support the promotion of Nigerian Reggae on the airwaves. By the mid-1980s the influence of British Reggae had grown to the point that there were now Reggae sound systems operating in Lagos. Among the sound systems were Champion Bubblers owned by Daddy C with the Late Great Ricky Zansky as the operator. The DJ line up was Lecturer 'Buchi' (who became Nigeria's No.1 Gospel-Reggae artist) and the famous Ras Kimono, among others. Champion Bubblers main competition was the sound system Mongruv Sound (later Realitee), owned by Daddy Pfizer. Reggae musicians like Majek Fashek, Daniel Wilson, The Mandators, or Evi Edna-Ogoli sang a more Nigerian stylised version of traditional Reggae. Evi Edna-Ogoli's 'Happy Birthday' even became a quasi-national anthem in the 1980s. Majek Fashek created an Africanized Reggae sound he called Pangolo, which sounds like Reggae, Bob Marley style, with an African twist in the lyrics and sound. Majek first became popular on national television as a member of the Benin-based Reggae group Jastix together with Ras Kimono and others.

This spiritual awakening was also occurring in the urban ghettos of Lagos like Ajegunle. The road to Boundary bus stop – the gateway to Lagos' urban ghetto Ajegunle – is rugged, irregular, and rowdy. But it fits Ajegunle's nickname: Jungle City. Here, the musician Daddy Showkey developed a Ragga/Reggae style distinct from Jamaican Reggae and West Indian dancehall: Galala. This is a syncretised hybrid of Rastafarianism and Old Testament Christian expression. Ajegunle Galala draws symbolism from Roots Reggae (dreadlocks, scarves, and caps in Rasta colours) without any engagement to the religious ideals of Rastafarianism. The Ajegunle Rasta musicians use Rasta terms like 'Irie', 'Jah', 'Babylon' in their lyrics in combination with 'Hallelujah', 'Jehovah', and 'Hosanna'. Underlying Galala is an obvious musical influence from Fuji music that was also popular in Ajegunle. The Galala dance was promoted as the official ghetto dance step by musicians like Daddy Showkey, African China, and Baba Fryo who all came from Ajegunle.

An ear to the street: the modern 9ja sound

With the deteriorating economy many musicians left Nigeria. The massive exodus of musical talent included The Mandators, Majek Fashek, Mike Okri, and Ras Kimono. But the period following the mass 'checking out' of musical talent from Nigerian shores also ushered in a new dawn in Nigerian music in the early 1990s. The situation created a second golden age for Nigerian popular sound. During this period a lot of musicians that were not able to leave the country started to frequent close-by Ghana. This country had better recording studios and a more organised music ecosystem that was still functional despite the economic downturn.

The Ghanaians have historically always been a source of inspiration for Nigerian musicians, and Hiplife—a Ghanaian musical style that fused Highlife and Hip-Hop, and was influenced by Dancehall and Reggae recorded in the Ghanaian Akan language—provided the perfect template for the transition from Nigerian 1980s Reggae to a modern sound that was to be called Naija pop or 9ja pop, after slang terms for Nigeria or Nigerian. This was to become the most popular dance music genre in almost all of Africa and Nigeria's most successful cultural export internationally since Fela Kuti. Taking a cue from the Ghanaians that had introduced a Pidgin English version of Rap, the new Nigerian producers also started experimenting with choruses and hooks in local languages. The resulting modern 9ja sound is an evolution of African rhythms mixed with a blend of Western and Caribbean genres. It comes out sounding like Dancehall and House meet R'n'B with an African melody, including local Nigerian code switched Rap and Nigerian Funk that harks back to the time of Segun Bucknor and Joni Haastrup.

The economy at the time no longer supported big bands, and studio time became prohibitively costly. For example, Reggae music, which was the toast of the 1980s and is structured typically around a band concept, became an expensive musical option. Many musicians re-invented themselves as producers/musicians with the help of modern digital technology. These new artists/producers cared less about mastering any musical instrument except the keyboard, which was needed to programme new software-based tracks. The new producers emerging on the scene were taking advantage of the democratisation of sound production with Digital Audio Workstations and sampled-based synthesizer beats became the core source of the modern 9ja sound.

These new producers had no apparent musical tutelage with old genres like Jùjú and Fuji music, except the use of the Yorùbá language in their lyrics. They were mostly in their early to mid-twenties and not at all musically dexterous in terms of instruments like the musicians of the 1960s-80s. What they had was a keen ear that understood what the street wanted. They were post-independence, military-government era kids, so they came with no Pan-African flavouring, or ethnic or religious struggle colouring.

Their music was about 'connecting', and they did this with street vernacular and sound that resonated with the common man.

Eventually, due to unfavourable economic conditions in the West, Nigerian musicians in the European diaspora started looking for musical opportunities in Nigeria. So, a new breed of musicians made its way back home. The musicians that had returned from the diaspora wanted to take part in the entertainment revival, so Nigerian DJs and VJs emerged, pioneered by DJ Jimmy Jatt. Meanwhile in Nigeria, the General Ibrahim Babangida military regime had deregulated media, and private radio emerged. The new radio and television station needed entertainment content, and there was a renewed push to reignite the Lagos music scene. At the same time, product brands like Benson & Hedges cigarettes saw sales opportunities in partnering with media content around entertainment. So, in 1995 music talent talk shows like the 'Benson & Hedges Grab Da Mike' contest emerged, where later 9ja stars like P-Square, Sound Sultan, and 6 Foot Plus were discovered. In the same year, Nigerian Breweries launched the 'Star Talent Hunt', where later stars like Nigga Raw and KC Presh first appeared.

The biggest producer of this era was Babatunde 'OJB Jezreel' Okungbowa. He was behind numerous hits from Ruggedman (who showcased Igbo language Rap music) and 2Face Idibia (who sang a Reggae based R'n'B sound) to Jazzman Olofin (who sported Yorùbá/Pidgin English Rap), and others. At this time ID Cabasa and Nelson Brown were also significant. ID Cabasa, producer of Loded Tunes was behind the acts Lord of Ajasa[17] and 9ice. Lord of Ajasa, whose real name is Olusegun Osanyi, is an indigenous Yorùbá Hip-Hop act and an early pioneer alongside AY and the late Dagrin of the use of indigenous Nigerian languages (without code switching) in Rap. Lord of Ajasa—through his style of free flowing, laidback Rap flows delivered in unadulterated Yorùbá—laid the foundation of popular Nigerian Rap stars like Olamide or Phyno that have taken the indigenous Rap genre mainstream. 9ice, who started out with Fuji music, is quoted as saying: 'English language has been imposed on us but God graciously gave Yorùbá language to us.' Born

17
Cf. Titilope Adeuja, 'Late Dagrin, Olamide, Phyno, Reminisce Are Enjoying What I Started—Lord of Ajasa', Nigeriafilms.com, 9 May 2015, <http://www.nigeriafilms.com/news/33117/69/late-dagrin-olamide-phyno-reminisce-are-enjoying-w.html> accessed 17 November 2015.

Alexander Abolore Adegbola Alapomeji Ajifolajifaola, 9ice's unique style is anchored with his mastery of the Yorùbá language in a code switch mix of Yorùbá proverbs with English, Pidgin English, Hausa, and Igbo.

Meanwhile, ID Cabasa's producer and colleague Nelson Brown created the sound of the Plantashun Boys, who were a pivotal group of this era and featured, alongside band members Blackface and Faze, a young 2face Idibia, who later became a solo star. The early modern Nigerian sound, showcased by the Plantashun Boys who disbanded in 2004, experimented with code switching techniques in different Nigerian languages other than Yorùbá in a bid to create a new sound—a trend that is very consistent in all albums of the music of 2face Idibia.

By far the biggest catalyst on the modern 9ja music scene was the influence of the production company and label Kennis Music and their own Ray Power FM Radio. The famous on-air personalities 'Keke' Ogungbe and Dayo 'D1' Adeneye were the hosts of the very popular 1990s Hip-Hop TV show 'AIT Jamz' on Africa Independent Television, which later morphed into 'Prime Time Jamz'. They were committed to promoting local music acts in the days when there was no social media. They showcased Nigerian music on their radio and television shows and packaged the modern 9ja sound in a way that increased its commercial demand like never before. In 1998, Ogungbe and Adeneye founded their own production company and label, Kennis Music, and signed the Gospel saxophonist Kunle Ajayi as their first act.

In 2004, the label made its biggest signing who became by far the most decorated and successful popular music artist in Nigeria today: Innocent Ujah Idibia, better known by his stage name 2face Idibia, a former member of the pivotal Plantashun Boyz. 2face's solo album with Kennis Music, *Grass To Grace* (2006), became an instant hit. The singer/rapper went on to receive, among others, four MTV Africa Music Awards, one MTV Europe Music Award, and one BET award for his musical work. In the course of this success Kennis Music became home to the biggest and best musicians from Nigeria at that time, including the aforementioned OJB Jezreel, Sir Shina Peters, Lagbaja, and Yinka Best. Kennis Music carved the path for many Nigerian independent record companies. Today a lot of music promotion in Nigeria is done via social media, and Kennis Music focuses more on artist development. Apart from Kennis Music, there was also a tremendous impact on the booming 9ja music scene by the re-emerging Nigerian entertainment journalism—for example the magazines *HipHop World Magazine* and *African Beats*, which focused on promoting Nigerian Hip-Hop.

—

Most of the new producers favoured the mass popular appeal for code switching/code mixing based on a combination of Standard English, Pidgin, Yorùbá, Igbo, or any other Nigerian language. The modern 9ja sound is a syncretic sound that took and appropriated whatever the street dictated. No Nigerian music form was left out, although some got appropriated more widely than others. Based on street demand and popularity, the new producers drew inspiration from the beats of Fuji music, that had continued to attract the younger generation and made Jùjú the most dominant and influential traditional Nigerian music genre. Young Fuji stars like Wasiu Ayinde Marshall (known as KWAM1 or K1 De Ultimate), Wasiu Alabi Pasuma, Alayeluwa 'King' Sule Alao Malaika, and King Saheed Osupa all played different, yet extremely popular, variants of Fuji music that attracted strong cult followings.

Despite the success of the 9ja sound, Fuji music had become the most innovative and creative popular music genre. The influence of Fuji music can be heard in the music of younger Nigerian Afro-Pop stars like Wande Coal, Wizkid, and Dammy Krane. With *Fuji Garbage* even the old Fuji master Sikiru Ayinde Barrister released a successful new record in 1995, which became an instant dance hit and was played at popular nightclubs to revive the dance floor. Fuji music's influence on the modern, internationally successful 9ja sound should not only be viewed in musical merit, but also in the fact that Sikiru Ayinde Barrister provided a platform where a lot of street-inspired musicians pollinated lyrical and musical ideas of popular sound. Fuji musicians did a lot of ghost writing for the modern 9ja sound and vice versa. For example, Daddy Showkey, the king of Galala, is a known Fuji music ghost writer.

Don Jazzy, reality TV and the internet: 9ja goes big

By the mid-2000s digital distribution (music downloads, smartphones, increased broadband et cetera) began to take centre stage in Lagos. There was a great push by an increased number of radio personalities and Lagos radio stations to promote the modern 9ja sound. By law the Nigerian Broadcasting Corporation (NBC) regulated that the airplay ratio between indigenous and imported music productions should be 60:40, favouring local music over foreign content. But surprisingly the radio stations brazenly refused to play Nigerian beats and played 70 percent foreign songs instead. Two reasons were put forward for this reaction. Firstly, the radio stations complained that there was not enough 9ja music content available to rotate on radio. Secondly, they said the available content was not of sufficient quality. Indeed, in 2005, when MTV Base was launched in Africa from Lagos, there were not many Nigerian videos of good enough quality to be on the platform. However, the station launched the video clip of 2face Idibia's 'African Queen' which was beamed to nine international markets and instantly put 2face, now known as 2Baba, on the international scene of contemporary African music. With this level of exposure, the song was eventually used on the soundtrack of the Hollywood movie *Phat Girlz* (2006).

By the mid-2000s a new producer and his label were defining the direction of the Lagos popular sound. The producer's name was Michael 'Don Jazzy' Collins Ajereh, and his label was appropriately called MoHits Records. Don Jazzy's influence on the modern 9ja sound is legendary. *Forbes* magazine rated him as the thirty-sixth 'Most powerful celebrity in Africa', due to the cultural impact of his musical production. For example, in 2006 Don Jazzy produced Weird MC's 'Ijoya'. Weird MC (Adesola Adesimbo Idowu) is one of the few female Nigerian Rap artists, and her 'Ijoya' [time to dance] was a massive success. Later, Don Jazzy produced tracks for, and among others, megastar Dapo 'D'Banj' Daniel Oyebanjo, whose 2012 summer hit 'Oliver Twist' topped the African charts and was a top 10 hit in the UK singles chart. D'Banj is arguably Don Jazzy's biggest product.

Don Jazzy also collaborated with Jay-Z and Kanye West on their album *Watch The Throne*, released in 2011. With a large Nigerian youth population that is hugely influenced by music created by Don Jazzy, it was not long before the numbers started to attract big music businesses, like Kanye West's label G.O.O.D. Music[18] and Jay-Z's Tidal company[19] that aim to distribute and aggregate the 9ja sound. In fact, despite rampant piracy, the demand for 9ja sound has tripled from 2011 to 2015, a feat that has not gone unnoticed by South African's MTN group. MTN, one of the world's largest telecommunications companies (operating in 21 countries in Africa and the Middle East), has become the largest distributor of music in Nigeria.[20] By this time 9ja music had become available on online platforms like Spinlet, Jaguda, and Naijapals.

But the big moment to introduce 9ja music to the whole African continent came when African reality TV, through the Big Brother Nigeria show beamed from Lagos. The Nigerian local producers insisted that three quarters of the music played during the show be Nigerian. This, together with channels like MTV Base and Channel O, provided a cross-African platform and created an eruption in the Lagos and Nigerian music scene. 9ja music is now a great influence on African youth culture at large. With several million album sales and sold out concerts in stadiums across Africa, from Accra in Ghana to Nairobi in Kenya, from the Democratic Republic Of Congo to Tanzania, Nigerian music exports like P-Square, 2face, and D'Banj have proven that the modern 9ja music was not only popular but a strong cultural force within Africa. For example, the public uproar that followed in South-West African Namibia after a P-Square concert had been cancelled at the height of the Ebola crisis required a special hearing in Parliament to grant a waiver for the concert to proceed.

All roads lead to Lagos: Afrobeats

By 2014, the impact of ID Cabasa's stable of Yorùbá influenced rappers (Olamide and Reminisce) and their knock-on effect on

18 Mfonobong Nsehe, 'Kanye West Signs Nigerian Artists to G.O.O.D. Music', Forbes, 17 June 2011, <http://www.forbes.com/sites/mfonobongnsehe/2011/06/17/kanye-west-signs-nigerian-artists-to-g-o-od-music/> accessed 17 November 2015.

19 Ibukun Yinka and Dulue Mbachu, 'Nigeria's Answer to Spotify Lures Investors from MTN to Jay-Z', Bloomberg Business, 20 October 2015, <http://www.bloomberg.com/news/articles/2015-10-20/nigeria-s-answer-to-spotify-lures-investors-from-mtn-to-jay-z> accessed 17 November 2015.

20 Amilare Opeyemi, 'MTN Group Is the Largest Distributor of Music in Nigeria', Ventures Africa, 21 October 2015, <http://venturesafrica.com/mtn-group-is-the-largest-distributor-of-music-in-nigeria/> accessed 17 November 2015.

Mermaid, Lagos, 2018, photo: Mike Calandra Achode, Tommaso Cassinis

Artist, Lagos, 2018, photo: Mike Calandra Achode, Tommaso Cassinis

The Shrine, Lagos, 2018, photo: Mike Calandra Achode, Tommaso Cassinis

Wafflesncream, 1004 Estate, Lagos, 2018, photo: Mike Calandra Achode, Tommaso Cassinis

The Shrine, Lagos, 2018, photo: Mike Calandra Achode, Tommaso Cassinis

other indigenous rappers like Phyno had become apparent. *Time Magazine* named Reminisce 'one of the seven world rappers you should meet' in its 12 July 2014 article 'Forget Eminem: World Rappers You Should Meet'.[21] A new hybrid sound derived from Fela Kuti's Afrobeat was slowly emerging, later to be called Afrobeats, with the plural 's', which was a fusion of the funky sound of the original Afrobeat, Hip-Hop, and Fuji music. Afro-Pop had evolved into Afrobeats. Afrobeats starboy Wizkid released his hit anthem 'Ojuelegba' (2014) which attracted the attention of British Grime rapper Skepta and Canadian rapper Drake, who both featured on a remix of the hit song one year later. With the emergence of Afrobeats came the growing influence of DJs, among the most notable DJ Spinall, DJ Neptune, DJ Coublon, and Masterkraft.

By October 2015, the world had started taking Afrobeats seriously. Ice Prince Zamani dropped a video of his hit track 'Boss', which became the first African music video to premiere on Tidal, Jay-Z's music streaming application. At the fifth edition of the MTV Africa Music Award, staged July 2015 in Durban, South Africa, Nigeria's Yemi Alade won the best female award and Nigeria's David 'Davido' Adedeji Adeleke, won the best male award.[22] In 2016, major music company Sony Music opened a shop in Nigeria and signed a worldwide deal with Davido. But overall, 2016 was Wizkid's year. He not only became the first Nigerian artist to top the US Billboard Hot 100 Chart; Wizkid also guest featured on Drake's song 'One Dance' from the Canadian's successful fourth album, *Views*. The song topped the UK Singles Chart for 15 consecutive weeks and the US Billboard Hot 100 for 10 non-consecutive weeks. By 2017, Wizkid's flavour of Afrobeats had become the dominant sound in Nigerian nightclubs, with artists from his own Starboy Entertainment label like Mr Eazi, R2Bees, and Maleek Berry dominating airplay.

Six years earlier, in March 2011, the musical *Fela!* about the life and music of Fela Anikulapo-Kuti had come to Lagos at the prestigious Eko Hotel's New Expo Centre. The show, which had finished its Broadway run, was a smash box-office success in London and the US. In addition to the rave reviews from critics, *Fela!* won several awards and received standing ovations from personalities such as former first lady Michelle Obama and actors Denzel Washington and Robert de Niro. The musical's lead act was the US actor Sahr Ngaujah who played Fela Kuti. To the great surprise, and a bit of shock, of the Lagos crowd, the music of *Fela!* was performed by more US artists, the group Antibalas. For many Nigerians the worldwide success of the show was still a kind of validation of the Nigerian contribution to music worldwide–straight from Lagos.

Bibliography

Adedayo, Festus, 'Ayinla Omowura: 35 years after', *Nigerian Tribune*, 2 August 2015, <http://tribuneonlineng.com/ayinla-omowura-35-years-after> accessed 17 November 2015.

Adeuja, Titilope, 'Late Dagrin, Olamide, Phyno, Reminisce Are Enjoying What I Started–Lord of Ajasa', *Nigeriafilms.com*, 9 May 2015, <http://www.nigeriafilms.com/news/33117/69/late-dagrin-olamide-phyno-reminisce-are-enjoying-w.html> accessed 17 November 2015.

Balogun, Sola, 'Independence Concert: Tafawa Balewa Inisisted That I Must Play on That Day–Victor Olaiya', *Nigeriafilms.com*, 7 September 2010, <http://www.nigeriafilms.com/news/8674/3/independence-concert-tafawa-balewa-inisisted-that-.html> accessed 17 November 2015.

Collins, John, *Music Makers of West Africa* (Open Library: Passeggiata Press, 1985).

Folami, Takiu, *A History of Lagos, Nigeria: The Shaping of an African City* (Florida: Exposition Press, 1981).

Marx, Ben, 'How the Sony Walkman Changed the Way We Listen to Music Forever', *Allday.com*, <http://allday.com/post/4587how-the-sony-walkman-changedthe-way-we-listen-to-music-forever/pages/2/> accessed 17 November 2015.

N.N., 'Highlife Piccadilly–African Music on 45 rpm records in the UK, 1954–1981', *Musical Traditions*, <http://www.mustrad.org.uk/articles/african.htm> accessed 17 November 2015.

Nsehe, Mfonobong, 'Kanye West Signs Nigerian Artists to G.O.O.D. Music', *Forbes*, 17 June 2011, <http://www.forbes.com/sites/mfonobongnsehe/2011/06/17/kanye-west-signs-nigerian-artists-tog-o-od-music/> accessed 17 November 2015.

Omobola, Odejobi Cecilia, 'Influence of Yorùbá Culture in Christian Religious Worship', *International Journal of Social Sciences & Education*, vol. 4 (2014).

Omojola, Bode, *Yorùbá Music in the Twentieth Century: Identity, Agency, and Performance Practice* (Suffolk, England: Boydell & Brewer, 2012).

Omojola, Bode, *The Music of Fela Sowande. Encounters, African Identity and Creative Ethnomusicology* (Music Research Institute: MRI Press, 2009).

Opeyemi, Amilare, 'MTN Group Is the Largest Distributor of Music in Nigeria', *Ventures Africa*, 21 October 2015, <http://venturesafrica.com/mtn-group-is-the-largest-distributorof-music-in-nigeria/> accessed 17 November 2015.

Oti, Sonny, *Highlife Music in West Africa: Down Memory Lane* (Nigeria: Malthouse Press, 2009).

21
N.N., 'Forget Eminem: World Rappers you should meet', Time Video, 12 July 2014 <http://time.com/2977682/forget-eminem-world-rappers-you-should-meet/> accessed 17 November 2015.

22
Fumnanya Agbugah, 'Three Reasons Nigeria Will Continue to Outshine at The Mama Awards', Ventures Africa, 22 July 2015, <http://venturesafrica.com/three-reasons-why-nigeria-will-continue-to-outshine-at-the-mama-awards/> accessed 17 November 2015.

Pareles, Jon, 'Babatunde Olatunji, Nigerian Drummer, Dies at 76', *The New York Times*, 9 April 2003, <http://www.nytimes.com/2003/04/09/obituaries/09OLAT.html> accessed 17 November 2015.

Ricketts, Olushola, 'Victor Olaiya was against a national band for independence', *New Telegraph Newspaper*, 3 October 2015, <http://newtelegraphonline.com/victor-olaiya-was-against-a-national-band-forindependence/> accessed 17 November 2015.

Thomas, Isaac B., *Life History of Herbert Macaulay, C.E* (Tika-To[r]e Press, 1946).

Ajayi Thomas, T., *History of Jùjú Music: A History of African Popular Music from Nigeria* (Jamaica, NY: Thomas Organization, 1992).

Obiora Uzokwe, Alfred, *Surviving in Biafra: The Story of the Nigerian Civil War* (Bloomington, IN: iUniverse, 2003).

Veal, Michael, *Fela: The Life and Times of an African Musical Icon* (Philadelphia: Temple University Press, 2000).

Yinka, Ibukun and Mbachu, Dulue, 'Nigeria's Answer to Spotify Lures Investors from MTN to Jay-Z', *Bloomberg Business*, 20 October 2015, <http://www.bloomberg.com/news/articles/2015-10-20/nigeria-s-answer-to-spotify-lures-investors-from-mtn-to-jay-z> accessed 17 November 2015.

Circadian Rhythms – The Many Layers of Lagos

Mallam Mudi Yahaya

Just after Nigeria's Independence in 1961, the novelist Cyprian Ekwensi published his satirical book, *Jagua Nana*. It tells the story of the restless prostitute of the same name, who is a high roller and a habitué of the sordid Club Tropicana.[1] Ekwensi's character Jagua Nana is an apt metaphor for Lagos, Nigeria's commercial and cultural centre. Indeed, like the prostitute Jagua Nana, the city has many sides to its nature, character, and language. But Jagua Nana might also be regarded as a prototype of the attendees in the intense and chaotic life of Lagos: The good life complete with financial stability might be an attractive factor to a life of prostitution – and it might also be regarded as an apt description of the reason why people of any background migrate to Lagos. The plural and myriad soundscapes of Lagos function as a complex entity, where everyone takes part in the unfolding peep show that has become part of the life and identity of Lagos. This is a city where the production and consumption of social showmanship are guaranteed across all social brackets.

In a sense, the story of urban Lagos is a story of give and take, sacrifice, transaction, and struggle at all costs between notions of success and traditions as they evolve with concepts of modernity. It's a story of how these elements battle for prominence, relevance, and value while carving an identity for the city. This identity has at least two sides. In Lagos, there exists a dichotomy of official culture and subculture/counterculture uncommon in most African cities. The official culture is based on the national vision of what a modern African state should look like – while the subculture/counterculture harks back to the history and tradition of resistance of Lagos as a once independent colony and city-state. That is to say, in the city of Lagos there is always the official way and the 'Lasgidi' way, as Lagos is called in popular slang.

The Portuguese name, Lagos, was given to the city by the explorer Rui de Sequeira on account of the many lagoons, which formed the archipelago that he found here.[2] The Benin and Awori people – who were migrant fishermen and the first settlers in what is today Lagos – founded the settlement at the end of the fourteenth century. They called it 'Eko'. The Lagos narrative is a classic tale of the evolution of a small fishing village into a thriving megacity of over fifteen million people. The chaotic, dysfunctional nature of Lagos had, by the turn of the twenty-first century, earned the city the reputation of an immoral urban nightmare – complete with traffic gridlocks, urban decay, population explosion, poor regulation policies, and high crime rates. Despite all the amplified negatives about the city, its vibrancy, energy, and cultural diversity sustain Lagos as the cultural production capital of West Africa. The ironic contradiction of it being a functional-dysfunctional city is tied to Lagos and is a result of the city's rapid population growth.

Like other African cities, Lagos finds itself between the conversation of urban life and modernity. In many ways this determines the urban arrangement of cultural sound. Any visitor of Lagos would not easily forget the cacophony that makes up the city's character. This relentless din is a cocktail of competing market loudspeakers, religious public address systems, music vendors, and bus conductors all jostling to define their space and identity in a city that continuously reinvents and redefines its urban form. The sound of Lagos and the music that comes out of it are agents and not objects of modernity. The sound acts for the city without defining its modernity. The sound is refashioned as a set of values in the modernisation procedure. These values serve as guidelines

---

1   Cyprian Ekwensi, *Jagua Nana* (London: Heinemann, 1961), 91–94.

2   Kristin Mann, *A Social History of the New African Elite in Lagos Colony, 1880–1913* (Stanford: Stanford University, 1977), 10–50.

for negotiating contact zones that recognise a relationship between African spirituality, cultural history, customs, and exposure to Western culture. And the codes are constantly re-modified.

The typical Lagosian relates to the urban landscape of Lagos in deciphering its underlying soundscape, which offers a unique sonic time signature. The cultural potential of Lagos does not have to be imagined as an object but rather experienced as a performance. This is because Lagos does not function as several invisible cities in one, but rather as a spontaneous creative archipelago of several cities that are not concealed from sight, depending on slant and perspective.

Pax Britannica and the dual city

Lagos consists of several islands linked to a mainland. The main island, Lagos Island, lies in the Lagos Lagoon and accommodates the city's commercial district. Lagos Island is also where the Colonial government buildings, main Christian cathedrals (Catholic and Anglican), and Central Mosque are located. It is connected to the mainland districts by three large bridges (Carter, Eko, and Third Mainland Bridge) and is also linked by bridges (Falomo, Five Cowrie Creek) to the neighbouring Ikoyi and Victoria Islands. Like many African cities, the colonial legacy made Lagos a dual city: one part ring fenced European quarters complete with complimentary architectural style, and the other part 'native' quarters, devoid of urban planning and left to evolve by itself. This set the background for redefining the traditional versus the modern – reimagining the colonial city into a metropolitan city.

Lagos operated as a slave trade outpost and was ceded in 1862 by King Dosunmu, the Oba of Lagos, to Queen Victoria as a British 'colonial possession'. This occurred after having been administered under several territorial configurations and in the wake of the 1851 demolition of Lagos by a British naval bombardment in support of British anti-slavery measures.[3] Lagos functioned as a city-state and operated as an independent colony until 1906, when it was merged with the surrounding former Southern Nigeria Protectorate. In 1914, Lagos became the capital of the protectorate of amalgamated Nigeria. In the period between 1815 and 1914, which is referred to by historians as the British 'imperial century'[4], many parts of the world saw Britain enjoy unchallenged marine power and emerge as a global hegemon that controlled most of the key sea trade routes worldwide. This era of Pax Britannica [the British peace] brought suppression of piracy and slavery. By 1833, when slavery was abolished in all British territories, the fortified Island of Lagos, which was a major slave port, was not exempt. By 1872 Lagos had become a cosmopolitan town-trading outpost with a population of about 60,000 people.[5] Africans born in the colony were British subjects, while Africans born in the later protectorates of Southern and Northern Nigeria were citizens under the jurisdiction of their traditional rulers. This duality of identity framed the nature of the hybrid culture that would evolve in postcolonial, independent Nigeria. Nigeria gained partial Independence from Britain on 1 October 1960, and total Independence as a republic in 1963, after the declaration of Independence was signed.

The site for the Independence Day ceremonies was a former racecourse on Lagos Island. In 1972, it was constructed into a square and named Tafawa Balewa Square, after Nigeria's first Prime minister, Sir Abubakar Tafawa Balewa. Symbolically, Tafawa Balewa Square can be considered the apex space for musical performance in Lagos. Situated in the centre of Lagos city, the site, which is circumscribed by the Lagos skyline and historic monuments, is the city's congregation ground for Christian religious festivals as well as a legendary, mythical shrine for Yorùbá religious cult worship or 'Eyo' and 'Egungun', Yorùbá carnival masquerades. This duality continues

---

3   Cf. Timothy H. Parsons, *The British Imperial Century, 1815–1914: A World History Perspective (Critical Issues in World and International History)* (Lanham, MD: Rowman & Littlefield Publishers, 1999).
4   Ibid.
5   Michael J. C. Echeruo, *Victorian Lagos: Aspects of Nineteenth Century Lagos Life* (London: Macmillan, 1977), 10–35.

in the square that once served as a major military parade ground for Independence Day celebrations as well as a prestigious wedding venue for the powerful elite. For musicians, Tafawa Balewa Square is a space that validates musical reputations and followership with a capacity of over 50,000 people for concerts.

In many formerly colonised African countries, music played a significant role in the Independence ceremonies and celebrations of the new sovereign states. As the Union Jack was lowered for the last time in the space now known as Tafawa Balewa Square, the apparent link between political and economic independence was underlined by the sound of African rooted music (African-American Jazz, Congolese Rumba, and Nigerian Highlife) as a post-colonial form of revalorisation. From the moment of the declaration of Independence in Nigeria, music was used as an artistic symbol that challenged European hegemony – and the main production centre of this music in Nigeria was Lagos. The emerging postcolonial Lagosians employed the reinforcing power of music as a conscious creative force. They aimed to mould the new Nigerian identity through strategic and politically conscious messages within the lyrics of songs. The result was that Nigerians would constantly be reminded of their emerging identity through music which they embraced in all aspects of their lives, from naming ceremonies, weddings and funeral services, to sports activities and underground traditional religious rituals.

But as a legacy of the colonial construct, post-Independence Lagos also operated a peculiar system of geographies of exclusion. These hierarchies further encouraged a duality in the city and its zones of exchange. There existed hierarchies of exclusion between white reserved areas and areas where regular Nigerians lived. For those that lived on the popular non-European 'government reserved areas (GRA)', the National Stadium in the sprawling, medium-density Surulere area (also known as 'New Lagos') provided a music entertainment space and venue. The concrete stadium originally held a capacity of 45,000 and was the second largest in Nigeria. It was a multi-use stadium that was built in 1973 for the All-Africa Games. The stadium's capacity was expanded to 55,000 in 1999. Even though these days the stadium is rarely used for sporting events, it still is a venue for music and entertainment alongside the various street vagrants and squatters that live within its premises.

Government official spaces like the Tafawa Balewa Square or the National Stadium were of course not the only zones where the different social strata from Lagos met. Exclusive spaces like the Federal Palace Hotel, which was where the Independence declaration was signed, became historic music venues for the post-colonial Lagos elite and the expatriate community. In reality, the Federal Palace Hotel was exclusive only in perception, because operationally it attracted all social strata for different levels of functionality. This constantly reminded patrons of the moral fluidity of the city as it operated as a court of contact for prostitution. In the 1970s, several musicians operated nightclubs that celebrated a new Nigeria and spoke about Lagos' role in a modernised country. These musicians' notion of nightclubs as modern identity outposts came from their experiences of nightclubs in Europe and the US, which they had seen when travelling abroad on tour. For most of Lagos' musicians, modernity suggested enjoyment, escape, and exoticism. And this could be seen in how they presented themselves.

The Jùjú music maestro Ebenezer Obey played on Mondays and Thursdays at the Obey Miliki Spot [*miliki* translates to 'enjoyment' in Yorùbá]. In a similar spirit, Caban Bamboo was the legendary musician at Bobby Benson's space for music and entertainment with its exotic name suggesting enjoyment as well as Lagos style modernity.[6] Bobby Benson's Hotel Bobby, where the Caban Bamboo nightclub was located, was probably the first indigenous-owned, Western styled venue in post-independence Lagos. It combined hotel lodging with night clubbing and attracted a mix of politicians, diplomats, military top brass, and business moguls as well as students and simple music lovers. Hotel Bobby is said to have had 'correct sophisticated ladies'[7] in its patronage – women that had benefitted from Western education and attitudes and/or were socially liberated. For patrons, it was important to dress and appear successful. The men wore lace African attires, suits, and tuxedos, while the unaccompanied 'sophisticated' ladies wore body revealing tight clothes. In contrast, the more traditional 'correct madams', as they were called, wore lace outfits, matching what their partners wore. It was a place where intellectuals, like the later Nobel laureate Wole Soyinka, contributed satirical subtext to lyrics of the music performed by Bobby Benson. In fact, the famous song 'Taxi Driver I Don't Care', ascribed to Bobby Benson, was inspired and composed by Wole Soyinka.[8]

Before Hotel Bobby there were other spots like the Empire Hotel. Here Fela Ransome-Kuti[9] operated his resident nightclub, the African Shrine (previously known as the Afro Spot), where he played songs that championed Pan-Africanism and spoke about the challenges and potentials of a truly independent Africa and the pivotal role of Lagos as a city. The African Shrine was a unique and one of its kind Lagos nightclub, where it was not uncommon for Fela and his band to play Afrobeat music until dawn in the midst of marijuana smoke, gyrating scantily clad female dancers (two of whom would typically be suspended in cages above the stage), and a score of singers moving to the beat.

Unlike Caban Bamboo, the African Shrine was not only about having a good time, but also about social discourse on public ethics, good governance, and anti-corruption. The Shrine's subtext was political criticism, where the government of the day was never spared for any unpopular policy or action. The African Shrine was also a space where Fela, who changed his surname from a more English sounding Ransome-Kuti to a more African Anikulapo-Kuti, performed traditional Ifá religious rituals, with music as a backdrop. Fela promoted the Ifá logic while he criticised Western religion and the role it played in the politics of what should be independent Nigeria. Ifá is an ancient Yorùbá religious system based on divination and verses of the literary corpus *Odù Ifá*. Ifá disciples cherish this belief system as the way of their Yorùbá ancestors, which serves as a system of identity, ethics, and guidance.

With equal solidarity, 'African' Christian churches also became sites of protest and confrontation. Already early Nigerian statesmen like Herbert Macaulay had questioned the white missionaries' exclusive racial policies. This stimulated and influenced the local society to reimagine a unique modern African identity. The European missionaries had discouraged the production and performance of African indigenous music and suggested that the music was 'offensive' and not worthy for use in holy worship. 'African' churches had adopted the Western Christian faith – but preferred to have an African feel to their worship. In this way, the church had emerged as a major site of opposition to European power, with music as the weapon of choice. Prior to Independence, transnationally successful Congolese music like Rumba or Soukous, widely connoted with Pan-Africanism as well as political and economic aspirations, influenced the popular music in Lagos. The 'African' churches promoted the tangent from African hymns to Highlife music and further on to Jùjú or Apala music. Today this is considered as the process which ushered in the birth of contemporary Nigerian popular music.

6   Jossy Idam, 'Bobby Benson', Online Nigeria Community Portal of Nigeria, 18 May 2008, <http://nm.onlinenigeria.com/templates/?a=12216> accessed 17 November 2015.
7   Bisi Lawrence, '*Caban Bamboo *Bobby Benson', *Vanguard*, 8 August 2009, <http://www.vanguardngr.com/2009/08/caban-bamboo-bobby-benson/> accessed 17 November 2015.
8   Obi Nwakanma, *Christopher Okigbo 1930–67: Thirsting for Sunlight* (Suffolk: Boydell & Brewer, 2010), 177.
9   Cf. Michael Veal, *Fela: The Life and Times of an African Musical Icon* (Philadelphia: Temple University Press, 2000).

Open sores and gated communities – the mosaic city

The Nigerian Civil War from 1967 to 1970, which is also known as the Biafran War, broke out after the secession of Eastern Nigeria that referred to itself as 'Biafra'.[10] The secession was caused by nationalist yearnings of the Igbo tribe of Eastern Nigeria. Members of the Igbo considered themselves marginalised by the Nigerian Military government of the time, which they felt was dominated by officers from Northern Nigeria. Additional reasons were the differing perspectives and arguments of what an ideal modern African state should be, in terms of constitution, inclusion, development, and vision. The Nigerian civil war not only changed the history of Nigeria but also redefined the purpose and operation of spatial legacies and urban hierarchies in Lagos. During the war, Lagos served as the capital of Federal Nigeria and the poster city of a peculiar perspective on what new African modernity should look like. The war provided ample arguments for what is essential for a modern country and its modern capital, demanding better inclusion and less of the colonial style exclusivity in a city. Post-war Lagos adjusted to these arguments.

The city had been spatially developed by the colonialists purely to secure and protect the export trade and commerce enterprise facilitated by the ports. But unlike many other African colonial cities, Lagos' historical past is not only colonial, but also that of a highly frequented slave trade outpost. It was a melting pot of numerous indigenous and foreign cultures that have shaped its peculiar aesthetic. After the slave trade had been abolished by Great Britain, a substantial repatriation movement emerged between the 1840s and the 1860s among ex-slaves from Cuba and Brazil. Most of these repatriates were of Nigerian origin, and quite a number of these were of Yorùbá descent. These returnees chose to establish themselves and seek prosperity in West Africa's largest port city, Lagos. The Brazilian and Cuban returnees, who were collectively called Aguda or Amaro, which translates from Yorùbá as 'those who have been away from home', were accomplished skilled artisans.

The majority of slave trade returnees from Brazil settled on the central Lagos Island, which is where up to this day the Brazilian quarter is located. Here they built what was considered modern European architectural buildings that served as a demonstration of a modern aesthetic option for the benefit of the native population. The Agudas built elaborate two-storey structures with Brazilian Latin stucco facades that eventually evolved to become the colonial aesthetics style of choice for large public buildings and private residences. A fine example of the latter is Water House on Kakawa Street, where piped water supplied to the house was sold to the community for profit. It was owned by the richest man in Lagos at that time, Candido Da Rocha, who was popularly called Baba Olomi [old man that sells water]. Candido was the son of João Da Rocha, who was abducted as a child in 1850 and sold into slavery in Salvador da Bahia, Brazil. The subsequent colonial architectural design of Lagos was configured by British, Brazilian, and traditional architecture. This mixture heavily influenced the visual production of cultural semiotic systems that uphold the cultural identity of Lagos.

But the Lagos tradition of spatial urban design with an emphasis on community and common identity was rudely interrupted and forever changed as the sound of sporadic gunfire become part of the city's soundscape. The sound came from crime syndicates, which manifested in Lagos as a consequence of the proliferation of small arms from the Nigerian Civil War. They introduced armed robbery and big-time crime. A reaction to this social interruption was the introduction of gated communities to Lagos – to a city that was otherwise open.

10 Cf. Luke Nnaemeka Aneke, *The Untold Story of the Nigeria-Biafra War* (New York: Triumph Publishing, 2007).

The birth of armed robbery partly caused the demise of cabaret style big band nightclubs. For this required one to go out at night – at the risk of being waylaid by armed robbers. Lagosians rediscovered the 'Owambe' parties, a type of excessively grand party that required streets to be cordoned off while loud music (typically Jùjú), dancing, and feasting carried on. The name Owambe [Yorùbá for 'Its there'] comes from an old Yorùbá party tradition from the early days of Jùjú music, where women wore waist beads with their undergarments that rattled when dancing.[11] Needless to say, Owambes are perfect settings to observe the morally fluid, transactional character of the city. In this instance, the partygoers would sit out at the party from late afternoon to the next day when the party would end, without the risk of a chance encounters with robbers.

The barricaded streets and roads became a space where the Lagos culture and tradition of showmanship could be extended. For example, 'spraying', a tradition of plastering money on a person dancing or playing music, was a characteristic of Owambes. Spraying became an integral part of most Nigerian cultures during the oil boom of the early 1970s. This period coincided with a time where oil profits, a successful economy and abundant infrastructural development, translated into an added ability to be opulent. With the rise of armed robbery as fallout of the Nigerian civil war, Owambes typically took place in the daytime and less often at night. The practice of closing off the roads to accommodate the seating capacity of merrymakers that overflowed from the main reception area to adjoining streets, provided a measure of security against armed robbers for all attendees.

In spite of rising crime rates, Lagos was redefining itself – and embracing many forms of openness. For example, the western psychedelic modern spirit of sexual liberation did not bypass Lagos. So, in 1970 the nation's most widely read newspaper, *The Punch*, followed the footsteps of the British tabloid newspaper, *The Sun*, and started featuring topless glamour models on page three of its print edition – complete with body statistics and even contact telephone numbers. The local demand for risqué sensation was so high that one of Lagos' oldest Newspapers, the *Daily Times*, had a publication specially focused on hot and sordid sexual stories, titled *Lagos Weekend*. Indeed, weekends in Lagos became occasions of 'accesses' to all forms that spontaneously attracted armed robbery.

After post-civil-war armed robbery had been firmly established, the fractal urban dichotomy and informalisation of Lagos became more obvious. It became clear that Lagos was increasingly becoming a mosaic of different, independent, informal, and self-organising communities. The gated communities introduced a type of exclusion that prompted the emergence of informal settlements connected to, but independent of, these gated communities. For every Victoria Island, highbrow, upmarket residential area, there was now a nearby Makoko slum that provided low cost accommodation and lodgings for domestic staff and workers that earned money on Victoria Island.

This ugly phenomenon, which could also be observed between the upmarket area of Apapa and its adjacent slum Ajegunle, was further complicated by the 1973 oil crisis and the OPEC oil embargo that raised the price of crude oil. Overnight, Lagos, the main terminal for Nigerian trade and oil exports, became a highly solvent container port city. The evolving and complex spatial phenomena attracted both the rich and the poor. The needy sacrificed everything for money from the rich by soliciting for illegal and legal patronage in terms of facilitating crime and vice at little or no cost. Drugs, robbery, and prostitution were everywhere. So, decisions had to be made by

---

11 For more information about Owambe parties as well as the various music genres of Lagos, please see Mallam Mudi Yahaya's article about music in Lagos in this book.

Lagos' authorities on how to contain the impending synthesis of urban density while still providing a secure, functional, and modern African metropolis.

The solvency of this period in Lagos was highlighted by Wole Soyinka in his book *The Open Sore of a Continent: A Personal Narrative of the Nigerian Crisis*.[12] Soyinka observed that in a bid to stall the urban migration from what felt like every Nigerian village to Lagos, politicians came up with an ambitious, but rather disingenuous nationwide federal housing project for low-income earners. This created a cement armada that choked up the ports of Lagos with shiploads of cement. Such was the scale of this jamboree that, as Soyinka observed, 'the parade of vessels that stretched out from Lagos harbour into miles and miles of international waters … were such a sight that pilots on commercial airlines would deliberately fly over the flotilla … whose strings of lights transformed Lagos harbour into the most scintillating, extensive, and expensive Christmas tree in or out of season'.

—

It is against this backdrop that the praxis of annexed areas in the periphery and survival constructions in slums and informal settlements like Mushin or Ajegunle emerged. Due to the rapid, unstructured development and the sudden urban displacement in Lagos, people looked for survival tools to navigate their new reality. One of these survival tools, which was brought into existence by the infamous Lagos harbour cement armada, was music. In the case of the informal settlements in Mushin and Ajegunle, this music took the form of Fuji music, which offered philosophical advice and anecdotes about life in its lyrics. Fuji music can be described as amplified dance music based on a rhythmic combination of talking drums, drum set, sekere [gourd rattle], bells, and claves, set to vocals in the form of poetry with influences from Yorùbá Blues, Apala, and Jùjú. It was immensely popular among blue-collar workers and people in trade. Fuji music came on the scene after the Nigerian civil war, which ushered in a season of reflection on ethnic nationality. With ethnicity came the politics of religion. It was during this period that the Muslim derived Fuji started to evolve. Historically, Lagos was predominantly a Muslim majority city and Islam flourished abundantly in the informal settlements.[13]

With the cement armada came traffic jams, called 'go-slow', due to cement haulage trucks trying to navigate to and from the ports on narrow roads that were not originally planned for high-density traffic. The 'go-slow' jams gave birth to 'go-slow' markets with street hawkers selling their goods directly to car drivers gridlocked in heavy traffic. This produced new patterns of distributing music. In this neoliberal, alternative economy new cultural gatekeepers or cultural intermediaries emerged: taxi drivers, auto mechanics, printers, and traders who now all defined a distinctive post-metropolis Lagos aesthetic, and provided a mimesis of their own cultural reality that was determined on the streets. This is evident in the abundant production, distribution, and display of colourful and graphic cultural propaganda posters and stickers that adorn all available spaces in the informal settlements of Mushin or Ajegunle.

The posters and stickers promoted cult followings of musical cultural icons that are well patronised by the new gatekeepers. This cultural phenomenon is best observed in the popularity, consumption, and demand of Fuji music. The new gatekeepers promoted Fuji music as a populist and inclusive music genre that broke down social barriers. Fuji was considered low art and traditional, as opposed to Jùjú music which was considered high art, modern, and music for the exclusive elite. Fuji music became a tool for appropriating space and defining a new aesthetic of

12 Wole Soyinka, *The Open Sore of a Continent: A Personal Narrative of the Nigerian Crisis (W.E.B. Du Bois Institute)* (Oxford: Oxford University Press, 1996), 80–81.

13 Michael J. C. Echeruo, *Victorian Lagos: Aspects of Nineteenth century Lagos Life* (London: Macmillan, 1977), 10–35.

enjoyment within a decolonised identity. The new gatekeepers ensured that Fuji music occupied all available spaces – from public transport and barbing saloons to urban infrastructure and public spaces, which were also used for cultural production. These new patterns of consumption were closely linked to the social groups in high-density, informal areas as well as formal areas.

—

The gains from the petrodollars not only stimulated population growth in Lagos via migration and established new cultural gatekeepers. The money also helped finance official governmental platforms to position Lagos as a major cultural hub for Nigeria. One of these platforms was the festival FESTAC'77, another was the National Theatre, where large parts of this festival took place. The National Theatre was built in 1976 under the military regime of General Olusegun Obasanjo by a Bulgarian construction company based on a design of a sports hall in Varna, Bulgaria. Its exterior is strangely shaped like a military peak cap. Inside there is a main hall which seats 5,000 with a collapsible stage, and two 700–800 capacity cinema halls, equipped with translation facilities for eight languages. FESTAC'77, the Second World Black and African Festival of Arts and Culture, partly took place in the National Theatre. Nigeria hoped to outdo Senegal, who, under the leadership of their intellectual president, Leopold Senghor, had hosted the first festival of this kind. The event was presented as a Pan-African celebration of music, dance, and theatre with debate sessions to discuss pan-African cultural policy and identity.

Through FESTAC'77 the world learnt more about the music of, among others, King Sunny Ade, Sonny Okosun, or Fela Anikulapo-Kuti, who ran an alternative venue at his nightclub, the African Shrine. Ironically, just before FESTAC'77, Fela, whose increasing popularity with the common man worried and angered the Nigerian government, had been raided by the authorities. This incident created a media buzz that attracted even more international visiting artists and music loving people to the African Shrine. The club was jammed packed every night and proved to be more critically popular among performing musicians than most official FESTAC'77 events that focused mostly on theatre and dance. In fact, during FESTAC'77, Fela and his band increased their regular performances of one or two shows per night to four shows per night due to popular demand.

The poetics of decay – the terminal city

The big money fiesta of the late 1970s and early 1980s ran the country into the ground. The toll of the governmental politics of those days, facilitating an urban culture of crime, vice, and zero responsible public ethics fuelled by corruption in all sectors of society, finally set in. Between 1983 and 1986, Nigeria applied for IMF and World Bank loans in a structural adjustment programme (SAP) that aimed to reduce the country's fiscal imbalances. This programme required fundamental changes that included privitisation, deregulation, and the reduction of trade barriers.[14]

The first social sign of cultural decay was the disappearance of Owambes. The Nigerian government no longer had any interest in promoting 'frivolous' ideas. Culture as well as culture-related fields were no longer seen as strategically important enough or as contributing to national productivity. So, the government stopped funding culture. The National Theatre in Lagos fell into disrepair. Traditional big venues like Tafawa Balewa Square were no longer accessible, as the government, which controlled these spaces was not interested in promoting cultural production. In general, public venues for hosting musical events began closing down. Lagos was badly hit.

14   Brian-Vincent Ikejiaku, 'Africa Debt Crisis and the IMF with a Case of Nigeria: towards Theoretical Explanations', *Journal of Politics and Law*, vol. 1, no. 4 (2008), 2–6.

The hardship and sacrifices of the SAP required a drastic restructuring of the country's economy. The programme caused mass unemployment, a rise in food prices, and an inflation spiral that affected many businesses, leading to their eventual liquidation. The economy's disposable income that supported the creative arts and culture was also hit hard. This austere situation caused a migration of creative talent out of Lagos to different parts of the world, especially to the global West. The economic downturn in Lagos was so critical that virtually anyone and everyone who had the means or qualifications left Lagos for greener pastures. Record labels closed, as the music business wound down. The SAP made Lagos a terminally ill city.

But at the same time, as life became tougher for Lagosians, music became the drug of choice for many to escape reality. Its effect was more evident in shared experiences. People looked for and constructed spaces to share their stories through music. The unavailability of big venues, despite the obvious public dependency and demand for music for survival, triggered the de-traditionalization of sites of hybrid identities (the office, the home, and the church) as the new sites for 'clubbing'. In particular, the Christian song-based praise worship tradition was a perfect channel for people to recalibrate and make meaning of the hardship they were going through. This promoted the blurring of the difference between secular and non-secular music. Once again, the church became a place of resistance – but this time through popular music production, and with the difference that this time it was not the old 'African' churches but the new popular Pentecostal churches.

It was especially in the high-density areas where Pentecostal Christianity spread, as the toll of economic reforms hit Lagos hard. Like Fuji music, Pentecostal roots in Lagos lay at the behest of the poor and the needy, unlike other organised Christian religions that are not populist in nature. The Lagos Pentecostal churches positioned themselves as agents of modernity and crafted a message of success. And this was formulated through music. Taking advantage of the mass appeal of Fuji music (as a traditionally Islamic inspired sound) the churches appropriated the speech-act performance of Fuji and connected it to Sacred Pop (popular commercial Gospel music). With this new, hybrid marriage between Gospel and Fuji music, the church also became the venue for popular dance – the new 'nightclub' in town. It became tradition that every Friday night, young 'clubbers' would now troop to a night vigil prayer worship service that lasted all night long. But even the church could not quarantine itself from the transactional nature of Lagos: many young Jagua Nanas found these churches fertile hunting grounds. To sum up, the churches had everything: great music, electrifying atmosphere, and husband-seeking young ladies. Which nightclubs could beat this?

The battle for the soul of the common man moved to new arenas. As Christianity became widely seen as the modernising religion, and money was the reward for being religious, some churches started presenting sexy adverts that showcased a life of luxury and enjoyment. There were new battles of roadside churches versus mega churches versus megaphone-churches. In the markets there were now mobile churches that brought the sound of the Lord to the people. Gospel secular music flourished. All these factors, the music plus success preaching and the attraction of modernity, caused a great number of former Muslims to convert to the Christian faith.

In reaction to this Christian invasion, the Muslim cultural intermediaries in Mushin, Ajegunle, and other informal urban slums extended their spiritual and musical inclinations to high-density contact zones. This came, among others, in the form of mobile billboards on public mass transit vehicles like motorcycles, tricycle motorbikes, Molues [a local mass transit bus], and Bolekajas [Yorùbá for 'come down let's fight']—a rowdy half-metal, half-timber bus construction. It was aided by unregistered social networks like savvy street hawkers, who created new 'musical' arenas that echoed popular lyrics, slang, and graphics from Fuji music, or 'area boys' (a local street subculture group of gangsters). It further institutionalised street hawking as a cultural infrastructure and an established commodity chain for music promotion, distribution, and marketing.

Street hawking, which is organised and run by a cartel, became a fast way of distributing products to the mass market. The process empowered the members of these unofficial networks by revalorising their sense of participation and inclusion as citizens of the city. Interestingly, the potency of these informal networks got the notice of Lagos politicians. The politicians started to invest in the creation and destruction of subcultural groups in the city. For example, many area boys found employment as easily mobilised thugs for political groups and government officials. When their services were needed, the area boys would be brought on. They would be returned to the street once debriefed, adequately rewarded, threatened, and warned against disclosure.

—

In the late 1980s, while all this was happening, another process was evolving in the high-density urban area of Ajegunle, the 'Jungle City'. This slum is where all the hard criminals live and hang out, like the infamous One Million Boys gang of robbers that attacked their victims with locally fabricated firearms and machetes. It is where all the real stories of the hardship of the city can be heard. It is a place that was spontaneous with its tactics and strategies for surviving Lagos. It is a place that resisted the city. According to Ajegunle's resident philosopher, poet, musician, and activist, Aj Dagga Tolar, 'Ajegunle has become a metaphor for the entirety of the Nigerian nation.' And: 'It is in this part of the country that you meet the poor of the poorest, and we try to survive day in and day out.'[15]

But Ajegunle is also an example of how failure generates opportunity given a certain form of creativity and necessity. It is in Jungle City that Lagos began its cultural regeneration after SAP, because Ajegunle became the main site for emerging new musical creativity, dance, and performance that was all held together by its own distinctive sound. At the time the Ajegunle sound was Galala, a blend of Roots Reggae, Fuji, and street slang lyrics. The lyrics of this sound were always about survival, success, and salvation that spoke directly to the heart of the common Lagosian.

In Lagos, what resonated with the larger urban landscape always came from the poor social bracket. It is like this here, in Ajegunle, where cultural intermediaries like the Galala musician Daddy Showkey defined the musical taste, dance, and fashion of all of Lagos. For example, Daddy Showkey sagged his jeans and so did all area boys. Many area boys also adopted dreadlocks in homage to the musician. Cultural intermediaries from Ajegunle like Daddy Showkey to Fuji star Wasiu Alabi Pasuma became role models for urban style and swagger. The Italian designer denim jeans and t-shirts they wore became the urban dress code. In the end, the area boys measured their sartorial taste based on standards of being hip set in Milan or Naples.

'Eko oni baje'—the exopolis city

As Lagos started its cultural regeneration in Ajegunle, its economic revitalisation came in a strange manner. On Monday, 19 October 1987, stock markets around the world crashed. Suddenly Lagosians in the diaspora, Lagosians that mainly left because of the IMF and World

15 Ofeibea Quist-Arcton, 'Out of a Nigerian Slum, a Poet Is Born', *NPR*, 27 June 2007, <http://www.npr.org/templates/story/story.php?storyId=10826005> accessed 17 November 2015.

Bank's structural adjustment programme (SAP), started thinking of repatriating what remained of their investments abroad back to Lagos. As unemployment in the global West increased, it became clear that, as they said in Yorùbá, 'Eko oni baje' [Lagos wasn't bad after all].

With the inflows of cash remittance that this movement triggered, the urban landscape of Lagos had come full circle; it now functioned as an 'exopolis' – a term in postmodern urbanism that refers to a simulacrum, an exact copy of an original that never existed.[16] Its image and its reality were confused. New, fantasy urban spaces were constructed in upscale areas like Victoria Island, Parkview estate or Lekki Peninsular. The Lagosian returnees desired a Lagos based on dreams; a post-metropolis that was disconnected with a community and bore an 'unimagined sameness',[17] lacking ties to any specific space. The new diaspora of Lagos appeared as a massive, dysfunctional living marketing advertisement, complete with Western paranoia about African society and its seeming absence of security, regulation, and urban planning. These new hyper-realities reintroduced urban hierarchies and exaggerated realities.

The thirst for exaggerated realities took hold in many different areas. For example, new contact zones which offered hard drug cocktails emerged. At these joints one could get anything, from marijuana to crack cocaine to the increasingly popular dried Lizard dung that, apparently, had a potency that surpassed the combined high of heroin, cocaine, and loud (a mixture of marijuana and heroin). Sanusi Fafunwa Street in highbrow Victoria Island became known as 'the hookers' lane', because it was here where prostitutes lined the entire stretch of the street every evening. They came equipped with a change of clothes to fit any type of evening outing that might be required. The location of Sanusi Fafunwa Street, with its close proximity to the richest neighbourhoods in Lagos, hinted to the nature of the clientele. Very close to Sanusi Fafunwa was a new gay club that not only serviced Lagos' shy and expatriate gay community, which was the usual clientele, but also gay Lagosian returnees who had come out of the closet.

From Victoria Island's Sanusi Fafunwa Street many clients took a five-minute drive to close by Kuramo Beach. Here, for an entrance fee of less than one Euro, people were ushered into a vaudeville heterotopia, complete with Michael Jackson dancing monkeys, grilled fish kebabs, and hardcore pornography, beamed onto large screens as visitors paid for raffia mats to have sex on the beach.[18] Kuramo Beach was also a home for smoking weed and other illicit drugs like heroin. The prostitutes at Kuramo Beach referred to themselves as hustlers and came from all parts of the country. While it lasted, Kuramo Beach was the cheapest nightclub on Victoria Island. It was washed away by ocean erosion in August 2012.

The early 1990s generally saw the sex boom as a citywide business. Famous red-light districts like Obalende, which traditionally serviced the exclusive Ikoyi residential area, were eclipsed by areas like Ipodo. The latter became the busiest red-light district in the city, where every house is a brothel of sorts. What Sanusi Fafunwa Street is to the rich is what Ipodo is to the blue collared common man, to people like bus conductors or area boys. Religion and commerce play a critical role in the social fabric of Ipodo. Spiritual oaths are made to a shrine dedicated to Satan, here known as Ojubu Esu. It is at this shrine that even underage young girls are forced into prostitution in a bond with the devil. According to an independent poll from 2012, conducted by a non-governmental organization, Sympathy Worldwide Foundation, which tackles the needs of sex workers, 13,680 prostitutes operated in Lagos every night.[19] Eventually threatened by the surge of indecency and moral decay in the city, the Lagos State government instituted a ban on indecent dressing.

16 Ray Hutchison, 'Exopolis', Sage Knowledge, <http://www.sageereference.com/view/urbanstudies/n98.xml> accessed 17 November 2015.

17 Michael Dear and Steven Flusty, 'Postmodern Urbanism', in Michael Pacione (ed.), The City – Critical Concepts in the Social Sciences, Vol. 1: The City in Global Context (London, New York: Routledge, 2002), 197.

18 Cf. News Admin, 'Kuramo Beach: Where Sex Sells Like Hot Cake!', The Street Journal, 2 June 2012, <http://thestreetjournal.org/2012/06/kuramo-beach-where-sex-sells-like-hot-cake/> accessed 17 November 2015.

19 Jerry Obidike, '13,680 Prostitutes operate in Lagos every night', Daily Sun, 8 January 2012, <http://odili.net/news/source/2012/jan/8/500.html> accessed 17 November 2015.

In the late 1990s, many returning New York Wall Street and London City finance industry workers sought to recreate their New York or London experiences in Nigeria. Thus, they often financed lounge and karaoke bars, retrofitted with diffused lighting, soft leather sofas, abstract artwork, and projector displays, with an open, breathable, plush, and relaxed modern lounge look. The lounge bars represented the new cash in town and the new patrons as well as gatekeepers of entertainment, music, and enjoyment. The 1990s were also the period of the 'Yahoo Boys' – young Nigerians who had returned from Europe or the US and opened up shop in Lagos as internet con artists, using tricks to obtain millions of US-dollars and Euros from their foreign victims.

The Yahoo Boys were easily identifiable; they wore outlandish designer clothes, complete with gold chains and medallions, drove expensive and exclusive cars, and never missed an opportunity to show off. They were the main patrons that kept the new, modern lounge and karaoke bars in business, spending big money on champagne and liquor. Different variants began to emerge in the Yahoo subculture – among them a very sinister variant called 'Yahoo Plus', who tricked their victims into sacrificial human blood rituals triggered by greed and the alleged opportunity to make money. The Yahoo Boys were so present on the clubbing circuit that the musician Olu Maintain released a song and popular dance step in 2007 he called 'Yahooze'.

With the advent of the lounge bar almost every song on the Lagos airwaves mentioned 'club life' in their lyrics. 'Clubbing' became an advertising buzzword – and a surreal anything-is-possible-construction of 'modern living'. This irony is noteworthy, as no Western-style club scene exists in Lagos on a broader scale. But still, 'clubbing' became synonymous with upward mobility. The new crowd from the diaspora brought the sound and music of the West to their new lounge spaces. So karaoke bars only offered Western pop music on their playlists. Electronic music genres like Techno and House began to appear in these spaces – and their influence became audible in Lagos' contemporary popular music. They became so widespread that even indigenous genres like Fuji music, which was traditionally a completely acoustic sound with little or no amplification other than the microphone's, started to introduce electronic dance music arrangements.

—

In 1994, Lagos finally became officially connected to Western pop culture. In that year, South African cable TV provider MultiChoice and Channel O came to town. MTV Base set up shop in Lagos as well. The internet and cable television became the new 'nightclubs' of choice; now it mattered more for Lagos' musicians to appear on TV shows than to hang out in clubs. This coincided with the democratisation of music recording by way of digital music production and rising internet bandwidth, which easily made it possible for Nigerian musicians to follow trends in Western music. Lagos cultivated a screen identity that interacted with music production, videos, and clubbing. The diaspora exopolis – here meaning a city that no longer conveys the traditional qualities of cityness – reinforced this, where new dance steps were learnt online rather than on the dance floor. In this sphere it was not strange to listen to a musician speak in a Western accent with no prior direct contact with, or experience of, Western culture, except through TV and internet. The new Lagos 'nightclubs' of choice were increasingly the reality shows and entertainment red carpet events shown on cable TV.

These events started to reshape the physical club scene in Lagos, which increasingly took its aesthetic cues from the screen and the internet. Even the unofficial social networks of street vendors and area boys began to cultivate a taste for a hybrid sound of code-switched Pidgin English and electronic dance music, mixed with Yorùbá or Igbo languages, championed by musicians like Phyno or the late Da Grin. But internet and cable TV also empowered musicians. They started cultivating an internationally conscious worldview. And music from Lagos began to shape public cultural opinion in vast parts of Africa in more ways than Fela could have imagined.

The influence and reach of this new hybrid of music, television, and internet activities did not escape the notice of major corporations headquartered in Lagos. So lounge bars, music talent shows, and web advertising became the most effective option for huge enterprises like telecommunication providers or beverage producers to maximise their sales and profits. Global brands also saw the opportunity in targeting the growing club-music and clubbing middle-class, which saw itself as up to date, sophisticated, and cultured. It influenced Lagos' culture, lifestyle, and invariably its consumption patterns. A scene that was less about dance culture and music and more about hanging out and lifestyle. So, their lounge bars became targets for global brands like Heineken and the English Premier League.

Lagos' popstars, realising this new interest in brand association and social status, began including brand names in their songs, copying the African American Rap star model. Local sports 'tribes' in lounge bars adopted lyrics of songs and appropriated them for their sports idols. A good example is the song 'Igwe' ['high chief' in the eastern Nigerian Igbo language] by Nigerian music superstar D'banj which was associated with Thierry Henry from the London football club, Arsenal.

Parallel to this, a new MTV and YouTube generated consciousness of body, gender, and sexuality politics began to spread from the centre to the periphery. Area boys suddenly wore earrings and had tattoos. A special signature touch to tattoo subculture in Lagos were young boys showcasing pink lip tattoos and shaved eyebrows, which they felt made them more sexually appealing to women. Women, especially prostitutes, requested solid pink or red ink tattoos on their labia and clitoris at Lagos' tattoo parlours, which was thought to increase sexual prowess and vivaciousness. At the same time, Nollywood films and Nigerian Hip-Hop openly cross-referenced to LGBT culture for the first time, influenced by the diaspora exopolis.

Lagos for show – the cosmopolitan city

Key to the new 'nightclubbing' was mobility for patrons to move from one lounge or karaoke bar to the next red carpet event. So, cab drivers tuned into traffic radio stations to navigate the city's gridlocks in order not to miss out on the action. Okadas [motorbike taxi shuttles] were stationed in front of all clubs, lounges, or church venues awaiting passengers. These Okada bikes, often decorated with graffiti showing street slang and messages, were mostly operated by indigenes from Northern and North-Eastern Nigeria. But with the recklessness of the Okada drivers and the rising terrorist threat of Boko Haram in the North Eastern part of the country, where the majority of the Okada riders came from, Lagosians became afraid of the motorbikes' potential threat to life and deployment for sinister purposes. This lead to Okadas being banned as a security and health hazard by the Lagos State authorities.

The ban on Okadas coincided with the advent of the increasing popularity of the gaming company Baba Ijebu. This company offered a bingo-like gambling that promised to provide alternative means of financial support for the lower blue-collar working classes. Baba Ijebu offered a lifeline to the out of work Okada drivers who make remittances to their North East homes. This lottery game and several variants, which requires skills in 'forecasting' target numbers and dream numbers, is an underground phenomenon in Lagos; an open secret on the streets. It is common to hear phrases like 'Three Direct', 'Two Sure', 'One against one' on street corners, phrases that describe winning strategies for Baba Ijebu and its derivatives. A significant percentage of the proceeds from this gambling are donated to churches to invest in a spiritually better life.

It is important to note that one would be hard-pressed to find a significant number of Lagosians that do not believe in any concept of God. Historically, Lagos was a Muslim city in Victorian times.[20] The coming of Christianity into Lagos was of mixed reactions due to strong resistance from high-density urban areas where Islam had already made substantial inroads. The determination of church missionaries preaching the 'modernising' capacity of Christianity made the Christianisation of Lagos possible. Next to the Muslim faith and other belief systems the trend of the 1980s, when Christian churches had first become venues for music and dance production in the wake of the SAP's hardships, continued into the 2000s. But it took another dimension. Increasingly the notion caught on that being 'born again' was a progressive practice in line with a secular, modern, and cosmopolitan worldview (an opinion that the Western mind might find puzzling).

Pentecostal faith relies on experience rather than dogma and doctrine, which facilitates its easy traction in Lagos – it tapped into a deep layer of spirituality and emotional intensity common in traditional Lagos society. A Pentecostal 'experience' is part religious service, part performance and spectacle with grooving and rocking. The worshippers are dressed in expensive suits or haute couture costumes bedecked with stunning jewellery – their God is not a poor God. Like in the African American churches religious music plays a central role. This music is rich with riffs, arpeggios, and impulsive embellishments. It prepares the congregation to enter the spirit. The congregation begins by swaying in a slow yet measured fashion, the tempo increases with clapping to the music and dancing in stylised steps, in an apparent subconscious limbo, eyes closed, heads hung down. Worshippers move to the central aisle, crying 'Hallelujah!'. The church cameras move in to capture the emotional rapture for audiences at home to share the spiritual fervour of the moment. Just like the city of Lagos, Pentecostalism is about excitement and emotion. It is about the show and showmanship.

Today Lagos has the highest population of Christian Pentecostals in Africa. The Pentecostal churches have grown into industrial enterprises, including twenty-four-hour media products like their own television channels, and the distinct lines between religion, wealth, and status have been blurred. Spiritual modernity has aligned with US style materialism. And Nigerian style Christian Pentecostal worship is being exported to every part of the African continent. This phenomenon might, in part, explain the increased demand for Nigerian music in Africa. In a sense this is about the amount of music produced in the city and in Lagos' Pentecostal churches.

Most of the famous music producers in Lagos began their careers in Pentecostal churches. Don Jazzy, for example, the most influential urban pop producer in Lagos, began playing musical instruments in a Pentecostal church. In Lagos, it is common knowledge that the best session musicians are found in the white garment churches – African Celestial Church and the Cherubim and Seraphim Church ('white garment' because the entire congregation wears white gowns to

---

20 Michael J. C. Echeruo, *Victorian Lagos: Aspects of Nineteenth Century Lagos Life* (London: Macmillan, 1977), 10–35.

worship). So, no wonder that, as MTV and visual online media created alternative music spaces, the vacuum left in the real world was easily filled by equally media-savvy Pentecostal organisations. They appropriated all available, free public space for their activities.

Lagos' Pentecostal church, House on The Rock, took the lead with its annual music festival 'Experience', which brings Lagos to a standstill once a year. The 'Experience' show is free to the general public and comes with a mixture of popular African American and Nigerian Gospel music stars. Virtually the whole city attempts to get into 'Experience'. It takes place in no other venue than Tafawa Balewa Square, which has become commercialised after military rule and the change of seat of government from Lagos to Abuja. The new, live 'clubbing' Christian rave experience is branded as a social good that benefits urban neighbourhoods. To Lagosians, this was not hard to sell as this was just a natural, cosmopolitan, and 'modern' progression from the traditional practice of Owambe marathon street parties. Live music was always the first choice for Lagosians. They embraced it as a practice that impacted on the identity and vitality of urban communities.

In appreciation of the 'raves' supporting to build communities, the Lagos state authorities began to recognise the power that producing music has. Due to this the authorities began to look at the power of music produced in Lagos for their own bread and circuses and political benefit. As a consequence, it introduced state-sponsored carnivals on the streets of Lagos like the Fanti Easter Festival and a people-friendly version of the famous Eyo Festival.[21] These festivals were aimed at uniting the people of Lagos and building harmony for political stability. The Lagos state government increasingly recognised music as a cultural product that could be packaged and commoditised for Africa-wide consumption and to the diasporas.

To this effect the Lagos state government invested in the Fela Museum and encouraged the Broadway show *Fela! On Broadway* to perform in Lagos by underwriting the Lagos production and subsidising tickets. But the *Fela!* show subsidy was an elitist gesture as the location of the show was Eko Hotel, one of the most exclusive hotels in Lagos. The tickets, although they were subsidised, were clearly out of the reach for the common man like the Okada motorbike taxi drivers who could only afford the gate fee to Fela's original Shrine nightclub. On the other hand, the majority of the middle-class and upper-class audience from 'the Islands' had probably never been to the original Shrine. Its location on the mainland, which they associate with lower-classes and crime, would have been too discouraging for them to venture.

—

In most religions practised in Africa, music plays some role or the other. But the parallels between the Christian church services and nightclubbing are uncanny, especially in the case of Lagos' Pentecostal churches. They run all night, on several days of the week just like nightclubs. Both the church and club are sites where people meet, shout, dance and, at times, take mind-altering substances before they go off with one another. It comes as no surprise that with the decline in church going in the Western world, nightclubs sometimes occupied their space. What is critical to this appropriation is the layout of churches as they correspond to the layout of nightclubs and, in a sense, to the aspiration of the people. In this process in the West, we see pews replaced by dance floors, pulpits by DJ-booths, organs by sound systems, and the vestry replaced by toilets.

With regards to their function, Lagos' Pentecostal churches could best be compared to a rave arena, with the most striking difference being the absence of sideshows, open alcohol consumption

21   Cf. Isiguzo Destiny, 'Eyo festival: The true face of Lagos', *National Mirror*, 16 July 2015.

and advertising (the churches have their own money). But Lagos' Pentecostal churches have abandoned the traditionally Western borrowed forms. The urban landscape, politics of architecture, and the desires of the people demand a peculiar type of spatial triad.

Lagos' Pentecostal churches borrow their visual vocabulary and aesthetic gaze from big business, sports arenas, shopping malls, and multi-national corporations – many of the churches have branches all over Africa. Their buildings are grand and superlative architectural statements that are embellished with rare marble stone and granite flooring, crystal chandeliers, climate-controlled air-conditioning, state of the art lighting, and reinforced walls full of speakers. Rarely do these churches have Christian symbols or Christian iconography embedded into their structures. This omission is an intentional effort of not reminding potential congregations of traditional Christianity – and rather opt for a more amiable and friendly, non-church-like ambience. After all, the overriding message is success, not salvation.

If traditional Christian churches are to be regarded as a symbol of the colonial-inherited, European society model, the Pentecostal church buildings stand for their favoured US-American society model. The tension between both is clearly visible in Lagos' urban landscape. Lagos Island, the old part of the city, has traces of a European style urban design including church spires and a cathedral, while the mainland and other newer districts of the city clearly display the effect of globalisation on Lagos and the influence of China.[22] This conflict could be seen as symbolic of the problems that plague Lagos as it is struggling with its own aesthetic identity and architectural vernacular.

Also on Victoria Island, the globalised architecture is already being established. Lagos' main representative is the new, Dubai-like Eko Atlantic project.[23] This is an ambitious project of creating a Lagos Manhattan on reclaimed land from the Atlantic coastline. Its visual language demonstrates the Lagosian fascination with Dubai and how, through commercial connections, and through old Lagos Lebanese families and Islam, Lagos is connected to the Arab world as well as the global economic and cultural system. This attempt to transit from the old to the new, from the colonial to the post-colonial, and from traditional to the modern can also be seen as a transition from the problems of the past to the problems of the future.

'Great Wall of Lagos' – The mega city and the encroaching water

Architecture of urban Lagos serves as an instrument that transforms old ideas to solve modern problems. As Lagos is a city in constant flux and transition, Lagosians find themselves living in an age where, on a daily basis, time accelerates at an increasing rate which determines the circadian rhythm of Lagos' peculiar time signature. The Dutch architect Rem Koolhaas echoed this observation when he wrote, 'The longer I work on it. The less I know why… Lagos is a mystery that is intensifying because of its oil, it is a very rich place but everybody is very poor. Since the 1960s the average income has decreased systematically. I don't think you can be in Lagos without becoming aware of its potency; when Lagos gets itself organized it will be extremely powerful; and already – without organization – it is very powerful.'[24] Koolhaas was intrigued about how Lagos self-organised its urban space, and commented on '… the ability of the population to take its fate into its own hands, and to survive by its own wits'. To Koolhaas, all this would not be possible '… if Lagos had not modernized according to fairly conventional vision of what a modern city should look like in the 1970s'.[25]

---

22 These buildings are glass and steel constructions which are not properly suited for the African climate but readily promoted by the Chinese all over Africa.
23 Tolu Ogunlesi, 'Eko Atlantic City – A Mammoth New Development on the Coastline of Lagos', *CNN Edition*, October/November 2012, <http://edition.cnn.com/WORLD/africa/africanawards/pdf/2013/tolu-ogunlesi/tolu-ogunlesi-eko-atlantic-story.pdf> accessed 11 November 2015.
24 *Lagos Wide and Close – An Interactive Journey into an Exploding City*, (dir.), Bregje Van der Haak (2005).
25 Ibid.

King Sunny Ade, Chicagofest, Chicago, Illinois, 1983, photo: Paul Natkin

Recording Studio, Lagos, 2009, photo: unknown

King Sunny Ade in concert at New World Nigeria, Stratford, London, 2012, photo: Robert Covell

Album cover I.K. Dairo M.B.E. & His Blue Spots, *Ashiko Music Vol. 2*, 1972

Fela Kuti, Stratford, London, 1983, photo: Bernard Matussiere

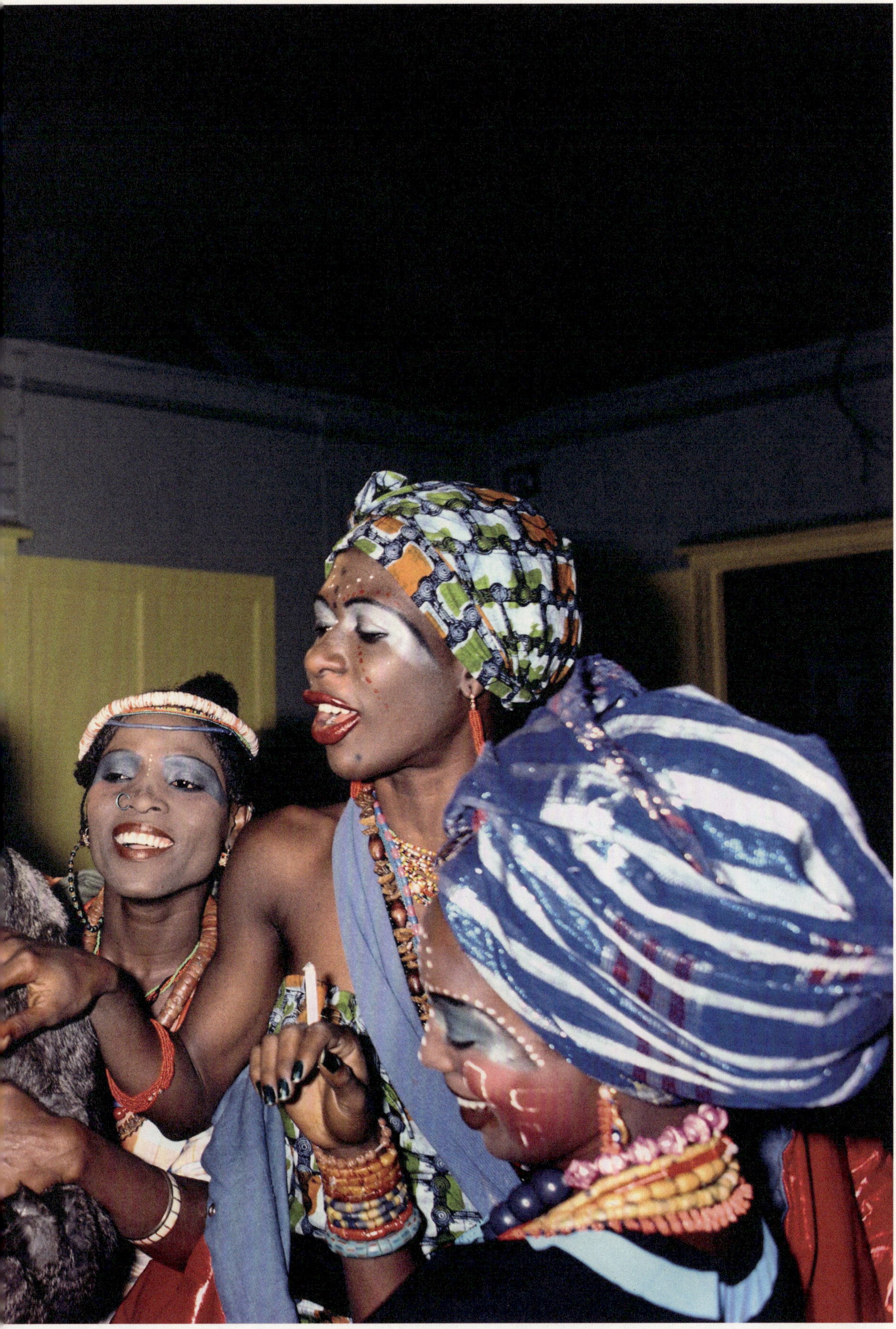

Album cover *Alhaja Queen Salawa Abeni And Her Waka Moderniser, Mo Tun de Bi Mo Se Nde*, 1986

Album cover *Sir Shina Adewale And The Superstars International*, 1978

Fela Kuti, Stratford, London, 1983, photo: Bernard Matussiere

Album cover Fela Kuti and Africa 70, *Zombie*, 1976

The New Shrine opened shortly after Fela Kuti's death in 1997, Lagos, 2011, photo: Martin Waalboer

Deciphering Lagos' soundscape is a step in the right direction, in comprehending the entropy that comes from a chaotic urban situation. Lagos is best described as an exclamation. It is a city that requires an understanding of what one sees as the difference between the cutting edge and the subtle surrounding – depending on what city one decides to see. Today Lagos' gridlocks have somewhat disappeared, and in its wake a sudden infatuation has come with the visualisation of Lagos as a modern 'mega city' of global importance. This incomprehensible interest in the charged nature of the word 'mega city' is discernible from a bird's eye view: A 'Great Wall of Lagos', packaged by the Eko Atlantic project and currently being erected, is needed to protect the coastline from the encroaching Atlantic, which is bringing the sea ever closer to the city's financial centre.

Bibliography

Aneke, Luke Nnaemeka, *The Untold Story of the Nigeria-Biafra War* (New York: Triumph Publishing, 2007).

Destiny, Isiguzo, 'Eyo festival: The true face of Lagos', *National Mirror*, 16 July 2015.

Echeruo, Michael J. C., *Victorian Lagos: Aspects of Nineteenth Century Lagos Life* (London: Macmillan, 1977).

Ekwensi, Cyprian, *Jagua Nana* (London: Heinemann, 1961).

Hutchison, Ray, 'Exopolis', *Sage Knowledge*, <http://www.sageereference.com/view/urbanstudies/n98.xml> accessed 17 November 2015.

Idam, Jossy, 'Bobby Benson', *Online Nigeria Community Portal of Nigeria*, 18 May 2008, <http://nm.onlinenigeria.com/templates/?a=12216> accessed 17 November 2015.

Ikejiaku, Brian-Vincent, 'Africa Debt Crisis and the IMF with a Case of Nigeria: towards Theoretical Explanations', *Journal of Politics and Law*, vol. 1, no. 4 (2008), 2–6.

Lawrence, Bisi, '*Caban Bamboo *Bobby Benson', *Vanguard*, 8 August 2009, <http://www.vanguardngr.com/2009/08/caban-bamboo-bobby-benson/> accessed 17 November 2015.

Mann, Kristin, *A Social History of the New African Elite in Lagos Colony, 1880–1913* (Stanford: Stanford University, 1977).

Nwakanma, Obi, *Christopher Okigbo 1930–67: Thirsting for Sunlight* (Suffolk: Boydell & Brewer, 2010).

N.N., 'Kuramo Beach: Where Sex Sells Like Hot Cake!', *The Street Journal*, 2 June 2012, <http://thestreetjournal.org/2012/06/kuramo-beachwhere-sex-sells-like-hot-cake/> accessed 17 November 2015.

Obidike, Jerry, '13,680 Prostitutes operate in Lagos every night', *Daily Sun*, 8 January 2012, <http://odili.net/news/source/2012/jan/8/500.html> accessed 17 November 2015.

Ogunlesi, Tolu, 'Eko Atlantic City – A Mammoth New Development on the Coastline of Lagos', *CNN Edition*, October/November 2012, <http://edition.cnn.com/WORLD/africa/africanawards/pdf/2013/tolu-ogunlesi/tolu-ogunlesi-eko-atlantic-story.pdf> accessed 11 November 2015.

Pacione, Michael (ed.), *The City – Critical Concepts in the Social Sciences, Vol. 1: The City in Global Context* (London, New York: Routledge, 2002).

Parsons, Timothy H., *The British Imperial Century, 1815–1914: A World History Perspective (Critical Issues in World and International History)* (Lanham, MD: Rowman & Littlefield Publishers, 1999).

Quist-Arcton, Ofeibea, 'Out of a Nigerian Slum, a Poet Is Born', *NPR*, 27 June 2007, <http://www.npr.org/templates/story/story.php?storyId=10826005> accessed 17 November 2015.

Soyinka, Wole, *The Open Sore of a Continent: A Personal Narrative of the Nigerian Crisis (W.E.B. Du Bois Institute)* (Oxford: Oxford University Press, 1996).

Veal, Michael, *Fela: The Life and Times of an African Musical Icon* (Philadelphia: Temple University Press, 2000).

BRISTOL

MUSIC/SPACES
A Village Dancing to its Own Beat

Dub-rooted Values in a Tightly Knit Music Scene

Tony Benjamin

▶ P.437

SPACES/POLITICS
Bristol Mixes

Underground, Identity, and the City

Rehan Hyder and Michelle Henning

▶ P.459

A Village Dancing to its Own Beat – Dub-rooted Values in a Tightly Knit Music Scene

Tony Benjamin

It's indoors, mostly, and crammed into a small arched vault throbbing with a rich bass pulse. It's summer 2014, and there are maybe a hundred people spilling in and out of this underground bar, endlessly passing up and down the stairs and onto the road, meeting and greeting and getting their heads together. There's no guest list or VIP access, but the familiar pair of security guys at the door recognise most faces as they arrive. There is a party mood and the tunnelled backroom pounds to classic Jungle rhythms, tisking hi-hats, and growling sub-bass funnelled by the rounded ceiling. On the makeshift-looking decks, DJ Flynn is pushing forward with Reggae flavours, while a live saxophone player and a guitarist add hints of a long-lost Kingston sound, and a score of jostling dancers drink to the beats in the dark. Even in this gloom, one figure stands out, the nodding, knot-haired silhouette of Grant Marshall – better known as Daddy G, founding member of the internationally famed Trip-Hop band Massive Attack – his head and shoulders rising above the rest.

Around the corner, in the crowded bar area where the sound is muted just enough for conversation, are Die and Krust, core members of the Full Cycle DJ crew, whose award-winning Reprazent project, led by Roni Size, put UK Drum'n'Bass on the world's music map. They mingle easily, as friends among friends, while the distinctive bandana-bound dreadlocks of DJ Ray Mighty (one half of the seminal Dub production duo Smith and Mighty) slip past, en route to taking his turn at the decks. In due course Krust and Die will make their musical contribution as well, pleasing the dance floor with specially made cuts, but for now, they're all at the party, equal citizens of this community of friends, held together by music for over twenty-five years.

The venue is Cosies, an incongruous little wine bar at the edge of the St Pauls area of Bristol, a hard-pressed corner of the inner city that has been home to Bristol's African Caribbean community since they began arriving in the 1960s. Managed from the mid-1990s by Queen Bee – a former Bristol pirate radio DJ who became the regular DJ for Massive Attack's increasingly global touring schedule – Cosies soon became the crucial meeting point for the Bristol dance music world. Queen Bee brought the best new DJ talent and locally produced sounds to the city's party people. In many ways, the place inherited the role of the long-closed club Dug Out – a similar underground meeting place where Bristol's young people from different ethnic and musical communities had freely mixed since the 1970s.[1]

The Dug Out's open-minded culture was regarded as the late 1980s melting pot that allowed Massive Attack, Tricky, Soul II Soul's Nellee Hooper, and others to fuse Reggae, Rock, Soul, and Hip-Hop into what would become known as the 'Bristol Sound'. That club's successor, Cosies, boasts a built-in Reggae-style sound system with hidden sub-bass speakers made by Krust's uncle. Over the years it has handled every kind of dance music from Hip-Hop and Jungle to Dubstep and Techno; all these genres, as well as associated DJs, producers and fashions, have had their time.

Through all the changing fashions, the one constant was Reggae – brought to Bristol in the 1960s by newly-arrived Jamaicans and shared with a wider, dance-hungry audience through sound systems in underground clubs and Carnival side streets, until becoming hard-wired into the city's musical identity. For Bristol's dance music community, Cosies' weekly helpings of Roots Reggae have long been as much a Sunday necessity as the traditional English roast dinner, but the music has a much wider significance. In a story that runs from early Hip-Hop through Trip-Hop, Jungle, Drum'n'Bass, and on to Dubstep, Grime and beyond, Bristol's distinctive contribution has been to bring the values of Dub Reggae – spacious open mixes, layered collages of sounds, and, crucially, viscerally physical basslines – to each new genre.

This particular summer's night is a memorial for Flora, Flynn's DJ partner since the 1980s Jungle scene, who has just passed away. Unsurprisingly, there's an emotional charge to the gathering, a reflective quality, but overall it's a sense that life is to be celebrated, that the pulsing sub-bass heartbeat of the city must go on and they will continue to play their part in making that happen. It's especially significant that even the most globally recognised of Bristol's musicians rarely move away and, like Daddy G, Krust, and Die, remain part of this community, both socialising with it and sharing music that is as local as it is international. Like the generation before and the generations that follow, these people are what make that distinctively Bristolian sound endure each new phase of dance music culture.

The city: inclusive culture and independent attitude

Bristol is such a small place you can get anything done for practically nothing. You can always walk across town if you have to and you can always get things to happen. You just had to know someone who had a studio.[2]

When compared to London, Birmingham, or Manchester, the city of Bristol is not huge. With a population of just over 600,000 makes it the tenth largest conurbation in the UK. But it is by far the biggest place in the south-west of England. Unlike the major towns in the north of England, Bristol has no neighbours to rival it for size, employment, or economic power and its thriving harbour made it the

---

[1] Please see Rehan Hyder and Michelle Henning's contribution in this book for learning more about the Dug Out and other important places of Bristol's music scenes.

[2] DJ Krust, in an interview with the author (2014).

regional centre for trade long before the industrial revolution. People from the outlying towns and countryside have always come into Bristol for business and pleasure, and the city has always profited from both. Surrounded by rich food-producing farmlands and with a long-established Atlantic port bringing wine, tobacco, coffee, and cocoa beans Bristol's comfortable self-sufficiency as a regional capital feeds an independent attitude that can quickly tip into complacency.

Being the biggest fish in its regional pond has always given Bristol an ambivalent relationship with London. The latter may be the capital city and the centre of politics and finance for the whole country, but it is a long way off and is thought to do little for Bristolians. The disdain is mutual: viewed from London, Bristol is a provincial backwater whose rural accent suggests comical pirates or farmhouse cider, stereotypes still largely unchallenged in the mainstream national media where west country voices are rarely heard. Most Bristol citizens feel their home city has all the conveniences of cosmopolitan urban living without being overwhelming – while London, by comparison, is not to be trusted: too big, too fast, too impersonal.

So, when the London media finally noticed Bristol's music scene in the early to mid-1990s, thanks to the emergence of ground-breaking debut albums from Massive Attack, Tricky, and Portishead, Bristolians generally rejected the labels of 'Bristol scene', 'Bristol sound', and 'Trip-Hop' that outsider journalists used to pigeonhole the music. From their local perspective, the music simply came from the life of the city where it belonged, it was what it was, and if others appreciate it, then that was what good music deserved. There was plenty of local pride in the on-going supply of quality musical innovation coming from Bristol. But the consensus was that it didn't need approval from London to make it good.

Bristol may be built like a city, but its comparatively small size enables the musical community to think like a village. Things happen because people know people, they meet on the street in passing as often as by appointment. If you have an interest in something, it will not be long before you know (and will be known by) nearly all the Bristolians who share your interest. These real social networks are especially visible around music, traditionally reinforced through gathering places like record shops, music venues, recording studios, and clubs. Musicians, DJs, and producers from all genres across the city know each other, check out gigs and tunes, and sit in on recordings. This generates a collaborative network that often shares resources and ideas in a culture of independent 'make do and mend' music. Of course there is rivalry, but on the whole, musicians say that it is respectful – people want to impress their peers by outdoing them, and they know what it takes.

This inclusive and supportive culture, combined with the continuing diversity of live music in the city, is what draws musicians from around the world to settle in Bristol, giving the city's live scene rich flavours of West African kora playing, Zimbabwean Jit-Jive, Balkan Gypsy dance music, and many other traditions. However, it is interesting to note that the greatest achievements of Bristol dance music since the early 1980s have nearly all been down to people born-and-bred there, whose roots lie firmly in some of the city's most hard-pressed neighbourhoods. And, significantly, they are nearly all still living in Bristol, still to be bumped into in clubs and bars, or spied in the crowd at the annual St Pauls Carnival. It is not a scene, it is a community and, musically, it is an ongoing party where the distinction between the audience and performers is often imperceptible.[3]

—

The story of this party begins with the arrival of significant numbers of Caribbean immigrants through the 1960s, attracted by government-led campaigns to boost the UK workforce as the post-war economy began to grow. In Bristol, this new and distinctive community largely gathered in the run-down, low rent, inner city district of St Pauls. They brought with them the Ska and Rocksteady music that would later become Reggae and, as they grew more settled, they began to build Jamaican-style sound systems for their own entertainment. These powerful amplification rigs with their huge speaker boxes optimised bass sounds to a physical level, and their crews established a DJ culture in backstreet 'blues' parties – unofficial gatherings for drinking and dancing often held as 'rent parties' in private houses – that eventually emerged onto the streets of St Pauls for an annual Carnival. The sound systems mostly played imported records, but by the late 1970s British-based Reggae musicians were beginning to establish themselves, and Bristol Reggae bands like Talisman and Black Roots soon gained national recognition through radio play and appearances on the summer festival circuit.

By the mid-1980s, Bristol had a new generation who had been schooled in the Jamaican Dub production style but were caught up in the whole culture of US Hip-Hop with its similarly deconstructed approach to beats and breaks. This evolving style was forged in a lively network of house parties and warehouse raves in abandoned industrial buildings across the city, while producers like Rob Smith, Nellee Hooper, and Dave McDonald were perfecting homegrown music in rudimentary home studios. Originally made as dubplates for the local party scene, these 'Bristol fashion' fusions began to receive national acclaim: the first to hit the charts in 1989 were the Fresh Four, signed by Virgin Records, then the Wild Bunch emerged, leading to Massive Attack and Tricky, along with Portishead, in the early 1990s. With their great success in singles and albums, as well as in clubs across the UK and beyond, these three acts were bracketed as 'the Bristol sound'; a chilled and often dark version of Hip-Hop driven by growling Reggae basslines.

While these acts celebrated their national and international recognition another new dance culture was already

---

3   This has been well observed in Peter Webb, *Exploring the Networked Worlds of Popular Music: Milieu Cultures* (New York and Abingdon: Routledge, 2007).

taking hold in the city, as the Fresh Four's DJ Krust began exploring the sped up beats of Jungle with Roni Size. Their Full Cycle crew, formed with DJs Die and Suv, evolved into Reprazent, reshaping Drum'n'Bass, the music succeeding Jungle, with their album *New Forms*, winner of the prestigious Mercury Music Prize in 1997. Even they were only part of a wider Drum'n'Bass wave sweeping Bristol into the new millennium with further breakbeat experimentation from acts like Kosheen and Boca 45. For ten years it seemed that the urgency of 160 beats per minute (BPM) dance music was calling the shots on the dance floors, until the acute ears of Rob Ellis, aka DJ Pinch, caught the beginnings of Dubstep. At first, only a south London scene, once Pinch introduced the slower, more spacious groove to a Bristol nightclub, it proved a perfect fit with the city's bass-hungry Dub-rooted tastes and soon inspired a fresh young generation of production talent. From 2007 onwards, young producers like Guido, Joker, and Gemmy were just some of the talent making Bristol UK Dubstep's second city, their self-styled 'Purple' sound bringing a psychedelic melodic dimension to Dubstep and becoming another local genre to get national recognition. By 2014, Joker would go on to play a major role in reviving the faster electronic glitch of Grime after mainstream pop had all but smothered it. These names are just some of the most prominent to emerge from what has always been a busy network of independent producers.

Roots and foundations: the 1960s and 1970s

By the end of the 1960s, the centre of Bristol was changing fast. The new big container ships could now only be loaded at the out of town docks, leaving the city's disused harbour area to crumble away. Bomb-damaged sites left from the Second World War were cleared and developed for commercial property and teeming inner-city streets were demolished, as families moved to newly built tower blocks and residential estates outside the central area. The effect was to create an unpopulated space at the city's heart, a place where, by day, people came to work or shop and returned to eat, drink, and enjoy themselves by night. With the rise of discotheques featuring DJs playing records rather than live bands, the mid-1960s saw the nightclub scene in Bristol proliferate, mainly with clubs playing chart music and US Soul. The Mecca organization, a powerful national investor, opened The New Bristol Centre, a massive multi-million-pound leisure complex right in the city's heart, with bars, cinemas, an ice rink, a casino, and a 2000-person capacity ballroom.

It's fair to say that, though Bristol had a thriving local Rock'n'Roll scene and was an important national hub for the 1960s Traditional Jazz revival, local musicians had not made a significant impact outside the city. The two most celebrated musical acts to emerge from Bristol had been Russ Conway, a Honky-Tonk pianist and early TV star who had two number one hits in the early 1960s, and Acker Bilk, a Jazz clarinettist whose 1961 slow instrumental 'Stranger on the Shore' spent an entire year in the UK charts and was the first British record to achieve number one in the US Billboard charts. The next time a Bristol-associated act would gain national fame, however, would be in 1966 when self-styled 'Scrumpy and Western'[4] band Adge Cutler and the Wurzels released 'Drink Up Thy Zider', a self-parodying drinking song that probably did more than anything to perpetuate the stereotype of a slow-witted rural 'yokel' [peasant] still often associated with the West Country accent. The record reached number forty-five on the charts and remains an anthem throughout the cider-producing countryside of Somerset around Bristol to this day.

While the centre of Bristol housed many nightclubs, by the early 1970s, it was not seen as a welcoming place for everyone. As a young woman who enjoyed dancing, Gill Loats – who would eventually become the first female DJ at the celebrated Dug Out club – avoided it as much as possible, choosing a club up on the outskirts of the central area instead:

> When I was fifteen I used to go to Tiffany's – I would go every night, three different nights: that's why my music taste is so varied, I couldn't understand the idea of listening to just one kind. The good thing was, it was up the road and I thought going downtown was a bit scary. In those days there were gangs like the Redland Boot Boys, the Muller Boys, there'd always be fighting in the streets.[5]

These roaming, aggressive skinhead gangs were the tip of an iceberg of racial hostility that made central Bristol particularly unsafe for the city's rapidly growing West Indian community. Largely crammed into the run down back streets of the impoverished St Pauls area, they were often not welcomed into other public spaces, though DJ Derek, a white Bristolian, remembers a local exception:

> Most (pubs) had the signs 'No Irish, no dogs, no blacks', But the white guy running The Criterion saw the potential and welcomed the West Indian community. He even had a Jamaican DJ in playing music. That was the one thing that started the community spirit (in St Pauls). I loved the music and fell in love with the people.[6]

Derek was not alone in discovering this musical import. By the early 1970s their exclusion had generated a mix of official and unofficial places where the black community of St Pauls could socialise. Officially there were clubs like the famed Bamboo Club and Western Star Domino Club as well as pubs like the Criterion, The Inkerman, and the Star and Garter, all of which featured DJs playing Caribbean dance music including Ska, Reggae, and Calypso. Then there were unlicensed rent parties known as 'blues' held in people's homes where, for a small entrance fee, you could buy drinks and dance through the night. While the facilities could be as

---

4 Traditionally made cider is called 'scrumpy' in South West England.
5 Gill Loats, in an interview with the author (2014).
6 DJ Derek, in an interview with the author (2014).

basic as 'just cans of Special Brew and a Dansette (record player) in the corner' (Gill Loats) the most popular Blues featured the city's first Jamaican-style sound system, with imposing hand-made speaker boxes delivering musical power unheard of outside the Caribbean. Future Reggae musician, Jabulani Ngozi – like many Jamaicans he has reclaimed a name reflecting his African ancestry before slavery – was still at school in 1972 when he joined Tarzan, one of the first and best of Bristol's sound systems, run by Hector Thaws, whose grandson Adrian Thaws would later find international fame under the name of Tricky:

> I became involved in Tarzan sound system – Tarzan the High Priest. They always needed help to move the boxes when they used to play the Bamboo Club, or house parties, every night from Thursday to Sunday from 8pm to 7am. I couldn't stay after ten o'clock ... They could see you were a school kid so you had to go. Then we came back in the morning to get [the boxes] out.[7]

This acoustic technology had its craftsmanship and Jabulani's brother Kwesi had a reputation as a master builder:

> My brother Kwesi and Baggy (who got shot) were the best at building speakers. You have to build each speaker on its own and you need a lot of knowledge to do that. A lot of youths used to try to build their own but they didn't know – you need screws and glue, you have to have both. They would use nails and as soon as the music started they would shake to pieces![8]

The blues parties' reputation soon spread among white Bristolians looking for entertainment, a late drink, or other stimulations, yet unwilling to get involved in the city centre nighttime melee. These outside faces were almost always received easily into the St Pauls party scene, as long as they paid their entry fee and behaved respectfully, and for this, they were rewarded with the sounds of Ska, Rocksteady, and Reggae, which would be hard to find elsewhere. The real bonus was hearing them on proper sound systems, and as Jabulani says: 'You have to hear it on the box. If you want to hear Reggae you have to hear it on a system.'

—

By the mid-1970s, the UK had several successful Reggae bands including Matumbi and Aswad from London, Birmingham's Steel Pulse, and others. Jabulani Ngozi remembers early Bristol Reggae bands like Sonic Invaders and The Untouchables, but it was Matumbi's multi-instrumentalist producer, Dennis Bovell, who was responsible for the first proper Reggae release from Bristol. Bovell spotted the young Joshua (now known as Jashwha) Moses performing at the Bamboo Club's annual talent competition:

> In those days, every year there would be a singing competition and there would be a festival. That was how I got to record my first song because this particular year, I think it was '75, '76, there was a group called Matumbi which consisted of Dennis Bovell and others. They were the ones who were actually going to back up these local singers and that's when I first sang a song that I had written called 'Africa', It just happened, it just worked. Next thing I knew, I recorded 'Africa'.[9]

Joshua Moses' first single 'Africa Is Our Land' was recorded in a London studio with Bovell himself playing all the instrumental parts and was released in 1978 on the short-lived London-based More Cut label. About this time Jabulani Ngozi was also starting to get a seven-piece Reggae band together with a view to making records:

> By 1979 we had started Black Roots and we played our first gig at Bath Pavilion. We wanted to record our tunes so we did a session at (downtown nightclub) Romeo & Juliet's and a benefit at Trinity (Arts Centre) to raise money for an EP and it felt like the whole community turned out for us.[10]

Black Roots' 'Bristol Rock' EP, released on the independent Nubian label in 1981, made an immediate impact with two of the most important institutions in UK music at the time, the Caribbean community newspaper *Black Echoes* (whose reviewer John Futrell wrote that 'Black Roots are the next great hope for reggae in this country'[11]) and Radio 1 DJ, John Peel whose comment became almost legendary: 'If anyone tells you that there is no such thing as good British Reggae, first tell them that they are a herbert and then make them listen to the Black Roots album.'[12]

The four tracks showcased the band's tight rhythms, instrumental flair, and conscious lyrics, with the title track a specific response to the 1980 riots in St Pauls that the band had seen at first hand, thanks to a habit of rehearsing in Albert Villas. This local community centre, which also housed a legal advice service, is right on what became known as 'the front line' of Grosvenor Road, St Pauls, where the rioting was at its most intense:

> We made that track 'Bristol Rock' the same week as the riots. We used to rehearse in Albert Villas three nights a week. The riot happened on a Thursday night, we didn't know what was happening – came out to find blacks fighting with police, shops on fire, rioting all over the place. Somebody knew (singer and poet) Bunny Marrett had lyrics so we brought him down straight away. It was easy to add them, the Bristol Reggae sound was warm, easy to get the feel. I never looked on it as a race riot, though, because sixty per cent of those rioters were white. It was a poverty rebellion, not a race thing.[13]

The other principal Reggae band from Bristol originally formed in 1977 as Revelation Rockers, until they received alarming warnings from another band with a similar name. So, they relaunched as Talisman. The inclusion of two white

7 Jabulani Ngozi, in an interview with the author (2014).
8 Ibid.
9 Alex Cater, 'The People: Joshua Moses', Bristol Archive Records, October 2011, <http://www.bristolarchiverecords.com/people/people_Joshua_Moses.html> accessed July 2014.
10 Jabulani Ngozi, in an interview with the author (2014).
11 Bristol Archive Records, 'Discography: Black Roots', Bristol Archive Records, <http://bristolarchiverecords.com/bands/Black_Roots.html> accessed July 2014.
12 Ibid.
13 DJ Derek, in an interview with the author (2014). DJ Derek goes even further on that subject, saying: 'One of the things that broke (racial tension) down was the riots: all the people banded together against a common enemy.'

musicians in their six-person line-up was considered groundbreaking, and they soon acquired a strong live reputation for their melodic sound; reminiscent of Birmingham's already popular UB40. Talisman released two successful singles on the Recreational Records label – a Bristol based, independent label in the influential Revolver Records shop that employed the young Grant Marshall (later known as Daddy G from Wild Bunch/Massive Attack). Their 1981 debut EP 'Dole Age/Free Speech' was picked as single of the week by the music magazine *NME* and the band famously played as support when the Rolling Stones performed at the Bristol City football ground in 1982.

—

From 1976 onward, a vibrant wave of Punk bands sprung up across Bristol, including The X-Certs, The Cortinas, Stingrays, Social Security, Chaos UK, The Media, and The Pigs. The Pop Group, centred on the wayward musical imagination of Mark Stewart, is still understood to be a seminal influence by the likes of Indie-Rock star Nick Cave[14] and others. Interestingly, their debut album *Y* (1979) was produced by Reggae producer Dennis Bovell, indicative of how the burgeoning Punk and Reggae scenes had become closely intertwined, possibly because both represented 'outsider' cultures whose musical styles and style of dress were largely unwelcome in mainstream town centre venues.

Many Punk musicians and their fans lived in squats, often in the St Pauls and Montpelier areas, where the black community was concentrated, and both communities were suffering unemployment and poverty from the 'Dole Age' recession of the late 1970s. An active political campaign – Rock Against Racism – organised gigs where both black and white bands would play and other campaigning organisations like the Campaign for Nuclear Disarmament (CND) and Anti-Apartheid also promoted benefit gigs that brought the two musical cultures together. Black Roots and Talisman were much in demand for these, as Jabulani recalls: 'We (Black Roots) did many Rock Against Racism gigs, did Miners (strike support) gigs, we did the major CND events and a lot of Anti-Apartheid ... that Bob Geldof thing. We did the first Glastonbury (festival) through CND.'[15]

On a practical level, Punk bands desperate for venues prepared to let them perform, found the Caribbean community offering them a space to play. Thus, more of the white community began to discover clubs like the Bamboo, Western Star Domino, and Tropic and enjoyed the music they usually played. Gill Loats recalls this period: 'I used to love the Western Star Domino Club for the music they played after the bands. It was Calypso music and I loved it. Sometimes I didn't much want the (Punk) band to play so we could get to it sooner.'[16] Eventually, even when Punk bands played elsewhere, the music mix remained the same. Mike Chadwick, who worked in the Revolver Records shop, found himself much in demand: 'I used to have an amazing Reggae collection because I was into Reggae in the 1970s. During the Punk thing in the '70s, I was a Reggae DJ in Bristol. We used to play with all of the Punk bands.'[17]

Punk culture wasn't just about live music and safety pins, however. Crucially it was based on a rejection of corporate business systems in favour of do-it-yourself methods, including hand-made posters and magazines, self-promoted gigs, and independent record production. By the beginning of the 1980s, Bristol had half a dozen 'indie' labels like Fried Egg, Cup of Tea, Heartbeat, and Recreational plus an erratic handful of fanzines including *Future Days*, *Loaded*, *Keep Upright Do Not Bend*, and *Out West* (the latter destined to morph into *Venue*, a fortnightly listings and news magazine for Bristol and Bath that would run for nearly thirty years).

In hindsight, it seems clear that all these elements – the social mixing, the self-reliance of the blues parties, sound systems, Punk, the do-it-yourself aesthetics of fanzines and record labels, the rise of squatting, and the sharpening political pressure of recession and resistance – added up to a potent opportunity for something unpredictable and innovative.

Hip-Hop forms at Dub Reggae speed: the 1980s

After Punk's flailing energy and the emergence of Roots Reggae, the early 1980s also saw a momentary resurgence of Jazz-influenced dance music in Bristol. In 1981, The Pop Group disbanded (they would later explain this as a consequence of being 'so young and volatile'[18]) and members variously joined a trio of bands each playing their own brand of danceable Post-Punk Jazz/Funk. Both the irrepressibly funky Maximum Joy and the more artful Rip Rig and Panic boasted vigorous female vocalists (the latter fronted by stepdaughter of famed avant-garde Jazz trumpeter Don Cherry, Neneh Cherry, who would go on to great success as a solo artist, including her international hit '7 Seconds', a duo with Senegalese superstar Youssou N'Dour) but both had folded by 1983. At that time Cherry was in a relationship with former Pop Group drummer Bruce Smith, the father of her child Naima, and this connection brought her into the Bristol music scene where she would be an influential presence right through the 1980s.

The most commercially successful – eventually – of these 'New Jazz' dance bands was Pigbag, originally from nearby Cheltenham, whose jaunty instrumental Boogie 'Papa's Got A Brand New Pigbag' (1981) would become a national club hit, thanks to 'Getting Up', a 1982 remix by Trance producer, Paul Oakenfold. Oakenfold's canny production emphasises a remorseless Disco beat throughout the tune's clattering Samba percussion, tight Funk-style brass riff and sequence of Jazz-Funk solos, resulting in a Post-Punk tribute to the James Brown sound. The subsequent reissue of the original, on prestigious independent label Stiff, took it to

---

14 This is widely quoted, but Nick Cave expresses his regard for The Pop Group in this video, 'Nick Cave on The Pop Group', YouTube, <https://www.youtube.com/watch?v=BUC2GmzJpGY> accessed July 2014.

15 Jabulani Ngozi, in an interview with the author (2014). As well as being one of the biggest events in the world, the Glastonbury Festival, which happens on a farm some 40 km from Bristol, has always been associated with social justice causes.

16 Gill Loats, in an interview with the author (2014).

17 Larry LeBlanc, 'Industry Profile: Mike Chadwick', Celebrity Access, 1 August 2012, <http://www.celebrityaccess.com/news/profile.html?id=619> accessed July 2014.

18 Press release from the band after reforming in 2010, Clash, 'The Pop Group Reform', 12 July 2010, <http://www.clashmusic.com/news/the-pop-group-reform> accessed 12 January 2015.

number three in the UK single charts in March 1982, just before the band split up. The tune was much sampled and somehow became an enduring favourite chant with football crowds.

But if it seemed that anarchic Jazz-flavoured dance music had had its day in Bristol, two more long-lasting musical units were coming together that would prove hugely influential in the development of the city's dance music culture: the DJ crew known as The Wild Bunch and the production duo of Smith and Mighty. In 1983, Restriction, another popular Bristol Reggae band, finally released what would be their only record: The 'Action' EP had the distinction of being mixed in London by Mad Professor, a former acolyte of Jamaican studio legend Lee 'Scratch' Perry. It was a Dub-infused mix of conscious toasting lyrics and richly arranged instrumentals, with Jamaican trombonist Vin Gordon making a guest contribution, yet its release bizarrely heralded the end of the band. Restriction guitarist Rob Smith recalls the decision: 'Restriction had gone as far as it could go. We'd made a single with the Mad Professor, but nobody outside was taking any notice of Bristol in those days and London was a mystery to me. The guy managing us did his best but we got nowhere.'[19] Smith's ambitions as a musician had been inspired by rock guitar heroes, but he had soon realised he was not destined to be a great player:

I was in a couple of Punk bands, but I never got good enough. I'd grown up with (David Bowie's guitarist) Mick Ronson and Jimi Hendrix and I knew I'd never be that good. I was good enough for Reggae though! I heard about this scheme, a Youth Opportunity thing based on a Reggae show 'Reggae Lives', We were called Zion Band and we played the music. Leroy from Talisman was the musical director and he showed me how to tighten up the (guitar) chops. We went on tour round the UK and we even played in Berlin and then we did some recording sessions and I realised what I really wanted to do: I started mucking about with eight-track (recordings) putting in echo and dub – it was so much fun.[20]

The musician's first encounters with Reggae came when he was eleven, hiding out at school:

Everybody played football at lunchtime but I wasn't interested so I looked around and found this common room where some older Jamaican girls were listening to a record player. I just sat at the back and listened and I couldn't believe it when they flipped each record over – they had the instrumental version on the back. I kept coming back and eventually I asked them to get me one. They got me one by I-Roy and then this bloke played me 'Dread Locks Dread' by Big Youth and I was sold.[21]

Smith had been fascinated by the way the producer stripped out the sound for the Dub version, stretching and echoing the ingredients. Before he got his first guitar, he bought an effects pedal – delay and equalizer – and began experimenting with the family record player, making Dub effects of his own. Even before the Zion Band experience, he had begun cutting and splicing tapes to make his own music. After the demise of Restriction, Smith was invited to join another band called Sweat:

That band was amazing, a little bit funky/punky/apocalyptic. We only ever did one gig but the rehearsals were amazing. Nellee Hooper was the drummer in the first line-up but his timing wasn't up to it. We kicked him out and got a Drumatix drum machine, then a (Roland) 707. I was writing all the drum programmes, I got good at using reverb on the sounds until it sounded brilliant.[22]

Short-lived it may have been but Sweat made a lasting contribution to Bristol music history (and, arguably, British dance music development) because it introduced Rob Smith to keyboard player Ray Mighty, and once the band had disbanded the production team of Smith and Mighty[23] was born. With what limited resources they could find, the pair began assembling a recording studio in Ray's flat, calling it Three Stripe after a sound system they were connected to (and whose massive speakers were at the heart of it). As they began experimenting with a mix of the newly fashionable Hip-Hop and their deep-rooted love of Dub Reggae, a posse of rappers and vocalists soon gathered around them, keen to get recorded. According to Smith, Three Stripe's initial goal was pretty straightforward: 'Our one ambition was to get a record out and get it on John Peel.'[24]

—

Certain aspects of the musical life of Bristol in the 1980s have become famous and one of these is the Dug Out club. Originally a Jazz club in the 1960s, by the early 1970s this small subterranean venue had acquired its own outsider identity. If mainstream clubs belonged to business and the blues parties belonged to the older St Pauls community, then it was not clear who the Dug Out belonged to. Certainly, it did not enforce an identity on the membership, permitting any kind of dress code and apparently oblivious to skin colour (sadly still a real issue at that time). Situated slightly away from the main centre and a stiff uphill walk from St Pauls, it was nearest to the affluent Clifton area, but the club's dinginess and aura of danger made it out of place there. The music policy reflected this lack of ownership too, permitting almost anything on the decks – something Gill Loats was quick to exploit as the club's first female DJ in the late 1970s:

Ah, the Dug Out, unique and never cloned, a club for non-clubbers, where chatting was easy and Disco scorned. Where Indie could be mixed with Reggae and (Punk band) Glaxo Babies back to back with (old school dance band composer) Joe Loss: 1979 (I did it first!).[25]

19 Rob Smith, in an interview with the author (2014).
20 Ibid.
21 Ibid.
22 Ibid.
23 Rob Smith was part of the 'Ten Cities' recording project for which producers and musicians from all ten involved cities in Africa and Europe cooperated to record electronic club music. The results have been released as the compilation 'Ten Cities' (Soundway, 2014).
24 Rob Smith, in an interview with the author (2014). For decades, John Peel was arguably the UK's most influential radio DJ.
25 Taken from Gill Loats' contribution to Bristol Archive Records page about Wavelength Records, Gill Loats, 'Archive Record Labels: Wavelength Records', Bristol Archive Records, April 2000, <http://www.bristolarchiverecords.com/archiveRecordLabels/wavelength_records.html> accessed July 2014.

The Dug Out was an early adopter of the use of two record decks, which meant the DJ didn't have to talk between the records, and one track could lead neatly into the next. For Gill Loats, in the 1970s, that meant being able to mix genres for surprising effects but other musical developments were on the way from the US that would use two decks for different purposes—and when the time came she was ready to hand over her DJ slot for Hip-Hop: 'No way was I getting into that scratching business and ruining my vinyl! (Anyway some geezers calling themselves The Wild Bunch seemed to have that all sewn up).'[26]

By 1983, Revolver Records worker Grant Marshall's regular night at the Dug Out had become the place to be, thanks to the loose collective known as The Wild Bunch. The early Hip-Hop crew initially included scratch DJs Nellee Hooper and Milo with Daddy G (as Marshall became known) taking MC duties. This core later gained graffiti artist 3D (Robert Del Naja) and MC Willie Wee as rappers and Andrew 'Mushroom' Vowles as DJ and tech wizard. At some point, they were also joined by the Tricky Kid (or Tricky, for short). Contrary to popular myth, the Wild Bunch did not come together in the Dug Out—they were already active around the city, particularly at illegal warehouse parties and on the house party scene—but the Dug Out probably gave them a crucial audience. Their sets, that combined classic Funk, Soul, and Reggae with new Hip-Hop material, all scratched, mixed, and overlaid with MC chatter and pre-composed raps, with the occasional self-produced dubplate, would always be a highlight. They weren't the only crew around Bristol at the time—others included 2 Bad, City Rockers, and UD4—but they were soon recognised as the best, and some of their parties, which featured graffiti and B-Boy break dancers, as well as the music, became Bristol legends.[27]

The first clue the world would have about this Bristol phenomenon was when Neneh Cherry, former vocalist of Bristol-based Rip Rig and Panic, name-checked them in her guest rap for Morgan/McVey's 1986 track 'Looking Good Diving With The Wild Bunch', effectively the prototype for her big 1988 hit 'Buffalo Stance'. Between the two releases she persuaded the Bunch to go to Japan in 1987, to play for some fashion shows and, while out of Bristol, some dissension happened leading to 3D's premature return to the UK, effectively quitting the crew. On returning from the Japan trip, Milo and Nellee Hooper moved to London, signing a deal with Island Records as The Wild Bunch and releasing two singles—'Tearin Down the Avenue' (1987) and 'Friends and Countrymen' (1988). Though these might well have been the first Rap records produced by British artists, they were only released in the United States on the Fourth & Broadway label. Shortly after this, Hooper became involved with the London-based Soul II Soul collective, Milo relocated to Japan, and The Wild Bunch name—so revered in Bristol—simply disappeared.[28]

Meanwhile, back in the city, Daddy G, 3D, Willie, and Mushroom found a name of their own—Massive Attack—and a manager in the shape of Cameron McVey, by now Neneh Cherry's partner. The first place they went was to the Three Stripe Studio (aka Ray Mighty's front room) where Smith and Mighty introduced them to Carlton McKay, one of many singers and rappers now in the Three Stripe orbit. The result of this introduction was the first ever Massive Attack record, 1988's 'Any Love' (featuring Daddy Gee and Carlton), a version of a song, originally by Rufus, sung in a sweetly soulful Lovers Rock style over bustling Hip-Hop samples and a pounding beat. The disc, credited as 'co-produced by Massive Attack, Smith & Mighty', must be one of the few records that Rob Smith has ever been associated with, that has no discernible bassline.

Smith and Mighty were still hoping to fulfil their ambition to catch radio DJ John Peel's ears with their own tracks, but it was apparent that people in London weren't interested. They pinned their hopes on a radical reinterpretation of the song by US composer Burt Bacharach 'Anyone (Who Had A Heart)' featuring the measured vocals of singer, Jackie Jackson (who Smith had met doing the Reggae Lives show) over complex percussion, breakbeat intrusions, and an insistent sequenced bassline. Smith recalls playing it for Daddy G, who liked it and suggested they approach Revolver Records, now a part of the national independent record distribution cartel based in the Bristol record shop. Smith remembers: 'So we took a cassette up to Revolver. The first guy, Mike, just wanted to show us out but (the other guy) Lloyd thought it was great and asked us, "Have you got a B-side?"'[29]

Smith and Mighty paid for 1000 copies to be made and, to their delight, they all sold 'just like that' and immediately got them noticed: 'It was number one in the dance charts for weeks and John Peel did play it, actually, but by then we were a bit overwhelmed because we needed to raise the money to print the next 1000.'[30] After that, the elusive 'people from London' finally started to come down to see what Smith and Mighty might have to offer, and the duo was signed up just as another significant project arrived on their doorstep.

The Fresh Four were a young crew from Knowle West, a tough public housing estate in the south of the city, and schoolmates (when he bothered to turn up) of the Tricky Kid. Brothers Krust and Flynn had befriended Suv and Judge in their early teens, and the four discovered Hip-Hop culture through their elder brother's music collections and the film *Wild Style*, a Warholesque semi-documentary drama from the South Bronx graffiti, rap, and dance scene. Krust remembers the instant effect that watching the movie had on them and their generation:

> What changed it was *Wild Style*—we put it in the VCR and didn't take it out for months. It was the blueprint; we were copying the moves, then the (graffiti) tagging. It was raw stuff, the code—how to be a B-Boy: loyalty, ethos.

---

26 Ibid.
27 A video promo for the Wild Bunch, made in 1985 by Bristol director Steve Haley, captures the rich multimedia mix of their shows. YouTube, 'Wild Bunch Crew – Original 1985 Promo', April 2008, <https://www.youtube.com/watch?v=uQ2j2OV-6aM> accessed July 2012.
28 This whole episode is thoroughly covered in the excellent book: Phil Johnson, *Straight Outa Bristol* (London: Hodder and Stoughton, 1996). Here, the author transcribes long and revealing interviews with Milo and 3D.
29 Rob Smith, in an interview with the author (2014).
30 Ibid.
31 DJ Krust, in an interview with the author (2014).

Becoming an individual – you didn't bite (copy ideas) – the biter is the lowest form.[31]

Though mostly out deejaying at parties and working on a cappella vocals, they were also experimenting with tape editing, cutting up cassettes, and reassembling the music. To earn money, they set up a cycle courier business, but mainly hung around in squats endlessly practising their turntable technique. When they eventually called on Rob Smith and Ray Mighty at Three Stripe on Ashley Road, St Pauls, it was their first venture into a recording studio; a product of the developing collaborative community of Hip-Hop devotees in Bristol as Krust recalls: 'We'd done parties with Smith and Mighty, Massive Attack, and those guys, and Suv knew Rob's brother. So we went to Ashley Road and they were really helpful.'[32]

What happened next was pure serendipity. Rob Smith recalls that it started with Flora (who would later become Flynn's regular DJ partner) who wanted to do a version of 'Wishing On A Star', by the US Funk/Soul band Rose Royce, and knew the singer Lizzie E. Putting her cool reading of the slow tune together with the Fresh Four's mix of a James Brown beat and breaks, a brief rap from Flynn, and a signature Three Stripe Dub-inspired bass motif produced something amazingly fresh yet still faithful to the original. The Four had only intended to get a one-off dubplate together for party purposes. But after Smith played the tape to manager Erskine Thompson the music industry professional saw its commercial potential and contacted the major label Virgin Records. A deal was struck and 'Wishing' was eventually released, accompanied by another of Steve Haley's *Wild Style*-inspired promotional videos filmed at one of the Fresh Four's famed warehouse parties. In September 1989, the single reached number ten in the UK charts.

By the end of the 1980s those three singles – Massive Attack's 'Any Love', Smith and Mighty's 'Anyone', and Fresh Four's 'Wishing' – had set the pace for dance music in Bristol by taking Hip-Hop forms down to slower Dub-Reggae speeds. The decade ended with two of those acts signed to Virgin with the promise of albums to come. Smith and Mighty, the production team behind all three records, had also been approached by Virgin but had opted instead for a deal with London Records. At last, it seemed that the imagination and taste of this Bristolian generation was turning its homespun, lo-fi resources into something poised to launch onto a much bigger stage.[33]

Into the Jungle: the 1990s

If the big time music business was now ready for the Bristol crews, it didn't necessarily follow that the crews were ready to play the game. Whereas Fresh Four, Smith and Mighty, and Massive Attack had always been pretty hard working, it had been on their terms and at their pace. Studio time is cheap if the studio is your own front room, and release dates and promotion schedules hardly matter when you're simply making dubplates for your next party. The record companies had brought them promises of big money but there were strings attached, and things started to go wrong relatively quickly.

Like any bunch of lads from a downtrodden housing project, the Fresh Four thought that getting hold of a fat cheque meant time for fun, rather than knuckling down to making more records. The company expected new products to be delivered on deadlines but the crew was too busy enjoying themselves, as Krust recalls: 'I was nineteen-years-old and we didn't know what we were doing. It was pure naivety. We didn't fulfil the contract – so we got dropped.'[34]

For Smith and Mighty, however, the problem was not lack of productivity. With their stable of vocalists and rappers and a back catalogue of unreleased projects, they should have had no problem with meeting any company's expectations. Their trouble was one of taste because, despite having signed them, it seemed that London Records subsidiary FFRR (named from the Full Frequency Range Recording technique pioneered by Decca Records in the 1950s) were not that interested in their music, and this had serious financial consequences, as Rob Smith explains:

It was a half million (pound) deal but we didn't realise it was segmented so they would only pay us bits of it when they released stuff. And they wouldn't release the stuff we did. We kept offering tracks and they kept refusing them. They even asked us, 'Do you know what dance music is? Can you do House music?' We compromised, did weak versions, but they still refused it. In the end I was ready to give up music altogether.[35]

The one thing FFRR did accept was *The Call Is Strong*, the album debut of Three Stripe vocalist Carlton, but on its 1990 release, initial press response was not enthusiastic, and sales were not high. With hindsight, it has often been recognised as a lost classic by dance music aficionados and it showcases how the Dub-derived Three Stripe style could combine well with the added gloss of a high production major release. But while in Bristol, Smith and Mighty had always been at the controls of their own equipment in their own time, they were now expected to sit in bigger London studios telling tape operators and engineers what to do; an unnecessarily disabling process that made everything more difficult to the point of impossibility. A friend of the duo described this clumsy and unproductive process 'like trying to open a door with a stick'. Eventually only one other track was approved for release – a version of the Diana Ross classic 'Remember Me' – but even that was dropped at the last moment. In the five years of their contract with London Records, that was the nearest Smith and Mighty got to making a record.

Massive Attack fared better, however. Rather than head for London, they were put into the Coach House, a state-of-the-

---

32 Ibid.
33 Another book with revealing interviews about this period of Bristol dance music (and its relationship with graffiti art) is Chris Burton and Gary Thompson, *Art & Sound of the Bristol Underground* (Bristol: Tangent Books, 2009).
34 DJ Krust, in an interview with the author (2014).
35 Rob Smith, in an interview with the author (2014).

art studio in affluent Clifton just up the road from the Dug Out club (by this time sadly closed). Any pressure on them to make music came from the more familiar faces of Neneh Cherry and Cameron McVey (credited on their first album as 'Booga Bear'). The band was able to develop ideas from their Wild Bunch years into new material, through a process of collective writing and production that dragged on for months. The first single 'Daydreaming' was eventually released in October 1990, and its ingredients of Shara Nelson's easy Soul vocals, urgently understated raps from Tricky and 3D, as well as an incessant looped bass and drum drive made it a perfect teaser for the album that would be released shortly after. Sales of that single were unimpressive, but when the critically praised *Blue Lines* appeared it made number thirteen in the UK album charts and Massive began to live up to their name.

—

The collapse of the Fresh Four had left Krust, Flynn and Suv free to throw themselves into the big outdoor rave scene of illegal dance music nights that was developing around the country, especially in the South West. The new musical influences were taking hold of the dance scene in Bristol, too, with DJ Tintin and Nick Warren starting the city's first Acid House night, selling out one of the bigger city centre nightclubs from the outset. Musically there was no doubt that things had begun speeding up – down at Three Stripe Studio, schoolboy brothers Jody and Sam Wisternoff were exploring influences of House and Techno with DJ Die under the name True Funk. Meanwhile, the out-of-town Tribal Gathering raves brought Krust into contact with Ryan Williams, another young producer from Bristol, soon to be more widely known as Roni Size. By 1992, the first sounds of the Reggae-meets-Techno dance music, that would become Jungle, were creeping into rave culture and Krust, Roni Size, Die and Suv all saw it as the way forward. Krust explains their motivation:

> We were just experimenting, trying to figure things out, pushing boundaries, trying to get free of the 'Bristol sound'. Of course we were influenced by all of that but we were also hearing the Jungle thing and tempos started rising. People would say 'the beats are too fast' and we would say 'Really?' We got to 160 (beats per minute) and levelled out.[36]

This was the birth of the Full Cycle crew, another collective, but this time a more stable one, with each working on their own material alongside the collaborations. They started a record label WTP ('Where's The Party?') as well, releasing the first single in 1993, a double A-side with DJ Krust's 'The Resister' backed by Roni Size and DJ Die's 'Music Box'. The former's classic Bristolian doom-laden opening drones on for nearly a minute before a fast Jungle drumbeat tells you that there's a new sound in town.

By 1994 WTP had become Full Cycle and the Jungle sound had been refined, thanks to a moment of exhausted inspiration in the studio, recalled by Krust: 'One night it got to 7am and we were still in the studio. It just didn't come right and then we took the kick drum out (of the mix) and it was like the sun came out. No more flat beat – the whole sound just lifted.'[37] By losing the 'four to the floor' insistence of a pulsing bass drum that made Techno and Acid House music so frenetic, the Full Cycle crew had given their music a new, spacious quality that allowed for much more creative freedom. In fact, it meant a return to Dub values, leaving the bottom end of the sound for bass and sub-bass.

By this time the Jungle scene in Bristol had really taken off, thanks to the club night Ruffneck Ting, that started in 1993, with DJ Dazee putting her stamp on things from the start, as part of the Ledge crew with Substance and other local DJ-producers. A surge of locally produced records and dubplates emerged to feed this new scene, with many distinguished by a combination of eclectic sound samples and visceral Dub basslines that harked back, through Massive Attack and Smith and Mighty, to their sound system roots. Early successes at Full Cycle Records included Flynn and Flora's debut 'String 4 String', a bass-busy workout, mixed at Three Stripe, featuring unexpected sweeps of harp, and Size and Die's spacious 'Music Box' with its psychedelic guitar and xylophone interlude.

By 1994 Bristol was becoming recognised as a centre for Jungle music, with Krust and Roni Size running a popular weekly pirate radio show that caught the attention of London-based junglists Brian Gee and Jumping Jack Frost. Their V Records was to become one of the UK's most influential stables of Jungle talent, and the label's first release was the 'Fatal Dose' EP by The Deceivers (aka Krust and Roni Size). In 1994, V Records subsidiary Philly Blunt also released the classic 'Warning' by Firefox (Roni Size) and '4-Tree', a much more Reggae-flavoured Jungle track woven around the seductive 'Sleng Teng' bassline, famously the first Jamaican Reggae *riddim* to make use of computers and which would inspire the development of the electronic Ragga style of Reggae.

The younger generation may have turned up the speed, but it would be the (slightly) older guard that made 1994 the most successful year ever for Bristol-made dance music. Not only did Massive Attack release their second album *Protection* (Virgin) to instant acclaim and a number four position in the UK charts, but also an entirely unknown act appeared from the same Coach House studio with an atmospheric album of filmic Hip-Hop that went to number two. No one had ever seen Portishead as a DJ crew or a live band for the simple reason that they had never performed in public. Their debut album *Dummy* (Go! Beat, 1994) was a studio project created by the unknown Geoff Barrow who, as a young unemployed person, had been acting as an unpaid studio intern when Massive Attack was making *Blue Lines*.

36 DJ Krust, in an interview with the author (2014).   37 Ibid.

A Hip-Hop devotee from the unpromising coastal satellite town of Portishead, he had been a bedroom DJ since his early teens, endlessly absorbing the lore of Hip-Hop from records. He met Blues singer Beth Gibbon on a work-training day for unemployed people and discovered she had lyrics for songs she had written – just as he had tunes without words. As they began putting the two together, Geoff called in Jazz guitarist Adrian Utley, who also used the Coach House. Geoff's radical insight as a producer was to record original instrumental music, breaks and so on, onto vinyl records so that he could scratch them back into the mix alongside found samples. This provided an atmospheric structure, around which Beth could build her emotive torch songs, the narratives of her poetic lyrics needing more space than the repetitive conventions of dance music would typically have permitted. In theory, none of these ingredients should have fitted with each other, but Barrow's production somehow steered this collision of Jazz, Blues, Hip-Hop, and Rock to produce a perfectly integrated musical soundscape (though whether you could dance to it was always debatable).

Massive Attack's *Protection* was less of a surprise, being a more polished development from their debut, thanks to the shrewd contribution of Nellee Hooper as co-producer. Veteran Jamaican Reggae vocalist, Horace Andy's contribution 'Spying Glass' kept the band's Roots Reggae credibility, while Tracey Thorn – the already successful vocalist of pop-friendly Everything But The Girl – contributed a spellbinding delivery of the title track. Her artlessly sincere voice over a crisply simple drumbeat, guitar samples, and shimmering keyboards made 'Protection' a successful single. Tricky's last Massive Attack appearance was captured on 'Karmacoma', a typically dark and unrelenting narrative unfolding over clanking percussion and electronics, courtesy of Bristol art-rock duo The Insects – an early example of the kind of artistic entrepreneurialism the band were developing as creator/producers.

—

The almost simultaneous arrival on the national radar of two such distinctive albums from Bristol flagged that in Bristol 'something was happening' and prompted a flurry of journalists hurrying westward to find out what it was. The mixture thickened further with the multi-layered sound collage of 'Aftermath', Tricky's brooding, self-produced single, released by Island Records on Fourth & Broadway, to prepare the way for the February 1995 arrival of his debut album *Maxinquaye* (Island). It was around this time, that the label of 'Trip-Hop' began to be applied to what was being called the 'Bristol scene' or the 'Bristol sound',

Though Trip-Hop was never formally defined, the implication was that its slacker pace and spacier sound represented a kind of psychedelic 'tripped out' version of Hip-Hop. The term soon went around the world in the review pages of *Rolling Stone*, *Mojo*, *NME*, *New York Times*, and others, but it was never happily accepted by Bristol's party people and the musicians themselves, who generally resented being pigeon-holed by outsiders – especially those from London. An early live appearance in the capital by Tricky (supported by Smith & Mighty) included a celebrated incident when Tricky asked the crowd 'Do you want some Trip-Hop?' They cheered approval, but he responded: 'Well you can all fuck off then!'[38] But whatever the labelling, the positive global response, to the now three albums, meant that by 1995 Massive Attack, Portishead, and Tricky were all transforming their studio creations into live performances and setting off on tours around the world.

All that media excitement overshadowed another significant release for the Bristol dance scene, as Smith and Mighty were finally freed from their contract with FFRR Records and celebrated by releasing the album *Bass Is Maternal* (1995) on their own More Rockers label. According to Rob Smith: 'We'd salvaged some Dub things we liked and just did what we wanted to do.'[39] As a flavour of what might have been released five years earlier the album's music is a brilliant and complex mix of ideas that clearly deserved a much wider audience, though even now the iTunes review still seems baffled by its experimentation.[40] However, its release was followed immediately by *Dub Plate Selection Volume One* (1995), an album by More Rockers, the duo of Rob Smith and DJ Peter D. Rose who had been working in Bristol clubs throughout the 1990s. As the plates progress, it is evident how much Smith's approach prefigured the Jungle template, as he acknowledges:

> I thought Jungle was amazing: to me it was a cousin of Reggae. Some people say I was doing that five years before. (Our 1992 EP) 'Steppers Delight', if you pitched it up, it is Jungle. I went to this rave with Flynn, somewhere off the M25, and he was saying, 'Come on, come on – you got to hear this,' They were playing our tune pitched up![41]

By this time Bristol's Jungle community was running at full steam, producing a string of classic dance tracks that pushed the envelope, including Ruffneck Ting's Substance and Dazee's the 'Ledge Project' EP which featured the upbeat 'Rude Girls' defiantly female riposte, to the more usual rude boys with its early use of vocal stretching and powerful sub-bass drop. *Native Drums*, Flynn and Flora's 1996 album on their Independent Dealers label, with loosely psychedelic tracks like the hypnotic 'You Are Sleeping', continued to break new ground. By this time Krust and Roni Size had even created a new label – Dope Dragon – and new identities – Gang Related and Mask, respectively – for their more experimental purposes, as Krust recalled:

> It was about making tunes for the weekend. For Full Cycle a new track would take a week – epic! Dope Dragon

---

38 It's an oft-repeated anecdote but might have first been noted in Phil Johnson, *Straight Outta Bristol* (London: Hodder and Stoughton, 1996).

39 Rob Smith, in an interview with the author (2014).

40 'Unfortunately, there's too much experimentation and not enough hooks on Smith & Mighty's long-awaited album debut. The duo simply don't find a happy medium between Jungle and Reggae on *Bass Is Maternal*, recorded for their own More Rockers label.' iTunes album review, accessed August 2014.

41 Rob Smith, in an interview with the author (2014).

tracks could be done in an hour. We just wanted to have fun doing it, but some of our biggest tunes came out that way, some were better than the ones we'd spent weeks on.[42]

Their 'Tear It Up' (1996) was a case in point, a banging break-driven feast with shuddering bass drops, but just to show what can be done with a bit more care, Krust also went on in 1997 to craft what may have been his masterpiece. The endlessly remixable classic 'Warhead' is a textbook case of 'less is more'; building tension through a remorseless hi-hat cymbal, and a progressive bassline that takes its time arriving. Very little happens, but it all happens at just the right time and the lack of unnecessary flashiness shows the confidence of a musician who feels he has it right.

—

Jungle was big, but it wasn't the only story in Bristol in 1996. Breakbeat duo Way Out West – Acid House DJ Nick Warren and former True Funk teen prodigy, Jody Wisternoff – turned club approval into UK chart success with their racing Techno house anthem 'The Gift' on the Deconstruction label. On a different track altogether, Andy Scholes and Jack Lundie had launched Two Kings, a Reggae-based label dedicated to preserving 'roots and culture philosophy' while benefitting from contemporary developments. Recording as Henry and Louis, their 'Beulah' figured on *Dub Out West Volume One*, a crucial compilation of Bristol dubplates, released on Nubian Records that year. Sifted through the breakdowns of Dub production, Beulah's high-tech electronic gloss still holds a futuristic science-fiction feel, like Kraftwerk on holiday in the Caribbean.

Behind his lighter Dope Dragon releases, Roni Size was already working on something much bigger, drawing together all of Full Cycle's talents for what would be both a studio concept and live band called Reprazent. Using his Coach House studio connections, he contacted Portishead founder, and guitarist, Adrian Utley, who recommended Portishead's drummer and session musician, Clive Deamer. Size called him up with an idea to sample his drum breaks but, coincidentally, Deamer had recently discovered the trick of playing the demanding rhythms of Drum'n'Bass and was keen to contribute as a live drummer:

Once I realised I could do (Drum'n'Bass rhythms), I'd started working at it, and then Adrian (Utley) rang me up and said Roni Size was interested. I remember (Roni) was sceptical that I could play 160/180 (beats per minute), but I was very fit then, doing martial arts and focusing on that independence of body. By the second or third day Roni realised I could give him exactly what he wanted – and more – so he began switching off the machines and putting things back in real time. It was really exciting, a really unique moment and we all felt it.[43]

Incorporating Deamer's live drumming, vocals from singer Onallee and Si John's acoustic double bass as well as fronting up with MC Dynamite gave Reprazent a combination of machine precision and human warmth that were realised at the highest studio production standards on *New Forms* (Talkin' Loud). The 1997 double album dropped an astonishing twenty-three tracks, including the seminal 'Brown Paper Bag' and 'Watching Windows', which immediately took Drum'n'Bass way beyond the dance audience that had grown up from the Jungle days. The album's mainstream appeal was such that *The Guardian* newspaper reviewed it favourably, and it beat albums by superstars Radiohead, The Chemical Brothers, and The Prodigy to win the prestigious Mercury Music Prize that year. Interestingly, Roni Size donated the almost 30,000 Euro prize money back to the Basement Project – the music project in a Bristol youth club that had helped him begin to learn the basic skills of dance music production.[44]

After the critical and commercial success of Reprazent and *New Forms*, Roni Size embarked on Breakbeat Era, a revival of an earlier R'n'B flavoured project with DJ Die and vocalist Leonie Laws. The band's 1999 album *Ultra Obscene* saw some commercial success, but this was to be a one-off effort. At about the same time, Ruffneck Ting's stalwarts Decoder and Substance teamed up with vocalist and songwriter, Sian Evans, to form the longer-lasting Kosheen, which achieved early success in 2000 with the anthemic 'Hide U' which went to number six in the UK charts (and in Romania even achieved number one). Kosheen has continued to produce albums but, sadly, the Ruffneck Ting club night died in 1999, marking a definite cooling in Bristol's passion for Drum'n'Bass.

Dubstep weighs in: the 2000s

In 1998, a new shop opened among the very independent leftfield traders of Bristol's Gloucester Road: Rooted Records, a specialist vinyl shop with an eye to dance culture. By the year 2000, it had established itself as the welcoming hub at the heart of the city's network of DJs and dance music lovers, not least thanks to the friendly presence and musical enthusiasm of manager Tom Ford. Significantly, the new millennium also saw the closure of Revolver Records, previous employer to Massive Attack's Grant 'Daddy G' Marshall, after over thirty years as Bristol's flagship independent music vendor. It seemed like a baton was being handed over, albeit with a challenge. Bristol's reverence for gut-wrenching basslines had run from sound system Dub through the Hip-Hop years, to Jungle and Drum'n'Bass, but in the new century it seemed unclear where fresh, ground-breaking creativity would appear. Nevertheless, Full Cycle was continuing to make excellent records for the now-dwindling Drum'n'Bass market, the Two Kings revival of classic Roots Reggae continued, the indomitable sound system clashes rumbled from time to time, and Smith and Mighty released a new album, courtesy of

---

42 DJ Krust, in an interview with the author (2014).
43 Clive Deamer, in an interview with the author (2014).
44 The Basement Music Project was started by youth worker Graham Baker in response to the young Ryan Williams (Roni Size) and friends being kicked out of school. This project, Roni Size told the Mercury audience, kept him out of serious trouble. The project is still running in Bristol, with Dubstep producers Joker and Biggsy having also benefitted from its encouragement.

Berlin-based !K7 Records. The surprisingly melodic, song-led collection *Big World, Small World* (1999) featured a range of vocalists, with Tammy Payne's contribution to the epic 'Same2' a particularly haunting torch song with sumptuous synths, unflinching breaks, and squelching sequenced bass.

A new label, Hombre Records had been started in the late 1990s by Jamie Eastman, with the aim of breaking the mould of Bristol dance music and returning to more classic Hip-Hop styles. The label featured One Cut, a production duo, specialising in sample-heavy, Funk-driven breaks with a retro feel (*Grand Theft Audio* album, 2000) and Aspects, a trio of MCs whose *Correct English* album (2001) rolled their gently Bristolian accent over classic-sounding break-beats. Though many Hombre Records were well received beyond the city, its backward-looking sound did not seem to catch on with the local dance music scene and the label would fold in 2003. Any musical legacy has unfortunately been overshadowed by Hombre's sleeve designs, which had been provided by now-legendary graffiti artist, Banksy. These have destined the discs to be hot property on the auction websites forever.

But there was already something new afoot, and it is possible to date the next phase of Bristol dance music quite precisely, because, in 2003, Rob Ellis (aka DJ Pinch)[45] discovered Dubstep, a visceral new form of deconstructed, bass-driven dance music, in a tiny scene centred on the FWD>> club night in Shoreditch, East London. After several exhausting motorway slogs to FWD>>, Ellis knew he had to establish Context, Bristol's first Dubstep night. The Dubstep style was still in its infancy, and with so few tracks available Pinch had to dilute the new bass-heavy Two-Step music with old school Dub and Jungle out of necessity. Things started quietly but as word got around, Context morphed into Subloaded, which quickly snowballed into one of the city's busiest dance nights, ramming out the famously dingy backroom of The Croft, a small eclectic club and bar in the anarchic Stokes Croft area. Subloaded's success soon established itself as an essential meeting place for a new generation of independent music producers, and thus it became a catalyst for a fresh wave of bass-heavy Bristolian creativity. As with Dub Reggae, Dubstep's spacious rhythm gave dancers a choice – go fast with the main beat or chill out to the 'half beat', the latter a marked contrast to the often frantic moves of Drum'n'Bass, Hip-Hop or House. Pinch was never surprised by the new music's success, saying (with hindsight): 'I knew straight away that this was a sound that would fit perfectly in Bristol. There is a lot of tension in the music that carries a satisfactory darkness with it but it's also lazy music. You don't have to dance hard to move with it. It was born with a reefer in its gob.'[46]

The shop Rooted Records would soon become the daytime centre for Dubstep action in Bristol and the showcase for the latest local products after Pinch launched his Tectonic label in 2005 and Rooted shop manager, Tom Ford (aka DJ Peverelist), started his label Punch Drunk in 2006. Pinch's own debut (with P Dutty) 'War Dub' was a cheeky warm-up to Bristol's latest bass infatuation, gradually creeping in from an inaudible murmur towards a lethal sub-bass drop, retreating and then repeating, while Peverelist's 'Roll With The Punches' had a beguiling melodic dimension that blithely ignored its scattershot percussion and assertive bass. The Worcester-based Planet Mu Records also released Pinch's 'Qawwali' that year, a trance-like evocation of Indian traditional devotional music under which a crisp bass exploration slowly emerges. None of these tracks are a straightforward piece of Dubstep, yet all three have a clear heritage in the kind of Dub experimentation previous Bristol dance music producers had favoured. Their arrival on the decks at Subloaded was, therefore, an open invitation to others to join the party and, perhaps unsurprisingly, one of the first to appear was Rob Smith:

I'd heard about Pinch doing a night – I'd been invited but hadn't gone. I used to go to Rooted to buy stuff and Tom recognised me, it was him that invited me to the night. Then Flynn came round one day, heard some stuff I was mixing and said 'How long have you been doing Dubstep?' and I realised it was what I was doing. To me it's still doing Breakbeat Dub, just pitched up to 140 (beats per minute). I went down to Tom and took him four sides and he put them out straight away.[47]

That batch, which included the thumping double A-side 'Corner Dub/Pretty Bright Light' (Punch Drunk, 2007), marked the arrival of RSD, the new identity picked by Smith for Dubstep purposes: 'It was so fortunate that this arrived. Dubstep saved my musical life! It was perfect for me, it has everything I love about music: space, a bit dark, deep bass, loosely based on Reggae.'[48]

Around about this time, another key Dubstep player arrived in Bristol – Appleblim, who had been co-running the groundbreaking London-based Skull Disco label with FWD>>'s Shackleton. Appleblim had moved down from London to study Creative Music Technology at nearby Bath Spa University, an influential training course that encouraged several producers who would later emerge on Bristol's Dubstep radar. Following regular appearances as a DJ in Bristol, alongside Peverelist and others, he settled in the city and established a third Dubstep record label: Apple Pips. So, Rooted Records' bass-heavy shelves soon gained tracks like 'Over Here' (2008), his collaboration with Peverelist. Later Bristol artists on Apple Pips would include Komonazmuk ('Dance Too', 2010), Al Tourettes ('Dodgem', 2009) and Orphan 101 ('Propa', 2011).

—

45 Rob Ellis was, together with Rob Smith, also part of the 'Ten Cities' recording project.
46 Gutterbreakz, Liner notes for *Worth the Weight – Bristol Dubstep Classics* (Bristol: Punch Drunk, 2010).
47 Rob Smith, in an interview with the author (2014).
48 Ibid.
49 'I'd met an MC called Shadz, and I rang him to play him a song down the phone when I was about fifteen or sixteen. He goes, keep playing the tune "cos I'm going to play it to my DJ", so he played it to Joker, and then Joker said, "Let's meet this evening and swap a CD." So we met at a chip shop, swapped a CD, and he played me some of his ideas on *Reason 3.5* or whatever it was back then.' Richard Carnes,

Now that a fresh scene was up for the taking it was inevitable that a younger generation would appear, and, by 2007, a crop of new names began to make waves. An early sign was the light-hearted gangster parody of TC's 'Deep' (D-Style, 2007), which featured Jakes, a former Drum'n'Bass MC, who was now one of the emerging Dubstep crew HENCH ('Hard Earned Never Caught Hustling') that also included Temo and Headhunter (aka Addison Groove). Joker, another one of the newcomers, was just sixteen when he mixed Dubstep and Grime influences on his 2007 'Kapsize' EP producing something he called 'Dirty Dubstep', a hybrid dance style ponderous with sinister bass-weight yet capable of suddenly lifting with skipping snare drums or waves of rich string textures.

Interestingly, one factor that had helped Joker hit the ground running so young was the encouragement and guidance from The Basement Project, the youth music facility that gave Roni Size his start as a producer, back in the 1980s. But it was when Bristol's legendary dub-plate cutter, Henry Bainbridge, directed Pinch to some of Joker's demo tracks, that things really started to happen for him. Pinch immediately booked him for the Subloaded club nights as well as the Dubloaded nights he co-hosted with Peverelist, and then came the inevitable offer of releasing the four-track 'Kapsize' EP on Pinch's new Earwax label.

This fruitful connection with Pinch also put Joker in touch with Multiverse Music, an electronic music collective based in Bristol, and set up by post-Techno producer James Ginzburg (aka Ginz of concept duo Emptyset), who had set up Tectonic Records with Pinch. As well as promoting the development of new kinds of electronic music for listening and dancing, Multiverse promoted the use of this music in film and game soundtracks, advertising and other media – a sign of how business-savvy the independent music business had become. Having started as a Techno-centred DJ team Emptyset were now evolving their increasingly randomised minimal electronic music, often linked to video images, that was taking them from club nights into art gallery spaces. Initial collaborations between Joker and Ginz led to the 2009 tracks 'Re-Up' and 'Purple City', the latter an exercise in hard-loping rhythm, minimalist restraint, and old school wonky synth sounds.

The 'Purple' thing from the latter EP's title became a theme for Joker, and – though in true Bristol fashion he denounced it as a media construction that was foisted on him – his association with two other young Dubstep pioneers Gemmy and Guido was widely dubbed the 'Purple Trio'. Another early Punch Drunk signing, former Hip-Hop MC Gemmy released his hypnotic 'Bk 2 The Future' (2008), which the label quickly followed with Guido's 'Orchestral Lab' (2009). Guido's style was markedly different to the other two, deploying intricately arranged synth washes in clever multi-layered contrasts and cinematic sweeps. Guido and Joker first hooked up as teenagers when the latter overheard some music Guido was playing to a mutual friend over his phone and they all arranged to meet at the local fish and chip shop and swap tracks.[49] Guido's album debut, *Anidea* (2010), marked a high water mark for Bristol Dubstep, with the off-centre Jazz orchestra feel of 'Mad Sax' that became an instant classic.

After just five years of non-stop local action in the clubs and studios, by 2010 there was enough in the back catalogues of the various Bristol Dubstep labels for Peverelist to confidently release a double-CD compilation: *Worth the Weight*. Justifiably subtitled 'Bristol Dubstep Classics', the two albums represent an enormous breadth of musical style, stretching the notion of Dubstep almost to the point of meaninglessness yet still, somehow, having a coherence that makes complete sense (to a Bristolian at least). The influential *Resident Advisor* site called the collection 'near perfect' and scored it 4.5 out of 5, not least for Peverelist's DJ sensibility in sequencing the twenty-six tracks. New Yorker, Andy Battaglia, writing for the equally influential *Pitchfork* site, scored it 6.9 out of 10, while noting that: 'For better and (sic) worse, *Worth the Weight* sounds almost fixated on the formidable. Everything on *Worth the Weight* is, in ways that can't be escaped, very heavy indeed.'[50]

It is an accurate observation and, given the album's title, it is obviously far from unintentional. It makes the point that Bristol's Dubstep revolution may have shaken walls elsewhere but has merely perpetuated an appetite for visceral bass-hungry dance music that has run through the home city's dance culture since the first sound systems arrived. The collaborative spirit of the album, which Peverelist could have simply turned into a Punch Drunk retrospective collection, reflects another Bristolian continuity: that as a musical community, whose collective commitment to making music is based on mutual respect. There is a sense that all the artists featured on *Worth the Weight* can be proud to be considered alongside their peers here, that the statement it makes about the Dubstep world they had collectively created in the city was as much of an achievement as their individual contributions.[51]

However, as with the later Multiverse compilation *Purple Legacy* (WOW, 2012), which drew together most of the key tracks from Joker, Gemmy, and Guido among others, there is also a feeling that *Worth the Weight* represents a summing up of an era that had already begun to recede in time, its work done. The key players had mostly begun to move on musically, Rooted Records was a shop selling beads, and The Croft had become a craft ale bar. While plenty of creative energy was still going into making new music, the idea of a vigorous network was harder to justify and, indeed, even the key Purple player Joker was about to be lured to London by a deal with respected label 4AD. While there was no doubt that Dubstep had defined itself as a serious genre, both for those who made it and those who enjoyed dancing (or at least nodding along) to it, where it was going next remained to be seen.

49 'Joker, Gemmy and Guido: Bristol's Next Generation', *Resident Advisor*, 16 September 2009, <https://www.residentadvisor.net/features/1093> and <http://subbass.blogsport.de/xmlrpc/page/46/> accessed July 2018.

50 Review of *Worth the Weight*: Andy Battaglia, 'Worth the Weight: Bristol Dubstep Classics', *Pitchfork*, 16 November 2010, <http://pitchfork.com/reviews/albums/14865-worth-the-weight-bristol-dubstep-classics/> accessed August 2014.

51 A number of excellent video documentaries have been broadcast about the Bristol Dubstep scene and its place in the story of Bristol dance music. These are available to watch online, including James Jessett, *Bristol: Bass Oddity* (Channel 4/www.dazeddigital.com), Howard Johnson, three-part *Sounds of the West*, and Jack Losh, *Dubbed Out In Bristol*.

Grime, Deep House, and Techno revealed: the present

By 2010 it had been widely acknowledged that Bristol Dubstep had made its mark in shaping and extending the genre, not least in giving it a depth of bass and a breadth of style. It was a local flavouring that echoed the previous periods of Bristol dance music based on Hip-Hop and Jungle. As with each of those phases, a peak moment of local action and national attention had been followed by a kind of meltdown as producers continued to explore, innovate and extend the boundaries of their genre. For the Bristol Dubstep community this all took place against the hard-times backdrop of the international financial crisis and the ensuing recession, which saw the loss of The Croft and The Tube, two particularly significant club venues. Even more disastrous was the 2010 closure of Rooted Records, by that time the last independent specialist dance music record shop in the city, and the point of contact for producers and DJs. It was a shocking development, not least for those local labels still making vinyl records. It led Chris Farrell, of the small Techno label Idle Hands, to open a shop of the same name with a focus on Bristol-made dance music and 'others from farther afield that might have influenced it'.[52]

This decline in visibility of Dubstep meant that other genres being produced in the city were revealed, notably Deep House, Techno and Grime. Grime was a Hip-Hop-based offspring from UK-Garage, a form of dance music that had evolved, like Dubstep, in response to the speed and hardness of late-1990s Drum'n'Bass music. By slowing things down to 130 beats per minute, UK-Garage had established an easier dance culture and a more commercial sound. Over time this developed into the less mechanical rhythms of Two-Step Garage, with stars like Craig David and Artful Dodger, and a Jungle-influenced version with raps that would become known as Grime. In Bristol, Grime had seemed overshadowed by the success of Dubstep, but the compatibility of the two styles meant that producers like Joker could move between the two. By 2010, young DJ/producers Kahn and Neek had taken their Sureskank Convention club night to increasingly large venues in Bristol, notably the newly opened Crash Mansion in central Bristol.

With support from the Multiverse promotion agency, Bristol-based Dutchman DJ October had started his Caravan label back in 2007, releasing records by Emptyset as well as his own productions. Increasingly linked with Idle Hands, it was no surprise when in 2010 he co-launched an Idle Hands residency at Crash Mansion. By 2011, his collaborations with young protégée Borai were also being released on Appleblim's Apple Pips. Borai himself was then picked up by the Chicago-based Tasteful Nudes label, with his debut 'Moonlight On The Malago', released in 2013. That title is a typical Bristol in-joke, relating to a polluted ditch running near his childhood home, while the music is a bright and brisk House/Techno number that evolves with patience over its 7 minutes. For Borai, growing up in the shadow of such a strong local Drum'n'Bass culture was initially a problem for him as a producer of House and Techno: 'I always thought I wasn't good enough because I felt I was competing against Roni Size: that's because I saw him about, we went to the same record shop. And I really admired Krust, Full Cycle, all that–but I knew I'd never get into it.'[53] The mid-1990s Dubstep thing happened at just the right time for Borai, opening creative possibilities that freed him up as a producer:

What I loved was this ability to throw absolutely anything into it – you could play with it. The basic rule was 140 (beats per minute) but after that anything goes. Drum'n'Bass had become locked down but we were all having fun. I got my stuff played a few times at Dubloaded alongside Joker, Tom (Peverelist) and Rob (Pinch) and I felt 'Yay!'[54]

Hooking up with October moved his sound on, however, into slower, deeper House grooves that eventually darkened into Techno: 'I even like it a bit faster now, but not so nosebleed you can't listen to it a bit.'[55]

—

While Techno had always had a presence on Bristol's club scene (if not so much in the studios), Grime really hadn't seemed to catch on with either promoters or producers in the city, until the Young Echo crew emerged through the Sureskank Convention night, offering a Dubstep/Grime fusion of their own making. The Sureskank nights began in Cosies bar, Bristol's long-established test bed for new musical ideas, and it was primarily the emerging Grime-merchants Kahn and Neek who initially pulled together the loose Young Echo collective. The choice of name indicated the group's understanding of a musical heritage that they respected, and the music reflected that. Kahn and Neek's 'Percy' (Bandulu, 2012), for instance, was a highly successful slice of stripped back retro-Grime with a no-nonsense mix that bullied dancers into submission. Controversially, they had insisted that their music should only be released on vinyl and not as a download. This inevitably led to charges of elitism, but they were adamant in their adherence to the practice, releasing singles in batches of 1000, much as Smith and Mighty first did back in the 1980s.

That comparison is also interesting because the pair has another identity as Dub Reggae producers, Gorgon Sound, making speeded up and wonky Electro Dubs like 'Find Jah Way' (Peng Sound, 2012), backed with an ace version by local veterans Dubkasm. The pair has admitted to making tunes 'to send to Rob Smith – dubs for Rob'. They are also making dubplates – one-off discs specially cut with a new sound system version that allows the DJ to play something unique – something developed by the original Reggae

52 Taken from: Idle Hands, 'About Idle Hands', <www.idlehandsbristol.com> accessed August 2014.
53 Borai, in an interview with the author (2014).
54 Ibid.
55 Ibid.

Postcard of Police Operation occupying St Pauls, Bristol, 1987, photo: Mark Simmons

Young Skinhead, High Wycombe, 1980, photo: Gavin Watson

The Atlantic Rollers and manager Tony Bullimore, c. 1970, photo: O. W. Oldham

Black Roots: (top row from left to right) Jabulani Ngozi, Charles Bryan, Cordell Francis and Carlton Smith; (bottom row from left to right) Derrick King, Errol Brown, Kondwani Ngozi and Anthony 'Drumtan' Ward, 1988, photo: unknown

Lead singer from Punk band Chaos, Cardiff, 1982, photo: N. P. Whitehead

Wild Bunch Decked Out, Camden, London, 1985, photo: Beezer

systems and continued through Jungle producers like Full Cycle. Impressively, Gorgon Sound has invested in the Roots Radical sound system, a new set-up, built and refined to the best old standards by DJ selector Beavis over many years. Gorgon Sound is providing new dubplates for Roots Radical as well as contributing to its construction costs.

Interestingly, Techno and House producer, Borai, also has a thing about dubplates that he takes very seriously, not least for maintaining the exclusivity of a local music scene:

> I'm building up my DJ set with dubplates. My plan is to cut (my music) all onto dubplates to play in clubs. I can't do a live show but this is like the Jungle boys playing sets of dubplates at Ruffneck Ting. The local residents always would bring them in, and that's what I want to do. I'm working with Henry Bainbridge at Dub Studio learning how to make them. I'm doing an apprenticeship and in the end, I want to do my own labels, but cutting them myself.[56]

The Young Echo collective's most remarkable achievement to date has been the *Nexus* album (Norman Records, 2013), a thirteen-track collaborative effort that ranges from abstract Electro beep musings, to dark, shambling vocal tracks and acerbic Dubstep. Despite the eclectic styling, there is a surprisingly consistent flavour to this coming together of Bristol's newest generation and, at times, the brooding disquiet of *Nexus* manages to evoke an atmosphere that recalls the sound of 1990s Tricky or Portishead. But the *Nexus* set is also very much of its own time and, just like its Bristolian Trip-Hop predecessors, it is still arguable whether you could dance to much of it.

By contrast, the Deep House creations of producer Julio Bashmore have taken dance floors by storm way beyond the city, with his 2012 'Au Seve' one of that summer's anthems for the holiday club scene in Ibiza. The disc's classic four-to-the-floor House sound and use of a sample from The Real Thing's 'You to Me Are Everything' all hinge on a bubbling synth bassline that hints at the music's birthplace. Though his record label, Broadwalk, is named after a downtown Bristol shopping mall, demonstrating local bonds, Bashmore took the still unusual step (for a Bristol musician) of relocating to London in 2013. This move possibly reflects the persistent marginalisation of House music among Bristol producers.

—

One of Bristol's most successful dance music acts of the new decade seemed to emerge from nowhere: Koan Sound. Jim Bastow and Will Weeks were school classmates when 'Clowny' (2009), their first track under this name, was signed by a US record label, as Jim Bastow recalls:

> We were pretty heavily into the Dubstep sound, just making tunes in our bedrooms and putting them up on Myspace and on forums. It was more of a hobby. Then someone picked it up, this small label somewhere in America. It's a bit amazing when you're sixteen and still at school![57]

After that recognition, the pair began to develop their sound in earnest, with the 'Max Out' EP (Inspected, 2011) ultimately catching the ear of US Grammy-winning electronic dance music superstar Skrillex, who signed Koan Sound to his OWSLA label just as they left school. Their OWSLA debut – 'Funk Blaster' (2011) – is a masterpiece of sound design, the EP's restless creativity unified by its studio sheen. With variable tempos and a range of textures from the dirtiest of bass grinds, to almost beatless washes of ambient strings, it is hard to categorise their music in a genre (though Beatport pigeonholed it as 'Glitch-Hop'). As with Young Echo's *Nexus*, Koan Sound's 2014 EP 'Dynasty' (OWSLA) is a richly individualistic fusion that chimes with Bristol's thirty-year history of mashing up the rule book. Any local influence must have been subliminal, however, as Jim Bastow says that they had not known about their musical forebears until very recently:

> I wasn't aware of Bristol music at first. I didn't have an older sibling to show me, so it's been a bit of a discovery for me. It was quite eye-opening to realise that a lot of the Drum'n'Bass and Dubstep I was into had been made in Bristol. We aren't much connected to other Bristol producers. We were too young to start with, when Dubstep was kicking off in Bristol, too young to get into the right clubs and a lot of those guys were older, had a broader knowledge of electronic music.[58]

They did pay their dues as DJs, though, playing 'graveyard sets' to dwindling numbers of tired clubbers at 3am in dance clubs like Lakota and Blue Mountain, even on school nights. So, when the OWSLA exposure led to touring opportunities, they were quick to take them. After succeeding major shows in North America, Australia, Europe, and South Africa, they were beginning to extend their live act:

> We were getting uncomfortable going out in big places in front of big crowds of people with just headphones and a USB so we're now incorporating live elements: Will has a drum pad and I have a keyboard. The stuff we're making now lends itself to that sort of performance.[59]

Bristol's producer, Guido, has already taken that step even further, forming a proper live band to perform the music from his 2013 album *Moods of Future Joy* (Tectonic). For him, it is important that the music really is live, rather than computer generated by popular software programmes such as Ableton Live, Cubase, and others:

> I don't rate laptop live shows from Ableton templates. Sorry, but they aren't really live shows. If I'm playing live, I want three or four people there with me, all of us playing together. If we make mistakes, then that's cool, it's part

---

56 Ibid.

57 Jim Bastow, in an interview with the author (2014).
58 Ibid.
59 Ibid.

of the process. It makes it feel more immediate for whoever is watching and listening.[60]

This distinction – between live music and software – has also been recognised by Joker, newly back in Bristol after his pop excursion with 4AD records, explaining his return to using old analogue synthesizers for his album *The Mainframe* (Kapsize, 2015): 'Hardware and software is like manual gear stick versus automatic Tiptronic. It's not like one is better, but people have their preference.'[61]

There is no doubt, however, that while dark Techno and Deep House are a presence in Bristol, Grime is the defining sound for the producer scene, with the Young Echo collective at the heart of things, and they are stripping back to older methods and formats. At the moment of writing this text, they run monthly Young Echo nights in the basement of The Exchange, the larger and dingier downtown club, run by the crew from The Croft, and have established No Corners, a label producing new music, exclusively in cassette or vinyl formats. Meanwhile, Kahn and Neek have revived the concept of using phone numbers on flyers and voicemail messages to promote their Hotline Recordings label and linked Hotline club nights, fusing Grime and Dancehall Reggae on tracks like 'Backchat' (complete with Dub version on the B-side).

So, where is it all heading? The Irish guy behind the counter in Idle Hands records shrugs, then neatly sums up most of what they are selling: 'Look – it's 140, low-end, powerful Bristol music.' He grins through his hipster beard. 'It's great!'

Collectives and continuity: past, present, and future

It has been twenty-five years since the Fresh Four single 'Wishing' warned the outside world that Bristol was cooking up its own approach to dance music. As the city's underground music industry emerged in the 1980s, the new producer-led ideas of Hip-Hop became fused into the sonic structures and spaciousness of sound system Reggae, brought to the city some twenty years earlier. As the 1990s unfolded, the unhurried Dub-heavy beats of local heroes, Smith and Mighty, Massive Attack, Tricky, and Portishead produced a shift in the relationship between electronic dance music, Rock, and Reggae that reverberated worldwide. Then, while global attention fell on what mainstream media had dubbed 'Trip-Hop', the first generation of Bristol Jungle producers were already taking that Dubwise template and reshaped their own music into Drum'n'Bass, preparing the way for Roni Size, Krust, and the Reprazent collective into the pre-Millennium limelight. When the new century saw the birth of Dubstep, Bristol magpies, like Pinch and Peverelist, were quick to seize on its potential for local adaptation, inspiring another wave of original bass-driven music that radiated out of the city and around the world. Subsequently, Grime began to dominate the hipper dance floors, and it was inevitable that Bristol's musical community would make their own locally flavoured variety.

Since those early days, back in the 1980s, when the young Krust and Rob Smith were spending hours cutting up samples from cassette tapes, the development of accessible music technology has transformed everything. Back then, musicians needed to know somebody with studio equipment and the skill to work it (Smith recalls the Wild Bunch greeting him: 'You're Rob Smith … you've got some gear, haven't you?'). It was this development of homespun, independent music production and distribution, that ultimately allowed Bristol's musicians to forget about London and just do it themselves. Clusters of artists and musicians gathering at studios like Three Stripe and The Coach House resembled the creative flux around Studio One, in Jamaica, more than the professionalised corporate machinery of London's major labels. Ironically, it would be these collectives that finally made the mainstream music industry bring their chequebooks out west.

Now accessible software and internet communication mean that two schoolboys with a home computer, like Koan Sound, can build market-ready music for instant global distribution via the US. The reach of the internet can give anyone a worldwide audience. Of course, it was not affordable technology that made Koan Sound such a success, it was their artistry. It is possible for outsiders to measure their success in music sales, media attention, or global reach. But ultimately, as for all their predecessors, it will be the dance floors of Cosies and other Bristol venues that make it real.

Importantly, for each chapter of this story, local collectives of like-minded individuals supporting each other, have fostered the best new music. Over the years the creative strength of collaborations like Three Stripe Studio, Wild Bunch, Full Cycle, Reprazent, Young Echo, and others, have broadened the potentially individualistic activity of studio-based dance music production. While they may have always had their eye on national or international success, their first task has been to please the local dance community, testing the music through one-off dubplates in clubs like the Dug Out, Cosies, Subloaded, and Sureskank Convention and then releasing their product in record shops like Revolver, Tony's, Rooted Records, and Idle Hands – the latter all daytime social gathering places for the city's dance community.

A close relationship between producer and audience is, of course, not unique to Bristol, but there is something about the city's size that seems to have made it particularly inclusive. Even when someone's music goes global, the most important approval still comes from close to home, which could explain why most of Bristol's most celebrated dance

---

[60] Guido, in an interview with Lauren Martin, 'I don't rate laptop live shows from Ableton templates', *FACT Magazine*, 20 November 2013, <http://www.factmag.com/2013/11/20/i-dont-rate-laptop-live-shows-from-ableton-templates-bristols-guido-opens-up-on-playing-live-and-new-album-moods-of-future-joy/> accessed August 2014.

[61] Paul MacInnes, 'Joker: "If you really want to make music, sign on … go and live at mum's"', *The Guardian*, 25 March 2015, <https://www.theguardian.com/music/2015/mar/25/joker-the-mainframe-purple-grime-album-interview> accessed 30 March 2015.

music makers – Rob Smith, Massive Attack, Portishead, Krust, Roni Size, Pinch – have stayed living and working in the city. This inclusiveness and continuity might well account for the way those Dub-rooted values have been handed down through what amounts to five or six musical generations, without showing signs of exhaustion. They might also explain the energy behind what *Resident Advisor*, the UK's definitive dance music website, has described as 'one of the planet's most thriving music scenes … bass music hotbed Bristol'.[62]

Bibliography

Battaglia, Andy, 'Worth the Weight: Bristol Dubstep Classics', *Pitchfork*, 16 November 2010, <http://pitchfork.com/reviews/albums/14865-worththe-weight-bristol-dubstep-classics/> accessed August 2014.

Burton, Chris and Gary Thompson, *Art & Sound of the Bristol Underground* (Bristol: Tangent Books, 2009).

Cater, Alex, 'Joshua Moses', Bristol Archive Records, October 2011, <http://www.bristolarchiverecords.com/people/people_Joshua_Moses.html> accessed July 2014.

Carnes, Richard, 'Joker, Gemmy and Guido: Bristol's Next Generation', *Resident Advisor*, 16 September 2009, <https://www.residentadvisor.net/features/1093> and <http://subbass.blogsport.de/xmlrpc/page/46/> acccessed July 2018.

Johnson, Phil, *Straight Outa Bristol* (London: Hodder and Stoughton, 1996).

LeBlanc, Larry, 'Industry Profile: Mike Chadwick', *Celebrity Access*, 1 August 2012, <http://www.celebrityaccess.com/news/profile.html?id=619> accessed July 2014.

Loats, Gill, 'Archive Record Labels: Wavelength Records', Bristol Archive Records, April 2000, <http://www.bristolarchiverecords.com/archiveRecordLabels/wavelength_records.html> accessed July 2014.

MacInnes, Paul, 'Joker: "If you really want to make music, sign on … go and live at mum's"', *The Guardian*, 25 March 2015, <https://www.theguardian.com/music/2015/mar/25/joker-the-mainframe-purple-grime-album-interview> accessed 30 March 2015.

Martin, Lauren, 'I don't rate laptop live shows from Ableton templates', *FACT Magazine*, 20 November 2013, <http://www.factmag.com/2013/11/20/i-dontrate-laptop-live-shows-from-abletontemplates-bristols-guido-opens-upon-playing-live-and-new-albummoods-of-future-joy/> accessed August 2014.

Resident Advisor, 'Profile: Julio Bashmore', <http://www.residentadvisor.net/dj/juliobashmore/biography> accessed August 2014.

Webb, Peter *Exploring the Networked Worlds of Popular Music: Milieu Cultures* (New York and Abingdon: Routledge, 2007).

---

62 *Resident Advisor*, 'Profile: Julio Bashmore', <http://www.residentadvisor.net/dj/juliobashmore/biography> accessed August 2014.

436 BRISTOL MUSIC

Bristol Mixes – Underground, Identity, and the City

Rehan Hyder and Michelle Henning

In May 2013 a new play opened at the Tobacco Factory Theatre in Bristol, in the south-west of England. The play was named after, and set inside, Bristol's most influential nightclub, the Dug Out. It juxtaposed two different moments in the city's history, which centre around intercultural and interracial mixing in Bristol. In 1944, a violent conflict, between black and white American troops on a nearby street, led one black GI to hide in the building with a young British Women's Auxiliary Air Force member. Thirty years later, a diverse group of young clubbers gather in the club in the aftermath of an IRA bombing. By privileging these stories in this particular space, the play reproduced established narratives about music and identity in Bristol. It attracted audiences who remembered the Dug Out fondly, and for whom the image of Bristol, as a site of cultural and racial mixing, is a flattering rather than a challenging one. Most importantly for this essay, it showed how the nightclub, for many, continues to play a significant part in the self-image of this city.

The Dug Out is important because of its reputation as a site of origin for what has become known as the 'Bristol Sound'. It is said to have nurtured a number of internationally acclaimed musical performers, DJs, and producers, such as Massive Attack, Portishead, Tricky, Nellee Hooper, and Smith & Mighty, whose work has popularised the perception of the Bristol Sound.[1] Today this notion is mobilised for promotion and cultural redevelopment within the city, describing music influenced by an eclectic mix of Dub Reggae, Punk and Soul, Jazz, film soundtracks and Hip-Hop, and characterised by a heavy bass and laid-back beat. However, the term 'Bristol Sound' articulates not only a particular musical style, but also concepts of urban inter-ethnic mix and syncretism, that underpin the city's claim to musical and cultural uniqueness. Hyder argues that hybridity and syncretism are central concepts for understanding the development of popular music in Britain, and it is clear that they characterise the underground club culture and music of this South-Western, British city.[2] The inter-ethnic makeup of bands like Massive Attack and the rich fusion of genres and styles suggest the importance of social and musical cross-pollination in shaping the distinct musical identity of Bristol.

Although the idea of the Bristol Sound helped put the city on the map of Britain's musical heritage, alongside Manchester and Liverpool, a number of musicians and writers question the usefulness of the term. For instance, Phil Johnson, in his landmark account of Bristolian music, *Straight Outa Bristol: Portishead, Tricky and the Roots of Trip-Hop* suggests that there was no Bristol Sound music scene.[3] Geoff Barrow, from the band Portishead, said that, 'The Bristol scene exists mostly in people's minds.'[4] Urban theorist, Alan Blum, has pointed out that scenes are characteristically elusive, especially for the new arrival: 'There is an esoteric aura connected with any scene which often makes knowledge of its whereabouts a problem for outsiders or for those new to the city.'[5] Histories of music in Bristol since the 1960s emphasise the role of clubs, especially, the Dug Out, in enabling the mix of genres such as New York Hip-Hop, Dub, Reggae, Funk, Soul, and Punk, that predicted the music that would emerge from the city in the early 1990s.[6] This does not indicate the existence of a unified, 'underground' scene, but suggests instead an

---

1. Please read about the Bristol Sound and its evolution in Tony Benjamin's contribution to this book.
2. Rehan Hyder, *Brimful of Asia: Negotiating Ethnicity on the UK Music Scene* (Aldershot: Ashgate, 2004).
3. Phil Johnson, *Straight Outa Bristol: Massive Attack, Portishead, Tricky and the Roots of Trip-Hop* (London: Hodder and Stoughton, 1996), 27.
4. Cited in John Connell and Chris Gibson, *Sound Tracks: Popular Music Identity and Place* (London: Routledge, 2003), 101.
5. Alan Blum, *The Imaginative Structure of the City* (McGill-Queen's University Press, 2003), 167.
6. See Peter Webb, 'Interrogating the production of sound and place: The Bristol Phenomenon, from Lunatic Fringe to Worldwide Massive', in *Music, Space and Place: Popular Music and Social Identity*, S. Whitley and A. Bennett (eds.), (Aldershot: Ashgate, 2004) and Sean O'Hagan, 'Blue Lines: Massive Attack's Blueprint for UK Pop's Future', *The Observer*, 28 October 2012, <http://www.guardian.co.uk/music/2012/oct/28/massive-attack-blue-lines-remaster> accessed 24 January 2013. For a taste of the range of music played by The Wild Bunch (who went on to form Massive Attack) see <http://www.allmusic.com/album/the-wild-bunch-story-of-a-sound-system-mw0000662655>.

oddly un-scene-like scene characterised by the diversity of the music played, and the social, ethnic, and subcultural diversity of the participants. Daddy G. (Grant Marshall) of Massive Attack who deejayed with The Wild Bunch at the Dug Out in the early 1980s, claims that: 'Especially back in '77 when it was like punks, bikers, dreads, you know just a whole cacophony of people in this one place. It's surprising how so many mixtures of people in that one place don't actually erupt.'[7]

Past scenes are easily mythologised, and the Dug Out play capitalises on the nostalgia in Bristol for this moment in its clubbing history. The Bristol Sound has become an opportunity to market the city, both outwardly as it competes with other cities for tourism and industry, and inwardly, in terms of the self-identity that has been built. Nostalgia for the Dug Out goes hand in hand with the celebration of street art, expressed in the recent adoption of the Bristolian graffiti artist, Banksy, as the city's favourite son. As Blum suggests, such marketing conveniently forgets the original tension between the scene and the city.[8] In the case of Bristol, this is also a spatial tension between a historically intolerant public space and the more tolerant space of the underground club, hinted at in the play.

In the following text, we draw on interview materials and historical research to restore some sense of this tension. How does a particular form of nightlife emerge and how is it then understood? We can look at how cultural practices are facilitated (or limited by) social and economic conditions, but we should also consider how these practices reshape the city. Will Straw suggests that, instead of asking how cities produce scenes, we ask 'how the activities transpiring within scenes produce urban culture as a set of institutions and textures'.[9] Romanticised or not, the notion of the Bristol Sound plays a significant role in official narratives of the city, and musical and social activities in Bristol. The Dug Out in its 1980s heyday has come to symbolise a cultural exchange and inter-ethnic creativity that actively continues to inspire, provoke, and shape the city, from the contemporary Bristol underground club scene, to the marketing of the brand Bristol. The clubbing and music scene has shaped present-day Bristol – both by reconfiguring urban space and by providing an identity and image for the city.

—

Globalisation, pushes cities to distinguish themselves from their perceived 'competitors' and formulate a collective identity. The 'uniqueness' of Bristol's ethnic and musical mixing in the 1980s, is reiterated by numerous interviewees in the 2009 book *Art and Sound of the Bristol Underground*, although in the same book, graffiti artist FLX does point out:

Other parts of the country had similar histories, like Camden where my cousins grew up. In the '80s it was very multicultural and that's where Soul II Soul kind of came out of. I went to college in Birmingham and that also had a scene of students living in the poorer areas going to the 'Blues' and underground clubs.[10]

Bristol's claim to uniqueness, like the claim made by other cities, is clearly problematic, but this is, as Blum has argued, 'a contested process through which groups make and remake the city'.[11] By presenting itself as distinctive or unique, the city sets itself a challenge – to become exactly that.

Bristol's music is part of its larger self-construction as a creative city. According to a number of studies, 'the presence of many artists in a city is itself a major contributor to a thriving economy'.[12] In the case of Bristol, there are a high number of artists and musicians, and many organisations associated with the 'creative industries' (including BBC Bristol, Aardman

---

[7] Daddy G. interview with Peter Kirk, 2004, published at Bristol Archive Records, <http://www.bristolarchiverecords.com/> accessed 28 June 2013.

[8] Blum, *The Imaginative Structure of the City* (see n. 5), 182.

[9] Will Straw, 'Cultural Scenes', in *Loisir et société/Society and Leisure*, 27: 2, (2004), 413.

[10] Chris Burton and Gary Thompson, *Art and Sound of the Bristol Underground*, (ed.), Richard Jones (Bristol: Tangent Books, 2009), 24.

[11] Blum, *The Imaginative Structure of the City* (see n. 5), 22.

[12] Nigel Thrift writes 'As cities are increasingly expected to have "buzz", to be "creative", and to generally bring forth powers of invention and intuition, all of which can be forged into economic weapons, so the active engineering of the affective register of cities has been highlighted as the harnessing of the talent of transformation. Cities must exhibit intense expressivity.' Nigel Thrift, 'Intensities of Feeling:

Animations, and Endemol). However, Bristol's self-marketing also engages subcultural activities such as popular music, nightlife, and graffiti. The notion of the 'creative city' is given a distinct twist by being overtly connected to its reputation for alternative culture in general, including links with alternative lifestyle and ecological practices. Bristol was an early adopter of recycling, alternative currency and bartering systems, organic farming, sustainable transport, self-build, and environmentalism. The Soil Association is based in Bristol, as is the Environment Agency, the BBC's natural history unit is headquartered there, and Sustrans (the sustainable transport organisation which founded the national cycling network) originated in Bristol. In 2008, despite its heavy traffic and hills, it was named England's first 'cycling city', and in 2013 it became the European Green Capital for 2015. A local guidebook emphasises the greenness (i.e. the availability of green spaces), but also its 'reputation for sustainability, environmental awareness, and action'[13] The city capitalises on its reputation as a free (slightly anarchic), creative, and 'laid-back' place despite the fact that, as in most European cities, the majority of Bristolians do not participate in alternative lifestyles.

To some extent, both the music that was categorised as Bristolian 'Trip-Hop' (notably Massive Attack, Portishead, and Tricky) as well as the graffiti art of Banksy, has offered a temporary solution to this problem by enabling the city to present this self-image to a broader audience. Although all of these also exhibit a dark side (nihilistic, socially critical, downbeat, and aggressive) which makes them unusual and challenging material for the construction of a marketing profile, they provide a more 'urban' and multi-ethnic vision that arguably, allows the city to deal with more difficult aspects of its history—such as the 1980 riot, or even the involvement of the city traders in slavery—and incorporate them into the collective experience of the city.[14]

In what follows, we pay attention to the productive myth of Bristol's inter-ethnic creativity, to the mix of people and musical genres in the clubs, and the way the alternative or underground musical nightlife produced and sustained certain communities. We combine academic accounts of Bristol's social and historical development with larger analysis of urban development and subcultures, and chronicles of the lived experience of clubbing and music-making in the city. These are reports provided in interviews commissioned by ourselves and Bristol Archive Records, and conducted by researcher Alex Cater. They provide a fine-grained sense of the ways in which the city and its club culture have developed.

Black Bristol

Bristol is the UK's seventh largest city, with a population of around half a million, located 190 km west of London. Like many port cities, it has a long history of inward and outward migration. Since the Middle Ages, migrants from other regions of Britain and Europe helped to shape its economy and culture.[15] Beginning in the sixteenth century, the Bristol's wealth came from the 'West India Interest', a trading relationship dependent on the trade in slaves from Africa to the West Indies, though few slaves were actually brought to the city.[16] The trade meant there were a small number of African residents, and eighteenth century Bristol church records document the marriages and deaths of black families from the 1720s, but they did not constitute a distinct community.[17] There is no continuity

        Towards a Spatial Politics of Affect', *Geografiska Annaler, Series B: Human Geography*, 86 (1), (2004), 57–78, here: 58.
13 See Alastair Sawday, *Bristol: A Guide for Good Living* (Bristol: Alastair Sawday Publishing Co. Ltd., 2010), 6.
14 One objection to the use of alternative and underground culture to market the city is that this is seen as a kind of co-option or incorporation (Hebdige 1979) of the radical: a way of turning creativity into commerce, although it has been argued that any scene or subculture is always to some extent already commercial (Blum, 2003) (see n. 5).
15 Madge Dresser and Peter Fleming, *Bristol: Ethnic Minorities and the City 1000–2001* (London: Phillimore and Co. Ltd., 2007).
16 Due to the nature of the so-called 'triangular trade' (where ships left Bristol full of goods to be sold in Africa, which were replaced by slaves to be sold in the West Indies before returning home with cargoes of sugar, tobacco, and cocoa) no large numbers of African slaves passed through the city. A small number of black Africans did arrive in the city either as slaves gifted to captains and first mates of slaving vessels or as free men who had won their liberty after serving in the armed services. Dresser and Fleming (2007) have been able to document just one hundred people of African descent settled in Bristol in the period 1688–1835 and although actual numbers were almost certainly greater than this figure, the size of this population was undoubtedly small (see n. 15).
17 Some of these early (forced) migrants are memorialized in the city's heritage trails, notably 'Scipio Africanus' and 'Pero'. Scipio was the servant of the ▶

between this population and the current black population. Throughout its history, the city docks attracted mainly white migrant labourers from Britain and Ireland, but it wasn't until the late 1940s, after the Second World War, that Bristol gained a larger non-white community. 'New Commonwealth'[18] citizens arrived from both the West Indies (mainly Jamaica) and South Asia (Pakistan, India, and Bangladesh). The West Indian population is now predominantly associated with the St Pauls area of the inner city, while Easton is home to the largest British Asian community.[19]

Although there is no direct connection between the city's slaving past and the current black community, commentators on the 'Bristol Sound' refer to this history to reinforce a sense of the 'racially diverse' and 'multi-ethnic' nature of the city.[20] For example, in an article on Bristol Trip-Hop and the scene of the early 1990s, journalist Nick Hasted writes:

> *The nature of the city helped make the scene unique. With its past in the slave trade, it was also a port with one of Britain's oldest West Indian populations, a West Country Liverpool. This was the most genuinely multi-racial scene since Coventry's 2-Tone, a decade before. With its easy use of Dub and Hip-Hop for millennial torch songs such as Massive Attack's 'Unfinished Sympathy', its musical miscegenation was, if anything, still greater.*[21]

Compared to other major British cities, Bristol actually has a relatively small black community. Historians Madge Dresser and Peter Fleming argue that the black population of Bristol is 'consistently overestimated'. At the time of 'Unfinished Sympathy' (1991), just over 5 per cent of Bristol's population were identified as non-white. This rose to 8 per cent in the 2001 census compared to 27 per cent in London and 29 per cent in Birmingham. Today, the picture has changed due to a rapidly growing Somali population. The percentage of people who described themselves as belonging to black and minority ethnic groups doubled to 16 per cent, but according to the census, Black Caribbeans still constitute less than 2 per cent of the city's population. The concentration of non-white people in the St Pauls and Easton areas of the inner city certainly contribute to the perception that these are 'black areas', but a closer look at patterns of ethnic and racial identity in these areas reveal a more diverse reality. St Pauls is generally regarded as the heart of 'Black Bristol' and has historically operated as a gateway for new arrivals. Even here, non-white residents only made up 30.5 per cent of the community in the 1991 census.[22]

The outside perception of Bristol as multi-ethnic may be linked to the repeated stigmatisation of Easton and St Pauls in the press and by politicians. Bristol hit the national headlines in 1980 when it was the site of the first of several inner-city riots in Britain. The St Pauls riot was characterised by the press as a 'race riot' by black youth, ignoring the involvement of white residents and other age groups. In 2002, the home secretary, David Blunkett, described Stapleton Road in Easton as one of the top ten 'crime spots' in the UK, and in 2002–2003 the press vilified St Pauls as a dangerous and lawless area after a drug gang confrontation in the Black and White Café, the place where the riots of 1980 had started. The riot was provoked by a police raid for illegal alcohol at the Black and White Café on Grosvenor Road, St Pauls.[23]

—

The visibility of its music and club scenes have also raised the profile of the West Indian settler community in Bristol and contributed to the perception that this community is larger than it is. St Pauls has been the centre of the development of the music and club scene in the city. Several of those who migrated as teenagers in

Earl of Suffolk, whose grave in North Bristol is a reminder of the presence of slaves and ex-slaves in the city. A lament to Scipio can be heard in the chorus of the Bristol Reggae band Black Roots' song 'Bristol Rock' (1981). Pero was bought, as a twelve-year-old child, by Bristol merchant and plantation owner, John Pinney. In 1999, the City Council named a new footbridge after the slave at the heart of the Bristol's dockside redevelopment area – see 'PortCities Bristol', PortCities Bristol, (1999) <http://discoveringbristol.org.uk/>.

18 This phrase refers to newly independent (largely non-white) nations who had previously been under British imperial control during the high point of colonial power in the nineteenth and early twentieth centuries. The loose 'league of nations', nominally headed by the British Queen, has continued to function up until the present day (2014).

the 1950s, including Reggae musician Bunny Marrett and Reggae and R'n'B singer Popsy Curious, had already begun to perform music in Jamaica.[24] The generation associated with the Bristol Sound includes the children and grandchildren of West Indian migrants who already had an active role in Bristol's nightlife.[25] For first-generation settlers from the Caribbean, music in Bristol began as a means of self-expression, sociability, and recreation but became the meeting ground for a wider range of social groups.

A good example of this is the St Pauls Carnival, founded in 1968 as a multi-cultural event to raise the profile of the city's Caribbean and Asian settler communities. Initially, the carnival juxtaposed different cultural performances focusing on the cultural diversity of the area. Dresser and Fleming claim that the 1980 St Pauls riot – the culmination of on-going tensions between the local police and second-generation West Indians – played a key part in the increasingly West Indian character of the carnival.[26] Gradually, it took on a specifically West Indian identity until it more closely resembled Caribbean carnivals such as the much larger event in London's Notting Hill. While the procession itself was primarily for children, the sound systems went on late into the night. In 1991, the carnival was renamed the St Pauls African-Caribbean Carnival. It increasingly attracted people from a wide range of ethnic and cultural backgrounds across the city, and played a significant role in establishing West Indian music and culture as a central feature of Bristol's cultural identity. The mix of racial politics and elements of heavy Dub sound system culture shaped the distinctiveness of the carnival and its uneasy relationship with the authorities, as reflected by the temporary cancellation of the event in 2012 due to concerns over crowd safety, and the antagonisms produced by the city council's increased formalising of the carnival.[27]

As we have shown, the tendency in writing about Bristol's music scene has been to overestimate the size of the West Indian population, as if the scale of that population produced the ethnic mix of the Bristol music scene. However, the opposite is more likely to be the case, white DJs such as Zion, from the UD4 crew, found the 1980s Hip-Hop scene in Bristol more accepting than in London, where 'the underground scene was more predominantly black. People would look at us two white guys like "Who the fuck are you!" or "Who let you in!".'[28] In other words, the smallness of the Hip-Hop and sound system scene in Bristol made it more hospitable

---

19 The city also has a large population of university students and white-collar workers drawn to the engineering, financial, and creative industries in the city, and people from Eastern Europe and Somalia, who have mostly arrived since 2001. Alongside these are the people who migrate to the city from the rural areas surrounding it: Bristol is the largest city in South West England.

20 Milo Miles, 'Trip-Hop'. *Salon*, 12 November 1995. See also Vivien Goldman, 'Local Groove Does Good: The Story Of Trip-Hop's Rise From Bristol', The Record: Music News from NPR, <http://www.npr.org/blogs/therecord/2012/01/31/142607358/local-groove-does-good-the-story-of-trip-hops-rise-from-bristol> accessed 19 July 2013. Goldman writes: 'Bristol fed off its slave port for hundreds of years; now it's one of Britain's blackest cities, culturally and socially.'

21 Nick Hasted, 'Bristol Time: The return of a trip-hop legacy', *The Independent*, 11 April 2008.

22 This summary is based on Madge Dresser and Peter Fleming, *Bristol: Ethnic Minorities and the City 1000–2001* (London: Phillimore and Co. Ltd., 2007), 157; Tom Slater and Ntsiki Anderson, 'The reputational ghetto: territorial stigmatisation in St Paul's, Bristol', *Transactions of the Institute of British Geographers*, 37/4 (2011), 530–46, here: 535; Pryce 1979; and the 1991 and 2011 censuses. Pryce pointed out that most of the West Indians in Bristol did not actually live in St Pauls. The 2011 census recorded 4,947 people living in the city who were born in Somalia, the largest number of Somali-born residents outside London and Birmingham. In 2011, 5 per cent of all schoolchildren in Bristol were from Somali families.

23 For press and political coverage see Matt Clement, 'Bristol: "civilizing" the inner city', *Race and Class* 48/4 (2007), 97–105; and Slater and Anderson, 'The reputational ghetto: territorial stigmatisation in St Paul's, Bristol' (see n. 22), 538–9.

24 Interviews with Popsy Curious: Alex Cater, 'Popsy Curious', Bristol Archive Records, <http://www.bristolarchiverecords.com/people/people_Popsy_Curious.html>; Bunny Marrett: Alex Cater, 'Bunny Marrett', *Bristol Archive Records*, January 2012, <http://www.bristolarchiverecords.com/people/people_Bunny_Marrett.html>.

25 Tricky's grandfather, Hector Thaws, owned the Tarzan sound system, and Daddy G. recalls his parents and their friends holding 'blues parties' when he was a small child. See interviews with Bunny Marrett (see n. 24) and Daddy G.: Peter Kirk, 'Daddy G.', Bristol Archive Records, August 2004, <http://www.bristolarchiverecords.com/people/people_Daddy_G.html>.

26 Dresser and Fleming, *Bristol: Ethnic Minorities and the City 1000–2001* (see n. 22).

27 In the view of Buggs Durrant, the carnival has become 'just a market to sell stuff'. Alex Cater, 'Buggs Durrant', Bristol Archive Records, April 2012, <http://www.bristolarchiverecords.com/people/people_Buggs_Durrant.html>. For others, the atmosphere of St Pauls itself has changed since the mid-1980s. Popsy Curious says: 'The community broke up. I don't know why but there is no longer a St Pauls community like there used to be … They move to Fishponds or Filton so the community is something of the past' (see n. 24).

28 Burton and Thompson, *Art and Sound of the Bristol Underground* (see n. 10), 113–4.

to white participants. Evidence from other British cities suggests that Bristol had no more or less thriving black or West Indian music scene, but that the smallness of the scene and its consequent openness to non-black participants[29] were significant factors in facilitating the hybrid scene and sounds, and also perhaps, in attracting interest from a predominantly white national media.

Ethnic and musical mixing in Bristol's nightclubs

> When my parents came over in the late 50's from Barbados and there was a lot of West Indians in Bristol, there wasn't anywhere for them to go. The British culture really hadn't really catered for the new influx of West Indians... there wasn't any social infrastructure for them. So they made their own parties you know what I mean, they which became, called Shabeens (sic) and blues parties and you used to get the whole neighborhood turn up on Fridays and Saturdays at somebody's house.[30]

Reflecting on the lack of welcoming social spaces catering for black Bristolians in the 1950s and early 1960s, Massive Attack's Daddy G recalls the important role that blues parties (sometimes referred to simply as 'blues') played in the cultural life of West Indian settlers in the city. At these parties, black Bristolians could mingle, socialise, and listen to music styles and genres imported from the Caribbean such as Ska, Bluebeat, and Reggae. As the reputation of blues parties spread, they offered the opportunity for an increasing ethnic mix of Bristolians to be exposed to Caribbean music. By the early 1970s, many of these parties had established reputations. Blues clubs such as Ajax on Ashley Road and Valentines on St Nicholas Road (both in the St Pauls area) became central to the development of sound system culture in the city. In particular, the Ajax and Tarzan sound systems were critical in fostering the development of Reggae in Bristol.

The blues parties were unlicensed, supposedly private parties, rather than clubs, where members of the West Indian community could meet and enjoy themselves free from the threat of racial aggravation. Other clubbers were also increasingly attracted by the prospect of cheap late night (and early morning) drinking. For musician Mike Crawford, the blues would be the last leg in an evening of clubbing around the city: 'At 2am when they threw you out so somebody would say, "well let's go down the blues." There wasn't much to do there except for drink, listen to some Reggae, and maybe shuffle around a bit. It was just a way of not having to go to bed yet.'[31] Reggae singer Joshua Moses remembers, 'the makeup of blues has always been mixed. I've never been to a blues that was all black and all white. It was always a mixture because that was the community that I lived in and it always reflected the community.'[32]

Other spaces where the sound systems played included halls and youth clubs, such as Ventures Youth Club, situated between Easton and Lawrence Hill, both working class neighbourhoods to the east of the city centre. Dave Fisher, of the Enterprise sound system, attributes the popularity of dances at the club in the mid-1970s to the fact that 'we never had anything else'.[33] The club was filled with three to five hundred people. 'The music was playing, the bassline pumping and with people in the hall dancing the place is hot – the walls were sweating.'[34]

The first official (i.e. fully licensed) black music venue was the Bamboo Club which opened in St Pauls in 1966. It was established by a white Bristolian, Tony Bullimore (later to become better known as an around-the-world yachtsman) and catered specifically for the West Indian community. The Bamboo Club conferred a sense of permanence and belonging on black settlers in

---

29 Phil Johnson has suggested that the small size of Bristol's black population helped facilitate more open inter-ethnic exchange than in other UK cities, as illustrated in his comments about schooling in the city: 'In Bristol there was no dominant school serving the areas with the most black residents, and the overall cultural values were largely white Bristolian ones,' Phil Johnson, *Straight Outa Bristol: Massive Attack, Portishead, Tricky and the Roots of Trip-hop* (London: Hodder and Stoughton, 1996).

30 Peter Kirk, 'Daddy G.' (see n. 25).
31 Alex Cater, 'Interview with Mike Crawford', Bristol Live Independent Music Archive (BLIMA) at the University of the West of England, 2013.
32 Alex Cater, 'Interview with Joshua Moses', Bristol Live Independent Music Archive (BLIMA) at the University of the West of England, 2013.
33 Alex Cater, 'Papa Roots Dave Fisher & Thabiti', Bristol Archive Records, <http://www.bristolarchiverecords.com/people/people_Papa_Roots.html> accessed 2012.

the city, but it also acted as a point of intercultural meeting. Bullimore, who was married to a West Indian woman, intended the Bamboo to be a means of introducing white Bristolians to Jamaican music and culture.[35] Yet, while it retained a strong Caribbean identity, the club welcomed a wide constituency, drawn from different ethnic backgrounds across the city and further afield.[36] Club member, Roy Hackett (who moved to Bristol from Jamaica in 1957), emphasises its inclusivity: 'It was for everyone; old people, middle-aged people and young people. The only people who weren't allowed in were under-aged people.'[37] White clubbers, used to mixing with black Bristolians at the blues parties, attended the Bamboo's mainstay Reggae and Soul nights, but the club also catered to other musical styles attracting a majority white audience. This included regular Jazz nights and concerts by a range of local and national Rock bands.

Of all of the live performers that appeared on the roster of acts at The Bamboo Club, two stand out as particularly significant, both in terms of the development of new musical forms and notoriety. In 1973, Bob Marley and the Wailers appeared at the Bamboo, marking an important moment in the club's place in Reggae history. A few years later, in 1977, the Sex Pistols were due to play the club shortly before the venue burned down – never to be re-opened, adding a hint of notoriety and mystery to the club's demise. On the surface, these two genres seem to be poles apart but the Bamboo was as happy to accommodate a mainly white Punk audience as it was to cater for the local black community, as singer Mike Crawford (who moved to Bristol from Glasgow) remembers:

The vibe was very good, they were all very accepting. Punk bands started to play down there and as I gradually became interested in the whole Punk thing it was a good place to see them. We would all turn up in safety pins and they didn't mind us, we never got any unpleasantness from them. From that point of view they were extremely accommodating. They must have wondered what the hell was going on.[38]

Several writers have suggested that the close relationship between Punk and Reggae fraternities in the UK in the mid- to late 1970s was due to their shared sense of disaffection. In particular, subcultural theorists like Dick Hebdige have emphasised the importance of the interaction between white and black youth in the development of British youth culture from the 1950s to the present day.[39] His claims are supported by interviews with people who frequented the Bamboo during the late 1970s. Mike Crawford suggests that the common economic and cultural outsiderism, of both Punks and ethnic minorities, gave rise to a sense of affinity inside the club: 'Nobody ever voiced it but there was a sense that the Jamaican guys were at the bottom of the economical (sic) scale and so were we. We liked their music – I'm pretty sure they didn't like our music – and so they were generous enough to invite us in.'[40]

How much cross-fertilisation between different musical genres such as Punk and Reggae took place at this time is difficult to gauge. Recent studies emphasise the fluidity and permeability of post-1970s British subcultures, challenging established notions of subcultural identities as

34 Ibid.
35 Interviewed by the BBC in 1967, Tony Bullimore claimed that, 'from a sociological point of view, the West Indian in Bristol feels that he is now on a more equal footing to Bristolians who have their own clubs and they feel quite proud of the fact that the club is done out in the same way as an English club and takes away this inferiority complex… that we haven't got anywhere to take our English friends. Now they can take them here.' BBC (2012), *Bristol on Film*, first broadcast on BBC4 on 20 May 2012. Bunny Marrett says: 'In those days the management had a committee who planned its development and it could be quite formal – you couldn't go in there without a suit and tie!' in Alex Cater, 'Bunny Marrett', (see n. 24).
36 Joshua Moses described the club as 'the heart of entertainment for Black people in the west country, not just Bristol'. Alex Cater, 'Joshua Moses', Bristol Archive Records, October 2001, <http://www.bristolarchiverecords.com/people/people_Joshua_Moses.html> accessed 2012.
37 As Joshua Moses recalls, 'in those days, my peer group, we weren't into the pubbing and drinking thing. We were into the music and, like all young boys growing up, girls and establishing ourselves, but for us it wasn't about having booze up. It was about having a night out with good music and meeting other people – sometimes from all over the country. It would attract people from other places or other parts of the country. It was a good social hub' Alex Cater, 'Interview with Joshua Moses', (see n. 32).
38 Alex Cater, 'Interview with Mike Crawford' (see n. 31).
39 In his influential book *Subculture: The Meaning of Style*, Hebdige argues that: 'We can watch, played out on the loaded surfaces of British working-class youth cultures, a phantom history of race relations since the war.' Dick Hebdige, *Subculture: The Meaning of Style* (London: Routledge, 1979), 45.
40 Alex Cater, 'Interview with Mike Crawford' (see n. 31).

sharply defined and distinct.[41] However, Mike Crawford's reminiscences suggest that Punk music was tolerated rather than enjoyed by the West Indian clientele of the Bamboo Club. Listening to one another's music may have been based more on economic necessity than pleasure; for club owners, Punk bands brought in much-needed business and for the down-at-heel Punk fans, the Bamboo offered a cheap place to listen to music, hang out, and drink, as Alex Carter remembers:

> Punk sets were really short. The band would be off and then the DJs would take over and the Jamaicans would reclaim it. You might stay around and get into the groove but once you had paid to get into one place you didn't really have the money to go anywhere else so you would try to stick it out.[42]

As well as the Bamboo Club, there were a number of other nightclubs and live music venues that started to cater to West Indian tastes during the 1970s and 1980s. The Western Star and Domino Club near Broadmead, the main shopping centre of the city, catered to middle-aged Jamaicans, combining dances and dominoes. On Stokes Croft, a street linking the centre to the area of St Pauls, the Tropic and the Moon Club also played Ska, Reggae, and later Hip-Hop. Generally, the audience would select the night rather than the club, according to the type of music played. Joshua Moses says of the Bamboo Club: 'It catered to the community and whatever type of music was popular at the time. If we had an interest we would go but if it wasn't our sort of thing then we wouldn't. People would go along to the nights that they were interested in.'[43]

—

As we have suggested, the venue with the most famously diverse audience was the Dug Out, distinctive for both the mix of people and the range of music played by the various DJs. As Joshua Moses recalls, the common factor at the club was based on the danceability of the music played, rather than any allegiance to a particular genre or sound: 'The Dug Out was based on dance music so it didn't matter what kind of music it was. As long as it was sweet and for dancing then it was okay.'[44] However, the combination of musical styles played at the Dug Out included music which would not be categorised as 'dance music' today. DJ Gill Loats remembers her own role in this:

> In my experience, most clubs ... had certain nights for certain types of people. Clubs would play Soul all night or Funk, and I mixed it up. I know that people used to think, 'that's a bit weird'. I would do things like play Swan Lake halfway through the night, which doesn't sound very exciting now because everybody does that, but nobody did then. One of my favourite tracks was the Maigret[45] Theme by Joe Loss and his orchestra, which was a hit in the 1960s with old women who liked that sort of thing. I used to put that stuff on in the middle of Reggae, Soul, Funk, Ska, Disco, Indie. I would play a bit of everything; everything I liked. There were no other clubs that would have played indie in the beginning. They would all play stuff that they had heard on Radio 1.[46]

The location of The Dug Out on Park Row, a street linking the more affluent northern area of Clifton to the less prosperous east, where Easton and St Pauls are located, is often cited as a significant factor in helping generate the diverse mix of music and clientele at the club. This helped mark out the Dug Out as an in between or liminal space, as Mike Crawford reflects:

> The reason the Dug Out was seen as important was because it was half way between Clifton and Redland and not that far from St Pauls. It wasn't a posh club so lots of people went there and lots of cultures rubbed up against each other.[47]

---

41 Sarah Thornton, *Club Cultures: Music, Media and Subcultural Capital* (Cambridge: Polity Press, 1995); David Muggleton, *Inside Subculture: The Postmodern Meaning of Style* (London: Berg, 2000).
42 Alex Cater, 'Interview with Mike Crawford' (see n. 31).
43 Alex Cater, 'Interview with Joshua Moses' (see n. 32).
44 Ibid.
45 A popular television detective series based on the George Simenon series of novels, broadcast by the BBC between 1960 and 1963.
46 Alex Cater, 'Interview with Gill Loats', Bristol Live Independent Music Archive (BLIMA) at the University of the West of England, 2013.
47 Alex Cater, 'Interview with Mike Crawford' (see n. 31).

Sapphire, a well-known clubber in the 1980s, talks of moving from the gay club Oasis to the Dug Out wearing a dress and feather boa.[48] As a black cross-dresser, Sapphire stood out, but 'nobody was being offensive'. He also found the crowd very mixed:

> The dress code was 'wear what you like' and the crowd was very different. You had your black men in trilby hats and their nice smart suits, you had funky ones with trainers and the street look, then you had the working girls. There wasn't any prostitution going on in the Dug Out but a lot of the girls when they finished working would go to the Dug Out. There was a great mix of people and then you would have your students. The Dug Out was a lot of people's first experience of clubbing.[49]

The mixture of black and white clubbers at the Dug Out is often emphasised. Gill Loats estimated the white to black ratio at the club to be around 60/40. However, evidence from clubs like the Bamboo and other underground spaces and parties suggests that such inter-cultural or inter-ethnic mixing was not uncommon amongst Bristol's clubbers and music lovers. Clubber Tim Williams remembers his experiences of Funk and Soul nights run by Steve and Adrian Ashby[50] at Bristol's Guildhall Tavern:

> From my earliest nights out in town, when we would go to the Top Rank and places like that, there was always plenty of black people present. That was the norm and the Guildhall was no different. Kids from all parts of town would come down. Obviously it was black music, there were plenty of black kids going to the Guildhall, probably 5–10 per cent. … If you went to the Dug Out the story from the middle class side of town was that the Dug Out was great because it was multi-racial. Well that wasn't unusual to us at all. Our shock about the Dug Out wasn't its multi-racial element because that was something we had always got used to. It was more the fact that you could be all scruffy and hippy and be in there.[51]

The implication is that it was the mix of classes rather than skin colours at the Dug Out that surprised Williams and his friends. At the Guildhall Tavern, the clientele – better known as the 'Avon Soul Army' – were primarily working-class and drawn from outlying working-class neighbourhoods:

> We were all working class kids. The kids that went to The Guildhall came from all over Bristol and were primarily working class. There were one or two infiltrators from Clifton but basically it was people from Knowle, Lockleaze, Brislington, Filton and Henbury. Usually there were warring factions from different parts of the city. Mostly fights would be between kids from different areas like, Southmead kids or Knowle West kids or something of that nature. Yet people got on, that was what was astonishing about it.[52]

Dressed in 1950s-style pegged trousers, mohair sweaters, and plastic 'jelly' sandals, those heading into town to the Guildhall Tavern experienced the club as part of an assertion of individualism and symbolic creativity, which appears to have been shared by a range of 'alternative' nightclubbers:

> You didn't want to be like anybody else. You wanted to be ahead of the mob. It was a really good time. If you had made your way in on the bus, in what was considered to be quite an outlandish style, and then you got there and there were other people who were dressed in the same way; it had a sort of brotherhood to it. People tended to get on,

---

48 'I am going to check out the Dug Out and everyone says, "you can't go down there, you will get beat up." I said "I will go down there and see if I get beat up," … I went in and had a lot of few strange looks but nobody was being offensive.' Alex Cater, 'Sapphire', Bristol Archive Records, October 2011, <http://www.bristolarchiverecords.com/people/people_Sapphire.html> accessed 2012.

49 Ibid.

50 Along with fellow DJs John Stallard, Steve Phillips, Jason Lumber, and Paul Alexander, the Ashby brothers continue to run the successful Soul Train club night which has played in a number of nightclubs around the city since the early 1990s.

51 Alex Cater, 'Interview with Tim Williams', Bristol Live Independent Music Archive (BLIMA) at the University of the West of England, 2013.

52 Ibid.; In his memoir of football hooliganism, music and fashion titled *Bovver*, Chris Brown reflects on the limits of 'brotherhood' in the Avon Soul Army which could not withstand the fierce rivalry between fans of the two Bristolian football league clubs, Rovers and City. Brown – a dedicated Rovers fan – recalls: '… a brawl that culminated in a vicious glassing of an ex-City player in the Guildhall Tavern' Chris Brown, *Bovver* (London: John Blake Publishing Ltd, 2002), 232.

which wasn't the case in pubs and clubs in town generally.[53]

This sense of underground or alternative togetherness found among people who dressed differently from the norm, is connected to the way that women may experience underground clubs as less of a 'meat market' (i.e. pick-up joint) than the larger commercial city centre clubs. Furthermore, clubbers distinguish between the 'underground' clubs such as the Dug Out and the city centre venues according to the music played. The big city centre venues played, what was perceived to be, safe and standardised mainstream music. This can be seen as a shared sensibility among the clubbers, DJs, and performers that continues today.

This notion of distinctiveness and separation from the mainstream has played a major role in subcultural and post-subcultural theories. While early accounts of British working-class subcultures (Cohen 1972, Hebdige 1979) emphasised tightly knit groups, who could be easily identified by their stylistic appearance, more recent work has identified a more fluid and flexible sense of subcultural identity, defined primarily by a common sense of distinction and opposition from the mainstream. Writers like Sarah Thornton and David Muggleton have suggested that subcultural appearance and affiliation is much more fluid and contingent. Rather than pledging allegiance to a common set of stylistic rules bound to a particular subcultural group, the subcultural terrain is inhabited by diverse individuals who share a common sense of being outside the mainstream. Although they might not all be dressed identically or even share the same taste in music, the collective sense of outsiderness helps foster a certain affinity.[54] In Bristol, clubbing produced a shared 'underground' sensibility, which cut across ethnic, class, and genre boundaries, and a sense of community marked out against the mainstream consumption of music.[55]

Although music writers have tended to extrapolate from Bristol's underground music scene, painting a picture of a tolerant, multi-ethnic city, black Bristolians found racial prejudice and hostility to be part of the everyday experience of their working day. In this context, locations like the Bamboo Club were important sites of community and leisure where like-minded people could gather. One thing white members of subcultures such as Punk had in common with these people was that they could experience the city as a hostile place where their appearance could have negative and potentially harmful consequences. Mike Crawford remembers:

Back then (in the late 1970s) people were still quite violently opposed to the way you looked. It's hard to imagine anyone getting excited about anything nowadays but I remember getting spat on in the street by people – women sometimes – for looking disgusting, they thought. So punks were the opposite of threatening. We were constantly being chased by other youth groups: teds, skins, football supporters. You would go out hoping that no one was going to lamp (i.e. hit) you but still wearing absurd clothes.[56]

In a similar vein, Lewi, from the B-Boy crew City Rockas, describes the threat of racism on Bristol's streets in the mid-1980s:

Bristol was funny back then, I mean, we would never really travel outside of central areas really. We always thought of South Bristol as being racist, there was no reason to go there. The outskirts of Bristol (and even some central parts) were really racist – skinheads who really wanted to kill you or do some serious damage would literally chase you down.[57]

For people whose appearance marked them as 'outsiders', the city centre was often a no-go

---

53 Alex Cater, 'Interview with Tim Williams' (see n. 51).
54 Muggleton's research with subculturalists in Brighton in the 1990s uncovered evidence that individuals did not seek to fit neatly into prescribed subcultural identities (such as 'Punk' or 'Mod') but constructed a more independent sense of identity and style that he describes as 'distinctive individuality'. David Muggleton, *Inside Subculture: The Postmodern Meaning of Style* (see n. 41).
55 This affinity was reflected by shared and derogatory slang terms identifying mainstream youth in Bristol. Names like 'Bedmies' (after the south Bristol district Bedminster) or 'Blads' were used to mark out members of the mainstream, as Tim Williams recalls: 'We didn't want to be like Blads, which I think was short for bladders. God knows why that was their name. Blads were your regular joes who wore flares and jumpers with stars on – or whatever it might have been at that time that we considered passé,' in Alex Cater, 'Interview with Tim Williams' (see n. 51).

area that was associated with and policed by more 'mainstream' youth. This undoubtedly made clubs located on the periphery of the city centre more attractive. Blues parties like Ajax and clubs like the Bamboo, both located in St Pauls, became safe refuges. Mike Crawford reflects on the Bamboo:

> It became somewhere that you could go, where you didn't have to go into town. Town was tricky on a weekend because there were so many beer monsters out there looking for funny looking people to beat up. You kind of gravitated towards places you felt relatively safe.[58]

West Indian clubs were not always straightforward 'safe spaces'. The loud, bassy sound systems that marked out both the official and informal spaces of the carnival and which were used in the West Indian clubs had long been competitive. At dances in the 1970s there would be two sound systems, sometimes from different cities, playing against one another, as Dave Fisher, from Enterprise Soundsystem and Bristol Dub Club (a Roots Reggae sound system night), explained: 'Whoever plays the best music would win. That is what it is all about. That's how your sound system is rated, do you play good music?'[59] By the early 1980s, the atmosphere at the dances had changed, the style of music had shifted away from Roots Reggae towards Ragga and Rub-A-Dub, and this competition between systems had become violent. Fighting in the clubs and the changed atmosphere made the dances less appealing, especially for women. Thabiti from Bristol Dub Club said:

> They knew every time they went to a dance all they were going to see, sooner or later, was a gang of men flow from one corner to the other corner. They knew what was going on. Soon the clubs stopped hiring out and stopped calling up the sound systems because it was being predominantly followed by undesirables.[60]

The change in atmosphere in St Pauls around 1980 affected the club culture too, but although the sound systems continue in Bristol, they changed. For example, in December 2013 at The Trinity Centre in Easton, Bristol's Lionpulse sound system went head to head with London's infamous Channel 1 sound system, at Teachings in Dub. Bristol's Lionpulse was a relatively new sound system on the scene (their launch was in April 2013), and they were going up against Channel 1, which had dominated dances for over thirty years and had also been a staple at the Notting Hill Carnival. DJ Max Pearce, who was present at the event, points out that:

> Although the tensions between the two sound systems at Teachings in Dub connote thoughts of competitiveness, militancy and destruction, there is also a sense of unity in the audience due to the fact that two tribes from different areas are brought together to share the feelings that listening to hypnotic music through good quality speakers can bring.[61]

During the late 1980s and early 1990s, the arrival of Acid House changed the dynamic between 'mainstream' (i.e. city centre) and underground clubs. Raves and unofficial festivals outside the city drew large numbers of clubbers, but were then suppressed through the Criminal Justice Act of 1994. The notorious example of the 1992 free festival at nearby Castle Morton, a fifty-minute drive from the city, which produced a widespread media outcry, is often cited as one of the drivers behind the drafting of the Act.[62] Larger clubs such as Lakota on Stokes Croft (which opened in 1989) thrived through the 1990s on the popularity of House music. Initially, this new club culture blurred the lines between underground and mainstream. According to promoter Tim Barford, who promoted Club Yeyo in the early 1990s, the arrival of Acid House had a radical effect on Bristol's club culture: 'Before long plasterers, students, bank clerks, and football hooligans were united in their love of House and

56 Alex Cater, 'Interview with Mike Crawford' (see n. 31).
57 Burton and Thompson, *Art and Sound of the Bristol Underground*, (see n. 10), 21.
58 Alex Cater, 'Interview with Mike Crawford' (see n. 31).
59 Alex Cater, 'Papa Roots Dave Fisher & Thabiti' (see n. 33).
60 Alex Cater, 'Papa Roots Dave Fisher & Thabiti' (see n. 33).
61 Pearce currently hosts *Kelan's Selection* on Bristol based internet station Passion Radio.
62 Meg Aubrey, Paul Chatterton, and Robert Holland, 'Youth culture and nightlife in Bristol', (Newcastle: Centre for Urban and Regional Development Studies and Department of Sociology and Social Policy University of Newcastle upon Tyne, 2001). Available online at <http://research.ncl.ac.uk/youthnightlife/bristolrep.pdf>.

Techno, and the existing clubs weren't big enough to contain it.'[63] Eventually, though, the national crackdown on impromptu and illegal raves and parties paved the way for more formalised and mainstream club nights which significantly undermined the underground status of Acid House. Both Collin and Thornton point to an increasingly commercialised club scene developing in the wake of Acid House.

Networks and mobility

Although Bristol is often identified as having its own distinctive set of musical sensibilities, the underground club culture is undeniably embedded in a series of movements and flows which have drawn in influences from around the world. In the late 1960s and 1970s, the Bamboo Club played host to a range of live Reggae acts originating from around the UK as well as Jamaica, as Roy Hackett remembers:

> It also had special one-off gigs when artists from [all] over Britain or maybe the world would come to play … when they were in England a lot of Soul artists from America or Jamaica would appear there because it was one of the few black clubs in England. Even though it was a small and compact club a lot of famous artists and big names passed through there. Two thirds of the bands were Jamaican bands, some were based here in England. We have a variety of music and a variety in the kinds of customers and supporters we had.[64]

Later on, during the 1980s, American Hip-Hop and Funk became part of an increasingly diverse musical mix at clubs like the Dug Out and The Moon Club.[65] Media enabled exposure to new styles: Charlie Ahearn's 1983 Hip-Hop film *Wild Style* is often cited as particularly influential in Bristol.[66] In the 1980s, Bristol crews, notably the Wild Bunch, played in Japan and New York. Jungle and Drum'n'Bass were also syncretic, arguably responding to the increasing commercialisation of club culture, these genres combined the new rave culture with Bristol's underground musical heritage. Bristol journalist, John Mitchell, says that: 'Bristol and Drum'n' Bass were natural partners… there were great nights like Ruffneck Ting (at the Lakota) – a melting point between the energy of rave and the more dubby sound system thing.'[67]

Throughout this period, clubbers would travel to other cities and towns and bring back new influences. Tim Williams remembers the links between the 1970s Soul and Funk scene in Bristol, Bournemouth (on the south coast), and London, and reflects on the creative impetus inspired by both mimicry and rivalry:

> We were going to London quite a lot. We went to Bournemouth quite regularly for bank holidays too. In Bristol you would get whole gangs of people coming down from London for the weekend. There was a kind of one-upmanship to it. We were taking our lead from the London clubs. Each week one or two parties would have been up to London at the weekend and maybe got some different clothes. They would bring things back, maybe even the dance moves, which might have changed subtly.[68]

In some cases, DJs and producers imported new styles and genres to Bristol clubs after experiencing them in London. Today, Bristol's reputation as a club city ensures that this is more of a mutual exchange, as the example of Channel 1 going head to head with Lionpulse at Bristol's Trinity Centre suggests. In a 2011 interview, Dubstep producer Pinch[69] explained why he had ended up promoting a Dubstep night in Bristol: 'I wanted it here that bad. I liked going up to FWD>> and everything but it would be nice not to have to do that two and a half hour drive back at two in the morning.'[70]

DJ-producers like Pinch and Peverelist have ensured that Bristol has become established as one of the most important locations for the development of Dubstep, with labels such as

---

63 Burrows, 'When the West went Dayglo', *Venue*, 2011.

64 Alex Cater, 'Interview with Roy Hackett', Bristol Live Independent Music Archive (BLIMA) at the University of the West of England, 2013.

65 Despite concerns about damaging her vinyl collection, Gill Loats recalls the period in the early 1980s where Hip-Hop began to make its mark in Bristol: 'People started scratching and I wasn't having any of that because I didn't want to ruin my records. So I just said, "I am not doing that," which was the biggest mistake I've probably made in my life because everybody went from £8 (10–15 Euro) for deejaying for an evening to loads of money and I didn't. Scratching actually moved it into Hip-Hop but before that I was playing Grandmaster Flash and some American imports of Hip-Hop. That was definitely the next thing coming. It was close to Funk, so I just started playing a bit of that.' Alex Cater, 'Interview with Gill Loats', (see n. 46).

H.E.N.C.H, Context, and Apple Pips as well as Pinch's Dubloaded and Subloaded nights. The BBC claimed that in 2008, 'Bristol is as significant artistically as London and this (Dubstep) could be the most thrilling chapter in an epic sonic journey spanning nearly twenty-five years of dance music across the city.'[71]

The global spread of Hip-Hop and Dub are particularly good examples of the way that underground music moves via established trade and communication networks, linking together geographically distinct musical communities. As George Lipsitz has written, this interchange uses routes opened up and maintained by the culture industries. These networks help to connect like-minded groups and individuals; particularly those that share common musical or cultural sensibilities. 'Families of resemblance' are fostered by the recognition of 'similarities to the experience and culture of other groups' and help produce syncretic musical identities.[72] In Bristol, the interchange between music makers and clubbers with places as far-flung as Tokyo, Kingston, and New York, but also other British regions, was a key part of the night-time creativity of the city. Additionally, as an urban hub in a predominantly rural part of England, situated very close to South Wales, the city has acted as a magnet for young musicians and DJs. Max Pearce, who moved to Bristol in 2011, says: 'I am from a small town in South Wales, where our only music scene was our own replication of the events in London and Bristol that we had heard or read about.'[73]

These processes, by which musical influences and scenes are transformed and reinvented, are by-products of globalisation. In other ways, though, globalisation is a threat to the club culture of the city. This is expressed most explicitly in the tensions over Stokes Croft. Stokes Croft is a central area for Bristol's more alternative club culture, on the edge of St Pauls.[74] Stokes Croft is seen as nurturing 'creative sensibilities' and cultural activism, but is at risk of being 'undermined' by neoliberalism.[75] It became notorious, nationally, after protests against the establishing of a Tescos supermarket in the street in 2011 turned into rioting, sparked by the attempt to evict a squatter from the Telepathic Heights building opposite the site. Since about 2007, Stokes Croft has become increasingly gentrified, but in uneven ways: it remains a relatively hospitable space for drug and alcohol addicts (as well as dealers) and rough sleepers, but the number of squats have been reduced and it is increasingly populated by cafés which cater to more middle class clientele.[76]

Campaigns and activist organisations such as The People's Republic Of Stokes Croft and the No Tesco In Stokes Croft campaign set out to protect Stokes Croft from this, and to challenge the homogenising effects of globalisation. One way in which they do this, is to present the street as a distinctive city quarter, competing with several other parts of the city for the title of the city's 'creative quarter', notably the area around the city's main rail terminus and North Street in Southville, a rapidly gentrifying area in the south of the city. The contradictions are evident on The People's Republic of Stokes Croft's website, which sets out its aims to promote 'the interests of the area', particularly 'the notion of Stokes Croft as a Cultural Quarter, as a destination', to 'generate prosperity', preserve what is 'valuable in the historic fabric of Stokes Croft', and to 'acquire freehold property in Stokes

---

66   Burton and Thompson, *Art and Sound of the Bristol Underground* (see n. 10).
67   Burrows, 'When the West went Dayglo' (see n. 63).
68   Alex Cater, 'Interview with Tim Williams' (see n. 51).
69   Pinch was part of the 'Ten Cities' recording project for which producers and musicians from all ten involved cities in Africa and Europe cooperated to record electronic club music. The results have been released as the compilation *Ten Cities* (Soundway, 2014).
70   BBC Radio 1, 'Story of Dubstep Episode 2: Pinch & Peverelist on Bristol Dubstep', available online at: <http://www.bbc.co.uk/programmes/p00ghtgv> accessed 4 August 2013.
71   Benjamin Slinger, 'Bristol: Rise Up', <https://www.bbc.co.uk/radio1/maryannehobbs/bristol.shtml> accessed 29 June 2013.
72   George Lipsitz, 'Cruising around the Historical Bloc: Postmodernism and Popular Music in East Los Angeles', in *Cultural Critique*, no. 5, University of Minnesota Press (1986), 157–177.
73   Max Pearce, correspondence with the authors, December 2013.
74   Clubs such as the Moon Club, the Tropic, the Blue Mountain Club, and Lakota are situated there. Newer cafés and bars with live music include the Arts House, the Attic Bar, the Bank Tavern, and The Canteen.
75   M. Buser, C. Bonura, M. Fannin and K. Boyer, 'Cultural activism and the politics of place-making', *City*, vol. 17, no. 5 (2013), 606–627.
76   Sharon Zukin, *Loft Living: Culture and Capital in Urban Change* (Baltimore: Johns Hopkins University Press, 1982). Such as The Canteen, Pieminister, The Arts House, The Runcible Spoon, Take 5 Café, and Café Kino. As in classic accounts of gentrification artists have been the avant-garde, moving into low rent buildings.

Croft'.[77] In the case of Stokes Croft the anti-capitalist, anti-corporate groups can, themselves, be perceived as part of a gentrification process by established working-class residents. They promote a distinctiveness of place against corporate homogenisation, but ironically, this also part of the capitalist marketisation of cities, since it is globalisation itself that produces the imperative for cities and their 'quarters' to brand themselves as 'creative' in the first place.[78]

Formal and informal spaces

Nevertheless, the commercialisation of Stokes Croft is potentially a threat to the club culture currently centred around that street since one of the characteristics, which has historically made a city hospitable to a thriving underground club culture, is the availability of informal nightlife spaces, often in the cheaper, more derelict, or peripheral parts of the central city. Straw has argued that the development of a significant cultural scene in the city of Manchester demonstrates the relationship between the scene, population surplus, and 'limited formal opportunities'.[79] As in other cities, Bristol's underground music scene seemed to thrive when the national economy was relatively bleak.

The period we are particularly interested in, club culture in the city from 1960 to the present day, coincides with the period that Saskia Sassen has characterised as the era of transformation in the world economy.[80] Although economically protected, to some extent, by the presence of nearby aerospace industries and by its proximity and transport links to London, Bristol has experienced periods of high unemployment. During the 1980s, under Margaret Thatcher's government, unemployment in Bristol was as high as it had been during the Depression of the 1930s.[81] The Enterprise Allowance Scheme of the late 1980s and early 1990s was supposed to remove unemployed people from the official statistics by subsidising the start of their own businesses. The scheme had the unanticipated side-effect of launching the careers of a generation of musicians and artists, often lower-middle-class graduates, partly by putting them in touch with one another; members of Bristol bands Portishead and Startled Insects met via the Enterprise Allowance Scheme.[82]

77 Buser et al. argue that 'the unevenness of gentrification results in contradictory effects (of resistance and recuperation) through which cultural activism must be understood.' But perhaps the tensions between globalisation and defense of the local, or between gentrification and cultural activism cannot be fully understood in terms of resistance and recuperation. See <http://www.prsc.org.uk/mission/>.

78 Sharon Zukin, *Loft Living: Culture and Capital in Urban Change* (Baltimore: Johns Hopkins University Press, 1982). In 1977 Stokes Croft was part of a 'ring of dereliction' according to city planners. In 2007, together with St Pauls it was described by planning documents as 'an inward-looking and isolated area with a degraded public environment' (Buser et al. 2013). In fact Buser et al. see the 'narratives of dereliction and deprivation' as one reason why 'Stokes Croft has not been affected by the development-led 'urban renaissance' present in other parts of Bristol' (though in fact we could name many parts of the city unaffected by this).

79 Will Straw, 'Cultural Scenes' (see n. 9).

80 Saskia Sassen, *The Global City* (Princeton: Princeton University Press, 2001).

81 This figure was still lower than in other British cities with a larger manufacturing base; Ian Archer et al., 'Unemployment Statistics, 1910–1997', Bristol Historical Resource, <http://humanities.uwe.ac.uk/bhr/Main/index.htm> accessed 12 June 2013; The 'dismantling of powerful industrial centres' and the internationalisation of the financial industry have left their impact on Bristol. Bristol industrialised later and de-industrialised earlier than other British cities, only industrialising when the abolition of the slave trade forced it to. In 1984, Bristol was 'generally regarded as facing a brighter economic future than any other British city-region of similar size' (Lovering 1985). Financial and aeronautical industries attracted what J. Lovering describes as 'elite labour groups' who express 'locational preference' for the Bristol region (Lovering 1985, 98), perhaps because of the prior presence of other members of this class, but also because the Bristol location is associated with a certain kind of lifestyle, not too much 'visible dereliction' and 'a good stock of inexpensive housing in Victorian suburbs or quasi-rural villages within easy access of the city centre' (Lovering 1985). Taken together, this fits with a larger picture of the period in Britain: high working-class unemployment, a growing white-collar labour force of office-workers, a declining manufacturing base, and a growing financial sector. These changes have been characterized in terms of the shift from 'Fordism' to 'flexible accumulation' and in relation to globalisation and the development of the global city—see J. Lovering, 'Regional intervention, defence industries, and the structuring of space in Britain; the case of Bristol and South Wales', *Environment and Planning D: Society and Space*, vol. 3, issue 1, 1985; David Harvey, *The condition of postmodernity* (Oxford: Blackwell 1990); Saskia Sassen, *The Global City* (see n. 80).

82 Straw touches on something similar: the Canadian government's Local Initiatives Project youth employment scheme, which, in the early 1970s, facilitated a national network of artist-run centres (Straw, 419). Straw also says: 'Scenes take shape, much of the time, on the edges of cultural institutions which can only partially absorb and channel the clusters of expressive energy which form within urban life. Just as they draw upon surpluses of people, scenes may be seen as ways of "processing" the abundance of artefacts and spaces which sediment within cities over time.' Scenes take place in relationship to what Gaonkar and Povinelli (2003) have called the 'edges of forms', the assemblages of things, places, technologies, and artefacts along which people move and live (Straw, 416). Will Straw, 'Cultural Scenes' (see n. 9).

Greenway Boys, Bristol, 1983, photo: Beezer

Massive Attack, from left to right: Mushroom, Daddy G, Shara Nelson and 3D, 1991, photo: unknown

Portishead, Hollywood, 2008, photo: Wendy Lynch Redfern

Ruff Neck Ting, Malcolm X Centre, Bristol, photo: Mark Simmons

Diggin' The Dug, Dug Out, Bristol, 1985, photo: Beezer

DJ Mushroom at The Crypt, St Pauls, Bristol, 1985, photo: Beezer

Wild Bunch Decked Out with Daddy G, Willie Wee, Nellee Hooper, Milo Johnson, Camden, London, 1985, photo: Beezer

Virgin Records & Tapes Broadmead, Bristol, photo: Beezer

Graffiti artist 3D, member of Massive Attack and of Wild Bunch, Bristol, 1985, photo: Beezer

No State Control, Bristol, photo: Beezer

Mass Dole, Broadmead, Bristol, 1982, photo: Beezer

The economic hardship and mass unemployment of the 1970s and 1980s meant that limited financial resources also played a part in shaping the club culture of the city. If a sense of camaraderie, felt within and across different subcultural groups, underpinned the social and cultural mixing in the clubs, so did the simpler desire of clubbers to find cheap alcohol. The search for cheap drinks by cash-strapped young clubbers was a significant factor in mapping out the night-time activities of many people. The UK's restrictive licensing laws meant that pubs stopped serving at 11pm. Since a lot of musical activity took place in the relatively informal spaces of local pubs, live performances and DJ sets were curtailed at 11pm. As Tim Williams remembers: 'In those days it was considered a night out if you went into town, went to a pub and then got the last bus home. People were pretty satisfied with that.'[83]

During weekends, a common experience for clubbers in Bristol was the quest for an after-hours drink, and mainstream city-centre nightclubs were pricey and had a strict dress code. Mike Crawford remembers…

> … the desperate search for a late night drink. You could get thrown out of a pub at 10:30pm and you didn't want to finish then, especially because a lot of us were on the dole. We didn't exactly get up that early. You would look everywhere and anywhere. Of course dressed like we were dressed we wouldn't even get into a proper club so we were looking for a place that would accept us. It was quite hard to get into places because they were very much aware you were just after a late drink.[84]

To extend an evening's drinking beyond 11pm meant seeking out semi-legal or illicit sites where alcohol could easily be obtained, such as blues parties or the small number of pubs well-known for their notorious after-hours 'lock-ins'. The Jamaican-run Star and Garter in Montpelier (the district adjoining St Pauls) was one, best known for fostering the early career of DJ Derek, renowned Reggae DJ and local Bristol hero.[85] Other establishments used their restaurant status to facilitate the continuation of alcohol sales. The Grecian Kebab House on Gloucester Road was a well-known after-hours venue, as was Jamaican Good Food on Ashley Road, in the heart of St Pauls, as remembered by clubber Becci Golding: 'For me it was a place to go and get beer and leave, though you could sit in and eat. Quite often what they would do, if there were loads of people sitting around drinking, is they would bring out some free plates of curry.'[86]

—

During the late 1980s and early 1990s, pubs and after-hours drinking establishments were part of a network of official, semi-legal, and informal sites of club culture where socialising, drinking, dancing, and listening to music continued long into the early hours. These clubs, restaurants, or pubs could act as pivotal nodes in the night-time network that might eventually lead revellers to the relatively informal space of a house party (meaning, in this context, a party in somebody's house), as clubber Becci Golding says:

> For me it was the Old E (Old England Pub). They would call last orders around 11pm or even 10:30pm on a Sunday. Then in the last hour there would be a bit of a buzz going about where people would be saying, 'where's the party tonight?' There was always a party somewhere.[87]

The transitory and informal spaces of parties represent a seldom-documented part of Bristol's musical nightlife and club culture. Some of these were impromptu, but as Golding remembers, music was central to the successful staging of any party and often took on a surprisingly formal and well-organised character:

> Either it would be someone's record player, or a bigger party where you would organize

---

83 He adds, 'It was only at weekends that people felt they maybe needed to go on to a secondary location to feel they had that night out.' Alex Cater, 'Interview with Tim Williams' (see n. 51).

84 Alex Cater, 'Interview with Mike Crawford' (see n. 31).

85 The status of DJ Derek has grown beyond the local area as reflected by the release of the compilation *DJ Derek Presents Sweet Memory Sounds* in 2006 on the legendary British Reggae record label Trojan.

86 Alex Cater, 'Interview with Becci Golding', Bristol Live Independent Music Archive (BLIMA) at the University of the West of England, 2013.

87 Ibid.

some DJs. When I moved out of home in 1986–1987 in Cotham, I lived in a house full of bedsits at 30 Aberdeen Road. It was quite notorious. One time everybody in all the bedsits decided to have a party on the same night. It was a massive party. In the bedsits we took all of their belongings and put them in other rooms that we locked. It was a three or four storey house and we had a DJ on in every level. Mark Stewart came and played. Gary Clail, from On-U Sound System, lived next door and he came and played. The police arrived at some point and sealed off both ends of the road and came to clear the party out.[88]

Graffiti artist FLX recalls:

Apart from going to the Wild Bunch at the Granary on Saturday afternoons for under-21s, I didn't ever go to town centre clubs. The venues for the parties were usually free – house parties, abandoned houses, or squats and warehouses. So all this made the parties more intimate if people got to know each other who probably would never talked to each other outside of the scene. People just seemed more relaxed in these venues.[89]

Pubs were also important spaces for DJ culture in the city, as Joshua Moses recalled: 'They would play Reggae singles and dubplates but not in a competitive way. Every Jamaican pub had a DJ as I remember it.'[90] While some DJs were associated with a particular club or venue, others would move around the city during any given week, playing in pubs and clubs on genre specific 'nights'. So, any one might host Hip-Hop one night, Reggae the next. Furthermore, any one of these nights might include a live Indie Rock band, an indication of the intermixing sounds and audiences in the night-time leisure economy. For black Bristolians, moving around the city to play their records in different places was an opportunity to spread their musical culture to a wider audience, as Joshua Moses reflects:

Particular days might be for particular clubs. Tuesdays might be for Top Rank, Thursday for the Dug Out, Friday for Locarno, and Saturday for The Bamboo. We would all be there every week at the venues when they had the nights we were interested in. We used to have to carry our own records to the venue for them to play because they didn't know anything about our kind of music.[91]

The large-scale organised house parties did not survive for very long. Graffiti artist FLX sees the Criminal Justice Act as killing the large-scale house parties and displacing them with more commercialised alternatives, such as two of Bristol's biggest nightclubs, Oceana, located on the regenerated dockside area, and The Syndicate 'superclub' in the centre of town on Nelson Street:

Even though the Bill (later the 1994 Act) was more to stop 'Acid House' warehouse parties that were starting to take over, it also killed the original house party thing. It actually all became too big to be sustained in this way, warehouse party survived by turning into more organized and profitable 'raves' and that was that.[92]

Another side effect of the popularity of Techno and House music, particularly among students at the time, was that small live music events were failing to gain a new, young audience. In a 2001 report on Bristol nightlife, Aubrey et al. claim that a decline in the young adult population, the increased popularity of commercial chart music, the growth in large areas, and the commercialisation of bars meant that 'small scale live music in many city centres has disappeared'.[93] According to Mintel, clubbing in general also appeared to become less popular among younger people by the end of the 1990s, while 'the over-25 "rave generation" continued to visit clubs'.[94] Aubrey et al. noted 'continuing

---

88 Ibid.
89 Burton and Thompson, *Art and Sound of the Bristol Underground* (see n. 10), 25.
90 Alex Cater, 'Interview with Joshua Moses' (see n. 32).
91 Ibid.
92 Burton and Thompson, *Art and Sound of the Bristol Underground* (see n. 10), 25.
93 'Live music is seen by many commercial operators as cutting into drinking space and profit margins. In other words, live music literally takes up space in the form of a band stage and a dance floor, thereby cutting down on vertical drinking space.' M. Aubrey, P. Chatterton, and R. Holland, 'Youth culture and nightlife in Bristol', (see n. 62), here 64.
94 Mintel, *Pre-Family Leisure Trends* (London: Mintel International Group, 2000), 45.

polarisation' between wealthy and poorer young people affecting their ability to access urban nightlife.[95]

Recoveries and continuous cultures

Despite this, since 2008, Bristol's club scene has recovered, with Dubstep continuing to be important and a resurgence in House and Techno music at events such as Just Jack, Housework, and Room 237.[96] The music continues to evidence the syncretic elements within Bristol's club culture, with new forms mixing with older styles. For example, the Young Echo club night featured a mixture of 'Asian and Middle Eastern Club Music, new and old Dub and Dancehall flavours, Dubstep, Chopped and Screwed R'n'B, American Hip-Hop, and more ambient and avant-garde based sounds'.[97]

The mobile sound system culture that began in the early years of the West Indian settlement also continues today.[98] While in other British cities the sound systems struggle to find clubs that do not already have their own in-house system, in Bristol, according to Dave Fisher, four venues continue to use sound systems: Malcolm X, Trinity, Black Swan, and Motion. Although the audience has changed, sound system culture continues to reflect the patterns of diversity and cultural exchange that have characterised much of Bristol's club culture. Dave Fisher and Thabiti say that…

> … when we first started off playing sound systems the audience was predominantly black and now it has reversed. Actually what we are starting to find now is that it's not just white people, even Asians are coming in large numbers now. It's inclusive, which is what we wanted.[99]

Bibliography

Archer, Ian et al., 'Unemployment Statistics, 1910–1997', *Bristol Historical Resource*, <http://humanities.uwe.ac.uk/bhr/Main/index.htm> accessed 12 June 2013.

Aubrey, Chatterton, and Holland, Paul, 'Youth culture and nightlife in Bristol', (Newcastle: Centre for Urban and Regional Development Studies and Department of Sociology and Social Policy University of Newcastle upon Tyne, 2001). Available online at http://research.ncl.ac.uk/youthnightlife/bristolrep.pdf

BBC (2012), *Bristol on Film*, first broadcast on BBC4, 20 May 2012.

BBC Radio 1, 'Story of Dubstep Episode 2: Pinch & Peverelist on Bristol Dubstep', broadcast 13 December 2010, <http://www.bbc.co.uk/programmes/p00ghtgv> accessed 4 August 2013.

Blum, Alan, *The Imaginative Structure of the City* (McGill-Queen's University Press, 2003).

Brown, Chris, *Bovver* (London: John Blake Publishing Ltd, 2002).

Burrows, 'When the West went Dayglo', *Venue*, 2011.

Burton, Chris, and Thompson, Gary, *Art and Sound of the Bristol Underground*, Richard Jones (ed.), (Bristol: Tangent Books, 2009).

Buser, M., Bonura, C., Fannin, M. & K. Boyer, 'Cultural activism and the politics of place-making', *City*, vol. 17, no. 5 (2013).

Cater, Alex 'Interview with Mike Crawford', BLIMA (Bristol Live Independent Music Archive) (University of the West of England, 2013).

Cater, Alex, 'Buggs Durrant', Bristol Archive Records, April 2012, <http://www.bristolarchiverecords.com/people/people_Buggs_Durrant.html> accessed 2012.

Cater, Alex, 'Bunny Marrett', Bristol Archive Records, January 2012, <http://www.bristolarchiverecords.com/people/people_Bunny_Marrett.html> accessed 19 July 2013.

Cater, Alex, 'Joshua Moses', Bristol Archive Records, October 2001, <http://www.bristolarchiverecords.com/people/people_Joshua_Moses.html> accessed 2012.

Cater, Alex, 'Papa Roots Dave Fisher & Thabiti', Bristol Archive Records, <http://www.bristolarchiverecords.com/people/people_Papa_Roots.html> accessed 2012.

Cater, Alex, 'Popsy Curious', Bristol Archive Records, <http://www.bristolarchiverecords.com/people/people_Popsy_Curious.html> accessed 19 July 2013.

Collin, Matthew, *Altered State: The Story of Ecstasy Culture and Acid House* (London: Serpent's Tail, 1997).

Connell, John, and Gibson, Chris, *Sound Tracks: Popular Music Identity and Place* (London: Routledge, 2003).

Clement, Matt, 'Bristol: "civilizing" the inner city', *Race and Class* 48/4 (2007), 97–105.

Dresser, Madge, and Fleming, Peter, *Bristol: Ethnic Minorities and the City 1000–2001* (London: Phillimore and Co. Ltd., 2007).

Goldman, Vivien, 'Local Groove Does Good: The Story Of Trip-Hop's Rise From Bristol', *The Record: Music News from NPR*, <http://www.npr.org/blogs/therecord/2012/01/31/142607358/local-groove-does-good-the-story-of-trip-hops-rise-from-bristol> accessed 19 July 2013.

Harvey, David, *The Condition of Postmodernity* (Oxford: Blackwell 1990).

Hasted, Nick, 'Bristol Time: The return of a trip-hop legacy', *The Independent*, 11 April 2008.

Hebdige, Dick, *Subculture: The Meaning of Style* (London: Routledge, 1979).

Hyder, Rehan, *Brimful of Asia: Negotiating Ethnicity on the UK Music Scene* (Aldershot: Ashgate, 2004).

Johnson, Phil, *Straight Outa Bristol: Massive Attack, Portishead, Tricky and the Roots of Trip-hop* (London: Hodder and Stoughton, 1996).

---

95 M. Aubrey, P. Chatterton, and R. Holland, 'Youth culture and nightlife in Bristol' (see n. 62), here 64.
96 Pearce in correspondence with authors (see n. 73)
97 Pearce in correspondence with authors (see n. 73)
98 As Max Pearce reflects: 'Regular events such as Teachings in Dub run by local UK Steppa's artist Stryda and Bristol Dub Club present the Jamaican tradition of sound system clashes to an audience of both new faces and original veterans.'
99 Alex Cater, 'Papa Roots Dave Fisher & Thabiti' (see n. 33).

Kirk, Peter, 'Daddy G.', Bristol Archive Records, August 2004, <http://www.bristolarchiverecords.com/people/people_Daddy_G.html> accessed 28 June 2013.

Lipsitz, George, 'Cruising around the Historical Bloc: Postmodernism and Popular Music in East Los Angeles', *Cultural Critique,* no. 5 (University of Minnesota Press, 1986), 157–177.

Lipsitz, George, *Dangerous Crossroads: Popular Music, Postmodernism and the Poetics of Place* (London: Verso, 1997).

Lovering, J., 'Regional intervention, defence industries, and the structuring of space in Britain; the case of Bristol and South Wales', *Environment and Planning D: Society and Space*, vol. 3, issue 1 (1985).

Miles, Milo, 'Trip-Hop'. *Salon*, 12 November 1995. See also Goldman, Vivien, 'Local Groove Does Good: The Story Of Trip-Hop's Rise From Bristol', *The Record: Music News from NPR*, <http://www.npr.org/blogs/therecord/2012/01/31/142607358/local-groove-does-good-the-story-oftrip-hops-rise-from-bristol> accessed 19 July 2013.

Mintel, *Pre-Family Leisure Trends* (London: Mintel International Group, 2000).

Muggleton, David, *Inside Subculture: The Postmodern Meaning of Style* (London: Berg, 2000).

O'Hagan, Sean, 'Blue Lines: Massive Attack's Blueprint for UK Pop's Future', *The Observer*, 28 October 2012, <http://www.guardian.co.uk/music/2012/oct/28/massive-attack-blue-lines-remaster> accessed 24 January 2013.

'PortCities Bristol', *PortCities Bristol*, (1999) <http://discoveringbristol.org.uk/> accessed 12 June 2013.

Richardson, Mike, 'Trade Unionism and Industrial Conflict in Bristol: A Historical Study', *Bristol Historical Resource*, <http://humanities.uwe.ac.uk/bhr/Main/index.htm> accessed 12 June 2013.

Sassen, Saskia, *The Global City* (Princeton: Princeton University Press, 2001).

Slinger, Benjamin, 'Bristol: Rise Up', <https://www.bbc.co.uk/radio1/maryannehobbs/bristol.shtml> accessed 28 June 2013.

Slater, Tom and Anderson, Ntsiki, 'The reputational ghetto: territorial stigmatisation in St Paul's, Bristol', *Transactions of the Institute of British Geographers*, 37/4 (2011).

Straw, Will, 'Cultural Scenes', *Loisir et société/Society and Leisure* 27: 2 (2004), 411–422.

Thornton, Sarah, *Club Cultures: Music, Media and Subcultural Capital* (Cambridge: Polity Press, 1995).

Thrift, Nigel, 'Intensities of Feeling: Towards a Spatial Politics of Affect', *Geografiska Annaler, Series B: Human Geography* 86(1) (2004), 57–78.

Webb, Peter, 'Interrogating the production of sound and place: The Bristol Phenomenon, from Lunatic Fringe to Worldwide Massive', *Music, Space and Place: Popular Music and Social Identity*, S. Whitley, and A. Bennett (eds.), (Aldershot: Ashgate, 2004).

'The People: Bristol Archive Records', Bristol Archive Records, <http://www.bristolarchiverecords.com/people/people.html> accessed 12 June 2013.

wayneyates09, 'THE BRISTOL SOUND', YouTube (2009), <http://www.youtube.com/watch?v=V34aBj4txCc> accessed 12 June 2013.

Zukin, Sharon: *Loft Living: Culture and Capital in Urban Change* (Johns Hopkins University Press, 1982).

LISBON

MUSIC/SPACES

The Soundtrack of a City, the Pulse of a Country

From Yé-Yé to African Lisbon

Rui Miguel Abreu ▶ P.487

SPACES/POLITICS

Time Capsule Lisbon

Revolution, Hangovers, Hedonism

Vítor Belanciano ▶ P.509

The Soundtrack of a City, the Pulse of a Country – From Yé-Yé to African Lisbon

Rui Miguel Abreu

In the 1960s, Lisbon was still the capital of an empire. This does not mean that its streets and clubs were filled with an effusive mix of sounds and styles imported from its colonies, like Paris, which had for a long time been a magnet for Jazz musicians, or London, where artists like Nigeria's Fela Ransome Kuti learnt their craft on stages brimming with musical fusion. Controlled by a dictatorship, the Portuguese imperial capital watched television and listened to radio channels where little room was given to any popular cultural manifestation other than Fado or Nacional-Cançonetismo.[1] However, the winds of change were blowing across Europe. Thanks to the social revolutions following in the wake of the phenomena of Elvis Presley and The Beatles, in Lisbon the young were creating a space for themselves as well. In Portugal the effects of this social upheaval began, very slowly, to be tolerated by the authorities.

Yé-yé and internationalisation: the 1960s

When, in 1960, the first avowedly Rock music EP produced in Portugal was commercially released, the doors opened to a new form of a more rebellious and more international expression. To be among the artists of the compilation *Caloiros da Canção* [song newcomers] (a 7-inch vinyl with two songs on each side) was the first prize in a competition held by the radio station Rádio Renascença. This competition ended with a draw, and so songs by both Daniel Bacelar as well as Os Conchas [The Shells] were included. Portugal had thus embarked on the international revolution, which – through music in particular – empowered the baby boomers' adolescents, born in the immediate aftermath of the Second World War. However, prior to this first record reaching the shops, Rock'n'Roll culture made its debut in the local underground scene. This was especially true in film, with a series of movies linked to the history of this music genre. *Blackboard Jungle*, which included Bill Haley's famous song 'Rock Around the Clock' and which caused hysteria in cinemas in the US, was first shown in Portugal in 1955. In the following year, *Rock, Rock, Rock* with music by Chuck Berry reached Lisbon's cinemas, next to, and among others, *Rock Around the Clock*, a 'rockxploitation' film, featuring Bill Haley. The new rhythm exploding across the US first reached those places in Lisbon which were frequented by US sailors: port bars, night clubs, and gambling dens.

The 1960s were a time of profound social change across the globe. But in Portugal the national dictator António de Oliveira Salazar[2] tried his best to steady the reigns of the old colonial empire. While the colonial war broke out in Africa, spreading rapidly from Angola to the other Portuguese colonies, Captain Henrique Galvão, with the support of General 'Fearless' Humberto Delgado, organised a major coup against the regime by commandeering the transatlantic liner, Santa Maria. The political climate quickly began to alter in this country of mild manners, and the war led students to close ranks[3] against a regime, which refused to countenance progress, pushing thousands to slip away across the border. Luís Pinheiro de Almeida noted that, 'at the time, Portuguese youth were more likely to have a machine gun in their hands than a guitar'.[4]

However, and as strange as it may seem, Salazar's regime did not actually try to suppress the nation's young rockers – at least during the 1960s, when a teenage and politically inoffensive aura still dominated the essence of Portuguese Rock music. According to Luís Pinheiro de Almeida:

---

1. A type of light Portuguese music with lyrics about traditional Portuguese values and the ideas and principles of the fascist dictatorship.
2. Salazar (1889–1970) was Portugal's prime minister from 1932 to 1968 and leader of the authoritarian dictatorship of the so-called Estado Novo [new state].
3. 1962 was a turbulent year in this particular respect.
4. Rui Miguel Abreu, '1955–1969: Quando a febre em Portugal Era o Yé-Yé', *Blitz* (July 2008).

The dictatorship affected every part of Portuguese society prior to 25 April,[5] and Portuguese music, Rock included, was no exception. In terms of lyrics in particular, it limited freedom of expression – or incentivized it in the so-called 'protest music' that came later. Moreover, due to the colonial war, compulsory military service was a barrier to the advancement of a band's career. These came to an end – with rare exceptions – when their members were called up.

Curiously, it was also due to the dictatorship and its institutions, the National Women's Movement (MNF) in this case, that Yé-Yé, or Rock, flourished in Portugal. In 1965 and 1966, more than 300 bands entered the Yé-Yé contest held at the Monumental Theatre in Lisbon. This was organized by the MNF for the Portuguese armed forces then fighting in various operations in the so-called 'Portuguese overseas territories'. Notable right-wing figures were invited to the jury, amongst them Martins da Cruz, the future Foreign Minister of the Social Democratic Party (PSD).[6]

In his 1984 book, *A Arte Eléctrica de Ser Português: 25 Anos De Rock'n Portugal*, a work of true importance for its systematic portrayal of the history of Rock music in Portugal up to the beginning of the 1980s, António Duarte recognises the importance of the musical explosion in the 1960s:

> Portugal is not a country with Rock roots, so we have to admit the extraordinary importance of this musical import for the birth, in this land of seafarers, Fado and football, of a movement which gradually gained independence and personality, albeit subject, almost completely, to the direct influences of Anglo-American Rock music. Portugal only began to develop its own style of Rock in the 1960s, when the famous but brainless Yé-Yé movement exploded, popularized by the holding of countless competitions to choose the best bands of the moment.[7]

With the lack of a specific circuit of concert venues, cinemas provided young musicians with the ideal spaces to perform live. The spreading of talent shows did the rest. Despite the rapid propagation of the Yé-Yé phenomenon, the local record industry took its time to realise the importance of Rock'n'Roll. Record releases were very sporadic and concentrated, above all, on the EP format. Edgar Raposo, Luís Futre, and João Carlos Callixto, three specialists on the era who held an exhibition, 'Nova Vaga', that resulted in a catalogue with varied information about this period, mention that only three Portuguese Rock albums were recorded in the country in the 1960s: 'The LP from 1966 by Conjunto João Paulo that was "falsely" claimed to have been recorded live at the Monumental (in fact it was recorded in the studio and the clapping added later), the LP by the Pop Five Music Incorporated and "Epopeia" by Filarmónica Fraude, both from 1969.'[8]

—

In this period, one group almost managed to achieve the status of a phenomenon in Portugal, rivalling the popularity of The Beatles. 'The Sheiks', tells band member, Paulo de Carvalho, 'were a group of friends who basically wanted to imitate the British and American bands they heard on records and the radio. That's how we learnt the songs, by ear, that we later played at our concerts.'[9] After the first recordings with Moreno Pinto at the Rádio Renascença studios for the programme *23ª Hora*, they were signed by the label Valentim de Carvalho, which did a better job of turning them into a success. The Sheiks' career, however, was cut short by the demands of their studies and compulsory military service, so the group did not survive the 1960s.

Band member Paulo de Carvalho recalls: 'My best time as a drummer was after the Sheiks

---

5   On 25 April 1974 a mostly peaceful military coup overthrew the regime, the so-called 'Carnation Revolution', which started the democratization of Portuguese society and the state's withdrawal from its African colonies.
6   Rui Miguel, '1955–1969', (see n. 4).
7   António Duarte, *A Arte Eléctrica de Ser Português: 25 Anos de Rock'n Portugal* (Lisbon: Livraria Bertrand, 1984), 48.
8   Edgar Raposo, Luís Futre, and João Carlos Callixt, in an interview with the author (2010).
9   Rui Miguel Abreu, 'Paulo de Carvalho: Uma Voz Única', *Blitz* (April 2011).

when I joined Thilo's Combo. It was a time when I learnt a lot, after all I was a kid of twenty playing with forty-year-old musicians with lots of experience.'[10] Thilo's Combo was led by Thilo Krasmann and recorded a series of EPs that were full of rhythm. It worked as a session group for several stars of Canção Nacional such as Simone de Oliveira. At the group's headquarters in Lisbon's Avenida da Liberdade, in the nightclub Galeria 48, Thilo's Combo adopted a fluid line-up inspired by the more modern sounds arriving from the US. For de Carvalho, this meant greater creative freedom:

> In the Sheiks, I was always on the receiving end. It was always three against one when it came to choosing songs to cover. The Beach Boys, for example ... it was very difficult to convince the Sheiks to play any of their songs because they were very complicated in vocal terms, especially the harmonies. Another singer that I loved and whose songs we never played was Steve Winwood and the things he did with the Spencer Davis Group. With the Sheiks we played some Beatles covers and they had to be the easiest ones. Interestingly, we never played anything by the Stones – musically it was very basic, but they had so much energy it was really hard to carry it off properly.[11]

Paulo de Carvalho joined Thilo's Combo towards the end of the band's career, in 1968, a year before the group disbanded. Next to his band membership he was able to play on records by people like the Angolan Ruy Mingas for example, and ensure the cachet of earning good money by playing at Galeria 48 each night. Being part of the Combo also provided de Carvalho with the experience of playing with US musicians like Van Dickson and Tyree Glenn Jr., who filled Lisbon nights with Soul. De Carvalho recounts:

> I had a very sharp voice, something I'd developed with the Sheiks. In the concerts played by Thilo's Combo, I'd sing three or four songs, stuff by Aretha Franklin mainly. One night, a black man walked into the room, and one of the American musicians who played with us gave him a really warm welcome. I think it was Tyree Glenn, who was the son of Louis Armstrong's trombonist. Anyway, he came in and I don't know if Thilo did it on purpose, but he asked me to sing a blues number by Aretha Franklin. One of the other band members was José Luís Simões, a great musician who played guitar and also doubled up on trombone. For that song, he was in the brass section and had put down his guitar. And the guy who'd walked into the room started to get excited and came over and picked it up.[12]

Today, Tyree Glenn Jr. continues to make music in Germany, his adopted home. His official website made getting in touch easy. The question, 'what do you remember about your time in Portugal?' was enough to prod his memory to the same night described by de Carvalho: 'The great saxophonist King Curtis, now dead, was my friend and in 1968 came to play in Estoril at a private party,' explains Glenn, referring to one of the famous events organised by the millionaire Antenor Patiño, who brought many European aristocrats and Hollywood stars to Portugal. 'When I learnt he was in Lisbon, I phoned him at his hotel and told him I was playing at Galeria 48, and he promised to drop by after his concert. We were playing with Thilo and at midnight he appeared, with Georgie Fame!'[13] exclaimed the musician, still amazed that Curtis would turn up in the Avenida da Liberdade accompanied by a British popstar. The saxophonist explained to King Curtis, who he knew from the New York club circuit, that he was living in Portugal, performing with Thilo and also playing basketball for Benfica, who he was with for two and a half years and still describes today as his one true club. Glenn goes on:

> King picked up the guitar and started to play 'Hey Joe', and we followed what he was

10   Ibid.
11   Ibid.

12   Miguel Abreu, 'Paulo de Carvalho', (see n. 9).
13   Ibid.

doing. Then Paulo, who only sang R'n'B songs by Aretha Franklin, Wilson Pickett and the like, started singing. He had, and still has a tremendous Soul voice. So King turned and started to look at the singer playing the drums. You have to realize that the songs Paulo was singing were, in several cases, originally played by King Curtis – the sax solo in 'Respect', for example, was by him. And he couldn't believe what he was hearing – a fantastic voice by a Portuguese drummer! The night ended with King Curtis inviting Paulo to go to the US.[14]

Paulo de Carvalho recalls the episode similarly:
King Curtis had a huge success with 'Memphis Soul Stew' which we also played. I still remember the drum break I used to play as an intro for the others. After the song, King Curtis was really impressed by seeing a white guy singing like that and offered to take me to America, but my wife had just had a baby, my military service was coming up, and I didn't have a passport, so I wasn't about to do anything crazy.[15]

Musically speaking, the late 1960s in Portugal were an extremely rich and exciting period, thanks to groups like Quarteto 1111, Psico, Pop Five Music Incorporated, and Objectivo. Their music held the kernel of what would mark a lot of the music produced in the 1970s, a decade that was revolutionary beyond the political.

Revolution and electric guitars: the 1970s

The atmosphere in Portugal at the beginning of the 1970s was not especially supportive to the free development of youth culture. For that very reason, international musical innovations – above all those by the Black Sabbath/Led Zeppelin axis that formed Rock's harder edge – had only a limited impact when they reached Portugal. Júlio Pereira, one of Portuguese pop music's seminal figures who influenced groups like Petrus Castrus and Xarhanga in the 1970s, notes that there was virtually no Rock music scene in Portugal before 25 April 1974: 'Being involved in Rock music at that time was difficult as it often led to clashes with family, school, neighbours and … especially the police.'[16] In fact, as early as 1970, the authorities' hard attitude towards music was made clear. In the summer of that year, a festival in the small town Oeiras near Lisbon, where several Rock bands and singers like José 'Zeca' Afonso were to perform, was closed down by the police.

Zeca was heavily involved in the trade union movement that had been encouraged during the early years of the new government of Marcelo Caetano and he had just released *Traz Outro Amigo Também*, an album recorded in London in early 1970 that earned him a press award in recognition of its major contribution to reinventing Portuguese popular music. For the authorities, it all spelled trouble. For that very reason, and to try and prevent the festival, which had brought several thousand young people to the small town of Oeiras, the police were ordered to charge. History proved, however, that you cannot hold back time, and in the following year Vilar de Mouros held the first Rock Festival in Portugal. It proved there was a new generation moving to the electric rhythms of Rock.

The foundation of a more Heavy-Rock-oriented Portugal are the band Os Chinchilas and their singer Filipe Mendes, also known as 'Phil Mendrix', a true icon of the 'electric art of being Portuguese', as the aforementioned book title goes. The Chinchilas were short lived and released only very few records – but they were the first platform for the talent of Filipe Mendes who went on to form the mythic Heavy Band at the beginning of the 1970s. 'My influences were The Beatles and The Stones and later Cream and Jimi Hendrix,' said Mendes,[17] who passed away in 2018. Innovative in his use of the guitar

---

14 Ibid.
15 Ibid.
16 Rui Miguel Abreu, 'Rock Em Portugal Nos Anos 70: Uma História Quase Secreta', *Blitz* (January 2007).
17 Ibid.

and with a style similar to Jimi Hendrix (hence the nickname), Mendes became a true believer in Portugal's Rock cause.

In 1971, he released the single 'Barbarella' – which Mendes still regards today as his best song from the 1970s – with Os Chinchilas. The band's powerful trio line-up had a major influence on him and was something he would continue to explore with Heavy Band, a group he formed in 1972 with Zé Nabo and João Heitor. This band would earn mythical status for accounts of wild concerts and because the two singles they recorded were only released in Angola, a factor which contributed to a certain rarity and consequent demand. Mendes recognizes that the Heavy Band had some effect on the Portuguese music scene: 'I have an idea I had followers from my style of music to even the type of record player I used.'[18] Mendes was also part of the band Psico (that would leave its mark on posterity with the single 'AI' from 1978) and of Roxigénio, who would release their debut record at the end of the decade in 1980.

Close contemporaries of the Chinchilas were the Beatniks, consisting of João Ribeiro and, later, Rui Pipas, Mário Ceia, and José Diogo (at which point they added a 'c' and became known as the Beatnicks). The Beatnicks added a certain psychedelic reverence to the counterculture ethos of the pre-revolution era through the more 'druggy' side of Beat culture and its reflections in Rock music. In 1971, their single 'Cristine Goes to Town' mirrored the heavy influence of Black Sabbath and obliged the long-haired fans who came to their concerts to headbang to the blasts of electric guitars. The Beatnicks were one of the less visible bands at the Vilar de Mouros festival, but also one of the heaviest. Filipe Mendes describes the Beatnicks – along with Zé Nabo's band Objectivo – as the 'hardest Rock band in Portugal in the 1970s'.[19]

Júlio Pereira may have played a leading role in the generation of musicians who set off to discover the traditional roots of Portuguese music, but before he gave the cavaquinho [a small Portuguese guitar] a new lease of life, it was the electric guitar that was his best friend. When asked about his early career, Pereira says, 'I practically only listened to Rock. And I liked to play what at the time was called "Hard Rock". I had a "classical" training: the bass, guitar and drums. I only discovered Jazz and other music when I was about twenty.'[20] Pereira was part of the now historic group Petrus Castrus, who released one of the decade's landmark LPs, *Mestre*, in 1973. The record was full of Psychedelic Prog Rock and politics with a famous poem by Ary dos Santos titled 'S.A.R.L.' (an acronym for the Portuguese expression for 'Anonymous Society of Limited Responsibility') providing the words to Júlio Pereira's heavy riffs. The powers that be were not impressed, and the band was subject to pressure from the censors who, as José Cid says, 'silenced' some of their work. Júlio Pereira was only part of the line-up that recorded *Mestre*, leaving soon after to set up Xarhanga, a group that left two singles to posterity: 'Acid Nightmare' or 'Wish Me Luck', and 'Great Goat' or 'Smashing Life'. At the time, the Portuguese used to sing in English – not so well, but loudly. The revolution of 25 April 1974 was approaching and would bring massive change.

'The 25 April was a key moment for the Portuguese. But for Rock, it was a step backwards because people associated this Anglo-American style of music with imperialism,' said the singer Filipe Mendes.[21] His peer Júlio Pereira has a different perspective: 'Until then, I had hated popular Portuguese music. And we didn't listen to Fado at home. The 25 April gave us the chance to hear the instruments and voices that were part of our musical tradition.'[22] Another thing the revolution brought, of course, was freedom, without which, JC Serra, a founding member of the band Aqui d'El Rock, explains that Punk would never have happened in Portugal: 'NO

18 Ibid.
19 Ibid.

20 Ibid.
21 Ibid.
22 Ibid.

WAY. In capital letters. Before 25 April, a group like Aqui d'El Rock couldn't have existed. Only with the freedom that 1974 brought was it possible for a group like ours to appear. Before that it couldn't have happened because no real musician would accept having their work censored.'[23] The first single by Aqui d'El Rock from 1978 was titled 'Há Que Violentar O Sistema' [you must violate the system], and it was one of the first products of Punk's revolutionary style in Portugal.

It is important to realise that, for some time, attempts were made to compare the impact of the so-called 'Portuguese Rock boom' to the Big Bang. The 1970s represented the void, but the dawn of the 1980s saw an incredible explosion in talent and energy that even gave us a godfather of Portuguese Rock: Rui Voloso. The real story is, of course, very different. When the LP *Ar De Rock* by Rui Veloso e A Banda Sonora reached the record shops in 1980, Filipe Mendes already had over a decade of crazy solos behind him, Sérgio Castro had already left Psico to form Arte & Ofício (who preceded the better known Trabalhadores do Comércio), and Punk had already scratched at the still fresh varnish of post-25 April Portuguese society. There was, indeed, a boom in the 1980s – but a boom in releases and commercial success. The creative roots of this generation, however, were firmly buried in the decade when Portugal changed course, thanks to a political revolution and lots of electrical noise.

Boom, Punk, and experiments: the 1980s

A quick glance at the lists of record releases in Portugal in the May/June 1979 issue of the historic magazine *Música & Som* shows that, as far as Portuguese Rock was concerned, there was a giant gap. Not just in terms of records. Accounts from the time also point to a relative lack of places to play and listen to music. The 1978 debut concert of Xutos E Pontapés, for example, took place at the famous Alunos de Apolo association in Lisbon's Campo de Ourique area, usually home to dancing of another kind.[24]

Of all the records – singles and LPs – released onto the market at this time by labels such as Imavox, PolyGram, Rádio Triunfo, Rossil, Telectra, and Valentim de Carvalho, not one could be described as Portuguese Rock music. Of course, generally speaking, there was a Rock scene in Portugal in the 1970s, but the record releases in this period were too sporadic for there to be anything called a real movement. Despite this, the process that would ultimately lead to the creative and recording explosion at the start of the 1980s was already underway. The international Punk movement had arrived in Portugal, and the aforementioned Aqui d'El Rock had even already released a record in 1978, placing itself at the vanguard of a scene that was only just starting to take shape: 'In the context and at the time, I think besides Aqui d'El Rock you could call Faíscas, UHF, Xutos E Pontapés, Minas, and Armadilhas Punk bands. It was at that point that you could start to talk about a scene, what came to be called the "Portuguese Rock boom",' explains JC Serra, drummer of Aqui d'El Rock.[25]

Rui Pregal da Cunha, who took his first steps with the band Heróis do Mar, draws a map of Lisbon's nightlife in the late 1970s and early 1980s: 'Pedro (Ayres Magalhães) used to go to Brown's a lot, close to the Centro Comercial Roma, but we would all meet up at Trumps at the end of the night.'[26] Brown's was an important place, and it was there, at the end of 1978, that the band, UHF, first played live at a concert also featuring Aqui d'El Rock and Faíscas de Dedos Tubarão, also known as Pedro Ayres. The Faíscas' manager at the time was Zé Pedro, from Xutos E Pontapés. The following year, UHF released their first record, the EP 'Jorge Morreu'. It came out on the same Metro-Som label as Aqui d'El Rock, which bridged the tiny

---

23 Ibid.
24 The place was, and still is, a venue for ballroom dancing.
25 Abreu, 'Rock Em Portugal Nos Anos 70', (see n. 16).
26 Ibid.

Punk scene of the late 1970s and the boom of the early 1980s, to which UHF again contributed decisively with the follow-up single 'Cavalos de Corrida' [Racing Horses], (1980). António Manuel Ribeiro, the singer of UHF, explains:

> For me the Ramones and the Sex Pistols were major influences because they were so uncomplicated. We were coming to the end of the 1970s and the Prog Rock period, which scared people because when you looked at the stage with all the expensive synthesizers and very elaborate sets you lost all hope of being able to form a band. And when the Ramones appeared, the message was the opposite – simple, street style, direct language. And it was very political, providing an outlook on life. The protest music generation was a bit lost after the revolution and we had a different view of things.[27]

UHF were at the front line of the 'Portuguese Rock boom' because, when the single 'Cavalos de Corrida' came out, they already had a long history of playing gigs all around the country. This had created a solid fan base, which, in some cases, still follows them to this day. 'Xutos', band member Zé Pedro explains, 'loved being able to play with UHF because it meant the gig was going to be done right'.

But the story of this boom would have been very different if Mrs. Emília Veloso had not had enough faith in her son's talent to pick up some of his recordings and take them to the label Valentim de Carvalho. The episode is told in the book *Os Vês Pelos Bês*, the authorized biography of Rui Veloso, written by Ana Mesquita:

> [The producer] António Pinho was amazing. He was very polite, listened to the tape and said he thought he was really good. He asked me if he also sang in Portuguese and I answered that I didn't know if Carlos Tê, who wrote the lyrics, was willing to write in Portuguese. All of the recordings were in English, but António Pinho continued listening until (the song) 'Chico Fininho' came up and it was at that point that he said he wanted to sign Rui.[28]

Emília Veloso had no doubt about it and encouraged Rui: 'Son, there are trains to Lisbon every day. It's time to sort your life out.'[29]

In July 1980, music changed in Portugal with the release of *Ar de Rock*, Rui Veloso E A Banda Sonora's first album, produced by António Pinho (who had been a member of Banda do Casaco). With Zé Nabo on bass and Ramon Galarza on drums – the two members of Banda Sonora – Rui Veloso created a Rock album sung, shamelessly, in Portuguese. António Pinho's insistence on singing in the 'not very Rock-like language of Camões',[30] as António Duarte wrote at the time, paid obvious dividends, especially the song 'Chico Fininho' [skinny guy] that quickly became a serious success in terms of sales and social identification. In just one song, 'speed', 'shit', 'heroin trip', and 'acid with loads of strychnine' were mentioned. This was Rock music recognising and describing drugs to enhance the portrayal, as the song goes, of a 'freak from Cantareira'. Other songs from the album *Ar de Rock* were given air time as well: 'Rapariguinha do Shopping', 'Donzela Diesel', and 'Sei de Uma Camponesa'.[31]

Rui Veloso's debut album confounded all expectations. Veloso recalls: 'It was predicted to sell around 5,000 copies and it sold over 30,000, which was a lot for a time when there were only a few record players in the entire country. We were a bit third world in that respect. But when this happened the other labels suddenly thought "Oh, you can make money from this kind of music!" and the race to sign bands took off.'[32] There started to be more concerts, too. Rui Veloso was also the first act to play in the new venue Rock Rendez-Vous in Lisbon, which opened on 18 December 1980, and soon became legendary.

---

27 António Manuel Ribeiro, in an interview with the author (2008).
28 Rui Veloso and Ana Mesquita, *Os Vês Pelos Bês* (Cascais: Prime Books Sociedade Editorial, 2006), 121.
29 Ibid., 122.
30 Duarte, *A Arte Eléctrica* (see n. 7), 72.
31 'Little girl from the shopping mall', 'Diesel maiden', and 'I know about a country girl'.
32 Rui Miguel Abreu, 'Rui Veloso, 35 Anos de Carreira: Como Tudo Começou', *Blitz* (May 2010).

'All of this happened', notes Francisco Vasconcelos from the label Valentim de Carvalho, 'because there was a revolution in the media at that time. There was space to do things and a greater willingness to take risks.'[33] Vasconcelos is referring here to the introduction of FM radio and to programmes like Luís Filipe Barros' *Rock em Stock* [rock in stock] and Júlio Isidro's famous 'Febre de Sábado de Manhã' [Saturday morning fever], both on the Rádio Comercial station. 'I opened up "Febre de Sábado de Manhã" to a wave of new Portuguese Rock music which at the start of the 1980s was a very clear movement,' explains Júlio Isidro.[34] Describing the Portuguese Rock boom as a snowball gaining speed and size, Isidro modestly says: 'I went in search of bands that were already out there. I just echoed what they were doing and the big contributors to that were the other media which also promoted the programme a lot and gave us extra exposure.'

In April 1979, Rádio Comercial had also aired the programme *Rock em Stock* with Luís Filipe Barros. 'At the start, I only played British and American music on my programme, but then I began playing songs by bands like Ananga Ranga and UHF. I played "Cavalos de Corrida" even before anything by Rui Veloso,' recalls Barros.[35] The percentage of Portuguese music on *Rock em Stock* grew as the audience began to react favourably to it. 'At that time, radio listeners weren't passive and would often phone the station to say what they thought about the programmes.' If they didn't phone, they'd actually go there in person: 'Xutos used to come to my programme every day. They had pins in their ears and I thought they were really funny. Later, when the song "Sémen" was banned at Rádio Renascença, I used to play it even more just because of that.'

Rui Reininho, singer of the band GNR (Grupo Novo Rock [New Rock Group]), reflects: 'We were anti-Blues. We didn't like solos and jams and just refused them. We knew exactly what we didn't want to do. Rui Veloso had had a lot of exposure. We were from the same town but from different neighbourhoods. And style wise, we didn't have a lot in common.'[36] In fact, one of the features of the Portuguese Rock boom was the extreme variety of styles that appeared at the time. To explore every possible avenue to success, record companies signed practically everyone who could play guitar and sing in Portuguese. 'They released a lot of crap,'[37] admits António Pinho, who, after working for Valentim de Carvalho, joined the record company PolyGram where he produced and recorded bands like Heróis do Mar [Heroes of the Sea] and Táxi. 'Just bet on whatever sells. It was a time when you sold a song and then got rid of the group – "chew'em up and spit'em out," as Táxi used to say.'

But memory can be selective, and the GNR singer, Rui Reininho, has different recollections: 'I saw things happening very spontaneously, with records and concerts and the street all mixed together. And it was in the street that things started to take hold.'[38] He confesses to having been 'dragged along by the momentum': 'I started performing with the lads in the band after they had already started.' Reininho disentangles the knotted ball of memory: 'Language was the big thing at the time. Rock had always been played at parties, but it was always sung in other languages.' Especially in English, according to António Pinho: 'The Portuguese were looking more to Britain musically.'[39] Rui Veloso had started by singing in English and various other bands did so too, like Táxi: 'When I heard them play I told them they had to start writing in Portuguese,' explains Pinho, who remembers that, for example, the band Chiclete [chewing gum] was called Cloud 9 before taking on a new Portuguese name.

—

One thing that all the people involved in this story seem to have in common is a sense that they were all in it together, as if they were all

33 Francisco Vasconcelos, in an interview with the author (2008).
34 Júlio Isidro, in an interview with the author (2008).
35 Filipe Barros, in an interview with the author (2008).
36 Rui Reininho, in an interview with the author (2008).
37 António Pinho, in an interview with the author (2008).
38 Rui Reininho, in an interview with the author (2008).
39 António Pinho, in an interview with the author (2008).

aware that what they were doing was going to change the course of musical history in Portugal. 'There was a certain sense of togetherness with bands like Xutos E Pontapés, for example,' says Rui Reininho. 'We'd meet up with Zé Pedro (Xutos singer) at international concerts. And then there were bands like the Street Kids – who were a bit more posh – or Heróis do Mar, though sometimes we'd fall out because of girlfriends,' he says.

In the autumn of 1981, Heróis do Mar, with a line-up featuring Rui Pregal da Cunha, Pedro Ayres Magalhães, Carlos Maria Trindade, Paulo Pedro Gonçalves, and António José de Almeida, released what can still be considered one of the best albums ever made in Portugal: the self-titled *Heróis do Mar*, with tracks like 'Brava Dança Dos Heróis' [Brave Dance of the Heroes] and 'Saudade' [Longing]. It was slammed when it came out and was very controversial for its overt nationalism. Singer Rui Pregal da Cunha explains: 'For me, it was a huge jumble of references that mixed Portuguese history with the Japanese adventure stories we saw at the cinema and Thor and Baldur – not from Norse mythology but from Marvel Comics!'[40]

Rui Pregal da Cunha admits that he 'lived in another world' with a set of friends who moved between the Lisbon nightclubs Jamaica (in the Cais do Sodré area), Yes (in Arieiro), Rockhouse (in Bairro Alto), and Trumps (in Rua da Imprensa Nacional). They charted the future of a national pop scene that, back then, refused to accept a Portugal marooned in time. 'In 1980, all the signs coming from abroad created a real hunger. So when one of us got a record', explains the singer, 'we'd take it with us when we went out at night and ask the DJ, wherever we were, to play it so our friends could hear it.'[41] As the memories start to return, Pregal refers to a sense of community, important for what would follow, that was at the heart of Heróis do Mar's line-up: 'People shared the music and ideas – they'd go to each others' houses to get dressed to go out at night, for example. There was an energy, a real appetite for discovery.'

Lisbon's cult gay nightclub, Trumps, 'our very own kind of Studio 54', as Rui Pregal notes ironically, was frequented by all sorts of people, seduced by the sounds of Disco and some electronic New Wave stuff that had started to make inroads on the dance floor. 'I was supposed to have been the first DJ at Trumps', recalls Pregal, 'and I even bought its first set of records, but I wasn't what they were looking for. They wanted hardcore Disco and I'd bought some Disco stuff, but other records too that were completely different.' Pregal suggested João Vaz, today the voice of the evening show on Rádio Comercial. Through his time at Trumps he developed him into a seminal DJ, who became an influential figure for many now established names on the Portuguese dance music scene.

'I was on the dance floor at Trumps and Pedro came up to me and asked if I wanted to come to their rehearsal room in Benfica because he was forming a new group,' explains Rui Pregal, who admits that the invitation to become a member of Heróis do Mar arose because of the way he looked: 'I was pretty serious about clothes at that time – I remember going to lessons dressed in a three-piece suit from the 1940s one day and the next turning up dressed like a Caribbean pirate with a sword and everything.' The main idea Rui Pregal da Cunha conveys about these early days of Heróis do Mar is of a very united and disciplined band that took decisions together: 'We were very tightknit. We practised eight hours a day. We'd go to the cinema together to see stuff we thought was important – what came out of it belonged to all of us.'[42]

The whole recording process was closely followed by the band's circle of friends, and an excitement started to grow. 'I think the record company realised it had something special on its hands,' says Rui Pregal. 'At the time, its bestseller was the album by Táxi, and ours was

---

40 Rui Miguel Abreu, 'Heróis do Mar: Uma Lenda Por Contar', *Blitz* (September 2008).
41 Rui Pregal da Cunha, in an interview with the author (2008).
42 Ibid.

clearly heading in a different direction, so there was an expectation building.' This expectation was the result of the anticipation of the public and press reactions to what Pregal describes as 'all that mixture–of African, Disco, and pop music and God knows what else'. In other words, there was excitement and expectation, but, as Rui Pregal da Cunha himself confesses, 'there was nothing that could have prepared all those people for what followed'. What followed were months of intense controversy.

In the same month that Heróis do Mar released the maxi-single 'Amor' in 1982, Manuel Reis opened the dance bar Frágil in Rua da Atalaia in Lisbon's Bairro Alto. That was the same year GNR released their debut album, *Independança*, and António Variações brought out his first single, a maxi with the songs 'Povo Que Lavas No Rio' [People who are Washing in the River] and 'Estou Além' [I am Beyond]. This created a situation which allowed Frágil to become a reference point not just in terms of nightlife, but the culture of the capital city and the whole country: Frágil fed off these creative minds, but it also nourished them with ideas and a very special energy.

Since 1998, Manuel Reis has overseen the destiny of Lux, another seminal Lisbon nightspot, and he has recaptured this energy on the website, *fragil.luxfragil.com*, which contains an important photographic and documentary archive; a portal back to the past. On hundreds of photos taken by José Soares and Nica (from 1982 to 1983), Mónica Freitas (with collaboration from Jaime Laranjeira and Carlos Ramos), and Luísa Ferreira (who took photos in the period from 1990 to 1998 on which she 'occasionally collaborated' with José Manuel Ribeiro, Paulo Rascão, and Daniel Rocha, according to the credits on the website) the story is told of a place where musicians, actors, painters, and poets as well as people from the world of politics and from society in general came together in a daily exercise of real democracy; everyone shared the same space and everyone listened to the same music.

Frágil was in a position comparable to where, for example, Rui Vargas started out, who, to this day, remains to be one of the most important DJs in the country and a name closely linked to Lux. Frágil always played the latest club music and witnessed the transition from Disco and New Wave at the dawn of the 1980s to early House music, for which it became one of the hot spots in Lisbon, bringing important DJs like UK-legend DJ Harvey to the country. Frágil has always had a close relationship with music and that is why so many and such a variety of musicians choose to play there; in search of inspiration, of course, but also in search of a place where they fit in naturally. From António Variações, Rui Reininho, and Rui Pregal da Cunha to people like João Peste, Adolfo Luxúria Canibal, and João Paulo Feliciano and their announcement of the arrival of a new generation, Frágil proved to be a magnet for the pacemakers of the country's modern pop scene.

At that time, Portuguese music started to open up to new influences, and this change was introduced by people such as Heróis do Mar and António Variações, another regular at Trumps who was ahead of his time. Variações moved in different circles, a fact which alone spoke of his desire to succeed in music. He had connections to the fashion and art worlds, but also to theatre and different areas of music. At the time he could just as easily enter the offices of the Valentim de Carvalho label, through Carlos Quintas, as immerse himself in the then nascent Punk scene.

In January 1979, Carlos Barroco, of the Galeria Novo Século, held an event at Alunos de Apolo to mark the 25th anniversary of Rock'n' Roll–a legendary night when Faíscas with Pedro Ayres Magalhães literally passed the baton to Xutos E Pontapés, who played their first ever live gig. António Variações was there, cutting hair, contributing to the curious colours of the time that foresaw the coming of a new era in Portuguese music. The Faíscas became Corpo Diplomático, the staging post before Heróis do Mar, the band which, along with Variações, contributed most to changing the course of pop in Portugal.

Someone else who also made it his business to go against the grain of Portugal's traditional conservatism was Nuno Rodrigues, a member of the group Banda do Casaco, who, in 1978, joined the A&R department of Valentim de Carvalho and pursued a parallel career as a music publisher. He remembers:

> When I got my independence and A&R was divided between me and Mário Martins, I started to study the artists we had in the pipeline and one caught my eye – 'António Ribeiro, 30 something, barber by profession'. At the time the record António had made with the conductor Jorge Machado was ready, but it left me cold so I set up a meeting with him to discuss other options.[43]

Nuno Rodrigues, today the head of the Companhia Nacional de Música and responsible for the recent release of two box set anthologies of Banda do Casaco, was at pains to stress that he had nothing against the legendary conductor, Jorge Machado, with whom he worked later, but that he felt that it wasn't the right direction for the artist: 'That single had nothing to do with Rock or pop.' Rodrigues recalls:

> When António turned up to talk to me, I realized that he must have made all of the traffic in Chiado screech to a halt. Which confused me even more: how could a man who looked the way he did be preparing to release a record of Easy Listening music? It just didn't make sense. The musicians around António didn't seem right to me so I chose some others to work with him. On the first single, it was Tó Pinheiro da Silva and Celso de Carvalho, both from Banda do Casaco. And also Ricardo Camacho, before he joined Sétima Legião, played with him.[44]

Rodrigues explains that his independence at Valentim de Carvalho at the time allowed him to go ahead without having to ask for opinions about the choice of music. Amália, who originally sang the aforementioned song 'Povo Que Lavas No Rio', was the label's treasure and protegée, but the producer didn't hesitate when the singer proposed recording the song: 'I had a lot of respect for Amália, but it never entered my head that I was desecrating some sacred repertoire.'

The boom, on the one hand, and on the other the explosion of creativity by bands like GNR and Heróis do Mar, and artists like António Variações, prepared the way for another scene. At the end of the 1980s this scene was creatively led by the band Pop Dell'Arte and their head João Peste. The first master recording by Pop Dell'Arte was made at Musicorde in Lisbon's Campo de Ourique area. From the master, the only song to stand the test of time was 'Turin Welisa Strada',[45] which was included on the compilation *Arriba! Avanti!* from 1991. 'The rest was never released and the master was eventually lost,' admits João Peste. 'The very next day we delivered a copy of the master to Rui Pego who had a Portuguese music programme on the radio. And two or three days after recording it, we were played on the radio for the first time.'[46]

The master from Musicorde saw Pop Dell'Arte qualify for the second edition of the festival Concurso de Música Moderna do Rock Rendez-Vous [competition of modern music of Rock Rendez-Vous] at the legendary club Rock Rendez-Vous (RRV) in 1985. João Peste has clear memories of performing at the historic and now defunct venue: 'I had a few drinks too many before the concert at the RRV. To calm the nerves. I recall having a cream cake for the performance and I remember coughing, but everyone thought it was part of the show. It went okay.' The group ended up winning the prestigious Award for Originality at the event – for

---

43 Rui Miguel Abreu, 'A História Secreta de António Variações', *Blitz* (September 2017).
44 Ibid.
45 No translation possible, made up words, a reference to dada art.
46 João Peste, in an interview with the author (2010).

which the prize was a simple amplifier – and were invited to record a single for the music competition label Dansa do Som. Given the prospect of having to shelve the aforementioned song 'Turin Welisa Strada', Peste declined the invitation and decided to create his own record label. 'I started to think that maybe it wasn't all that hard to create your own label,' says Peste. 'I knew how to book a studio and we met other bands at our concerts. So it didn't seem all that complicated.'

With the help of Maria João Serra, his sister's friend who was studying business at the time, Peste set up the label Ama Romanta. This published recordings by Mão Morta, Mler Ife Dada, Anamar, Telectu, Sei Miguel, and Nuno Canavarro, out of a portfolio of twenty-two bands, from 1986 to 1991. 'I was still a kid, full of energy, and the truth is that I didn't really know what I was getting myself into,' Peste admits. 'But we were a group of friends and everyone helped out. Ama Romanta was a collective project, even though I was the managing partner and face of the company.' The label Ama Romanta, like Fundação Atlântica, marked an Indie generation that followed the boom of the early 1980s, but despite this João Peste doesn't see himself as an agent of change. In fact, he mentions the surprise he felt when 'Querelle', Pop Dell'Arte's debut EP from 1987, was not added to Rádio Renascença's playlist. Then came their debut album, *Free Pop*, nowadays seen as a milestone of Portuguese 1980s pop – which was, once again, hammered by the critics at the time:

> There were some scathing reactions to Free Pop. *But we ended up thinking that it was actually positive, from a marketing perspective. After the Aula Magna concert, (the journalist) Manuel Neto wrote a full-page article for the* Diário Popular *newspaper with a heading in very bold letters that read: 'The Bad, the Ugly and the Awful – The buffoonery paving the way for the Carnival'. Viriato Teles also trashed the record, which he said was an example of how you shouldn't sing, write, produce, design a cover, and so on.*[47]

Nonetheless, João Peste sees *Free Pop* and the later *Sex Symbol* (1995) as the best of Pop Dell'Arte's work, which amounts to very little by normal pop standards – their fifth album of original material, *Contra Mundum*, has only just been released in 2010 – but it consists of important material in terms of originality. 'The aim was to never repeat ourselves,' says Peste. 'We never wanted to rework our last album. There was always a certain continuity of course, but our attitude was always that if you're going to create something, then it has to be new.' Interestingly, from early on, Pop Dell'Arte's music contained echoes of the two major revolutions that would mark the 1990s: Hip-Hop – they recorded with the first signed Portuguese rapper, General D, before he even performed under his own name – and House, both underlining the avant-garde and visionary aspects of João Peste's group.

Hip-Hop and House: the 1990s

The history of Portuguese Hip-Hop has yet to be written, since it is still playing out. Of course, certain aspects go back well over a decade, and these have already been documented. But the underlying driving force motivating the artists, agents, publishers, and revolutionaries behind the success of what has, today, become an inevitable genre, still has to be identified. One thing is for certain, in just twenty years things have changed radically. In 1997 Emanuel Ferreira and António Contador published the book *Ritmo e Poesia* which – unusually written as events were still unfolding[48] – gave an account of the culture's local and external roots. Right at the beginning of the book they identified a series of parameters that are very different from those governing the movement today:

> *Why write a book about Rap? Why write a book about an inconvenient musical genre*

---

47   Ibid.
48   This effort to document an ongoing phenomenon in the country is rare in Portugal.

Bodybuilding theme party at Frágil, Lisbon, 1983, photo: José Soares e Nica

31 de Dezembro de 1986

Invitation for New Years Eve at Frágil, Lisbon, 1986

New Years Eve, mask party, Lux Frágil, Lisbon, 2004, photo: Luisa Ferreira

Fashion designer Filipe Faísca at Lux Frágil, Lisbon, 2002, photo: Luísa Ferreira

Actress Anamar, Frágil, Lisbon, 1984, photo: Mónica Freitas

navigating through the troubled waters of political incorrectness? What makes Rap, from a social and media perspective, an opaque and consequently low-profile genre within the musical panorama? What is so particular about Rap lyrics that the only thing people discuss about them is how controversial they are? Why does it seem to have such a linear rhythm and no melody? How do you define a rapper and what type of qualities do they have that makes them stand out unambiguously from any other type of artist/musician?[49]

Some of these questions raised in 1997 still make sense today. But others have definitively become redundant over time, and they show how innocent this genre was in Portugal back then. Some twenty years ago, rappers were drawn to Hip-Hop out of militancy and love, knowing that not even the music papers would notice them. Today, rappers can aspire to write soundtracks for soap operas, be nominated for MTV awards and receive a barrage of interviews in the music press. Much has changed. Returning to *Ritmo e Poesia*:

> Miratejo is to Rap in Portugal what the Bronx is to Rap in the US. In sum, it is a Mecca for Portuguese aesthetes of rhythm & poetry in this, its early phase. It is a copy of its older American brother in search of a clearer realisation that it will go through a decisive Black English phase. American rappers find a receptive audience for their message here, especially given that these potential MCs can clearly see the similarities between life in the South Bronx and the cities on the south bank of the Tagus. The lack of resources is key to the low profile of what is said in loud voices, but it is not enough of a barrier to stop people speaking out. In fact, the opposite is true. The use of beat-boxing and other improvised techniques is dictating the current crucial development of the grassroots, the key backbone to Rap anywhere. Wherever it is, Rap begins underground. Portugal is no exception.[50]

It certainly isn't. The culture's origins in Portugal are profoundly linked to the towns on the south bank of the Tagus river or in Portuguese: Tejo river – towns which are the Portuguese equivalent to the Bronx. Due to the in-flows of migrants, since at least the 1980s, enabled this revolutionary US culture to reach Portuguese shores and the African communities there. But this was not the only channel. In the US there is a well-established Cape Verdean community in Boston as well as Portuguese communities in Newark and in Paris, France. These communities were important because it was through them that cassettes with recordings of radio programmes, that focused on Hip-Hop, began to arrive in Portugal. These cassettes were the first main conduit for the spread of this virus.

We have to recall the breakdance phenomenon in the 1980s, which spread around the world via Hollywood movies like *Beat Street*. The Portuguese also fell for these films, and there was a string of breakdance crews throughout the country in the 1980s, dancing to Hip-Hop music. But it was by means of the previously mentioned cassettes that Rap really started to emerge. In the early 1990s, the seeds had been sown for a movement whose form would take shape with the release of General D's debut EP 'PortuKKKal e um Erro' [PortuKKKal is a Mistake] in 1994, and the compilation *Rapública*. The latter especially showcased many of the movement's frontrunners who are still active today, among them Boss AC, Melo D, and D-Mars, not to mention Black Company, who had the first Portuguese Hip-Hop mega success with their song and compilation contribution 'Nadar'. Vítor Belanciano[51] wrote, in the *Público* newspaper in 2000, about the then still 'nascent' Portuguese Hip-Hop scene:

> The release of the compilation Rapública in 1994 seemed to suggest that Portugal had woken up to the Hip-Hop sensation. But,

---

49 António Concorda Contador and Emanuel Ferreira, *Ritmo e Poesia – Os Caminhos do Rap* (Lisbon: Assírio & Alvim, 1997), 6.
50 Ibid., 8.
51 To learn more about the places and audiences of Lisbon's music scenes please see Vítor Belanciano's essay in this book.

despite records in recent years by Da Weasel, Mind da Gap, Black Company, Boss AC, Ithaka and General D – all with, not always readily assumed, links to the genre – the feeling one gets is that Hip-Hop's profile at that time was somewhat extemporaneous after all.... A certain naivety by some of the people involved, the lack of tradition in Portugal of listening to 'black music', the fact no small labels existed which could develop the genre, and the near inexistence of a musical circuit comprising DJs and record shops are some of the possible explanations why Hip-Hop never really took off in Portugal. However, in recent years, the scenario has changed.[52]

In fact, after Black Company's success, which led to the group releasing their debut album *Geração Rasca* in 1995, Hip-Hop almost disappeared back into the underground. This going underground of Portuguese Hip-Hop was also a reaction to the almost mythical attention given to the *Rapública* generation. The only exception was the work of the Nortesul label in the second half of the 1990s. This label released tracks by Mind Da Gap and Boss AC, as well as Cool Hipnoise (formed by Melo D after Family) and Ithaka (a project by the US rapper Darin Pappas). These projects were low profile, but everything else dwelled below the radar.

The second half of the 1990s was an era of mixtapes by DJs like Bomberjack, Assassino, and Kronic and long freestyles, which later gained exposure on the Marginal radio station on the *Hip-Hop Don't Stop* programme. Then, most importantly, there was the work of José Mariño, later director of Antena 3, who unified this culture nationwide on the radio show *Rapto*. This is where, for example, the first tracks by Mind Da Gap and by all the other future artists of this movement were played. With its own circuit of shows and mixtape distribution, the Hip-Hop movement grew in Portugal. In 1999, another crucial step was taken in its development: the release of the first albums by the rapper Sam the Kid, *Entre(tanto)*,[53] as well as the crew Filhos de um Deus Menor's [Sons of a Lesser God] *A Longa Caminhada* [The Long Walk], and Micro's *Microestática*. These three records proved to the movement that there was creative space to explore the album format, a more contemplative format than that of the mixtape freestyles and gave rise to the movement's second phase at the turn of the century.

Though established, the genre didn't take Lisbon's nightclubs by storm. Most of the memories of the late 1990s are of the mythical nights at the club Trópico headed by artists like Pacman from Da Weasel, or sporadic programmes at venues like Johnny Guitar, a club that filled the void after Rock Rendez-Vous disappeared and which was much more Rock oriented. Hip-Hop punctuated the sets of DJs in Lisbon's Bairro Alto area at clubs like Frágil, Três Pastorinhos, and Sudoeste – but always as a sort of warm up to the main event: House music.

—

The DJ, record seller, musician, and activist Tó 'DJ Vibe' Pereira remembers the first steps in an intricate tapestry of clubs, DJs, labels, parties, and raves that marked the introduction of contemporary club culture to Lisbon and the rest of the country. Tó Pereira began by playing Rock at clubs in the Avenida 24 de Julho before the House sound, exported from Chicago, first took over Britain, then Ibiza, and finally many other parts of Europe and the world. Besides Tó Pereira, there was another activist who had a huge influence on the success of House music in Portugal: António Cunha, co-founder of the influential label Kaos Records at the beginning of the 1990s. About him and his musical publishing work, Vítor Belanciano wrote the following at the time of his premature death in 2012:

The origins of his actions have to be put into the context of the Acid-House movement

---

[52] Vítor Belanciano, 'O Hip-Hop Está No Ar', *Público* (21 January 2000).

[53] A play on words, it can mean 'meanwhile' or 'among so much'.

that began in Britain at the end of the 1980s. If Punk was all rage and provocation, Acid-House was about community and hedonism. The children of the sixties generation had learnt from the illusions of their parents. They didn't want to fight for vague future ideas. They wanted to realize their idea of happiness in the present, even if they had to hold illegal parties in places in the heyday of raves. Suddenly, Britain and, by extension, Europe adopted the rhythms of House music and sought new ways to experience them. It was all so explosive that it was bound to die out fast. In 1992, the British government conveyed the idea that there was a direct correlation between drug use and dance music, almost completely shutting down the movement, which, from that point onwards, began to have greater impact in the rest of Europe. And that's what happened in Portugal.[54]

Lisbon's first House parties started to occur around 1991, in abandoned warehouses in the Xabregas area, then still far from the energy that is emitted today. At the time, a culture started to form between few clubs on the Avenida 24 de Julho and in the Bairro Alto area, such as Kremlin and Frágil, as well as Bimotor dos Restauradores, the record shop where Tó Pereira worked. It was here that Cunha and Tó Pereira, the future DJ Vibe, first met. Rui da Silva (future 'Doctor J') also appeared on the scene at this downtown venue. Belanciano wrote:

> Vibe was already the best-known DJ in Portugal. He had been part of (the alternative electronic band) LX-90 and was leaving a legacy as a DJ at places all over Lisbon, like Plateau, Alcântara-Mar, and, in particular, Kremlin, throughout the 1990s. Rui da Silva, after several years as a sound engineer at the radio station TSF, started working full time in music production with DJ Vibe, forming the Underground Sound Of Lisbon. With Cunha, they opened Kaos in 1992 that would become the first Portuguese label focusing on electronic dance music.[55]

The movement that emerged out of these rave parties animated by this new sound caught the world's attention. In 1993, the British magazine *Muzik* printed an issue about the Portuguese music scene with a cover and an article that left no doubt: 'A New Paradise Called Portugal'. International interest was largely spurred by the impact of 'So Get Up', a track by the Underground Sound of Lisbon included on the inaugural Kaos-EP 'Chapter One' with vocals by Darin Pappas. This Californian rapper and poet living in Portugal would later set up Ithaka – a Hip-Hop project that released an album on the Nortesul label which became a staple of the sets of several open-minded international DJs such as Junior Vasquez and Danny Tenaglia.

The second half of the 1990s was the first time that the DJ cabins in Lisbon and the rest of the country were truly synchronised with what was going on throughout the rest of the world. The beat was the same and, after António Cunha's untimely disappearance, the movement was led, as Vítor Belanciano pointed out in the pages of the *Público* in 2012, by 'a posse of established DJs (Vibe, Tó Ricciardi, Rui Vargas, Luís Leite, DJ Jiggy, Mário Roque, XL Garcia), projects (Urban Dreams, Kult Of Krameria, Paul Jays, Alex Fx, J. Daniel), companies (Kaos, X-Club), and labels (I Kaos, Warning Inc, Question Of Time, and Squeeze)'.[56]

Hip-Hop's breakthrough and African Lisbon: the new millennium

Portuguese Hip-Hop quickly grasped that there was a void to be filled, as a new decade and century dawned. More gigs, more frequent mixtape releases, and the whole atmosphere surrounding the movement suggested that this was going to be the genre's decade. With a more attuned media, there was an opportunity to step up. The first to do so seriously was the

---

54 Vítor Belanciano, 'António Cunha e o Paraíso da Dança em Portugal', *Público* (19 January 2012).
55 Ibid.
56 Belanciano, 'António Cunha', (see n. 54).

rapper Chullage in 2001, with the release of his debut album of *Rapresálias… Sangue, Lágrimas, Suor* [Raprisals… Blood, Tears and Sweat] on the first national Hip-Hop label: Lisafonia. This was the first label set up by the Hip-Hop industry for the Hip-Hop industry – and also the first to recognise the hurdles it would have to face. Chullage explained the problems of creating music in Portugal at the time:

> First, people start by saying you can't make a Hip-Hop album, or they say nobody's going to listen to it. Then you have to get a lot of money together to use a studio, money which you don't have. You have to get it from all over the place and always begrudgingly because nobody really believes you're going to manage to make a Hip-Hop album. And there's one really bad thing: the sound technicians never treat Hip-Hop with respect. As far as they're concerned, a Hip-Hop song always sounds fine and they don't put as much effort into it as they do for something they like. That's really bad. Then there's the problem with the labels: they don't really promote an album and it's difficult to get it into the shops. With Hip-Hop, you have to fight in a way that you don't with other types of music.[57]

Other publishers quickly followed Lisafonia such as Loop:Recordings (opened in 2001) and the Kombate collective (2002). Other labels, like Matarroa (2003), also came to prominence in this decade.

On the occasion of his then new album, in 2003, the rapper Boss AC still complained about the public's lack of interest: 'You can sense it right through the album. It's a disillusionment at every level, with the press, radio, the labels, concerts, venues … It's really hard to survive by doing what you enjoy when things are like this.'[58] But in 2006, the discourse changed. AC's persistence attained the success his talent had deserved for a long time and saw Portuguese Hip-Hop finally reach the top of the charts. The years from about 2010 onwards, have been the most important and dynamic in the short history of Portuguese Hip-Hop. These have been the years of more frequent record releases that have finally broken down the barriers as far as the media are concerned. They have seen artists like Sam the Kid and Boss AC perform on the main stages of the country's summer music festivals. They have seen Hip-Hop become mainstream. But success has not gone to the head of any of the artists, who have never forgotten where they come from.

It would have been unthinkable a few years ago, that there would be several Hip-Hop-centred events at the same time on the same night in venues like Musicbox, Titanic Sur Mer, Lux, Park, or the newly opened Time Out venue. This reflects the growth of the genre through the power of the social networks that award the creativity of these artists with millions of views on streaming platforms. It is near impossible in Lisbon to go out today and not hear rappers like ProfJam, Holly Hood, Sam The Kid, Mundo Segundo, or Piruka. The line-up at Lisbon's music festivals like Super Bock Super Rock, Lisboa Dance Festival, Nos Alive, and Sol da Caparica also echo this.

Today there is also a new important set of coordinates on the contemporary musical map of Lisbon as the city now has its own (electronic) beat. This beat started to emerge midway through the last decade with the band Buraka Som Sistema and the discovery of an African Lisbon. Since the decolonisation in 1975 this social sphere had been bubbling below the surface with secret parties in the housing estates at the city's periphery. A decade ago, Buraka's explosive gigs at tiny clubs in Lisbon's pre-gentrified Santos era, announced a grassroots movement that rapidly took hold. When they presented their music as 'progressive Kuduro',[59] the reaction of many people was as strong as if they had described themselves as 'Afro-Xula'.[60] But in a city before the days of the neo-Kuduro

---

57 Chullage, an interview with the author (2002).
58 Boss AC, an interview with the author (2003).
59 For more about Kuduro music and other music from Luanda/Angola please see Ângela Mingas' and Marissa J. Moorman's essays in this book.
60 Xula is a traditional dance from Portugal, so Afro-Xula is a fusion.

label Príncipe Discos and DJ Marfox, before the Portuguese-Angolan producer Batida, and before 'internet sensations' like Deejay Telio, the truth is that Buraka already represented the real 'underground sound of Lisbon'.

Let me explain. What Buraka offered to the modern world was a perspective. More interesting than producing electronic music in well-established Lisbon areas like Bairro Alto, Damaia, Almada, or Sacavém, and making a strenuous effort to eliminate the physical and conceptual boundaries separating the city from New York, Detroit, London, or Berlin – and therefore actually erasing any characteristics that set us apart. What band members Lil John/Branko, Blaya, Conductor, Kalaf, and DJ Riot managed to do was to take these differences and create something original based on what was common. The sound of the CD-Rs sold in Praça de Espanha, the beat emanating from the cars in endless traffic jams on the motorway IC19, the rhythms that made the little speakers jump on the computers which conjured up the revolution from disadvantaged neighbourhoods from Pontinha to Quinta do Mocho, from Arrentela to Cova da Moura, and from Rio de Mouro to Buraka after which the band named itself.

Buraka Som Sistema has managed to generate outside interest in this vision. They presented another Portugal to the world, other than Fado and similar clichés, which sparked an interest in Lisbon among the most influential avant-garde urban music magazines – and along the way even confirmed Kalaf as a distinct intellectual voice and Lil John/Branko as a true 'globetrotting' producer able to move in the same circles as the Diplos of this world. Their label Enchufada opened doors, altered perceptions, created opportunities, and initiated dialogues with other places far from the centre.

One result is Globaile, the festival event the band created in 2016 on the Lisbon City Council's invitation. Another result is this new and vibrant Lisbon that has turned the city periphery into the new centre and has broken down barriers and resistance: Lisbon as a new Lisbon – and not a new Barcelona, London, or Berlin. Lisbon as a place of integration and dialogue, as an advanced laboratory of new social dynamics. Lisbon as a stage for new heroes, new accents, new rhythms. Lisbon as a future and no longer just as a glorious past. This is the Lisbon that Buraka today bequeaths the world.

The events organised by the young label Principe Discos are the ultimate consequence of the birth of this new Lisbon, which, just like the US that succumbed decades ago to the sound of its inner cities, has also learnt to dance to the sound of its own beat. Lisbon's equivalents to these inner cities lie at its periphery, which has generated an electronic whisper that has also carried the new identities of the city beyond Portugal's borders. To a certain extent, the city's mayor, Fernando Medina, has acknowledged this by permitting Buraka Som Sistema to end their farewell tour in the city where they grew up with a concert in the Gardens of the Tower of Belém.[61] Interestingly, the council's acknowledgment does not extend to Lisbon's electronic music community.

The itinerant Boiler Room, a global electronic music broadcasting platform which hosts and shares online electronic music shows, returned to Lisbon for a show in the summer of 2016. Its line-up was curated by Buraka Som Sistema, who selected the Brazilian DJ Marky and the Peruvian band Dengue Dengue Dengue, as well as Batida, DJ Nervoso, DJ Firmeza, DJ Lilocox, and DJ Maboku from Portugal. As soon as the line-up was announced, the social networks exploded with criticism: 'What the hell kind of a line-up is that?'; 'That doesn't represent the Lisbon sound'; 'This isn't Techno or anything else', It was undisguised racism in many of the comments and an inability to recognise that it is not by seeking to copy the sound of London and Berlin that Lisbon will make its mark, but rather by identifying and developing

---

61 This is the same Tower of Belém where 'explorers' set off to the world several centuries ago.

its own unique DNA – genuinely created at home but with the obvious potential for global explosion. First Buraka and Enchufada and then Príncipe have managed to do so, with great talent.

Thirty years ago, people imagined what would happen if the German electronic band Kraftwerk and the US Funk band Parliament were stuck in an elevator together with only a synthesizer to make noise. What followed was the Techno explosion with direct links from the music's birthplace, Detroit, to all over the world – nowadays resulting in official recognition of this once underground music by the Detroit city council. Perhaps, a few years from now, Lisbon, the city of Fado and Rock and Rap, will, like Detroit, also get its own Rhythm Week with an official pronouncement in City Hall and civic honours for Branko and Kalaf, Conductor, Riot, Blaya and Marfox, Batida and DJ Nervoso, and all those who deserve it. Only time will tell.

Bibliography

Abreu, Rui Miguel, 'Rock Em Portugal Nos Anos 70: Uma História Quase Secreta', in: *Blitz* (January 2007).
Abreu, Rui Miguel, '1955–1969: Quando a febre em Portugal Era o Yé-Yé', in: *Blitz* (July 2008).
Abreu, Rui Miguel, 'Heróis do Mar: Uma Lenda Por Contar', in: *Blitz* (September 2008).
Abreu, Rui Miguel, 'Rui Veloso, 35 Anos de Carreira: Como Tudo Começou', in: *Blitz* (May 2010).
Abreu, Rui Miguel, 'Paulo de Carvalho: Uma Voz Única', in: *Blitz* (April 2011).
Abreu, Rui Miguel, 'A História Secreta de António Variações', in: *Blitz* (September 2017).
Belanciano, Vítor, 'O Hip-Hop Está No Ar', in: *Público* (21 January 2000).
Belanciano, Vítor, 'António Cunha e o Paraíso da Dança em Portugal', in: *Público* (19 January 2012).
Contador, António Concorda and Ferreira, Emanuel, *Ritmo e Poesia – Os Caminhos do Rap* (Lisbon: Assírio & Alvim, 1997).
Duarte, António, *A Arte Eléctrica de Ser Português: 25 Anos de Rock'n Portugal* (Lisbon: Livraria Bertrand, 1984).
Veloso, Rui and Mesquita, Ana, *Os Vês Pelos Bês* (Cascais: Prime Books Sociedade Editorial, 2006).

Time Capsule Lisbon – Revolution, Hangovers, Hedonism

Vítor Belanciano

Good conversation has creative possibilities, as artist and dilettante, Andy Warhol once said. Good conversation not only needs people who are fully capable of producing it, but also an environment; a place. Places for good conversations that have become part of urban history have almost always followed ideals of leisure and cultural production linked to pleasure. Most of these places have attained symbolic meaning as they have become more than simply localities where people would meet up to talk, dance, and communicate. They have become icons. They have acted as incubators of ideas by reflecting their time and helping to transform it. People, concepts, ideas, fashion, art, images, or music have all interacted with each other or collided between the walls of these places, pushing for new dynamics and creating new possibilities in one cultural flux, night after night. In some places this only happened for a few nights, in others for years, or even decades.

Pleasure is often (mis)understood as frivolous and profane. So, places of socialisation through pleasure must be careful with regards to established norms. The rules are simple: the audience can have fun, but within certain limits. In these venues, most of the times, the most superficial debates and the deepest discussions of life went hand in hand. But why do we feel attracted to these places? Each and everyone has their own story. Some are impelled to escape the mundane. Others look for new social or sensual experiences. Others have even found an ideal for a different urban life here. But the story of each one of those places is also a chronicle of the social. A universe of hedonistic sharing that interrogates and questions many of the current social norms of the respective city and time.

If we understand a nightclub as a place where people meet, socialise, and dance while listening to music, it becomes hard to define where and when this phenomenon may have started. Places according to this definition have practically existed since the beginning of human culture. The Greek gods for example certainly understood a thing or two about the importance of escapism. But club culture as we perceive it today, in a narrower sense, might be said to have had its genesis in the 1920s, its germination actually began 1950s' youth culture, and it first really culminated in the 1960s.

The 1960s: Yé-yé on the Avenidas Novas

In Lisbon, most cultural movements and bohemian dynamics have always been related to the life of their respective neighbourhoods. The concept of neighbourhood itself, that is, as an urban ensemble where buildings are made according to a single project, became popular in Lisbon during the Industrial Revolution. But even before that, housing was already being built following a certain order with small urban clusters within the city, for example, in the historical neighbourhoods Alfama, Bairro Alto, or Bica. But in the 1960s, the city's nightlife was essentially happening uptown, in the so-called 'Avenidas Novas' [New Avenues], that had been part of an urban expansion project. Those years were marked by the dictator António de Oliveira Salazar's fascist regime. Lisbon was stuck in a time capsule and separated from the rest of the world. In the US and the rest of Europe, youth culture and Rock'n'Roll were thriving. But they came to Portugal from remote places and very belatedly – also because the colonial war made many young people go to battlefields in Africa where they were unable to directly follow these developments.

The pioneers of Rock music in Lisbon were children from wealthy families that could travel abroad and buy records and instruments. Rock started to be played at balls, college parties, hotel bars, and mostly in the now gone Monumental movie theatre in the Saldanha district. It was at sessions like The Great Contest of Yé-yé,[1] where Portuguese bands would present instrumental versions of songs by The Beatles, The Rolling Stones, Kinks, or The Shadows.

Groups like Os Conchas, Conjunto Mistério, Os Ekos, Quarteto 1111, or Sheiks recorded music that showed a hint of international youth culture, and Victor Gomes E Os Gatos Negros even displayed a little Rock'n' Roll boldness onstage. Young people were having fun, while intellectuals were plotting against the old regime. They would conspire it at poet Natália Correia's house, in Lisbon's Marquês de Pombal district, during poetry reading sessions that turned into evening gatherings with music in the background. This continued until Natália opened the bar O Botequim in the Graça neighbourhood in 1971.

The intellectuals also plotted in cafés with coffees, cigarettes, and endless conversations in informal meetings. Those were the places after work, through the night, or on weekends, where Lisbon's 1960s were settling. It was mainly men, under clouds of smoke, with suits and skinny ties. The Brasileira and Leitaria Garrett in Chiado, as well as the Martinho da Arcada in Rossio were the usual spots, but they were losing their prominence to cafés in the aforementioned 'New Avenues'. In the café Bocage on Avenida da República or in the Monte Carlo in Saldanha, people from film and theatre, intellectuals, and students from college protest movements would gather through the night. But it was essentially in Vá-Vá on the Avenida de Roma, where it was all happening. It was there

[1] 'Yé-yé' is a Portuguese term for early Beat and Rock'n'Roll music. To learn more about the club and dance music of Lisbon please see Rui Miguel Abreu's essay in this book.

that a new creative generation was thinking, discussing, dating, and creating a political opposition – thus projecting a new city.

At the same time, the first gay bars in the city were opening, like Antiquário in Campo de Ourique, Bar Z near the Glória elevator, or Bric-a-Bar in Príncipe Real. There were other possibilities for people not only interested in drinking but dancing, like Porão da Nau in Saldanha, which opened in 1965. In its first year, its dark navy-decor cellar welcomed superstars like Ella Fitzgerald and Duke Ellington, with theatre artists, journalists, or radio and advertising people in the crowd. Young people from wealthier and more select surroundings would prefer the Caruncho in Lumiar, where they could see, on some nights, live acts like Sheiks, while more bohemian people would go to Hot Clube in Praça da Alegria and listen to Jazz on more eventful nights, or to Ritz Clube nearby in Rua da Glória.

In 1967, the artist Francisco Relógio opened O Relógio in the Lapa neighbourhood, an elitist discotheque that would later become the famous Stone's disco in 1970. A couple of years before this transformation, in 1968, the Ad-Lib opened in Rua Barata Salgueiro on the seventh floor. For more exclusive nights there would only be Van Gogo in Cascais, half an hour's drive from Lisbon, where exiled European aristocrats and the country's most powerful families would gather.

Then came 27 July 1970, an important mark in the history for Portugal's future. On this day the old autocrat Salazar died at eighty-one years. The country was about to change.

The 1970s: revolution, hangover, and disco hedonism

On 25 April 1974 a military coup overthrew the government by Marcelo Caetano, who had succeeded Salazar. Portugal went through a phase of complete political and social commotion. During this transition Portuguese people were slowly becoming aware of what was happening throughout the rest of the world. Slowly. For example, in the UK during the second half of the 1970s, Punk was on the cover of all newspapers. But in post-April-25 Portugal, the music and movement were practically unheard of. Instead, political protest singers like José Afonso, José Mário Branco, and Sérgio Godinho, who had been banned during the decades of the dictatorship, would now reign, along with local cover bands. Information on what happened beyond the borders was almost completely unavailable – and records were hard to attain. The only way to get them was to ask people who were traveling to buy them.

Still, some sheltered places escaped these circumstances. With the rise of democracy, the impulse of wanting to live everything at once became even bigger. Discussing ideas would bring constant intellectual confrontation between young people in the most diverse places, rapidly transforming these places into live concert venues. That was the case, for instance, with many high school gymnasiums.

Generally, unlike working class youth cultures in the UK, in Portugal wealthier and well-educated young people were those who were most interested in international trends. This was understood as a desire for emancipation while, at the same time, stepping away from a scene that was dominated by Portuguese popular music. The minority of people were aware of what was happening in the world, like musicians Pedro Ayres Magalhães and Paulo Pedro Gonçalves, who came from middle-high class bourgeoisie and neighbourhoods like Alvalade. In 1977, they founded the Faíscas, one of the first Portuguese Punk groups. Two years later, they started Corpo Diplomático, and in the 1980s they rose to fame with Heróis do Mar. Later, in 1985, Ayres Magalhães would form the band Madredeus.

Next to their contemporaries, Minas E Armadilhas and Aqui d'El Rock, Faíscas were the closest thing to Punk that was happening in Portugal at the time. They were willing to make a difference. The band started to organise live concerts outside the main circuit, eventually creating their own: at Brown's disco, at places like the National Society of Fine Arts, or during Saturday matinees at Alunos d'Apolo philharmonic society – thus inspiring the birth of other groups like Zé Pedro's Xutos & Pontapés, who were connected to the Faíscas.

After the revolution, at the end of the 1970s, a shock-induced hangover became manifest in Lisbon and, at the same time, a sense of desperation over the lack of swiftness in the dreams of change becoming reality. Still, in some places, small bands could invent their own utopias. In this context, parties in private homes or garages became more important and were becoming an alternative to official places like Stone's. Younger generations that were more connected to international trends were exchanging experiences in these informal environments. It was a necessity that partly came from a contingency, as most places for a night out (even more popular ones like Stone's or Bananas, with only few exceptions like Trumps in Príncipe Real) would overlook the most exciting things that were happening in the world. For those who longed to escape apathy, the solution was to create small casual places where one could delve into a particular universe.

All this happened with a hedonist attitude that was an echo of the 'Disco' trend happening almost everywhere on the planet back then. While the 1960s sub-cultures were primarily based on a noisy and dramatic 'no', Disco culture would unleash a euphoric 'yes'. No aggressive positions towards the world could be found. Instead, Disco people tried to ignore reality and build their own cosmos. God, the State, work, and family would be ignored – but unlike Punk there was no nihilism involved, only an attempt to create a space of happiness. Thus, several minorities and social groups built their own universes in informal places with almost no connections to the hostile world outside.

The 1980s: the rise of Bairro Alto and the birth of Frágil

In a way, the attempt to create a place of well-being beyond existing norms would prompt the transformation of Bairro Alto [The high district] into Lisbon's cultivated new shelter for the bohemian. A new generation in fashion, architecture, design, art, film, music, literature, and journalism was in the starting blocks. But they did not have a place that would allow for a network of communication and where they could meet informally. Bairro Alto became that place. And in a way, contemporary Portugal was born there. The generation that holds today's power and is influential in many areas, from arts to politics, met in that neighbourhood of narrow streets, secular houses, and small traditional stores and restaurants.

The neighbourhood Bairro Alto was built between the end of the fifteenth century and the beginning of the sixteenth century as an orthogonal grid. Until the middle of the twentieth century, it was the location of the country's biggest newspapers and printing offices, as well as sailors' taverns and ill-famed brothels. In the 1960s and 1970s, the Bairro Alto was already a place of meetings and social gatherings, but what happened in the 1980s was something new. The country had gotten rid of its dictatorship half a dozen years ago and wanted to open up to modernity. The neighbourhood was turning into the place where everyone would come and meet. Velvet sofas, glittering mirrors, and dubious music prevailed. The hegemonic model from the 1970s had been Stone's in Lapa, and Bananas in Alcântara. But in 1982, at the heart of Bairro Alto, Frágil was born, and everything changed.

For most people of the late 1970s and early 1980s, a night out meant nothing more than going out and having some drinks. But for others, this practise was starting to carry a new and different meaning, with the birth of new groups, social configurations, culture, and ideas. Culture was seen as something that was created by practising it and that could be built through cultural spaces of identity. In the 1980s, going to Frágil required making a choice and taking a stand. It was about having a model for a city, a lifestyle, patterns of taste, and the way one felt entering the venue. Some people would accept this. Others wanted to be part of it but were not accepted. Many would reject it.

Frágil's fame was composed of many elements. It was a meeting place for new creative agents. It became notorious for barring entrance to many people, with its bouncers even making their way into the city's hall of fame. It became known for its musical selection that followed the emerging genres of the time like Post-Punk, House, or Hip-Hop. It regularly changed décor. Behind all of this was architect Manuel Reis, greeting regular clients with a kind gesture almost every night.

For many, the Frágil was an elitist place, a network of close relations between groups of people that knew each other. Ultimately, Frágil became a utopia of being among peers. It was the most talked about place. But its fame was only possible thanks to other important nightclubs that were settling around it, such as Três Pastorinhos, Café Concerto, Artis, Nova, Keops, Ocarina, and Rockhouse (later Juke Box), turning an area of the city that was, until then, seen as marginal, into one of its focal points.

In Bairro Alto, Fado houses now existed next to nightclubs with contemporary design. It was as if tradition and innovation did not come in absolute forms and had to interact, thus reconstructing the city's identity map. This map was now changing. Bairro Alto became the most eloquent example of how a forgotten area of the city could renew itself with a bohemian environment made of different cultural consumption patterns. During the day, clothing and record stores, cafés, art galleries, and restaurants created a dynamic on the streets. At night, taverns, restaurants, and bars were filling up with people. Black clothes, antique trench coats, spiked hair and a carefully absent posture were dominant.

The city's artists would go down the streets arm in arm, walking through the popular Lisbon from Cais do Sodré and Mercado da Ribeira. They would eat, discuss projects, and party until morning. There was a feeling that one was participating in a new dynamic. The area's corridors and inner courtyards would fill up, and people would dance to the sounds of Talking Heads, De La Soul, Prince, and music from African countries. Music offered a place of belonging, an alternative way of reflecting and experimenting with the world. So, Portuguese groups such as Sétima Legião, Pop Dell'Arte, Mler Ife Dada, URB, Croix Sainte, Anamar, and Ocaso Épico were born, joining the ranks of Xutos & Pontapés, Rádio Macau, and António Variações.

It was also the time when Portuguese Rock music was established. In a short period of time, Rock Rendez-Vous in Rua da Beneficiência in the Rego neighbourhood turned into a cult live venue where newly emerging act would play. By the time it opened, in December 1980, it was the only Lisbon venue for modern Portuguese music, producing live concerts and scouting talent. In the ten years of its existence it held six important music contests. Practically every Portuguese Rock group has played there, as well as foreign groups like Killing Joke, Teardrop Explodes, Chameleons, and The Danse Society.

Suddenly, in the first half of the 1980s, Portugal seemed to be less isolated. The Clash were playing in Pavilhão Dramático de Cascais, half an hour's drive from Lisbon. One could go to see Siouxsie & The Banshees or Echo & The Bunnymen in Pavilhão do Restelo or Durutti Column in Aula Magna. At the Superior School of Fine Arts in Chiado or at the António Arroio School in Alameda, Portuguese bands were evolving, influenced by British and US Post-Punk and New Wave. It was an era that gave birth to inspiring characters, idea producers, and people who were able to build their own utopias, acting as catalysts and contributing, in their own way, to change the world around them.

Singer, António Variações, was an influential figure in the late 1970s and early 1980s, until his death in 1984. When he walked up the streets, necks would turn to catch a glimpse of a long-bearded man wearing extravagant clothes in a city of suits and ties. He did not dress himself that way in order to provoke. It was a statement. He was genuine. Variações is still seen as one of the country's best musicians, with a unique voice that transcends generations and genres. In Portugal, he was one of the first people to make dance music when there was still no purpose for it.

Zé da Guiné, from Guinea-Bissau, who had come to Lisbon in the second half of the 1970s, was another one of those creative people. One would see him walking the streets of Chiado and Bairro Alto; tall and elegant, with a loose walk, warmly greeting those who'd pass him by, actors, artists, musicians, mundane people, as well as also elderly people or idlers. He seemed to know everyone as he smiled, with his hat or cap on, wearing a suit and an impeccable pair of creased pants from Feira da Ladra or Madame Bettencourt's house, where he would buy second-hand clothes. Opening the club Souk at the end of the 1970s, Zé da Guiné was one of the first people to go into Bairro Alto's real territory, the prostitute houses and ill-famed taverns. He then embarked on a new project called Rock House (later Juke Box) and helped the area's regeneration. But the most striking project Zé da Guiné was committed to was Noites Longas, in Largo do Conde de Barão in the Santos area. This venue was located in a decadent yet charming small palace from the seventeenth century that would later house the club B. Leza. The building is now abandoned.

Bairro Alto was a place of diversity. People from different origins, colours, and social situations would party together. Many people from ex-Portuguese colonies influenced by Zé da Guiné would go there, also because clients from other centres of Lisbon's African nightlife, like the disco A Lontra, would end up there. In that sense, Noites Longas was one of the most successful and unique democratic experiences of Lisbon's nightlife.

The 1990s: a new industry and a new nightlife zone

When electronic dance music came to Europe at the end of the 1980s, it opened up new ways for artistic and cultural movements. In 1987, the Acid-House revolution started in Ibiza and the UK. In Portugal new electronic music projects appeared like Armando 'Balla' Teixeira's Ik Mux and Golpe de Estado. The syncretism between electronic and Rock music would give birth to projects like LX-90 or Repórter Estrábico. In 1992, political powers in the UK would imply that there was a direct correlation between the use of addictive substances and electronic dance music, thus shutting down almost all 'rave' events. This would have an impact on the rest of Europe.

In Lisbon, like the rest of the country, this kind of event had its heyday in the middle of the 1990s, usually taking place in abandoned locations. Refusing a secretive approach, they were publicised with advertisements, sponsors, and even supported by official entities, who hoped that this phenomenon would attract tourists. It was a liberating but also alienating period. Portugal had joined the European Union in 1986, and investments made with EU funding would give the impression – mostly an illusion, as one would later understand – that this was the most adequate way of development. There was a feeling of optimism that would favour new activities.

For many of those who would had exclusively listened to Rock music, the discovery of electronic dance music's spirit – more than its sound – would begin here. No one was afraid to celebrate in a huge abandoned barrack and to show off a confident mood, as if they were staying at a friend's place. In 1991, the first parties to bear some resemblance to the famous English 'raves' were happening in Xabregas in Eastern Lisbon. These parties captured some of that 'rave' spirit, even though they were essentially different from what happened in the UK. After Bairro Alto finally went to sleep each night, thousands of people would go to Xabregas, which might have been known to them through word of mouth or by flyers that had been handed to them in the street on the same day.

New records labels sprang up like Warning Inc. or Question of Time. One of the most important labels was Kaos. Its founders, in 1992, were the charismatic House and Techno DJs and producers António Cunha, DJ Vibe, and Rui da Silva. One year after its foundation Kaos released the debut EP 'Chapter One' by the project Underground Sound of Lisbon (comprised of DJ Vibe and Rui da Silva) with the hit song 'So Get Up', featuring the voice of US poet and singer Darin 'Korvonjuowrong' Pappas. Months later, this record reached the hand of the New York star, DJ Junior Vasquez, and was thereafter reissued for the international market by the US record label Tribal, prompting remixes by Vasquez and Danny Tenaglia. In a short period of time, Underground Sound of Lisbon would sell more than 20,000 copies and reach the number one spot in dance charts on both sides of the Atlantic. For electronic dance music culture in Portugal, without much international visibility at the time, it was a moment of great recognition. As with everything else, anything seemed possible in Portugal back then.

In the middle of 1990s, the UK magazine *Muzik*, at the time the world's most important dance music publication, put the Lisbon scene on its cover and called Portugal 'the new paradise of dance music' and an alternative to Ibiza. In the following years new companies (X-Club) and other protagonists (DJ Jiggy, Mário Roque, XL Garcia) stepped into the light. House or Techno were not the only new dance music genres to become more visible in Lisbon in this era. This was also the case with Hip-Hop, thanks to the seminal compilation *Rapública* (1994), as well as musical expressions associated to Jazz or Drum'n'Bass. In other words, a new industry based on dance music was born.

The new economic surge also prompted the birth of a new nightlife zone in the city as an alternative to Bairro Alto. This was found in the Avenida 24 de Julho in the Santos neighbourhood by the Tejo river. The Bairro Alto was associated with vanguards and more transgressive ideas. An example was Galeria ZDB, a multidisciplinary space for live concerts, performances, or art–a kind of alternative and independent cultural centre. In the middle of the 1990s, Frágil, forever a symbol of the Bairro Alto, no longer had the same aura. Something was lost.

On Avenida 24 de Julho the nightspots were much bigger than those in Bairro Alto, and in most of them things were different. There was a longing for sophistication, even opulence, that suited the economic upswing at the time. If Bairro Alto was associated to new artistic dynamics, Avenida 24 de Julho welcomed those who were experiencing the country's development surge, young people who seemed materially comfortable and saw nightlife as a diversion instead of a cultural dynamic.

Still, there were two nightclubs where everyone would meet late at night: Alcântara-Mar in Alcântara, and many went to Kremlin in Escadinhas do Duque. In Kremlin, people would dance until morning. It was the quintessential hedonistic place of the time, with a powerful sound system, a large dance floor, and several DJs who were aware of the best things that were happening in Techno and House music at the time. Until then, the DJ as an artist was yet to be recognised. But since the middle of the 1990s, people would go out at night to, especially, attend certain DJ sets, for example DJ Vibe's famous Saturday night sessions in Kremlin that went on for five hours.

In December 1995, something happened. Captain Kirk was born in 121 Rua do Norte. Few may have realised it at the time, but this place embodied a desire for change, as an expression of truth that had already existed but had not yet been revealed. Frágil had become famous for realizing the idea of a bohemian cultural bar, but at the same time it was also something else. Trendy places of that period, especially on Avenida 24 de Julho, showed a desire for sumptuousness and also for a larger institutional control. Kirk was about informality and vulgarity, which was, after all, also an aesthetic statement. It was the result of a wish to develop something different with artistic tendencies and social behaviours. Even though the place's raw energy did not always clarify what its founders and audience were really hoping for.

Kirk was not a large place. But its influence could not be measured that way anyhow. Its particular elements were not new. For example, there would be film sessions at the end of the day, and the DJ's role was recognised more than anywhere else during that era. But these elements consolidated the wishes of those who thought Bairro Alto had stalled, of a younger generation, whose adolescent energy wanted the world; now, immediately. It is not surprising that Kirk only lasted a couple of years. But that does not mean it left without a trace.

Kirk's owners had restored an old house, known as 'the dancer's tavern', and turned it into a dancing bar. On the right side, a pinball machine, on the left, some tables that surrounded a circular dance floor, a long counter, and eight TV sets. It was not very sophisticated, but its clients–who also went to other places in Bairro Alto like Majong, Três Pastorinhos, Targus, or Frágil–did not mind. Kirk's first year was a success, bringing together people from the arts, dance, film, journalism, and fashion. In the beginning, evening film programmes turned the place into something more than a bar. At seven in the afternoon, one could almost watch complete retrospectives of notorious filmmakers. One would go to Kirk, as is the case with any other place that carries a particular symbolic weight, to see and to be seen.

At the time, a group of DJs were moving around places in Bairro Alto, in search of legitimate new soundscapes, which went beyond the prevailing functional logic of electronic dance music. Kirk was like a catalyst. Several household names of today's Portuguese DJ culture such as Tiago Miranda (former member of the bands Loosers, Dezperados, Pop Dell' Arte, Slight Delay), Dinis, Nuno Rosa (from the band Dezperados, also known as Pinkboy or Gunrose), Johnny, or Rui Murka were discovered here or had the chance to evolve. CoolTrain Crew collective also started off in Kirk before their residence in Ciclone (ex-Johnny Guitar) in the Santos neighbourhood and their spreading of soundscapes like Drum'n' Bass nationwide.

All of these names built Kirk's sonic image, a mixture of languages that were then settling from Drum'n'Bass to more danceable Jazz, turning into even more eclectic nights where anything could happen. Kirk was a place that released an excessive energy, and like many other places whose time frames depend on the spontaneity that they released, it did not last long.

The 1990s were a time of transition for Bairro Alto. The area recreated its 1980s heritage and gave back a new energy—forecasting, at the same time, a new era. Its impoverished phase coincides with its occupation of the streets; instead of from the inside, Bairro Alto was now being experienced from the outside, on the streets. In the process of this change the area's mysterious aura, and any chance to feel surprised when entering a place, were lost. But the democratisation of Lisbon's nightlife, which had started in Avenida 24 de Julho, eventually came back to Bairro Alto. New and small places devoid of any cultural dynamic were opening, spots that were confined to selling drinks. Streets filled up with people with glasses in their hands. Tensions between residents and visitors rose. According to some people, Bairro Alto was decaying.

At the same time the city's self-esteem was high. It had been 1994's European Capital of Culture, a moment of recognition for Portuguese culture that connected the city to the international arts circuits. In 1998, the World Exposition (Expo' 98) opened its doors in Lisbon. This was a one-year event of great cultural vitality that prompted an architectural revolution, as well as an urban renewal of a significant part of Eastern Lisbon (although in the end not much was left for local culture).

In this context, Manuel Reis, Frágil's helmsman since the beginning of the 1980s, made a decision; he decided it was time to leave Bairro Alto. In 1998 his new adventure after Frágil, Lux, opened its doors in Cais de Pedra, in front of the Santa Apolónia train station. It was based in a 1910 concrete building, formerly used as a stowage company's workshop. Then in 1999, in the small palace where As Noites Longas had opened back in the 1980s, Baile was born, later known as B. Leza. Two places that would become highlights of the following years.

The 2000s: diversity and reconstruction

In the 1980s Frágil had earned a reputation for elitism. In the beginning, its successor Lux was accused of the same thing, although for some, compared to Frágil, it was much too inviting. But it was neither one thing nor another. Rather than being exclusive, it was a place where compatible differences came together. In Frágil, it was easy to sense a utopia of being among peers. But because of its much bigger size, Lux had to be something else. Architects, Margarida Grácio Nunes and Fernando Sanchez Salvador were the authors of this project. They created a discotheque on the ground floor, a bar on the first floor, and a terrace upstairs. The place quickly became iconic. It was a bar, a discotheque, as well as a venue for live music, performing arts, exhibitions, and book launches. An ambiguous place, but it projected something real—a contemporary ideal of leisure, of cultural production and consumption associated with socialisation and pleasure.

Lux transformed over the years. Today it is still an identity setter. A place where trends are foretold. A living laboratory. But it is also being increasingly enjoyed in more indifferent ways. New generations have desacralized it. It is still attended by cultural elites that come see regular live concerts (for example Prince, LCD Soundsystem, Jamie Lidell, and Animal Collective have played there over the years) or important DJ sessions by international or resident DJs like Rui Vargas, Tiago, Nuno Rosa, or Dexter. But the place is, now, also visited by a bigger, anonymous audience.

Besides its regular day-to-day activity, Lux also became important for what it stood for. Of course, in the last decade many smaller places like Incógnito, Galeria ZDB, Lounge, Frágil, MusicBox, or Mini-Mercado eventually played an important part in galvanising the dance music circuit. But Lux was its main stimulator, for its identity was, and still is, linked to several tendencies, genres, scenes, and phenomena in electronic dance music. Thus, it contributed to the inclusion of Portuguese bands (Gala Drop), collectives (Discotexas, Sonic), and DJs and producers (Tiago, Xinobi, Moullinex, Photonz, Zentex, or Kaspar) in today's global movement of electronic music. At the same time, Lux ignited the transformation of an abandoned area into a lively zone of shops, galleries, and restaurants, thus creating a new pole in the city to attract further nightlife.

If Lux represents a cosmopolitan Lisbon that is aware of global tendencies and references, B. Leza, in Largo do Conde Barão in Santos, was a place where cultural miscegenation between Africa and Europe, throughout the decade, was not an illusion. Other discotheques such as Mussulo or Comvento belonged to strictly African circuits, be them Angolan, Cape Verdean or Mozambican. But in B. Leza there was a profound mixture of colours and origins, even though most of its crowd had its roots in Portuguese-speaking African countries.

It was here that, for many years, bodies swung sensually to the rhythm of musical expressions like Funaná or Morna, and white Lisboners had their first contact with a lot of African music from the likes of Lura, Nancy Vieira, Tito Paris, or Tcheka. There is still a lot to do with regards to the connection between Portuguese, Brazilian, and Portuguese-speaking African music. But without B. Leza, it wouldn't even exist. It was during the B. Leza's nights where a new generation, open for surprises, was mixing African, Portuguese, and transnational soundscapes, feeling as comfortable with Lux's electronic sounds as they felt with Jazz or songs from African origins in B. Leza.

A group of people (musicians or DJs, self-taught or former Jazz students, black or white) shared the same type of sensibility, leading to label experiments like Nylon, Kami Khazz, or Meifumado, to producers like Journeys, and musicians and projects such as Spaceboys and Melo D

Margarida Martins, Frágil, Lisbon, 1983, photo: unknown

Entrance of Frágil, sailor party, Lisbon, 1983, photo: José Soares e Nica

Frágil birthday party at Convento do Beato, Lisbon, 1996

Invitation for a Japanese party at Frágil, Lisbon, 1984

View on Lisbon, 2000, photo: Stefan Schneider

Façade of Frágil, Lisbon, 1982, photo: José Soares e Nica

Invitation for New Years Eve at Frágil, Lisbon, 1988, photo: unknown

PLATES

LISBON

Rui Reininho and António Variações, Frágil, Lisbon, 1983, photo: José Soares e Nica

Dancer at Lux Frágil, Lisbon, 2007, photo: Luísa Ferreira

Margarida Martins and Mário Marques, Absolut Citron Party, Frágil, Lisbon, photo: unknown

Frágil, Lisbon, 1983, photo: José Soares e Nica

Zoe Melo, Frágil, Lisbon, 1993, photo: Luísa Ferreira

(both coming from an older group called Cool Hipnoise), or even Loopless, Shelter Av., Type, or Precyz. All of these agents came from a post-Hip-Hop generation and a transversal range that was more interested in assimilating every type of music around it than limiting its influences. Most of them believed in a mixed sound based on Funk, Jazz, Soul deviations, and the urban reality of African diasporas.

Never did Lisbon's social landscape change as quickly as in the first decade of the 2000s. It was an opportunity to create new languages, imaginary worlds, and other kinds of experiences. It was becoming clear that the city was increasingly inhabited by people of different colours, roots, and experiences. Still, the majority of those people were, and are, looked down upon by most of Portuguese society as immigrants. But most of them are not immigrants. They're just Portuguese – with skin tones, family stories, and customs that are different from the romantic image that Portugal still has of itself. Indeed, this change began with the immigration from Portuguese-speaking African countries, followed by Brazil and Eastern Europe. Slowly, the traditional Lisbon of Fado, popular festivities, marches, and roasted sardines, based on very idealised concepts of what tradition was supposed to be, was merging with other realities. In recent years, several creative agents who work in different artistic practises, especially music, have reflected on this development.

    The strongest example for this would be Buraka Som Sistema. But there are other examples like Batida,[2] DJ Marfox, DJ Nigga Fox, Macacos Do Chinês, Kilu, or Ritchaz & Kéke, all of them produced new Portuguese music that came from the descendants of the second generation immigrants. They are all different. From different generations, origins, cultural capitals, and motivations. They do not want to be a symbol for anything. None of them want their art to be trapped within their identity. But they unwittingly reflect a city from Southern Europe, Lisbon, with the Atlantic Ocean by its side, and its privileged connections to Brazil, parts of Africa, and the rest of Europe, knowing that they can filter that vast legacy. Especially because recent years have shown that Lisbon's language is already made of Portuguese and Creole, of Fado and Kuduro, of Lux but also B. Leza, blacks and whites and mixed races.

    Lisbon is a hybrid and diverse city in the making. When walking around historic neighbourhoods like Bairro Alto, Chiado, Santos, Bica, Mouraria, Intendente, or Cais do Sodré, that reality is present. Observers often do not realise it is there. Because they try to legitimise differences, people often use expressions like 'Lusophone', 'second-generation immigrants', or 'Luso-Africans' – not realising that they are actually establishing separations, and divisions.

But new Lisboners' range of references is wider. They bring new elements, promote diversity, and use different languages, like Hip-Hop,

[2] Batida aka Pedro Coquenão was part of the Ten Cities recording project.

popular Portuguese music, Kizomba, or Kuduro, in a non-hierarchical way. They do not reject anything, whether it is their parents' culture or global culture. They are not easy to categorise because most of them want to understand and assimilate everything that is around them.

If one band embodies all of Portugal's transformations in the last few years, that band would have to be Buraka Som Sistema and their completely untameable, plural, and under-construction sound. Instead of separating, they have always preferred to agglutinate things. When they appeared, they met an increasingly receptive international environment, that started to accept urban languages like Brazilian Baile Funk or South African Kwaito. Buraka Som Sistema came from the creative cauldron of Enchufada, a studio, record label, and creative unit that also gave birth to bands like 1-UIK Project. They were composed of two Portuguese (João Barbosa and Rui Pité) and two Angolans (Kalaf Ângelo and Andro Carvalho, ex-Conjunto Ngonguenha) who had been living in Portugal for a long time.

Buraka Som Sistema started their career with their 2006 sessions in Clube Mercado. There, with no previous releases, people started to talk about them, which immediately established them as a project from Lisbon. The band would have been different had it been born in Luanda, São Paulo, or in any other part of the world. But the two Portuguese's backgrounds, whether from Rock or House, met with the Angolans' knowledge of African music. All this only made sense in Lisbon.

Especially in the international press, Buraka Som Sistema were sometimes referred to as 'Angolan' or 'African'. Maybe this attribution appeared because there was still some difficulty – inside and outside of Portugal – to understand the changes of a country now inhabited by people of different colours, origins, and experiences. But now the change is there. With new generations and a wide array of references. With parents who have inherited traditional African cultural forms, but who also have been socialised in Portugal, and who are aware that they are living in a global culture and belong to a transnational space. No other contemporary music reflects Portugal and especially Lisbon – the streets' reality instead of their own romanticised image – as much as the one from Buraka Som Sistema.

The band's success did not come easily. They moved in a territory of ambivalent identities, despite having become the most internationally recognised Portuguese act of all time, outside of the Fado circuit. Still, its musical perspirations could not defy all stereotypes. They were challenging the view of Portuguese people. In 2016 the band took a hiatus from performing. It might still be too soon to understand the real impact that they had on cosmopolitan and post-colonial Portugal.

But things have already changed. A current example for this would be the monthly Príncipe record label nights in MusicBox, in the Cais do Sodré area. For this label and platform youngsters from Lisbon's periphery are currently making, with their own hands, some of the most exciting new Portuguese music of today. They produce this electronic dance music in their bedrooms or living rooms, later to be danced to at parties where people of different colours, ages, clothing styles, and wealth gather. It is all based on this music. Music that can be Kuduro, Afro-House, Funaná, or Tarraxinha – or all of it at the same time.

On these nights at the MusicBox, 'perifery' and 'centre' come together without remission in sweaty, festive nights. MusicBox is perhaps the most symptomatic case of how some bohemian and cultural places have been diversifying in the last decade. With the increasing popularisation of Bairro Alto other neighbourhoods such as Bica, Cais do Sodré, and, more recently, Intendente have become more central.

The importance of cultural neighbourhoods

Cultural neighbourhoods exist in many cities. Their model changes, but usually they are areas that have been reconverted into creative and informal environments, offering a mixture of cafés, bars, art galleries, clubs, and live music venues. Here, emerging artists can experiment. Sometimes these neighbourhoods' borders are undetermined. But inside, one feels one has entered a cultural community and may interact with it. In Lisbon, there have been two such areas since the 1980s, according to sociologist Pedro Costa[3]: Bairro Alto and neighbouring Chiado. Both complement each other, as autonomous systems. Bairro Alto represents a more nocturnal side, linked to transgression and emergent activities. Whereas Chiado, where one can find the largest concentration of bookstores in the country, stands for the daytime.

The Bairro Alto-Chiado axis is one of the city's most important centres for nightlife, performing arts, fashion, antique stores, literature, audio-visual production, and visual arts. It is known for its many cultural activities, and especially for the development of a creative field that favours information exchange and the spreading of innovation, and for how tolerant and warmly even the most alternative cultural presentations are welcomed. This is a centre that works as a basis for a production system of cultural activities. But it also has a specific self-governing system and its own system of representations.

In Bairro Alto, in the 2000s, places that were former landmarks of the 1980s and 1990s, like Frágil or Captain Kirk, have lost their iconic value. There are still some places that stand out, for example bars like Maria Caxuxa, Clube da Esquina, or Purex, dancing bars like Bedroom, 49, or art galleries such as ZDB. But nowadays most things happen outdoors, on the streets and crossroads and squares. Until now, there has been a sort of self-adjustment process in the neighbourhood. However, excesses, from venues as well as from their punters, may lead to its collapse, after which the area might regenerate itself once again.

[3] Cf. Pedro Costa, *A Cultura em Lisboa* (Lisbon: Imprensa de Ciências Sociais, 2007).

A cultural neighbourhood is a complex ecosystem. It lives on an unstable balance. It requires careful public action, with more guidance and less intervention. Proactivity often has counter-productive effects when ignoring these places' specificities. In Bairro Alto's case, as ironic as it may sound, tensions between residents and visitors, traditional trade and new activities, or daytime and night-time clubbers, were precisely what gave it some salubrity.

Bairro Alto is the kind of place that lends a human dimension to lifestyle. Most stable cities have something comparable. But compared to similar places in Europe, it is unusual for such an area to remain important for so many years. Eventually, gentrification processes occurs, prompting the city's cultural agents to reorganise themselves, on their own or together with public agencies, looking for new central positions in the city. This is exactly what is happening in Lisbon now. Several public policies try to diversify new areas, namely Cais do Sodré but also the Martim Moniz-Mouraria-Almirante Reis-Intendente axis.

So, could Lisbon have more areas with the characteristics of a cultural neighbourhood like Bairro Alto? There have been attempts and experiments. For instance, in the industrial strip of Alcântara by using LX Factory, a closed industrial space that gave way to offices, stores, and nightspots. In Santa Apolónia with its proximity to Lux and Clube Ferroviário. In Santos for its private initiative design district. In Cabo Ruivo, where the reactivation of unexplored spaces is still possible, or in Baixa and Avenida Almirante Reis and their cheap rents. But in Cais do Sodré these attempts have been most eager and intense. They will only succeed if they can resist the temptation of eliminating the area's popular environment. Only then can a new cultural and bohemian axis grow in the city. The overcrowded Bairro Alto would be thankful.

Today, cities, rather than countries, are competing for attention, investments, creativity, and tourism flows. For this competition, monuments, museums, operas, or symphony orchestras are no longer sufficient. Nowadays, cities need dynamic cultural environments with their own narratives, stories, and vibrations. There are many ways to promote a city. Not necessarily through sophisticated marketing campaigns, but through authenticity. Through identification processes. That is why local music scenes are relevant. An exciting music scene, a community that is able to assimilate alternative lifestyles, integration policies, and socially creative agendas, shows an open city that is able to assimilate differences and attract the most diverse kind of people.[4] To enable this, alternative forms of life and work must be able to follow their own path.

Lisbon, due to its characteristics and neighbourhoods, is hoping for social regeneration movements to revitalise many areas through artists and their activities. The city has almost everything. It has traces of

[4] Cf. Richard Florida, *Who's Your City – How the Creative Economy Is Making Where to Live the Most Important Decision of Your Life* (New York: Basic Books, 2008).

timelessness, but it does not care much for its patrimony. It has futuristic traces, but it lacks the consistency of stable cities. It has its own light, the river and the sea's vicinity, but its inhabitants still have to truly experiment with the street's vibrations and enjoy open air spaces. The city is welcoming more and more people from other latitudes with more diverse life options, but the pleasures, as well as the conflicts of true intercultural relations, are yet to come.

Maybe Lisbon needs a new narrative. For many decades after 25 April 1974, Portugal seemed to have been divided between European spaces and others with connections to Portuguese-speaking African countries, as well as to Brazil. In recent years at least parts of Lisbon's music scene have understood that society will be more capable of creating wealth at all levels – and to become more European through that process – if it manages to nurture creative affinities of exactly those regions of the world. More and more music and places are showing a happy and jubilant mixture of all references which have come to this city. The result is truly genuine and alive music that has the potential to overcome Portugal's problem of always trailing behind foreign models.

The most attractive cities of our time are those that are able to be culturally significant, assimilate their differences, and authentically express their singularity. Lisbon can do this. It is already doing it.

Bibliography

Contador, António Concorda, *Cultura Juvenil Negra em Portugal* (Oeiras: Celta Editora, 2001).
Costa, Pedro, *A Cultura em Lisboa* (Lisbon: Imprensa de Ciências Sociais, 2007).
Eshun, Kodwo, *More Brilliant Than the Sun – Adventures in Sonic Fiction* (London: Quartet Books, 1998).
Ferro, José Paulo, *Roll Over, Adeus Anos 70* (Lisbon: Documenta, 2012).
Florida, Richard, *Who's Your City – How the Creative Economy Is Making Where to Live the Most Important Decision of Your Life* (New York: Basic Books, 2008).
Huq, Rupa, *Beyond Subculture – Pop, Youth and Identity in a Postcolonial World* (New York: Routledge, 2006).
Leloup, Jean-Yves, and Renoult, Jean-Philippe, *Global Tekno – Voyage initiatique au coeur de la musique électronique* (Rosières-en-Haye: Éditions du Camion Blanc, 1999).
Lipsitz, George, *Footsteps in the Dark – The Hidden Histories of Popular Music* (Minneapolis: University of Minnesota Press, 2007).
Lloyd, Richard, *Neo-Bohemia – Art and Commerce in the Postindustrial City* (New York: Routledge, 2006).
Miller, Paul D., *Rhythm Science* (Cambridge: MIT Press, 2004).
Muggleton, David and Weinzierl, Rupert, *The Post-Subcultures Reader* (New York: Berg Publishers, 2003).
Poschardt, Ulf, *DJ Culture* (London: Quartet Books, 1995).
Sabatier, Benoît, *Nous sommes jeunes, nous sommes fiers – La culture jeune d'Elvis à Myspace* (Paris: Hachette Littératures, 2007).
Smith, Raven, *Club Kids – From Speakeasies to Moombox and Beyond* (London: Black Dog Publishing, 2008).
Thornton, Sarah, *Club Cultures – Music Media and Subcultural Capital* (Oxford: Polity Press, 1995).
Vilela, Joana Stichini and Mrozowski, Nick, *LX60 – A Vida em Lisboa Nunca Mais Foi a Mesma* (Alfragide: Dom Quixote, 2013).

In the Labs of the Century – Part 2: Spaces/Politics

Johannes Hossfeld Etyang

The party, the dancefloor, the rave: these are the labs where the twenty-first century nervous systems assemble themselves.
Kodwo Eshun

At first glance, clubbing seems to be just another part of everyday life: celebrating, dancing, a time of leisure. It is a fleeting practice. In the morning there is nothing left but a few, faint traces: the empty dance floor, scattered remnants of the night, a bare quiet, and a hangover. The spaces where clubbers gather to dance are often small, insignificant and frequently short-lived or temporary. Very little about them seems to be of enduring relevance. Yet this observation is congruous with another: clubs and cultures they birth are essential in many people's lives. Clubs are places 'that cast a spell'.[1] The Tresor in Berlin, the Dug Out in Bristol, Jackie's in Cairo, Mandy's in Johannesburg, Xlib in Kyiv, Obey Miliki Spot in Lagos, the Soundspaces in the musseques of Luanda, the Diamond Dog in Naples, the Frágil in Lisbon, or the Starlight in Nairobi, where Obama's father danced: these names are portholes to vibrant city histories. While some of these clubs only briefly flared, and now no longer exist, they have achieved importance and permanence in the collective memory. They are remembered as spaces that were life changing and vitally important. Far from being commonplace and quotidian, these clubs were experienced as sites of the extraordinary and existential. In some instances, they have achieved the status of myth in the life of the clubbers and in the psychogeography of their cities. (For our understanding of 'clubs' and 'club culture' see the first part of this essay.)

The second essay series in this book – marked by the running header 'Spaces/Politics'[2] – takes these thoughts as its starting point. Whereas the first series of essays cover music and music spaces, the second series of essays interpret that which is forged in the sonic spaces. Although not always explicit in stating such, this second grouping of essays engages clubs as laboratories for forms (or ways) of life and thus as (micro-)political spaces; that's why they cast a spell in peoples lives. This introductory essay explores the basic assumptions that are alluded to in the individual essays, but form a common background.

The form of this essay thus unfolds in two steps. First, the essay explores the question of what can be meant by the term 'political' in the context of club cultures, offering the metaphors of 'laboratory' and the 'prism'. It may seem strange to propose club cultures as political, as one of the basic concepts of conventional political thought, the 'public sphere', is clearly dissonant to a social practise such as clubbing. Instead, the essay draws attention to an understanding of public spheres that stem from an alternative intellectual constellation, formed since 1960, when our music histories begin. From the point of view of this constellation, club cultures can be seen as unique public spheres with their own 'tactics of sound'.

Concurrently and inextricably, public spheres are spatialized, its practices exist as spatial practices, in the city. This leads to the second step in this essay's unfolding line of thought. This book is not called *Ten Cities* for nothing: It explores club cultures not only as laboratories of the political, but also as laboratories in the city. With this second step, the essay takes a critical distance to the concepts of urban theory (as before from conventional political theory) and suggests music histories as an approach to urban research. The essay concludes with a theme that, in this point of view, appears as particularly relevant: club cultures' fight for space, safety and control in often oppressive, gendered, policed and surveilled cities.

This line of enquiry (decidedly biased, in contrast to the book's general proposition) is mainly backed up by authors from a Black radical tradition, especially from African cities, and in particular, as in the first part of this essay (Music/Spaces), by authors from within the circle of the legendary magazine

---

1
Cf. Dave Haslam's apposite introduction to *Life after Dark. A history of British Nightclubs and Music Venues* (London: Simon and Schuster, 2015), vii, xii.

2
See the essays of Tobias Rapp, Rehan Hyder and Michelle Henning, Ali Abdel Mohsen, Sean O'Toole, Kateryna Dysa, Mallam Mudi Yahaya, Vítor Belanciano, Ângela Mingas, Mukami Kuria, Peter Wafula Wekesa, and Joyce Nyairo as well as Vincenzo Cavallo and Iain Chambers.

Drum, published in Johannesburg in the 1950s (see also Sean O'Toole's essay in this book).

Laboratories and prisms

Can Themba is remembered as '*Drum*'s wiliest, most mischievous reporter'.[3] Towards the end of the 1950s, Themba's parties in his apartment–known as the 'House of Truth' and located in Johannesburg's district of Sophiatown–were legendary. One night the great star of the age, Dolly Rathebe, performed in Themba's apartment, accompanied by pianist and composer Todd Matshikiza.

> *Instantly the stone-faced figures round the room sprang to life like puppets lifted off their perch ... Twenty other bodies were now up and jiving on the floor, hopping to and from each other, grinning and gasping in a crazy silent conversation ... I sat in my corner, watching this mass of dancing bodies. Everything was changed. The green peeling walls seemed insubstantial, swaying in time with the music. Grandma in the oval frame took on a new expression of tolerance and sympathy. The room became vast, its sharp right-angles vague and distant. The jivers seemed not solid ... The music throbbed on, issuing mysteriously from the wobbling bodies, steady as a record ... The singing stopped: not the end of a record, but the current switched off. The jiving stopped. The clapping stopped. Everybody separated and sat down.*[4]

At this house party in Sophiatown, music created an inner sphere of sound; but here it was not just the space that was transformed as soon as music filled it, like that of the 'stingy room' that had been transformed in the Queenstown Marabi party, remembered by Matshikiza (see the first part of this essay).[5] In Themba's apartment 'everything was changed'. The jivers were no longer 'solid'. The House of Truth became a fluid, moving world in contrast to the everyday outside world. It was the house of *another* truth.

This other truth is a shared truth made public. Themba did not sit alone in his living room and listen to music. At the moment of the party, his house was a place of assembly and encounter. In the bubble of vibrations, the clubbers grew into a temporary sound-family, a temporary social world with its own code of social communication. The communication did not only consist of talking. In the soundscape of the club a 'crazy silent conversation' takes place – in another language that works by sound, embodiment, displays, performances, and passions. It is the wordless all-language[6] conversation of clubbing.

This social world of the club sound-sphere has a far-reaching meaning. Lewis Nkosi, another *Drum* author and a well-known clubber in his time, who briefly lived with Themba, recalls the early 1950s in Sophiatown as follows:

> *Stories began to filter to the press of mixed racial couples taking part at university dances; of white youths from the rich white suburbs defying the law and roaming black townships by night, of new clubs and Jazz haunts where free racial mixing took place on an unprecedented scale ... Under the cloak of darkness, groups of us, without obtaining police permits for white members of our convoys, drove into the sealed-off African townships, dodging police patrols, assisting young white girls over fences in badly lit township alleyways ... How was a mother to address a white girl whom her son brought home after dark, under the cover of darkness, from the university, from a Liberal Party meeting, from COD, or the Jazz club?*[7]

What was happening in and around the clubs of Sophiatown, and the other townships, was not mere leisure, fun and making friends. It was more. Nkosi sums this up when he remembers a night in February 1959, in an Indian club, at the after party for the performance of the legendary Jazz opera *King Kong*, composed by Matshikiza and held in Wits University's Great Hall: '... the party assumed again the proportions of a vast conspiracy against the state. It might as well have been, for many of those present were the same people who were later to be arrested for treason.' Nkosi remembers this as 'a time when it seemed that the sound of police gunfire and jackboot would ultimately become ineffectual against resolute opposition and defiance'.[8] When Nkosi speaks of conspiracy, opposition and

---

3
Lewis Nkosi, *Home and Exile* (London: Longman, 1965), 8.
4
Dolly Rathebe sang the hit song 'Into Yam'. The passage is taken from the memoirs of the then publisher of *Drum*, Anthony Sampson, *Drum* (London: Hodder & Stoughton, 1983), 117–118.
5
Todd Matshikiza, 'The Stars of Jazz', *Drum*, June 1957, 37–41.
6
'All Language Club' is the programmatic name of the music club that plays a central role in Cyprian Ekwenzi's legendary novel *People of the City* from 1954. In the novel, the metaphor of the 'All Language Club' signifies a political laboratory from whence 'the spirit of fellowship created here would take root and expand' cf. Cyprian Ekwensi, *People of the City* (London: Heinemann Educational Books, 1963), 38f.
7
Lewis Nkosi, *Home and Exile* (see n.3), 29; 11; 'COD' is the Congress of Democrats, see e.g. Gail M. Gerhart, *Black Power in South Africa. The Evolution of an Ideology* (Berkeley: University of California Press, 1978) 112.
8
Nkosi, *Home and Exile* (see n.3), 17–18. Nkosi calls Sophiatown a 'symbol of defiance', e.g. in his introduction to the memoir of his *Drum* colleague Bloke Modisane from 1963: *Blame Me on History* (London: Penguin, 1990), xviii.
9
This on the other hand is exactly what the high school teacher-turned-freedom fighter (and jitterbug dancer) Cornelius Molapo does in Nkosi's political thriller *Underground People* (Cape Town: Kwela Books, 2002).
10
Nkosi, *Home and Exile* (see n.3), 16, 18
11
Nkosi, *Home and Exile* (see n.3), 17. At the same time, Nkosi is well aware of the 'dual experience' of this 'fringe society' and its ambiguity; on this aspect, (see n.28).
12
Maik Nwosu, *Alpha Song* (Lagos: House of Malaika & Beacon Books, 2001), 88. (Most references in this essay relate to the 1950s and 1960s, but Maik Nwosu's 2001 novel describes the craving for the 'life in the nights' in Lagos with such ambiguity that it would be wrong not to include it here.) In the novel, Nwosu hints ironically at subcultural studies, when he lets Tamuno have a sociology degree with the (ghost-written) thesis *The Ends of Popular Culture* which he puts up on the walls of his clubs. Rainald Goetz puts the question like this: 'Thema: das Leben. / Die Menschen. / Ein jeder. / Und dein Leid und meines'. [Subject: Life. / People. / Every single one. / And your pain and mine] cf.

defiance, he does not suggest the explicit political planning.[9] It's about experimenting with forms (or ways) of life. It's about 'black and white artists … co-operating' and parties 'where white men danced with black women and black men danced with white women'.[10] The practice of the clubbers and musicians at parties, clubs, Jazz haunts and university dances in 1950s Johannesburg, under the cloak of darkness, inside the sphere of sounds, contrasting with the sound of police gunfire and jackboot, pointed to nothing less than the experimentation with a 'new "fringe society" coming together in a spirit of tolerance and occupying a "no-man's-land"'.[11]

In this view, the practice of clubbing is about life being reshaped, about experiments with other, non-solid, defiant and deviant forms (or ways) of life. As the club impresario Tamuno says in Maik Nwosu's 2001 novel *Alpha Song* with which we ended the first part of this essay, 'Some people think the nightclub is all about dancing and people connecting. It is a language too, and that's important. It should give you a feeling of flotation that says to you: what's this grand act telling me about my life, about the largesse of life?'[12] Club cultures give space for this question to be posed, and offer the opportunity to experiment with possible answers[13] – in a 'public rite'[14], with a 'communal goose bump'[15], in a new fringe society of sound with re-assembled nervous systems, under conditions that make the odds more favourable than in other cultures not defined by music (for instance, where people sit, drink coffee and talk). When club cultures happen to offer such a space, this inner sphere of sound is perceived as filled with an explosive power. C.L.R. James noted that, as he watched the clubbers at his favourite club, the Apollo in Harlem, New York, in the 1940s, 'All the power is hidden in them there. It's waiting to come out. And the day … it takes political form, it is going to shake this nation as nothing before has shaken it.'[16] This is the first proposition that we argue in this book: clubs can be laboratories of the political.[17]

Even if the possibility of experimentation is not realized – and even for those who cannot imagine clubs as laboratories of the political – club cultures are still politically relevant in another way. Even if a club might not (or not only) be a laboratory, it will always be a prism, for the very reason that not everything in it is transformed. Apartheid did not cease to exist in the sound spheres, it pervaded the rooms of the Marabi party in 1930s Queenstown, the Jazz clubs in 1950s Sophiatown, and Themba's House of Truth. *Drum*'s British editor, Anthony Sampson, who also attended Themba's house parties, would have less to fear from the South African police than his host, and the latter less so than his next-door neighbour who was not in the public eye. Club cultures tend to 'duplicate structures of exclusion and stratification found elsewhere'.[18] Exclusions made in the most blatant and hurtful ways due to race, class, gender or (dis)ability are a violent everyday reality in many club cultures. Hierarchies of power, structural advantages and privileges may persist, or may even be amplified in clubs. Club cultures are characterized by overlaps and equivalences between inner sphere of sound (at night) and its elsewhere, its outside, the daylight society (an ambiguity that cannot be ignored).[19] In the club things will not always be all different or better, but they will be clearer and more readable.[20] Maybe we will see societies and cities in a clearer light if

Rave (Frankfurt am Main: Suhrkamp, 1998), 70.
13
This also means that, in the inner sphere of sound not everything is necessarily going to be different or better. Clubs are spaces of possibilities. Possibilities either arise (as they do in the view of Nkosi) or they don't; answers to the questions of life are experimented with or not. On the aspect of the *potential* of popular culture to be 'active sites of resistance' or not, as it is cf. Lawrence Grossberg, *We Gotta Get out of this Place* (London and New York: Routledge, 1992), 87.
14
Ralph Ellison, who wrote about Jazz culture on the other side of the Atlantic in the 1950s, described the 'institution' of public Jazz dance as a 'public rite' cf. Ralph Ellison, *Living with Music* (New York: The Modern Library, 2001), 46. According to Ellison, a 'feeling of communion' was 'the true meaning of the public jazz dance' cf. 46; 59. On the idea of Rave as communion see Simon Reynolds' brilliant book cf. Simon Reynolds. *Energy Flash* (London: Faber & Faber, 2013).
15
This is how Binyavanga Wainaina describes a party with Congolese dombolo dance in Kenya in his memoirs *One Day I Will Write About This Place* (Minneapolis: Graywolf Press, 2011), 140.
16
James liked going to the Harlem Clubs during his US time as much as his friend Ralph Ellison. See the unpublished notes cited in Scott McLemee's introduction in *C.L.R. James: On the 'Negro Question'* (Jackson: University Press of Mississippi, 1996), xxxiii; James' thoughts often revolve around classical music and on one occasion he described the revolutionary effect of its distribution in the media. See *Special Delivery: The Letters of C.L.R. James to Constance Webb, 1939–1948* (Oxford: Blackwell Publishers, 1995), 52.
17
On the term 'the political' (with its tense relationship to 'micropolitics') cf. Oliver Marchart, *Post-Foundational Political Thought: Political Difference in Nancy, Lefort, Badiou and Laclau* (Edinburgh: Edinburgh University Press, 2007).
18
About the British Rave scene cf. Sarah Thornton, *Club Cultures: Music, Media, and Subcultural Capital* (Cambridge, UK: Polity Press, 1996), 25.
19
The gendered worlds of club cultures are a striking theme that is repeatedly discussed in the club scenes. The under-representation of women on the production side has already been mentioned (see the first part of this essay), but this also applies to writing about women as clubbers. Maria Pini uses the example of UK Rave to point out that women in club cultures are 'relatively invisible', although they do indeed have a 'heavy presence' cf. Maria Pini, *Club Cultures and Female Subjectivity* (Basingstoke: Palgrave Macmillan, 2001); this is already evident in Matshikiza's aforementioned article from *Drum* about the Marabi Party, and in all the novels written from a male perspective which this essay refers to – from Ekwenzi to Nwosu. On the sexualized images at Matshikiza cf. Dorothy Driver, 'Drum magazine (1951–99) and the spatial configurations of gender', in Kate Darian-Smith and Sarah Nuttall (eds), *Text Theory Space* (London and New York: Routledge, 1996), and Brett Pyper, 'To Hell with Home and Shame!', *Gender and Sexuality in South African Music*, eds. Chris Walton and Stephanus Muller (Stellenbosch: SUN ePReSS, 2005), 19–26. The work of authors such as Angela McRobbie, Maria Pini, Fiona Hutton, and Rebekah Farrugia make the far-reaching meanings of the dance floor for the lived experiences of women visible, which is correspondingly ground-breaking. This book – with its short contributions and the respective perspective of the authors – certainly does not continue this with the emphasis it deserves. Much more research is needed here.
20
Cf. George Lipsitz, *Footsteps in the Dark* (Minneapolis: University of Minnesota Press, 2007), xv.

we look at them at night, and in particular at their sound spaces.[21] This is the second proposition that we take in this book: that clubs are prisms.[22]

Clubs as prism and laboratory of the political: these two perspectives on club cultures form an underlying and shared background to the second series of essays in this book.[23] Whereas club music and it's spaces are covered in the first series of essays, the second series of essays expounds on this. This second grouping of essays interprets that which is forged in the sonic spaces of club cultures. It engages the dance floor as a (micro-)political space. This understanding of club culture as political requires contextualisation and theoretical elaboration.

Dancing and thinking

There is a history of understanding club cultures as political.[24] For some it is almost a truism, but for most, it is a provocation. The sceptics, those who may still regard clubs as prisms, but certainly not as laboratories of the political, have always been in the majority. Club cultures were essentially suspect as far as political thinking was concerned: political activism and the ecstatic have always had a difficult relationship. The authors of *Drum* were among the first to express these doubts. Themba described himself and his coterie of friends as 'cavaliers of the evanescent, romantics who turned the revolt inwards upon our bruised spirits'.[25] Nkosi concluded his memories of 1950s Johannesburg saying: 'Alas, we didn't realise how small and powerless we were.'[26] The fact that black and white South Africans danced together in these moments, as experienced and extolled by Nkosi, can be cast in a very different light: 'We are fighting for the full rights of Africans. We do not fight to dance and sit with Europeans.'[27] (See also Sean O'Toole's mention of the later bomb attack on Club Pelican in Soweto by students affiliated to the ANC's underground network in his essay on Johannesburg in this book.) The romantic cavaliers are symptomatic of a dual experience[28] and of an ambiguity, which always leaves a sense of doubt: is this politics or romanticism, fight or flight, disguise or deceit, a genuine position or a charade, rebel subculture or mere subcultural distinction?[29]

Another example. About twenty years after Sophiatown, Disco, captivated the music world from the mid to late 1970s. Disco was a political laboratory for clubbers. Perhaps nobody described this better than Richard Dyer when he wrote in 1979 that Disco had the power to facilitate experience, and that was the basis of the political.[30] At the same time, a racist and homophobic society saw disco as a 'metaphor for the end of humanism and the decline of the West', which culminated in the Disco Demolition Night of 1979.[31] What is interesting is that Disco was hated not only on the right but also on the (white) left. 'All my life I've liked the wrong music … And since I became a socialist, I've often felt virtually terrorized by the prestige of Rock and Folk on the left … It's not just that people whose politics I broadly share don't like disco, they manage to imply that it's politically beyond the pale to like it,' writes Dyer. It's no coincidence that this defence of Disco is printed in the magazine *Gay Left* and originates from a community that has always known more about the relationship between politics and dance culture than many others.

A decade later this ambivalence (abetted by mainstream moral panic) continued in the scenes of Rave and Techno. In 1990, Hakim Bey's manifesto *The Temporary Autonomous Zone* concludes with the following passage: 'Let us admit that we have attended parties where for one brief night a republic of gratified desires was attained. Shall we confess that the politics of that night have more reality and force than those of, say, the entire U.S. Government?'[32] But at the same time, it seemed obvious to dismiss Rave and Techno in the 1990s[33], as an inconsequential immersion in and absorption with sound.[34] Just as it seemed plausible to view the subcultures of the neo-liberal, isolationist 1990s as a sell-out to exploitative capitalism and an exercise in post-Fordist individualism.

Dance music (or club music, as we use these terms interchangeably) itself hardly gives any reason to regard it as political. With other music, this connection was more obvious. The most direct approach has always been the verbal statements: the authors, their voices, their text, and their messages. Thus, political protest music could be clearly identified (such as the political Folk mentioned by Dyer). This book also contains songs with

21
Especially in the novels from the African cities, the club and bar often serve as an observation point and prism. In addition to the sources already cited in this essay, one should think of the Tropicana in Ekwenzi's *Jagua Nana*, Groppi's in Waguih Ghali's *Beer in the Snooker Club*, or the Club Cambana in Wole Soyinka's *The Interpreters* in the 1960s or, in more recent years, of the Bar Credit Gone West in Alain Mabanckou's *Broken Glass*, the Club *Tram 83* in Fiston Mwanza Mujila's novel of the same name, or the Bar Mateso Bila Chuki in Billy Kahora's *The Cape Cod Bicycle War*.

22
It was Walter Benjamin, writing with reference to the Parisian ballrooms of the 1920s such as the Grande Chaumière, the Closerie des Lilas and the open-air Bal Mabille, who formulated this function of the prism: 'nothing in La vie parisienne is as Parisian as the transparent nature of that nonsensical nightlife in which not the logical but certainly the moral order makes its appearance'. Benjamin adds: 'Of course, it does not come to judge; it comes as protest and evasion, as cunning and as mollifying gesture: in a word, as music'. Benjamin says this after attending a lecture by Karl Kraus who has been reading Offenbach's *La vie parisienne* cf. Walter Benjamin, 'Karl Kraus Reads Offenbach', *Selected Writings*, vol. 2, part 1 (Cambridge, MA: Harvard University Press, 1999), 111.

23
Whether clubs are perceived as laboratories or prisms or as both varies accordingly from one of this book's authors to the next.

24
The history of writing about pop and politics is too extensive to be summarized here; further down in this text, part of a prehistory from around 1960 is recapitulated. For electronic dance music the contributions on the excellent websites <dj.dancecult.net> or <https://norient.com> can also be recommended.

25
Can Themba writes in his 1961 essay 'The Bottom of the Bottle', *The Will To Die* (Capetown and Johannesburg: Africasouth Paperbacks, 1982), 111.

26
Cf. Lewis Nkosi, *Home and Exile* (see n. 3), 17.

27
Cf. Gail M. Gerhart: *Black Power in South Africa*, 220, quoting a public speech at a Pan Africanist Congress public meeting in Cape Town in the late 1950s.

lyrics that play a political role, such as 'Kaffir' by the South African Kwaito musician Arthur Mafokate, 'Traffic Cop' by Kwaito band Brothers of Peace, 'Unbwogable' by the Kenyan band Gidi Gidi Maji Maji, or 'Figli di Annibale' by the Dub band Almamegretta from Naples.[35] But often dance music is without explicit political messages. Sometimes lyrics are just appropriated, such as 'Dancing in the Street', Marvin Gaye's song for Martha and the Vandellas, which became a civil rights anthem in 1964,[36] but with most dance music that's difficult too: 'Pump Up the Jam', 'Everybody in the Place', 'Hyper Hyper'. Music with a definite 'attitude' was always easier to understand politically. The dance pose did not really count. In dance cultures, pleasure and hedonism, the camp, the spectacle, not to speak of the openly commercial, often reign supreme. The dance-club cavaliers are all too easily perceived not as rebels, but rather as posers and quitters, the 'evanescent' as the inane, as 'not solid' but vacuous.

Although dance cultures have always had a difficult political status, the connection with the political does not disappear. The relationship between dance cultures and the political has always been marked by a tension 'where it is recognized that in some complicated way something political is at stake'.[37] But it is by no means clear what this tension is and how it is best dealt with.

The public sphere

The understanding of club cultures is a complex subject because of the lack of available concepts and theories. Political theory has minimal terminology for nocturnal ways of life.[38]

Which concepts could be applied? One notorious concept from the vocabulary of classical political theory offers a useful place to start: the 'public sphere'. In 1960, when the music histories in this book begin, the term was reinvigorated when philosopher Jürgen Habermas wrote his habilitation thesis, entitled *The Structural Transformation of the Public Sphere*.[39] Published in 1962, Habermas' book has had a strong impact in shaping the notion and making the term 'public sphere' a key concept for political theory. If clubs are to be understood as temporary political spheres and conceptualised with the tools of political theory, the term public sphere cannot be avoided.[40]

According to Habermas, a public sphere is an arena of communication, in which citizens articulate opinions and values, form ways of life, and establish political positions and oppositions. Habermas demonstrates this with the example of the citizens of England, France, and Germany during the seventeenth and eighteenth century. Their public sphere was a 'sounding board'[41] on which the citizens could experiment on their ways of life and find their voice against an authoritarian feudal state. It is formed through communication as sonic spheres of speech.[42] These sonic spheres were established in spaces that were everyday, semi-private, protected, sometimes commercial, cultural spaces such as literary or political salons and coffee houses. This example indicates how closely club cultures are linked to the concept of the public sphere, although in club cultures the sonic spheres are not established by speech but by sound and music. The mental leap from the more than 3,000 coffee houses in

28
For Achille Mbembe, Congolese Rumba creates a 'dual experience' 'of sadness, anguish and loss on the one hand and radiant happiness and emotional expressiveness on the other'. Achille Mbembe, *Variations on the Beautiful in the Congolese World of Sounds* (Vlaeberg, South Africa: Chimurenga Magazine, 2009), now in Sarah Nuttall (ed.), *Beautiful/Ugly: African and Diaspora Aesthetics* (Durham: Duke University, 2006), 63.
29
On this subject and at the same time as a defence of the political possibility of subcultures cf. Mark Greif, 'Positions', in Greif, Ross, and Tortorici (eds.), *What Was the Hipster? A Sociological Investigation* (New York: n+1 foundation, 2010).
30
Richard Dyer, 'In Defense of Disco', *Gay Left*, vol. 8, (Summer 1979).
31
Andrew Kopkind, 'The Dialectic of Disco', *The Village Voice*, 12 February 1979, as well as *The Thirty Years' Wars: Dispatches and Diversions of a Radical Journalist, 1965–1994* (London: Verso, 1995), 308.
32
Hakim Bey, *The Temporary Autonomous Zone, Ontological Anarchy, Poetic Terrorism* (New York, NY: Autonomedia, 2008), 132.
33
As a summary of a sceptical discussion with a UK focus cf. George McKay, *Senseless Acts of Beauty* (London: Verso, 1996), chapter 4.
34
For instance, in his anthropology of spheres, Peter Sloterdijk is obviously fascinated by club cultures and apparently has the Berlin Loveparade in mind (which was becoming a mass phenomenon at the time of writing), but sees this 'integristic music therapy' psychologically, not politically; it is a devotion he claims to 'yield little profit for the participants' medial competence in the sobering periods that follow' cf. Peter Sloterdijk, *Spheres. Volume 1: Bubbles* (Los Angeles: Semiotext(e), 2011), 527f.
35
Joyce Nyairo provides paradigmatic examples for Kenyan song lyrics in her book *Kenya@50: Trends, Identities and the Politics of Belonging* (Nairobi: Contact Zones NRB, 2015).
36
Marvin Gaye said about Martha and the Vandellas: 'they captured a spirit that felt political to me', in David Ritz, *Divided Soul: The Life of Marvin Gaye* (Cambridge, MA: Da Capo Press, 1991), 107.
37
On the problem see also Angela McRobbie, *In the Culture Society* (London and New York: Routledge, 2013), 133: 'Our critical vocabulary seems sadly lacking'. The works of Georgina Born and Tia DeNora are particularly noteworthy for their attempts to explore the relation between music and society.
38
On the relationship of concepts and ways of life cf. Rahel Jaeggi, *Critique of Forms of Life* (Cambridge: Harvard University Press, 2018).
39
Jürgen Habermas, *The Structural Transformation of the Public Sphere* (Cambridge, MA: MIT Press, 1991).
40
Paul Gilroy pioneered the concept of soundsystem parties as alternative public spheres already in 1987 cf. Paul Gilroy, *There Ain't No Black in the Union Jack* (London: Hutchinson, 1987), 210, 215, 223.
41
Jürgen Habermas, *Between Facts and Norms* (Cambridge, MA: MIT Press, 1998), 359.
42
Of course, music also belonged to the media in the bourgeois salons. Habermas himself refers to this (see n. 39, 34). The transition from 'occasional music' to 'music not tied to a purpose' (see n. 39, 39) serves as an example to explain the transition from the representative to the bourgeois public. But music is just the excuse for the gathering here. It is merely 'an accompaniment of people's humming', as Theodor Adorno says about salon music in his essay 'On the Fetish-Character in Music and the Regression of Listening' from 1938, in *Essays on Music* (Berkeley: University of California Press, 2002), 300. The non-verbal soundscape of music is not thought of as a public sphere itself. In this tradition, the public sphere is and remains an essentially verbal-dependent project.

London around 1710 to the almost 1,000 music clubs today – with the bridge of coffee bars with jukeboxes in the 1950s – is far, yet it seems plausible.[43]

Or maybe not? The public sphere, this laboratory of European bourgeois citizens, as conceived by Habermas, was a sphere of practical reason, made up of the triad of language, consensus and rational distance (of the fully self-assured rational self). Its time was daytime or the early evening, and its intoxicant was coffee. It was, as Oskar Negt and Alexander Kluge state, 'a republic of scholars'.[44] The laboratories of the clubbers and ravers are very different. The sound is the affective vibrational materiality of club music; the club itself feels like a drug.[45] It's a space for experiments with becoming different, of a different, less self-assured self in altered states.

In this sense, the classical bourgeois concept of the public sphere really is entirely dissonant. The republic of clubbers and the 'republic of scholars' are not comparable. The concept of the public sphere is based on the latter, the bourgeois citizen. This particular form or way of life is conceived on an abstract level as ideal and universal (an operation that has been comprehensively exposed by postcolonial theory), and as such it is asserted as an 'ideal type for all modern political processes', as Paul Gilroy puts it.[46] In this way, the bourgeois public sphere dominates the global knowledge economy and determines which spheres can be heard at all in connection with the political. Other forms (or ways) of life and their practices appear as dissonant and irrelevant, excluded from the legitimate spectrum of the political. Among its first victims are perhaps club cultures, which are seen as a threat to the public sphere. Marshall McLuhan saw a Manhattan disco and said with reference to the Gutenberg Galaxy: *'Ceci tuera cela'* [this will kill that].[47]

1960 – A constellation of thought

Around 1960, when Habermas was developing his writings on the public sphere at the Institute for Social Research in Frankfurt, a time at which the histories in this book begin, alternative positions of practice and thought were being developed and proposed by authors in Africa and Europe. Concretised around the years 1958–1960, in cities south and north of the Mediterranean, this constellation of thought challenges the bourgeois citizen's claim to universality. It opens up a different horizon in which it is reasonable to associate dance cultures and the political. This vibrant body of critical theory is as crucial to our book as the constellation of music at the same time.

In the late 1950s, changes of historical scale and global significance were taking place in the global South[48]. On the African continent, people fought against European colonialism and imperialism. Take the examples offered by the five African countries in this book. In Nigeria, after a long history of resistance to British rule, the Eastern, Western, and Northern regions attained self-government in 1958; independence followed in 1960. In Kenya, Dedan Kimathi was hanged in Kamiti Prison in 1957, there was an effort to break the Mau Mau resistance and the colonial government was still trying to cover up its brutality,[49] but the road to independence was unstoppable.[50] In Angola, the Baixa de Cassanje region rose against the Portuguese colonialists; the liberation struggle was to last until independence in 1975. In South Africa, the apartheid regime bulldozed Sophiatown, while in Sharpeville it massacred black protesters, ending the period from the mid-1950s that Nkosi had described as hopeful; the ANC and PAC were proscribed, and the struggle intensified. In Egypt, Nasser nationalised the Suez Canal against the influence of England and France, and placed the country on the path of Arab socialism. But models for this resistance against European colonialism are older. One goes back to the era that Habermas takes as an example for the emergence of the bourgeois public sphere.

When urban Europeans met in coffee houses in the 1800s, to debate and to consolidate their social advancement, they did so on the basis of the economic system of exploitation that was colonial trade, including coffee. The journals they read in the coffee houses also reported on the slaves' struggle for freedom and independence on the coffee plantation island of Haiti from 1791 to 1804. This revolt was 'one of the great epics of revolutionary struggle and achievement'[51], but it was hushed up by the

43
On the number of coffee houses in the first decade of the eighteenth century cf. Habermas, (see n.39), 32.
44
As Oskar Negt and Alexander Kluge noted already in 1972 cf. Oskar Negt and Alexander Kluge, *Public Sphere and Experience: Analysis of the Bourgeois and Proletarian Public Sphere* (Minneapolis: University of Minnesota Press, 1993), 9.
45
This is how the heroine Jagua feels about her favourite club in Lagos in Cyprian Ekwenzi's 1961 novel: 'The Tropicana to her was a daily drug, a potent, habit forming brew' cf. Cyprain Ekwensi, *Jagua Nana* (London: Heinemann 1975), 13.
46
Paul Gilroy, *The Black Atlantic. Modernity and Double Consciousness* (London: Verso 1993), 77.
47
Umberto Eco recalls this sentence by McLuhan in Geoffrey Nunberg, *The Future of the Book* (Berkeley: University of California Press, 1997), 295; McLuhan alludes to Victor Hugo's novel *Notre-Dame de Paris*, in which the archdeacon of Notre-Dame compares the new medium of the printed book with the cathedral and says this very sentence: the book will kill the cathedral. McLuhan's book on the Gutenberg Galaxy dates from the same year as Habermas' book – perhaps Habermas would have agreed with the image.
48
On the 'labile signifier' for the 'outside to Euro-America' cf. Jean Comaroff and John L. Comaroff, 'Theory from the South: Or, how Euro-America is Evolving Toward Africa', in *Anthropological Forum* (2012), vol.22, no.2, 127.
49
Caroline Elkins, *Imperial Reckoning: The Untold Story of Britain's Gulag in Kenya* (London: Pimlico, 2005), 340.
50
On the political songs of the liberation struggle cf. E.S. Atieno Odhiambo, 'Kula Waya: Gendered Discourses and the Contours of Leisure in Nairobi, 1946–63', in Tiyambe Zeleza and Cassandra Vaney (eds.), *Leisure in Urban Africa* (Trenton, NJ: Africa World Press, 2003).
51
Cf. C.L.R. James' books from 1938: *The Black Jacobins* (New York: Vintage Books, 1963), ix; and *A History of Pan-African Revolt* (Oakland, CA: PM Press 2012), 37f; C.L.R. James had written his books *The Black Jacobins* and *Toussaint L'Ouverture* with the intention 'to stimulate the coming emancipation of Africa' cf. 'Preface to the Vintage Edition', iiix.

European intellectuals of the day.[52] Yet, around the 1960s, the movements for independence on the African continent mirrored Haiti's model. The resistance also included what Amilcar Cabral called 'cultural resistance'.[53] This was increasingly articulated and developed. The Black radical tradition accrued a rich corpus of multifaceted political thought; the South African journalists writing for *Drum* in the 1950s are a part of this. There are also explicitly theoretical forms, as an African critical theory gained ground and reached its peak in the years around 1960.[54] It key proponents included W.E.B. Du Bois, C.L.R. James, George Padmore, Richard Wright, and Aimé Césaire. Major works in this period were written or published by Amilcar Cabral, Es'kia Mphahlele, Léopold Senghor, Kwame Nkrumah, Wole Soyinka, Kofi Abrefa Busia, Albert Memmi, Samir Amin, and Frantz Fanon.[55]

In 1958, Fanon made his intervention from the podium of the All-Africa Peoples' Conference in Accra, which in 1961 would become the first chapter of *The Wretched of the Earth* (*Les Damnés de la Terre*) that he was working on in Tunis.[56] This corpus of texts from a Black radical tradition contains implicit or explicit theories of the public sphere and the political. Often, these theories go beyond merely looking at public spheres in terms of language. Paul Gilroy summarized a characteristic of the Black Atlantic as 'tactics of sound, developed as a form of black metacommunication in a cultural repertoire increasingly dominated by music, dance, and performance'.[57] In Africa, the Caribbean, and the Americas, social and political theory has long recognized and articulated an awareness of the tactics of sound.

In Europe as well, other schools of thought (and practice) were emerging at the same time. Three manifestations of this thought that coincide with the chronology and geographic focus of this book bear scrutiny.

New public spheres: In England, the first anti-nuclear march took place in Aldermaston. The new social movements, which took their cue from the Afro-American civil rights movement, became a new social force in Europe. In Eastern Europe, movements of dissident civil societies formed. Multiple, small, but transnational public spheres came into being that hardly fulfilled the ideal of the bourgeois public sphere. The experiences gathered through these movements formed new theories that confronted the traditional theory with its exclusions and its 'bourgeois masculinist ideology'.[58]

The everyday and urban space: In 1958, Henri Lefebvre wrote: 'Man must be everyday, or he will not be at all.'[59] Alienation was no longer seen exclusively in economic contexts but in all areas of life, including everyday life, which Lefebvre had been researching since the 1940s. The everyday was understood as political. The theory later formed its own jargon, which was deployed against traditional political theory. 'Micropolitics' became one of the magic words.

In this fusion of politics and everyday life, the urban space became particularly interesting. The ordinary spaces of everyday urban life, as this perspective made clear, could prove to be extraordinary, because they allowed for the emergence of situations that make everyday life political. One can search for and create such zones of experience, even if they are only temporary.[60] In 1958 the first issue of the *Journal of the Situationist International* in Paris (of whom, around that year, Lefebvre was an ally) published the iconic manifesto for this notion titled: 'Formulaire pour un urbanisme

52
On the reception by European intellectuals of the liberation struggle on Saint-Domingues, Haiti cf. Susan Buck-Morss, *Hegel, Haiti, and Universal History* (Pittsburgh, PA: University of Pittsburgh Press, 2009), 17ff.
53
Amilcar Cabral, 'National Liberation and Culture' and 'Identity and Dignity in the Context of the National Liberation Struggle', both in *Return to the Source: Selected Speeches of Amilcar Cabral* (New York and London: Monthly Review Press, 1973).
54
On the 'articulation' of practice cf. Cedric Robinson, *Black Marxism: The Making of the Black Radical Tradition* (Chapel Hill, NC: University of North Carolina Press, 1999), 5; on the programmatic postulation to perceive this corpus of the Black Radical Tradition as critical theory see; Reiland Rabaka, *Against Epistemic Apartheid* (Lanham, MD: Lexington Books, 2010).
55
They are also the years in which two of the most important authors on the correlation of politics and the public sphere with music and pop culture write on the other side of the Atlantic: C.L.R. James had repeatedly thought about the connection between pop and politics during the time he spent in the US before his expulsion in 1953, and had clearly anticipated positions of what was to become Cultural Studies cf. *American Civilization* (Cambridge: Blackwell, 1993), written as a prospectus around 1949. Some ten years later James writes his cultural study of cricket (as a public sphere), which is published in 1963: C.L.R. James, *Beyond a Boundary* (London: Hutchinson, 1963). In the same year, Amiri Baraka published his *Sociology of Blues*, which builds on an essay from 1961: Amiri Baraka, *Blues People: Negro Music in White America* (New York: William and Morrow, 1963). On Ralph Ellison's criticism of the book in the 1964 *New York Review of Books* see Ralph Ellison, 'Blues People', *Living with Music* (see n. 14), 120–132.
56
Cf. Fanon's report in the Algerian newspaper *El Moudjahid* in December 1958, 'Accra: Africa Affirms Its Unity and Defines Its Strategy', now in Frantz Fanon, *Toward the African Revolution* (New York: Grove Press, 1964), 153f.
57
Gilroy, *The Black Atlantic* (see n. 46), 201; 'Haiti was the original Black Power', Linebaugh and Rediger write: 'If the distinctive accomplishment of the English working class was its labor press, the singular achievement of the black freedom struggle was its music.' cf. Peter Linebaugh and Marcus Rediker, *The Many-headed Hydra. Sailors, Slaves, Commoners, and the Hidden History of the Revolutionary Atlantic* (Boston: Beacon Press, 2002), 334.
58
On 'bourgeois masculinist ideology' cf. Nancy Fraser, 'Rethinking the Public Sphere', in Craig Calhoun (ed.), *Habermas and the Public Sphere* (Cambridge, MA: MIT Press, 1992), 137; the discussion is expansive. One of the most important criticisms of the 'ideal' version of this concept of the public sphere comes from feminist theory, e.g. from Nancy Fraser, Johanna Meehan, and Joan B. Landes who in the 1990s begin to point to the exclusions from apparently ideal inclusive spheres. In a certain way and ironically, the exclusion (on the production side) and the invisibility of women in many public spheres of sound (on the reception side) will continue within club cultures.
59
Henri Lefebvre in a preface to a new edition of his 1947 book *Critique of Everyday Life*, vol. 1 (London and New York: Verso, 1991), 127.
60
For the notion that spaces are made from sound, however, we had to look across the Atlantic to Toronto around 1960: to McLuhan's Communications Group. This idea was later integrated into Sound Studies by R. Murray Schafer.

nouveau'.[61] Factory Records owner Tony Wilson later borrowed the name for his legendary club, the Haçienda in Manchester, from the manifesto.

Subcultural studies, pop and politics: While the minutes of the Situationist *dérive* [drift] did occasionally mention bars as hubs of the city, they were largely silent on pop music spaces. Guy Debord, the head of the Situationist International, had been fixated on world revolution and obsessed with his group's singularity; in his view, pop music subcultures had always fallen for the spectacle. The connection between micropolitics and music youth cultures was not on his radar. Indeed, no one else thought of it, even though in 1958 at the latest, these 'absolute beginners', who received their education in the clubs[62], could hardly be ignored any longer.

In 1958, the cover of the British journal *Universities & Left Review* featured two Teds.[63] Stuart Hall, the journal's editor, remembers: 'Everybody asked us, "Why? What has this to do with socialism?"'[64] These were not political subjects, after all, just deviant teenagers, and that was exactly how the journal dealt with them, in line with the sociology of deviance and outsider/counterculture/subculture literature of the time: youth music cultures only featured as a problem.[65] This view would however soon begin to change, tellingly thanks to the work of people from the Situationist fringe, who were influenced by the Black radical tradition.[66] From there, the impulse would trickle down into pop culture via promoters like Tony Wilson and Malcolm McLaren.[67] In due course, subculture theory would change along the same lines. From the mid-1970s the Centre for Contemporary Cultural Studies (CCCS), in Birmingham, began a programme of research into the connection between pop and politics. During this time, Stuart Hall, who had put the Teds on the title page of *Universities & Left Review* a few years earlier, led the CCCS.[68]

Stuart Hall was about the same age as Jürgen Habermas, but drew on a very different personal and thematic constellation. At the CCCS people were familiar not only with Marx and Gramsci, but also with the Black radical tradition around 1960, which had anticipated the field of Cultural Studies. The CCCS understood the Rudies, Rastas, Mods, and Punks as political subjects.[69] It explored their complex processes of appropriation of music, identity, and space, and read their practices as language, as acts of symbolic, ritualistic resistance, 'expressed obliquely'.[70] This conflation of pop and the political has been highly significant: as an impulse, a challenge, and a school of thought. Other spaces and other public spheres were opened up to political analysis, including the musical public spheres that transcended language and nation. Paul Gilroy saw the sound system parties in the UK as alternative public spheres that brought together the Black political countercultures of the world and their sound tactics in a shared history of the Black Atlantic.

Collectively, this intellectual constellation around 1960 made it possible for music cultures to be examined more closely. The public and political spheres could be seen as diverse and multifaceted. In contrast to the bourgeois understanding of the public sphere articulated by Habermas, the emergent paradigms referred to above viewed the public sphere not just as a space for the expression of practical reason, typically in words, but as a zone to do with everyday life, in which music and its cultures played an integral role. The party, the dance floor, the rave could also be spaces of the political (as per Kodwo Eshun's quote at the beginning of this essay). Thus, at the beginning of the period covered in this book, there was not just a specific constellation of musical cultures, but – importantly – also of practice and thought, both in the global South and North, giving rise to a project that continues to this day.[71] This book sees itself as part of this on-going project. It was conceived around 2010, some five decades after the intellectual seeds for rethinking the public sphere were sown, and functions as a kind of 'shout-out' to this critical theory.

… and everything changes

It is central to the formulation of this book that the party, the dance floor, the rave – when the opportunities arise – are not mere meeting places where activists gather and relax from the real political work, which happens elsewhere. Clubs are not merely spaces of suspended from reality or escape. The essays in this book, read as a whole, make clear that the opposite is true.

61
Ivan Chtcheglov wrote the text in 1953. It appeared prominently in the first issue of the movement's newspaper in 1958, when its author had already been excluded from the Situationist International (SI). Gilles Ivain (Ivan Chtcheglov) 'Formulaire pour un urbanisme nouveau', *Internationale Situationniste 1* (June 1958), 17–18, trans. in Ken Knabb (ed.), *Situationist International Anthology* (Berkeley: Bureau of Public Secrets, 1981).

62
1958 is also the setting of Colin MacInnes' youth culture novel *Absolute Beginners*, published in 1959: 'my university, you might say, and that's the Jazz clubs', the novel's narrator says – connecting the 'Jazz world' with a political vision of absolute equality 'when you come in the Jazz club door' cf. Colin MacInnes, *Absolute Beginners* (London: Allison & Busby, 2011), 83.

63
This Rock'n'Roll-listening working-class and racist youth subculture was a topic of early subcultural studies. See also the portrait in MacInnes, *Absolute Beginners* n. 62), 54–57 and 231f; and its review by Stuart Hall, 'Absolute Beginnings. Reflections on The Secondary Modern Generation', *Universities & Left Review* no. 7 (1959), 24: 'The Teds and the bottle-throwers lurk in the background — and at the end of the novel, which is set graphically in the Notting Hill riots, they emerge to take their proper place in the roll-call of urban violence.'

64
Cf. Stuart Hall, 'Politics of Adolescence?', *Universities & Left Review* no. 6 (1959).

65
Howard S. Becker, Herbert Marcuse, and Theodore Roszak and, in German-speaking countries, Walter Hollstein and Rolf Schwendter, for example, relate music cultures and political action to each other only in passing and indirectly.

66
In London in 1966, Charles Radcliffe wrote an article entitled 'The Seeds of Social Destruction' for his magazine *Heatwave* (a song title by Martha and the Vandellas) where he claimed that Teds, motorcycle riding Coffee Bar Cowboys, Jazz fans, Rockers, and Mods were political rebellious forces. The year before, Franklin Rosemont, founder of the Chicago Surrealist Group, who Radcliffe collaborated with, had published the pamphlet '*Mods, Rockers & the Revolution*' in Chicago cf. Franklin Rosemont and Charles Radcliffe, *Dancin' in the Streets!: Anarchists, IWWs, Surrealists, Situationists & Provos in the 1960s* (Chicago: Cahrles H. Kerr, 2005), 127–131; 301–392.

Radcliffe was, together with Christopher Gray, admitted into the Situationist International, but the discrepancy to Debord's theory was

'For these people, the music and the dancing were not a dream and an escape, but an assertion', says the protagonist Toby in a party scene from Nadine Gordimer's 1958 novel, *A World of Strangers*. The novel draws on Gordimer's experience of the bohemian circles of Johannesburg and unmistakably features *Drum* authors as fictional characters.[72] In his memoirs about this period, Lewis Nkosi seems to reference Gordimer when, at the opening night party for *King Kong* in 1959, he beholds a 'South African underground' that is 'no longer a fantastical dream conjured up in some daring novel'.[73] Writing in 1963, *Drum* author Bloke Modisane, recalling a Sophiatown party, stated that it seemed to him as if the clubbers were transported into another existence, one that had nothing in common with white South Africa any longer. Crucially, it is not the clubbers who appear to be in a trance or a fictional world; rather, for Modisane, it is as if white South Africa is otherworldly – 'another planet in another galaxy and apartheid becomes a sound in a nightmare'.[74] The experience of the clubbers is concrete and real, but also temporary, small, ambivalent, indirect, micropolitical. The political action consists precisely in the experimental life forms in the club. It consists of the assertion, the 'crazy silent conversation', the lived practice.[75] The club itself *is* the place of the political.

The relationship between these different modes of the political sphere is always complex and opaque: between the inner sphere of the musical bubble and the outer spheres, between the club and the street, between the micropolitical public spheres of sound and the explicitly political spheres, alliances, movements, or even political parties of the daylight society. Even if they are connected,[76] the differences between these two frameworks of the political is unavoidable. As Sean O'Toole says in his essay on Johannesburg in this book: 'Dancing bodies late at night express a different solidarity to bodies tightly packed in a political march.'

In its historical development, this relationship may have to be understood as distant, slow, mediated, and indirect, something that 'flows or flees'[77] rather than act directly. Peter Wafula Wekesa and Vítor Belanciano in this book offer us two different examples during two different periods. Peter Wafula

too obvious. Radcliffe bails out after almost a year, Gray is excluded. The Londoners and the Chicagoers were much more influenced by radical Black theory and practice. Radcliffe got his decisive influences from the Blues, about which he wrote in London for anarchist magazines. Rosemont, on the other hand, studied with St. Clair Drake, the influential African-American scholar, at Roosevelt University in Chicago. By then, Drake had returned from Ghana, where he had been head of the Sociology Department at University of Ghana since our key year 1958. In 1945 Drake and Horace Cayton published the book *Black Metropolis* on the black city life in Chicago, in which music places also play a certain role as places of public life.
67
In the circles of successor groups like King Mob in London, people like Malcolm McLaren and Tony Wilson, who later ran the Factory Records label, begin to watch and listen carefully and bring this impulse to British pop culture. On Malcolm McLaren and Tony Wilson as 'fans' of the Situationists, see Simon Reynolds, *Totally Wired. Post-punk Interviews and Overviews* (New York: Soft Skull Press 2010), 75; Greil Marcus suggests a continuity across these ruptures by drawing a line of development from the European avantgardes like DADA via the Situationists to Punk, in his influential book *Lipstick Traces: A Secret History of the 20th Century* (Cambridge: Harvard University Press, 1989).
68
(See n. 63), 2.
69
The authoritative papers and books by Jefferson and Clarke, Iain Chambers, Stanley Cohen, Paul Willis, and Dick Hebdige are published between 1972 and 1979. The anthology *Resistance Through Rituals* is published in 1976. It contains the essay 'A Strategy for Living' by Iain Chambers, our author for Naples, in which he explores the appropriation of black music by white American and British youth, Stuart Hall et al. (eds.), *Resistance Through Rituals* (London: Hutchinson, 1991), 157–88.
70
As Dick Hebdige put it in his 1979 book *Subculture. The meaning of style*, (London and New York: Routledge, 2012), 17–18; 37; 133.
71
Of course, criticism of this constellation also belongs to this history after 1960. Can Themba's doubts about the romantic 'cavaliers of the evanescent' later return as an objection critically questioning the 'ritual as resistance' paradigm and the trope of micropolitics: critics asked whether their simple dichotomies (such as subcultures versus mainstream) correspond at all to the complexity of the subcultures, whether the analogies were not too easy to draw, and the terms too quickly at hand. If this project continues, then it must take

up this criticism. One of the most important points of criticism, which is important for the approach of this book, is the presumption that such simple mention of resistance would decouple the macro level of the political; for more recent work on the Micro-Macro Gap cf. Oliver Marchart, 'Bridging the Micro-Macro Gap: Is There Such a Thing as a Post-Subcultural Politics?', in David Muggleton and Rupert Weinzierl, *The Post-Subcultures Reader* (Oxford and New York: Berg Publishers, 2003); The concept of 'the public sphere' as a concept of a macro-political tradition of thought serves this book as an impulse not to let the relationship between the micro- and macro-level of the political break off.
72
Nadine Gordimer, *A World of Strangers* (London: Bloomsbury Publishing, 2002), 128; the key concept of 'assertion' is taken up by Es'kia Mphahlele, fiction editor at *Drum* until 1957, in an essay from 1964, in which he reflects on club cultures cf. 'The Fabric of African Culture', *Voices in the Whirlwind* (New York: Hill and Wang, 1972), 154); on Gordimer's novel cf. Es'kia Mphahlele, *The African Image* (London: Faber & Faber, 1962), 146–8.
73
Nkosi, *Home and Exile* (see n. 3), 18; On the ability of dance cultures (in Mbembe's case: Congolese Rumba), to disguise and dissimulate, but also to 'lie' cf. Achille Mbembe, *Variations on the Beautiful in the Congolese World of Sounds* (see n. 28), 92.
74
Bloke Modisane: *Blame me on History* (see n. 8), 118.
75
A programmatic formulation for this comes from the Situationists in 1962, with the question whether the Paris Commune had been a failure. See no. 11 of the 'Theses on the Paris Commune', by Kotányi Debord and Vaneigem, trans. in Ken Knabb (ed.), *Situationist International Anthology* (Berkeley: Bureau of Public Secrets, 1981).
76
For Ali Abdel Mohsen (cf. his essay in this book), on Tahir square in 2011, music and revolution were inseparable. As Walid Sharkawy said in one of Ali Mohsens reports from the revolution in Cairo in 2011: 'When Mubarak leaves,' he says, 'it will be to the beat of our drums' cf. Ali Abdel Mohsen, 'Revolutionary music: The noise from Tahrir', *Egypt Independent*, 8 February 2011, <https://www.egyptindependent.com/revolutionary-music-noise-tahrir/>. Accessed on 1 May 2015.
77
As Deleuze and Guattari say in a central passage in their theory of micropolitics, *A Thousand Plateaus. Capitalism and Schizophrenia* (Minneapolis: University of Minnesota Press, 1987), 216 cf. for an interpretation of music as the source of lines of flight cf. 11.

Wekesa has shown that during the colonial era the clubs in Nairobi were places where political movements and trade unions would also meet, but above all, they were places of experimentation for a new society. They 'represented a crystallization of different cultural, class, racial, and other categories that created an environment that was clearly heterogeneous'. To further quote Wafula Wekesa from his essay, here one could gradually explore and negotiate a Nairobi-specific 'broad multicultural and cosmopolitan reality' that was 'marked by intense diversities, new adaptations, and continuities'. Clubs became focal points for new ways of life that evolved after independence, laboratories on the way to a cosmopolitan society in Nairobi.[78]

Vítor Belanciano describes a similar indirect process in Lisbon. He tells the story of a slow opening of the social time capsule in which Lisbon lived until the mid-1970s. A cultural diversity, emanating mainly from the city's supposed periphery, began to shape modern Lisbon. This diversity was first lived in a club as a kind of social laboratory, then in a quarter of the city, before it changed Portuguese society as a whole. 'Bairro Alto became that place, and it was a founding era. In a way, contemporary Portugal was born there,' writes Belanciano in his essay. 'But in 1982, at the heart of Bairro Alto, Frágil is born and everything changes.'

Thinking about cities: An epistemic failure of imagination

Belanciano's remark highlights an important point: the political laboratory is localized; it occupies a specific place, a neighbourhood in the city. This is another aspect of the intellectual constellation around the year 1960. One cannot speak about the political without also talking about the spaces in which the political is spatialized. Social practices also exist as spatial practices – the spatial turn will develop it into a programme of its own right.[79] The city is thus a 'strategic site',[80] in which spatial and political cultures are to be considered together. The history of public spheres of sound is always one of the spaces in which they were produced, and which in turn produces them. This book is not called *Ten Cities* simply because it maps localized music histories, but because the stories of the political are always stories of space and stories of the city, and vice versa.

At this point it is necessary to shift the focus from the theme of the political sphere to that of space and the city. This is the second step in the essay's unfolding mentioned previously. The second essay series (with the running header 'Spaces/Politics') are connected by the keywords 'space' or 'city'. This book shares certain operations with urban research: It selects a limited number of cities, puts them in relation to each other, and offers imaginings of urban life. The operations of urban research – selecting cities, relating them to one another, offering imaginings – are seen as questionable by researchers, especially those from the global South (as questionable as using the concepts of traditional political theory to tackle the politics of club cultures). According to Sarah Nuttall and Achille Mbembe, they lead to an 'epistemic failure of imagination'.[81]

What exactly is this failure about? Urban theorist Mike Davis presents an example in his book *Planet of Slums* (2005). This book is part of a problem-oriented discourse on cities, where the selection process groups together cities that can be described as 'dysfunctional' according to the criteria of modern urban development. It puts cities in a category with the attribute of 'slum formation'.

> *Eight generations after Engels, shit still sickeningly mantles the lives of the urban poor ... Indeed, one can set Engels'* The Condition of the Working-Class in England in 1844 *side by side with a modern African urban novel, such as Meja Mwangi's* Going Down River Road *(1976), and ponder the excremental and existential continuities ... Today's poor megacities – Nairobi, Lagos, Bombay, Dhaka, and so on – are stinking mountains of shit that would appal even the most hardened Victorians.*[82]

It is well known that early urban research developed from the sensation of horror that slum regions such as London's East End aroused in polite Victorian society. The frightened citizens and early urban explorers knew as little about the cholera-ridden slums (and their subcultures) in the city's poor districts as they knew of 'the wilds of Australia or the islands of the South Seas,' noted Friedrich

78
This emerging society meant a breakdown of social barriers, as described by Peter Wafula Wekesa in this book, while at the same time creating a fragmented class society. On the fragmentation of class society since independence, taken from music and music cultures in Kenya cf. E.S. Atieno Odhiambo, 'From the "English country garden" to "Makambo mibale": Popular Culture in Kenya in the Mid-Nineteen Sixties', in James Ogude and Joyce Nyairo (eds.), *Urban Legends, Colonial Myths: Popular Culture and Literature in East Africa* (Trenton, NJ/Asmara: Africa World Press, 2007), 155–172.

79
Henri Lefebvre had the spatial-political experiences of Paris in May 1968 in mind when he wrote about 'Representational Space', one of the most important impulses for the spatial turn of the 1990s. Foucault (who ignored the Situationists), on the other hand, may not have thought of Paris at all when he coined the other magic word of spatial thinking, 'heterotopia'. He may rather have had the Tunisian political resistance in mind, when the students protested against the Bourguiba government and neo-colonialism in Tunis in 1966 and 1967. In Tunis, Foucault is politicized, it is here that he undergoes a 'true political experience' cf. Foucault in conversation with Duccio Trombadori in *Remarks on Marx* (New York: Semiotext(e), 1991), 134; 136; on Foucault's interpretation of the protest as a 'problem of neo-colonialism' cf. Michel Foucault, *Dits et écrits II* (Paris: Gallimard 2001), 806; Foucault does not list clubs among the heterotopias, although clubs – the gay clubs on Folsom Street in San Francisco, for example – played a decisive role in his own life. One would have liked to have read an explicit treatise on music clubs from Foucault that might, for example, have processed his visit to the Berlin club Dschungel in 1977. On the experiences beyond the 'middle-range pleasures that make up everyday life' see *Essential Works of Foucault*, vol. 1 (New York: The New Press, 1997), 129.

80
On the city as a strategic site for social processes cf. Saskia Sassen, *Territory. Authority. Rights* (Princeton: Princeton University Press, 2008), 281; see also 'The City: Its Return as a Lens for Social Theory', *City, Culture and Society* (2010), vol. 1, issue 1, 3–10.

Engels.[83] The accusatory, Protestant-reformist, as well as the sensationalistic, exoticizing and reductive discourse about the urban 'other' begins in the western city as an ethnography of the urban jungle. But in spite of its accusatory rhetoric, urban research often recovered complexity and depth, even when it functioned as reportage.[84]

Today, it often falls short as it produces simplistic images of narrow problem areas within highly diverse cities, for instance like Nairobi. This is spelled out by urban theorist Edgar Pieterse in his response to Davis' approach: 'My problem … is that such analyses flatten highly fluid, adaptive, contradictory, and to an extent open-ended social and institutional dynamics to the point where it obscures the ground on which a highly strategic, tactical, and opportunistic politics must be built because that is the terrain offered by our emergent cities.'[85]

For a city like Nairobi, however, there is an additional effect that depends on the knowledge economies of cities (parallel to the knowledge economy of music and politics discussed above and in the first part of this essay). While Davis may shock the reader in his book about Los Angeles,[86] there are still many alternative imaginings of Los Angeles available and in circulation in urban research, as well as in many other representations of the social imaginary. And it is exactly because the dominant narrative is so different that Davis' discourse of fear works so well. For a city like Nairobi, the situation is different. The Nairobians know their city and they hardly recognize their neighbourhoods in the simplistic stereotypes conjured by northern intellectuals.[87] But there is only a limited number of imaginings in global circulation, and these are usually not alternative accounts that reinstate complexity. They are more likely pictures of a 'vampiric machine' with an 'autistic lens'[88]: the visual clichés on the news on the one hand and the NGOs on the other. The widely available image of Nairobi is of a slum city, a place of 'shit' as Davis writes. It is worth taking a closer look at how such city discourses operate, as such flattened clichés apply not only to cities in the global South, but also to ordinary cities in the North, and are often no less reductive.

Comparative city discourses operate around an attribute. This attribute sets different cities in relation to each other, creating a subject area such as slum cities in Davis' book, for example. In addition to problem-oriented and developmentalist urban research, such discourses include narratives of world cities, global cities, or megacities. This kind of comparative thinking, which strategically connects cities with shared attributes, can be critiqued from three perspectives.

Firstly, it is reliant on spectacular attributes such as the extraordinary, exotic, sensational, the mega; the shockingly dysfunctional or, correspondingly, the attributes of successful cities which are said to be home to the urban *Weltgeist*. Cities without spectacular or exotic attributes fall through this grid. Thus, urban research overlooks the 'ordinary cities', as the urbanist Jennifer Robinson has postulated.[89]

Secondly, an argument based on sensational attributes runs the risk of overlooking or neglecting the ordinary aspects of cities – their everyday life. Setting an attribute reinforces the 'tendency to fix urban studies to a narrow range of questions and problems'.[90] When attention is focused on the urgent, the diversity and breadth of the subjects, as well as their complexity and ambiguity, is lost from view. One part (or attribute) determines the imagining of a whole;[91] whether that is a city or maybe even a region or a continent. All the more so if there are no counter-imaginings in circulation. Take Davis' piquant language: 'shit' stands for slum, the label 'slum' (or 'Kibera') for Nairobi, and 'Nairobi' most probably becomes a metonym for 'Africa'.

Thirdly, attributes do not just bundle cities into sets, they also introduce differences if the attribute works as a measure. The first difference the attribute introduces is that of time. Current normative theory arranges cities on a timeline from backward to developed and contemporaneous. The arrangement places cities on a linear track with 'progress' as the destination. In this diachronic order, progress is the projection of 'certain people's presents as other people's futures'.[92] It creates the second difference in the form of a spatial order: the spearhead of urban development is often located in the Northern hemisphere. The cities that have lagged behind, and that have not yet reached the here and now of the others, are often in the global South. In this hierarchy, African cities are the 'globalized allegory for failed

---

81
Achille Mbembe and Sarah Nuttall 'Writing the World from an African Metropolis', *Public Culture* 16, no. 3 (2004), 349.
82
Davis, Mike. *Planet of Slums* (London: Verso, 2007), 138.
83
Friedrich Engels quotes the preacher G. Aston in 'Die Lage der arbeitenden Klasse in England' [the condition of the working class in England], in *Marx-Engels-Werke*, vol. 2 (Berlin: Dietz Verlag, 1962), 261; on Henrys Mathews 'Cockney Polynesia' cf. Christopher Herbert, *Culture and Anomie. Ethnographic Imagination in the Nineteenth Century* (Chicago: University of Chicago Press, 1991), 204f.
84
Rolf Lindner, *The Reportage of Urban Culture: Robert Park and the Chicago School* (Cambridge, MA: Cambridge University Press, 1996).
85
Edgar Pieterse, 'Exploratory Notes on African Urbanism', Paper presented at the 3rd European Conference on African Studies, Leipzig, June 2009, <www.ebe.uct.ac.za/usr/ebe/calendar/AfricanUrbanismNotes.pdf>, 5.
86
Mike Davis, *City of Quartz: Excavating the Future in Los Angeles* (London: Verso, 1990) and *Ecology of Fear. Los Angeles and the Imagination of Disaster* (New York: Metropolitan Books, 1998).
87
Meja Mwangi's social study of Nairobi in the 1970s is far more complex than portrayed by Davis. Clubs and bars played a decisive role, such as the legendary Club Starlight. Cf. Meja Mwangi, *Going Down River Road* (Nairobi: East African Educational Publishers, 1993).
88
Okwui Enwezor, *Snap Judgments: New Positions in Contemporary African Photography* (Göttingen: Steidl, 2006), 13.
89
Jennifer Robinson, *Ordinary Cities between Modernity and Development* (London and New York: Routledge, 2006).
90
AbdouMaliq Simone, 'Ghostly Crack and Urban Deceptions: Jakarta', in Mohsen Mostafavi (ed.), *In the Life of Cities: Parallel Narratives of the Urban* (Basel: Lars Müller Publishers 2012), 123.
91
Robinson, *Ordinary Cities* (see n. 89), 123.
92
From the extensive literature on the temporal and spatial structure of modernity and its concept of progress, see especially: Peter Osborne: *The Politics of Time. Modernity and Avant-Garde*, (London, and New York: Verso, 1995), 17.

modernization', as Pieterse writes.[93] In Davis telling, the abyss that was the nineteenth-century English slum is coeval with the slums of early twenty-first-century Nairobi. The fact that Meja Mwangi's description dates back to 1976 does not change this time span in any way. In this view, the cities of the global South are in any event behind those of North by more than 150 years.

A planet of music

It is potentially problematic to think about cities like Nairobi, Luanda, and Lagos, but also Kyiv, Berlin, and Naples, within such comparative city discourses. Any thinking with attributes – for instance 'slum', 'mega', 'dysfunction' – risks flattening local complexities, creates hierarchies, and messes with coevalness. Although this book itself is not part of the discipline of urban research, its approach takes a position on this discourse. If possible, this approach aims to avoid the three discursive traps mentioned above. If we have certain operations in common with urban research (the selection of cities and a perspective for capturing images of urban life), here the approach should lead to imaginings of cities that take the ordinary, everyday life of the city into account, and restores its complexity. This book assembles several cities, hoping to avoid the thinking in hierarchies and the denial of coevalness. Key to this, or so we assume, is the attribute we apply in this book, to avoid these three pitfalls. We apply the attribute 'music'. In our view, music histories are 'a resource for understanding life and its potentials'[94] and can contribute to complex and rich city histories.

It is probably no coincidence that the concepts of the city developed by recent advances in urban research make frequent references to the trope of the invisible and elusive, as they act as a backlash against the all too rapid, all too obvious reductions of cityness. This can be seen in the work of urban theorists like Filip de Boeck and AbdouMaliq Simone. It is most certainly no coincidence that new approaches to the city are accompanied by a critique of seeing and its 'ocularcentric epistemology'. A greater emphasis is put on non-visual sensory approaches such as listening to the produced space of cities, as demonstrated by the discipline of sound studies.[95] Of all the sounds, music offers a particularly compelling access to a city. Lewis Nkosi wrote: 'Johannesburg, unlike Durban, was dense, rhythmic.'[96]

As an attribute 'club music' (or 'dance music') works in a very interesting way. This music and its culture make the effects of the differential logic of comparative city discourses (as described above) implausible because the criterion of club culture is not 'exceptional', but unpretentiously 'ordinary'. In Berlin, Bristol, Johannesburg, Cairo, Kyiv, Lagos, Lisbon, Luanda, Nairobi, and Naples, club music is produced and danced to, its value is measured by its function for its own audience. It is difficult to deny cities simultaneity and equality in this respect of their lives and history. Even if the pointless argument of size or economic centrality of music industries (as equivalents of the global-city and mega-city discourse) were used, cities such as Lagos and Johannesburg would not be worse off as places of music production and club culture than the large cities of the North. Provided, of course, that the investigation is open to the specificity, scope, and networks of the music industries of these cities in all their diversity and does not merely focus on what the cities of the North know as the 'music industry'.[97] It is certainly always possible to superimpose this narrative with a different one that reinstates the logic of progress and development and the difference of time by way of the technological theme.[98] But the attribute 'club music' makes this considerably more difficult. With club music as an attribute, it is not necessary to construct a counter-discourse, for example by inverting value systems or reversing teleologies.[99] Anything else but stories of coevalness is simply implausible.

This is the approach of this book: using the attribute 'club music' we select cities and enter urban histories that are not written from the narrow range of questions of the dysfunctional, colossal, urgent, or sensationalistic, but rather through the perspective of everyday life and urban space.

Bedroom, club, street

The imaginings that emerge, especially in the second essay series, are as varied as the approaches taken to writing; the motifs too

[93] Edgar Pieterse, 'African Cities: Grasping the Unknowable', in Edgar Pieterse and AbdouMaliq Simone (eds.), *Rogue Urbanism: Emergent African Cities* (Johannesburg: Jacana Media & ACC, 2013), 21.

[94] Simone, 'Ghostly Crack and Urban Deceptions', (see n. 90), 123.

[95] On this subject cf. Charles Hirschkind, *The Ethical Soundscape* (New York: Columbia University Press, 2013), (for 'occularcentric epistemology' cf. 18); and Georgina Born (ed.): *Music, Sound and Space* (Cambridge: Cambridge University Press, 2013), specifically the essay by Andrew Eisenberg, 'Islam, Sound and Space', 186–202.

[96] Nkosi: *Home and Exile* (see n. 3), 12. Lefebvre's fourth volume of his critique of everyday life, which takes the rhythm of the city as a conduit, is an important point of reference for such approaches in recent urban research cf. Henri Lefebvre, *Éléments de rythmanalyse* (Paris: Éditions Syllepse, 1992); see also 'The Right to the City' from 1968, in *Writings on Cities* (Oxford: Blackwell, 1996), 109: 'The city is heard as much as music'; Jane Jacobs compared the essence of social order in a city (i.e. people using the sidewalk) with a dance cf. Jane Jacobs, *The Death and Life of Great American Cities* (New York: Random House, 1961), 50.

[97] Mark Abrahams, for example, measures different cultural industries in the world against the standards of the major cities of the north and derives a ranking from them. Not surprisingly, this looks exactly like the economic ranking of the Global Cities theories cf. Mark Abrahamson, *Global Cities* (Oxford: Oxford University Press, 2004).

[98] See the *New York Times* article on Just A Band in the part one of this essay.

[99] Rem Koolhaas constructs a counter-argument for Lagos as a 'forefront of globalizing modernity', in Rem Koolhaas, 'Lagos', in Francine Fort and Michel Jacques (eds.), *Mutations* (Barcelona: ACTAR 2001), 653.

are numerous. This is not the place to recapitulate them; the essays are too specific and complex. But at least one topic is mentioned below: the way the essays in the series 'Spaces/Politics' deal with the availability and scarcity of city space. In all cities the stories of club cultures are also always stories of the difficult appropriation of urban space; not only of so-called 'public space', but of all productions of space in which public spheres can arise. This has to do with the operation of various binaries – inner/outer, open/closed, visible/secret, public/private – and the peculiar relationship between them.

The music spaces that appear in this book are not private: a bedroom where one listens to music alone,[100] or the basement of the house where Ralph Ellison's Invisible Man listens to music.[101] As 'private' spaces they would be misunderstood, because clubbing is ways of life made public (as conceived above). At the same time, however, the spaces are not simply the unprotected street, city squares, or bald 'public space'.[102] They are marked out by a bubble of sound and are often hidden, controlled, and protected from the 'sound of police gunfire and jackboot'.[103] They form an inner sphere that defines and encloses a space where weak public spheres encounter a 'protective clandestinity' that protects them from being controlled by the 'preponderance of assholes, yahoos, spoilers, whining neurotics, and police agents'[104] (not to forget, parents). Without these exclusions, there would be no control[105] over one's own space where experimentation with subjectivities and sexualities could take place.

This is a prerequisite for the described antagonistic (political) structure of the inner/outer spheres of club cultures. The retreat into the night, the small, the non-verbal, the withdrawal into the hidden, the ostensible exodus become evident not as an escape from the political, but as a precondition for this kind of political sphere. (At the same time, because of this, clubs are susceptible to be a stage of distinction and space of exclusion; the figure of the bouncer is the metaphor for this ambiguity, of the enfolding and demarcating spheres of club cultures.)

Oppressive cities, gendered cities

It is precisely this antagonism, this demarcation of one's own sphere and control over this sphere in the face of an exterior daylight society, which often translates itself directly as an urban history of conflict. The city authorities have always understood that what was happening in the club laboratories ought to be controlled and disciplined. In every city it has been all about spatial conflicts between club cultures and the official mechanisms of surveillance, policing and disciplinary coercion by the official city and its economies on the other. The appropriation of an urban space must always be fought for, and the space for the protective surreptitiousness must be wrested from the city.

In some cities, this has been easier. Berlin, for example, has been a city of protective niches and bubbles since the 1960s, where there was a greater scope for experimentation than anywhere else – first with the special West Berlin subculture model, then in a city of spatial experiments after the fall of the Berlin Wall, until subcultures became an integral part of the city (see Florian Sievers p. 289 and Tobias Rapp p. 311) and recognized as a creative class and driving forces of gentrification. In other cities at other times, it has been much more difficult to appropriate spaces, to define them with music, to exert control over them. Think of Lisbon during the Salazar dictatorship and Kyiv in times of the communist regime, which was marked by the 'constant monitoring and control of the sphere of culture' by the regime (see Kateryna Dysa p. 171), as well as the African cities during colonial times and apartheid. In the brutal colonial and apartheid regimes of rule and exploitation, the colonial cities were organized entirely on control and segregation, which can still be observed today in the form of a 'dual city' (see Mudi Yahaya p. 410, Ângela Mingas p. 359). Nairobi, for example, 'was a segregated city where Africans lived in the mud-pits on the edges of the city while the Asians and Europeans inhabited the city's proper and foliant/jacaranda suburbs'.[106] Here intricate topologies of spatial segregation and control can be observed in detail.

Nairobi was founded as a city of complex segregated zones and developed accordingly in the master plans of 1927 and 1948.[107] Urban planning justified and administered segregation. Urbanists and urban planners worked with legislators and police, who

100
Places of privacy naturally play a decisive role for subcultures. Not only as the proverbial bedroom studio for digital music production. It is therefore not surprising that in Kodwo Eshun's sentence, which opens this essay, the 'bedroom' comes first: 'The bedroom, the party, the dance floor, the rave: these are the labs where the twenty-first century nervous systems assemble themselves', as the complete quote reads, see Kodwo Eshun, *More Brilliant Than the Sun. Adventures in Sonic Fiction* (London: Quartet Books, 1998), 00 (-001). Angela McRobbie has shown the importance of bedroom cultures for the subcultural activity of girls, see Angela McRobbie, 'Settling Accounts with Subcultures', in Simon Frith and Andrew Goodwin (eds), *On Record: Rock, Pop and the Written Word* (London: Routledge, 1990).
101
It is the invisible man in his hideout who remembers Louis Armstrong before he decides to leave the basement in Ralph Ellison: *Invisible Man* (New York, NY: Random House, 1952).
102
In the legal sense or in the sense of completely and unconditionally inclusive spaces, music clubs are hardly even public spaces. The underlying assumption of a 'unitary public space' is a phantom, 'because its claim to be inclusive has always been an illusion'. So writes Rosalyn Deutsche (quoting Bruce Robbins) in, *Evictions. Art and Spatial Politics* (Cambridge, MA: MIT Press, 1998), xxiii; but this does not detract from the importance of the struggle for so-called 'public space'.
103
Nkosi: *Home and Exile* (see n. 3), 17.
104
Hakim Bey, *Immediatism* (Edinburgh and San Francisco: AK Press, 1994), 15.
105
On this subject cf. Ta-Nehisi Coates' memories of the clubs on Washington DC's U Street in the mid-1990s: 'On the outside black people controlled nothing … But in the clubs … under the spell of low lights, in thrall of hip-hop music, I felt them to be in total control of every step, every nod, every pivot.' Ta-Nehisi Coates, *Between the World and Me* (New York: Spiegel & Grau, 2015), 62.
106
E.S. Atieno Odhiambo, 'The Agrarian Question, Ethnicity and Politics in Kenya, 1955–1993', *Jahazi*, vol. 1, no. 4, (2011), 67.
107
Alfred Omenya, 'Island Urbanism. Spatial Segregation in Nairobi', in Philipp Heidkamp, Johannes Hossfeld, Jessica Stihl (eds.), *Learning from Nairobi* (Cologne: KISDedition 2010), 216–219.

enforced the pass laws, to form a spatial control system. Yet even in colonial times, cultures of everyday life nevertheless created spheres in which agency and control became possible, among them music spaces, as shown by Peter Wafula Wekesa on Nairobi before independence in 1963. The colonial government had understood that music spaces were better not left unchecked. But it failed even in the 'formal and closely monitored centres in the city … It is noteworthy however that instead of these social spaces performing their original colonial function of restricting and controlling Africans, they quickly emerged as the hotbed of entertainment and facilitation of other social and even political movements' (see Peter Wafula Wekesa p. 63). This is the foundation on which Nairobi's club culture developed further in the 1960s: 'Club music in 1960s Nairobi emerged from a clearly restrictive and controlled colonial arena in which Africans were expected to be passive participants', says Wafula Wekesa. After independence, the urban space of Nairobi remained a fiercely contested zone for an emerging urban class society.[108] Already by 1963, colonial segregation in Nairobi had been recast as an oppressive insular urbanism; Nairobi became a city in which the dispossessed were rendered powerless and the margin for appropriation of space was narrow and fragile.

Today large parts of the accessible spaces are privately owned while the 'public space' is contested by a myriad of actors vying for control (amongst them the police who regularly victimize clubbers). Safety and control are always precarious for club-hopping Nairobians. The temporary club zones, and the trajectories between them, are fragile. In response, clubbers gain control over their sanctuaries by establishing their own infrastructure (as conceived by AbdouMaliq Simone as an intersection of 'objects, spaces, persons and practices').[109] Most clubbers, especially those who do not have the privacy of their own cars, form their infrastructure of the night from groups of friends and confidants among the matatu touts, taxi drivers, bartenders, security guards, police officers, gangsters, open-air vendors, and club bouncers. In club zones such as Nairobi's 'Westie', a district west of the Central Business District (see Joyce Nyairo p. 75 and Mukami Kuria p. 78), this infrastructre is dense and provides a sanctuary for night communities. One of the well-known crews in Westie around 2009, when this essay was written, was the Hip-Hop band Ukoo Flani, who had their home base in the area between the clubs Rezorus and Skylux (both closed by now). In Swahili, *ukoo* means 'clan' and Flani is a contraction of the word *fulani* meaning 'some'. Thus, Ukoo Flani literally means 'a clan of some sort'. As such clubbers exert control over their zones: They form families of the night, communities, crews, cliques, and tribes that claim their space in the city by night. Band members Alai K and Richie Rich explain: 'That's how we live in our city. At night, we make this our territory.'[110]

Elsewhere in the city, where clubbers are less numerous, they gain space, safety, and control through other tactics, for instance, through temporary[111] and mobile spheres, often with the use of cars (the connection between mobility and club cultures, especially in African cities, is no coincidence). Nairobi's 'parking lot pimping', as Mukami Kuria describes it in this book, is an example. Or, in the case of Cairo, the way the clubbers from the area of Dar el-Salam wrested their temporary sound zone from the city of Cairo with tuk-tuks and Mahraganat music, as Ali Abdel Mohsen describes in his essay: 'a rare form of control over an oppressive city'.[112]

The weaker this protective infrastructure, the more exposed one is, especially to heterosexual male violence. Club zones like Westie are contact zones and at the same time zones of insecurity and vulnerability. This is especially true for members of the LGBTQ community and for women, as Mukami Kuria shows in her essay in this book:

> Just as queer bodies are rarely ever able to lay claim to leisure, public pleasure, and to occupy space, the freedom of women's bodies is equally limited. While nights in Nairobi are often described as fast-paced and hedonistic, young women are often on the receiving end of cautionary tales and warnings about safety in clubs. The city and its nightlife are therefore gendered, inextricably linked to patriarchy and the way in which it prescribes and restricts the actions of young women.

108
The great Kenyan historian E.S. Atieno Odhiambo deduced an emerging urban class society from song lyrics. One of the recurring themes in the 1960s music was that of the city and which of its spaces different classes felt entitled to: the rich elites aspire to live in a home with an English garden. E.S. Atieno Odhiambo, 'From the "English country garden" to "Makambo mibale"', (see n. 78), 155–172; on the 'Ideology of Order', which also represents a system of spatial order cf. E.S. Atieno Odhiambo, 'Democracy and the Ideology of Order in Kenya', in Michael Schatzberg (ed.), *The Political Economy of Kenya* (New York: Praeger 1987), 177–201,

109
For AbdouMaliq Simone, infrastructure constitutes more than the physical environment and facilities: It is 'a platform providing for and reproducing life in the city', an intersection of 'objects, spaces, persons and practices' cf. AbdouMaliq Simone, 'People as Infrastructure: Intersecting Fragments in Johannesburg', *Public Culture*, vol. 16, no. 3 (2004), 407–429.

110
Alai K and Richie Rich in conversation with the author (May 2009).

111
Tactics of hiding work across all times of day. After the coup attempt in Kenya in 1982, club cultures escaped state repression, which is always the strongest form of spatial control, through the tactics of temporal concealment: parties in clubs like the Starlight simply took place in the afternoon to avoid state surveillance. See Joyce Nyairo, *Kenya@50* (see n. 35), 99.

112
Cf. also Mamadou Diouf, 'Engaging postcolonial cultures: African youth and public space', *African Studies Review* (2003), vol. 46, 2, 1–12.

The sound spheres of the clubs create distinction and even proper exclusion. A particularly extreme example of the exclusion of women and their exploitation in large parts of club culture is Cairo, where Ali Abdel Mohsen gives a detailed account of Haram Street in his essay, written from a male perspective (see p.113). Nowhere else do women seem to be more blatantly excluded from the majority of public sound spheres.[113] Here clubs are shown to be public spheres whose political aspects are ambiguous: prisms of society whose structures permeate the clubs or are replicated within them.

Rhythm analysis

The essay aggregated under 'Space/Politics' header interpret club cultures as political. They explore the idea that club cultures can be seen as unique public spheres with their own 'tactics of sound' and can be understood as laboratories and prisms for the political. This entails, concurrently and inextricably, a perception of club cultures as cultures of spatial production. Clubs were said to 'cast a spell' – we suspect this is drawn from their function as laboratories and prisms for the political sphere and urban life. But it only becomes visible if one assumes a critical distance to the conventional concepts of the political sphere and urban theory, which often obscure certain expressions of the political and images of urbanity (just as they obscure forms of music).

From this critical distance, one could even argue that it is not possible to understand Nairobi's society, nor for that matter the city itself, without talking about the Starlight, Madhouse,[114] and Westlands, about *matatus*, Benga, and Ohangla, about Joseph Kamau, Ismail Jingo, Tedd Josiah, and Kalamachaka. You cannot know anything about Bristol unless you appreciate Smith & Mighty, Wild Bunch, and Pinch, the Bamboo Club, Dug Out, and St Paul quarter – in other words, until you take a look behind the Bristol myth. It is impossible to grasp Johannesburg unless one knows about Marabi and Kwela, Yvonne Chaka Chaka, Brenda Fassie, and Lebo Mathosa, the Bantu Men's Social Centre, Razzmatazz in Hillbrow, and Tandoor in Yeoville. The same can be said for Berlin, Cairo, Kyiv, Lagos, Lisbon, Luanda, and Naples. In *Ten Cities'* rhythm analysis, undertaken from the perspective of sound and night, club cultures appear to us as points of crystallization that allow for a different narration of the political and the city.

Bibliography

Abrahamson, Mark, *Global Cities* (Oxford: Oxford University Press, 2004).
Adorno, Theodor W., *Essays on Music* (Berkeley: University of California Press, 2002).
Atieno Odhiambo, E.S., 'Democracy and the Ideology of Order in Kenya', in Michael Schatzberg (ed.), *The Political Economy of Kenya* (New York: Praeger, 1987).
Atieno Odhiambo, E.S., 'From the "English Country Garden" to "Makambo Mibale": Popular Culture in Kenya in the Mid-Nineteen Sixties', James Ogude and Joyce Nyairo (eds.), *Urban legends, colonial myths: popular culture and literature in East Africa* (Trenton, NJ and Asmara: Africa World Press, 2007).
Atieno Odhiambo, E.S., 'Kula Waya: Gendered Discourses and the Contours of Leisure in Nairobi, 1946–63', Tiyambe Zeleza and Cassandra Vaney (eds.), *Leisure in Urban Africa* (Trenton, NJ: Africa World Press, 2003).
Atieno Odhiambo, E.S., 'The Agrarian Question, Ethnicity and Politics in Kenya, 1955–1993', *Jahazi*, vol.1, no.4, 2011.
Baraka, Amiri, *Blues People: Negro Music in White America* (New York: William and Morrow, 1963).
Benjamin, Walter, 'Karl Kraus Reads Offenbach', *Selected Writings*, vol.2, part 1, 1927–1930, (Cambridge, MA: Harvard University Press, 1999).
Bey, Hakim, *Immediatism* (Edinburgh and San Francisco: AK Press, 1994).
Bey, Hakim, *The Temporary Autonomous Zone, Ontological Anarchy, Poetic Terrorism* (New York, NY: Autonomedia, 2008).
Born, Georgina (ed.), *Music, Sound and Space* (Cambridge: Cambridge University Press, 2013).
Buck-Morss, Susan, *Hegel, Haiti, and Universal History* (Pittsburgh, PA: University of Pittsburgh Press, 2009).
Cabral, Amilcar, *Return to the Source: Selected Speeches of Amilcar Cabral* (New York and London: Monthly Review Press, 1973).
Coates, Ta-Nehisi, *Between the World and Me* (New York: Spiegel & Grau, 2015).
Jean Comaroff and John L. Comaroff, 'Theory from the South: Or, how Euro-America is Evolving Toward Africa', in *Anthropological Forum* (2012), vol.22, no.2.
Davis, Mike, *City of Quartz: Excavating the Future in Los Angeles* (London: Verso, 1990).
Davis, Mike, *Ecology of Fear: Los Angeles and the Imagination of Disaster* (New York: Metropolitan Books, 1998).
Davis, Mike, *Planet of Slums* (London: Verso, 2007).
Deleuze, Gilles and Guattari, Felix, *A Thousand Plateaus. Capitalism and Schizophrenia* (Minneapolis: University of Minnesota Press, 1987).
Deutsche, Rosalyn, *Evictions. Art and Spatial Politics* (Cambridge, MA: MIT Press, 1998).
Diouf, Mamadou, 'Engaging Postcolonial Cultures: African Youth and Public Space', *African Studies Review* (2003), vol.46, no.2.
Driver, Dorothy, 'Drum Magazine (1951–99) and the Spatial Configurations of Gender', in Darian-Smith, Kate and Nuttall, Sarah (eds.), *Text Theory Space* (London and New York: Routledge, 1996).
Dyer, Richard, 'In Defense of Disco', *Gay Left*, vol.8 (Summer 1979).

113
In Ali Mohsen's essay in this book, women often appear as prostitutes in many Cairo clubs, these male 'emergency clinics of sorts'. Ali Mohsen at least hints at emancipatory possibilities of participation, for example in Jackie's discotheque. Perhaps in the 'netherworld' of weddings there is also a female public. But to make this visible, we need further research and thorough descriptions from more, especially female, perspectives.
114
Joyce Nyairo, 'Fare thee well, Nairobi's home of song and sin', The Nation, 29 August 2014, <http://www.nation.co.ke/news/Florida-Night-Club-Demolition/1056-2434974-qlvoh7z/index.html> accessed on 1 September 2014.

Ekwensi, Cyprain, *Jagua Nana* (London: Heinemann, 1975).

Ekwensi, Cyprian, *People of the City* (London: Heinemann Educational Books, 1963).

Elkins, Caroline, *Imperial Reckoning: The Untold Story of Britain's Gulag in Kenya* (London: Pimlico, 2005).

Ellison, Ralph, *Living with Music* (New York: The Modern Library, 2001).

Engels, Friedrich, *Die Lage der arbeitenden Klasse in England* [The Condition of the Working Class in England], *Marx-Engels-Werke*, vol. 2 (Berlin: Dietz Verlag, 1962).

Enwezor, Okwui, *Snap Judgments: New Positions in Contemporary African Photography* (Göttingen: Steidl, 2006).

Eshun, Kodwo, *More Brilliant Than the Sun. Adventures in Sonic Fiction* (London: Quartet Books, 1998).

Fanon, Frantz, *Toward the African Revolution* (New York: Grove Press, 1964).

Foucault, Michel, *Conversation with Duccio Trombadori in Remarks on Marx* (New York: Semiotext(e), 1991).

Foucault, Michel, *Dits et écrits II* (Paris: Gallimard, 2001).

Foucault, Michel, *Essential Works of Foucault*, vol. 1 (New York, NY: The New Press, 1997).

Fraser, Nancy, 'Rethinking the Public Sphere', in Calhoun Craig (ed.), *Habermas and the Public Sphere* (Cambridge, MA: MIT Press, 1992).

Gerhart, Gail M., *Black Power in South Africa. The Evolution of an Ideology* (Berkeley: University of California Press, 1978).

Gilroy, Paul, *The Black Atlantic. Modernity and Double Consciousness* (London: Verso, 1993).

Gilroy, Paul, *There Ain't No Black in the Union Jack* (London: Hutchinson, 1987).

Goetz, Rainald, *Rave* (Frankfurt am Main: Suhrkamp, 1998).

Gordimer, Nadine, *A World of Strangers* (London: Bloomsbury Publishing, 2002).

Greif, Mark, 'Positions', in Mark Greif, Kathleen Ross, and Dayna Tortorici (eds.), *What was the hipster? A sociological investigation* (New York: n+1 foundation, 2010).

Grossberg, Lawrence, *We Gotta Get out of this Place* (London and New York: Routledge, 1992).

Habermas, Jürgen, *Between Facts and Norms* (Cambridge, MA: MIT Press, 1998).

Habermas, Jürgen, *The Structural Transformation of the Public Sphere* (Cambridge, MA: MIT Press, 1991).

Hall, Stuart (ed.), *Resistance Through Rituals* (London: Hutchinson, 1991).

Hall, Stuart, 'Politics of Adolescence?', *Universities & Left Review* no. 6 (1959).

Hall, Stuart, 'Absolute Beginnings. Reflections on The Secondary Modern Generation', *Universities & Left Review* no. 7 (1959), 2

Haslam, Dave, *Life after Dark. A History of British Nightclubs and Music Venues* (London: Simon and Schuster, 2015).

Hebdige, Dick, *Subculture. The Meaning of Style* (London and New York: Routledge, 2012).

Herbert, Christopher, *Culture and Anomie. Ethnographic Imagination in the Nineteenth Century* (Chicago: University of Chicago Press, 1991).

Hirschkind, Charles, *The Ethical Soundscape* (New York: Columbia University Press, 2013).

Ivain, Gilles (Ivan Chtcheglov), 'Formulaire pour un urbanisme nouveau', *Internationale Situationniste* vol. 1 (June 1958), 17–18, trans. in Ken Knabb (ed.), *Situationist International Anthology* (Berkeley: Bureau of Public Secrets, 1981).

Jacobs, Jane, *The Death and Life of Great American Cities* (New York: Random House, 1961).

James, C.L.R., *On the 'Negro Question'* (Jackson: University Press of Mississippi, 1996).

James, C.L.R., *Special Delivery: The Letters of C.L.R. James to Constance Webb, 1939–1948* (Oxford: Blackwell Publishers, 1995).

James, C.L.R., *A History of Pan-African Revolt* (Oakland, CA: PM Press, 2012).

James, C.L.R., *American Civilization* (Cambridge: Blackwell, 1993).

James, C.L.R., *Beyond a Boundary* (London: Hutchinson, 1963).

James, C.L.R., *The Black Jacobins* (New York: Vintage Books, 1963).

Knabb, Ken (ed.), *Situationist International Anthology* (Berkeley: Bureau of Public Secrets, 1981).

Koolhaas, Rem, 'Lagos', in Francine Fort and Michel Jacques (eds.), *Mutations* (Barcelona: ACTAR, 2001).

Kopkind, Andrew, 'The Dialectic of Disco', *The Village Voice*, 12 February 1979.

Kopkind, Andrew, *The Thirty Years' Wars: Dispatches and Diversions of a Radical Journalist, 1965–1994* (London: Verso, 1995).

Lefebvre, Henri, *Critique of Everyday Life*, vol. 1 (London and New York: Verso, 1991).

Lefebvre, Henri, *Éléments de rythmanalyse* (Paris: Éditions Syllepse, 1992).

Lefebvre, Henri, *Writings on Cities* (Oxford: Blackwell, 1996).

Lindner, Rolf, *The Reportage of Urban Culture: Robert Park and the Chicago School, Cambridge* (Cambridge, MA: Cambridge University Press, 1996).

Linebaugh, Peter and Rediker, Marcus, *The Many-headed Hydra. Sailors, Slaves, Commoners, and the Hidden History of the Revolutionary Atlantic* (Boston: Beacon Press, 2002).

Lipsitz, George, *Footsteps in the Dark* (Minneapolis: University of Minnesota Press, 2007).

MacInnes, Colin, *Absolute Beginners* (London: Allison & Busby, 2011).

Marchart, Oliver, 'Bridging the Micro-Macro Gap: Is There Such a Thing as a Post-Subcultural Politics?', in David Muggleton and Rupert (eds.), *The Post-Subcultures Reader* (Oxford and New York: Berg Publishers, 2003).

Marchart, Oliver, *Post-Foundational Political Thought: Political Difference in Nancy, Lefort, Badiou and Laclau* (Edinburgh: Edinburgh University Press, 2007).

Marcus, Greil, *Lipstick Traces: A Secret History of the 20th Century* (Cambridge: Harvard University Press, 1989).

Matshikiza, Todd, 'The Stars of Jazz', *Drum*, (June 1957).

Mbembe, Achille, *Variations on the Beautiful in the Congolese World of Sounds* (Vlaeberg, South Africa: Chimurenga Magazine, 2009), now in Sarah Nuttall (ed.), *Beautiful/Ugly: African and Diaspora Aesthetics* (Durham: Duke University, 2006).

Mbembe, Achille and Nuttall, Sarah, 'Writing the World from an African Metropolis', *Public Culture 16*, no. 3 (2004), 349.

McKay, George, *Senseless Acts of Beauty* (London: Verso, 1996).

McRobbie, Angela, 'Settling Accounts with Subcultures', in Simon Frith and Andrew Goodwin (eds.), *On Record: Rock, Pop and the Written Word* (London: Routledge, 1990).

McRobbie, Angela, *In the Culture Society* (London and New York: Routledge, 2013).

Modisane, Bloke, *Blame Me on History* (London: Penguin, 1990).

Mohsen, Ali Abdel, 'Revolutionary music: The noise from Tahrir', Egypt Independent, 8 February 2011, <https://www.egyptindependent.com/revolutionary-music-noise-tahrir/> accessed on 1 May 2015.

Mphahlele, Es'kia, *The African Image* (London: Faber & Faber, 1962).

Mphahlele, Es'kia, *Voices in the Whirlwind* (New York: Hill and Wang, 1972).

Mwangi, Meja, *Going Down River Road* (Nairobi: East African Educational Publishers, 1993).

Negt, Oskar and Kluge, Alexander, *Public Sphere and Experience: Analysis of the Bourgeois and Proletarian Public Sphere* (Minneapolis: University of Minnesota Press, 1993).

Nkosi, Lewis, *Home and Exile* (London: Longman, 1965).

Nkosi, Lewis, *Underground People* (Cape Town: Kwela Books, 2002).

Nunberg, Geoffrey, *The Future of the Book* (Berkeley: University of California Press, 1997).

Nwosu, Maik, *Alpha Song* (Lagos: House of Malaika & Beacon Books, 2001).

Nyairo, Joyce, 'Fare thee well, Nairobi's home of song and sin', The Nation, 29 August 2014, <http://www.nation.co.ke/news/Florida-Night-Club-Demolition/1056-2434974-qlvoh7z/index.html> accessed on 1 September 2014.

Nyairo, Joyce, *Kenya@50: Trends, Identities and the Politics of Belonging* (Nairobi: Contact Zones NRB, 2015).

Omenya, Alfred, 'Island Urbanism. Spatial Segregation in Nairobi', in Philipp Heidkamp, Johannes Hossfeld and Jessica Stihl (eds.), *Learning from Nairobi* (Cologne: KISDedition, 2010).

Osborne, Peter, *The Politics of Time. Modernity and Avant-Garde* (London, and New York: Verso, 1995).

Pieterse, Edgar, 'African Cities: Grasping the Unknowable', in Edgar Pieterse and AbdouMaliq Simone (eds.), *Rogue Urbanism: Emergent African Cities* (Johannesburg: Jacana Media & ACC, 2013).

Pieterse, Edgar, 'Exploratory Notes on African Urbanism', Paper presented at the 3rd European Conference on African Studies, Leipzig, June 2009, <www.ebe.uct.ac.za/usr/ebe/calendar/AfricanUrbanismNotes.pdf> accessed on 1 May 2012.

Pini, Maria, *Club Cultures and Female Subjectivity* (Basingstoke: Palgrave Macmillan, 2001).

Pyper, Brett, 'To Hell with Home and Shame!', in Chris Walton and Stephanus Muller (eds.), *Gender and Sexuality in South African Music* (Stellenbosch: SUN ePReSS, 2005),19–26.

Rabaka, Reiland, *Against Epistemic Apartheid, Lanham* (Lanham, MD: Lexington Books, 2010).

Reynolds, Simon, *Energy Flash* (London: Faber & Faber, 2013).

Reynolds, Simon, *Totally Wired. Post-punk Interviews and Overviews* (New York: Soft Skull Press, 2010).

Ritz, David, *Divided Soul: The Life of Marvin Gaye* (Cambridge, MA: Da Capo Press, 1991).

Robinson, Cedric, *Black Marxism: The Making of the Black Radical Tradition* (Chapel Hill, NC: University of North Carolina Press, 1999).

Robinson, Jennifer, *Ordinary Cities between Modernity and Development* (London and New York: Routledge, 2006).

Rosemont, Franklin and Radcliffe, Charles, *Dancin' in the Streets!: Anarchists, IWWs, Surrealists, Situationists & Provos in the 1960s* (Chicago: Cahrles H. Kerr, 2005).

Sampson, Anthony, *Drum* (London: Hodder & Stoughton, 1983).

Sassen, Saskia, 'The City: Its Return as a Lens for Social Theory', *City, Culture and Society*, vol.1, no.1 (2010).

Sassen, Saskia, *Territory. Authority. Rights* (Princeton, NJ: Princeton University Press, 2008).

Simone, AbdouMaliq, 'People as Infrastructure: Intersecting Fragments in Johannesburg', *Public Culture*, vol.16, no.3.

Simone, AbdouMaliq, 'Ghostly Crack and Urban Deceptions: Jakarta', in Mohsen Mostafavi (ed.), *In the Life of Cities: Parallel Narratives of the Urban* (Basel: Lars Müller Publishers 2012), 123.

Sloterdijk, Peter, *Spheres. Volume 1: Bubbles* (Los Angeles: Semiotext(e), 2011), 527f.

Themba, Can, 'The Bottom of the Bottle', *The Will to Die* (Capetown and Johannesburg: Africasouth Paperbacks, 1982).

Thornton, Sarah, *Club Cultures: Music, Media, and Subcultural Capital* (Cambridge, UK: Polity Press, 1996).

Wainaina, Binyavanga, *One Day I Will Write About This Place* (Minneapolis: Graywolf Press, 2011).

About the Authors

Rui Miguel Abreu is a Portuguese music journalist, lecturer, and DJ who has been writing about music since 1989. He has written for many newspapers and magazines such as *A Capital*, *Se7e*, *Independente*, *Público*, *Expresso*, *Dance Club*, and *Blitz*. He now runs his own electronic music and Hip-Hop digital magazine *Rimas e Batidas* (rimasebatidas.pt), which is also a daily radio show on Antena 3. He presents the show ELECTRIC AFRICA on state-owned RDP África, a radio station broadcasting to Lusophone African countries. He has worked on several documentaries for Portuguese TV on the history of Rock music in Portugal. Together with Rocky Marsiano, he created the music project Meu Kamba. Rui Miguel Abreu is regarded as one of the most active agents in the Portuguese Hip-Hop scene.

Vitalii Bard Bardetski is a leading Ukrainian booking agent, concert promoter, and a former FM radio and TV music channel programming director, electronic record label and underground nightclub owner, magazine editor, and music management teacher. His Promo Ocean agency represents over 150 international artists. He is currently working on a documentary film about the music scene in Ukraine in the 1970s. In 2018, he opened GRAM, the first audiophile bar in Ukraine.

Vítor Belanciano has been a journalist and music critic for the daily newspaper *Público* for about twenty years. He studied sociology, graduated with a degree in anthropology and returned to sociology for his PhD. Over the years he was also an actor, DJ, journalist, critic, teacher, consultant, and the editor of several music publications from *Fact Magazine* to *Vice Magazine* in Portugal. Over the years, he has followed the emergence of new musical genres and their relationship to politics, economy, society, arts, and ideas.

Tony Benjamin is a music writer and reviewer from Bristol, UK, who also programmes live music. He has been devoted to live music since attending the 1970 Isle of Wight music festival. For fifteen years, he was the Jazz and World Music editor for *Venue*, the weekly lifestyle and listings magazine for the Bristol and Bath area (now sadly defunct), and currently writes on the Bristol Jazz scene for *Bristol 24-7*, a monthly magazine and website. He also contributes live reviews to *Jazzwise*, the leading UK national contemporary Jazz magazine. For six years he curated The Jazz Lounge at the Glastonbury music festival, and for ten years he has curated the main stage at the annual Bristol Harbour Festival. He also programmes Jazz, roots and acoustic music for the Colston Hall, Bristol's premier music venue.

Sellanga Ochieng' (Blinky Bill) is a musician, producer, and DJ based in Nairobi. He is a TED Fellow, Red Bull Music Academy alumni, and a participant at the US State-funded One Beat Program and of the Goethe-Institut Nairobi's music co-production projects BLNRB and Ten Cities. He is a founding member of electronic and arts collective Just A Band with whom he has produced three albums. He has recently worked on two solo projects: *We Cut Keys While You Wait* (2016), and his latest release *Everyone's Just Winging It and Other Fly Tales* (2018). His music is a mix of futuristic African Beats meets, Funk, Hip-Hop, Electronica, and a hint of Jazz.

Danilo Capasso is an architect, artist, and DJ. He holds a PhD in urban planning. With his company Questions of Spaces, he is involved in several projects ranging from landscape and urban design competitions to tactical urbanism and photographic research. His theoretical research is mainly focused on emerging urban regeneration practices and liminality applied to urban spaces. As a cultural curator, he developed a strong experience and interest in digital art, new media, and public art, with specific knowledge of electronic music. As DJ Danylo, he has been part of the Neapolitan clubbing scene since the late 1980s.

Vincenzo Cavallo is an expert in participatory methodologies, online participation, urban culture, and participatory videos and has produced documentaries, feature films, and social campaigns in Africa, Latin America, and Europe. He holds a PhD in Communication and New Technologies. He is the founder of the BUS, a creative space for music and art in Nairobi, Kenya, and the co-founder of Cultural Video Foundation Kenya. Among his productions are: *Connection House* (2016); *WAZI?FM* (2013); *Pasos de Cumbia* (2013), a 12 episode TV series on Afro-Colombian music; an episode in the documentary *Napoli24* (2012); *Twende Berlin* (2010), a Kenyan musical documentary on gentrification; the documentary *24H in East Naples* (2006). Currently, he is working on his new film project *Bufis*. Most of his videos and documentaries can be watched on youtube or on www.vincenzocavallo.com.

Iain Chambers teaches Cultural, Postcolonial, and Mediterranean Studies at the University of Naples, 'Orientale,' and is presently the director of the Centre for Postcolonial and Gender Studies at the Orientale. Among his many publications are *Urban Rhythms. Pop Music and Popular Culture* (1985), *Migrancy, Culture, Identity* (1994), *Mediterranean Crossings. The Politics of an Interrupted Modernity* (2008) and *Postcolonial Interruptions, Unauthorised Modernities* (2017).

Kateryna Dysa is an Associate Professor of History Department at the National University of Kyiv–Mohyla Academy. She holds a PhD from Central European University, Budapest. Her research interests vary from historical anthropology of early modern Europe to the modern history of cities and travel. Currently, she is researching nineteenth and early twentieth century travel literature about Kyiv, such as tourist guides and travelogues. Some of her recent publications include: 'A Family Matter: The Case of a Witch Family in the Eighteenth-Century Volhynian Town,' *Russian History 40* (2013); 'Guidebooks as a reflection of taste: Aesthetic judgements in guidebooks to Kyiv at the turn of the 19th–20th centuries,' *Naukovi zapysky NaUKMA. Istorychni nauky*, vol. 194 (2017). She co-edited the book *Zhyvuchy v modernomu misti: Kyiv kintsia 19–serdyny 20 st.* [Living in the modern city: Kyiv of the late nineteenth and mid-twentieth centuries] (2016) with Olena Betlii and Olha Martyniuk. The short version of the essay in this book was pre-published in Ukrainian in *Naukovi zapysky NaUKMA. Istorychni nauky*, vol. 182 (2016): 56–61.

Maha ElNabawi is a writer and a co-founder of the Cairo-based, independent media company, Mada Masr. After graduating from the American University in Washington, DC in 2005, Maha began her dual career between writing and digital media in New York and later, back home in Egypt. Maha's work has a particular focus on youth-driven, sub-cultural music from the Middle East and North Africa region with much of her writings published in *The Wire UK*, *The Guardian*, *Spex*, *Playboy*, and *Beehype*. Maha is currently working on a collection of fiction short stories that centre on music in Egypt. Her work can be found on www.clippings.me/mahaelnabawi and via twitter: @MahaElNabawi.

Michelle Henning is Professor of Photography and Media at the University of Liverpool. Her research focuses on photography, everyday life, and museums and exhibitions. She also works as an artist and photographer, designing album covers and tour merchandise. With Dr. Rehan Hyder, she established BLIMA (Bristol Live Independent Music Archive), a hub for research into Bristol's live and independent music culture. Her publications include *Museums, Media and Cultural Theory* (2006), and with Rehan Hyder, 'Locating the "Bristol Sound": archiving music as everyday life' in Sara Cohen, Robert Knifton, Marion Leonard, Les Roberts (eds.), *Sites Of Popular Music Heritage* (2014).

Rangoato Hlasane is a cultural worker, writer, DJ, educator, and co-founder of Keleketla! Library in Johannesburg and the annual Molepo Dinaka/Kiba Festival in Polokwane. He is a faculty member at Wits School of Arts and a PhD candidate in African Literature, University of the Witwatersrand. Rangoato Hlasane is a guest author with Malose Malahlela for the 2014 book *Creating Spaces: Non-formal Art/s Education and Vocational Training for Artists in Africa Between Cultural Policies and Cultural Funding,* edited by Nicola Laure Al-Samarai. He recently contributed a reflective, multi-authored case study of Keleketla! Library in the Brazil-based journal, *Mesa* (No. 3: Publicness in Art). His research and writing into South African music histories are published in two books published in 2013, in Dorothee Kreutzfeldt and Bettina Malcomess (ed.): *Not No Place. Spaces and Fragments of Time* (2013), and Marie-Hélène Gutberlet (ed.): *Space Between Us* (2013).

Johannes Hossfeld Etyang is the director of the Goethe-Institut, Nairobi, Kenya. He worked at the Goethe-Institut South Africa in 2006 and was already the director of the Goethe-Institut Kenya from 2007 to 2013. In 2014, he was a fellow at the Bayreuth Academy of Advanced African Studies. From 2015 to 2019 he was the Head of the Department for Film, TV, and Radio at the headquarters of the Goethe-Institut, Munich, Germany. Recently he edited: *Kiluanji Kia Henda – Viajando ao Sol durante a Noite / Travelling to the Sun through the Night*, Göttingen: Steidl, 2018.

Rehan Hyder is Senior Lecturer in Media and Cultural Studies at the University of the West of England, Bristol. His research focuses on youth culture, ethnicity, and popular music. Along with Professor Michelle Henning, he established BLIMA (Bristol Live Independent Music Archive), a hub for research into Bristol's live and independent music culture. He is the author of *Brimful of Asia: Negotiating Ethnicity on the UK Music Scene* (2004). Recent publications include 'Black music and cultural exchange in Bristol' in John Stratton & Nabeel Zuberi (eds.): *Black Popular Music in Britain Since 1945* (2014) and with Michelle Henning, 'Locating the "Bristol Sound": archiving music as everyday life' in Sara Cohen, Robert Knifton, Marion Leonard, Les Roberts (eds.), *Sites Of Popular Music Heritage* (2014).

Mukami Kuria is a Kenyan writer and freelance editor living and studying between Cambridge, Nairobi, and London. She is a founding member and co-convenor of The Gathering, and has worked for 1:54 Contemporary African Art Fair, Tiwani Contemporary, and Addis Fine Art and edited the book on Just A Band in the Contact Zones Nrb series, published in Nairobi. She is a graduate of the London School of Economics and Political Science and holds an LLM in International Law at the University of Cambridge.

Ângela Mingas is an Angolan architect and is the director of the CEIC Arquitectura (Centre for Studies and Scientific Research) and of the Faculty of Technological Sciences at the University Lusiada of Angola, where she held different positions in her the fields of architecture, pedagogy, and academic administration. She studied architecture, pedagogy, and anthropology at the Escola Superior de Belas Artes de Lisboa and the Royal Academy of London and holds a PhD from Universidade Lusiada, Oporta, Portugal. She gained experience as an architect and consultant in various venues, both private and public. Since 2006, she has curated the Fórum de Arquitetura de Angola. From 2017 to 2018, she was the Secretária de Estado para o Ordenamento do Território of the Angolan Government.

Ali Abdel Mohsen is the Digital Content Editor at the Institute of Contemporary Art, University of Pennsylvania. He was a journalist in his hometown Cairo for several years, working as a reporter for the *Egypt Independent*, the English edition of *Al-Masry Al-Youm*. In addition to covering politics and culture for numerous international publications, Ali Abdel Mohsen also ran a documentary production company with offices based in Cairo and Beirut. His paintings, drawings, videos, and installations have been featured in numerous solo and group exhibitions across the Middle East, Europe, and North America.

Marissa Moorman is an Associate Professor of African History and of Cinema and Media Studies at Indiana University. Moorman has published on music, fashion, film, radio, and urban space. She is on the editorial board of *Africa is a Country*, the blog that is not about Bono, famine, or Obama, where she is also a regular contributor. She is the author of *Intonations: a Social History of Music and Nation in Luanda, Angola, 1945-Recent Times* (Ohio University Press, 2008) and writing *Powerful Frequencies: Radio, State Power, and the Cold War in Angola, 1933–2002*.

Joyce Nyairo is the Managing Director of Santuri Media Limited, a publisher of biographies and other cultural memory projects. A regular columnist at the *Daily Nation*, her latest book is *Kenya@50: Trends, Identities and the Politics of Belonging* (2015). It includes an interlude titled 'Clubs, Clothes, and Class' which constitutes her contribution to the essay 'A Matter of Salvation. Politics of Music and Space in Nairobi' in this book.

Bill Odidi is the Head of the English Service radio at the Kenya Broadcasting Corporation (KBC) in Nairobi and has twenty years of experience in radio and television, print, and online journalism. Bill Odidi also writes on the music industry for the *Business Daily* in Kenya, and various online publications. He has also worked as a researcher for the independent music production house, Ketebul Music, and reports on Kenyan music for the programme, *Music Time in Africa*, on the Voice of America. He served for two years as a board member of Music in Africa Foundation.

Sean O'Toole is an author, critic, journalist and editor based in Cape Town. His essays, cultural journalism, and reviews have appeared in numerous books, newspapers, and magazines. He is the founding editor with Tau Tavengwa of *CityScapes*, a bi-annual magazine project of the African Centre for Cities at the University of Cape Town. He has published one book of fiction, *The Marquis of Mooikloof and Other Stories* (2006), and co-edited two volumes of essays, both with Lien Heidenreich-Seleme, *Über(W)unden: Art in Troubled Times* (2012) and *African Futures* (2016).

Tobias Rapp is a journalist with the German weekly news magazine *Der Spiegel*. He studied comparative literature studies. Before working for *Der Spiegel*, he was music journalist with the daily newspaper *taz* and a DJ. His book *Lost and Sound: Berlin, Techno und der Easyjetset* (2009) is one of the essential books on the Berlin Techno and club scene.

Florian Sievers is a trained journalist for economics, contributing regularly for business magazines, but he likes as well to write about cultural issues, from architecture to music. Residing in Berlin he is an enthusiastic clubber, appreciating the city's electronic music from Techno to Bass music as much as these genres' African roots. He has researched the latter on many trips to Africa's urban centres from Lagos and Dakar to Nairobi and Addis Ababa. In Berlin, Florian Sievers has compiled *Mandarinenträume – Electronic Escapes from the Deutsche Demokratische Republik 1981–1989*, a CD with electronic music from the former Socialist East Germany, has co-published the book *Pop 16 – 100 Jahre Produzierte Musik*, and runs the party series *Bomayé!* with electronic music from African countries. He was one of the editors of *Groove*, the magazine for electronic music and club culture, and regularly writes for publications like *Dummy*, *enorm* and *Spex* magazine.

Peter Wafula Wekesa is a senior lecturer in the Department of History, Archeology and political studies at Kenyatta University, Nairobi. He holds a PhD in History from Kenyatta University (2007) and has published several articles on the history of border community relations, border resources, identity politics, popular music, and nationhood. His articles have appeared in *Africa Development*, *Journal of Third World Studies*, *East African Social Science Review*, *Journal of East African Studies*, *Chemichemi*, and *Jahazi*, among others. He has also contributed several book chapters as well as being a co-editor (together with Kimani Njogu) of *Kenya's 2013 General Elections: Stakes, Practices and Outcomes* (2015).

Mallam Mudi Yahaya is a writer, cultural activist, filmmaker, photographer, and founder of independent record label Tarbaby Records. Mudi Yahaya works mainly on long-term, self-assigned projects. As a photographer, he has exhibited in London, New York, Berlin, Lagos, Bamako, Harare, and Johannesburg. Mudi Yahaya's work was featured in several publications such as the book *Lagos: A City At Work* (2005), *Artist Of Nigeria* (2012) as well as the *London Times*. He exhibited in *A Perspective of Contemporary Nigerian Photography* (2009) and *Reconstruction In Reverse* (2010), both at the Omenka Gallery, Lagos. In 2011, he had a solo show at Centre for Contemporary Art, Lagos. In 2015, he was selected for the Pan African Exhibition of the tenth Edition of the *Rencontres de Bamako*. Mudi Yahaya's interest in music began at a young age with formal classical piano training in the former Soviet Union.

Thanks

Rui Miguel Abreu, thanks to all the musicians, singers, DJs, producers who have contributed fire to all the dance floors that kept Lisbon a vibrant city up to this very day. Thanks to my family, Fatima and Inês, the main inspiration for every word I write.

Vitalii Bard Bardetski, thanks to Pasha, Ivan, Taran and Asja.

Tony Benjamin, thanks to DJ Krust, Gill Loats, Daddy G, Clive Deamer, Queen Bee and Tintin, Chris Farrell and all the other people who chipped in with off the record chats, and Phil Johnson for his excellent book *Straight Outta Bristol*. Special big thanks to the mighty Rob Smith and a sad tip of the hat to the late DJ Derek.

Danilo Capasso, thanks to the people who contributed to this work, in particular for the interviews that took place between 2013 and 2014: Ivan Maria Vele, Salvatore Magnoni, Giancarlo Lanza, Danilo Vigorito, Augusto Penna, Adriano Casale aka Bostik, and Lino Monaco. Thanks to Marco Basile, Giovanni Calemma, Alessandro Zak David, Lucio Luongo, Francesco Quarto, Salvatore Toti Ruggeri, Paolo Traverso. Thanks to Iain Chambers and Vincenzo Cavallo with whom we invented and discussed the concept for describing clubbing and music under Vesuvius. I also thank all those with whom I could not speak, and would have liked to, and everyone that has been quoted, or not, and has contributed over the years to making the city what it is. Finally, I wish to thank Alessandro Buffa and Iain Chambers for their editorial assistance.

Vincenzo Cavallo, thanks to Iain Chambers, Danilo Capasso, the Goethe-Institut Nairobi; thanks to Napoli and its cultural scene without it I would not be who I'm today.

Iain Chambers, thanks to the Goethe-Institut for an extremely instructive experience in Nairobi.

Kateryna Dysa, thanks to Tatyana Yezhova and Mick Dziuba for sharing their memories and for indispensable information. Thanks to Olena Betlii, Yulia Nazarenko, Maria Chorna and Lesyk Yakymchuk for their help and support.

Maha ElNabawi, thanks to Mervat El Sangak, Faty Saad, Lina Attalah, Mahmoud Refat, Nevine Soliman, Tarek El Kashef.

Rangoato Hlasane, thanks to Senyaka Kekana (RIP), Kagiso 'Gwyza Diseko', Solly Mathosa, Esther 'Esta M' Mathebula, all members of Thath'i Cover Okestra.

Johannes Hossfeld Etyang, thanks to all the authors, to my co-editors Joyce Nyairo and Florian Sievers, and to Anne König, Jan Wenzel, Markus Dreßen and Adriaan Van Leuven at Spector Books; for editing my essay Joyce, Florian, Iain Chambers and Sean O'Toole. Thanks to Abbas Kubaff, Adam Lucas, Alai K, Andi und Hannes Teichmann, Andrew Tshabangu, Angelika Diegel, Anne Peter, Anyiko Owoko, Batida, Bert Rebhandl, Billy Kahora, Blinky Bill, Boniface Mwangi, Buddha Blaze, Christiane Schulte, Christine Buchheit, Mbutch Muhuni, DJ Raph, DYMK, Eliphas Nyamogo, Evgenij Konovalenko, Francis Gay, Franziska Lukas, Fred und Evelyne, Friederike Claußen, Gabriel Gitau, G-Money, Georg Milz, George Gona, Gerriet Schultz, Ghada El-Sherbiny, Günther Hasenkamp, Hesbon Alphayo, Irene Bibi, Isaac Anyanga, Jacob Barua, Jahman Oladejo Anikulapo, James Chege, James Muriuki, Jay Routledge, Jim Chuchu, Joachim Bernauer, Johannes Ebert, John Sibi-Okumu, Jonas Helbig, Jörg Süßenbach, Judy Ochieng, Jürgen Bock, Kamaru, Katharina von Ruckteschell, Kevin Mwachiro, Kilian Crone, Kiluanji Kia Henda, Kimani Njogu, Klaus Krischok, Leon Erasmus, Lien Heidenreich-Seleme, Mahmoud Refat, Marc-André Schmachtel, Mark, Maurits Heumann, Mbũgua Wa Mũngai, Mechack Muendo, Moritz Kasper, Nadine Siegert, Nazizi, Njane Mugambi, Noemie Njangiru, Okwui Enwezor, Oren Gerlitz, P.O.P, Parselelo Kantai, Patrick Wangila, Paul Munene, Peter Muli, Peter Musole, Phil Johnson, Pinch, Richie Rich, Rob Smith, Robin Sättele, Sauti Sol, Sam Hopkins, Sasha Perrera, Serge Dubrovsky, Sharama, Silvia Gioiello, Simon Njami, Smiso Zwane, studio ang, Susanne Gerhard, Tabu Osusa, Tom Odhiambo, Tony Ogaga, Tshepang Ramoba, Ulf Vierke, Zelalem; the Academy of Advanced African Studies/Bayreuth University; Carol, Amai and Ajaa Hossfeld Etyang.

Rehan Hyder and Michelle Henning, thanks to, Alex Cater, Bristol Archive records, Max Pearce, and to all the musicians and producers interviewed by Alex for this project.

Mukami Kuria, thanks to Blinky Bill for graciously inviting me on this journey of sonic exploration; to Kahira Ngige, B.M., Ndinda Kioko, Keguro Macharia; the team that has laboured many years to bring together all our visions of our distinct cities; lastly to this city, Nairobi and its inhabitants, for all your fervour, energy, courage and boldness, shukran.

Marissa Moorman, thanks to Ângela Mingas.

Joyce Nyairo, thanks to Sam Kahiga and Kenneth Watene, generous with their time and knowledge and still unrecognized for their role in the development of Kenyan pop music.

Bill Odidi, thanks to my entire clan.

Sellanga Ochieng' (Blinky Bill), thanks to Mukami Kuria.

Sean O'Toole, thanks to Matthew Krouse, John Nankin, Jürgen Schadeberg, Warrick Sony, Nigel Vermaas.

Florian Sievers, thanks to my friend Johannes Hossfeld Etyang for igniting the spark to this project and to my co-editor Joyce Nyairo. To Andi Teichmann for the initial introduction to Johannes. To Sasha Perera, Gerriet Schultz, Oren Gerlitz, Hannes Teichmann, Lucio Aquilina, Marco Messina, Rob Smith and Pinch for our trips in Africa together. To Marc-André Schmachtel, Emeka Bob-Anyeji, Mudi Yahaya, Christiane Schulte, Rita Soares, Moritz Kasper, Franziska Lukas and Sam Hopkins for big fun in Lagos, Luanda, and Nairobi. To Heiko Hoffmann and everybody at *Groove Magazin*, to everybody at *Spex*. And of course to the House and Techno music of my city of Berlin for bringing me to Africa in the first place. Most of all thanks for sharing my life to Matea, Alma, Artur.

Peter Wafula Wekesa, thanks to Kenyatta University for the resources that enabled me complete the research and to Ian Simiyu Wafula.

Mallam Mudi Yahaya, thanks to my father, the Late Air Vice Marshall Mahammodu Yahaya.

Photography Credits

© 2020 for the works reproduced:
the artists or their legal successors

p. 46 (top): President Records ltd
p. 47, 48 (bottom), 67, 69: Ketebul Music, Extracted from Shades of Benga: The Story of Popular Music in Kenya, all photos edited and retouched by Steve 64 Kivutia
p. 90: Manon Duclos Studio Le Carré
p. 96: courtesy of the Department of Special Collections, Stanford University Libraries
p. 212: Basil Breakey/Musicpics Africa cc Archive and Photo Collection
p. 213–214: Musa N'Nxumalo SMAC Art Gallery
p. 288 (top), 307–310, 329: tilman brembs/zeitmaschine.org
p. 232–233: Nina Fischer & Maroan el Sani/VG BILD-KUNST, Bonn
p. 255–256, 377, 383 (bottom): Anita Baumann/Camera Africa
p. 403–406: Mike Calandra Achode, Tommaso Cassinis/Crudo Volta
p. 451 (bottom): Gavin Watson/ Museum of Youth Culture
p. 454, 473, 476 (bottom), 477–480: Beezer Photos
p. 452 (top): Bristol Culture
p. 452: Black Roots/Nubian Records
p. 475: Wendy Lynch Redfern/Under the Radar Magazine
p. 499–528: frágil.luxfragil.com

Special thanks to all photographers and institutions who generously supported this project with their images:

Ali Abdel Mohsen, Jorge António, Royce Bett, Giovanni Calemma, Danilo Capasso, Erica Cevro-Vukovic, Alessandro David, Manon Duclos Studio Le Carré, Nina Fischer & Maroan el Sani, Kiluanji Kia Henda, Steve Kivutia (Ketebul Music), Andreas Langfeld, Lucio Luongo, Angela Maione, Tiago Manaia (frágil.luxfragil.com), Musa N. Nxumalo, Eva Maria Ocherbauer, Stefan Schneider, Mark Stratford (President Records ltd), Alfredo Vasquez (Black Roots/Nubian Records), Tobias Zielony

Front cover: Royce Bett, tilman brembs/zeitmaschine.org, Kiluanji Kia Henda

Back cover: Anita Baumann/Camera Africa; Royce Bett, Max Fonseca, Kiluanji Kia Henda, Eva Maria Ocherbauer, Jürgen Schadeberg, Chris Saunders

Colophon

TEN CITIES
Clubbing in Nairobi, Cairo, Kyiv, Johannesburg, Naples, Berlin, Luanda, Lagos, Bristol, Lisbon
1960 – March 2020

Editors
Johannes Hossfeld Etyang
Joyce Nyairo
Florian Sievers

Project Direction and Concept
Johannes Hossfeld Etyang/
Goethe-Institut

Image Research
Christin Krause
Andreas Langfeld
Adriaan Van Leuven

Translation
Jan Caspers (GER-EN: Hossfeld Etyang)
Christopher Foster (POR-EN: Belanciano)
Francisco Da Cunha De Eça Valente
(POR-EN: Abreu)
Andrea Cappellani (ITAL-EN: Capasso)
Dasha Posrednikova, Pavlo V. Pushkar
(UCR-EN: Bardetski)
Alicia Reuter (GER-EN: Sievers, Rapp)

Copy Editing
Elias Quijada Link
Wanda Meister
Alicia Reuter
Florian Sievers

Proofreading
Anne König

Graphic Design
Adriaan Van Leuven

Lithography
ScanColor Reprostudio GmbH, Leipzig

Production
Robert Stürzl
Jan Wenzel

Printing and Binding
optimal media GmbH, Röbel

Publisher
Spector Books
Harkortstraße 10
04107 Leipzig
www.spectorbooks.com

Distribution
• Germany, Austria:
GVA, Gemeinsame Verlagsauslieferung
Göttingen GmbH&Co. KG
www.gva-verlage.de
• Switzerland:
AVA Verlagsauslieferung AG
www.ava.ch
• France, Belgium:
Interart Paris
www.interart.fr
• UK:
Central Books Ltd
www.centralbooks.com
• USA, Canada, Central and South
America, Africa:
ARTBOOK | D.A.P.
www.artbook.com
• Japan:
twelvebooks
www.twelve-books.com
• South Korea:
The Book Society
www.thebooksociety.org
• Australia, New Zealand:
Perimeter Distribution
www.perimeterdistribution.com

The publishers have made every effort to identify the right holders of all works. Please notify the publishers of any errors.

© 2020 for all texts the individual authors, for all images the individual authors and their assignees; Spector Books, Leipzig

ISBN 978-3-944669-79-3

Ten Cities is a project of Goethe-Institut

GOETHE INSTITUT
Sprache. Kultur. Deutschland.